EARLY CHRISTIAN CREEDS

EARLY CHRISTIAN CREEDS

J. N. D. KELLY, D.D., F.B.A.

Principal of St Edmund Hall, Oxford

Third edition

LONGMAN

Longman Group UK Limited
Longman House, Burnt Mill, Harlow
Essex CM20 2JE, England
and Associated Companies throughout the world

Published in the United States of America
by Longman Inc., New York

Second Edition © J. N. D. Kelly 1960
Third Edition © Longman Group Limited 1972

First published 1950
Second edition 1960
Third edition 1972
First published in paperback 1981
Fifth impression 1991

British Library Cataloguing in Publication Data

Kelly, J. N. D.
Early Christian creeds. – 3rd ed.
1. Creeds – History
I. Title
238′.1   BT990   72-169389

ISBN 0-582-49219-X

Produced by Longman Singapore Publishers Pte Ltd
Printed in Singapore

PREFACE TO THE
THIRD EDITION

THIS third edition represents a much more extensive and far-reaching revision of the original text than did the second. In addition to making a host of minor adjustments and substituting references to more up-to-date editions and texts, I have introduced a large number of alterations of substance to take account of the considerable recent literature on ancient creeds (much of it, it can be fairly claimed, stimulated by the book itself). The most important of these are in Chapters X and XI, where the brilliant work of A. M. Ritter on the Constantinopolitan Creed has prompted me to rewrite certain vital pages; but many other sections (examples are those dealing with the Descent to Hell and the Communion of Saints) have undergone substantial modification. The Greek or Latin texts of certain creeds have also been slightly amended in the light of recent critical studies. It is my hope that as a result of these changes the usefulness of the book will be enhanced for presentday students.

As I explained in the Preface to the first edition, my reason for not including an exhaustive bibliography was that the late Père J. de Ghellinck's astonishingly comprehensive survey of literature dealing with the Apostles' Creed (*Patristique et moyen âge*, I) had just been published, and that if a proper bibliography of the Nicene Creed were to be compiled it would have to be on a comparable scale. A. M. Ritter's book goes some way towards meeting the latter need, but books and articles have continued to multiply since 1950 beyond expectation. While making no claim to anything approaching completeness, I have endeavoured, in revising the footnotes, to mention as many of these as possible, including several published in the past year or two.

As in the first edition, I should like to record my indebtedness to the pioneer work of scholars of the older generation, such as

A. E. Burn, B. Capelle, C. P. Caspari, F. Kattenbusch, J. Lebon, H. Lietzmann (under whom I worked for a period in Berlin), G. Morin, and E. Schwartz. The reader will come across the names of these, as of many others, on almost every page. Among my own contemporaries I should like above all to mention the Rev. Dr. F. L. Cross (now, alas, dead), whose encouragement meant much to me. The more recent scholars whose work has most influenced this fresh edition are G. L. Dossetti, A. M. Ritter, and I. Ortiz de Urbina. I am also grateful to many who made suggestions for the revisions which appear in it, especially to the Very Rev. H. Chadwick, Dean of Christ Church. Although their careful work has had many changes thrust upon it, I should again like to record my thanks to Mrs. C. F. W. R. Gullick, who compiled the original index, and to my sometime pupil, the Rev. D. L. Thawley, whose eagle eye read the proofs of the first edition. To my publishers I am grateful for their readiness to allow me to carry out a much more thorough revision than I at one time thought possible.

Oxford,
Michaelmas, 1971.   J.N.D.K.

CONTENTS

vii

SHORT BIBLIOGRAPHY

B. CAPELLE, *Le symbole romain au second siècle* (*R. Bén.* xxxix, 1927).

B. CAPELLE, *Les origines du symbole romain* (*Rech. théol. anc. méd.* ii, 1930).

H. J. CARPENTER, "*Symbolum*" *as a Title of the Creed* (*J.T.S.* xliii, 1942).

H. J. CARPENTER, *Creeds and Baptismal Rites in the First Four Centuries* (*J.T.S.* xliv, 1943).

O. CULLMANN, *The Earliest Christian Confessions* (E.T. by J. K. S. Reid), London, 1949.

F. T. DÖLGER, *Die Eingliederung des Taufsymbols in den Taufvollzug* (*Antike und Christentum* iv, 1934).

G. L. DOSSETTI, *Il símbolo di Nicea e di Costantinopoli*, Roma etc., 1967.

D. VAN DEN EYNDE, *Les normes de l'enseignement chrétien*, Paris, 1933.

J. DE GHELLINCK, *Patristique et moyen âge*, Tom. I, Brussels and Paris, 1946; 2nd ed. 1949.

A. HARNACK, *Apostolisches Symbolum* (Hauck's *Realencyk.* I, 741 ff.).

A. HARNACK, *Konstantinopolitanisches Symbol* (Hauck's *Realencyk.* XI, 12 ff.).

F. J. A. HORT, *Two Dissertations*, Cambridge, 1876.

J. LEBON, *Les anciens symboles à Chalcédoine* (*R.H.E.* xxxii, 1936).

H. LIETZMANN, *Symbolstudien* (*Z.N.T.W.* xxi, 1922; xxii, 1923; xxiv, 1925; xxvi, 1927).

H. LIETZMANN, *Geschichte der alten Kirche*, Bd. II, Berlin, 1936 (Ch. 4).

F. LOOFS, *Das Nicänum* (*Festgabe für K. Müller*, Tübingen, 1922).

A. M. RITTER, *Das Konzil von Konstantinopel und sein Symbol*, Göttingen, 1965.

ED. SCHWARTZ, *Das Nicaenum und das Constantinopolitanum auf der Synode von Chalkedon* (*Z.N.T.W.* xxv, 1926).

H. B. SWETE, *The Apostles' Creed*, London, 1894.

C. H. TURNER, *The History of the Use of Creeds and Anathemas*, London, 1906; 2nd ed. 1910.

I. ORTIZ DE URBINA, *El símbolo Niceno*, Madrid, 1947.

ABBREVIATIONS

A.C.O.	Ed. Schwartz, *Acta conciliorum oecumenicorum*, Berlin and Leipzig, 1914 ff.
Badcock	F. J. Badcock, *The History of the Creeds*, 2nd ed., London, 1938.
Bihlmeyer	K. Bihlmeyer, *Die Apostolischen Väter*, 2nd ed., Tübingen, 1956.
Burn	A. E. Burn, *An Introduction to the Creeds*, London, 1899.
Caspari *A. und N.Q.*	C. P. Caspari, *Alte und neue Quellen zur Geschichte des Taufsymbols und der Glaubensregel*, Christiana, 1879.
Caspari *Quellen*	C. P. Caspari, *Ungedruckte, unbeachtete und wenig beachtete Quellen zur Geschichte des Taufsymbols und der Glaubensregel*, Christiana, 1866–9.
C.C.L.	*Corpus Christianorum, Series Latina.*
D.A.C.L.	*Dictionnaire d'archéologie chrétienne et de liturgie.*
E.J.G.	E. J. Goodspeed, *Die ältesten Apologeten.*
Hahn	A. and G. L. Hahn, *Bibliothek der Symbole und Glaubensregeln der alten Kirche*, 3rd ed., Breslau, 1897.
H.E.R.E.	Hastings' *Encyclopaedia of Religion and Ethics.*
J.T.S.	*Journal of Theological Studies.*
Kattenbusch	F. Kattenbusch, *Das apostolische Symbol*, Leipzig, 1894.
Mansi	J. D. Mansi, *Sacrorum conciliorum nova et amplissima collectio*, Florence and Venice, 1759 ff.
Mon. Germ. Hist.	*Monumenta Germaniae Historica.*
Nachricht. Gött.	*Nachrichten von der Königl. Gesellschaft der Wissenschaften zu Göttingen.*
Opitz *Urk.*	H. G. Opitz, *Urkunden zur Geschichte des arianischen Streites* (in Vol. III of the Berlin Academy's *Athanasius Werke*, 1934–5).
P.G.	J. P. Migne's *Patrologia, Series Graeca.*
P.L.	J. P. Migne's *Patrologia, Series Latina.*
R. Bén.	*Revue Bénédictine.*
Rech. théol. anc. méd.	*Recherches de théologie ancienne et médiévale.*
R.H.E.	*Revue d'histoire ecclésiastique.*
Ritter	A. M. Ritter, *Das Konzil von Konstantinopel und sein Symbol*, Göttingen, 1965.
Th.L.Z.	*Theologische Literaturzeitung.*
Z.für KG.	*Zeitschrift für Kirchengeschichte.*
Z.N.T.W.	*Zeitschrift für die neutestamentliche Wissenschaft.*

Patristic references are usually to *P.G.*, *P.L.*, *C.C.L.*, the Berlin series *Die griechischen christlichen Schriftsteller der ersten drei Jahrhunderte* (= *G.C.S.*), or the Vienna *Corpus scriptorum ecclesiasticorum latinorum* (= *C.S.E.L.*).

CHAPTER I

CREDAL ELEMENTS IN THE
NEW TESTAMENT

1. *The Ancient Legend*

FOR hundreds of years Christians have been accustomed to understand by the word *creed* a fixed formula summarizing the essential articles of their religion and enjoying the sanction of ecclesiastical authority. It seems fitting that the opening chapter in a study of the origin and development of the chief Christian credal confessions should consist of an attempt to determine whether, and if so in what sense, it can reasonably be claimed that a creed existed in New Testament times. For more than half the Church's history no one had any doubts on this score: it was confidently assumed that the twelve Apostles had themselves composed and authorized the first summary of belief. The title "Apostles' Creed", or *symbolum apostolorum*, which first occurs in a letter[1] sent by the synod of Milan (390) to Pope Siricius and probably drafted by St Ambrose (he was one of its signatories), is symptomatic of an attitude which was general. A good illustration of the picture people had of the beginning of creeds is provided by the circumstantial story told by Tyrannius Rufinus, once the friend and now the embittered foe of St Jerome, in the exposition of the creed (almost the earliest we possess from the West) which he wrote towards 404. The Apostles, he relates,[2] having been equipped at Pentecost with the ability to speak different languages, were instructed by the Lord to journey forth and proclaim God's word to the several nations of the world:

As they were therefore on the point of taking leave of each other, they first settled an agreed norm for their future preaching, so that they might not find themselves, widely separated as they would be,

[1] St Ambrose, *Ep.* 42, 5 (*P.L.* 16, 1174).
[2] *Comm. in symb. apost.* 2 (*C.C.L.* 20, 134 f.).

giving out different doctrines to the people they invited to believe in Christ. So they met together in one spot and, being filled with the Holy Spirit, compiled this brief token, as I have said, of their future preaching, each making the contribution he thought fit; and they decreed that it should be handed out as standard teaching to believers.

Rufinus did not invent the story he quotes. On the contrary, it represented in his eyes an ancient and hallowed tradition. As a matter of fact, the tradition makes its first appearance in another North Italian document of the same period, the *Explanatio symboli ad initiandos*,[1] which probably consists of notes based on an extemporary discourse by St Ambrose,[2] and in the *Apostolical Constitutions*,[3] which also belongs to the latter half of the fourth century. In the latter the nameless compiler depicts the Twelve as recalling how, to meet the menace of heresy and to strengthen the hands of the episcopate, they had conferred together and had written out "this Catholic teaching", excerpts from which they then proceed to cite. When and where the story assumed the shape it here exhibits, we can only guess now. Much earlier, in the second half of the second century, it was taken for granted in Catholic circles that what was coming to be called "the rule of faith" (an outline summary of Christian teaching, used for catechetical instruction and other purposes) was ultimately traceable to the Apostles. The rule of faith must not be confused with the creed, but (as we shall later discover) the relationship between them was close. When recapitulating it, St Irenaeus, for example, explains[4] that it has been handed down from "the Apostles and their disciples"; and his remark[5] that if the Apostles had not bequeathed us any writings we should have had to follow "the rule of faith which they delivered to the leaders of the Church" is typical of the period. Tertullian similarly speaks[6] of "the rule of truth which descends from Christ, transmitted through His companions". Exactly the same assumption marked the thought at an earlier

---

[1] *P.L.* 17, 1193-6.
[2] R. H. Connolly greatly strengthened the case for an Ambrosian authorship. Cf. *J.T.S.* xlvii, 1946, 185 ff.
[3] 6, 14.
[4] *Adv. haer.* 1, 10, 1 (*P.G.* 7 549 ff.).
[5] *Adv. haer.* 3, 4, 1 (*P.G.* 7, 858).
[6] *Apol.* 47: cf. *De praescr.* 21; 37 (*C.C.L.* 1, 164; 202 f.; 217).

date still of St Justin, St Ignatius and the author of the *Didache*.[1]

Rufinus's hint that each of the Apostles made his personal contribution to the formula is later elaborated with picturesque detail. We see the legend in a developed form in the series of sermons *De symbolo*[2] falsely attributed to St Augustine. Thus we read in the first of them:[3]

On the tenth day after the Ascension, when the disciples were gathered together for fear of the Jews, the Lord sent the promised Paraclete upon them. At His coming they were inflamed like red-hot iron and, being filled with the knowledge of all languages, they composed the creed. Peter said "I believe in God the Father almighty . . . maker of heaven and earth" . . . Andrew said "and in Jesus Christ His Son . . . our only Lord" . . . James said "Who was conceived by the Holy Spirit . . . born from the Virgin Mary" . . . John said "suffered under Pontius Pilate . . . was crucified, dead and buried" . . . Thomas said "descended to hell . . . on the third day rose again from the dead" . . . James said "ascended to heaven . . . sits on the right hand of God the Father almighty" . . . Philip said "thence He will come to judge the living and the dead" . . . Bartholomew said "I believe in the Holy Spirit" . . . Matthew said "the holy Catholic Church . . . the communion of saints" . . . Simon said "the remission of sins" . . . Thaddaeus said "the resurrection of the flesh" . . . Matthias said "eternal life".

The setting, it should be noted, is deliberately borrowed from the narrative of *John* 20, 19, according to which only the Twelve received the outpouring of the Holy Spirit. The prestige of the creed was thus skilfully enhanced by attributing it to the direct action of the Spirit using the Apostles as instruments.

Thus dressed out the legend won almost universal acceptance in the middle ages.[4] This is all the more remarkable because it was no easy feat to squeeze exactly twelve articles out of the creed. St Thomas Aquinas, for example, found it a somewhat

---

[1] For the evidence cf. D. van den Eynde, *Les normes de l'enseignement chrétien*, Paris, 1933, 51 ff.; R. P. C. Hanson, *Tradition in the Early Church*, London, 1962, 64 ff.; 75 ff.

[2] In the Appendix to vol. v of Migne's edition.

[3] *Serm.* 240 (probably of the eighth century) in *P.L.* 39, 2189.

[4] Most writers, like St Maximus of Turin (*Hom.* 83: *P.L.* 57, 433 ff.), Cassian (*Con. Nest.* 6, 3: Petschenig I, 328), St Isidore of Seville (*De eccl. offic.* 2, 23: *P.L.* 83, 815 f.), etc., were content to assert the apostolic authorship; a few (e.g. St Priminius) assigned each clause to a separate Apostle.

embarrassing requirement, and preferred to distinguish seven articles relating to the Godhead and seven to Christ's humanity.[1] For the purposes of popular instruction, however, the Church found the story of the creed's apostolic origin, embellished with imaginative details, useful as reinforcing the authority of what had become a sacred formula. Sometimes it was given pictorial expression, as in the Liebfrauenkirche at Trier, where the twelve slender columns supporting the vaulting were in the fifteenth century adorned with representations of the Apostles and the articles they had severally contributed. It was a favourite subject for illuminations in psalteries and books of hours, and for windows of painted glass, each Apostle being depicted carrying an emblem emblazoned with his particular clause of the creed. A set of nine hexameters, alleged to be the work of St Bernard, has also survived[2] assigning twelve of its affirmations (the clumsy poet was obliged to omit two because he could not make them fit) to their presumed inventor. The verses evidently enjoyed a considerable vogue, no doubt because of their aptness for impressing the teaching of the creed on people's memories.

Though accepted as a piece of history right down to the fifteenth century, the story had all the air of being a pious fiction. It was not to be expected that it would stand up to the reawakening of the critical sense. The first serious questionings of the edifying tale became audible at the council of Florence (1438–45), which attempted a reunion between the Churches of East and West. At the beginning of the negotiations,[3] in 1438, when the fathers were still sitting at Ferrara, the Latin representatives invoked the Apostles' Creed. The Greeks would have nothing of this, and their leader, Marcus Eugenicus, metropolitan of Ephesus, peremptorily exclaimed, "We do not possess and have never seen this creed of the Apostles. If it had ever existed, the *Book of Acts* would have spoken of it in its description of the first apostolic synod at Jerusalem, to which you appeal." For one reason or another no further headway was made in the matter at the council. A little later, however, the

---

[1] Cf. *Summ. theol.* II, 2 Q. 1, art. 8.
[2] For text cf. Hahn 87.
[3] Cf. J. Hardouin, *Acta conciliorum* IX, 842E and 843A. Mansi gives too brief a résumé of Sessions XIII and XIV.

apostolic origin of the creed was sharply criticized by Lorenzo Valla, the scholarly propagator of renaissance ideas and doughty foe of the temporal power of the Popes.[1] Shortly afterwards a less brutal and theologically more skilful attack was made by Reginald Pecock, bishop of St Asaph (1444) and then of Chichester (1450). He denied the apostolic authorship of the creed and rejected the Descent to Hell.[2] Though suppressed for the moment (Valla had to recant, and Pecock was forced to resign his see in 1458), and in any case thrust into the background by the greater controversies of the Reformation, these ideas came into their own in the seventeenth century when G. J. Voss (1642) and Archbishop Ussher (1647) inaugurated the modern era of credal studies.

Once the question is squarely faced, the extreme unlikelihood of the Apostles having drafted an official summary of faith scarcely merits discussion. Since the Reformation the theory that they did has been quietly set aside as legendary by practically all scholars, the conservative-minded merely reserving the right to point out that the teaching of the formula known as the Apostles' Creed reproduces authentically apostolic doctrine. It has become plain that what we have to deal with is only a particular example of the recognized tendency of the early Church to attribute the whole of its doctrinal, liturgical and hierarchical apparatus to the Twelve and, through them, to our Lord Himself. So much may be freely conceded without prejudice to the question whether or not the spokesmen of second-century Catholicism were correct in their assumption that their rule of faith, as distinct from any official formula, was identical with the faith of the Apostles. During the nineteenth century, however, the critical argument was carried several stages further down the slope of scepticism. Doubts were expressed whether any creed at all, any organized body of doctrine, much less one compiled by the Apostles themselves, could have existed in the New Testament period. No unambiguous allusion to one, no plausible quotation from its text seemed to be discoverable in the apostolic literature. Had the

---

[1] For the story see D. G. Monrad, *Die erste Kontroverse über den Ursprung des apostolischen Glaubensbekenntnisses*, Gotha, 1881.

[2] *Book of Faith*, Pt. II, ch. V.

Church possessed such a formula, some trace of it must have survived, for its authority would surely have been immense. In any case, to postulate one would surely make nonsense of the known development of creeds in the second and third centuries. Finally, it was pointed out, it would involve a grave anachronism to trace creeds and fixed formularies back to the Church's infancy. The faith itself had not then attained the pitch of development at which it could be distilled into a creed, and the very notion of stereotyped definitions had yet to emerge.

The force of these and similar considerations is at first sight impressive. It is therefore scarcely surprising that during the great efflorescence of credal studies between 1860 and 1914 opinion hardened decisively against the tradition of a primitive creed. The prevailing temper, it must be remembered, under the influence of men like Harnack, was dominated by a peculiar theory of Christian origins. A sharp antithesis was often drawn between the Spirit-guided, spontaneous New Testament phase and the second-century epoch of incipient formalism and institutionalism. So long as this was the accepted historical framework, there was no room for anything like a full-dress creed at the nursery-stage of Christianity. The majority of scholars (there were, it is true, some notable exceptions)[1] decided that formulated creeds in any admissible sense of the term did not come into existence until the middle of the second century, or possibly a little earlier. Before then, if anything approximating to a creed was in use in the Church, it can have been nothing more elaborate than the simple baptismal confession "Jesus is Lord" or "Jesus is the Son of God". The history of creeds was the history of the enlargement of these brief asseverations through the exigencies of controversy and the evolution of the mature theology of Catholicism.

2. *The Apostolic Tradition*

If the problem is posed in the form of the question, Did the apostolic Church possess an official, textually determined con-

---

[1] E.g., A. Seeberg, whose much neglected *Der Katechismus der Urchristenheit* (Leipzig, 1903) laid the foundations of an entirely new and much more profitable approach to the subject.

fession of faith or did it not?—there can be little doubt that the negative answer returned by the older investigators of credal origins was well grounded. What is less certain is that the choice of alternatives thus offered is a fair and reasonable one. To put the matter in another way, one wonders whether the dilemma propounded does not obscure the real issue. Neither general probability nor the evidence of the documents gives any colour to the supposition that stereotyped, verbally sacrosanct creeds of the kind that were later to become current existed in New Testament days. As a matter of fact, they did not make their appearance until several generations later: even the theory that they cannot be dated before the middle of the second century can be shown to be unduly optimistic. But agreement on that point does not in the least exclude the possibility that creeds of a looser sort, lacking the fixity and the official character of the later formularies but none the less foreshadowing them, were in use comparatively early. If the Church had a creed at all in the New Testament epoch, it can only have been something like this. It is worth examining what can be said in favour of this hypothesis.

In discussing this there are two considerations which should be borne in mind. First, the early Church was from the start a believing, confessing, preaching Church. Nothing could be more artificial or more improbable than the contrast so frequently drawn between the Church of the first century, with its pure religion of the Spirit and its almost complete absence of organization, and the nascent Catholic Church, with all its institutional appurtenances, of the late second century. Had the Christians of the apostolic age not conceived of themselves as possessing a body of distinctive, consciously held beliefs, they would scarcely have separated themselves from Judaism and undertaken an immense programme of missionary expansion. Everything goes to show that the infant communities looked upon themselves as the bearers of a unique story of redemption. It was their faith in this gospel which had called them into being, and which they felt obliged to communicate to newcomers. It would have been surprising if they had not given visible expression to it in their preaching as well as in their corporate life and organization. Like other religious groups with a saving message, they must have been driven by an inward impulse to embody it in their liturgy, their institutions and their propaganda, and to seize every opportunity of harping on it.

Secondly, the character of the apostolic literature, as scholarship since the beginning of the twentieth century has come increasingly to acknowledge, harmonizes with this assumption. The day has passed when the Gospels and Epistles could be treated as objective biographies and detached commentaries on topical happenings. The New Testament is a thoroughly propagandist miscellany, written "from faith to faith". The Gospels themselves are carefully elaborated expositions of certain dogmatic beliefs about Jesus which they seek to explain and justify. The other documents equally presuppose a background of faith shared by the author and those for whom he is writing. For all the differences of nuance and standpoint which they admittedly exhibit, they comprise a body of literature which could only have sprung from a community with a strongly marked outlook of its own.

In the light of these considerations it is impossible to overlook the emphasis on the transmission of authoritative doctrine which is to be found everywhere in the New Testament. In the later strata the references to an inherited corpus of teaching are clear enough. In *Jude* 3, for example, we read of "the faith once delivered to the saints"; later (verse 20) the author speaks of "your most holy faith", again using the word in the sense of an accepted body of beliefs. Similarly in the Pastoral Epistles such phrases as "model of sound words" (2 *Tim.* 1, 13), "the healthy doctrine" (2 *Tim.* 4, 3; *Tit.* 1, 9), "the deposit (τὴν παραθήκην)" and "the noble deposit" (1 *Tim.* 6, 20; 2 *Tim.* 1, 14), "the faith" in its concrete acceptation (1 *Tim.* 1, 19; *Tit.* 1, 13), and "the splendid teaching" (1 *Tim.* 4, 6) form a constant refrain. The writer of *Hebrews*, too, is frequent in his allusions to "the confession (τῆς ὁμολογίας)" to which he advises his readers to hold fast at whatever cost (3, 1; 4, 14; 10, 23). In another passage (6, 2), concerned with catechetical practice, he refers unmistakably to an elementary stage in Christian education which includes instruction in doctrine as well as in ethics and the sacraments.

An illuminating example of this insistence on traditional doctrine may perhaps be discerned in the first of the Johannine Epistles. In his tortuously expressed, baffling opening sentence (1, 1) the writer uses the phrase "the Word of life (τοῦ λόγου τῆς ζωῆς)". The most common interpretation of it has been that it refers to the Incarnate Logos, thus taking up the theme of the Fourth Gospel.[1] To another school of exegetes[2] the analogy of *Phil.* 2, 16 ("holding fast to the word of life") and of *Acts* 5, 20 ("all the words of this life") has suggested that the reference really is to the message of salvation announced by the Church. The solution of the difficulty lies in the recognition that neither of these aspects of Word excludes the other. The Incarnate Lord was assuredly, in the eyes of Christians, the true Word of God; while the gospel which they proclaimed was precisely that Word shown forth in His Person and His saving exploits. What St John is doing is to recall his readers, faced as they are with the caricatures of Christianity presented by heretics, to the pure and primitive message handed down in the Church, that message of which He was the embodiment. This gives point to the appeal to them to continue steadfast in the teaching they had heard from the beginning (2, 24).

The suggestion has sometimes been made that texts like these merely prove that the faith was tending to assume a hard-and-fast outline towards the end of the first century. St Paul himself, however, is a witness to the fact that the process was at work at a much earlier stage. Remonstrating with the Galatians (*Gal.* 3, 1), he reminds them that before their eyes Jesus Christ had been " openly set forth crucified ". In 2 *Thess.* 2, 15 he exhorts his correspondents to "hold fast to the traditions (τὰς παραδόσεις) which you have been taught." (the latter verb hints that he has doctrine in mind), and in *Rom.* 6, 17 he speaks explicitly of "the pattern of doctrine (τύπον διδαχῆς)" to which they have been committed. In 1 *Cor.* 11, 23 and 1 *Cor.* 15, 3 the same idea of tradition passed down (cf. the key-words παρέλαβον and παρέδωκα) and received recurs, in the one case with reference to the Eucharist and in the other to the narrative of the Resurrection.

---

[1] Cf., e.g., J. Chaine, *Les épîtres catholiques*, Paris, 1939, 141.
[2] So B. F. Westcott and A. E. Brooke in their commentaries. C. H. Dodd has supported the same exegesis in his edition in the Moffatt series (1946).

Nor are these, though among the best known, the only instances of such language in St Paul. What, for example, is "the gospel (τὸ εὐαγγέλιον)" which he declares that he preaches among the Gentiles (*Gal.* 2, 2), and which he mentions on other occasions (e.g. *Rom.* 2, 16; 16, 25; 1 *Cor.* 15, 1), unless the saving story of redemption? Another title by which he designates the same faith—one which has tended to monopolize attention in recent years—is "the preaching" or "the preaching of Jesus Christ" (τὸ κήρυγμα: cf. *Rom.* 16, 25; 1 *Cor.* 1, 21). Yet another, and more general, descriptive term is "the faith (ἡ πίστις)" and the related verb. Thus in *Col.* 2, 7 he admonishes his readers to "be established in the faith as you have been taught it"; in *Gal.* 1, 23 he reports the churches as saying that "the man who once persecuted us is now preaching the faith which he once ravaged"; and in *Eph.* 4, 5 he clinches his argument about the unity of the body by pointing out that there is "one Lord, one faith, one baptism". Finally, it is with an eye to the Gospel as the Church's witness that he speaks so frequently (cf. 1 *Thess.* 1, 6; 2 *Thess.* 3, 1; 1 *Cor.* 14, 36; *Gal.* 6, 6; *Phil.* 1, 14, etc.) of "the word of God" or "the word of the Lord". In contradiction to the view that St Paul was a daring doctrinal innovator, virtually the inventor of Catholic theology, all the evidence goes to prove that he had a healthy regard for the objective body of teaching authoritatively handed down in the Church.[1]

Nor was St Paul isolated in having this attitude. According to *Acts* 6, 4 the Apostles considered "the ministry of the word", that is, the proclamation of the message with which they were entrusted, to be their overriding duty. The author of 1 *Peter* recalls to his correspondents (1, 25) "the word which was preached to you", and which presumably formed the basis of their baptismal instruction. Examples could easily be multiplied, and the conclusion is inescapable that, however anachronistic it may be to postulate fixed credal forms for the apostolic age, the documents themselves testify to the existence of a corpus of distinctively Christian teaching. In this sense at any rate it is legitimate to speak of the creed of the primitive

[1] On this see the admirable study *Paul and his Predecessors* by A. M. Hunter (London, 2nd ed. 1961).

Church. Nor was it something vague and nebulous, without precision of contour: its main features were clearly enough defined. The Epistles and Gospels are, of course, rarely if ever concerned to set out the faith in its fulness: they rather presuppose and hint at it. Even so, it is possible to reconstruct, with a fair degree of confidence, what must have been its chief constituents.

Much attention has been devoted in recent years to this subject. The result has been, ironically enough, an almost general rallying to positions which it was formerly fashionable to dismiss as the last ditch of the ultra-conservative.[1] A pioneer in the field has been Paul Feine, whose researches[2] broke new ground in the most constructive way. His influence has been extensive, although it has usually (like that of A. Seeberg, whose book is mentioned above) remained without overt acknowledgement. Feine exposes himself to criticism, however, both by concentrating exclusively upon baptism and by apparently insisting on fastening a creed, in the sense of an official and textually determined formula, on the apostolic age.[3] More cautious, and on the whole more reliable, conclusions have been worked out by C. H. Dodd, and have been expounded and given currency in a series of well-known books.[4] By ransacking the Pauline epistles and the speeches embodied in the early chapters of *Acts* (which are stamped, he thinks, with traits pointing infallibly to their primitive character), he believes he is able to sketch the outline of the faith preached in the Church in the first two or three decades after the Resurrection. Its core, he argues, consisted in the proclamation that Jesus of Nazareth, of the lineage of David, had come as Son of God and Messiah; that He wrought mighty acts and gave a new and authoritative teaching or law; that He was crucified, died, and was buried; that He rose again on the third day and was exalted to the right hand of God, victorious over principalities and powers; and

---

[1] Up-to-date discussion about the apostolic kerygma makes little, if any, advance on what was familiar, e.g., to P. Batiffol (*L'église naissante*, 1909, ch. 2) and F. E. Brightman (cf. *The Early History of the Church and the Ministry*, 1918, 316 ff.).

[2] *Die Gestalt des apostolischen Glaubensbekenntnisses in der Zeit des N.T.*, Leipzig, 1925.

[3] Cf. Harnack's critical review in *Th.L.Z.*, 1925, 393 ff. J. Coppens gave a fairer, more balanced notice in *R.H.E.* xxii, 1926, 582 ff.

[4] Cf. especially *The Apostolic Preaching and its Developments*, London, 1936.

that He will come again to judge the living and the dead. The setting of all this was the conviction, openly announced, that the Apostles and those in fellowship with them constituted the new Israel of God, the heir of the ancient promises, and were marked out as such by the manifest outpouring of the Holy Spirit. Those who embraced this gospel, repented and believed in Christ, would receive the forgiveness of their sins and a share in the life of the coming age.

So far as it goes, this analysis of the propaganda of the apostolic Church could hardly be bettered. Such are the pattern and content of the credal themes which can be overheard by any attentive reader of the New Testament writings, and on which the synoptic Gospels are magnificently elaborated variations. The one defect from which it suffers is the consequence of the method of approach which has been adopted. Based as it is on the *preaching* of the early Church as reflected in St Paul's letters and *Acts*, it tends to convey a slightly one-sided picture of its corpus of beliefs. Preaching was only one of the spheres in which the faith of first-century Christians found an outlet, and in preaching, for obvious missionary reasons, the emphasis tended to be almost exclusively Christological. Yet the Church carried over from its Jewish antecedents a settled belief in God the Father, the maker of heaven and earth, the one God of the whole world; and the teaching of Jesus had assigned special prominence to the Fatherhood of God. The New Testament repeatedly underlines the place which this cardinal affirmation occupied in the thought of first-century Christians. But if attention is concentrated on the kerygma as it appears in sermons alone, it is easy to overlook this important item. Similarly the profoundly Trinitarian strain in early Christianity is liable to be ignored in the kind of approach which we are examining. The Trinitarianism of the New Testament is rarely explicit; but the frequency with which the triadic schema recurs (as we shall see in the following section) suggests that this pattern was implicit in Christian theology from the start. If these gaps are filled in, however, we are entitled to assume with some confidence that what we have before us, at any rate in rough outline, is the doctrinal deposit, or the pattern of sound words, which was expounded in the apostolic Church since its inauguration and which constituted its distinctive message.

3. *Fragments of Creeds*

That the Church in the apostolic age possessed a creed in the broad sense of a recognized body of teaching may be accepted as demonstrated fact. But it is permissible to take a further step. There is plenty of evidence in the New Testament to show that the faith was already beginning to harden into conventional summaries. Creeds in the true meaning of the word were yet to come, but the movement towards formulation and fixity was under way. Thus the reader of the New Testament is continually coming across creed-like slogans and tags, catchwords which at the time of writing were being consecrated by popular usage. In addition he lights upon longer passages which, while still fluid in their phrasing, betray by their context, rhythm and general pattern, as well as by their content, that they derive from community tradition rather than from the writer's untrammelled invention. To explain them as excerpts from or echoes of an official ecclesiastical formula, as used to be fashionable, is unnecessary and misleading. Since the very existence of a creed in the precise sense implied is pure hypothesis, and unlikely hypothesis at that, it is more natural to treat them as independent units and examine them on their merits.

Two points in this connection are worth noticing. First, these beginnings of crystallization did not take place haphazardly. They were provoked by particular situations in the Church's life. Particular occasions lent themselves to the exposition or declaration of Christian doctrine: they called for something like a creed. The one which has been most thoroughly investigated is baptism. Some kind of assurance of faith, and thus some sort of avowal of belief, was required of candidates seeking admission to the Church. But it is a mistake to concentrate exclusively on baptism, as scholars have sometimes been disposed to do. The catechetical instruction preceding baptism was also a moment sympathetic to the shaping of credal summaries. So was preaching: the method and style of different preachers doubtless varied, but the content and wording of their message must have tended to run along certain accepted lines. The day-to-day polemic of the Church, whether against heretics within or pagan foes without, provided another situation propitious to the production of creeds. Yet another was supplied by the liturgy : solemn expressions of faith, in the form of hymns, prayers and devotional cries, had a natural place there. An interesting special case is the rite of exorcism. The exorcism of devils was widely practised in the early Church, and the codification of suitable formulae of proved potency seems to have set in relatively soon. Nor should we overlook the formal correspondence of Church leaders with their flocks. In the ancient as in the modern world, letters, especially official ones (and it must be remembered that Christian letters were often intended to be read aloud at Church meetings), abounded in stereotyped turns of phrase, and sometimes these had something of the character of brief formal confessions.

Secondly, the *Sitz im Leben*, if this technical description of it is in place, did not only create the occasion for tentative creeds : it also to some extent determined their style, substance and structure. Sometimes diffuseness was appropriate, sometimes terseness and aridity. If a dry enumeration of Christ's redemptive deeds was suitable in a catechetical instruction, a more enthusiastic, fulsome utterance might be expected in an act of worship. In certain circumstances what seemed fitting was a Trinitarian or a binitarian ground-plan, the former emphasizing belief in the three Divine Persons, the latter belief in the Father and the Son. More often than not, a single-clause Christological statement was sufficient for the purpose in hand. This last division, based on underlying plan, has proved so significant that, in proceeding to survey the evidence for quasi-credal material in the New Testament, we shall catalogue it in accordance with the pattern it exhibits. At the same time we shall try, though not always with much hope of success, to indicate the situation in the Church's life in which the formulae under discussion have their roots.

First, then, let us glance at the formulary elements which consist of simple, one-clause Christologies. The most popular, as well as the briefest, in the New Testament is the slogan *Kurios Iēsous* (κύριος Ἰησοῦς = "Jesus is Lord"). St Paul states (1 *Cor.*

12, 3), "No one can say *Kurios Iēsous* except by the Holy Spirit", and again (*Rom.* 10, 9), "If with your mouth you confess *Kurios Iēsous* and believe in your heart that God has raised Him from the dead, you will be saved." He does not disclose the occasion on which these utterances were made, but the context of the first, with its reference to the alternative of saying *Anathema Iēsous* (="cursed be Jesus"), seems to suggest that it is an hour when the Christian's loyalty is tested (by persecution possibly, but not exclusively) that he has in mind.[1] This harmonizes well with the stress laid by early Christians on the sinfulness of denying Christ when challenged,[2] as well as with what we know of the practice of the civil authorities of trying to induce Christians haled before them to curse Christ.[3] The verse from *Romans* has been generally taken as an allusion to the acknowledgement of Christ's lordship made at baptism. The repeated description of baptism as "in the name of the Lord Jesus" (cf., e.g., *Acts* 8, 16; 19, 5; 1 *Cor.* 6, 11) certainly seems to imply that the formula "Jesus is Lord" had a place in the rite. The words occur again in *Phil.* 2, 11, where St Paul speaks of every tongue confessing that "Jesus Christ is Lord", the setting in this case being liturgical. Again, that the tag was handed out to converts as a convenient epitome of their faith is suggested by such passages as *Col.* 2, 6, "You received Christ Jesus as the Lord", and by the references in *Acts* to "believing on the Lord Jesus Christ" (e.g. 11, 17; 16, 31) and to "preaching the Lord Jesus" (cf. 11, 20). The *Martyrdom of St Polycarp*[4] reports that the imperial magistrate, doing his best to persuade the aged bishop to come to terms, asked him, "What harm is there in saying Caesar is Lord?" The acclamation *Kurios Kaisar* would seem to have been a popular one in the civic cult of the Roman empire, and Christians were no doubt conscious of the implicit denial of it contained in their own *Kurios Iēsous*.

Another formula, equally concise and ancient, though

---

[1] Cf. O. Cullmann, *The Earliest Christian Confessions* (E.T.), London, 1949, 27–30.
[2] Cf. *Mt.* 10, 33; 26, 34 f.; 1 *Jn.* 2, 22; 2 *Tim.* 2, 12.
[3] Cf. *Martyrdom of St Polycarp* 9, 3, where St Polycarp asks "How can I curse my king?"; and Pliny, *Epp.* X, 96, where he reports to Trajan how he tried to make Christians curse (*maledicere*) Christ.
[4] 8, 2 (Bihlmeyer, 124).

destined to be superseded when its original Messianic significance was forgotten, is "Jesus is the Christ". 1 *Jn.* 2, 22 testifies
to its use ("who is the liar, except he who denies that Jesus is the
Christ?"), as does *Mk.* 8, 30 ("Peter said to Him, Thou art the
Christ"). Yet another which often crops up is "Jesus is the Son
of God". A striking example of its use as a baptismal confession
is the story of the baptism of the Ethiopian eunuch at the hands
of St Philip, narrated in *Acts* 8, 36–38. According to the reading
of the Western text (for our purpose it makes no difference
whether it is original or an interpolation), the eunuch sealed his
faith by declaring, "I believe that Jesus Christ is the Son of
God". The author of 1 *John* makes much of it, arguing (4, 15)
that "Whosoever confesses that Jesus is the Son of God, God
abides in him and he in God", and later asking (5, 5), "Who is
the conqueror of the world, but the man who believes that
Jesus is the Son of God?" As used by him the words, while
embodying a primitive Christian affirmation, have a certain
polemical colouring, being directed against the Docetists whom
he is attacking. This comes out in a more self-consciously
polemical formula (4, 2), "Jesus Christ has come in the flesh".
The same statement that Jesus is the Son of God, without any
hint of heresy-hunting, is quoted in *Hebr.* 4, 14. It reappears in a
very different setting in *Mk.* 5, 7, where the devil whom the
Lord is about to exorcize cries, "Jesus, thou Son of God most
high, I conjure thee", and in *Mk.* 3, 11, where the demons
salute Him with the words, "Thou art the Son of God".
Possibly these passages give a clue to the exorcistic formulae
current in the first-century Church.[1]

So far we have been glancing at miniature creeds, hardly
more than catchwords. Side by side with them there are many
examples of fuller and more detailed confessions in the pages of
the New Testament. In 1 *Cor.* 15, 3 ff., St Paul reproduces an
extract from what he describes in so many words as "the
gospel (τὸ εὐαγγέλιον) which I preached to you and which you
received": he adds that, so far from its being his gospel, he in

---

[1] The same slogan found pictorial expression in the widely popular symbol of
the fish: the letters of the Greek ᾽Ιχθύς spelled out "Jesus Christ, Son of God,
Saviour". Cf. F. J. Dölger, *Ichthys*, I, 248, 259, 318 ff. Cf. also the second-century
inscription scratched up in San Sebastiano (Rome) and referred to in *Z.N.T W.*
xxi, 1922, 151.

his turn had received it, presumably from the Church. The fragment quoted runs:

For I passed on to you in the first place what I had myself received,
 that Christ died for our sins according to the Scriptures,
 and that He was buried,
 and that He was raised on the third day according to the Scriptures,
 and that He appeared to Cephas,
 then to the Twelve,
 then to more than five hundred brothers at once . . .
 then He appeared to James,
 then to all the apostles. . . .

This is manifestly a summary drawn up for catechetical purposes or for preaching: it gives the gist of the Christian message in a concentrated form. A defensive, apologetic note becomes audible in the impressive array of witnesses with which it terminates. Along with it we should probably class the more closely knit theological statement of *Rom.* 1, 3 f:

Concerning His Son,
 Who was born of David's seed by natural descent,
 Who was declared Son of God with power by the Spirit of holiness
 when He was raised from the dead,
Jesus Christ our Lord,
 through Whom we have received grace,

as well as the briefer extracts in *Rom.* 8, 34:

  Christ Jesus Who died, or rather
  has been raised from the dead,
  Who is on the right hand of God,
  Who also makes intercession for us,

and 2 *Tim.* 2, 8:

  Remember Jesus Christ,
  raised from the dead,
  of the seed of David (according to my gospel).

Odd sentences scattered throughout the epistles seem to echo catechetical formulae like these, e.g. *Gal.* 1, 4 ("Jesus Christ, Who gave Himself for our sins"); 1 *Thess.* 4, 14 ("If we believe that Jesus died and rose again"); and 1 *Thess.* 5, 9 (". . . through our Lord Jesus Christ, Who died for us"). So, too, the lengthier, more freely expressed passage in 1 *Pet.* 3, 18 ff:

> For Christ also suffered for sins,
> > the just for the unjust, to bring us to God,
> slain indeed in the flesh but quickened in the Spirit,
> > in which He went and preached to the spirits in prison
> . . . through the rising again of Jesus Christ,
> Who is on the right hand of God,
> having ascended to heaven,
> angels, authorities and powers having been subjected to Him,

reads like a part-paraphrase and part-quotation of an instruction preparatory to baptism. The insertion in verses 20 ff. of a short account of the meaning of the sacrament bears this out.

The plan of these Christological kerygmas is simple: they are built up by attaching to the name of Jesus selected incidents in the redemptive story. An underlying contrast between flesh and spirit, son of David and Son of God, humiliation and exaltation, can often be detected. The most impressive example of it is the well-known Christological passage *Phil.* 2, 6–11, which is entirely modelled on the antithesis between Christ's self-emptying and His elevation to glory as Lord of creation. So far from being Pauline, it is almost certainly an ancient Christian hymn, probably of Palestinian derivation, which was already arranged in rhythmic strophes by the time it fell into St Paul's hands. Scholars[1] have hazarded the guess that it must be an excerpt from some primitive eucharistic liturgy, but this is pure conjecture: nothing in the language or in the movement of ideas gives the least support to it. The most that can be claimed is that its setting was undoubtedly cultic, and that it is a fine example of the early crystallization of liturgical material. Another

---

[1] So H. Lietzmann, *Z.N.T.W.* xxii, 1923, 265, and E. Lohmeyer, *Kyrios Jesus* (*Sitzungsberichte der Heidelberger Akademie der Wissenschaften*, Phil. Hist. Kl. 1927–8), 65 f. Also the latter's *Philipper* (Göttingen, 1928), *ad loc.*

hymn-like scrap, setting out the essentials of the *paradosis* in rhythmic lines, is 1 *Tim.* 3, 16:

> Who was revealed in the flesh,
> was justified in the Spirit,
> appeared to angels,
> was preached among the Gentiles,
> was believed on throughout the world,
> was taken up in glory.

The same type of kerygma, much abbreviated, of course, was used at exorcism and for healing. Thus St Peter (*Acts* 3, 6) cured the lame man at Beautiful Gate by solemnly adjuring him, "In the name of Jesus Christ, the Nazoraean, walk." A little later, when asked to explain the miracle (4, 10), he elaborates the formula into "In the name of Jesus Christ, the Nazoraean, Whom you crucified, Whom God raised from the dead."

So much for single-clause, purely Christological formulations of the doctrinal deposit of the apostolic Church. They were manifestly not the only type: contemporaneously with them the doctrinal deposit was taking shape in semi-formal confessions of a bipartite structure based on the parallel ideas of God the Father and Jesus Christ His Son. One of the most important instances of these is St Paul's (1 *Cor.* 8, 6)

> We, however, have one God the Father,
> from Whom are all things, and we to Him,
> and one Lord Jesus Christ,
> through Whom are all things, and we through Him.

The formulary character of this is unmistakable, and is emphasized by the careful parallelism and the artificial construction. Theological motives are in part at work, for St Paul is concerned to bring out the cosmic roles of Father and Son, but polemical ones are for the moment uppermost. St Paul is asserting the unity of the Christians' God as contrasted with the "many gods and many lords" of paganism. A closely related passage, looser in expression but built upon the same plan, is 1 *Tim.* 2, 5 f:

> For there is one God,
> likewise one mediator between God and men,
> the man Christ Jesus,
> Who gave Himself as a ransom for all. . . .

Another familiar two-clause confession, the creed-like character of which leaps at once to the eye, occurs in 1 *Tim.* 6, 13 f :

> I charge you in the sight of
> God Who gives life to all things,
> and Christ Jesus Who witnessed the fine confession
> in the time of Pontius Pilate,
> that you keep your commission spotless,
> without reproach, until
> the manifestation of our Lord Jesus Christ.

It hardly requires much imagination to discern behind this loose paraphrase a formal confession of belief in God the Father, the Creator of all things, and Christ Jesus His Son, Who suffered (this is surely the true sense of μαρτυρήσαντος τὴν καλὴν ὁμολογίαν) under Pontius Pilate, and will come again in glory.[1] The situation to which it belongs would seem to be the doctrinal preparation for baptism. A fragmentary creed of similar type is cited in 2 *Tim.* 4, 1 as a solemn adjuration :

> I charge you,
>   in the sight of God,
>   and of Christ Jesus, Who is going to judge living and dead,
>   and by His coming-again and His kingdom. . . .

Here the Second Coming, usually included in the list of saving exploits ascribed to Christ, appears as a coordinate article of faith.

A passage witnessing to a binitarian formula of a slightly different type is *Rom.* 4, 24 :

> because of us . . . who believe
> on Him Who has raised
> Jesus our Lord from the dead,
>   Who was delivered up for our transgressions
>   and was raised for our justification,

where the creed-like note is unmistakable. Passages with exactly the same structure and content occur with great frequency, as is shown by *Rom.* 8, 11 ; 2 *Cor.* 4, 14 ; *Gal.* 1, 1 ;

---

[1] For this interpretation cf. C. H. Turner in *J.T.S.* xxviii, 1927, 270 f. We are not, of course, required by it to draw the improbable conclusion that ὁμολογίαν must have stood in the original quoted by the writer. For μαρτυρεῖν="suffer", cf. 1 *Clement* 5, 4; 5, 7.

1 *Thess.* 1, 10; *Col.* 2, 12; and *Eph.* 1, 20. Nor are they confined
to St Paul. The author of 1 *Peter* addresses his correspondents
(1, 21) as

> You who through Him [i.e. Jesus] believe on
> God, Who has raised
> Him from the dead
> and has given Him glory.

Whatever was the situation in which it took shape, it is clear
that "God, Who has raised the Lord Jesus from the dead" had
become a stereotyped tag or cliché before the third generation of
the first century.

These comprise the examples of bipartite confessions in the
New Testament to which appeal is generally made. But they
by no means exhaust the list: they can be abundantly supplemented if the search for formulary elements is conducted on a
wider basis. Practically every one of St Paul's letters, for
example, opens with the conventional greeting, "Grace and
peace be to you from God the Father and the Lord Jesus
Christ".[1] Evidently it was a stock form. Nor was it an idiosyncrasy of Pauline usage. Closely similar greetings feature in
the Pastoral Epistles (1 *Tim.* 1, 2; 2 *Tim.* 1, 2; *Tit.* 1, 4) and
2 *Peter* (cf. 1, 2, "in the knowledge of God and Jesus our Lord");
also in 2 *Jn.* 1, 3 ("grace, mercy, peace from God the Father
and Jesus Christ the Son of the Father"). Again, the expression
"the God and Father of our Lord Jesus Christ" had also hardened into a stereotyped formula, as its use in *Rom.* 15, 6; 2
Cor. 1, 3; 11, 31; *Eph.* 1, 3; 1 *Pet.* 1, 3 shows.[2] Its original setting,
if we can judge from *Rom.* 15, 16 ("that you may unitedly with
one mouth glorify God . . .") as well as from its frequent
employment as a blessing, was probably liturgical. Apart from
such special contexts, however, numberless other passages serve
to illustrate the way in which the men of the apostolic Church
acquiesced instinctively in the coordination of Father and Son.
It was almost a category of their thinking. Thus St Paul prays
in 1 *Thess.* 3, 11, "May our God and Father, and our Lord
Jesus Christ, make our way straight to you"; while in 2 *Thess.*

---

[1] Cf. *Rom.* 1, 7; 1 *Cor.* 1, 3; 2 *Cor.* 1, 2; *Gal.* 1, 3; *Eph.* 1, 2 (cf. also 6, 23); *Phil.* 1,
2; 2 *Thess.* 1, 2.
[2] So W. Bousset in *Jesus der Herr*, Göttingen, 1916, 36 n.

2, 16 he expresses the hope that his correspondents may be comforted and strengthened by "our Lord Jesus Christ and God our Father". St James describes himself (1, 1) as "the servant of God and the Lord Jesus Christ", and St Peter (1 *Pet.* 2, 5) speaks of "spiritual sacrifices acceptable to God through Jesus Christ". The Apocalyptist too describes himself (1, 2) as having borne witness "to the word of God and the testimony of Jesus Christ". The catalogue could be extended almost indefinitely. The items contained in it, the reader scarcely needs to be reminded, are not creeds; but they are highly significant as instances of the codification of fundamental theological ideas in the apostolic age, and they help to explain the lines along which creeds proper developed.

The binitarian schema, it is evident, was deeply impressed upon the thought of primitive Christianity; so, it would appear, was the Trinitarian. Explicit Trinitarian confessions are few and far between; where they do occur, little can be built upon them. The two most commonly cited are St Paul's prayer at the end of 2 *Corinthians* (13, 14), "The grace of our Lord Jesus Christ, and the love of God, and the communion of the Holy Spirit, be with you all", and the baptismal command put by St Matthew (28, 19) into the mouth of the risen Lord, "Make disciples of all nations, baptizing them in the name of the Father and of the Son and of the Holy Spirit". These are not the only examples, however, of such formulae in the New Testament, although preoccupation with them has sometimes caused others which, while perhaps less obvious, are in reality no less significant to be overlooked. Amongst these may be reckoned 1 *Cor.* 6, 11, "But you were justified in the name of our Lord Jesus Christ and in the Spirit of our God"; 1 *Cor.* 12, 4 f., "There are varieties of talents, but the same Spirit, varieties of service, but the same Lord, and varieties of effects, but the same God Who effects everything in everyone"; 2 *Cor.* 1, 21 f., "It is God Who confirms us along with you in Christ, Who has anointed us and sealed us and given us the earnest of the Spirit"; and 1 *Thess.* 5, 18 f., "For this is the will of God in Christ Jesus for you: quench not the Spirit". The triadic schema is again clearly visible in such a context as *Gal.* 3, 11–14, "It is obvious that no one is justified in the sight of God by the law . . . Christ has redeemed us from the curse of the law . . . that you may receive the promise of the Spirit through faith." An excellent instance of it is to be found in 1 *Pet.* 1, 2, ". . . according to the fore-knowledge of God the Father, by the consecration of the Spirit, unto obedience to . . . Jesus Christ", and another in *Hebr.* 10, 29, "Of how much worse vengeance will he be thought worthy who has spurned the Son of God . . . and has insulted the Spirit of grace?" A host of other passages stamped with the same lineaments might be quoted.[1] In all of them there is no trace of fixity so far as their wording is concerned, and none of them constitutes a creed in any ordinary sense of the term. Nevertheless the Trinitarian ground-plan obtrudes itself obstinately throughout, and its presence is all the more striking because more often than not there is nothing in the context to necessitate it. The impression inevitably conveyed is that the conception of the threefold manifestation of the Godhead was embedded deeply in Christian thinking from the start, and provided a ready-to-hand mould in which the ideas of the apostolic writers took shape. If Trinitarian creeds are rare, the Trinitarian pattern which was to dominate all later creeds was already part and parcel of the Christian tradition of doctrine.

4. *The Original Pattern*

The preceding section has provided a survey, not necessarily complete but sufficient for our purposes, of the credal elements embodied in the New Testament. The reader should be wary of drawing hasty or extravagant conclusions. Often the words "creed", "confession" and "formula" have been used to describe the material; but they have been used loosely, for lack of more precise designations. It cannot be too often repeated that, in the proper sense of the terms, no creed, confession or formula of faith can be discovered in the New Testament, with the possible exception of such curt slogans as *Kurios Iēsous*. What is manifest on every page is a common body of doctrine, definite in outline and regarded by everyone as the possession of no

[1] Cf., e.g., *Lk.* 24, 49; *Rom.* 1, 1–4; 5, 1–5; 14, 17 f; 15, 16 and 30; 1 *Cor.* 2, 10–16; 6, 13 ff.; 12, 3; 2 *Cor.* 3, 3; *Eph.* 1, 3; 1, 11–13; 1, 17; 2, 18–22; 3, 3–7; 3, 14–17; 4, 4–6; 4, 30–32; 5, 18–20; *Phil.* 3, 3; *Col.* 1, 6–8; 2 *Thess.* 2, 13–15; *Tit.* 3, 4–6; 1 *Pet.* 4, 14; *Jud.* 20 f. The *comma Johanneum* (1 *Jn.* 5, 7 f. in the A.V.) is not admissible as evidence, being a 4th cent. Spanish interpolation.

individual but of the Church as a whole. At the New Testament stage this corpus of teaching was beginning to crystallize into more or less conventional patterns and forms, and sometimes set types of verbal expression were becoming current. Generally, though the underlying structure was hardening, the language still remained fairly fluid.

In our account we have given prominence to the fact that the specimens of the kerygma which are discernible can be classified according as their ground-plan consists of one, two or three members. A view which was once widespread, and which still finds adherents to-day, is that fragmentary creeds such as these are really extracts from or reminiscences of a full-dress apostolic creed constructed on the Trinitarian basis universally favoured by later ages. We have already pointed out how difficult it is to sustain such a thesis. There is no allusion anywhere to a primitive formula of the kind supposed, and no trustworthy evidence that one ever existed: the hypothesis is the result of an anachronistic reading-back of subsequent practice into the life of the early Church. From what we know of ecclesiastical conditions in that age, it is hard to conceive of one being developed. Our conclusion must be that one-membered, two-membered and three-membered confessions flourished side by side in the apostolic Church as parallel and mutually independent formulations of the one kerygma; and this is a datum of prime importance. It is worth noting that there is abundant confirmation of it in the documents of the second century. As we shall see when we come to examine them, they too witness to the contemporaneous use, for different purposes, of all three types of confession.

A rather different kind of misapprehension has held the field in recent years. It will have been noticed that the confessions which crop up most frequently in the New Testament are the single-clause Christological ones. On the basis of this it has been argued that single-clause creeds represent the authentic faith of the primitive Church, and that two-clause and three-clause confessions were the result of the progressive enlargement both of the Church's theological conceptions and of its propagandist requirements. No doubt the three types existed side by side at the period of the composition of the New Testament writings, but at the earliest stage of all the simple statement that Jesus was Lord (or something like it) expressed the beliefs of Christians in epitome. Both R. Seeberg,[1] for example, and J. Haussleiter[2] advocated theories of this sort. A bare Christological affirmation, they contended, constituted the Judaeo-Christian nucleus, while a confession of several articles was gradually developed to meet the needs of Gentile converts. O. Cullmann has recently presented the thesis in a slightly different, more precise form, and has tried[3] to show that the bipartite formulae took their origin in the Church's struggle with paganism. At first, when those entering its ranks were all converted Jews, a short Christological creed was all that was necessary. But when it became a question of introducing pagans to Christianity, it seemed desirable, before coming to faith in Christ, to make sure that they were sound on the Judaeo-Christian belief in God the Father, and for this purpose a confession based upon the Jewish *Shema*[4] was devised. All the bipartite formulae in the New Testament, Cullmann has declared, appear in contexts where paganism is being consciously opposed. Tripartite confessions in their turn developed out of bipartite because of the association of the Holy Spirit with baptism. At the primary stage, he has suggested, an explicit mention of baptism (cf. *Eph.* 4, 4) was added to the two-clause creed: then for ONE BAPTISM was substituted, as more suitable for mention in the creed alongside the Father and the Lord Jesus Christ, the gift believed to be bestowed in baptism, viz. the Holy Spirit.

This picture of the evolution of credal formulae has, on the surface at any rate, a certain attractive plausibility. It is indisputable that, so far as explicitly formulated credal confessions are concerned, those of the single-clause, Christological pattern seem to have been far and away the most popular in the apostolic age. Binitarian ones were apparently much rarer and Trinitarian ones rarer still. But the theory propounded to explain this phenomenon is dangerously misleading. To take one or two relatively small points first, it is just not true that all the

---

[1] Cf. *Lehrbuch der Dogmengeschichte* (4th ed. 1953), I, 217 f.
[2] Cf. *Trinitarischer Glaube und Christusbekenntnis in der alten Kirche*, 1920, 41.
[3] Op. cit. 30 ff.
[4] Composed of *Deut.* 6, 4–9 ("Hear, O Israel, the Lord our God is one Lord"), *Deut.* 11, 13–21 and *Num.* 15, 37–41.

New Testament specimens of binitarian confessions occur in contexts where paganism was envisaged as the enemy, or even where the needs of Gentile Christians were being specifically catered for. I *Cor.* 8, 6 may be represented as conforming to this analysis, but the majority of them cannot. The most important, I *Tim.* 6, 13 f., is almost certainly to be connected with baptism, and there is little to be said for Cullmann's strained attempt to interpret it as referring to a judicial process. In particular, the oft-recurring tag, "God, Who has raised the Lord Jesus from the dead", seems to suggest that the binitarian formulation of the faith was prior to the requirements of the Gentile mission. As for Trinitarian confessions, the proposal to interpret the third article as replacing an original mention of ONE BAPTISM is far-fetched in the extreme and depends upon an ingenious guess. The text cited as evidence, *Eph.* 4, 4, really contains a seven-fold affirmation, and cannot be taken as illustrating how the two-clause formula was expanded by the addition of a mention of baptism. In any case, the Holy Spirit stood for much more in the eyes of Christians of the first two generations than the gift they had received in baptism.

Criticisms such as these can be successfully urged against the details of the hypothesis we are examining. But it is open to attack along a rather broader front. The pages of the New Testament make it abundantly plain, as we have had occasion to observe, that the binitarian and Trinitarian schemas were much more deeply impressed on the mind of primitive Christianity than O. Cullmann and scholars of his outlook have been prepared to admit. The juxtaposition of the Father and the Lord Jesus Christ as parallel realities and the collocation of the Father, the Son and the Holy Spirit had become categories of Christian thinking long before the New Testament documents were written down. To confine our attention for the moment to the former, examples of the binitarian formula are to be found in a great variety of contexts, including many (as the Pauline letters show) designed for a predominantly Jewish-Christian audience. To posit a Gentile-conscious milieu for their emergence is purely gratuitous. In the case of certain of them, indeed, there are strong reasons for supposing that the background against which their two-clause structure developed must have been thoroughly Jewish. We have already commented on the stereotyped character of the liturgical formula "Blessed be the God and Father of our Lord Jesus Christ", and have pointed to the frequency with which the expression "God, Who has raised the Lord Jesus Christ from the dead" recurs. For all its Christian dress, it is easy to descry behind the former the influence of the numerous liturgical blessings, so similar in general pattern, which figured, in St Paul's day as to-day, on almost every page of the Jewish prayer-book. So, too, W. Bousset was probably right in claiming [1] that the latter was a reminiscence, adapted to the historical facts of the Christian revelation, of the solemn description of God as "Who raisest the dead" which formed part of the Shemoneh Esreh, [2] or series of benedictions prescribed for thrice-daily repetition, and which must have rung in the ears of every Jew.

The truth of the matter would seem to be that the scholars whose theories we are criticizing have been mesmerized by the evolutionary axiom that the less complex must always precede the more complex, and that there must be a line of progressive development. Consequently they have assumed that at the first stage there must have been some elementary confession, like "Jesus is Lord" or "Jesus is the Christ". More elaborate confessions must have come later, and reasons for the successive elaborations must be sought in the pressure of external circumstances. What more natural than to find a solution in the Church's relations with Gentile converts and in the intrinsic requirements of the baptismal rite? Yet as an explanation of the origin of two- and three-clause creeds the theory is quite gratuitous. In the first place, whatever may be said of explicit three-clause confessions, there can be no doubt that confessions based on the binitarian pattern were deeply rooted in the earliest phase of Christianity. The Church's beliefs about Jesus only acquired significance in the setting of its belief in God the Father, Whose Son He was and Who had raised Him from the dead. If examples are called for, we need only appeal, as we have already done more than once, to the tag, cited alike by

[1] *Jesus der Herr*, 36 n.
[2] It is probable that these prayers were already in use early in the first century. Cf. I. Elbogen, *Der Jüdische Gottesdienst in seiner geschichtlichen Entwicklung*, Leipzig, 1930, 30.

St Paul and St Peter, "God, Who has raised the Lord Jesus from the dead". In the second place, it did not need conscious opposition to pagan polytheism to induce Christians to set forth their belief in God the Father. The doctrine was central in Judaism, from which the Church had emerged with the conviction that it was the true heir of the faith as well as the promises of Israel. It was central also in the teaching of Jesus; and if St Paul's language is to be taken seriously, the cry *Abba* (="Father") was a quasi-liturgical cliché on the lips of Christians.[1] The belief in the Holy Spirit, too, was clearly part of the doctrinal apparatus of men who realized that they were living in the Messianic age and who felt themselves under His sway. It may be true that often, perhaps usually, the semi-credal confessions which achieved currency in the earlier decades did not give expression to this framework but were content to announce the purely Christological kerygma. It was, after all, natural and inevitable that the initial proclamation of the gospel should emphasize the distinctively Christian, entirely novel and revolutionary element in the divine revelation. But the framework was there. It was always presupposed; and the firmness with which it was apprehended is evidenced by the extraordinary way in which the binitarian and Trinitarian patterns wove themselves into the texture of early Christian thinking. In due course, with the development of catechetical teaching and of more systematic, comprehensive instruction generally, as well as with the evolution of liturgical forms giving fuller expression to the faith, these vital aspects of it came to receive more regular and formal acknowledgement in creeds and semi-credal summaries. But this was not in response to any challenge or prompting from without: it was simply that binitarian and, ultimately, Trinitarian summaries were inevitably, the Christian faith being what it was, more adequate vehicles for conveying its message. The impulse towards their formation came from within, not from without; and at the New Testament stage we can observe the process in full swing, with confessions of all three types co-existing and interacting.

---

[1] Cf. *Rom.* 8, 15; *Gal.* 4, 6. C. Fabricius has an interesting essay on this subject, entitled *Urbekenntnisse der Urchristenheit*, in the *Reinhold Seeberg Festschrift*, Leipzig, 1929, I, 2. ff.

Thus we are brought back by devious routes to our starting-point. The story that the Twelve, meeting in solemn conclave, composed an "Apostles' Creed" is no doubt a pious fiction. But the second-century conviction that the "rule of faith" believed and taught in the Catholic Church had been inherited from the Apostles contains more than a germ of truth. Not only was the content of that rule, in all essentials, foreshadowed by the "pattern of teaching" accepted in the apostolic Church, but its characteristic lineaments and outline found their prototypes in the confessions and credal summaries contained in the New Testament documents.

CHAPTER II

CREEDS AND BAPTISM

1. *The Role of Declaratory Creeds*

WE saw in the last chapter that a number of situations in the life of the apostolic Church lent themselves to the production of semi-formal confessions of faith. Baptism, worship, preaching, catechetical instruction, anti-heretical and anti-pagan polemics, exorcism—all these provided occasions for giving concrete expression, along lines determined by the needs of the moment, to the cardinal articles of Christian belief. From any one, or all, of these, as the liturgy settled down in fixed moulds, stereotyped formularies might be expected in due course to develop. In point of fact they did develop from several of them, as anyone can discover at a glance who surveys the mass of sacramental rites and services which have been handed down in the Church. In this book, however, our concern is not with any and every type of fixed formulary, but with creeds in the technical acceptation of the word, such as the Apostles' Creed. What we want to ascertain is the environment in which declaratory statements of faith like this originated and the motives which prompted Christians to draw them up. And here we are confronted with an all but universally accepted answer. Creeds proper, it is alleged, took their rise in connection with the rite of baptism. "It is indisputable", remarked Hans Lietzmann,[1] "that the root of all creeds is the formula of belief pronounced by the baptizand, or pronounced in his hearing and assented to by him, before his baptism."

This is a subject which calls for rather careful examination. There can be no doubt (the argument of the present chapter should serve to substantiate it) that creeds have, historically speaking, been intimately associated with baptism. On any

---

[1] *Die Anfänge des Glaubensbekenntnisses*, Tübingen, 1921, 226. This short essay formed part of a *Festgabe* presented to A. von Harnack.

view, moreover, it must be admitted that there was an extremely close connection between their formulation and the admission of neophytes to the Church. But the precise kind of relationship and the exact character of the connection need to be defined. It is no exaggeration to say that in the past there have been considerable confusion and misunderstanding on these points. The investigation which it is proposed to carry out in this chapter will of necessity be somewhat cursory. But it should assist in throwing light both on the emergence of credal formulae in the Church and on the ways in which they have been employed in the baptismal liturgy.

Perhaps it will make a useful starting-point if we set down, in all its crudity, the popular theory of the relation between creeds and baptism. In their present form creeds are declaratory, that is to say, they are short statements, couched in the first person, asserting belief in a select group of facts and doctrines regarded as vitally important. Declaratory creeds of this sort have for centuries played a prominent role in baptism. In the Roman ritual prior to 1969,[1] for example, after the ceremonies at the church door, the priest led the party to the font and, as he went, recited, along with the sponsors, the Apostles' Creed and the Lord's Prayer. So in the Eastern Churches,[2] after the exsufflation, or exorcism of certain parts of the candidate's body, and after his triple abjuration of Satan and triple declaration of adhesion to Christ, he is bidden to recite the Nicene, i.e. Constantinopolitan, Creed. Some such declaratory profession of faith, it is commonly assumed, must always have formed an element in the service of baptism. In fact, it was precisely the need for a formal affirmation of belief to be rehearsed by the catechumen at baptism which instigated the Church to invent creeds in the first place. Whatever other uses they may have been put to in the course of history, the true and original use of creeds, their primary *raison d'être*, was to serve as solemn affirmations of faith in the context of baptismal initiation.

Broadly speaking, and subject to certain reservations which will be mentioned later, this account is correct enough so far as

---

[1] The revised (1969) rite has no declaratory creed.
[2] Cf., e.g., F. J. Goar, Εὐχολόγιον sive Rituale Graecorum, Lutetiae Parisiorum, 1647, 338.

concerns the use of creeds in the fourth century and the long period subsequent to it. The baptismal liturgies, Eastern and Western, which have come down to us are jungle-like in their complexity: their very variety, too, presents formidable obstacles to anyone who tries to hack his way through them. But the general ground-plan which they exhibit is fairly clear at least as regards the candidate's affirmation of his faith. Two moments, apparently, stand out in the ritual of baptism when he might be expected to make his affirmation. One was the very act of being baptized, at the climax of the whole ceremony. As he stood in the water of the font, he was invited to assent to three successive questions whether he believed in the Father, in the Son and in the Holy Spirit. As he replied "I believe" to each of them, he was plunged in the water, three times in all, and his baptism was complete. In addition to this, however, much earlier in the service or even in the course of the ceremonies preparatory to the baptism itself, there was another occasion when he was expected to affirm his faith. This time it was not a case of assenting to interrogations, but of reciting a declaratory creed. It is this rite which was technically known as the "rendering" of the creed (Lat. *redditio symboli*; Gk. ἀπαγγελία τῆς πίστεως), and which marked the culmination of the catechetical training leading up to the sacrament.[1] At a certain stage in the training (the exact date varied, but it signalized their transition to the superior grade of *competentes* or φωτιζόμενοι) the bishop formally "delivered" the creed (this was the *traditio symboli*) to the more advanced catechumens. It was then their business to learn and assimilate it, so as to be able to reproduce it as their own spiritual possession on the eve of their initiation. The theory was that the creed was a secret formula which could not be written down but must be memorized by the faithful. In many churches there would seem to have been more than one reddition. This was the case in the East[2]; and St Augustine[3] indicates that there was a preliminary reddition on the occasion of the delivery of the Lord's Prayer, i.e.

---

[1] For this rite in the fourth century cf. *Peregrin. Ether*. 46 (Geyer, 97 f.); St Hilary, *Lib. de syn.* 91 (*P.L.* 10, 545); St Augustine, *Confess.* 8, 2, 5 (*P.L.* 32, 751).

[2] Cf. L. Duchesne, *Christian Worship* (Eng. trans. 1931), 332.

[3] *Serm.* 59, 1; 213, 8 (*P.L.* 38, 400; 1064 f.). Cf. L. Eisenhofer, *Handbuch der Katholischen Liturgik*, Freiburg im Breisgau, 1933, II, 249 f.

eight days after the delivery of the creed. But in most rites (the Gallican was an exception) a specially formal reddition was provided for on the day of the baptism itself.

Some impression of how all this actually worked out can be gained from the picture of baptism as practised in Jerusalem in the middle of the fourth century which has survived in St Cyril's *Catechetical Lectures* (delivered either in 348, when he was still a priest, at the instance of his bishop, or possibly[1] after his own consecration as bishop). The preliminary instruction took place, as everywhere in those days, throughout Lent, and at a certain point in the course of it (not directly indicated, but probably at the end of the fifth week) the creed was delivered to the cate-chumens.[2] The remaining two weeks before Holy Week were occupied in expounding it. The baptism itself was administered by night, on Easter Eve, and St Cyril describes[3] how the can-didates were conducted into the forecourt of the baptistery (εἰς τὸν προαύλιον τοῦ βαπτίσματος οἶκον), and there, turning westwards, in four separate acts renounced Satan, his works, his pomp and his worship. Then turning eastwards, towards the region of light, they made their profession of faith, "I believe in the Father, and in the Son, and in the Holy Spirit, and in one baptism of repentance". We may confidently surmise that this represents an abridgement of the more detailed formula which St Cyril had commented on clause by clause, but which he may have felt some compunction about setting down. Their next step was to enter the baptistery proper, where they stripped off their clothes, were anointed with exorcized oil and descended naked into the water-tank. Here they were severally asked whether they believed in the name of the Father and of the Son and of the Holy Spirit, and as they made their "saving con-fession (τὴν σωτήριον ὁμολογίαν)" in reply they were plunged three times in the water. St Cyril's account is confirmed and supplemented by that of the Aquitanian lady Etheria, who about forty years later visited Jerusalem and made a tour of the holy places, noting down liturgical and ecclesiastical practices

---

[1] So J. Mader, *Der hl. Cyrillus von Jerusalem*, Einsiedeln, 1891, 2 f.
[2] *Cat.* 5, 12 (*P.G.* 33, 520 ff.).
[3] For this account see *Cat.* 19, 2–9 and 20, 2–4 (*P.G.* 33, 1068 ff. and 1077 ff.), which St Cyril delivered to the newly baptized in the following Easter week.

with devout curiosity. She reports[1] that the catechumens had the creed delivered to them by the bishop at the beginning of the sixth week of Lent, and "rendered" it (this would be the first, less significant reddition, not the one mentioned by St Cyril) a fortnight later, on Palm Sunday.

The seventh book of the *Apostolical Constitutions* (written towards the close of the fourth century and reproducing Syrian liturgical usage) tells a similar story. No mention is there made of the tradition of the creed, although it is clearly presupposed in the emphasis laid on an exhaustive pre-baptismal instruction in the faith.[2] But it recounts at length the catechumen's renunciation of Satan and declaration of adhesion to Christ, and immediately after that represents him as rehearsing a full-dress declaratory creed. The actual baptism is narrated without any hint of an interrogatory creed, but that there was one seems to be implied in the description[3] of the anointing which followed the declaratory creed as "a preparation for the baptismal confession (προπαρασκευὴν ὁμολογίας βαπτίσματος)". Most of the Eastern rites conformed to this pattern. St John Chrysostom, for example, preaching on 1 *Cor.* 15, 29 about 396 at Antioch, quotes a fragment from what was apparently a declaratory creed uttered before the candidates stepped into the water.[3] A generation or so later John Cassian, upbraiding the heresiarch Nestorius (the date is 430 or 431) with having abandoned the creed he had professed at his baptism, backed his argument with extracts from the declaratory creed used for baptismal purposes at Antioch.[5] The recently recovered *Catechetical Lectures* of Theodore of Mopsuestia (*c.* 350–428) carefully expound the creed, a variant of the Constantinopolitan formula, which, according to the author, was recited "before our baptism".[6] As recited on the day of baptism itself, the customary position of the declaratory creed was immediately after the abjuration of the devil.

At the same time there is abundant evidence, as has already been hinted, that these Eastern rites also prescribed a second affirmation of faith, in the form of the assent given to a triple

[1] *Peregrin. Ether.* 46 (Geyer, 97 f.).
[2] Ch. 39 (pp. 440 ff. in the edition of F. X. Funk, 1905).
[3] Ch. 42 (p. 448 in Funk).   [4] *P.G.* 61, 348.
[5] *Con. Nestor.* 6, 3 (Petschenig I, 327).
[6] Cf. *Hom.* xii, 25–28 (ed. Tonneau and Devreesse in *Studi e Testi* 145, 361 ff.).

interrogation, at the very instant of baptism. A good example occurs in the Syrian *Testamentum Domini* (a post-Nicene rehash of St Hippolytus's *Apostolic Tradition*, probably dating from the fifth century). The directions given here provide for the renunciation of the devil ("I renounce thee, Satan, and all thy worship, thy shows, thy lusts and all thy works") and for the anointing of the candidate. He is then instructed to turn to the East and declare his adhesion to Father, Son and Holy Spirit. Then follows[1] the description of the actual baptism:

Let the baptizands stand naked in the water. A deacon should step down in like manner into the water with the baptizand. Thus when the baptizand has stepped down into the water, the baptizer should place his hand upon him and say, "Dost thou believe in God the Father almighty?" and the baptizand should reply, "I believe". At once let him baptize him for the first time. Then the priest should say, "Dost thou believe also in Christ Jesus the Son of God, Who came from the Father, Who is with the Father from the beginning, Who was born from the Virgin Mary through the Holy Spirit, Who was crucified under Pontius Pilate, died, rose again on the third day reanimated from the dead, ascended into heaven, sits at the right hand of the Father, and will come to judge the living and the dead?" And when he answers, "I believe", let him baptize him a second time. Then he should say, "Dost thou believe also in the Holy Spirit, in the holy Church?" And the man who is being baptized should say, "I believe". Then let him baptize him a third time.

An at first sight perplexing feature about the *Testamentum*, for its date, is the absence of a declaratory creed. Probably it was passed over in silence because of the convention which decreed that such formulae should be regarded as secret. There is evidence that one figured in the Roman liturgy from the fourth century at any rate, and that a prominent place was assigned to it. Rufinus, for example, reports[2] that in the Church of Rome (he was writing at the end of the fourth century) it was customary for those who were about to be baptized to recite the creed in the hearing of the people. The ceremony must have been more than usually impressive, for it struck Rufinus as having been instrumental in preserving the text of the Roman

---

[1] P. 128 f. in the edition of I. E. Rahmani (Mainz, 1899): I have translated his Latin.

[2] *Comm. in symb. apost.* 3 (*C.C.L.* 20, 136).

creed from alteration. St Augustine, too, tells a story which brings out the spectacular, almost dramatic character of the "rendering of the creed" at Rome. Recalling the baptism of the famous convert Victorinus, he reveals that Roman catechumens on the point of being baptized were expected to recite the creed, in a set form of words which they had memorized, from a lofty position (*de loco eminentiore*) in full view of the congregation.[1] So St Leo, in a sharp letter to Palestinian monks whose Christological views he considered to have gone grievously astray, rebukes them[2] for forgetting "the salutary creed and confession which you pronounced in the presence of many witnesses". None of them, unfortunately, lets us into the secret of the precise point in the liturgy at which this impressive scene was enacted. The gap is filled, however, by the extremely interesting discussion of the arrangements for the catechumenate penned by the Roman deacon John about 500.[3] Here it is clearly stated that the recitation of the Apostles' Creed fell outside the actual rite of baptism, before the anointing of the *Effeta*.

Though it seems to have loomed larger at Rome than elsewhere, this solemn rehearsal, or reddition, of the creed before baptism was universally observed in the West. It was treated as the occasion for a special sermon, and a number of such discourses have come down to us. St Augustine testifies to the importance it assumed in Africa. Not that he suggests that it was the only, or even the most prominent, affirmation of faith at baptism. The declaratory recital of the creed, as his references to it make plain, was the concluding stage in the catechumenate, whereas the confession at the moment of baptism was in the form of answers to interrogations. It was the same in other Western churches. For example, the fourth-century treatise *De Sacramentis*, which consists of six short addresses delivered by a bishop (almost certainly St Ambrose himself)[4] to the newly

---

[1] *Confess.* 8, 2 (*P.L.* 32, 751).
[2] *Ep.* 124 *ad monach. Palaest.* (*P.L.* 54, 1067 f.).
[3] *Ep. ad Senarium* 4 (*P.L.* 59, 402).
[4] The view that it consists of notes of addresses of St Ambrose's taken down by a *notarius*, put forward by F. Probst (*Liturgie des vierten Jahrhunderts*, Münster, 1893, 232 ff.), has been widely accepted. Cf. G. Morin in *Jahrbuch für Liturgiewissenschaft* viii, 1928, 86–106, and Dom R. H. Connolly's privately published pamphlet, *The de Sacramentis, a work of Ambrose*, Downside Abbey, 1942. For the text see *P.L.* 16, 417–62.

baptized, and which claims[1] to follow Roman models as far as possible, reproduces the interrogations in detail. According to it, the candidate entered the font and renounced, first, the devil and his works, and then the world and its pleasures.[2] Then the speaker goes on to recall:

> You were questioned, "Dost thou believe in God the Father almighty?" You said, "I believe", and were immersed, that is, were buried. Again you were asked, "Dost thou believe in our Lord Jesus Christ and His cross?" You said, "I believe", and were immersed. Thus you were buried along with Christ; for he who is buried along with Christ rises again with Him. A third time you were asked, "Dost thou believe also in the Holy Spirit?" You said, "I believe", and a third time were immersed, so that your threefold confession wiped out the manifold failings of your earlier life.[3]

The closely related work of St Ambrose, the *De mysteriis*,[4] which seems to be largely dependent on the *De sacramentis*, gives a similar account, mentioning[5] the renunciation of "the devil and his works, the world and its luxury and pleasures" after the candidate has entered the baptistery, and briefly recalling,[6] in language throwing the three separate answers into high relief, his affirmations of belief in the Father, the Son and the Holy Spirit. It is probably this act of faith which St Leo had in mind when he remarked,[7] "at our regeneration . . . we renounce the devil and express our belief in God", and again,[8] "He is not in agreement with God who is out of harmony with the profession he made at his regeneration, and who, unmindful of the divine contract, is found remaining attached to what he renounced while departing from what he said he believed".

A place is given to both types of profession in the Gelasian Sacramentary, which is considered to reflect Roman liturgical practice in the sixth century. Here the renunciation of Satan appears, as we might expect, at an early point in the service, and is carried out with the thrice-repeated cry "I renounce (*abrenuntio*)". Then comes the creed in its declaratory form. As child baptism was by now all but universal, the rubric enjoins it

---

[1] 3, 1.   [2] 1, 2.   [3] 2, 7.
[4] *P.L.* 16, 389–410. The Ambrosian authorship, despite F. Loofs (*Leitfaden der Dogmengeschichte*, 4th ed., Halle, 1906, 470), is securely established.
[5] 2.   [6] 5.
[7] *Serm.* 63, 6 (*P.L.* 54, 357).   [8] *Serm.* 66, 3 (*P.L.* 54, 366).

to be said by the priest with his hand on the children's heads.[1] All this happens outside the actual baptistery, and is followed by a series of prayers and liturgical acts. Then in the baptistery the font is elaborately blessed, and the rubric continues:[2]

> After the blessing of the font you baptize each one of them in order as you ask them these questions (*sub has interrogationes*), "Dost thou believe in God the Father almighty?" *Resp.* "I believe." "Dost thou believe also in Jesus Christ His only Son our Lord, Who was born and suffered?" *Resp.* "I believe." "Dost thou believe also in the Holy Spirit, the holy Church, the remission of sins, the resurrection of the flesh?" *Resp.* "I believe." Then at each turn you plunge him three times in the water (*deinde per singulas vices mergis eum tertio in aqua*).

This has been, of necessity, a rapid and incomplete review of a confusing array of evidence. There is no task in the field of liturgies which deserves higher priority to-day than the sorting out of the baptismal and associated rites, and the elaboration of a constructive theory of their evolution. What has been said, however, should be sufficient to prove that declaratory creeds had an assured position in the baptismal service (understanding this in the widest sense) at any rate from the fourth century. It can even be claimed that their importance becomes progressively enhanced. In the Eastern Churches the questions and answers at the moment of baptism eventually disappeared: all that remained was the triple sprinkling with the words "So and so is baptized in the name", etc. The Constantinopolitan Creed after the abjuration of the devil is the only profession of faith which survives in the service, and its form is of course declaratory. In the West this never happened, though occasional hints crop up that the importance of the questions and answers diminished (e.g. they might sometimes be dispensed with in the case of a sick baptizand who had already recited the declaratory creed),[3] and in the end they were detached from the immersions. Here too, however, the declaratory creed, the recitation of which had in olden days often taken place outside the

---

[1] Cf. H. A. Wilson, *The Gelasian Sacramentary*, Oxford, 1894, 79.
[2] Cf. op. cit. 86.
[3] Cf. the letter of St Fulgentius of Ruspe (first half of sixth century) to Ferrandus (*Ep.* 12, 16: *C.C.L.* 91, 371).

actual service, succeeded in establishing itself securely in the baptismal liturgy itself. Thus far the popular theory whose credentials we are examining may be considered to have justified itself.

The warning was given, however, at the beginning that its vindication, even so far as concerns the period subsequent to the fourth century, would have to be subject to certain reservations. The first of these is that, for the early centuries at any rate, the declaratory creed was not the only nor the most significant profession made at baptism. The "questions on faith (*interrogationes de fide*)" and the answers to them, as we have seen, constituted another. Indeed, forming as they did the kernel of the rite, it is hard to escape the suspicion that the avowal of belief which they enshrined was regarded as the essential one. This is in fact borne out by much of the language used by writers belonging at all events to the earlier section of our period. St Cyril of Jerusalem, for example, uses the words [1] "You confessed the saving confession (ὡμολογήσατε τὴν σωτήριον ὁμολογίαν)" of the declaration of belief made at baptism, and it is the answers to the "questions on faith" that he has in mind. In the *Apostolical Constitutions* [2] the designation "confession of baptism" *par excellence* is applied to them. So, too, the great weight attached by St Basil [3] and other Greek fathers to the triple immersion and the triple interrogatory confession bound up with it suggests that for them this was the confession which stood out. It was the same in the West. St Augustine, for example, inquires, [4] "Who is unaware that it is no true Christian baptism if the evangelical words of which the symbol consists are missing?"; and elsewhere [5] speaks of "the necessary interrogation framed in a few words". In the Gallican ritual, as we have seen, this was the only profession of faith made on the actual day of baptism.

And this leads us to a further point underlining the secondary role of declaratory creeds. They were not really part of the

---

[1] *Cat.* 20, 4 (*P.G.* 33, 1080).
[2] Ch. 7, 42 (Funk, 448).
[3] Cf. *De Sp. sancto* 15, 35 (*P.G.* 32, 132). Also St Greg. Naz., *Or.* 40, 41 (*P.G.* 36, 417), and St Greg. Nyss., *Orat. in bapt. Christi* (Jaeger 9, 229).
[4] *De bapt. con. Don.* 6, 47 (*P.L.* 43, 214).
[5] *Ibid* 1, 13 (*P.L.* 43, 121). Cf. also *De fid. et op.* 9, 14 (*P.L.* 40, 205 f.) and *Ep.* 98, 5 (*P.L.* 33, 361 f.).

baptism itself at all. By right they belonged rather to the cate-chetical preparation preceding the sacrament: their recitation logically formed its concluding stage. This comes out clearly in the ritual of the tradition and reddition of the creed, which in origin have nothing to do with the baptism as such. In most rites the formal reddition of the creed took place some days, or at least some hours, before the baptism. According to Gallican usage there was no further declaratory creed in the baptismal service itself. One appeared, as we saw, in the usage of certain Eastern churches immediately after the renunciation of the devil, but it may be suspected that this is, as it were, a bridge between the rites of the catechumenate and of the baptism. Even so, the group of rites and ceremonies in the Orthodox prayer-book in which the declaratory creed is to-day embedded is clearly demarcated off from the baptismal service and labelled "Prayer for making a Catechumen".[1] It is not without signifi-cance that the declaratory creed, in all the rites of which we have descriptions, was pronounced before the candidate actually entered the baptistery and came to the water. The pro-cess of its amalgamation with the baptismal liturgy proper can be studied most instructively in the Roman usage. In the earlier centuries its *raison d'être* was clearly to provide the culmination of the catechetical preliminaries: its position in the "scrutinies" emphasizes this. Later, with the virtual disappearance of adult baptism, the baptismal rite underwent a drastic alteration, many of the ceremonies properly belonging to the catechumen-ate being squeezed into the service of baptism. It is to this pro-cess of adjustment that we ought to attribute the presence of the declaratory creed in the prominent position it occupies in the Roman service-books after the sixth century.

2. *The Baptismal Interrogations*

So far, in examining the popular belief that declaratory creeds were in origin a direct offshoot of the baptismal liturgy, we have deliberately confined our attention to the fourth cen-tury and the period subsequent to it. It is now time to inquire what light the first three centuries have to throw on our prob-lem. It is all the more urgent to investigate their evidence as to

[1] Cf. F. J. Goar, op. cit. 334.

the use of creeds in view of our discovery that even after the fourth century declaratory creeds were not the only or the most important professions of faith employed at baptism. Our procedure will be to glance first of all at the indications furnished by the New Testament, and then to turn to the writers of the second and third centuries. The distinction between declaratory creeds proper and mere declarations of assent in answer to questions is one which must be borne in mind.

As regards the New Testament stage, there is no doubt that belief was considered the indispensable precondition of baptism from the earliest times. So much is clear from the essence of the rite as constituting admission to the Church. And to be assured of belief a profession of faith of one kind or another must have been demanded. The most circumstantial New Testament narrative illustrating this is that of the baptism of the Ethiopian eunuch in *Acts* 8, 36–8. As the story runs, the eunuch was so affected by St Philip's sermon on the Suffering Servant that he asked, "Look, there is water. What is to prevent me from being baptized?" St Philip's reply, according to the reading of the Western text (which gives a clue to primitive Christian practice even if it is not original), was, "If you believe with all your heart, it is permissible". The eunuch then confessed his faith, "I believe that Jesus Christ is the Son of God", and St Philip straightway baptized him.

Several other passages in *Acts* imply that a declaration of belief was required at baptism. For example, in *Acts* 16, 14 f. Lydia is baptized at Philippi after attending to St Paul's preaching, and she sums up the event in the words, "You judged me to believe in the Lord". Evidently she was understood to have given some token of the instruction imparted by the Apostle. So, too, the panic-stricken gaoler at Philippi was told by St Paul that if he wanted to be saved he must believe in the Lord Jesus: he then had the gospel preached to him and, presumably after assenting in some form to what he had heard, was baptized.[1] There may perhaps be a more explicit allusion to the baptizand's act of declaring his faith in the account of his own baptism put into St Paul's mouth: Ananias, he recalls,[2] had said to him, "And now

[1] *Acts* 16, 30 ff.
[2] *Acts* 22, 16.

why delay? Get up, be baptized, and wash away your sins, calling on His name." In *Acts*, moreover, as in other books of the New Testament, baptism is described as being administered "in the name of the Lord Jesus": according to *Matt.* 28, 19 and *Didache* 7 it was in the threefold name. It has been conjectured that a declaration of belief must have been forthcoming corresponding to this formulary, and the conjecture is abundantly borne out by the Church's practice in regard to the formulary in succeeding generations.

There are suggestions elsewhere in the New Testament of an affirmation of faith made at baptism. 1 *Pet.* 3, 21 is often cited in this connection, but the true meaning [1] of the words συνειδήσεως ἀγαθῆς ἐπερώτημα εἰς θεόν seems to be "the pledge to God of a good conscience". On the other hand, it is highly probable, as was pointed out in the previous chapter, that St Paul's remark,[2] "If you confess Jesus as Lord with your mouth, and believe in your heart that God has raised Him from the dead", should be referred to baptism: if so, we probably have a fragment of the baptismal confession as well. The actual confession made seems to be overtly mentioned in 1 *Tim.* 6, 12 (τὴν καλὴν ὁμολογίαν), as well as in *Hebr.* 4, 14 ("Let us hold fast our confession—κρατῶμεν τῆς ὁμολογίας"). Another interesting passage, sometimes overlooked, is *Eph.* 1, 13, "In Whom having believed you were sealed with the Holy Spirit of promise": belief, and so, we are entitled to infer, some verbal manifestation of it, precede baptism.

These and other passages (there is no need to cover the familiar ground in detail) substantiate the hypothesis that a confession of faith was normally expected at baptism at the time when the documents quoted were written. But they do not by any means necessitate—and this is what primarily concerns us—that the confession was in form declaratory. The account of the eunuch's baptism stands alone in suggesting that it was: the other texts can all be interpreted with equal success as postulating a simple assent to questions addressed to the candidate. When we turn to the famous description of baptism given by

[1] Cf. E. G. Selwyn, *The First Epistle of St Peter*, 1946, 205 f.; J. N. D. Kelly, *The Epistles of Peter and of Jude*, 1969, 162 f.
[2] *Rom.* 10, 9.

St Justin [1] about the middle of the second century, our doubts regarding the declaratory form of the confession demanded are reinforced. He remarks:

All those who have been convinced and who believe that our instruction and our message are true, and promise that they are able to live according to them, are admonished to pray and with fasting to beseech God for pardon for their past sins; and we pray and fast with them. Then they are conducted by us to a place where there is water, and are reborn with a form of rebirth such as we have ourselves undergone. For they receive a lustral washing in the water in the name of the Father and Lord God of the universe, and of our Saviour Jesus Christ, and of the Holy Spirit. . . . Over him who has elected to be reborn and has repented of his sins the name of the Father and Lord God of the universe is named, the officiant who leads the candidate to the water using this, and only this, description of God. . . . The name for this lustral bath is "enlightenment", the idea being that those who receive this teaching are enlightened in their understanding. Moreover, it is in the name of Jesus Christ, Who was crucified under Pontius Pilate, and in the name of the Holy Spirit, Who through the prophets announced beforehand the things relating to Jesus, that the man who is enlightened is washed.

Plainly St Justin's church had orderly arrangements for instructing converts in Christian doctrine and for satisfying itself that they had properly absorbed it. But in spite of the frequent attempts which have been made to reconstruct one, there is no unambiguous allusion here to a declaratory baptismal creed. That one may have been uttered is conceivable, but St Justin's language seems much more consistent with a profession of faith in the form of answers to a questionnaire. A revealing light is thrown on the actual procedure by his casual remark that it was the officiant who pronounced the name of God the Father (which presumably implies that he also used the words "Jesus Christ, Who was crucified", etc., and "the Holy Spirit, Who announced", etc.). It is very unlikely that what is here referred to is a formula of baptism ("I baptize thee in the name of", etc.), partly because it cannot be proved and is not at all likely that such formulae were in use at this early date, and more

---

[1] *Apol.* 1, 61 (E.J.G., 70 f.). The book was written at Rome.

decisively because when they did come into use they were much briefer than the ones suggested here would have been. The suspicion is unavoidable that what St Justin had in mind was a series of interrogations about belief similar to those which we observed to be a regular feature in later baptismal rites.

Tertullian is a writer from whom we should naturally expect useful information on the subject of baptismal creeds. He wrote a full-length treatise concerned wholly with baptism (defending it against detractors, it must be admitted, rather than delineating its ritual), and his works abound in illuminating glimpses of baptismal procedure. Yet here, too, popular assumptions about the relationship between declaratory creeds and baptism fail to find confirmation. Kattenbusch observed[1] long ago that the ceremony of "rendering the creed", the chief occasion for a declaratory profession of faith and so conspicuous a feature in later African and Roman usage, had apparently no place in his accounts of the administration of the sacrament. To judge by the hurried recapitulation of what happened given in *De corona*,[2] the liturgy passed straight from the renunciation of the devil in the body of the church to the threefold questions and immersions in the baptistery. Nowhere, indeed, is a declaratory creed unmistakably hinted at. On the other hand, whenever he has occasion to refer to the Christian's affirmation of his faith at baptism, he does so in language which harmonizes much more easily with the assent given to a questionnaire than with a declaratory profession. Several times he employs the metaphor of a soldier of the imperial army taking his military oath.[3] There must have been a close parallelism between the procedures involved, and since the soldier's oath was generally rehearsed in his hearing while he simply indicated his assent, the obvious deduction is that much the same must have happened at baptism. There is a well-known sentence in his treatise *De spectaculis*[4] which points to the same conclusion: "When we entered the water and affirmed the Christian faith in answer to the words prescribed by its law (*in legis suae verba profitemur*), we testified with our lips that we had renounced the devil, his pomp

[1] II, 60–62.
[2] Ch. 3 (*C.C.L.* 2, 1042 f.).
[3] Cf. *Ad mart.* 3; *De cor.* 11 (*C.C.L.* 1, 5; 2, 1056).
[4] Ch. 4 (*C.C.L.* 1, 231).

and his angels." The passage from the *De corona* which has already been referred to is similar in its bearing: "Then we are three times immersed, making a somewhat fuller reply than the Lord laid down in the gospel (*amplius aliquid respondentes quam Dominus in evangelio determinavit*)." It is just possible to extract from this an allusion to a declaratory creed pronounced at the moment of immersion, but the singularity of such a profession at this point in the service makes the interpretation far-fetched. The "reply" is much more naturally understood of the baptizand's responses (probably, as in the later liturgies, a curt "I believe") to the officiant's three interrogations, each one of which was by now fuller and longer than the simple formulae implied in the Lord's command in *Matt.* 28, 19. That this was the procedure familiar to Tertullian is shown by his remark elsewhere,[1] "For we are baptized, not once but thrice, into the three persons severally in answer to their several names". The weight he attached to these responses can be inferred from another statement[2] of his to the effect that "the soul is bound, not by the washing, but by the candidate's answer".

The only conclusion a fair-minded critic can draw[3] is that Tertullian knew nothing of a declaratory creed used in baptism. No one accustomed to working through early baptismal liturgies can doubt that the sole creed he would have acknowledged was the baptizand's assenting "I believe" in answer to the questions put by the baptizer. A remarkable confirmation of this is provided by the *Apostolic Tradition*, written about 215 by St Hippolytus and probably reflecting Roman liturgical practice at the end of the second and the beginning of the third century. Among the most precious features of this document is the detailed account it furnishes of the catechumenate[4] and of the baptismal service.[5] Not only is there no mention in all this of the tradition or reddition of the creed, but there is not the slightest suggestion of a declaratory creed to be found in the genuine

---

[1] *Adv. Prax.* 26 (*C.C.L.* 2, 1198).
[2] *De resurr. mort.* 48 (*C.C.L.* 2, 989).
[3] It was drawn by Kattenbusch in the passage referred to above. The case was well re-argued by F. J. Dölger in *Antike und Christentum* iv, 1933, 138 ff.
[4] Ch. xvi–xx in the edition of G. Dix (London, 1937).
[5] Ch. xxi. Cf., e.g., the discussion by H. Lietzmann in $Z.N.T.W.$ xxvi, 1927, 76 ff. The original Greek of the *Tradition* is lost: it survives in Latin (only fragmentary), Sahidic, Ethiopian and Arabic versions.

text. A creed which is declaratory in form can be read in the Ethiopic and Sahidic versions, but experts are satisfied that it is a late intruder into the text.[1] The only profession of faith in fact required is apparently the one which the candidate makes as he stands naked in the water. It conforms to the pattern which should now be familiar to readers:

> And when he who is to be baptized goes down to the water, let him who baptizes lay hand on him saying thus, "Dost thou believe in God the Father almighty?" And he who is being baptized shall say, "I believe". Let him forthwith baptize him once, having his hand laid upon his head. And after this let him say, "Dost thou believe in Christ Jesus, the Son of God, Who was born by the Holy Spirit from the Virgin Mary, Who was crucified under Pontius Pilate and died, and rose again on the third day living from the dead, and ascended into the heavens, and sat down on the right hand of the Father, and will come to judge the living and the dead?" And when he says, "I believe", let him baptize him the second time. And again let him say, "Dost thou believe in the Holy Spirit, in the holy Church, and the resurrection of the flesh?" And he who is being baptized shall say, "I believe." And so let him baptize him the third time.

The realization that this threefold affirmation of the baptizand constituted, for Tertullian and St Hippolytus, the sole baptismal confession should enable us to read certain important third-century texts with unclouded eyes. St Cyprian, for example, argued forcefully in one of his letters[2] against the Novatianist heretics and their claim to possess a valid baptism:

> But if anyone in opposition should contend that Novatian observes the same law as the Catholic Church observes, baptizes with the same symbol (*eodem symbolo*) as we, acknowledges the same God the Father, the same Christ His Son, the same Holy Spirit, and that he has the power to baptize because he does not seem to deviate from us in the baptismal interrogation—whoever thinks that this contention should be put forward should realize in the first place that the schismatics and we do not have one and the same law of the symbol and one and the same interrogation. For when they say, "Dost thou believe in remission of sins and life eternal through the

---

[1] Cf. R. H. Connolly in *J.T.S.* xxv, 1924, 132 f.
[2] *Ep.* 69, 7 (Hartel I, 756).

holy Church?" the question they put is a lying one, for they do not possess the Church. . . .

The word "symbol" in this passage has often been taken to refer to a declaratory creed. Yet "to baptize with the creed", in the sense of a declaratory creed, is an extraordinary, not to say impossible, manner of speaking: at no point in the history of the baptismal liturgy was the declaratory creed conceived of as playing this role. It should be obvious[1] that in this context "symbol" and "baptismal interrogation" cover much the same ground, "symbol" possibly including the immersions as well as the triple interrogations.[2] In a later letter[3] included in the Cyprianic collection, St Cyprian's correspondent Firmilian relates how a crazed woman had the temerity to baptize people:

Among the other deceptions by which she took multitudes in, she had the face to pretend that she was sanctifying bread by a tremendous invocation and was celebrating the eucharist . . . and baptized many, using the customary and established words of the interrogation (*usitata et legitima verba interrogationis usurpans*), so that she might not appear to deviate at all from the rule of the Church. What then are we to say about her baptizing . . .? Surely Stephen and his supporters must approve it, especially as neither the symbol of the Trinity (*symbolum Trinitatis*) nor the established and churchly interrogation was lacking.

Here again it is inappropriate to translate "symbol of the Trinity" as a declaratory creed: it is more natural to take the words as referring to the baptismal questions,[4] or perhaps to the questions in the setting of the triple immersion.[5] The passage brings out with extreme clarity the overriding role of "the customary and established words of the questioning". If further proof of this were required, one need only cite the pathetic story related by Dionysius of Alexandria in a letter[6] to Pope Xystus about the man who came to him in great distress: he had himself been baptized in heretical circles, and had just witnessed a

---

[1] See the brief but excellent remarks of O. Casel in *Jahrbuch für Liturgiewissenschaft* ii, 1922, 133 f.
[2] Cf. H. J. Carpenter, *J.T.S.* xliii, 1942, 7 f.
[3] *Ep.* 75, 10–11 (Hartel I, 817 f.).
[4] Cf. O. Casel, op. cit.
[5] Cf. H. J. Carpenter, op. cit.
[6] Quoted by Eusebius, *Hist. eccl.* 7, 9 (Schwartz, 276).

Catholic baptism and heard "the questions and answers (τῶν ἐπερωτήσεων καὶ τῶν ἀποκρίσεων)," and it had dawned upon him that there had been nothing like this in his own baptismal initiation. Or one might recall the language [1] of the inquiry presented to the council of Carthage (shortly after 342) [2] as to whether it was permissible to rebaptize a man who had already been down once to the water "and had been questioned in regard to the Trinity (*interrogatum in Trinitatem*) according to the faith of the gospel and the apostles' doctrine".

This completes our study of the use of creeds in connection with baptism in the first three centuries. The conclusion to which the impressive array of evidence points stares us in the face: declaratory creeds of the ordinary type had no place in the baptismal ritual of the period. If in the fourth century and thereafter their role was, as we saw, secondary, prior to the fourth century they had no role at all. An affirmation of faith was, or course, indispensable, but it took the form of the candidate's response to the officiant's interrogations. [3] Occasionally (cf. the eunuch's confession) he may have uttered an explicit declaration of faith: there was no set rule about such things in the Church's infancy. Most frequently he would indicate his assent by a simple "I believe". Not only was this the sole profession of faith used at the service, but there is much that goes to suggest that, in conjunction with the triple immersion, it was regarded as the central and operative feature in the whole baptismal action. Many liturgical experts [4] are inclined to go further and contend that, at this early stage in the evolution of the rite, the baptismal questions and answers occupied the place and performed the function of the later baptismal formula ("I baptize thee in the name", etc., or "So and so is baptized in the name", etc.), the first unambiguous appearance of which is comparatively late. Of declaratory creeds, statements of faith in the first person in a more or less fixed form of words, there is no trace at all in the early liturgies.

---

[1] Mansi, III, 153.
[2] For this date, see E. Schwartz, *Z.N.T.W.* xxx, 1931, 4 n.
[3] So R. H. Connolly in *J.T.S.* xxv, 1924, 131 ff. Others have followed suit, but the case has been most fully argued by H. J. Carpenter in *J.T.S.* xliv, 1943, 1 ff.
[4] Cf., e.g., O. Casel, op. cit. and P. de Puniet, *D.A.C.L.* II, 343. Against them, however, see J. Brinktrine's article in *Ephemerides Liturgicae* xxxvi, 1922, 328 ff.

Startling as these results may appear to adherents of the widespread popular view which is being examined, they enable us to survey the evolution of baptismal rites and the ceremonies leading up to them in a clearer perspective. The double recital of creeds, one declaratory and one interrogatory, has always been something of an anomaly. The explanation is that the declaratory creed was really bound up with the ritual of the tradition and reddition of the creed, and this logically cohered with the catechumenate, not with the baptism itself. The only creed properly belonging to the baptism as such was the interrogatory one. Scholars have often assumed that the ceremonies of the tradition and reddition of the creed were established from the earliest times. But the catechumenate itself, in its evolved and fully articulated form, was a relatively late development. The gulf between the catechetical arrangements presupposed by St Justin, for example, and those envisaged in the rubrics of St Hippolytus's *Apostolic Tradition* is enormous :[1] even so the process was not complete. The tradition and reddition of the creed, as the absence of these ceremonies from the *Apostolic Tradition* shows, belong to the heyday of the fully mature catechumenate, that is, to the second generation of the third century at the earliest. The whole conception of the creed as a secret formula, not to be written down but to be solemnly imparted by the bishop to the catechumens of tried loyalty, also implies that the emergence of the tradition and reddition must have taken place in the third century. It was at this epoch (we shall examine the evidence in Chap. VI) that what has come to be known as the *disciplina arcani*, the treatment of the sacraments and the creed as mysteries to be disclosed only to proven churchmen, flourished. If, therefore, declaratory creeds, as employed at baptism, were logically connected with this phase in the preparation leading up to it, it would be hazardous to look for them in the baptismal liturgy prior to the third century.

3. *The Catechetical Setting of Creeds*

Our object in pursuing the lengthy investigation carried out in the two foregoing sections was to ascertain the part played by

---

[1] This has been carefully studied by B. Capelle in an important article in *Rech. théol. anc. méd.* v, 1933, 131 ff.

baptism in the formulation of so-called baptismal creeds. The discussion was mainly taken up with their use in the liturgy of baptism, but we should now be in a more favourable position to tackle the real issue before us. The striking fact has been brought to light that for the first few centuries at any rate the only creed, if creed is the right designation for it, directly connected with baptism was the baptizand's assent to the minister's questions regarding his beliefs: even when they found their niche within the liturgy, the function of declaratory creeds proper long remained secondary.

What, then, shall we say of the origin of these brief statements of belief couched in the first person? It should be obvious that a wider background must be sought for them than the actual ceremony of baptism itself. Their roots lie not so much in the Christian's sacramental initiation into the Church as in the catechetical training by which it was preceded. Declaratory creeds, conceived in the setting of their original purpose, were compendious summaries of Christian doctrine compiled for the benefit of converts undergoing instruction. The German scholar A. Seeberg was working along sound lines when he stated:[1] "The primitive Christian creeds are simply and solely the recapitulation, in a formula based upon the Trinitarian groundplan, of the basic catechetical verities." Our own English historian C. H. Turner put the same point in different words:[2] "The creed belongs, not indeed to the administration of the rite of baptism, but to the preparation for it."

We saw in the first chapter that even at the New Testament stage the Church's central message, the kernel of its doctrinal deposit, was beginning to harden into semi-stereotyped patterns, and that catechetical instruction was one of the fields in which this process was earliest in getting under way. The process was in full swing in the second century, and in the next chapter we shall be passing in review some of the forms in which the "rule of faith" or "canon of the truth", as it came to be called, found expression in that period. It is obvious that teachers must always have felt the need for concise summaries, approximating as closely as possible to formulae, and that the

---

[1] *Der Katechismus der Urchristenheit*, Leipzig, 1903, 271.
[2] *The Use of Creeds and Anathemas in the Early Church*, London, 2 ed. 1910, 17.

increasingly elaborate and official character of the Church's arrangements for instruction must have made the need all the more urgent. What is significant is that when we first come across declaratory creeds, their express purpose is to subserve the ends of popular instruction. When the bishop has "handed out" the creed in the later weeks of Lent, he proceeds to comment on it clause by clause, while the catechumens are required to learn it by heart as a convenient synopsis of what they are in duty bound to believe. Similarly they are expected to "give it back" on the eve of their baptism, their ability to recite it being a demonstration that they are now sufficiently grounded in the faith. This original function of creeds, as well as their later role in the service of baptism itself, is well illustrated by the words with which Eusebius of Caesarea prefaced the creed which he produced at the council of Nicaea with a view to his doctrinal rehabilitation:[1] "As we have received from the bishops before us, both in our catechetical training and when we received the baptismal bath . . . so we now believe and bring our faith forward to you."

Declaratory creeds may therefore be regarded as a by-product of the Church's fully developed catechetical system. At the same time, as Eusebius's remark helps to remind us, the traditional bridge joining them to baptism should not be ruthlessly demolished. It would be false as well as misleading to minimize the connection between them: it was in fact extremely intimate. The catechetical instruction of which declaratory creeds were convenient summaries was instruction with a view to baptism. The catechumen was all the time looking forward to the great experience which would set the crown upon all his intensive preparatory effort. So closely did the catechetical instruction dovetail into the ceremony of initiation which was to be its climax that the single word baptism, in an extended sense, could be used to cover them both taken together. Thus St Irenaeus could speak[2] of "the rule of the truth . . . which he received through baptism (διὰ τοῦ βαπτίσματος)". Furthermore, the catechetical preparation was dominated by those features of the

---

[1] Cited by St Athanasius in the appendix to *De decret. Nic. syn.* (for the text, see *P.G.* 20, 1535 ff: also Opitz, *Urk.* 22).
[2] *Adv. haer.* 1, 9, 4 (*P.G.* 7, 545).

impending sacrament which constituted its essence, the three-fold interrogation with the threefold assent, and the threefold immersion. Consequently the instruction deliberately aimed (some illuminating illustrations will be found in St Irenaeus's handbook, the *Epideixis*[1]) at elucidating and expounding the three aspects of the Divine Being in Whose triune name the baptism was to be accomplished, and the catechetical summaries whose formation it prompted were inevitably cast in the Trinitarian mould. Left to themselves or to other influences, cate-chetical summaries might well have evolved along quite different lines. There were powerful tendencies in the early Church towards the production of single-clause or two-clause formulations of the faith; but the impact of the baptismal command, not to mention the intrinsic genius of Christianity, was decisive. Finally and most important, over and above the Trinitarian framework, the verbal content of the new declaratory creeds was in large measure borrowed from the baptismal interrogations. These latter themselves had by the third century become, as Tertullian had occasion to observe,[2] somewhat fuller than the Lord's command might seem to have warranted, and the additional material had been derived from the catechetical stock-in-trade. When declaratory creeds came to be developed, the influence was in the reverse direction. New clauses might be, and were, considered necessary, and other alterations might have to be introduced. But the basis on which they were constructed normally consisted of the ancient baptismal questions linked together as a continuous statement and couched in the first person.

4. *The Name "Symbolum"*

A striking illustration of the close ties binding declaratory creeds, despite their catechetical provenance, to the baptismal liturgy is provided by the name which eventually came to be applied to them, first in the West and later in the East as well. This name was "symbol": *symbolum* in Latin and σύμβολον in Greek. There is a well-known passage of Tertullian[3] which is

---

[1] Cf. especially Ch. 6, 7, 100 (in the edition of J. Armitage Robinson, London, 1920), where he dwells on the "three points" or "articles" of Christianity.
[2] *De cor.* 3 (*C.C.L.* 2, 1042).
[3] *Adv. Marc.* 5, 1 (*C.C.L.* 1, 664).

often quoted as supplying the first allusion to this designation of the creed. In his hectoring way he is challenging the heretic Marcion, who had made a fortune as a shipmaster in the Black Sea, to show what right he had, in view of his rejection of the Old Testament and *Acts*, to accept St Paul as an apostle. "I should like you to inform us," he jeers, "ship-captain from Pontus, with what warrant (*quo symbolo*) you have taken the Apostle Paul on board your vessel?" The word *symbolum* here means no more than the documentary authority for embarking a passenger, but some have suspected that Tertullian's choice of it was suggested by its use as a title of the creed. This is most unlikely,[1] however, for Tertullian cannot have the creed in mind: his appeal is to the Scriptures which Marcion had refused to recognize. Apart from this, the earliest Western instance of this use of *symbolum* is agreed to be the sentence of *Ep.* 69 of St Cyprian which was reproduced in the section before the last, though its significance there may cover more than a mere profession of faith. In the East the customary description of the creed was "the faith ($\dot{\eta}$ $\pi\dot{\iota}\sigma\tau\iota\varsigma$)" or "the teaching ($\tau\dot{o}$ $\mu\dot{a}\theta\eta\mu a$)", and we have to wait for a hundred years after St Cyprian, until the so-called canons of the council of Laodicea,[2] for the appearance of $\tau\dot{o}$ $\sigma\dot{\upsilon}\mu\beta o\lambda o\nu$ in this sense. The seventh of these (their claim to the title they bear is highly doubtful) laid it down that heretics should be required "to learn the symbols of the faith ($\tau\dot{a}$ $\tau\hat{\eta}\varsigma$ $\pi\dot{\iota}\sigma\tau\epsilon\omega\varsigma$ $\sigma\dot{\upsilon}\mu\beta o\lambda a$)" In view of this, and the fact that the designation did not become regular until the fifth century, it seems reasonable to suppose that it originated in the West.

In modern times the most widely accepted interpretation of *symbolum* has been one which can be traced back to Rufinus. In the preface of his exposition of the creed,[3] when telling the familiar story of its joint composition by the Twelve, he observes that in Greek the word *symbolum* can signify either "token (*indicium* or *signum*)" or *collatio*, i.e. a whole towards the making of which several people have made contributions. Though it made

---

[1] Cf. J. Brinktrine, *Theol. Quartalschrift* cii, 1921, 163; H. J. Carpenter, *J.T.S.* xliii, 1942, 3 f.

[2] For text see Mansi II, 563 ff. They probably represent a compilation made by a private individual. Cf. the article by A. Boudinhon in *Comptes rendus du congrès scient. internat. des cathol.*, 1888, II, 420–7 (summarized in Hefele-Leclercq, *Hist. des conciles* I, 992 ff. and *Dict. de théol. cathol.* VIII, 2611 ff.).

[3] Ch. 2 (*C.C.L.* 20, 134 f.).

a great appeal to subsequent writers, the latter explanation can be dismissed out of hand: it depends on faulty philology (the Latin *collatio*=the Greek συμβολή, not σύμβολον), and is obviously inspired by the fanciful tale of the apostolic authorship of the creed. Rufinus dwells at length, however, on his derivation of the word from the idea of a token. The Apostles realized, he says, that there were Jews going about pretending to be apostles of Christ, and it was important to have some token by which the preacher who was armed with the authentic apostolic doctrine might be recognized. The situation was analogous, he says, to one which often arises in civil wars, when the rival partisans might easily make the most disastrous mistakes of identity were it not that the opposing commanders hand out distinguishing emblems, or passwords (*symbola distincta*), to their supporters: thus if there are doubts about anyone, he is asked for his token (*interrogatus symbolum*), and at once betrays whether he is friend or foe. This is the reason too, Rufinus goes on, why the creed is never written down, but is committed to memory and is thus maintained as the secret of apostolic churchmen.

Two important passages of Tertullian have usually been hailed[1] as anticipating Rufinus's line of thought. In his *De praescriptione*[2] he makes a point of the bond uniting the Roman and the African churches, coining the term *contesserare* to describe it. This verb, like the noun *contesseratio* which he improvises in his second passage[3] (here his theme is the unity of the Catholic churches generally), is derived from *tessera*, which in this context stands for the tally or token which guest-friends living far apart might rely upon as a means of recognizing each other.[4] Here the token conceived of as uniting the churches and expressing their mutual relationship is their common apostolic faith, or what he calls "the unique tradition of one and the same mystery (*eiusdem sacramenti una traditio*)". But though the ideas involved are not dissimilar and *tessera* and *symbolum* to a certain extent overlap, Tertullian is not thinking precisely of a creed or creeds: indeed, in the former passage what he has in view is the common faith and practice of the Church in the

---

[1] E.g. Kattenbusch II, 80 n.; Burn, 49.
[2] Ch. 36 (*C.C.L.* 1, 216 f.).
[3] Ch. 20 (*C.C.L.* 1, 202).
[4] For a lively example see Plautus, *Poenulus* V, ii 87 f.

widest sense, including Holy Scripture, the sacraments and martyrdom. Moreover, although Rufinus's theory that *symbolum* originally meant sign or token was taken up by a number of other Fathers,[1] it was by no means the only or the most widely favoured exegesis. We have already noticed the popularity of the rather wild guess that it was selected as being equivalent to *collatio*, or a joint composition. St Augustine lent the weight of his authority to another, much more plausible explanation. The creed is called a symbol, he suggested,[2] on the analogy of the pacts or agreements which businessmen enter into with one another. *Symbolum*, it should be noticed, was an ancient Latin borrowing, and in secular usage had meanings ranging from a signet-ring[3] or the impress of a seal[4] to a legal bond or warrant.[5] That the last mentioned was well to the fore in Christian times is proved by its occurrence in Tertullian.[6] St Augustine's derivation of the title of the creed thus harmonized with current linguistic usage, and it did not stand alone: it had the support of a whole school of writers both before and after his day.[7]

Baffled perhaps by the variety of explanations sponsored by the Fathers, modern students have sometimes sought a solution in an entirely different field. It has been proposed[8] to derive the Christian application of *symbolum* to the Church's creeds from the practice of the mystery religions. Stereotyped formulae, disclosed only to members of the cult, were often employed in these at the initiation ceremonies and as tokens by which the devotees might identify each other; and there are solid grounds[9] for holding that they were technically known as

---

[1] Cf., e.g., St. Aug., *Serm.* 214 (*P.L.* 38, 1072); St Maximus of Turin, *Hom.* 83 (*P.L.* 57, 433).

[2] Cf. *Serm.* 212 (*P.L.* 38, 1058) and *Serm.* 214 (*P.L.* 38, 1072). In the latter the ideas of pact and password are combined. The passages are discussed by B. Busch in *Ephemerides Liturgicae* lii, 1938, 440 f.

[3] Pliny, *Hist. nat.* 33, 1, 4.

[4] Plautus, *Pseudolus* I, i, 53; II, ii, 55; etc.

[5] Cato (*ap.* Front., *Epp. ad Anton. imp.* i, 2).

[6] Cf. *symbolum mortis* in *De paenit.* 6 (*C.C.L.* 1, 331).

[7] Cf. Nicetas Rem., *Explan. symb.* 13 (*P.L.* 52, 873); St Peter Chrys., *Serm.* 57, 58, 59 (*P.L.* 52, 360 ff.); *Explan. symb. ad init.* 13 (*P.L.* 17, 1155); St Fulgentius Rusp., *C. Fab.* 36, 1 f. (*C.C.L.* 91A, 854 f.); Theodore Mops., *Hom.* xii, 27; etc.

[8] Cf., e.g., F. Nitzsch's article in *Zeitschrift für Theologie und Kirche* iii, 1893, 332–41.

[9] Cf. A. Dieterich, *Eine Mithrasliturgie*, Leipzig and Berlin, 1923, 64 n.

symbols (σύμβολα). Plutarch, for instance, has a sentence[1] referring to "the mystic symbols of the Dionysiac orgies which we who are participants share with one another". St Clement of Alexandria, ridiculing the Attis cult, reproduces[2] some of its sacred formulae and calls them symbols. That the word was familiar, in this sense of cult slogans, to Latin-speaking authors is shown by Firmicus Maternus's remark,[3] at the opening of a discussion of such tags :

> I should like now to give an account of the signs, or symbols (*quibus . . . signis vel quibus symbolis*), by means of which the wretched rabble identify one another in the midst of their superstitious ceremonies. For they have their special signs, their special answers, which have been imparted to them at their sacrilegious gatherings by the devil's instruction.

So, too, Arnobius applies[4] precisely the same term *symbola* to the crude formulae which the initiates were expected to recite in the rites of Eleusis. There is obviously a certain parallelism here with Christian creeds, and it is not surprising, particularly when we remember the extent to which the Church's teachers were prepared to exploit the terminology of the mystery cults, that some scholars should have inferred that *symbolum* was among the words which they appropriated.

Before attempting to arbitrate between the conflicting theories, it may be advisable to glance once again at those key passages in the correspondence of St Cyprian in which the word is first used in connection with the creed. It will be recalled that in *Ep.* 69, 7 he was dealing with the claim of the heretic Novatian to be administering a valid baptism on the plea that "he baptizes with the same symbol as we Catholics, recognizes the same God the Father, the same Christ His Son, the same Holy Spirit, and . . . does not seem to differ from us in the baptismal interrogation", and in reply repudiated the suggestion that the schismatics could possibly have "the same law of the symbol and the same interrogation". Similarly Firmilian,

---

[1] *Consol. ad uxor.* 10 (=611D).
[2] *Protrept.* 2, 15 (Stählin, 13). In 2, 18 (Stählin, 14) and 2, 22 (Stählin, 17) the word stands for cult objects.
[3] *De error. profan. relig.* 18 (Ziegler, 43).
[4] *Adv. nat.* 5, 26 (*C.S.E.L.* 4, 198).

in *Ep.* 75, 10–11, of the Cyprianic corpus, discussing the baptism practised by a crazed woman, admitted that it lacked "neither the symbol of the Trinity nor the established and churchly interrogation". There is general agreement nowadays that in neither of these passages can symbol refer to a declaratory creed, for neither "to baptize with the creed" nor "creed of the Trinity" are natural forms of expression. Almost certainly what the writers had in view were the triple interrogations addressed to the candidate by the minister and his triple assenting answers:[1] possibly they were also thinking of the triple immersion or affusion.[2] This interpretation admirably fits the expressions "baptize with the symbol" and "symbol of the Trinity"; while Tertullian's remark[3] that "a law of baptism (*lex tinguendi*) was laid down and the form was prescribed: 'Go,' He said, 'teach the nations, baptizing them in the name of the Father and of the Son and of the Holy Spirit'," illustrates the use of "law of the symbol". An interesting confirmation is supplied by the ninth canon of the council of Arles (314),[4] which made the following ruling:

With regard to Africans, forasmuch as they practice rebaptism according to their own regulations, it is decided that if anyone comes to the Church out of heresy, they should address to him the symbol questions (*interrogent eum symbolum*). If they perceive that he has been baptized in the Father and the Son and the Holy Spirit, it will only be necessary for a hand to be laid upon him so that he may receive the Holy Spirit. But if on being questioned he does not answer with this Trinity (*non responderit hanc Trinitatem*), he should be baptized.

Here the phrase *interrogent eum symbolum* clearly seems to signify "put to him the baptismal questions". Exactly the same usage of *symbolum* is implied in the passage[5] of St Augustine which has already been mentioned, where he states that "it is no true Christian baptism if the evangelical words of which the symbol consists are missing".

[1] See above, p. 47.
[2] Both Kattenbusch (II, 189) and P. de Puniet (*D.A.C.L.* II, 293) understood the latter passage as referring simply to the immersions.
[3] *De bapt.* 13 (*C.C.L.* 1, 289).
[4] *C.C.L.* 148, 10 f.
[5] *De bapt. con. Don.* 6, 47 (*P.L.* 43, 214).

We may regard it as certain, then, that *symbolum* initially denoted the triple baptismal interrogations: for St Cyprian it may have covered the thrice-repeated dipping in the water as well. What precisely motivated the choice of the word remains a baffling mystery, though of course the answer to our question depends on the connotation it had for those who originally applied it to this purpose. Rufinus's suggestion that it meant a token or emblem is nowadays under a cloud in some quarters,[1] mainly because of the lack of evidence that the creed was ever used as a secret password. Yet it should be pointed out that what Rufinus emphasizes is the creed's role as an instrument for identifying people, and he only introduces the practice of armies in civil wars as an illustration. Similarly the mystery religion hypothesis has come under fire:[2] one would have expected the Greek-speaking churches, it has been said, to have taken the lead in designating the creed a symbol, and it is also curious that the normal Latin term for a cult formula was *signum*. Yet that the mystery devotees employed fixed slogans which they called symbols, that these performed functions strikingly similar to those of the credal questions, that the Church's language referring to baptism was much influenced by the jargon of the mysteries, and that Latin writers like Firmicus Maternus and Arnobius casually allude to cult formulae as symbols remain facts which have to be reckoned with. On the other hand, it has recently been argued[3] with considerable force that the reference lurking in the word is really to the great contract or pact between God and man accomplished in baptism, of which the baptismal questions, assents and immersions could, taken together, be regarded as the seal or token. This account of the matter would harmonize with a number of factors, notably (*a*) the regular use of *symbolum* with the meaning of warrant, contract or seal in Latin secular writers, (*b*) the repeated description of baptism as a pact and the association of *symbolum*, in the sense of the creed, in a whole series of Fathers, with the same idea and (*c*) the close analogy of the action of baptism, involving questions formally put and assents made, to the making of an agreement in proper legal form.

[1] Cf., e.g., H. J. Carpenter, *J.T.S.* xliii, 1942, 11.
[2] Cf. Kattenbusch II, 130 n.; H. J. Carpenter, op. cit. 6.
[3] By H. J. Carpenter, op. cit. 7–11.

Admittedly this last explanation has many attractions: it would be hazardous to rule out the possibility that it contains the key to our problem. Yet there are certain difficulties about it of which account must be taken. It may be doubted, for example, whether in the early centuries, Tertullian [1] apart, current theology consciously conceived of baptism as a covenant. No doubt the external forms of the sacrament were always calculated to suggest the act of making a commercial legal agreement, and the pact conception was eagerly embraced by many writers after the third century; but other ideas occupied the foreground of the stage in the period when symbol was being applied for the first time to the creed. Moreover, if the figure of a covenant was in fact so prominent at that epoch and if it really did inspire the choice of symbol as a term to describe the credal questions and answers, it is surely strange that the fourth- and fifth-century Fathers were so little alive to it. The most extraordinary, and from our point of view significant, thing is how completely in the dark they apparently were about the original import of the word. Again, however neatly the interpretation of symbol as the outward sign of a pact may suit certain contexts, it scarcely makes a satisfactory clue to the meaning of such a vitally important phrase as Firmilian's "symbol of the Trinity". To understand it as equivalent to "the pledge of a bond entered into with the Trinity" involves travelling a long way from the presumed original meaning of the word as a deed or warrant.

Whether or not objections such as these are decisive against a theory with so much to recommend it is a question which must be left to the reader's judgment: it is perhaps over-optimistic to look for a completely water-tight solution to a problem like this. On the other hand, one is tempted to inquire whether a more straightforward, if also more obvious, explanation of the choice of symbol cannot be found by looking to its basic meaning. It should never be forgotten that the primary idea which *symbolum*, in its Latin as well as its Greek form, conveyed was that of a sign, a token, a symbol: it stood for anything by which one was reminded of something else. This was the import which was always to the fore when the word was used, and which was never lost sight of even when its immediate reference was, for example,

---

[1] Cf. his description of baptism as a *fidei pactum* in *De pudic.* 9, 16 (*C.C.L.* 2, 1298).

to a signet-ring or a warrant. And if it was as meaning a sign or
a token that *symbolum* was enlisted as a title for the credal questions and answers, Firmilian's revealing phrase may provide a
pointer to its precise connotation. The questions and answers
were a sign, an expressive and portentous symbol, of the Triune
God in Whose name the baptism was being enacted and with
Whom the Christian catechumen was being united.[1] That the
symbol was a symbol of the Trinity seems to be hinted at by the
language of the canon of Arles which has been quoted; and
there should be no need to emphasize further the way in which
the questions and answers were regularly connected with the
Lord's command to baptize in the threefold Name. It is not impossible (though our theory by no means necessitates it) that the
fact that symbol was already the convenient term for a cult
slogan assisted, if it did not directly provoke, its application to
the formulae which had become the distinctive tokens of
Catholic orthodoxy. However that may be, it must be agreed
that Rufinus may not have been so widely astray as has sometimes been supposed in interpreting symbol as a distinguishing
sign or emblem. By his time, of course, the creed which was most
prominent was declaratory in form, consisting of a continuous
statement and entirely separated from the triple questions and
immersions. We can readily understand how he and other
patristic writers of the same epoch and afterwards were at a loss
to fathom the original bearing of the accepted description of it
as a symbol, and felt at liberty to improvise such explanations
as occurred to them.

But whatever the ultimate reasons for the selection of this
word, there can be no doubt that as used in the third century it
denoted the baptismal questions and answers. Later it became
the regular title of the declaratory creed. How this change came
about, and at what precise date, we cannot now determine with
certainty. The transference, however, was a natural and easy
one, for the kinship between declaratory creeds and the baptismal interrogations was extremely close: it probably coincided
with the introduction of declaratory creeds into the ceremonial

---

[1] So J. Brinktrine (though he thought of the baptismal formula rather than the
questions) in *Theologische Quartalschrift* cii, 1921, 166 f. O. Casel supported the view
sketched above in *Jahrbuch für Liturgiewissenschaft* ii, 1922, 133 f.

preparation for baptism. It was fully established by the middle of the fourth century, as we can infer from the allusions of Rufinus, St Augustine and others to the tradition and reddition of the creed. All this has great intrinsic importance, but it should have a special interest for us, engaged as we have been in exploring the relation of creeds to baptism. The grand discovery to which our lengthy discussion has led is that the classical name for baptismal creeds was itself in origin bound up in the most intimate way with the primitive structure of the baptismal rite.

CHAPTER III

THE MOVEMENT TOWARDS FIXITY

1. *The Creative Period*

THE object of this chapter is to examine the evolution of creeds (using the word in the elastic, non-technical sense adopted in the first chapter) in the period between the close of the first century and the middle of the third. The outside limits of the survey have not been chosen arbitrarily, but are determined by historical considerations. We have already glanced at the Church's credal activity, such as it was, in the apostolic age: for obvious reasons it forms a subject on its own, meriting separate discussion. After the middle of the third century, as has already been suggested, an entirely new situation arose with the introduction of the "handing out" and "giving back" of the creed, and the *disciplina arcani* with which they were connected. These ceremonies not only brought declaratory creeds into the foreground, but had the effect of tending to stabilize their wording. Our period can therefore claim to form a natural unit. That it is also one deserving the closest scrutiny must be manifest to anyone who reflects that these half-dozen generations were, institutionally, among the most creative in the Church's history. The outline plan of Catholicism had already been sketched in the first century, but it was in the second and third that the solid building reared itself. This generalization is as true of creeds and liturgies as it is of other expressions of the Catholic spirit.

As we pick our way through the confusing territory ahead of us, we shall be in danger of getting lost unless we have a clear idea of what we are looking for. The precise date and manner of the emergence of official summaries of faith, the development in particular of baptismal professions and their relation to other credal statements, the degree to which external factors such as the Church's struggle with paganism and heresy conditioned the content of early creeds—these are some of the subjects on which we shall be expected to throw light. They have long been under discussion among students of creeds, and certain conventional views hold the field. All too often, however, they are vitiated by being based on premises which must to-day be considered obsolete, and in consequence it is imperative to go over the ground again in detail. The lessons learned in the previous chapter, for example, involve a radical change in the perspective of credal studies. It is not unlikely that they will encourage, even compel, a complete reorientation of outlook in certain directions.

It would clearly be rash, for instance, to take it for granted nowadays that stereotyped official formulae emerged, even locally, at a relatively early date. With some exceptions the general tendency, among the classic historians of creeds, has been to regard the movement towards fixity as well under way, in individual churches at any rate, in the first half of the second century. The East may have been slower, but Rome, according to men like the German Kattenbusch[1] and the English Burn,[2] could boast of a firmly established, dominant credal form before the epoch of the heretic Marcion, that is, before the 'forties of the second century.[3] An hypothesis like this cannot be dismissed out of hand, but its plausibility largely depended on two tacit assumptions, first, that the "rule of faith" was identical with the creed, and, secondly, that a declaratory creed at all periods featured in the service of baptism. Once the precariousness of these assumptions is grasped, it becomes possible to approach the evidence without preconceived ideas and appraise it for what it is worth, without always suspecting the lurking presence of an official formula. In itself the theory of the sudden codification of the Church's belief, even in so go-ahead a community as that of Rome, shortly after A.D. 100 is improbable, especially in view of the extreme fluidity of the forms it assumed in the preceding decades and the gradualness with which other aspects of the liturgy settled down. Indeed, if the history of the liturgy provides a proper parallel, we should

---

[1] Cf. II, ch. 7.

[2] P. 64 ff.

[3] The sort of evidence adduced was Tertullian's remark (*Adv. Marc.* I, 20: *C.C.L.* 1, 460) that, according to his supporters, Marcion had not so much innovated on the rule of faith as restored it when it had been corrupted.

expect that the formulation of a number of distinctive types of confession, existing side by side in friendly competition and without any hard-and-fast rigidity of wording, would be the natural second stage in the development of creeds.

Another lesson driven home by the results of our previous inquiry is the comparative width and richness of the field which the student of creeds must explore. It was all very well confining his attention to the baptismal liturgy when the creed was assumed to be an embryo coming to birth within its womb and drawing all its substance from that one situation in the Church's life. We have seen, however, that, so far as baptism is concerned, it will be fruitless to look to it as a source of declaratory creeds in this period: attention should rather be devoted to the baptismal interrogations, so far as traces of them survive. The baptismal setting, it is clear, must be expanded so as to include the whole system of training leading up to the sacrament. It was the popular theology of the catechetical schools (perhaps "schools" is too grandiose a name for the instructional arrangements of the second century) which supplied creeds with most of their content. Nor should it be forgotten that there were all sorts of other situations in the Church's life which lent themselves to the proclamation of its faith. We are accordingly justified, when we look for influences bearing on the formation of creeds, in taking account of confessions of whatever kind wherever we come across them. In the second century, as we have already seen was the case in the first, the Eucharist, exorcism and many other formal or informal occasions in the experience of Christians may have made their contribution. In this connection it will be interesting to inquire, in the light of the conclusions of the first chapter, how far one-clause, two-clause and three-clause confessions continued to exist, side by side and in independence of each other, in the second century as they did in the first.

Lastly, there is one more aspect of credal formulae in regard to which it will be advantageous to keep an open mind, the choice of material for inclusion in them. A dogma widely encouraged in the past was that creeds expanded from brief affirmations to much longer, more elaborate ones solely under pressure of the desire to rebut or exclude heresy. Thus the description of God the Father as "maker of heaven and earth" was often thought[1] to betray an anti-Marcionite bias, Marcion having distinguished the God of heaven Whom Jesus revealed from the Demiurge who created the material order. Again, the insistence on the details of Christ's human career has frequently been attributed[2] to anti-Docetic polemic: the Docetists refused to admit the physical reality of His body. One German scholar went so far as to declare that "the baptismal creed of the Roman church was simply the precipitate of the struggle against Marcion".[3] Actually, many of the clauses pointed to as anti-heretical were commonplaces of Christian confessions at a time when the motives alleged were scarcely likely to have been operative. In any case, as we saw in the first chapter, the evolutionary approach to the development of creeds is beset with pitfalls. As we pass the evidence for creeds in the second and third centuries in review, we shall try to assess without prejudice the influence exerted on their content and on the emphasis of their several parts by polemical considerations. It must be obvious, however, that the primary aim of catechetical instruction (to select what we have reason to suppose was the most fruitful field of credal development) was a constructive one: it was to pass on to the inquirer or catechumen the wonderful story of the saving work which God had accomplished for man in His Son. No doubt the anti-heretical note is audible from time to time: it is shrilly emphatic in some of the passages of St Ignatius which will shortly be cited and which are sharply anti-Docetic in tone. Yet we should not rashly assume that it represents the only or the most important function of creeds, taking precedence over their original, and positive, function of setting forth the faith.

2. *The Apostolic Fathers*

The writings of the so-called Apostolic Fathers form the first stratum of our period. So far as creeds are concerned, they reveal a situation closely in line with the one we have already glanced at in the New Testament itself. There is no suggestion,

---

[1] Cf., e.g., J. Haussleiter, *Trinitarischer Glaube und Christusbekenntnis in der alten Kirche*, Gütersloh, 1920, 51.
[2] So J. Haussleiter, loc. cit.
[3] G. Krüger in *Z.N.T.W.* vi, 1905, 72–9. He was reproducing, with additional arguments, the thesis of A. C. McGiffert's *The Apostles' Creed*, 1902.

much less explicit mention, of a formal, official creed anywhere, and the attempts to unearth one have come to grief in exactly the same way as the efforts to discover a genuine Apostles' Creed in the New Testament. On the other hand, there is an abundance of quasi-credal scraps which show that the creed-making impulses of the Christian communities were alive and active. In their ground-plan and content these fragments fore-shadow illuminatingly the course which was to be taken by the later official formularies.

Sometimes these embryonic confessions exhibit an explicitly Trinitarian character. The *Didache*, for example, gives unmis-takable directions for the administration of baptism:[1] "After you have said all these things, baptize in running water in the name of the Father and of the Son and of the Holy Spirit." Two chapters later, laying down regulations about the people en-titled to participate in the Eucharist, the anonymous author describes them as "those who have been baptized in the name of the Lord", which is probably only a compendious way of referring to the longer, triune formula employed at the initiation service. In the liturgies, as we noted in the previous chapter, to baptize in the name of the Father, etc., meant asking the ques-tions "Dost thou believe . . .?" three times and plunging the candidate in the water in three successive immersions. As the *Didache* too envisages a triple sprinkling, an interrogatory creed of this kind (whether confined to bare, unamplified questions about the three Persons, we cannot of course say) is almost cer-tainly presupposed. The author of 1 *Clement* brings out a similar formula when, echoing a verse of St Paul,[2] he inquires of his readers,[3] "Have we not one God, and one Christ, and one Spirit of grace Which has been poured upon us?" The stress on *one—one—one* is prompted by his indignation at the divisive con-tentiousness to which the Corinthians have succumbed, but it is not improbable that he has the interrogatory creed of baptism in mind. His mention of the Spirit, Which was held to be be-stowed in baptism, and his reminder in the next line of their "one calling in Christ", seem to presuppose a baptismal setting and so to bear this out. It is perhaps not far-fetched to overhear

---

[1] Ch. 7 (Bihlmeyer, 5). [3] Ch. 46, 5 (Bihlmeyer, 60).
[2] *Eph.* 4, 4–6.

a hint of the same formula in the solemn, oath-like assurance in ch. 58,[1] "For as God liveth, and the Lord Jesus Christ liveth, and the Holy Spirit", especially as he immediately interjects the comment that this triune God is "the faith and hope of the elect", and as the general context is one admonishing his readers to repose "on the most holy name of His majesty", that is, on the great Name into which they were baptized.

If the background of these triadic confessions is liturgical, the famous injunction in the *Shepherd* of Hermas,[2] "First of all, believe that God is one, Who created and fashioned all things, and made all things come into existence out of non-existence . . .", plainly presents us with a sample of current catechetical teaching. Hermas was familiar with the triad Father, Son and Holy Spirit;[3] and this fact, taken in conjunction with the emphatic "First of all", suggests that the basic pattern of the catechesis of which this is a fragment was Trinitarian. On the other hand, while direct quotations of it are not forthcoming, we can detect unmistakable echoes of the special Christ-kerygma in both St Clement and Hermas. The former's allusion to "one calling in Christ"[4] may hint at this: so may such statements of his as "the creator of all things, through His beloved Son Jesus Christ . . . called us from darkness to light",[5] or "Through the blood of the Lord redemption will be given to all who believe and hope in God",[6] or "Jesus Christ our Lord, by the will of God, gave His blood on our behalf",[7] or again "Of which resurrection He has made the Lord Jesus the first-fruits, raising Him from the dead".[8] Hermas's references to it are more open. The law of God which is given to the whole world, he declares,[9] is "the Son of God preached to the ends of the earth", while Christians are those who have heard the kerygma and have believed in Him. The officers of the Church are entitled "the apostles and teachers of the preaching of the Son of God":[10] it is their business to preach the name of the Son of God, and to bestow baptism as the seal of it.[11]

---

[1] Bihlmeyer, 66.
[2] *Mand.* 1 (*G.C.S.* 48, 23).
[3] Cf. *Sim.* 5, 6, 2–7 (*G.C.S.* 48, 57 f.).
[4] 1 *Cor.* 46 (Bihlmeyer, 60).
[5] Op. cit. 59 (Bihlmeyer, 66).
[6] Op. cit. 12 (Bihlmeyer, 41 f.).
[7] Op. cit. 49 (Bihlmeyer, 62).
[8] Op. cit. 24 (Bihlmeyer, 49).
[9] *Sim.* 8, 3 (*G.C.S.* 48, 69).
[10] *Sim.* 9, 15 (*G.C.S.* 48, 89).
[11] *Sim.* 9, 16 (*G.C.S.* 48, 90).

The letters of St Ignatius have long been recognized as a peculiarly tempting country to the explorer of creeds. The Trinitarian pattern is occasionally observable in them, an example being *Magn.* 13,[1] where he invites his correspondents to walk, in all their actions, "in faith and love, in the Son and the Father and the Spirit, in the beginning and in the end", and, a few lines later, to be in subjection to the bishop and one another "as . . . the apostles to Christ and to the Father and to the Spirit". The very same letter[2] brings to light an informal confession of a recognizable two-membered type: "There is one God, Who revealed Himself through Jesus Christ His Son, Who is His Logos coming forth from silence." Nevertheless his most noteworthy quasi-credal passages are Christological in form and content, and provide some of the most convincing evidence for the separate existence of single-clause confessions. A sample of them is the summary statement in *Ephes.* 18, 2 :[3]

> For our God Jesus Christ
>   was conceived by Mary according to God's plan,
>   of the seed of David and of the Holy Spirit ;
> Who was born and was baptized
>   that by His passion He might cleanse water.

Another comes in *Trall.* 9 :[4]

> Be deaf when anyone speaks to you apart from Jesus Christ,
>   Who was of the stock of David,
>   Who was from Mary,
>   Who was truly born, ate and drank,
>   was truly persecuted under Pontius Pilate,
>   was truly crucified and died
>   in the sight of beings heavenly, earthly and under the earth,
>   Who also was truly raised from the dead, His Father raising Him. . . .

A third is *Smyrn.* 1, 1–2 :[5]

> . . . being fully persuaded as regards our Lord,
>   that He was truly of David's stock after the flesh,

---

[1] Bihlmeyer, 92.
[2] Ch. 8 (Bihlmeyer, 90 f.).
[3] Bihlmeyer, 87.
[4] Bihlmeyer, 95.
[5] Bihlmeyer, 106.

Son of God by the Divine will and power,
begotten truly of the Virgin,
baptized by John
    that He might fulfil all righteousness,
truly nailed in the flesh on our behalf under Pontius Pilate
    and Herod the tetrarch . . .
    that through His resurrection He might set up an ensign . . .
    in one body of His Church.

Researchers of the older school usually worked on the assumption that passages like these were freely paraphrased extracts from the baptismal creed used by St Ignatius. Theodor Zahn,[1] for example, pointed confidently to the expressions "professing faith" or "professing the faith ($\pi i \sigma \tau \iota \nu \ \dot{\epsilon} \pi \alpha \gamma \gamma \epsilon \lambda \lambda \dot{o} \mu$-$\epsilon \nu o \iota$)" and "professing to belong to Christ ($o i \ \dot{\epsilon} \pi \alpha \gamma \gamma \epsilon \lambda \lambda \dot{o} \mu \epsilon \nu o \iota$ $X \rho \iota \sigma \tau o \hat{\nu} \ \epsilon \hat{\iota} \nu \alpha \iota$)" in *Ephes.* 14, 2,[2] and claimed to discern an allusion to the underlying formula. The attempts to reconstruct "the creed of St Ignatius" have been numerous and audacious.[3] They were foredoomed to failure, however, for the martyr bishop himself never so much as breathes a hint of the existence of such a formula. The passage cited by Zahn envisages faith as an attitude, like love, not as a formulated body of teaching, and the three Christologies quoted above are manifestly independent units. What is true is that the outline of the primitive Christological kerygma is visible through the loose folds of St Ignatius's polemical style. The Ephesian text, with its dry-as-dust enumeration of facts, may well represent a cross-section of local catechetical teaching. The other two have a solemn, almost hymn-like character which has made some scholars[4] suspect the Eucharist or some other liturgical situation as their background. It is a distinct possibility, though the heightened style may be merely the by-product of the writer's intense excitement. A unifying feature in all three is their basic identity of theological outlook. They are all built on the same foundation idea of the antithesis between the Lord's humiliation and His exaltation, and exhibit the same scheme—according to the

---

[1] *Das apostolische Symbolum*, 1893, Erlangen-Leipzig, 42 f.
[2] Bihlmeyer, 86.
[3] Cf., e.g., A. Harnack in his *Anhang* to Hahn's *Bibliothek*; R. Seeberg in *Z. für KG*. xl (N.F. iii), 1922, 3.
[4] So, e.g., H. Lietzmann in *Z.N.T.W.* xxii,. 1923, 265.

flesh, according to the Spirit; son of David, Son of God. They stand in the line of tradition which leads back to *Rom.* 1, 3 and *Phil.* 2, 5–11. The second and third are remarkable for the pointedly anti-Docetic twist which the author, conscious of the menace of heretics denying the reality of the Lord's human experiences, has given to them.

Another witness to the lively persistence of the ancient Christ-kerygma is St Polycarp. In his *Epistle to the Philippians*[1] he rails against people who do not confess that Christ has come in the flesh and deny the testimony of the cross (τὸ μαρτύριον τοῦ σταυροῦ), saying that there is no resurrection and no judgment. He summons his correspondents to abandon the vanity of the many and their false teachings (ψευδοδιδασκαλίας), and to return to "the word delivered to us at the beginning (τὸν ἐξ ἀρχῆς ἡμῖν παραδοθέντα λόγον)". Beyond doubt it is the traditional teaching, compact in outline if plastic in verbal expression, that he has in mind. In an earlier chapter[2] of the letter we can catch an echo of it:

> . . . believing on Him
> Who raised our Lord Jesus Christ from the dead,
> and gave Him glory and a throne at His right hand,
> to Whom are subjected all things in heaven and earth,
> Whom every breath of wind serves,
> Who will come as judge of living and dead.

The structure of this confession is bi-membered, and it is interesting to observe that the lengthier member, concerned with the Christology, is subordinated grammatically to the shorter first member. Very likely it is a fragment of the routine teaching handed out to converts in the Smyrnaean church. The fact that it is a cento of tags from 1 *Peter*[3] deserves notice as throwing light on the way in which the body of catechetical tradition was built up.

3. *The Creeds of St Justin*

From the Apostolic Fathers we turn to St Justin Martyr. His first *Apology*, written at Rome 150–155 and addressed to the emperor Antoninus Pius, and his *Dialogue with Trypho the Jew*,

[1] Ch. 7 (Bihlmeyer, 117). [3] 1, 21; 3, 22; 4, 5.
[2] Ch. 2 (Bihlmeyer, 114).

written 155–160 and recalling a debate which took place at Ephesus some years earlier, are precious sources for liturgical practice in the middle of the second century as well as for the apologetic theology of the period. Their value to the historian of creeds is immense. Unlike the Apostolic Fathers, in whose writings we can only catch distant echoes of credal formulae, in St Justin we for the first time come across what can plausibly be taken to be quotations of semi-formal creeds. It is this fact which has created a special problem for students of creeds. They have been much exercised to determine what was the exact relationship between St Justin's formularies and the contemporary creed of the Roman church. So far as we are concerned, we shall find it more convenient to postpone the detailed discussion of this question to subsequent chapters, when we shall have acquired a fuller acquaintance with the so-called Old Roman Creed. Here it will be sufficient to observe that there are marked discrepancies between this (technically designated R) and the formulae which may be supposed to lie behind St Justin's language, and that in any case the hypothesis that Rome possessed a single official creed at this date is highly doubtful.

The majority of confessions found in St Justin exhibit the familiar three-clause ground-plan. It is indeed remarkable how deeply the pattern was imprinted on his mind. A multitude of minor contexts can be collected to illustrate this, such as *Apol.* I, 6, 2 :[1]

> But we revere and worship
> Him (i.e. the true God),
> and the Son, Who came from Him and taught us these things . . .
> and the prophetic Spirit;

or *Apol.* I, 65, 3 :[2]

> To the Father of the universe,
> through the name of His Son,
> and of the Holy Spirit;

or *Apol.* I, 67, 2 :[3]

> The Maker of all things,
> through His Son Jesus Christ, and
> through the Holy Spirit.

[1] E.J.G., 29. [2] E.J.G., 74. [3] E.J.G., 75.

The longest and most elaborate comes in *Apol.* I, 13:[1]

Thus we are not atheists, since we worship
    the creator of this universe . . .
and that we with good reason honour
    Him Who has taught us these things and was born for this
        purpose,
Jesus Christ,
Who was crucified under Pontius Pilate, the governor of Judaea in
    the time of Tiberius Caesar,
having learned that He is the Son of the true God
and holding Him in the second rank,
and the prophetic Spirit third in order, we shall proceed to demon-
    strate.

The setting of the second and third of these extracts is a description of the Eucharist: possibly they are summaries, somewhat
abbreviated, of prayers from the service. The last is obviously a
very free expansion, in the writer's own words, of the creed we
are about to discuss. Its circumstantiality and explanatory tone
are perhaps reminiscent of the lecture-room.

The two passages in St Justin which are of outstanding importance both relate to the service of baptism, and were quoted in
full in the last chapter. They have a striking similarity of wording, and this trait alone inclines one to suspect a more or less
settled liturgical form. The first[2] is quite brief and runs:

For they receive a lustral washing in the water in the name of the
Father and Lord God of the universe, and of our Saviour Jesus
Christ, and of the Holy Spirit. . . .

A few lines later we come to the second passage:[3]

Over him who has elected to be reborn and has repented of his
sins the name of the Father and Lord God of the universe is named,
the officiant who leads the candidate to the water using this, and
only this, description of God. . . . Moreover, it is in the name of
Jesus Christ, Who was crucified under Pontius Pilate, and in the
name of the Holy Spirit, Who through the prophets announced
beforehand the things relating to Jesus, that the man who is enlightened is washed.

The phrasing of the clause about God the Father is identical
in both, and appears again, without any significant change, in

---

[1] E.J.G., 33 f.   [3] *Apol.* I, 61, 10 (E.J.G., 70 f.).
[2] *Apol.* I, 61, 3 (E.J.G., 70).

Apol. I, 46.[1] Almost certainly, therefore, it reproduces an accepted baptismal form. The text of the second and third clauses is more fluid, but their content is broadly clear. There is nothing to show that the Christological section was in any material way fuller than our excerpts indicate. If anything is to be read, as has sometimes been thought, into the phrase "the things relating to Jesus", it must imply that a more or less developed Christology was appended to the clause about the Spirit. It was only to be expected that scholarship would feel justified in attempting to reconstitute what may be called "St Justin's creed". It is necessary, however, to understand clearly what one is about. St Justin himself explains that the formulae (for formulae they were) were uttered by the officiant and not by the candidate for baptism. The repetition of "in the name of" bears this out. As we have suggested, it is most unlikely that the baptismal formula proper ("I baptize thee in the name", etc.) was in use at this period. It would seem, therefore, as we argued in the preceding chapter, that what we have here is not a declaratory creed of the kind that scholars have usually reconstructed, but the baptismal interrogations. In St Justin's church the questions asked by the officiant had assumed a fixed outline and ran as follows:

Dost thou believe in the Father and Lord God of the universe?
Dost thou believe in Jesus Christ our Saviour, Who was crucified under Pontius Pilate?
Dost thou believe in the Holy Spirit, Who spake by the prophets?

Side by side with this strictly Trinitarian confession, St Justin could evidently draw upon a simple Christological kerygma of the type which, as we have seen, had had a continuous history since the preaching of the Apostles and the writings of St Paul. There are many passages in his works which reflect it, notable examples being:

We say that the Word, Who is the first offspring of God,
    was begotten without carnal intercourse,
    Jesus Christ our teacher,
    and that He was crucified,
    and died,
    and rose again,
    and ascended to heaven;[2]

[1] E.J.G., 59.

[2] *Apol.* I, 21, 1 (E.J.G., 40).

We find it proclaimed beforehand in the books of the prophets that
  Jesus our Christ would come to earth,
    be born through the Virgin and be made man . . .
  would be crucified and die,
  and be raised again,
  and ascend into heaven;[1]

But Jesus Christ, Who came in our times,
  was crucified, and
  died,
  rose again,
  has ascended into heaven and has reigned;[2]

He was conceived as a man of the Virgin,
  and was named Jesus,
  and was crucified,
  died,
  and rose again,
  and has ascended to heaven;[3]

For the rest you must prove that He consented to
  be born as a man through the Virgin according to His Father's
    will,
  and to be crucified,
  and to die, and also that after this
  He rose again,
  and ascended to heaven;[4]

For in the name of this very Son of God and first-begotten of all
  creation,
    Who was born through the Virgin,
    and became a passible man,
    and was crucified under Pontius Pilate by your people,
    and died,
    and rose again from the dead,
    and ascended to heaven,
  every demon is exorcized, conquered and subdued;[5]

You would not blaspheme against Him
  Who has come to earth and been born,
  and has suffered,
  and has ascended to heaven,
  and will also come again;[6]

---

[1] *Apol.* I, 31, 7 (E.J.G., 46 f.).
[2] *Apol.* I, 42, 4 (E.J.G., 55).
[3] *Apol.* I, 46, 5 (E.J.G., 59).

[4] *Dial.* 63, 1 (E.J.G., 168).
[5] *Dial.* 85, 2 (E.J.G., 197).
[6] *Dial.* 126, 1 (E.J.G., 246 f.).

Jesus,
Whom also we have recognized as
   Christ the Son of God,
   crucified,
   and risen again,
   and ascended to the heavens,
   Who will come again as judge of all men right
   back to Adam himself.[1]

It can scarcely be doubted that these excerpts have something of a formulary ring about them: they are echoes of the liturgy or teaching of the Church. At the same time it would be a grave error to treat them as belonging to a three-clause creed with a fully expanded Christological section of the type which later obtained the monopoly. There were occasions, such as the rite of exorcism or the eucharistic service, as well as the systematic exposition or preaching of the Christian message, when Christological confessions like these had a special appropriateness. The exorcistic formula cited above, for example, bears every sign of being a fairly close replica of one which was actually used. The shorter form given in *Dial.* 132, 1 is akin to it, although it adds a mention of the Second Coming. It is difficult to resist the conclusion that St Justin knew and, on occasion, had recourse to a developed Christological kerygma which already enjoyed a measure of fixity and which was still quite independent of the Trinitarian confessions.

The works of St Justin thus have considerable importance for the student of creeds. It is pure guesswork, unsupported by anything that he says, to postulate his acquaintance with an official declaratory creed used at Rome or in any other church. On the other hand, he provides the earliest direct evidence we possess for the emergence of relatively fixed credal questions at baptism; and he illustrates the continued existence of one-clause, purely Christological confessions alongside the Trinitarian ones employed at baptism and on other occasions. A fact which deserves notice is the fidelity with which these reproduce the primitive kerygma, without bending it to any appreciable extent to polemical or apologetic needs or colouring it with St Justin's own philosophical theology. It is interesting to observe,

---

[1] *Dial.* 132, 1 (E.J.G., 254).

in connection with the latter of the points just mentioned, that there is a contemporary of St Justin's who can also be claimed as a witness to the Christ-kerygma in the middle of the second century, the apologist Aristides. Some earlier scholars[1] jumped all too hastily to the conclusion, when the Syriac version of his *Apology* was discovered, that it testified to the existence of a full-dress, formal declaratory creed. Even if such optimistic claims must be rejected, it should be clear that ch. 2[2] of the Syriac text contains an illuminating paraphrase of the Church's tradition about Jesus. To attach this to the statements about God the Father in ch. 1 in the attempt to reconstruct a three-membered creed is to misconceive the argument of the *Apology*. The theological discussion in ch. 1 is quite separate, and in ch. 2 Aristides is drawing on traditional Christological teaching which existed in its own right and betrayed many points of resemblance with that of St Justin.

4. *St Irenaeus and his Rule of Faith*

Next in order after St Justin as a witness to the evolution of creeds comes St Irenaeus, the great Christian theologian and apologist of the second half of the second century. It was his constant claim that the Church's faith was everywhere one and the same. In a famous passage[3] he dwelt on the fact that, though it was scattered from one end of the earth to the other, it shared one system of belief derived from the Apostles and their disciples, and that while the languages of mankind were various "the substance of the tradition ($\dot{\eta}$ δύναμις τῆς παραδόσεως)" was identical in all places. His favourite term for designating this was "the canon of the truth", by which he did not mean a single universally accepted creed, or indeed any kind of formula as such, but rather the doctrinal content of the Christian faith as handed down in the Catholic Church.[4] This, he contended, was identical and self-consistent everywhere, in contrast to the variegated teachings of the Gnostic heretics. There are a number

---

[1] Cf. J. Rendel Harris, *Texts and Studies* I, 1891. 24 ff.

[2] Op. cit. 36 f. The corresponding chapter of the Greek version in *Barlaam and Josaphat* is 15 (op. cit. 110).

[3] *Adv. haer.* 1, 10, 1–2 (*P.G.* 7, 549 ff.).

[4] For "the rule of the truth" see D. van den Eynde, *Les normes de l'enseignement chrétien*, Paris, 1933, Pt. II, ch. vii; R. P. C. Hanson, *Tradition in the Early Church*, London, 1962, ch. 3.

of passages in which he alludes to it or even reproduces summaries of it, and we shall now have to examine them. Of the two treatises which are relevant, the *Epideixis*[1] and the *Adversus haereses*, the former is a popular, less controversial work, written as a compendium of Christian teaching for the benefit of converts under instruction, while the latter is of course St Irenaeus's polemical *magnum opus*. Our task will be to detect suggestions of formal or informal creeds and to observe the structure and interrelation of credal summaries.

Quite near the beginning of the *Epideixis*,[2] the author impresses on his reader (the book is addressed to a friend named Marcianus) the importance of faith and what it involves. "First of all," he says, "it bids us bear in mind that we have received baptism for the remission of sins in the name of God the Father, and in the name of Jesus Christ the Son of God, Who was incarnate and died and rose again, and in the Holy Spirit of God." There is another reference to the threefold name in ch. 7, where he explains that "the baptism of our regeneration proceeds through three points, God the Father bestowing upon us regeneration through His Son by the Holy Spirit". Precisely the same emphasis on the "three points", or "articles", of baptism recurs towards the end of the treatise.[3] The clear implication of his language is that he knew a series of baptismal questions which ran, at any rate roughly (there is no need to assume that his transcription of the text was necessarily full or exact):

> Dost thou believe in God the Father?
> Dost thou believe in Jesus Christ, the Son of God,
>> Who was incarnate,
>> and died,
>> and rose again?
> Dost thou believe in the Holy Spirit of God?

For a detailed exposition of the "three points", in a context likewise connected with baptism, we turn to ch. 6, where St Irenaeus writes:

This then is the order of the rule of our faith, and the foundation of the building, and the stability of our conversation: God the

---

[1] Found in an Armenian version in 1904. References will be to the English translation by J. A. Robinson, London, 1920 (S.P.C.K.).
[2] Ch. 3.   [3] Ch. 100.

Father, not made, not material, invisible; one God, the creator of all things: this is the first point of our faith. The second point is this: the Word of God, Son of God, Christ Jesus our Lord, Who was manifested to the prophets according to the form of their prophesying and according to the method of the dispensation of the Father: through Whom (i.e. the Word) all things were made; Who also at the end of the times, to complete and gather up all things, was made man among men, visible and tangible, in order to abolish death and show forth life and produce a community of union between God and man. And the third point is: the Holy Spirit, through Whom the prophets prophesied, and the Fathers learned the things of God, and the righteous were led into the way of righteousness; and Who in the end of the times was poured out in a new way upon mankind in all the earth, renewing man unto God.

Manifestly this is not the baptismal creed: it is rather a kind of short commentary on it. It gives the gist of the pre-baptismal catechetical instruction, and illustrates how it was modelled on the pattern of the baptismal questions.

Both these credal summaries from the *Epideixis* are three-clause Trinitarian confessions. So are the most important embodied in *Adversus haereses*. An example is the famous passage[1] in which St Irenaeus speaks of the orthodox churchman's "fully-orbed faith ($\pi \acute{\iota} \sigma \tau \iota \varsigma$ $\acute{o} \lambda \acute{o} \kappa \lambda \eta \rho o \varsigma$) in one God almighty, from Whom are all things; and his firm belief in the Son of God, Jesus Christ our Lord, through Whom are all things, and in His saving dispensations ($\tau \grave{a} \varsigma$ $o \acute{\iota} \kappa o \nu o \mu \acute{\iota} a \varsigma$ $a \grave{v} \tau o \hat{v}$) by which the Son of God became man; and . . . in the Spirit of God, Who in each generation discloses publicly among men the saving dispensations of the Father and the Son, as the Father wills". Though the second and third sections are very loosely paraphrased, it scarcely needs to be pointed out that this confession is deliberately modelled on the well-known Pauline one in 1 *Cor.* 8, 6. As regards doctrinal content, its kinship is close, for all its terseness, with the creed-commentary in *Epideixis* 6. Both stress the creative work of the Father and His oneness, both teach that the Son is the instrument of creation, and both dwell on the prophetic work of the Spirit down the ages.

The most notable credal passage, however, in St Irenaeus,

---

[1] *Adv. haer.* 4, 33, 7 (*P.G.* 7, 1077).

and the one most frequently cited, is constructed on a different plan. It is the passage to which reference was made at the beginning of this section, and runs as follows:[1]

For the Church, although scattered throughout the whole world as far as the limits of the earth, has received from the Apostles and their disciples, handed down, its faith in one God the Father almighty, Who made the heaven and the earth and the seas and all the things in them; and in one Christ Jesus the Son of God, Who was made flesh for our salvation; and in the Holy Spirit, Who through the prophets proclaimed the saving dispensations, and the coming, and the birth from the Virgin, and the suffering, and the rising again from the dead, and the incarnate taking-up into the heavens of the beloved Christ Jesus our Lord, and His second coming from the heavens in the glory of the Father to sum up all things and to raise up all flesh of all humanity, so that . . . He may make a just judgment among all men, sending into everlasting fire the spiritual powers of evil and the angels who transgressed and fell into rebellion, and the impious . . . among men, but upon the just . . . bestowing life and immortality and securing to them everlasting glory.

The peculiar feature of this is that it seems to be the result of an ingenious conflation of a short, neatly balanced Trinitarian confession with a more detailed and circumstantial Christology. The former, like the passage quoted in the previous paragraph, re-echoes, though more distantly, the Pauline formula of 1 *Cor.* 8, 6. The resemblance does not stop there, and in fact (despite the word-order "Christ Jesus", which recalls *Epideixis* 6) there is a close family resemblance between *Adv. haer.* 1, 10, 1 and *Adv. haer.* 4, 33, 7. The Christology, it is worth noting, does not form part of the second section, as would have been natural at a later epoch, but is linked up with the triadic creed as the subject-matter of the Spirit's prophesying. It has all the air of having once existed as an independent one-clause confession in which the several episodes here represented by nouns ("the coming", etc.) were doubtless expressed by finite verbs.

Alongside of these, however, there are many creeds of the two-article type to be found in St Irenaeus, and our study of his contribution would be incomplete if we did not take notice of them. Some of them are relatively simple tags, such as:[2] "And

---

[1] *Adv. haer.* 1, 10, 1 (*P.G.* 7, 549).
[2] *Adv. haer.* 3, 1, 2: in Latin (*P.G.* 7, 845 f.).

all these evangelists have handed down to us that there is one
God, maker of heaven and earth, announced by the law and the
prophets, and one Christ, the Son of God." Others are marked
by a fuller Christology, the mention of the Son being elaborated
with an extended kerygma. For example, he describes[1] tribes
of barbarians who possess no written Scriptures as having the
Christian tradition written in their hearts and believing

in one God, the maker of heaven and earth and of all the things
that are in them, through Christ Jesus the Son of God, Who because
of His outstanding love towards His creation endured the birth from
the Virgin, uniting in Himself man to God, and suffered under Pontius Pilate, and rose again, and was taken up in splendour, and will
come again in glory, the saviour of those who are saved and the
judge of those who are judged.

To these should be added a striking passage[2] aimed at Docetists
who distinguish the eternal Son of God from the human Jesus,
in which the Christology is loosely prefixed to a minute two-
membered creed reminiscent of 1 *Cor.* 8, 6:

He is Himself Jesus Christ our Lord, Who suffered for us and rose
for us and will again come in the glory of the Father to raise again all
flesh, and to show forth salvation and demonstrate the rule of just
judgment to all who have been made by Him. There is therefore one
God the Father . . . and one Christ Jesus our Lord.

This completes our survey of St Irenaeus. The evidence justifies us in drawing certain conclusions. First, he was familiar with
a short baptismal creed in the form of a threefold interrogation,
although it is impossible now to determine how hard-and-fast
its wording was or how far *Epideixis* 3 reflects its authentic
terms. Secondly, St Irenaeus also knew the traditional Christ-
kerygma, with its recital of the experiences and achievements of
the Lord. It is interesting to study the ways in which he was
prepared to combine it with, or insert it into, dyadic or triadic
confessions. Thirdly, he could further draw on two-article and
three-article summaries of Christian doctrine. Sometimes these

[1] *Adv. haer.* 3, 4, 2: in Latin (*P.G.* 7, 855 f.).
[2] *Adv. haer.* 3, 16, 6: in Latin (*P.G.* 7, 925).

were loose in their phrasing, as in *Epideixis* 6, while at other times their structure was fairly taut and formal, as in the opening words of *Adv. haer.* 1, 10, 1 and the two-article summaries cited above. None of them shows signs, any more than the Christological confessions, of being a creed in the strict sense of the word : they are formularies which have become more or less stereotyped. Fourthly, the impact of the Pauline text 1 *Cor.* 8, 6 deserves notice. Lastly, the influence of anti-heretical motives is, on the whole, surprisingly slight, especially when we consider the polemical nature of St Irenaeus's work. It would be rash to minimize it : the prominence given to the oneness and immateriality of God, to the identity between Jesus and the Messiah prophesied in the Old Testament, and to the reality of the incarnation in *Epideixis* 6, probably betrays the desire to rescue Marcianus from Gnostic fallacies. Such a trait as the emphatic "incarnate taking-up into the heavens" in *Adv. haer.* 1, 10, 1 is also anti-Gnostic in tendency. These are superficial features, however, and can be easily separated from the body of the time-honoured rule of faith. It is noteworthy that the polemical note is entirely absent from the brief baptismal questionnaire.

Perhaps this is the appropriate place to mention certain other formulae belonging to approximately the same period which illustrate St Irenaeus's creeds. Side by side with his two-article confessions, for example, we may set the avowal put into the mouth of St Justin (he suffered in the late 'sixties of the century) in the ancient account of his martyrdom :[1]

> Our worship is given to the God of the Christians, Whom we believe to have been at the beginning the sole maker of these things and the author of the whole world, and to the Son of God, Jesus Christ, Who has also been announced by the prophets as destined to come as a herald of salvation to the race of men and as a teacher of noble doctrine.

Similarly, Lietzmann[2] pointed out that the creed produced by

---

[1] *Acta Iustini* 2, 5. The first half of the above creed reproduces the text of P (Parisinus, 1470, A.D. 890). Most editions give a text which has been harmonized with later creeds. Cf. P. F. de' Cavalieri, *Studi e Testi* 8, 1902, 33 f., and F. C. Burkitt, *J.T.S.* xi, 1909, 66.

[2] *Z.N.T.W.* xxii, 1923, 271.

"the blessed presbyters" (possibly bishops[1]) of Smyrna in opposition to the heretic Noetus presents an exact parallel:[2]

> We also glorify one God,
>> but as we know Him;
> and we accept the Christ,
>> but as we know Him—Son of God,
>>> Who suffered as He suffered,
>>> died as He died,
>>> and rose again the third day,
>>> and is on the Father's right hand,
>>> and will come to judge living and dead.

Even more important is the creed which appears in the Coptic *Epistula Apostolorum*, an anti-Gnostic work probably written somewhere in Asia Minor shortly after the middle of the second century. Its opening chapters, in the Ethiopian version, consist of a discourse claiming to come from the Eleven, and including in it a description of some of the Lord's miracles. The disciples explain that the Five Loaves of the miraculous feeding are a symbol of our Christian belief, that is

> in (the Father *omitted by cod. A*) the ruler of the universe,
> and in Jesus Christ (our Redeemer *omitted by codd. A, C*)
> and in the Holy Spirit (the Paraclete *omitted by codd. A, B, C*)
> and in the holy Church,
> and in the forgiveness of sins.[3]

The impression left by the context, as well as by the whole style of the passage, is that it is a more or less stereotyped form. As it stands, the parallel with the Gospel miracle guarantees its division into five articles. Almost certainly it is a three-clause formulary, modelled on the baptismal interrogations, which has been expanded to five clauses by the tacking on of additional articles at the end.

5. *Tertullian's Creeds*

We must now turn to Tertullian[4] and inquire what light he has to throw on the emergence of credal forms. Students of

---

[1] Cf. C. H. Turner, *J.T.S.* xxiii, 1921, 28 ff.
[2] In St Hippolytus, *Con. Noetum* 1 (Nautin, 235–7).
[3] Ch. 5 (16) Ethiop. (C. Schmidt, *Gespräche Jesu mit seinen Jüngern*, 1919, 32).
[4] By far the fullest and most thorough discussion of Tertullian's credal formulae is to be found in the little-known article *La doble fórmula simbólica en Tertuliano*, by the Spanish Jesuit J. M. Restrepo-Jaramillo in *Gregorianum*, xv, 1934, 3–58.

creeds are united in believing that his evidence is of outstanding value; their divisions begin when the evidence has to be interpreted. We shall find it convenient, as a matter of method, to make the same distinction as we found so useful in regard to St Irenaeus. There are a number of contexts (we studied most of them, from a slightly different point of view, in the last chapter) where Tertullian makes reference to the baptismal questions and answers. He is, in fact, one of our leading authorities for this feature in baptism. At the same time, like St Irenaeus, he is familiar with a "rule of faith (*regula fidei*)" or "rule", and is repeatedly appealing to it. By the expression he means much the same as St Irenaeus means by his "canon of the truth", i.e. the body of teaching transmitted in the Church by Scripture and tradition. If anything, his conception of it is more precisely defined : he distinguishes more clearly the doctrinal content of the rule.[1] For this reason scholars have been led to infer that he is more closely dependent on a fixed creed than St Irenaeus. It will be advisable, as in the previous section, to make a careful separation between Tertullian's baptismal confessions and his allusions to the rule of faith in contexts without any direct bearing on baptism.

First, let us recall the specifically baptismal passages. In one[2] of these he says, "When we enter the water and affirm the Christian faith in answer to the words prescribed by its law." The "law", presumably, is the dominical command to baptize all nations in the threefold name. Elsewhere[3] he speaks of a man descending into the water and "being dipped to the accompaniment of a few words (*inter pauca verba tinctus*)". By these "few words" we have learned to understand the interrogations about belief addressed to him by the officiant. Another well-known passage[4] gives a clue to what they were : "Then we were thrice immersed, making a somewhat fuller reply than the Lord laid down in the gospel." The plain meaning of this is that the minister of the sacrament put three questions to the baptizand in the form, "Dost thou believe in God the Father?"—"Dost thou believe in Jesus Christ His Son?"—"Dost thou believe in the Holy Spirit?", but that these bare references to the three divine Persons were amplified by epithets or additional clauses not provided for

---

[1] Cf. D. van den Eynde, op. cit. 297.
[2] *De spect.* 4 (*C.C.L.* 1, 231).
[3] *De bapt.* 2 (*C.C.L.* 1, 277).
[4] *De cor.* 3 (*C.C.L.* 2, 1042).

by the Lord's command. The problem is to discover what items went to make up this supplementary matter. A tiny ray of light is supplied by another passage [1] from the same book. After speaking of the divine names of the Three Who are at once witnesses of our faith and guarantors of the salvation which we seek, he goes on :

> But after both the attestation of our faith and the promise of salvation have been pledged under the sanction of three witnesses, a mention of the Church is necessarily added ; for where the Three are, that is, the Father and the Son and the Holy Spirit, there the Church is too, which is a body composed of three.

We are not here concerned with the subtleties of Tertullian's theology of the Church, but we are concerned to observe that evidently the Church figured in the baptismal interrogations. It figured also, as we noticed earlier in this chapter, in the credal summary in the *Epistula Apostolorum*: we shall shortly come across it again as an article in the creed of the Dêr Balyzeh Papyrus and as a clause in the baptismal questions known to St Cyprian. Very probably REMISSION OF SINS had a place in Tertullian's questionnaire too. Such at any rate is the suggestion of a passage [2] in which, dealing with the problem of why Jesus Himself did not practise baptism, he inquires derisively what He could have baptized men into, finding reasons for dismissing each of the possible answers ("into the remission of sins?— which he bestowed verbally; into Himself?—Whom He concealed with humility; into the Holy Spirit?—Who had not yet descended from the Father; into the Church?—which the Apostles had not yet erected"). Many scholars would go much further and would wrest out of the words "a somewhat fuller reply" the suggestion of an elaborate formula akin to, if not identical with, the Old Roman Creed. The question of Tertullian's acquaintance with this ancient formula will have to be explored later. Here we must be content with pointing out that Tertullian's own language is quite unsuitable if he has a full-dress creed in mind. "A somewhat fuller reply" surely implies that the creed consisted of questions, and that the core and substance of these were constituted by the words laid down by the Lord, that is, the names of the three Divine Persons. We are

---

[1] *De bapt.* 6 (*C.C.L.* 1, 282).　　　[2] *De bapt.* 11 (*C.C.L.* 1, 286).

entitled to believe that Tertullian's interrogations contained other items than the mere mention of the Church, but what they were we can only guess. The likelihood is, however, that, added all together, they were not so numerous as to throw the simple triadic scheme completely out of balance.

So much for the baptismal passages: it should again be emphasized that these are the only ones where there is an unmistakable baptismal setting. For Tertullian's citation of the rule of faith we have recourse to four principal passages, and these will be given in chronological order. The first is from his *De praescriptione*,[1] written about 200, and runs:

> The rule of faith is . . . that rule by which we believe that there is one, and only one, God, and He the creator of the world, Who by His Word coming down in the beginning brought all things into being out of nothing; and that this Word, called His Son, appeared in manifold wise in the name of God to the patriarchs, made His voice heard always in the prophets, and last of all entered into the Virgin Mary by the spirit and power of God His Father, was made flesh in her womb and was born from her as Jesus Christ, thereafter proclaimed a new law and a new promise of the kingdom of heaven, wrought wondrous deeds, was nailed to the cross and rose again on the third day, was taken up to heaven and sat down at the Father's right hand, and sent in His place the power of the Holy Spirit to guide believers, and will come again in glory to take the saints into the enjoyment of life eternal and the celestial promises, and to condemn the impious to everlasting fire, both parties being raised from the dead and having their flesh restored.

Despite appearances, this is in effect a Trinitarian statement of faith and not a binitarian one, as has been alleged. The wording is extremely free throughout, and this excuses the inclusion of the belief in the Holy Spirit in a subordinate clause inserted into the lengthy Christology.

Our next two passages strike a more formal note. One, from a later chapter in the same treatise,[2] extols the common faith which the Roman church shares with the African:

> She acknowledges one Lord God, creator of the universe, and Christ Jesus, Son of God the creator from the Virgin Mary, and the resurrection of the flesh.

[1] Ch. 13 (*C.C.L.* 1, 197 f.).   [2] Ch. 36 (*C.C.L.* 1, 217).

The source of the other is *De virginibus velandis*[1] (dated 208–211):

> The rule of faith is one everywhere, alone incapable of alteration and reform—the rule which teaches us to believe in one God almighty, creator of the world, and His Son Jesus Christ, born from the Virgin Mary, crucified under Pontius Pilate, raised on the third day from the dead, taken up into heaven, now sitting on the Father's right hand, destined to come to judge the living and the dead through the resurrection of the flesh.

There is no mention of the Holy Spirit here, but it should be noticed that the Spirit figures largely in the following sentences.

The fourth quotation of the rule of faith occurs in *Adversus Praxeam*,[2] written after 213:

> We, on the contrary . . . believe that there is of course one God, but that according to the divine dispensation which we call economy there is also a Son of this one God, His own Word, Who came forth from Him, through Whom all things were made, and without Whom nothing was made. (We believe that) this Son was sent by the Father into the Virgin, and was born from her, man and God, son of man and Son of God, and was given the name Jesus Christ; that He suffered, that He died and was buried, according to the Scriptures, and was raised again by the Father, and was taken up to heaven, and sits at the Father's right hand, and will come again to judge the living and the dead: Who sent forth, as He had promised, the Holy Spirit, the Paraclete, from the Father, the sanctifier of the faith of those who believe in the Father and the Son and the Holy Spirit.

Here again, as in the first passage, we have a masked Trinitarian formula which might easily pass for a binitarian one. Another interesting feature of it is the way it terminates in a brief Trinitarian creed.

The first thing to be noticed about these excerpts from Tertullian's rule of faith is the way in which they mirror his polemical interests. The second and third passages, taken from contexts without any doctrinally controversial flavour, are stark summaries of essential Christian teaching. There is not a turn of phrase in them which is coloured by controversial or apologetic

---

[1] Ch. 1 (*C.C.L.* 2, 1209).   [2] Ch. 2 (*C.C.L.* 2, 1160).

bias. In sharp contrast the first passage abounds in traits which are clearly traceable to Tertullian's animus against and eagerness to refute the various sects attacked in the treatise. The oneness of God, for example, is set in high relief, and the suggestion of a second God is expressly denied; Jesus is identified with the Messiah of ancient prophecy and is declared to have experienced a genuine human birth from Mary's womb; and the resurrection of the flesh is heavily underlined. These were just the issues over which Church and Gnosis drew swords. Similarly the fourth passage, from a book devoted to exposing a heretic who confounded the Persons of the Father and the Son and gave it out that the Father had actually suffered, makes a special point of the separate existence of the two Persons. It was this Jesus Christ, it argues, sent from the Father, Who was born, as both God and man; and it was He Who suffered. The book was a product of Tertullian's Montanist period, and it is to this fact that we doubtless owe the special emphasis on the Spirit in the closing section. On the other hand, all this polemical matter is on the surface, clearly separable from the rule of faith, and has not contributed any lasting element to it.

The big question, however, is whether it can be claimed that the passages bear witness to the existence of a creed in the proper sense of the word. Clearly if there is a creed underlying them, Tertullian cannot have regarded its verbal expression as inviolable. Otherwise he would have felt some compunction about varying the language in which he clothed it to suit his passing purposes. Tertullian, it should be recalled, was a legalist: anything like an official form would have appealed to him. The theory of scholars like Kattenbusch, that he was deterred from writing down the official text by the convention that the creed was a mystery which could be revealed only to the initiated, has little to be said for it. It is improbable that the *disciplina arcani* exercised such an influence at this early date, and Tertullian himself had no hesitation about describing the ceremonies of baptism. It is impossible, therefore, on the basis of his citations of the rule of faith, to argue that Tertullian knew a single authoritative creed, even a local one.

At the same time it is difficult to resist the impression that some kind of formulary or formularies must lie behind these samples of the Church's belief. All four passages are closely similar in content and even language. The wording of the first and fourth is loose, being deliberately adapted to the writer's controversial ends; but when the controversial padding is removed, the natural structure beneath it is a creed-like summary of the faith. The creed-like character of the second and third passages (though the second is a mere fragment) is quite striking: the terse participial phrases of the third, in particular, have a definitely formulary ring. It should be noted that most of them reappear, with very few and slight modifications, in the other contexts. The most plausible solution would seem to be that, while Tertullian was not acquainted with any one official creed, he was drawing on formulae which had attained a fair measure of fixity. Perhaps what he had in mind in *De praescr.* 36 and *De virg. vel.* 1 was the baptismal questionnaire; several features in those passages would harmonize with such an assumption. Perhaps his language reflects more or less stereotyped summaries of belief employed for the purposes of catechetical instruction. In a later chapter there will be an opportunity for discussing this question more fully.

6. *The Growth of Fixed Forms*

From North Africa it is only a short leap, liturgically as well as geographically, to Rome. But before we make it, we should glance at an important creed text which has survived in a seventh-century papyrus hailing from Dêr Balyzeh, in Upper Egypt. It was discovered in 1907 by Flinders Petrie and W. E. Crum, and is now housed in the Bodleian Library at Oxford.[1] It consists of a number of fragments which, when pieced together, are seen to contain an ancient Egyptian prayer-collection. Towards the end a simple creed is included. As it stands it is declaratory in form, and the rubric directs that it be said by someone not specified (the newly baptized person, it has been conjectured). The text, with the abbreviations

[1] Cf. P. de Puniet, *R. Bén.* xxvi, 1909, 34 ff.; Th. Schermann, *Der liturgische Papyrus von Dêr-Balyzeh*, Leipzig, 1910 (*Texte und Untersuchungen*, 36); C. H. Roberts and B. Capelle, *An early Euchologion: the Dêr-Balizeh Papyrus enlarged and re-edited*, Louvain, 1949 (*Bibliothèque du Muséon*, vol. 23).

expanded and a few letters which have fallen out replaced, is as follows :

ὁμολογεῖ τὴν πίστιν λέγων ·	. . . confesses the faith, saying
Πιστεύω εἰς θεὸν πατέρα παντοκράτορα,	I believe in God the Father almighty,
καὶ εἰς τὸν μονογενῆ αὐτοῦ υἱὸν	and in His only-begotten Son
τὸν κύριον ἡμῶν 'Ιησοῦν Χριστόν,	our Lord Jesus Christ,
καὶ εἰς τὸ πνεῦμα τὸ ἅγιον, καὶ εἰς σαρκὸς	and in the Holy Spirit, and in the resur-
ἀνάστασιν ἐν τῇ ἁγίᾳ καθολικῇ ἐκκλησίᾳ.	rection of the flesh in the holy Catholic Church.[1]

An extravagantly early date has sometimes[2] been proposed for the Dêr Balyzeh euchologion, the beginning of the third or even the last decades of the second century being mentioned ; but the great liturgical expert F. E. Brightman was probably right in saying[3] that nothing warrants a date prior to the middle of the fourth century. The creed itself has several Egyptian parallels,[4] and may well be much more ancient than other items. Its position seemed odd when the service was taken to be eucharistic. A declaratory creed at the close of the rite is unexampled, and when a creed was eventually incorporated in the mass it was always the Constantinopolitan creed. It is now clear that the papyrus is a miscellany of prayers, and that the creed (which is preceded by a gap) belongs to a baptismal rite.[5] Whether it originated as a declaratory confession or in the form of questions put to the candidate, cannot now be determined : if we are inclined to take it back to a very early date, the latter becomes the more likely hypothesis.

Having noted this important formula, we are free to turn to Tertullian's Roman contemporary St Hippolytus. His *Apostolic Tradition* is the first document which shows us what appears to be a fixed creed in its integrity. Despite his title of saint, Hippolytus was a dissident bishop, and anti-Pope, at Rome in the first decades of the third century. He was a stickler for ecclesiastical precedent, and his *Tradition* is a summary account of the rites and ordinances of the Church as he knew them. His object in compiling it was "that those who have been rightly instructed may hold fast to that tradition which has continued until now,

---

[1] This reading, first proposed by J. A. Jungmann, *Z. für Kat. Theol.* xlviii, 1924, 465 ff., is preferable to ". . . and in the holy Catholic Church".

[2] Cf. Schermann, op. cit.   [3] *J.T.S.* xii, 1911, 311.

[4] H. Lietzmann, *Die Anfänge des Glaubensbekenntnisses*, 1921, 227.

[5] Cf. C. H. Roberts and B. Capelle, op. cit.

and fully understanding it from our exposition may stand the more firmly therein ".[1] A thorough conservative in matters of Church order, these words suggest that the liturgies he incorporated in his treatise were those in use at Rome in his day and earlier. Since the book was written in the opening years of the pontificate of St Callistus (217–222), or more probably towards the close of that of his predecessor Pope Zephyrinus (*circa* 198–217), we may confidently turn to it for information about Roman liturgical practice at the end of the second and the beginning of the third century.

We have already had occasion to refer to the baptismal creed of the *Tradition* : in citing it here we shall endeavour to give the reader a more exact picture of the facts. The restoration of the true text raises complicated problems, for the Greek original of the treatise is lost : we have to do what we can with a number of translations into Latin, Coptic, Ethiopian and Arabic, and with the revisions of the *Tradition* which appear in the Arabic *Canons of Hippolytus* and the Syrian *Testamentum Domini*. The basic authorities appear to be the Latin of the Verona Fragment (fifth century),[2] *Test. Dom.*[3] and *Can. Hipp.*[4] The sorting out of the conflicting texts has been taken in hand notably by R. H. Connolly,[5] R. Seeberg,[6] B. Capelle,[7] H. Lietzmann,[8] G. Dix,[9] B. Botte,[10] and J. M. Hanssens.[11] Below are printed the Latin of the Verona Fragment (with the first article, missing from the MS, restored from *Test. Dom.*), and a reconstruction of the probable form of the original Greek; the Latin is translated on p. 46, the Greek on p. 114. It will be observed that, with Seeberg, Lietzmann and Botte, we have adopted the reading THROUGH THE HOLY SPIRIT FROM MARY THE VIRGIN. This is supported by Lat. and *Test. Dom.* Copt, gives IN THE H. SP. FROM M., while *Can. Hipp.*, Eth. and Arab. suggest FROM THE H. SP. AND M. THE V. Connolly, followed by Capelle and Dix, preferred this, arguing that it agreed with St Hippolytus's

[1] Ch. i (cf. G. Dix, *The Apostolic Tradition*, London, 1937, 2).
[2] Cf. E. Hauler, *Didascaliae apostolorum frag. lat.*, Leipzig, 1900, 110 f.
[3] Cf. ed. of I. E. Rahmani, Mainz, 1899.
[4] Cf. ed. of W. Riedel, *Die Kirchenrechtsquellen des Pat. Alex.*, Leipzig, 1900, 200 ff.
[5] *J.T.S.* xxv, 1924, 131 ff.
[6] *Z. für KG.* xl, 1922, 6 ff.   [7] *Z.N.T.W.* xxvi, 1927, 76 ff.
[8] *R. Bén.* xxxix, 1927, 35 ff.   [9] Op. cit. lx f. and 36 f.
[10] *La tradition apostolique*, Paris, 1968.   [11] *La liturgie d'Hippolyte*, Rome, 1969.

personal theological usage elsewhere and with the anaphora of the *Ap. Trad.* itself. But (*a*) he was much more likely to set out his own theological ideas in the loosely worded anaphora than in the relatively fixed baptismal questions; (*b*) Lat. and *Test. Dom.* are agreed to be particularly reliable witnesses to this creed. It is more difficult, and also more important, to determine the wording of the third question. The majority of scholars favour the reading adopted below, viz. "in the holy church", with no mention of "resurrection of the flesh". P. Nautin[1] prefers "in the Holy Spirit [which is] in the holy church for the resurrection of the flesh". On the other hand, D. L. Holland,[2] after an exhaustive re-examination of the evidence, has added strength to the view that St Hippolytus's original is most accurately preserved in the Latin.

[Credis in deum patrem omnipotentem?]	Πιστεύεις εἰς θεὸν πατέρα παντοκράτορα;
Credis in Christum Iesum, filium dei,	Πιστεύεις εἰς Χριστὸν Ιησοῦν, τὸν υἱὸν τοῦ θεοῦ,
qui natus est de Spiritu sancto ex Maria virgine, et crucifixus sub Pontio Pilato et mortuus est [et sepultus], et resurrexit die tertia vivus a mortuis et ascendit in caelis et sedit ad dexteram patris, venturus iudicare vivos et mortuos?	τὸν γεννηθέντα διὰ πνεύματος ἁγίου ἐκ Μαρίας τῆς παρθένου, τὸν σταυρωθέντα ἐπὶ Ποντίου Πιλάτου καὶ ἀποθανόντα, καὶ ἀναστάντα τῇ τρίτῃ ἡμέρᾳ ζῶντα ἐκ νεκρῶν, καὶ ἀνελθόντα εἰς τοὺς οὐρανούς, καὶ καθίσαντα ἐκ δεξιῶν τοῦ πατρός, ἐρχόμενον κρῖναι ζῶντας καὶ νεκρούς;
Credis in Spiritu sancto et sanctam ecclesiam et carnis resurrectionem?	Πιστεύεις εἰς τὸ πνεῦμα τὸ ἅγιον ἐν τῇ ἁγίᾳ ἐκκλησίᾳ;

That this was a formal, fixed creed need not be doubted: an interesting echo of it can be overheard in another context of St Hippolytus, where he speaks of "confessing God the Father almighty, and Christ Jesus the Son of God, God Who became man, etc.".[3] The question is whether we are entitled to designate it the official creed of the Roman church. St Hippolytus's regard for tradition and his anxiety that ancient forms should be respected have already been mentioned. They make it certain that the rites he described so minutely reflect actual practice at Rome. But caution is necessary. Formal liturgical prayer was still in its infancy. The eucharistic prayer which St Hippolytus invites his readers to accept is manifestly his own composition

---

[1] See below, p. 153 n.   [2] *Z.N.T.W.* lxi, 1970, 126–44.
[3] Cf. *Con. Noet.* 8 (Nautin, 249).

and designedly gives expression to his anti-Monarchian theology.[1] Elsewhere in the book he concedes that in celebrating the holy mysteries the bishop is not absolutely bound to recite the prayers prescribed as though he had learned them by heart.[2] He admits that it is all to the good if a bishop has the ability to pray "suitably, with a grand and elevated prayer". The most he stipulates is that no one shall be prevented from using set forms if he wants to. In view of this it would be hazardous to assume that the goal of local uniformity had been reached in the matter of baptismal creeds, though they were no doubt more fixed than the eucharist. As Connolly remarked long ago,[3] "at the beginning of the third century the Roman creed was probably not so rigid in its formation but that the personal element may still have had some play". This is, if anything, a conservative estimate: we may well wonder whether, in the light of the evidence, we are not better advised to think of a number of semi-official forms than of a single authoritative Roman creed at this time. But the further discussion of this question must be deferred until we examine the Old Roman Creed itself in the next chapter.

It is interesting to observe that a slightly younger contemporary of St Hippolytus, Origen, writing at Caesarea in the late 'thirties of the third century, hints at what looks like a formal creed,[4] no doubt that of his native Alexandria. Commenting[5] on *St John* 13, 19, he has been pointing out that there are certain articles of faith which are absolutely essential ("the articles which, in being believed, save the man who believes them"), and has been saying that the Christian must believe the whole lot and must not pick and choose. Then, for the sake of clearness, he instances some:

First of all believe that there is one God, Who created and framed all things and brought all things into being out of non-being. We must also believe that Jesus Christ is Lord, and all the true teaching concerning both His godhead and His manhood. And we must

[1] Cf. G. Dix, op. cit., xliv.
[2] Cf. ch. x, 3–5 (in G. Dix's ed.).
[3] *J.T.S.* xxv, 1924, 137.
[4] On Origen's rule of faith, see G. Bardy, *La règle de foi d'Origène*, in *Recherches de science religieuse* ix, 1919, 162–96.
[5] *In ev. Ioann.* 32, 16 (Preuschen, 451 f.).

believe in the Holy Spirit, and that having free-will we are punished
for our misdeeds and rewarded for our good deeds. To take a case, if
a man should appear to believe in Jesus but should not believe that
there is one God of the law and the gospel, Whose glory the heavens
brought into being by Him declare . . . this man would be defective in a most vital article of faith. Or again, if a man should
believe that He Who was crucified under Pontius Pilate . . . (but
should not accept) His birth from the Virgin Mary and the Holy
Spirit . . . he too would be most defective . . .

Similar summaries occur elsewhere[1] in Origen's works, and
there is abundant evidence to show that he attached great importance to the ecclesiastical tradition of doctrine. When these
passages are surveyed, it is impossible to deny that what he had
before his mind was some kind of triadic formula giving expression to the kernel of the faith: the phrases "born of the Virgin
Mary and the Holy Spirit", "crucified under Pontius Pilate",
and the like, are typical. And since the form is Trinitarian, and
it is explicitly said that the articles are indispensable ones, without which a man cannot be a Christian, it may well have been
a formula which was employed at baptism.

We have no means of determining, of course, whether Origen
was thinking of an interrogatory or a declaratory confession.
We do know, however, that towards the middle of the third
century, at any rate in North Africa, the form of the baptismal
questions had become settled and had acquired official recognition. Our information about this is derived from the correspondence between St Cyprian and Firmilian to which reference was made in the preceding chapter. Firmilian, it will be
recalled, was able to speak[2] of an "ecclesiastical rule" of baptism, of an "established and churchly interrogation (*interro-
gatio legitima et ecclesiastica*)", and even of "the customary and
established words of the interrogation (*usitata et legitima verba
interrogationis*)". Nothing warrants us in assuming that these
things were exceptional or out of the way in his eyes. As Firmilian was bishop of Caesarea, it is natural to regard any inferences drawn from his remarks as applying equally to other

---

[1] Cf. *in Matt. comment. ser.* 33 (Klostermann-Benz 2, 61); *con. Cels.* 1, 7 (Koetschau
1, 60); *De princip.* 1, *praef.* (Koetschau, 9–16); *in Ierem. hom.* 5, 13 (Klostermann,
42); *in* 1 *Cor. hom.* 4 (cf. *J.T.S.* ix, 1908, 234).
[2] *Ep.* 75, 10–11 (Hartel I, 818).

churches of Asia Minor. The language of St Cyprian, too, reveals that extraordinary weight was attached to the precise form of the administration of the sacrament, and that Novatianist heretics were showing their cunning by imitating the Catholic practice down to the minutest detail.[1] He gives some indication of what was contained in the questions, mentioning God the Father, Jesus Christ His Son and the Holy Spirit, and going on to quote verbally what appears to be the remainder of the third article—"Dost thou believe . . . in the remission of sins and everlasting life through the holy Church?"

7. *Some Conclusions*

It cannot be claimed that the survey we have just conducted provides satisfactory answers to all our questions. Where the documents are so sparse and their precise bearing often so elusive, complete enlightenment is scarcely to be expected. Nevertheless there are certain concrete gains which can be marked down on the credit side. Now is the appropriate moment for us to draw up an account of them even if it must be at the cost of some repetition.

In the first place, it should be clear that there was no shortage of creeds, in the looser, less exact sense of the word, in the second and third centuries. As in the New Testament period, the Church's faith continued to find expression in semi-formal summaries adapted, in general structure, content and style, to the situations which called them forth. Many of the confessions at which we glanced were Trinitarian in their ground-plan; others were binitarian; still others were one-clause Christological statements. All three types, it would appear, existed independently of each other, and we have seen no reason for supposing that the latter two were really fragments of more fully developed Trinitarian creeds. The Christological group in particular merits attention: it carried on the ancient Christ-kerygma which had played such an important role in apostolic times. The principal items comprised in it were well on the way to becoming stereotyped: the sequence of Christ's birth from the Virgin Mary and the Holy Spirit, His suffering and death under Pontius Pilate, His resurrection on the third day, His session at

[1] *Ep.* 69, 7 (Hartel I, 756).

the Father's right hand and His future coming to judge the living and the dead, recurs with persistent regularity and in language which is more or less fixed. No doubt it had a secure niche in the exorcistic rite, in the anaphora of the Eucharist,[1] and in catechetical instruction. An interesting point is the variety of ways in which these different types of confessions were sometimes combined with each other. In St Irenaeus's *Adv. haer.* 1, 10, 1, for example, we saw how an elaborate Christology could be interwoven with the third article of a three-membered confession[2]; while the same author's *Adv. haer.* 3, 16, 6 and Tertullian's *Adv. Prax.* 2 provide examples of Christological kerygmas prefixed, in the one case to a two-article and in the other case to a three-article confession.

Having established this, however, what are we to say about creeds in the precise acceptation of the word? Here our reply will be calculated to disappoint many. Certainly nothing has come to light to upset the conclusion of the previous chapter that declaratory creeds, stereotyped in form and officially sanctioned by local church authorities, had no currency in the second and third centuries. Still less would there seem to be any warrant for speaking of "the creed of Rome" or "the creed of Antioch", as if each local community possessed a single acknowledged formula of its own. It is inconceivable that if, at any point in our period, such a thing as an official declaratory creed had been in existence in any church of which records have come down to us, it would have escaped without some mention, however indirect. The familiar explanation that reference to it was deliberately avoided for motives of cultic reticence rests on an anachronistic ante-dating of the operation of these motives. Admittedly great stress is laid on orthodox belief by many of the writers we have consulted, and they are all convinced that there is one, universally accepted system of dogma, or rule of faith, in the Catholic Church. But this is never unambiguously connected, even by theologians like St Irenaeus and Tertullian, with any set form of words. Though they frequently cite the rule

---

[1] The best early example is the canon of St Hippolytus's *Apostolic Tradition* (ed. of G. Dix, 7 f.).

[2] For other and later examples illustrating the long persistence of this type of conflation, see H. Lietzmann, *Anfänge des Glaubensbekenntnisses*, Tübingen, 1921, 231 f.

of faith, it is plain that their citations are neither formulae themselves nor presuppose some underlying formula. If their summaries of it have a concrete outline and a distinctive note, that is because they are giving expression to a clearly articulated common body of doctrine, and because there was an inevitable tendency to adopt conventional forms of language. By the beginning of the third century, of course, this tendency was far advanced; but even if some of the summaries current in the Church, especially the briefer ones, approximated to creeds, it is important to be on one's guard against applying this description to them too hastily.

There is one class of summaries, however, with regard to which such caution is not necessary, and these are the baptismal interrogations. Probably the most important lesson we have been taught as a result of our researches is the desirability of treating these apart as a category on their own. Because they were ensconced in the liturgy, these questionnaires easily outstripped creeds of other kinds in the race to acquire verbal fixity and the hallmark of official local recognition. As early as St Justin there was apparently something approaching a settled form for the baptismal questions. Similarly St Irenaeus and Tertullian clearly knew formularies which, while not necessarily sacrosanct in their wording, had an official character and a distinctive outline. By the middle of the third century the process of crystallization had gone a very long way: there were (and had been, we may conjecture, for some time) "customary and established words". The endorsement of the local ecclesiastical authority, it would seem, had been added. The framework of the questions was always and everywhere the Lord's baptismal command, the candidate being asked three several times whether he believed in the Father, the Son and the Holy Spirit. Gradually these bare interrogations were expanded, so that Tertullian could comment on the fact that they were in his day "rather fuller" than Christ had prescribed in the Gospel. The method of enlargement was to insert epithets or clauses descriptive of the three Persons, or to interpolate additional items in the third article. As early as St Justin God was described as the Father and Lord of the universe, Jesus Christ as our Saviour Who was crucified under Pontius Pilate, and the Holy Spirit as the organ of prophecy down the ages. The Christological article was still further enriched in the set of baptismal questions referred to in St Irenaeus's *Epideixis*. Jesus Christ is there designated the Son of God, Who was incarnate, died and rose again. This is particularly interesting as suggesting that the source of the enlargement was often the Christ-kerygma which, as we have seen, originated and existed quite independently of the Trinitarian baptismal confession. Tertullian testifies to a form in which the third article contained a mention of the holy Church and possibly other matters as well. The questionnaire in St Hippolytus's *Tradition* has a long, fully developed Christological section reminiscent, like St Irenaeus's second interrogation, of the separate Christ-kerygma, and includes the resurrection of the flesh as well as the holy Church in the third section.

As regards the choice of material for inclusion in creeds, the surmise we hazarded at the beginning of this chapter would seem to have received some support. It is scarcely a fair statement of the case to assert that creeds, whether regarded as baptismal questions or as looser, more informal summaries, owed their growth from brief to fully developed affirmations exclusively to the insertion of matter designed to rebut heresy. Admittedly writers like St Irenaeus and Tertullian felt at liberty to give a heavy polemical underlining to portions of the rule of faith when they were freely recapitulating it in the course of anti-heretical arguments. Admittedly, too, individual clauses (for example, as we shall later see, the adjective HOLY applied to the Church, and RESURRECTION OF THE FLESH) gave expression to an anti-heretical animus. But to single out this motive and concentrate wholly on it is to ignore the positive aspect of the Church's formulation of its faith. Such doctrines as the oneness and Fatherhood of God, invaluable as they proved to Christian apologists in their battle with Marcion and his followers, had their place in the Church's system of doctrine long before Marcion began disseminating his errors. Again, the recapitulation of the details of the Saviour's career, though it supplied a powerful weapon against the Docetists, had a continuous history ever since the Church's inauguration, and the second-century formulation of it did not materially differ from that current in the Church of the apostolic age. Important as was the part played by the orthodox campaign against Gnosticism in the shaping of credal formularies, their kernel always consisted of those primordial verities which it was the Church's *raison d'être* to proclaim to the world. A more exact account of the matter would be that part of the Catholic reaction to the Gnostic crisis was a renewed and enhanced insistence on the public, apostolically authorized deposit of doctrine which had been handed down in the Church from the beginning as the canon or rule of faith.

Finally, we may ask what factors, if not the desire for concise official formulae which would shut the gate against heretical innovations, were instrumental in bringing about that measure of uniformity and codification which were achieved in our period. A great change was wrought, though we may have appeared reluctant to recognize it, between the New Testament stage and the middle of the third century. Even if locally authorized creeds and formulae were not so early in the field as optimistic scholars have sometimes liked to imagine, we were able to observe a steadily progressing tendency for the baptismal questions to "freeze" (the process was not complete, of course) into rigid forms, and we noticed that the less formal summaries of doctrine comprised under the rule of faith had a more precise, determinate outline and a more settled phraseology at the beginning of the third century than at the end of the first. The answer must be the unsatisfying one that the responsibility cannot be assigned to any single cause. But a more profitable way of dealing with the question is to point to the general, and universally recognized, tendency of the liturgy in this period to assume a fixed shape. Creeds and credal formulae, as E. Norden [1] had the acumen to remark, and as H. Lietzmann [2] was never tired of reiterating, are part and parcel of the liturgy. They share the fortunes of the prayers and services in which they are embedded. We should, of course, beware of ante-dating the era of liturgical fixity. The language of the eucharistic service was still fairly pliable in the middle of the fourth century. [3] None the less, towards the end of the second, at any rate in the

[1] Cf. *Agnostos Theos*, Leipzig and Berlin, 1913, 263 ff.
[2] Cf., e.g., *Die Urform des apostolischen Glaubensbekenntnisses*, Berlin, 1919, 274 (in *Sitzungsberichte der Preuss. Akademie*).
[3] Cf. G. Dix, *The Shape of the Liturgy*, London, 6 ff.

first decades of the third, a bias in favour of set forms was making itself felt, and the prayers of the Church were being set down in writing. The most obvious illustration is provided by the *Apostolic Tradition* of St Hippolytus. In this movement, itself the product of causes deeply buried in the instinctive life of institutions and societies, we can perceive writ large the gradual codification of creeds which we are studying.

CHAPTER IV

THE OLD ROMAN CREED

1. *The Evidence for R*

THE third century was, from a number of points of view, a critical epoch in the Church's history. One among the many problems with which it had to grapple was the influx into its ranks of an ever-swelling multitude of converts from paganism. Every thoughtful observer must have been conscious of the grave threat to the integrity of the Church's traditional teaching: the Gnostic crisis had demonstrated how easily it could be swamped by a flood of incomers with incomplete or crassly misguided notions of the authentic content of Christianity. As a counter-measure a thorough reorganization and elaboration of the catechetical system was taken in hand: many signs of it are discernible in contemporary liturgies and in the writings of third-century fathers. St Hippolytus's *Apostolic Tradition* shows that the Roman church was earlier in the field than most with this overhaul. Henceforth most exhaustive arrangements were made both for grounding candidates for admission to the Church in the main articles of belief, and for testing their success in absorbing this teaching. One offshoot of this tightening up, and one which is of direct relevance to our studies, would seem to have been the development, some time or other in the third century and probably in Rome first of all, of the rites of the handing over, or *traditio*, and giving back, or *redditio*, of the creed as part of the immediate preparation for baptism. Once these conventions had established themselves, a declaratory formula became necessary, and the circumstances of its use by the bishop and of its being memorized and solemnly rehearsed by the catechumens were such as to surround it with immense prestige. The parallel development of the *disciplina arcani*, or rule of secrecy, with all that it carried with it of awe and reverence attaching to the central mysteries of Christianity, only served to magnify still further the sacredness of creeds.

The one selected for use by the local bishop must quickly have ousted all other summaries of belief current in the district, and must itself have acquired the position of the official symbol of faith. The era of declaratory confessions was now in full swing, and while it would be rash to suppose that the text was treated as inviolable, each local church henceforth had its own creed, which might be marked by distinctive divergences from those of its neighbours. As the third century wore on, this situation became, it would seem, universal, and persisted for centuries after the council of Nicaea had inaugurated a line of conciliar creeds claiming a more than merely local allegiance.

One of the earliest of local creeds to take shape and be canonized in this way was that of the Roman church. It is the purpose of this chapter to examine the document which has been identified as the ancient Roman baptismal creed (its conventional description is R), to investigate its credentials, and to give a bird's-eye view of its history so far as it is recoverable. No apology should be needed for allocating so much space to it. The descent of the Roman creed can be traced with some degree of confidence to the second century, at any rate to its closing decades. If this is correct, it should have a special interest as lifting the curtain a few inches from the obscure period studied in the last chapter when there were a variety of local types competing for a monopoly. Its outstanding importance on other grounds scarcely needs stressing. It became the direct ancestor of all other local creeds in the West, and its influence even on Eastern creeds was marked. The Apostles' Creed itself, which was later elevated to a position of unique authority as the baptismal formula of Rome and the West generally, is merely one among R's many descendants: it is in fact, as we shall later discover, the old creed of Rome enriched with matter which had become popular in the provinces.

Our primary source for the text of the Old Roman Creed, in its Latin form, is the treatise *Commentarius in symbolum apostolorum*[1] which the Aquileian priest Tyrannius Rufinus wrote towards 404. It was from this famous book that, in the first chapter, we culled the legend of the composition of the creed by the twelve Apostles. In it Rufinus comments, clause by clause,

[1] *C.C.L.* 20, 133–82.

on the baptismal creed of his own church, Aquileia, and compares it with that of Rome. His reason for this odd procedure was that, while he recognized that the Roman church preserved the original creed of the Apostles in its purity, he felt constrained (by natural piety, we may conjecture) to use the formula he had himself professed at baptism as his working basis. Since he scrupulously indicates the points at which the Aquileian creed diverges from the Roman, it has usually been regarded as an easy task to piece the latter together as it existed in his day. The text thus obtained is confirmed by the Latin creed which has been inserted, on the back of the last page but one (p. 226 *verso*), into the Graeco-Latin uncial MS Laud. Gr. 35 in the Bodleian Library. This is a sixth or seventh century MS, and is best known as Codex E (*Codex Antiquissimus*) of the *Acts of the Apostles*. Further confirmation is supplied by a Cottonian MS (2 A XX) of the eighth century, now in the British Museum.

Printed below in parallel columns are the Latin text of R as suggested by Rufinus and the MSS we have mentioned and an English translation :

Credo in deum patrem omnipotentem;	I believe in God the Father almighty;
et in Christum Iesum filium eius unicum, dominum nostrum,	and in Christ Jesus His only Son, our Lord,
qui natus est de Spiritu sancto et Maria virgine,	Who was born from the Holy Spirit and the Virgin Mary,
qui sub Pontio Pilato crucifixus est et sepultus,	Who under Pontius Pilate was crucified and buried,
tertia die resurrexit a mortuis,	on the third day rose again from the dead,
ascendit in caelos,	ascended to heaven,
sedet ad dexteram patris,	sits at the right hand of the Father,
unde venturus est iudicare vivos et mortuos;	whence He will come to judge the living and the dead;
et in Spiritum sanctum,	and in the Holy Spirit,
sanctam ecclesiam,	the holy Church,
remissionem peccatorum,	the remission of sins,
carnis resurrectionem.	the resurrection of the flesh.

Some sixty years before Rufinus wrote his book, a creed practically identical with the above, but in Greek, figured in the well-known apologia which Marcellus, bishop of Ancyra in Cappadocia, submitted to Pope Julius I at the synod held in

Rome in 340. An over-zealous exponent of Nicene orthodoxy, he had fallen foul of the Eusebian party and had been expelled from his see as being virtually a Sabellian. Like others in the same plight at this time, he took refuge in Rome, where he received a warm welcome. His apologia took the form of a detailed statement of his beliefs on the theological issues at stake: the idea was that his Roman supporters might have material with which to vindicate his innocence. In the middle of this document[1] a short creed crops up which is a replica, in all save a few relatively unimportant points, of the creed which can be reconstructed out of Rufinus's treatise. This was identified, towards the middle of the seventeenth century, by James Ussher,[2] the scholarly archbishop of Armagh (who had also been the first to disentangle the Latin text of R from Rufinus), as the contemporary creed of the Roman church. Its interpolation by Marcellus in his defence was, thought Ussher, an ingenious move designed to provide an absolutely unimpeachable proof of his orthodoxy by the innuendo that he considered the Pope's own baptismal confession the best expression of his faith; and we know from Pope Julius's allusion to it in his subsequent letter to the Eastern bishops that the plan succeeded.[3] Practically all scholars since Ussher's day have acquiesced in his identification. Marcellus's creed runs as follows:

πιστεύω οὖν εἰς θεὸν παντοκράτορα·
καὶ εἰς Χριστὸν Ἰησοῦν, τὸν υἱὸν αὐτοῦ τὸν μονογενῆ,
   τὸν κύριον ἡμῶν,
τὸν γεννηθέντα ἐκ πνεύματος ἁγίου καὶ Μαρίας
   τῆς παρθένου,
τὸν ἐπὶ Ποντίου Πιλάτου σταυρωθέντα καὶ ταφέντα,
   καὶ τῇ τρίτῃ ἡμέρᾳ ἀναστάντα ἐκ τῶν νεκρῶν,
   ἀναβάντα εἰς τοὺς οὐρανοὺς καὶ καθήμενον
   ἐν δεξιᾷ τοῦ πατρός, ὅθεν ἔρχεται
   κρίνειν ζῶντας καὶ νεκρούς·
καὶ εἰς τὸ ἅγιον πνεῦμα, ἁγίαν ἐκκλησίαν, ἄφεσιν ἁμαρτιῶν,
   σαρκὸς ἀνάστασιν, ζωὴν αἰώνιον.

[1] See St Epiphanius, *Pan. haer.* 72, 3, 1 (Holl III, 258).
[2] See his *De Romanae ecclesiae symbolo apostolico vetere aliisque fidei formulis* . . . *diatriba*, London, 1647.
[3] Cf. St Athan., *Apol. con. Ar.* 32 (*P.G.* 25, 302).

The text, it will be observed, exhibits several deviations from the Latin version suggested by Rufinus. The chief of these are the omission of FATHER (πατέρα) in the first article, and the addition of LIFE EVERLASTING (ζωὴν αἰώνιον) after RESURRECTION OF THE FLESH: a less important variation is the insertion of AND (καὶ) before ON THE THIRD DAY and SITS.

Marcellus's letter is not the only witness to the Greek text of the Old Roman Creed: a MS of considerably later date can also be cited. This is the collection of liturgical pieces known as the *Psalter of Aethelstan*, in the Cottonian Collection in the British Museum. The creed appears in the MS (Galba A XVIII: 9th cent.) at the end of the psalter proper along with other formulae, the Greek words by a curious trick having been transcribed in Anglo-Saxon characters. The contents agree exactly with the Latin R, and the text differs from Marcellus's in a number of minutiae (κρῖναι for κρίνειν, πνεῦμα ἅγιον for τὸ ἅγιον πνεῦμα, etc.), as well as in the points mentioned above.[1]

2. *The Tradition Defended*

The preceding section has given a sketch of the argument for supposing that Rufinus and Marcellus bear witness to the existence of a standard creed at Rome in the fourth century. Ussher's brilliant surmise seemed to be corroborated in a quite remarkable way when the true date and authorship of St Hippolytus's *Tradition*, with its interrogatory formula so closely similar to R, were established at the beginning of this century. Before proceeding further, however, we must subject his case to a more searching scrutiny. The Roman creed is such a key document in the history of creeds that absolute assurance as to its credentials is desirable. Moreover, while practically all scholars since Ussher's time have accepted the traditional identification, objections have been advanced against it by F. J. Badcock, whose work on creeds has had considerable influence in Great Britain. We must weigh his argument before passing to an investigation of the earlier history and pedigree of the Old Roman Creed.[2]

[1] It was Abp. Ussher who made use of *Psalt. Aethel.*
[2] For Badcock's views cf. *J.T.S.* xxiii, 1922, 362 ff. and *The History of the Creeds*, London, 1930 and 1938. They have not so far been fully discussed in print.

The pivot on which the whole orthodox theory turns is, of course, the belief that the contemporary creed of the Roman church can be reliably recovered from the hints given by Rufinus in his treatise. Badcock was accordingly not slow to draw attention to the fact that all Rufinus promised to give in his book was the creed of his native church Aquileia. Admittedly he singled out several striking divergences between it and the Roman creed, but we have no reason to suppose that his list was exhaustive. Unless we can be sure that it was, the attempt to reconstruct R with the aid of his casual remarks is foredoomed to collapse. Stress has also been laid on the fact that there are a number of respects in which the creed pieced together from the *Commentarius* differs verbally from what must have been the current Roman form. Thus Rufinus uses *in* with the ablative, not the accusative, when expressing belief in each of the three divine Persons. Again, for HIS ONLY SON in the second article he writes *unico filio eius* instead of the undoubtedly more plausible *filium eius unicum*. The accumulation of these and similar points tends to undermine confidence in the testimony of the *Commentarius* to the Roman creed.

Strictures like these betray a curious misunderstanding of the character and purpose of Rufinus's tract. If there is one thing which he makes crystal clear in his opening chapters, it is that he conceives of himself as commenting on the Apostles' Creed, the formula originally concocted by the Twelve, and not primarily on the creed of his own or any other local church. He several times refers, in general terms, to the "tradition of the creed" and the "tradition" which "was given to the churches", and declares[1] his intention, in contrast to the behaviour of the heretical commentator Photinus, of "restoring their plain and simple meaning to the apostolic words". In order to establish the authority of the creed, he relates the familiar story of how the Twelve severally contributed its clauses before departing from Jerusalem on their missionary enterprises. At the same time—and this is the next point he brings out[2]—he is convinced that the veritable creed of the Apostles is preserved in its integrity in the Roman church alone. He was apparently of the same mind as St Ambrose, who had

[1] Ch. 1 (*C.C.L.* 20, 133 f.).   [2] Ch. 3 (*C.C.L.* 20, 136 f.).

remarked[1] a few years previously on the way the Roman church had managed to maintain the Apostles' Creed inviolate (*intemeratum*) from the beginning. Elsewhere, he explains, additions had crept into the original text "on account of heretics (*propter nonnullos haereticos*)" against whose novel opinions precautions needed to be taken. At Rome, however, it retained its primitive form unimpaired, partly because no heresies had ever taken their rise there, and partly because the local baptismal custom of making candidates recite the creed publicly had acted as a safeguard against interpolation. Presumably the sensitive ears of those who had previously received baptism would have been quick to notice any variation in the traditional text, and they would at once have pounced upon it.

The only sensible inference from all this is that Rufinus must have failed lamentably to achieve his object unless he had given his readers a good general idea, to say the least, of the Roman creed. Admittedly he decided to follow the text of the Aquileian formula in his exposition. By interjecting the words "to which I pledged myself when I was baptized at Aquileia", he gives a pretty clear hint that his reason was that it was the creed which he had known longest and which had a particular claim on his regard. As he proceeds, however, he marks the places, almost apologetically, where the Aquileian form exhibits contrasts with the Roman. Since the Roman creed is in his eyes identical with the creed of the Apostles, and since it is the latter that he is concerned to expound, it is inconceivable that it contained other material deviations, whether in the way of interpolation or omission, which he has passed over in silence. On the other hand, his procedure does not oblige him to draw attention to purely verbal differences between the Aquileian and the Roman texts. He was not out to remark on points of accidence or word-order, but on points of substance involving a variation in doctrinal teaching. There is little to show that at this period importance was attached to minutiae of language in creeds or in the liturgy generally: in fact, all the evidence points the other way. If it had not been so, it is difficult to see how St Augustine, for example, could have based his Sermons 212, 213 and 214, delivered at Hippo in North Africa, on the creed of

[1] *Ep.* 42, 5 (*P.L.* 16, 1125).

Milan, which was broadly akin to the North African creed but by no means identical with it, and got away with it. Thus Rufinus had no motive for going out of his way to mention the Aquileian creed's preference for *in* with the ablative rather than the accusative, or even for the placing of the adjective *unico* before instead of after *filio eius*, or its substitution of *ex Maria* (FROM MARY) for *et Maria* (AND MARY). How unobservant of such trifling variations he was comes out clearly in such a passage as the opening words of ch. 4,[1] in which he says that almost all the Eastern churches have the form I BELIEVE IN ONE GOD, again putting the words ONE GOD in the ablative in spite of the fact that they are in the accusative in all Eastern creeds. From the point of view of his immediate purpose (he had not twentieth-century standards of scholarship), these were deviations of little or no importance, if indeed he was conscious of them at all.

Many other things might be said if there were space to widen the field of discussion. For example, we have already mentioned St Hippolytus's interrogatory baptismal creed. Whatever its exact relation to R (a question which will be gone into later), the resemblance between the two is extremely close, and some kind of kinship seems to be implied. A creed remarkably like R, to say the least, was current at Rome early in the third century, and this fact alone, quite apart from the kind of argument pursued by Ussher, might seem a strong presumption in favour of the claims he advanced on behalf of R. Yet the only creed our critic would acknowledge to have existed at Rome prior to 371[2] was the short formula prescribed by the Gelasian Sacramentary for the moment of baptism.[3] Enough has been said, however, to prove that only resolute scepticism could doubt that the Roman creed as it existed about 400 can be recovered, in substance at any rate, from *Comm. in symb. apost.* If this is agreed, we are entitled to carry it back more than one generation at the least, for Rufinus emphasized that the Roman church had retained the apostolic wording intact. If some of his theories were fanciful, he was not likely to be completely in error about

---

[1] *C.C.L.* 20, 137.
[2] Cf. Badcock, ch. ix.
[3] For its text see above, 38.

what happened in his own lifetime. It is therefore not surprising that the great majority of scholars, coming across a practically identical creed in Marcellus's letter, should have concluded that it, too, is none other than the creed of the contemporary Roman church.

Against this traditional rampart, too, the same critic has delivered a frontal assault. Archbishop Ussher, he argued, foisted upon the world a wholly misleading interpretation of Marcellus's apologia. Like Rufinus, he was simply quoting the creed of his own church, in this case Ancyra: the creed of Rome was not in his thoughts at all. In substantiation of this he cited Marcellus's explicit statement, "I thought it necessary . . . to write down faithfully in my own hand and to deliver to you my faith (τὴν ἐμαυτοῦ πίστιν), which I learned and was taught out of the holy Scriptures", and along with this his remarks towards the end of the letter, "This is the faith (ταύτην . . . τὴν πίστιν) which I received from holy Scripture, which I was taught by my parents in religion, and which I preach in the Church of God.[1]" The clear suggestion, if not direct assertion, of these sentences, it is argued, is that what he had in mind was the baptismal creed of his own diocese of Ancyra, which had been employed at his own baptism, and that this is to be identified with the short formal statement of faith which is inserted in the middle of the letter and which we hailed as the Roman creed. As a further proof of the falsity of our inference, it is pointed out that the word FATHER (πατέρα) does not occur in the first article, while the words LIFE EVERLASTING (ζωὴν αἰώνιον) appear in the third, and that there are certain other minor differences.

To anyone who has sat down quietly and worked through the original text of the letter, this must seem an astonishing, not to say preposterous, line of argument. We may leave on one side the suggestion, rejected by all experts,[2] that the creed quoted by Marcellus conforms to the general type of creeds from Asia Minor, and turn to the section of St Epiphanius's *Panarion* in which the letter is embedded. Marcellus, it may be confidently asserted, nowhere gives the slightest hint that he is appealing to

---

[1] St Epiphanius, *Panarion*, 72, 2–3 (Holl III, 257, 258).
[2] There is a brief but devastating critique of the suggestion by H. Lietzmann in *Z.N.T.W.* xxii, 1923, 258.

the creed of Ancyra. Not only is this the case, but the idea that his mentions of "my faith" and "the faith I was taught" refer to the short formulary under discussion, or to any formulary at all, is quite unfounded. He is referring to his faith in the wider sense of his theological position. His apologia is a lengthy and skilful one, taking up (apart from his prefatory remarks and the creed itself) three paragraphs or 45 lines in Karl Holl's Berlin edition, and it comprises both a counter-attack on his Arian detractors for their blasphemous misconceptions regarding the relation of the Father and the Son (the first paragraph), and a detailed, subtly argued exposition of his own constructive attitude (the remaining two). The statement of his "faith" which he promised at the beginning of the letter must be taken as covering the whole of the two paragraphs in which he develops his own theological views in a manner calculated to set his orthodoxy in high relief, and not just the little creed. Packed as they are with citations from Scripture, they bear out his boast that his teaching had a thoroughly Biblical basis. It is arbitrary to confine the reference to "my faith" and to "this faith" to a single small item in the lengthy passage which comes between these two key phrases. Quite obviously Marcellus was not thinking of a succinct formula (the formula quoted, it is worth pointing out, though doubtless useful as a device for capturing the Pope's good will, was scarcely sufficient in itself to rebut the allegations made against him), but of the general content of his beliefs regarding the consubstantiality of the Father and the Son.

What then are we left with? In his letter of defence Marcellus silently interpolates a creed which is all but identical with what we know to have been the creed of Rome some sixty years later. He nowhere says it is the creed of his own diocese, and indeed gives no clue as to where he got it. There can surely be little doubt what he was doing. Anxious to demonstrate his orthodoxy to the Roman pontiff and to establish the correctness of his theological position, he resorted to the expedient of quoting the Roman baptismal creed as if it were one which accurately summed up the tenets he stood for. As Kattenbusch pointed out long ago,[1] if he wanted to appeal to a creed to confirm his

[1] I, 73.

general orthodoxy in Roman eyes, there was none that he could appeal to with an equal chance of success. The practice of producing creeds as proofs of one's orthodoxy was, apparently, conventional in the fourth century, and agreed with the prevailing disposition to treat creeds as tests. Eusebius of Caesarea, as we shall see, followed it at the council of Nicaea, and so did Theophronius, bishop of Tyana (in Cappadocia), at the synod of Antioch in 341.[1] Marcellus went one better by quietly putting forward as his own the creed of those whose favour he hoped to win.

The fact that the text as it has come down to us exhibits several variations from what was probably the true Roman text need not perturb us unduly: it is unlikely that it worried anyone at the time, for the verbal expression of creeds was not then considered sacrosanct. In any case we are dependent for our knowledge of St Epiphanius's *Panarion* at this point on a single MS[2] of the early fourteenth century. As for the presence of EVERLASTING LIFE (ζωὴν αἰώνιον) in the final article, it is scarcely conceivable that the words are an unconscious reminiscence by Marcellus of some Eastern credal form. Much more probably they are to be explained as an interpolation, absent-minded or deliberate, on the part of some scribe who remembered the full text of the Apostles' Creed too loyally.[3] The only variant likely to cause difficulty is the omission of FATHER (πατέρα) in the first article. Archbishop Ussher hazarded the guess that it was "left out, as it would appear, by scribal carelessness". But this hardly merits consideration. It is worth noticing that there are two other places in this letter where Marcellus shows a predilection for the form "God almighty (θεοῦ παντοκράτορος)". One of the characteristic points of his theology was that the Word of God did not become Son until the Incarnation, His only generation being in the Virgin's womb, and that the title Son, like those of image, Christ, Jesus, life, way, etc., was only properly applicable to Him during the incarnate state.[4] It was logical that he should feel a certain

---

[1] Cf. St Athanasius, *De Synod.* 24 (*P.G.* 26, 724).
[2] J=*Jenensis* mscr. Bose 1 (A.D. 1304).
[3] Cf. the impressive array of such alterations in Caspari, *Quellen* III, 108 ff.
[4] Cf. Fragg. 4–7, 42, 48, 91, 109 in E. Klostermann's *Eusebius Werke* IV, 185–215 (*G.C.S.* 10).

reluctance about describing the eternal God, to Whom the Word belonged, as Father in His ultimate being. He was the indivisible, absolutely one Monad, and the Word resided in Him consubstantially (ὁμοούσιος) as an inseparable energy, not as a distinct hypostasis. It is therefore understandable that he should have preferred in certain contexts, such as the opening article of the creed, to avoid the term Father. Such a daring tampering with the text (his Roman judges, biased as they were in his favour, were perhaps inclined to turn a blind eye to it) was a manoeuvre as much in keeping with his character as with his theology.

3. The Original Language of R

We may take it as established that the formula referred to by Rufinus and quoted by Marcellus is none other than the Roman creed of the fourth century. We therefore possess it in two versions, Latin and Greek. The question arises which of them is the original one. It is a question which has been much discussed, not only to satisfy academic curiosity, but because of the bearing the answer has on the date and composition of the creed.

The practically unanimous verdict has been that the Greek text is the original and the Latin a translation: it is borne out by the presence in St Hippolytus's *Tradition* of a closely related creed whose original was Greek. A case has been advanced for the contrary thesis, however, the argument used[1] being that the Latin text reveals rhythmic qualities which are noticeably absent from the Greek. Some of the ancient authors, like Faustus of Riez,[2] even describe it as a *carmen* or hymn. It is assumed that the version which is built up with stylistic care must have the priority in time. But not everybody will find this reasoning convincing. In the case of liturgical pieces a rhythmic translation of an unrhythmic original is just as conceivable as the reverse. As a matter of plain fact, however, it is not possible to observe in the Latin text any of the rhythms fashionable in the artificial prose style of the empire. Whether the test of quantity

---

[1] Cf. H. Jordan, *Rhythmische Prosa in der altchristlichen lateinischen Literatur*, 1905, 33 ff., and J. Haussleiter, *Trinitarischer Glaube*, 92 ff.
[2] Cf. his phrase *symboli salutare carmen* in *De Spir. sanc.* 1, 1 (*G.S.E.L.* 21, 102).

or of accentual stress is applied, the results are equally negative, nor are there any of the favourite kinds of rhyme or assonance.[1] The word *carmen*, too, must not always be taken as meaning a rhythmic composition: it could be used in a wider sense to cover a solemn, liturgical formula.

It cannot be pretended that, so far as internal evidence goes, a compelling case can be made out for either the Greek or the Latin. Both of them are smooth-running, idiomatic pieces of prose. It has been pointed out that one or two features of the Greek, such as the placing of ON THE THIRD DAY ($\tau\hat{\eta}$ $\tau\rho\ell\tau\eta$ $\eta\mu\epsilon\rho\alpha$) before the verb ROSE AGAIN, suggest a Latin word-order. On the other hand, there are rather more features of the Latin text which might imply that it is a translation. For example, *omnipotentem* (=ALMIGHTY) and the Greek $\pi\alpha\nu\tau o\kappa\rho\alpha\tau o\rho\alpha$ are not exact equivalents; but whereas *omnipotentem* was the nearest available Latin translation of the Greek, a Greek translator would have found $\pi\alpha\nu\tau o\delta\upsilon\nu\alpha\mu o\nu$ ready to hand. The infinitive *iudicare* (=TO JUDGE) after WILL COME, while perfectly possible, is a Greek usage, and a Latin original would probably have preferred *ad iudicandos* or *ut iudicet* or something of the sort.[2] The word-order in the Christological section follows the Greek, un-Latin practice of thrusting the verb well forward. Lastly, *Christum*, which comes before *Jesum*, is here employed as a title, meaning Messiah: a usage common enough in Greek of the early Christian period, but thoroughly un-Latin.

None of these indications is decisive, or anything like it. On the whole, however, the scales are tipped slightly in favour of the priority of the Greek text, and the parallel Greek creed of St Hippolytus brings them down heavily. The Latin text need not, of course, be much younger. Indeed, there is everything to be said for F. Loofs's contention[3] that, from the chronological point of view, the two forms are almost contemporary. There must always have been catechumens for whom the formula had to be in Latin. The interesting corollary follows, however, that the original composition of R must have taken place at a time

---

[1] Cf. W. Meyer in *Gesammelte Abhandlungen zur mittellateinischen Rhythmik*, 1905, II, 241 Anm.

[2] Tertullian's use of the same infinitive in *De virg. vel.* 1 is a sign of the close connection of his creed texts with R.

[3] Cf. his *Symbolik*, 1902, 8.

when Greek was the official language of the Roman church. We are thus able to trace it back at least a hundred years before Marcellus. It is well known that Greek was used at Rome in the liturgy and for other purposes throughout the second century. The inscription [1] on the tomb of Pope Gaius, who died in 295,[2] reveals how long it survived as a formal convention. There were probably Greek-speaking communities in the Church until an even later date.[3] But Latin was coming into official use in the first and second generations of the third century. It therefore seems plausible to ascribe the composition of R to the opening years of the century at the latest. As a matter of fact, this is no more than we should have expected on other grounds, although it is useful to have the linguistic confirmation. The whole weight of the external evidence is also in favour of a very early date for R. The fact that St Hippolytus, for example, bears witness to the existence of an almost identical formulary in the first decades of the third century might by itself be held to be decisive. Moreover, R exercised a powerful influence, as the chapter after the next will disclose, on all the other local creeds of the West. This can only be explained on the assumption that its position was already firmly established by the middle of the third century.

4. R, Tertullian and St Hippolytus

Is it possible to say anything more precise about the origins of R than that they belong to the vaguely defined Greek-speaking period of the Roman church? The most obvious line of approach to this question is to inquire whether the credal forms witnessed to by Tertullian and St Hippolytus throw any light on the earlier history of R. As regards the former at any rate, it has been widely held that he had a direct acquaintance with the Old Roman creed. The reader will recall the famous passage in De praescriptione 36 where he

---

[1] Cf. C. M. Kaufmann, Handbuch der altchristlichen Epigraphik, 1917, 235.

[2] So (not 296) H. Lietzmann, Petrus und Paulus in Rom, 2 ed., 1927, 9.

[3] Cf. the interesting attempt of Th. Klauser, on the basis of M. Victorinus, Adv. Arium 2, 8 (P.L. 8, 1094), and Pseudo-Aug., Quaest. vet. et nov. test. 109, 20 f. (C.S.E.L. 50, 268), to show that the translation from Greek to Latin of the Roman liturgy of the Mass itself was carried out as late as 360–382 (Studi e Testi 121, 1946, 467 ff: in Miscellanea Giovanni Mercati I).

expatiates on the close relationship between the African churches and Rome.

"Let us examine", he cries, "what that blessed church (Rome) has learned, what she has taught, what she has shared (*contesserarit*) with the African churches: she acknowledges one God and Lord, creator of the universe, and Christ Jesus, Son of God the creator from the Virgin Mary, and the resurrection of the flesh."

Many have been tempted to regard this as a manifest allusion to, possibly even citation of, R. We have already suggested[1] that their exegesis is mistaken, and have argued that Tertullian was not thinking of an official formula. This will be the place to probe the possibility that he was familiar with R rather more thoroughly.

Let us start, however, with the baptismal creed of St Hippolytus's *Apostolic Tradition*, setting the two texts R and H (=the creed of the *Tradition*) side by side. It should be remembered, of course, that in its present form R is a declaratory creed. The probability is that if it was in current use in the first decade or so of the third century it consisted of three questions.

H	R
Dost thou believe in God the Father almighty?	I believe in God the Father almighty;
Dost thou believe in Christ Jesus, the Son of God,	and in Christ Jesus His only Son, our Lord,
Who was born by the Holy Spirit from the Virgin Mary,	Who was born from the Holy Spirit and the Virgin Mary,
Who was crucified under Pontius Pilate, and died,	Who under Pontius Pilate was crucified, and buried,
and rose again on the third day living from the dead,	on the third day rose again from the dead,
and ascended into the heavens,	ascended to heaven,
and sat down on the right hand of the Father,	sits on the right hand of the Father,
and will come to judge the living and the dead?	whence he will come to judge the living and the dead;
Dost thou believe in the Holy Spirit in the holy Church?[2]	and in the Holy Spirit, the holy Church, the remission of sins, the resurrection of the flesh.

The perplexing thing about these creeds is their combination of striking resemblances with a number of significant differences.

---

[1] See above, 87 f.   [2] See above, p. 91.

The resemblances leap to the eye at once, even in translation. They consist not only in the general pattern of the creeds, their agreement in stressing Christ's birth from the Holy Spirit and the Blessed Virgin rather than His pre-cosmic begetting, and their use of such characteristically Roman turns as CHRIST JESUS. They include also remarkable similarities of language which can be picked out at a glance in the original texts. But the discrepancies are obvious too. The first is the omission by H of the description of Jesus as ONLY-BEGOTTEN and OUR LORD. Secondly, while H probably defines His earthly birth as BY THE HOLY SPIRIT FROM THE V. MARY, R has the distinctive wording FROM THE HOLY SPIRIT AND THE V. MARY. Thirdly, R has AND WAS BURIED as against H's AND DIED (AND WAS BURIED of *Frag. Ver.* is not original). Fourthly, H interpolates the word LIVING before FROM THE DEAD. Fifthly, there is a difference between H's treatment of the Second Coming and R's: H probably had a participle (ἐρχόμενον), while R read WHENCE HE WILL COME (ὅθεν ἔρχεται). Sixthly, H has nothing to correspond (the variant texts which insert the words are of later date) with R's REMISSION OF SINS or RESURRECTION OF THE FLESH. Lastly, it has several minor differences of wording and the characteristic IN THE HOLY CHURCH.

The impression left by a comparison of R with Tertullian's excerpts from the rule of faith is even more baffling. The difficulty of assuming that he had any one formal creed in mind when he wrote was mentioned in the preceding chapter, but there are certain points which can be taken as settled. Thus the brief summary introduced in his *De praescriptione* 36 and quoted above indicates familiarity with the form CHRIST JESUS so characteristic of R and H. Again, the most formal of his creed extracts (*De virg. vel.* 1) agrees with R in singling out the Son's birth from the Virgin Mary rather than His eternal generation, and in mentioning His crucifixion "under Pontius Pilate". The Virgin birth also features in *Adv. Prax.* 2. In addition some of his better-known passages reveal unmistakable verbal coincidences with R, such as the word-order "on the third day resuscitated from the dead" in *De virg. vel.* 1, the sentence "sitting now at the right hand of the Father" in *De virg. vel.* 1 and "sits at the right hand of the Father" in *Adv. Prax.* 2, the mention of "buried" in *Adv. Prax.* 2, and the Greek-sounding infinitive "to judge (*iudicare*)" following the future participle *venturum* in *De virg. vel.* 1. and *Adv. Prax.* 2. Reading snatches like these one is tempted to agree with the older commentators who postulated here and elsewhere incontrovertible allusions to R. On the other hand, there are features which betray very different influences, and these cannot be ignored. The title FATHER is strangely absent from the first article in Tertullian's texts, and he consistently adds the adjective ONE (*unum* or *unicum*). On the strength of this it has sometimes been argued that the original Roman creed must have described God the Father as ONE, the word being deliberately excised during the controversy with the modalist monarchians. In itself this is a far-fetched hypothesis, and it rests on the dubious premises (*a*) that we have Tertullian's assurance that the African church derived its formal creed from Rome, and (*b*) that Rome in his day had a single official formulary. Another feature in Tertullian's creeds which runs directly counter to R is the persistent designation of God as "framer of the world (*mundi conditorem*)", or "creator of the universe (*creatorem universitatis*)". Here again, as in the use of the phrase ONE GOD, we have a markedly Eastern trait. Furthermore, in the second article he has no mention, any more than St Hippolytus has, of two of R's most distinctive features, the description of Christ Jesus as ONLY-BEGOTTEN and as OUR LORD. Occasionally,[1] too, he puts in a reference to the Son as "the Word of God" Who was the Father's agent in creation. In these same passages we look in vain for the words FROM THE DEAD, and for R's typical form WHENCE HE WILL COME.

An interesting attempt to solve the riddle of the relationship of R to the creeds of Tertullian and St Hippolytus has been made by the Benedictine scholar Dom Bernard Capelle.[2] His theory is that all three bear witness to the official creed of the Roman church, but at successive phases of its development. Thus Tertullian represents the creed at a slightly earlier stage than St Hippolytus, while by the time R appears on the scene it has undergone a still more radical revision. On this

---

[1] *De praescr.* 13; *Adv. Prax.* 2 (*C.C.L.* 1, 197; 2, 1160).
[2] Cf. his article in *R. Bén.* xxxix, 1927, 33–45.

hypothesis he thinks that both the similarities and the differences between the creeds are fully accounted for. In particular, the framers of R altered SON OF GOD in Tertullian and H to ONLY SON because they wanted a more Scriptural expression (cf. 1 *Jn.* 4, 9), and inserted OUR LORD so as to make the second article symmetrical with the first. Assuming on the basis of his reconstruction of the text that BURIED formed part of H, Dom Capelle explains the excision of DIED on the ground that it seemed superfluous after CRUCIFIED. LIVING ("on the third day rose living from the dead" in H) was also cut out as not adding much to ROSE AGAIN, and WHENCE HE WILL COME was substituted for COMES (probably the participle ἐρχόμενον in Greek) because it made a better join. REMISSION OF SINS was interpolated because a reference to baptism seemed appropriate in a formula designed for catechumens. The redaction of R on this theory may be ascribed to some indeterminate date in the second generation of the third century.

This is a neat analysis, worked out with considerable ingenuity. If only it could be taken for granted that about 200 the Roman church owned a single, official baptismal creed, it would doubtless be necessary to demonstrate the kinship of H and R, not to mention Tertullian's forms, by some such drastic methods. Dom Capelle, it should be noticed, seems to have precisely this assumption in mind throughout the course of his argument.[1] He never questions the premiss that all three must be versions of "the Roman creed". Somehow or other, therefore, R must be twisted and pulled about until it is revealed to be H after all in disguise. Unfortunately the keystone of the whole elaborate construction is an anachronism. We have seen that to speak of local churches as possessing, in any strict sense of the term, one sacrosanct formula at the beginning of the third century is to antedate a vital stage in the evolution of creeds. There is every likelihood that at Rome, as in other churches, several formulae were in current use at this time, and there is nothing to show that the language of any of them was religiously safeguarded. It is conceivable that H, R and Tertullian (if indeed he can be claimed as a witness to

---

[1] He seems to have altered his viewpoint in his later article in *Rech. théol. anc. med.* ii, 1930, 14.

Roman credal forms) all represent different contemporary traditions enjoying the blessing of Roman authority. This, or something like it, is by far the most probable hypothesis unless R's characteristic differences from H confirm Dom Capelle's view of their derivative status.

It can safely be said that they do not. So far from there being anything distinctively third-century about them, practically all of them represent material which might well have secured admittance to a Roman creed in the second century. This applies notably to the title OUR LORD, but it is true also of the clause THE REMISSION OF SINS, whatever the actual date of its insertion into Roman creeds. The former was a commonplace from the earliest times,[1] while the latter figured in the mid-second-century creed of the *Epistula Apostolorum*. There were, indeed, circles in the West which preferred, after the example of the Old Testament, to confine the title LORD to God the Father, and this possibly explains its absence from H and Tertullian's creeds. The adjective ONLY-BEGOTTEN ($\mu o \nu o \gamma \epsilon \nu \hat{\eta}$) may have owed its place to Scriptural precedent, as Dom Capelle argues, but there were probably dogmatic motives at work as well, and the date need not be so late as he suggests. The claim that Christ was the true Only-Begotten was being advanced by St Irenaeus against the Valentinian Gnostics long before the second century ended.[2] Its appearance in R is much more likely to indicate a polemical gesture than a reversion to Biblicism on the part of the Roman officials of the early third century. The other variations of language between H and R, which Dom Capelle dismisses so lightly, serve to emphasize the difference between the two creeds. It is difficult to believe, for example, that anything was gained by altering the precise BY THE HOLY SPIRIT FROM THE VIRGIN MARY,[3] which probably stood in H, to R's simpler FROM THE HOLY SPIRIT AND THE VIRGIN MARY, any more than by changing WILL COME TO JUDGE ($\dot{\epsilon} \rho \chi \acute{o} \mu \epsilon \nu o \nu$) to WHENCE HE WILL COME TO JUDGE ($\ddot{o} \theta \epsilon \nu \ \ddot{\epsilon} \rho \chi \epsilon \tau a \iota$).

The true solution of the problem presented by the similarities and differences between the creeds of Tertullian and

[1] Cf., e.g., *Rom.* 1, 5; 10, 9; St Iren., *Adv. haer.* 3, 16, 6; 4, 33, 7 (*P.G.* 7, 925; 1077).
[2] Cf. *Adv. haer.* 3, 16, 1; 2; 6 (*P.G.* 7, 920; 921; 925).
[3] N. B. Dom Capelle does not accept this reading: see *R. Bén.* xxxix, 1927, 35 ff.

St Hippolytus and R has already been foreshadowed. Several credal summaries were probably in use in the Roman church about 200. There is no reason to doubt that St Hippolytus introduces us to one of them, but there must have been others as well: the age of liturgical fixity and uniformity had not yet arrived. R may very well have been another. The striking resemblances between R and H are best explained on the hypothesis that, while both were in a sense independent forms, they were close relatives and jostled against each other like members of a family. Thus there must have been considerable mutual influence, especially as on our theory creeds were still fairly elastic in their verbal expression. Similarly Tertullian seems to have known R: some of his statements at any rate read like echoes of it. But he seems to have known, and to have frequently resorted to, other types of doctrinal summary too. One of these may have been H: there are points of contact between his language and that of H. Others were of the distinctively Eastern mould. This explanation is the only one which does justice to the fact that no one credal formula had apparently yet been granted a monopoly. If it rules out of court the neat but artificial theory of origin sketched by Dom Capelle, it at least enables us to carry back the history of R with confidence to the turn of the second century. If it is legitimate to follow up the hint contained in the polemical insertion of Monogenes as a description of Christ, we may be emboldened to peer still further back into the obscurity of the second century.

5. *The Holl-Harnack Hypothesis*

With this conclusion research into the pre-history of R might be thought to have reached a dead end. The attempts which were formerly popular to discern the shadowy outline of R hovering behind the credal formulae of St Justin proved sterile. True, his baptismal questions, as we reconstructed them, for a moment tempt us to discover pointers to the Old Roman Creed in the absence of the adjective ONE with God the Father and in the prominence given to Christ's crucifixion under Pontius Pilate. But the whole plan of the creed is in fact quite different, with its description of God as "the Father and Lord of the universe", its designation of Christ (*Jesus Christ*, be it noted) as "our Saviour", and its mention of the Spirit's prophetic ministry. A completely fresh line of investigation was, however, opened up in 1919 by a series of brilliant papers presented in that year to the Prussian Academy of Sciences by Karl Holl, Adolf von Harnack, and Hans Lietzmann. Some account must now be given of their pioneer work, the results of which have been acclaimed in many quarters as solidly established. The suggestions they put forward, if accepted, would have the effect of placing the composition and character of R in an entirely new perspective.

Holl[1] confined himself to an analysis of the second, or Christological, section of the creed. First, he noticed that there are two descriptive titles attached to Christ Jesus—(*a*) HIS ONLY SON and (*b*) OUR LORD. The Christology which follows, he then observed, breaks naturally into two separate passages, and each of these is introduced in the original Greek by the definite article (τὸν γεννηθέντα etc. and τὸν ἐπὶ Ποντίου Πιλάτου etc.). The first of these describes the birth of Jesus Christ from the Holy Spirit and the Virgin Mary. The second dwells on His crucifixion, burial, resurrection, ascension, session at His Father's right hand, and future coming in judgment. It is most unlikely, he urged, that this symmetrical structure, thrown as it is into sharpest relief by the reduplication of the definite article, is accidental. What it suggests is that each of these descriptive passages is a theological exposition of one of the preceding titles ascribed to the Saviour. Thus the former of them explains and justifies the divine Sonship along the lines of *Luke* 1, 35, where it is prophesied by the Angel that the Holy Spirit will descend upon the Blessed Virgin, and that *therefore* (note διό in the Greek) her offspring will be called Son of God (υἱὸς θεοῦ, the very title of the creed). Similarly the second would seem to interpret Christ's position as LORD as being the reward of His sufferings and death upon the cross. The theology is precisely that of St Paul in *Phil.* 2, 6 ff., where he makes the point that it was *because* (note διό again in v. 9) He humbled Himself to

---

[1] Cf. *Sitzungsberichte der Preussischen Akademie*, 1919, I, 2 ff. Cf. also his *Gesammelte Aufsätze* II, 115 ff.

death on the cross that God exalted Him and gave Him the name which is above every name, so that every tongue should confess that He is *Lord* (in the Greek, κύριος), the second title of the creed.

Holl's lecture did no more than break up R into its constituent elements. But if his argument is valid, a further step may logically be taken. R as we know it must be a derivative creed, a descendant of a more primitive form which once stood alone and did not contain the double Christology expanding the two titles attributed to Jesus. This was the inference which A. von Harnack[1] explicitly drew in his supplementary article contributed to the Berlin Academy one month after Holl's. The original skeleton creed must have run as follows:

> I believe in God the Father almighty,
>> and in Christ Jesus, His only Son, our Lord,
>> and in the Holy Spirit, the holy Church, the forgiveness of sins, the resurrection of the flesh.

This creed, he pointed out, bears the proof of its one-time independence on its face. Not only is it built upon a symmetrical pattern, three main articles with three subordinate members each (he treated THE FORGIVENESS OF SINS and THE RESURRECTION OF THE FLESH as going together), but a similar symmetrical correspondence can be observed in the flow of ideas.

A formidable difficulty confronting this hypothesis, as stated by Harnack, is that of fitting the two items THE FORGIVENESS OF SINS and THE RESURRECTION OF THE FLESH into the alleged ninefold scheme. Not everyone was prepared to accept Harnack's proposal to cut the knot by lumping them together as two complementary aspects of one conception, the fruits of the redemption enjoyed by believers. It was at this point that H. Lietzmann stepped in with his contribution to the symposium.[2] First, he argued with much force that it was simply impossible to treat the two sub-clauses as one. The true solution, he then suggested, was to omit THE REMISSION OF SINS as no part of the skeleton creed. In reality the primitive formula was a genuine nine-clause one, and he pointed to the creed[3] of the Dêr Balyzeh

---

[1] *Sitzungsberichte der Preussischen Akademie*, 1919, VII, 112 ff.
[2] Op. cit. XVII, 269–74.   [3] See above, 89.

Papyrus as a parallel. On his assumption that the third article reads "... and in the holy Catholic Church", this offers precisely that ninefold creed, divided into three principal clauses, which Harnack was looking for, and there is no mention in it of REMISSION OF SINS. Lietzmann was satisfied, in view of the acknowledged dependence of the Egyptian church on Rome for its liturgical forms, that the Dêr Balyzeh Papyrus had preserved the early-second-century Roman tradition. In a later study[1] he was able to marshal an array of other parallels from related Egyptian sources, all of them testifying to the existence of short nine-clause creeds. Amongst these were the creed of the ancient Coptic baptismal liturgy,[2] the creed of the Ethiopian translation[3] of St Hippolytus's *Tradition*, and a formula contained in the *Epistula Systatica* of the Alexandrian patriarch.[4] Still other examples of brief creeds harking back to an early epoch are to be found, he argued, in the Armenian baptismal ritual edited by Conybeare, in the *Epistula Apostolorum*, and in the Roman Gelasian Sacramentary.[5]

Such was the complex hypothesis unfolded in successive stages by the three German scholars. In passing judgment on it, full acknowledgment must be made of its brilliance and suggestiveness, as well as of the very real advance it has stimulated in our understanding of R's pre-history. Whatever else may be said, it has at least finally established the fact that R as we know it is a conflation, the result of the welding together of a short Trinitarian formula and of an originally independent Christological summary. A great debt is owed to Harnack and Lietzmann in particular for pointing out, what had escaped notice before their day but is in fact obvious once attention is drawn to it, how easily the Christology can be disengaged from the body of the creed. The reader has already had proof, in the evidence accumulated in Chaps. I and III, of the continued existence of an autonomous Christ-kerygma in the Church from the first to the end of the second century at least. He has also been apprised of the ways in which this tended to become

[1] *Die Anfänge des Glaubensbekenntnisses*, Tübingen, 1921.
[2] Cf. J. A. Assemanus, *Codex Liturgicus Eccles. Univ.*, Rome, 1749, I, 159.
[3] Cf. G. W. Horner, *Statutes of the Apostles*, London, 1904, 173.
[4] In E. Renaudot, *Liturg. Orient. Collect.*, Paris, 1716, I, 490.
[5] For references and documents, see *Anfänge*, 228 ff.

attached to Trinitarian formulae, being sometimes inserted into the second article, and sometimes (as in the famous passage of St Irenaeus, *Adv. haer.* 1, 10, 1) tacked on at the end. Lietzmann's demonstration of the abundance and variety of brief Trinitarian creeds, usually of nine clauses each, in the early centuries at once raises the question whether short texts of this type or fully developed ones resembling R should be regarded as the original. It is difficult to imagine motives for abbreviating a creed which already contained a fully expanded Christology, whereas the enlargement of a short formula with Christological additions scarcely calls for explanation. In the light of all the facts which have been mentioned, it cannot be doubted that R represents such an enlargement, carried out for motives which will be discussed in the following chapter, and that behind it, somewhere in the obscurity of the second century, stands a simple Trinitarian confession, cast in the form of questions addressed to the catechumen, which itself points back to the Matthaean baptismal command. This conclusion, it is worth noting, coheres with and derives support from the results of our investigations in the previous chapter, which established that short triple questionnaires based on the Lord's command recorded in the First Gospel were the earliest creeds to become crystallized.

If this point can be claimed as settled, the same cannot be said for the remainder of the hypothesis, which seeks to interpret the Christological section of R as intended to elucidate the two titles attributed to Jesus.[1] Some of the objections which have been advanced, it must be admitted, fail to carry conviction. R. Seeberg, for example, was convinced that he had undermined the whole theory by showing that it involved, indeed rested upon, a brand of Christology which could not be squared with second-century Roman theology. The tracing of Christ's divine Sonship, he contended, to His physical conception by the Holy Spirit was inconceivable at a time when every educated Christian was prepared to acknowledge the Son of God as a pre-existent being. The following chapter will be the

---

[1] For criticism of the hypothesis, see in particular R. Seeberg, *Z. für KG.* xl (N.F. iii), 1922, 1–41; B. Capelle, *R. Bén.* xxxix, 1927, 33 ff. and *Rech. théol. anc. méd.* ii, 1930, 5 ff.; J. Lebreton, *Rech. des sciences relig.* xx, 1930, 97 ff. In what follows I have been greatly helped by these articles.

appropriate place to examine the precise Christological views implied by R, and it may be that we shall decide that Holl's account of them is not the true one. But it is proper to point out here that Seeberg's language was extravagant: the Christology proposed by Holl did not necessarily exclude pre-existence, and theories of the type he had in mind were undoubtedly current in certain Roman circles. But the hypothesis has more serious objections to wrestle with than this. For example, contrary to what Holl's theory requires, it is extremely doubtful whether in fact the redactor of R can have been thinking of *Lk.* 1, 35 when he carried out his work. Nothing in the clause of the creed suggests the Lukan passage, and the language indeed seems reminiscent rather of *Mt.* 1, 20. Here we not only have the past participle BORN ($\gamma\epsilon\nu\nu\eta\theta\acute{\epsilon}\nu$), corresponding exactly with the creed, as opposed to the present ($\gamma\epsilon\nu\nu\acute{\omega}\mu\epsilon\nu\nu\nu$) of *Lk.* 1, 35, but we also have the very words of the creed FROM THE HOLY SPIRIT. Yet the divine Sonship is not linked up in the Matthaean passage with the conception from the Blessed Virgin.

Much more dangerous to Holl's hypothesis, however, is a consideration of its treatment of the title LORD and the section of R's Christology which is alleged to explicate it. In the first place, it is a curious and important fact that certain Roman creeds of the end of the second century apparently lacked the title LORD while nevertheless including a passage about Christ's suffering, glorification and Second Coming which closely approximated to that contained in R. The creed of St Hippolytus's *Tradition* is the most striking example which springs to mind, though it is noteworthy that Tertullian's "creed" also lacked LORD. It is hardly satisfactory to argue, as Lietzmann did,[1] that LORD was deliberately dropped from the creed in some Roman circles because it was deemed to belong more fittingly to God the Father. Writers like Novatian, who liked to apply "Lord" to the Father, were prepared equally to apply it to Christ[2]; and in any case the hypothetical exciser of LORD apparently made no attempt to transfer it to its rightful place in the first article. Neither H nor Tertullian's creed, as we have already tried to show, can be regarded as identical with R, but

---

[1] Cf. *Z.N.T.W.* xxvi, 1927, 89 f.
[2] Cf. *De Trinit.* 1 and 9 (*P.L.* 3, 913 and 927).

all three belonged to the same family and circulated in the same milieu. If much the same Christology appeared in H as in R despite the absence of LORD from H, it is hard to believe that that Christology was regarded by Roman theologians of the latter part of the second century as a gloss on the title.

In the second place, Holl's assumption that the words WHO WAS CRUCIFIED, etc. explain and justify the title LORD along the lines of *Phil.* 2, 6–11 cannot be accepted without question. For one thing, it would appear to rest upon a complete misapprehension of the chord which this vital section of the creed must have struck in the heart of the Christian reciting it. For him the significance of the words lay not so much in the glorious reversal of the Lord's fortunes as in his own assurance of redemption through the Saviour's triumph. Though the thought of His exaltation and lordship was no doubt present, it was the promise of His coming again to judge the living and the dead which loomed largest and most impressive in the catechumen's consciousness. For another thing, to acquiesce in Holl's interpretation we should have to be satisfied that the true reference of "the name which is above every name" was in the eyes of second-century churchmen to the title "Lord". To the majority of modern exegetes it seems indisputable that such was St Paul's meaning. The ancient fathers, however, thought differently. For them "the name which is above every name" was generally the sacred name Jesus; for some, like St Augustine, it was Son. Not a single trustworthy instance of their understanding by it the title "Lord" can be produced. The only passage to which Lietzmann was able to point in support of Holl was the oft-quoted chapter of St Irenaeus, *Adv. haer.* 1, 10, 1.[1] Here the author brings his recital of the rule of faith and of the saving deeds of Christ to a climax by indicating the dénouement in which they will culminate—"so that to Christ Jesus, our Lord and God and Saviour and King, every knee may bow, of things in heaven and things on the earth and things under the earth, and every tongue confess to Him". But here, as Dom Capelle has correctly emphasized,[2] what recalls the Pauline paean to St Irenaeus is not so much the enumeration he has just made of the terrestrial experiences of the Saviour as the

[1] *P.G.* 7, 549 ff.   [2] *Rech. théol. anc. méd.* ii, 1930, 17.

mention of His forthcoming Parousia and His final summing-up of all things, while "the name which is above every name" is clearly for him Christ Jesus.

These are very serious objections: they strike at the very roots of the suggestion that the Christological section of R is a twofold theological commentary on the preceding titles of Christ. The question arises whether in fact there is any compelling reason for accepting it. It is worth pointing out that no capital should be made out of the fact that the Christology dwells successively on two distinct phases of the Lord's experience, His earthly generation and then His passion and exaltation, as if their combination in a unified declaration in the creed were something crying out for explanation. Examples of the Christ-kerygma in which the birth from the Blessed Virgin and the passion are set side by side are forthcoming as far back as the letters of St Ignatius.[1] St Justin too, as we saw in the previous chapter,[2] is a witness to precisely the same type of kerygma. The creed of St Irenaeus's *Epideixis*,[3] with its reference to "Jesus Christ, the Son of God, Who was incarnate, and died, and rose again", stands out as the perfect forerunner of the kind of Christology we meet with in R. The only curious feature about R is the one which first attracted Holl's attention, the reduplication of the Greek definite article τόν (represented in Latin by the repeated *qui*), which seemed to him to throw the two divisions of the Christology into sharp relief. No one can determine now what was the redactor's motive in inserting this trait: perhaps he simply wanted to underline the two aspects of the divine mystery, the Lord's incarnation and His redemptive action. By itself, however, it is much too feeble a buttress to sustain so daring and far-reaching a construction as the hypothesis of Holl and his associates.

6. *Conclusion*

Even if so much of the three German scholars' complex theory must perforce be discarded, enough remains in their demonstration of R's composite character to signalize an

---

[1] Cf. the passages from *Trall.* 9 and *Smyrn.* 1 cited above, 68 f.
[2] Cf. the excerpts cited above, 73 f.
[3] See above, 77.

important advance in credal studies. The question which next rears its head concerns the date at which we may presume the simple, three-articled formula which underlies the Old Roman Creed to have been enlarged by the insertion of a fully developed Christology. So far as general considerations go, a date somewhere within the second half of the second century would seem most in accord with the available data. Anything later would be difficult to reconcile with St Hippolytus's use of a baptismal creed closely akin to R and incorporating a similar Christology. Moreover, St Hippolytus, we know, was a conservative who preferred to walk in old paths; it is antecedently probable that the liturgies he reproduces had the authority of at least a generation behind them. A date prior to 150 is exposed to special objections too. St Justin is an important witness for the existence of the Christ-kerygma; but the second of his baptismal questions, while mentioning the crucifixion, does not seem to have included a full-length Christological passage. The line of tradition in which he stands is not exactly that of R, but the suggestion of his formulae is that the first tentative experiments at interpolating Christological assertions into the second question were being made about the middle of the century. In any case it is hard enough to find fixed formulae of any kind prior to St Justin. The first example of a rather fuller Christological insertion comes in a document dating from a generation later, St Irenaeus's *Epideixis*. If the laconic words in his creed, "Who was incarnate, and died, and rose again," may be taken as standing for somewhat more detailed statements, it is not far-fetched to see in it an extremely close parallel to R so far as structure is concerned. Further pointers to the date of R's redaction are suggested by the possible motives in the minds of those who carried it out. If their object, or even one of their objects, was to provide a counterblast to Docetism by emphasizing the reality of Christ's experiences, this would supply additional confirmation of the date towards which the argument is tending. It was in the seventies and eighties of the second century that the Church's polemic against Gnosticism was beginning to take shape and becoming a force to be reckoned with.

There is one important piece of evidence, however, which

has not yet been quoted and which may seem to demand a rather later date. This is the well-known passage, often identified as a fragment of the *Little Labyrinth* and attributed to St Hippolytus, which has been preserved by Eusebius.[1] The author is examining the claim of his Adoptionist opponents to represent the primitive Christological tradition.

"For they declare", he says, "that all the older teachers, including the Apostles themselves, received and taught exactly the same doctrine as they give out now, and that the truth of the preaching was preserved inviolate ($\tau\epsilon\tau\eta\rho\hat{\eta}\sigma\theta\alpha\iota$ $\tau\dot{\eta}\nu$ $\dot{\alpha}\lambda\dot{\eta}\theta\epsilon\iota\alpha\nu$ $\tau o\hat{v}$ $\kappa\eta\rho\dot{v}\gamma\mu\alpha\tau o s$) until the times of Victor, who was the thirteenth bishop in Rome from Peter: but that from his successor Zephyrinus the truth was falsified ($\pi\alpha\rho\alpha\kappa\epsilon\chi\alpha\rho\dot{\alpha}\chi\theta\alpha\iota$ $\tau\dot{\eta}\nu$ $\dot{\alpha}\lambda\dot{\eta}\theta\epsilon\iota\alpha\nu$)."

Naturally the author rejects their plea, bidding them consult the writings of St Justin, Miltiades, Tatian, St Clement and the rest, "in all of whom Christ is proclaimed as God ($\theta\epsilon o\lambda o\gamma\epsilon\hat{\iota}\tau\alpha\iota$ $\dot{o}$ $X\rho\iota\sigma\tau\dot{o} s$)". But the terms he chooses to employ have seemed to some modern investigators to reveal the fact that the official Roman summary of faith, in other words the creed, was tampered with in the pontificate of Zephyrinus.[2] In particular, the words "the truth of the preaching was falsified", the verb $\pi\alpha\rho\alpha\chi\alpha\rho\dot{\alpha}\sigma\sigma\epsilon\iota\nu$ being taken in the sense of to corrupt or alter a text,[3] have seemed to bear this out. Hence scholars like W. M. Peitz, J. Haussleiter and K. Lake have united in regarding the incident reported in this veiled language as being none other than the interpolation of the long Christological section into the short Trinitarian formula which lies behind R. On this view the final redaction of the creed must be thrust well forward into the third century, the reign of Zephyrinus being 197–217.

The difficulty of supposing that one of the principal Roman summaries of faith was still an immature nine-clause formula in the first decade of the third century is obvious, but such an

---

[1] *H.E.* 5, 28, 3 ff. (Schwartz, 215 f.). The title *Little Labyrinth* is due to Theodoret. Most scholars to-day deny its connexion with St Hippolytus: cf. G. Bardy, *Paul de Samosate*, 2nd ed., Louvain, 1928, 490 n.

[2] Cf. W. M. Peitz, *Stimmen der Zeit* xciv, 1918, 553 ff.; J. Haussleiter, *Trinitarischer Glaube*, 1920, Gütersloh, 84 ff.; K. Lake, *Harvard Theol. Review*, xvii, 1924. 173 ff.

[3] Cf. for this use Eusebius, *H.E.* 5, 28, 19 (Schwartz, 218).

objection cannot count as decisive. More important is the close
kinship of R in its developed form with the baptismal creed of
St Hippolytus's *Tradition*. The hypothesis under discussion asks
us to believe that the dissident bishop allowed the Christological article of his creed, which as it stands has a full-dress
account of the exploits of Christ, to come under the influence
of a new-fangled addition to R introduced by his hated opponent and contemporary Zephyrinus. This is altogether too much
to credit. Equally important is the fact that the hypothesis rests
upon the premiss that at the beginning of the third century
there was a credal formula which could be designated the
official creed of Rome. There should be no need now to underline the fallacy of such an assumption. The really damning
criticism, however, is that the theory is involved in a totally
mistaken exegesis of the passage we are discussing. To put the
matter briefly, that document does not represent the anonymous
Adoptionists as talking about creeds or official formularies at
all. Their grievance is that "the truth of the preaching" has
been falsified, and by that they plainly mean the Christological
doctrine of the Church, not a creed. The Greek verb παραχαράσ-
σειν is equally capable of signifying "falsely expound" or "mis-
represent", as in a passage of Socrates[1] in which Eustathius of
Antioch is reported to have charged Eusebius of Caesarea with
misrepresenting, or caricaturing, the Nicene faith. That must
be the sense it bears here, since its object is not a document but
"the truth". Even had the author said that "the preaching"
had been falsified, there would still be no reference to a creed,
for κήρυγμα in this context, as always, means the content of the
Church's message and not the formula, if any, in which it is
officially embodied. He himself, a few lines further down,
defines the subject of discussion not as a formulary but as "the
Church's belief (τοῦ ἐκκλησιαστικοῦ φρονήματος)", and this
should put the question beyond all doubt.

This ill-founded conjecture having been demolished, we are
free to return with renewed confidence to the theory of a somewhat earlier date. J. Lebreton[2] hazarded the guess that the

[1] *H.E.* 1, 23 (*P.G.* 67, 144).
[2] Cf. *Histoire du dogme de la Trinité*, Paris, 1927–8, II, 161 ; *Recherches de science religieuse* xx, 1930, 97 ff.

pontificate of Victor (189-197) may well have witnessed the final redaction of R. What suggested this particular decade to his mind was the conviction that the theological bias of the creed was patently anti-heretical, and that Adoptionist Monarchianism as well as Docetism was the target of its attack. We know that it was in the early 'nineties that Adoptionism installed itself at Rome, and that Victor took vigorous action against its leading exponent, Theodotus of Byzantium. Conceivably Lebreton was right, though his case was a slender one and there is nothing at first sight distinctively anti-Adoptionist in the Christological article. On the whole, however (there will be further discussion of this in the following chapter), it seems more likely that he was exaggerating the element of polemic in the creed and identifying its objects more precisely than the facts warranted. If this is so, the claims of a slightly earlier date than the reign of Pope Victor deserve to be considered, especially as we know that the practice of expanding the second article of creeds had been in full swing since the times of St Justin. Yet the honest student is bound to be suspicious of dogmatism in this matter: he must be the first to confess himself frankly baffled by the lack of any really solid data to go upon. To console him, however, he has at least the satisfaction of being able to vouch for the antiquity and respectability of R's ancestry. The underlying formula on which it was based was in all probability a simple, three-clause interrogation modelled on, if slightly fuller than, the Matthaean baptismal command: thus it joined hands with the faith and practice of the first-century Church. The Christology which was later combined with it was a sample of that semi-stereotyped proclamation of the good news about Christ which second-century Christians had inherited practically unaltered from the Apostles.

CHAPTER V

THE TEACHING OF THE OLD ROMAN CREED

1. *The First Article*

It is fitting that we should pause at this point and examine the contents of the formulary we have identified as the ancient creed of the Roman church. So far our study of it has been, of necessity, almost exclusively literary and historical. But the creeds of Christendom have never been dry-as-dust documents asking only to be sorted out, catalogued and assigned accurately to their proper dating. They have been theological manifestos, shot through with doctrinal significance and sometimes deeply stained with the marks of controversy. R was no exception. Indeed, as we shall soon be discovering, it was nothing more nor less than a compendium of popular theology, all the more fascinating to us because we can still discern, crystallized in its clauses, the faith and hope of the primitive Church. To do justice to it we must approach it at a deeper level than has hitherto been practicable and seek to unravel this message. The reader should be warned at the outset against entertaining too optimistic expectations. A fully satisfactory study of R's teaching would call for something approaching a full-length history of Christian doctrine in the second century. Here we shall attempt nothing more ambitious than to lay bare, so far as it can now be done, the original bearing of the several articles of the creed at the time of its composition. Occasionally it will be profitable to refer, by way of illustration and contrast, to the meaning read into them by later generations of Christians, but anything like exhaustiveness in this direction will be out of the question. The reader must be prepared for this chapter to assume the aspect and character of a running commentary.

Let us make a start with the first article. As originally formulated in the second century, this consisted of the bare affirmation

I BELIEVE IN GOD THE FATHER ALMIGHTY. The Eastern precedent, as we shall observe in the next chapter, was for creeds to
open with an assertion of belief in ONE GOD. A brave attempt
was made by nineteenth-century scholars [1] to demonstrate, by
appealing to writers like St Irenaeus and Tertullian, that the
same tradition prevailed in the West as well. The word ONE,
they contended, was deliberately jettisoned because of its
liability to offer a foothold to Sabellianism. Such a theory may
be dismissed as improbable in the extreme. It is based on the
tacit, and erroneous, assumption that the authorities appealed
to were acquainted with and quoting from a formulated,
official Roman creed. As a matter of fact, there is plenty of
second-century creed-material (e.g. in St Justin's works) which
testifies to the existence of an affirmation of belief in God
without the epithet ONE at a time when Sabellianism had not
yet become a menace. The suggestion that the Church could
ever have dropped ONE from its creeds, once it was present in
them, because of its supposed encouragement of Sabellianism
is far-fetched. Christians could ill afford to discard, for any
price, so cardinal an article of faith. The Roman creed implies
and is based upon the belief in one God, but the belief is not
asserted in so many words.   The reason for this is that the
ground-plan of the formula is strictly dictated by the baptismal
command in *Mt.* 28, 19.

The first problem raised by these words I BELIEVE IN
GOD THE FATHER ALMIGHTY (εἰς Θεὸν πατέρα παντοκράτορα ;
in deum patrem omnipotentem) concerns the precise relationship of
FATHER and ALMIGHTY to each other and to GOD. Later Latin
sermons and commentaries on the Apostles' Creed generally
treat them as two coordinate descriptions of the First Person
of the Trinity. Modern exegetes [2] of the creed have on the whole
decided that FATHER ALMIGHTY are to be taken closely together as a single title. Against this it must be urged that there
is no authority whatsoever for such an honorific periphrasis for
God either in the Old Testament (Septuagint) or in the New.
In the Old Testament [3] by far the most frequent collocation is

---

[1] Cf., e.g., A. E. Burn, 57 ff.
[2] Cf., e.g., Kattenbusch II, 517 ff.
[3] Cf. Hatch and Redpath, *Concordance to the Septuagint*, Oxford, 1892-7, 1053 f.

"Lord Almighty (κύριος παντοκράτωρ=Hebr. *Yahweh Sabaoth*)" or "God Almighty (ὁ Θεὸς ὁ παντοκράτωρ)". Occasionally "the Almighty (ὁ παντοκράτωρ)" is to be found alone as a noun translating the Hebrew *El Shaddai*. In the New Testament "Almighty" hardly puts in an appearance at all. Where it does, as in 2 *Cor.* 6, 18 ("Lord Almighty". a cento of O.T. quotations), or in *Revelation*[1] ("Lord God Almighty"), it falls into line with the evidence of the Septuagint. The words are first found linked together in *Martyrium Polycarpi* 19, 2 and St Justin's *Dialogue with Trypho* 139, both books belonging to the middle of the second century. One or two possible passages in St Irenaeus,[2] two or three in St Clement of Alexandria,[3] and one in St Hippolytus[4] practically exhaust the list of references in the second and early third centuries. The fathers used "Almighty" very frequently, but always either alone (ὁ παντοκράτωρ) or combined with "God" (ὁ παντοκράτωρ Θεός; *deus omnipotens*). On the other hand, the combination "God the Father" was one which had abundant precedent in the New Testament. Time and again St Paul uses such phrases as "Grace and peace from God the Father" (*Gal.* 1, 3), "to the glory of God the Father" (*Phil.* 2, 11), or "in God the Father" (1 *Thess.* 1, 1). Other New Testament writers reflect the same usage[5]; and it is interesting to observe that in the original Greek the word "Father" is attached to "God" without any article, as in the creed. In the literature of the second and following centuries "God the Father" is so regular a description of the Deity that quotations illustrating it are superfluous.

We are thus led to the conclusion that, of the two descriptive predicates FATHER and ALMIGHTY, the one which is associated the more closely with GOD is FATHER. The basic, primordial verity in which belief is proclaimed is GOD THE FATHER. That this is the core of the first article need not occasion the least surprise: it is just what we should expect in view of the fact that the model was provided by the baptismal formula. The

[1] Cf. 1, 8; 4, 8; 11, 17; 15, 3; 16, 7; 21, 22.
[2] *Adv. haer.* 1, 3, 6; 2, 35, 3; 4, 20, 6—*deus pater qui continet omnia* (*P.G.* 7, 477; 840; 1037).
[3] *Strom.* 7, 2, 7; 7, 2, 8; 7, 3, 16 (Stählin 3, 7; 8; 12).
[4] *Con. Noet.* 8 (Nautin, 249).
[5] Cf., e.g., *Jam.* 1, 27; 1 *Pet.* 1, 2; 2 *Jn.* 3; *Jud.* 1.

further title ALMIGHTY must have been conflated with it very early, as a result no doubt of the influence of the language of the Septuagint on Christian theological usage.

Though this may seem a trivial point, it has some value as confirming the connection of the creed with the Matthaean baptismal command. Much more important is the question of the meaning of the two expressions FATHER and ALMIGHTY. In later ages the almost invariable tradition of patristic exegesis in the West was to interpret the former as referring to the special relation of the First to the Second Person of the Holy Trinity. The Father was Father of the eternal Word. As early as the middle of the fourth century St Cyril of Jerusalem[1] was explaining, in his discussion of the creed, that FATHER properly belonged to God in virtue of His relation to the Son, the very word suggesting the idea of a son to the mind : it could be taken as describing His fatherly relation to mankind, but only by a misuse of language ($\kappa\alpha\tau\alpha\chi\rho\eta\sigma\tau\iota\kappa\hat{\omega}\varsigma$). Taking up this cue, Rufinus comments :[2]

When you hear the word GOD, you are to understand a substance without beginning, without end, simple. . . . When you hear the word FATHER, you are to understand the Father of the Son, of that Son Who is the image of the aforesaid substance. For just as no one is entitled master unless he has either property or a slave to exercise lordship over, and just as no one is called tutor unless he has a pupil, so no one can be described as father unless he has a son.

This type of interpretation, and this identical argument to support it, became almost routine in subsequent centuries.[3]

At the same time there is evidence to suggest that the affirmation conveyed in some circles a warmer, less strictly theological message. St Augustine supplies a good example. In *Sermon* 213,[4] on the Tradition of the Creed, he exclaims, "Observe how quickly the words are spoken, and how full of significance they are. He is God, and He is Father: God in power, Father in goodness. How blessed we are who find that our Lord God is our Father!" When we recall the setting of baptism, charged

[1] *Cat.* 7, 4f (*P.G.* 33, 608 f.).
[2] *Comm. in symb. ap.* 4 (*C.C.L.* 20, 137 f.).
[3] Cf., e.g., a sermon ascribed to St Caesarius (*C.C.L.* 103, 48).
[4] *P.L.* 38, 1060.

with ideas about the believer's rebirth and adoption as a son of God, it is easy to surmise that thoughts such as those to which St Augustine was giving expression must often have been present in people's minds as they answered the credal questions. And we have proof of it in a fine passage of St Cyprian[1] commenting on the words "Our Father" in the Lord's Prayer:

A man renewed, reborn and restored to his God through His grace [i.e. baptized] says "Father" at the beginning of the prayer because he has now begun to be a son. . . . So the man who has believed in His name and has become God's son ought from this point to begin both to give thanks and to profess himself God's son, by declaring that God is his Father in heaven, and also to bear witness . . . that he has renounced an earthly and carnal father and has begun to know, as well as to have, as a father Him only Who is in heaven.

He goes on to show that only those who "have been sanctified through Him and restored by the birth of spiritual grace" are truly entitled to say "Our Father". Tertullian gives vent to similar sentiments in a passage[2] which may have given St Cyprian his model; and Origen expatiates[3] on the fact that, while the title "Father" as applied to God was of frequent occurrence in the Old Testament, it was the Christians who were first privileged to call God FATHER in the fullest sense of the word.

When we turn to the period of the creed's formation, it is clear that neither of these interpretations represents the whole, or even the most important part, of what was in the minds of its authors. It would be gravely misleading, of course, to exclude them. St Clement of Rome, for example, bids[4] his readers approach God in holiness of soul, "loving our gentle and compassionate Father Who has made us an elect portion unto Himself"; and more than one reference to God as the Father of Christians can be quoted from the second-century homily[5] known as 2 Clement. Equally there are plenty of second-century contexts (e.g. in St Ignatius) where the Fatherhood of God is

---

[1] *De domin. orat.* 9 and 10 (Hartel I, 272 f.).
[2] *De orat.* 2 (*C.C.L.* 1, 258).
[3] *De orat.* 22 (Koetschau 2, 346 ff.).
[4] Ch. 29 (Bihlmeyer, 51).
[5] Ch. 8; 10; 14 (Bihlmeyer, 74; 75; 77).

understood in relation to His Son Jesus Christ. That this was part at any rate of the intention of the creed is obvious from the language of the second article. Most often, however, where the term "Father" was used at this time, the reference was to God in His capacity as Father and creator of the universe. Thus St Clement of Rome could speak[1] of "the Father and creator of the whole universe" and of "the demiurge and Father of the ages", while St Justin was frequent in his references[2] to "the Father of all and Lord God" and "the Father of all things". A revealing text is that in which St Irenaeus declared that the universal creator was called Father because of His love (revealed in His creative activity), Lord because of His might, and our maker and framer because of His wisdom.[3] St Theophilus of Antioch has an interesting passage[4] describing God as "Father because of His being before the universe", while Tatian[5] speaks of Him as "Father of things perceptible and of things invisible". So, too, when Novatian expounds[6] the clause GOD THE FATHER AND ALMIGHTY LORD in his rule of faith, he paraphrases it as meaning "the all-perfect founder of all things". To Christians of the second century this was beyond any question the primary, if by no means the only, significance of the Fatherhood of God. It was a belief which they shared, as the third book of *Maccabees* and the writings of Philo prove, with Hellenistic Judaism[7] as well as with enlightened religious people generally.[8]

Naturally there was nothing controversial about this affirmation of the divine Fatherhood. Nor was there about the epithet ALMIGHTY which went closely conjoined with it. There was abundant authority for its use in the Septuagint, and in early Christian writers it recurs on countless occasions as a description of God's majesty and transcendence. The underlying meaning of παντοκράτωρ in Greek, however, and the meaning

---

[1] Ch. 19 and 35 (Bihlmeyer, 46 and 54).
[2] *Apol.* I, 12; 61; II, 6 (E.J.G., 33; 70; 82).
[3] *Adv. haer.* 5, 17, 1 (*P.G.* 7, 1169): cf. 2, 35, 3 f. (*P.G.* 7, 840 ff.).
[4] *Ad Autol.* 1, 4 (*P.G.* 6, 1029).
[5] *Or. adv. Graec.* 4 (E.J.G., 271).
[6] *De Trin.* 1 (*P.L.* 3, 913).
[7] Cf. III *Macc.* 2, 21; 5, 7; and Philo, *passim*.
[8] Cf., e.g., Epictetus, 1, 3, 1; 1, 9, 7; 1, 19, 12; 3, 24, 15 f. Also St Justin, *Apol.* I, 22.

taken for granted in the second-century Church, was by no means identical with that of "Almighty" in English or *omnipotens* in Latin. The exact equivalent of these would have been παντοδύναμος. Παντοκράτωρ is in the first place an active word, conveying the idea not just of capacity but of the actualization of capacity. More important, the basic conception involved is wider than that contained in "Almighty". Παντοκράτωρ has the meaning "all-ruling", "all-sovereign". This is brought out in numberless patristic contexts, but with particular force in the first few chapters of the second book of St Irenaeus's *Adversus haereses*.

"Either there must be one God," he argues against the Gnostic theory of a graded hierarchy of divine beings, "Who contains all things and has made every created being according to His will; or else there must be many indeterminate creators or gods . . . but not one of them will be God. For each one of them . . . will be defective in comparison with all the rest, and the name of 'Almighty' will come to nought (*solvetur omnipotentis appellatio*)."[1]

St Theophilus of Antioch makes the same point when he explains[2] that God is called almighty "because He rules and compasses all things. For the heights of the heavens and the depths of the abysses and the limits of the world are in His hand." Similarly Origen makes[3] the fact that God is almighty an argument for the necessary existence of a created order. "Thus God cannot be called even almighty unless He has subjects over whom to hold sway; and consequently for God to be shown to be almighty, the universe must necessarily exist." In a section[4] of his lectures devoted to discussing παντοκράτωρ St Cyril of Jerusalem remarks that the Almighty is

He Who rules all things, Who has authority over all things. People who say there is one Lord of the soul, and another of the body, imply that neither is perfect. For how could he who has authority over the soul, but not over the body, be almighty? And how could he who is master of bodies, but has no sway over spirits, be almighty? . . . But the divine Scripture and the utterances of the truth know only one God Who rules all things by His power.

[1] *Adv. haer.* 2, 1, 5 (*P.G.* 7, 712). Cf. also 2, 6, 2 (*P.G.* 7, 724 f.).
[2] *Ad Autol.* 1, 4 (*P.G.* 6, 1029).
[3] *De princip.* 1, 2, 10 (Koetschau, 41 f.).
[4] *Cat.* 8, 3 (*P.G.* 33, 628).

The alternative meaning, that underlying παντοδύναμος and now obviously present in the English translation, was not long in making itself felt. Thus we gather from Origen's *Contra Celsum* that the pagan philosopher, no doubt picking up scraps of Church doctrine, was under the impression that Christians taught that God could do anything. "He can assuredly according to us do anything," replied Origen,[1] "that is, anything that can be done without detriment to His divinity, His goodness or His wishes." Thus God can no more be unjust than a thing whose nature it is to be sweet can, in virtue of its natural quality, prove itself bitter. In another passage[2] concerned with the same difficulty, he contended that God could not do what was base: if He could, He Who is God could not be God, for if God does what is base He is no longer God. When Rufinus comes[3] to the word, he sticks to the older tradition, saying, "He is called almighty because He wields power over all things (*quod omnium teneat potentatum*)," and goes on to point out that he does this through the agency of the Son. St Augustine, however, was exercised about the problem of what God could and could not do. In *Sermon* 213,[4] for example, he remarks that we can expect all mercies from Him because He is omnipotent: to say that He cannot forgive all our sins is a blasphemous denial of His omnipotence. He is, in a word, omnipotent to perform everything that He wills. Yet he continues, "I can tell the sort of things He could not do. He cannot die, He cannot sin, He cannot lie, He cannot be deceived. Such things He cannot: if He could, He would not be almighty." On other occasions St Augustine combined the older view with the more philosophic one. In *Sermon* 214[5] he first of all teaches that the belief in God's almightiness is equivalent to believing that He is the universal creator: "Be mindful to believe God omnipotent in the sense that there is no creature which He has not created." Then a few paragraphs later he discusses the problem of divine omnipotence in a more speculative vein. Taking 2 *Tim.* 2, 13 ("He cannot deny Himself") as his text, he points out that the reason why God cannot do certain things is that He does

---

[1] *Con. Cels.* 3, 70 (Koetschau 1, 262).   [2] *Op. cit.* 5, 23 (Koetschau 2, 24).
[3] *Comm. in symb. ap.* 5 (*C.C.L.* 20, 140).   [4] *P.L.* 38, 1060 f.
[5] *P.L.* 38, 1066 ff.

not will to do them. "If God can be what He does not will to be, He is not omnipotent."

But the paradoxes and philosophical puzzles inherent in the notion of divine omnipotence were altogether foreign to the minds of the authors of the Old Roman Creed. The chief doctrine contained in the first article of their interrogatory formula was the creative Fatherhood of God, His majesty and transcendent sovereignty. It might appear that there was nothing distinctively Christian about such a belief, for the best Jewish and pagan thought of the age would have heartily endorsed it. But a special atmosphere surrounded the words as they were conned by the Christian catechumen in anticipation of his sacramental initiation. He knew, as Jews and pagans were not privileged to know, that the eternal Father of the universe was also the Father of Jesus the Christ, and had even vouchsafed to adopt him as His son by grace; and he knew that the sovereign power which God possessed by right had been signally manifest in the resurrection of His Son and in the redemption of His chosen people.

2. The Core of the Second Article

Detached from the special kerygma about Christ, the second article of the Old Roman Creed was extremely terse—AND IN CHRIST JESUS HIS ONLY SON OUR LORD (καὶ εἰς Χριστὸν Ἰησοῦν υἱὸν αὐτοῦ τὸν μονογενῆ τὸν κύριον ἡμῶν ; et in Christum Iesum filium eius unicum dominum nostrum). Even this form must represent an elaboration of the true original, for ONLY almost certainly secured its place in the latter at some date subsequent to its composition, and it is possible that LORD too was a late entrant. The unusual word-order CHRIST JESUS is a feature which pulls one up at once with a jolt. It reappears in the baptismal questionnaire of St Hippolytus's *Tradition*, in one at any rate of Tertullian's forms, and in the creeds of Rufinus (Aquileia) and St Peter Chrysologus (Ravenna[1]) : everywhere else it yields place to the normal JESUS CHRIST. The presence of the inversion is a proof of the primitiveness of the core of the Old Roman Creed. When it was put together CHRIST was not

[1] See below, pp. 173 f.

a mere name: something of its original significance as a title, the equivalent of Messiah or the Anointed, still hovered about it. St Paul was evidently conscious of the word's true implications, for he showed a marked predilection for the order Christ Jesus. But the most illuminating parallels are to be found in accounts of the apostolic preaching by the author of *Acts*. Thus St Peter is represented (2, 36) as declaring, "Let all the house of Israel know assuredly that God has made Him both Lord and Christ, this Jesus Whom you crucified." Later (5, 42) it is said of him and his companion apostles that "they ceased not to teach and to preach Jesus as the Christ". Apollos at Ephesus, we are informed (18, 28), "powerfully confuted the Jews, and that publicly, showing by the Scriptures that Jesus was the Christ". Evidently the nucleus of R joined hands with the ancient kerygma.

The authority behind this usage was, of course, the Old Testament. Ὁ Χριστός, the Anointed, was the regular Septuagint translation of the Hebrew *Mashîah*.[1] The Messianic category had been used by Jesus Himself, and it was natural for early Christianity, rooted as it was in Judaism, to appeal to it as an explanation of the significance of His Person. In the post-apostolic age other categories loomed into the foreground, and the historical associations of the older Hebrew title were less apparent to converts entering the Church from a Gentile environment. Hence CHRIST called for elucidation. St Clement of Rome uses the word more frequently with the article than without, and in some of his contexts[2] it is apparent that it retained for him something of its Messianic flavour. But St Justin, who was fully apprised of its proper connotation (as his *Dialogue*[3] shows), found it advisable to explain the enigmatic term to the Roman Senate. It applies, he said,[4] to the Logos, Who is alone properly to be called God's Son. "Being begotten in the beginning when God created and set in order all things through Him, He is called Christ in virtue of the fact that He has Himself been anointed and that God through Him has set

[1] See Hatch and Redpath, *Concordance*, s.v.
[2] Cf., e.g., 16, 1; 42, 1; 44, 3; 49, 1; 54, 2; 57, 2 (Bihlmeyer, 43; 57; 59; 61; 64; 65).
[3] E.g., 48 ff. (E.J.G., 146 ff.).
[4] *Apol*. II, 6 (E.J.G., 83).

all things in order." The name itself, he adds, contains an ineffable meaning (ὄνομα καὶ αὐτὸ περιέχον ἄγνωστον σημασίαν). In general it was the interpretation of *Christus* as "anointed" which was to persist when the specifically Messianic reference had faded into the background. Tertullian, for example, pointed out[1] that *Christus* was not properly a name but an appellation and signified "anointed (*unctus*)". He had been designated such as a result of "the sacrament of anointing". St Cyril of Jerusalem discussed both JESUS and CHRIST in his tenth *Catechesis*,[2] concluding that "He is called Christ, not as anointed by human hands, but as having been anointed by the Father eternally for a super-human priesthood". Recurring to the same name point a little later,[3] he summed the matter up by saying that "He bears two names, Jesus because He bestows salvation, and Christ because of His priesthood". Rufinus carried on the same tradition.

"He is called Christ," he remarked,[4] "from chrism, i.e. from anointing. . . . Christ is either a highpriestly or a royal name. For in the old days both high-priests and kings were consecrated by the anointing of chrism. But they, being mortal and corruptible, were anointed with an unguent of corruptible matter; but He is made Christ through the anointing of the Holy Spirit."

To CHRIST JESUS two further descriptions were attached—HIS ONLY SON and OUR LORD. The word ONLY (μονογενής; *unicus*) merits some discussion, particularly as it is probably a later accretion to the original nucleus. In the New Testament it is used by St Luke, St John and the author of *Hebrews*, but by no one else. Its proper meaning is clearly brought out in *Hebr.* 11, 17, where Isaac is described as Abraham's "only son", and in *Lk.* 7, 12, where the Lord raises the "only son" of the widow of Nain from the dead. As indicating the peculiar relation of Jesus to God it is confined to the Johannine writings.[5] There it stresses the uniqueness of Jesus alike in His Sonship (so different from the sense in which men can be the sons of God), in His intimacy with the Father, and in His consequent

---

[1] *Adv. Prax.* 28 (*C.C.L.* 2, 1200).   [2] Ch. 4 (*P.G.* 33, 664).
[3] Ch. 11 (*P.G.* 33, 676).   [4] *Comm. in symb. ap.* 6 (*C.C.L.* 20, 141).
[5] Cf. *Jn.* 1, 14; 1, 18; 3, 16; 3, 18; 1 *Jn.* 4, 9.

knowledge of Him. Its use in Christian writings before St Irenaeus, however, is most infrequent. St Ignatius approximates to it, calling [1] Jesus "His sole Son ($\tau o\hat{v}$ $\mu\acute{o}\nu o\upsilon$ $\upsilon i o\hat{v}$)", but the only certain instances of the term itself are St Justin, *Dial.* 105,[2] *Martyrium Polycarpi* 20[3] and *Ep. ad Diognetum* 10.[4] For this reason its sudden appearance in the creed calls for explanation. The key to the problem is almost certainly to be found in the fact that about the middle of the second century the word was becoming a cliché with the Valentinian Gnostics. Possibly inspired by the Fourth Gospel,[5] they were tending to monopolize it as a designation for their aeon Nous, making a sharp distinction between Monogenes and the historical figure Jesus. They even claimed St John as an ally in this way of thinking because of his statement, "We beheld His glory, glory *as of* an only-begotten".[6] It is interesting to note that St Irenaeus, in answer to extravagant teaching like this, vigorously marshalled authorities to demonstrate that, on the contrary, the true Monogenes must be identified with the Word Who, in obedience to His Father's behest, became flesh as our Lord Jesus Christ, suffered on our behalf, and rose again.[7] In all probability, therefore, the introduction of the word to the vocabulary of orthodoxy and its insertion into the credal questions are to be connected with this counter-attack.[8] If this be so, we may conjecture some date in the 'sixties or 'seventies for its incorporation in R.

An interesting corollary follows from this use of Monogenes. It has often been asserted that the Old Roman Creed was distinguished by its lack of interest in the pre-historical existence of Christ: its Christology centred in the supernatural character of His earthly begetting. It is doubtful, as we shall shortly see, whether this is a fair account of the teaching of the Christological section, but in any case the application of the title

---

[1] *Rom. praef.* (Bihlmeyer, 96).   [2] E.J.G., 221.
[3] Bihlmeyer, 131.
[4] Bihlmeyer, 147 (a quotation from 1 *Jn.* 4, 9).
[5] Cf. J. N. Sanders, *The Fourth Gospel in the early Church*, Cambridge, 1943, ch. 3; R. McL. Wilson, *The Gnostic Problem*, London, 1958, 128 f.; 194.
[6] Cf. St Clement Alex., *Excerp. ex Theod.* 7, 1 ff. (Stählin 3, 108).
[7] Cf., e.g., *Adv. haer.* 3, 16, 1; 3, 16, 6: also 1, 10, 3 (*P.G.* 7, 920 f.; 925; 556).
[8] So H. B. Swete in *The Apostles' Creed*, Cambridge, 1894, 25 ff., followed by H. Lietzmann, *Z.N.T.W.* xxvi. 1927, 90 f.

Monogenes to Jesus utterly destroys the theory. In the Johannine writings, with their explicit doctrine of the Word as the eternal Son of God, the suggestion of the pre-cosmic relationship of the Monogenes to His Father is never far from the surface. The single context of St Justin,[1] where the term crops up clearly, understands it of the Word's eternal generation. Finally, both the Valentinians' perversion of Monogenes and St Irenaeus's rejoinder to them imply that the question at issue concerned the identity of the historical Jesus with the eternal Only-begotten of the Father. The Old Roman Creed, therefore, takes its stand with those who believe in the pre-existence of Him Who became incarnate of the Blessed Virgin.

Neither of the two titles attributed to Christ Jesus, HIS SON and OUR LORD, could be adequately discussed without assigning more space to them than is practicable here. The former reproduces His own claim, so frequently attested in the Gospels,[2] to divine Sonship. The Church accepted the claim unquestioningly, and the word was a favourite one with the New Testament writers generally. The confession that Jesus was the Son of God became one of the earliest of Christian credal slogans.[3] What particular theology of Sonship was implied in the simple baptismal question underlying R, it is of course impossible now to determine. The acclamation of Jesus as Lord was likewise a distinctive element in Christian teaching and preaching from the first. St Paul represents[4] it as the typical utterance of the believer under the influence of the Spirit, and we noticed in Chapter I how the primitive community employed it as a stereotyped baptismal confession. How deep the roots of this title went is indicated by St Paul's quotation[5] of the Aramaic prayer *Maranatha* (="Come, our Lord"). It continued in use as a popular category for explaining the Person of Jesus, being aided in this because, although the regular Septuagint translation of the Hebrew Yahweh, it was not tied up with exclusively Judaistic associations. In *Phil.* 3, 8 we observe the usage "my Lord" creeping in, while in *Rom.* 15, 30 and 16, 18 and in I *Cor.* 1, 2 "our Lord" makes an appearance. The

---

[1] *Dial.* 105 (E. J.G., 221).
[2] Cf. esp. *Mk.* 13, 32; *Lk.* 10, 21 f.=*Mt.* 11, 25 ff.
[3] Cf. *supra*, p. 16. [4] I *Cor.* 12, 3.
[5] I *Cor.* 16, 22. Cf. *Didache* 10, 6 (Bihlmeyer, 6).

absence of LORD from H and from Tertullian's confessions encourages, though it by no means necessitates, the inference that it represents a later accretion to the original core of R.

3. *The Christological Insertion*

In the mature development of R the brief primitive affirmation of the second article did not stand alone, but ushered in a lengthy Christological statement stressing both the Saviour's birth from the Holy Spirit and the Blessed Virgin, and His sufferings, glorification and Second Coming. The Christ-kerygma, as we saw earlier, formed a stock feature of the apostolic propaganda: it was securely ensconced in the second-century Church's rule of faith and played a vital role in catechetical instruction. St Ignatius, St Justin and St Irenaeus [1] vouch for the existence of precisely that type of kerygma, dwelling on the Lord's birth and on His sufferings, etc., as parallel truths, which reappeared in the creed. Before proceeding to comment on it in detail, we should consider for a moment the motives which may have prompted the amalgamation of a full-blown Christology with the already existing triadic formula. In the preceding chapter we criticized recent suggestions that the Christological excursus should be regarded as a kind of theological exegesis of SON and LORD.

The most plausible alternative explanation is that the interpolation was inspired by the desire to exclude heresy. Long before its originally independent existence was admitted, many scholars [2] held that this portion of the creed was patently anti-Docetic. If they meant to imply that its several clauses were actually put together with this intent, they were mistaken. The Christ-kerygma was an original element in the Christian message, and it had reached a fair degree of stabilization in apostolic days. But the same hypothesis may be applied, with suitable modifications, to explain the incorporation of the Christology. The nerve of the argument lies in the insistence in this section of the creed on the reality of Christ's human

---

[1] See above, p. 126.
[2] Cf., e.g., A. C. McGiffert, *The Apostles' Creed*, New York, 1902; G. Krüger, *Z.N.T.W.* vi, 1905, 72 ff.

experiences—His birth, His physical sufferings, His death and burial. St Ignatius's polemic against Judaistic Docetism, it will be remembered, had resulted in precisely this emphasis on the reality of the incarnate life.[1] Much the same emphasis, though with a different twist because of the Gnostic distinction between Christ and the historical Jesus, recurs in St Irenaeus with almost monotonous regularity. The view of the heretics was that Christ's flesh was unreal, and that He was impassible: these were articles of faith with them (si enim quis regulas ipsorum omnium perscrutetur).[2] It is a commonplace that, as part of the Church's reaction to the Gnostic crisis, a marked stiffening in the formulation of doctrine took place and a deliberate appeal was increasingly made to the ancient, traditional rule of faith. The redrafting and strengthening of creeds of which the enlargement of R provides an illuminating sample may well have been the direct product of this movement.

If the redaction of R is agreed to have been carried through somewhere around the third quarter of the second century, the claims of this hypothesis are strong; it is hardly possible to deny a considerable element of truth to it. No one incorporating a Christology of this type in the pre-existing triadic formula could have been unconscious of its apologetic appositeness against Gnostic errors. But we must beware of exaggerating or concentrating exclusively on this motive. The anti-Gnostic bias imparted to the creed was in no way pronounced. St Ignatius underlined his points by the addition of emphatic adverbs ("was truly born", etc.); and a century or so later St Gregory Thaumaturgus adopted the same device in his profession of faith.[3] There were no similar tell-tale signs of a polemical intention in the creed. Strangely absent from it, too, were the other characteristic features of the anti-Gnostic campaign, such as the insistence, so frequent in St Irenaeus, on the oneness of God the Father and on His creation of both heaven and earth. It should be recalled, furthermore, that the expansion of the second article of creeds, without any perceptible anti-Gnostic arrière pensée, had been getting under way as far back

---

[1] Cf., e.g., Trall. 9; Smyrn. 1, 1–2 (Bihlmeyer, 95; 106).
[2] Adv. haer. 3, 11, 3 (P.G. 7, 882).
[3] Expos. fid.: P.G. 10, 935 (υἱὸς ἀληθινὸς ἀληθινοῦ πατρός).

as St Justin's time. Nor was the interpolated matter confined to items relevant to the Gnostic issue: it comprised, in addition to and logically connected with the facts of the incarnation, mentions of the Lord's glorification and of the Second Coming and Judgment. Taken all together, these considerations would seem to suggest that, while the combination of a Christ-kerygma with the creed undoubtedly reflected the self-conscious interest in and apologetic use of the rule of faith which the struggle against Gnosticism instigated, there were probably other, rather more ordinary and human motives at work as well. The *gesta Christi* had always, and necessarily, been a stock theme of Christian catechetical instruction. As the baptismal questions tended to become summaries of the course of teaching which led up to the sacrament, the need must early have been felt of including in them a somewhat fuller Christological statement. Mere convenience, too, must have encouraged the grouping together of the two independent, but logically interrelated, types of credal summary. Christians must have been conscious of a gap so long as articles like Christ's exaltation and coming in judgment, which loomed large in popular instruction, had no place in the credal interrogations. Thus if the controversial atmosphere of the age was propitious to R's enlargement, it would be unwise to overlook the other, more ordinary factors which were probably operating in the same direction.

The various statements comprised in the Christological section must now be submitted to a somewhat closer examination. The opening one is an affirmation of the Saviour's birth FROM THE HOLY SPIRIT AND THE VIRGIN MARY. As early as St Ignatius[1] the Virgin Birth figured in summaries of the kerygma, and the fathers fastened[2] on *Is.* 7, 14 ff. as its prophetic anticipation. It is a curious fact, however, that until the times of St Irenaeus Jesus was usually described as having been born simply from the Virgin, the Holy Spirit, despite the Gospel account, being passed over in silence. It is unnecessary to read too much into this, as if the Old Roman Creed were guilty of a startling innovation. Possibly the explanation lies partly in

---

[1] Cf. *Eph.* 18, 2; *Trall.* 9; *Smyrn.* 1 (Bihlmeyer, 87; 95; 106).

[2] Cf. St Justin, *Apol.* I, 33 (E.J.G., 48); St Irenaeus, *Adv. haer.* 3, 21, 1 (*P.G.* 7, 946); *Epideixis* 53 (Robinson, 116).

the fact that the Old Testament prophecy mentioned only a virgin, and partly in the uncertainty under which the majority of early writers laboured (we shall recur to this later) as to the identity and role of the Holy Spirit referred to by the Evangelists. In any case, the chief interest of the clause concerns the light which it may possibly throw on the kind of doctrine of Christ's Person envisaged by R's redactors. Harnack at one stage thought that the general drift of the creed was decidedly Adoptionist, and in this he was followed by Karl Holl. Arguing that the clause was designed to explain Christ's Sonship as originating with His human birth, Holl claimed that it gave no support either to a Logos theology or, for that matter, to any idea of eternal generation.[1]

Theories of this sort, it may be confidently asserted, are strangely wide of the mark. R was an influential creed, representing a powerful strain of Roman theological tradition: the date of its final composition can hardly be placed before the middle of the second century. It is paradoxical to assert that Christological views of the kind presupposed had any vogue in official circles at this epoch; while the out-and-out Adoptionists of the 'eighties and 'nineties preferred to concentrate on the Lord's baptism as the critical moment of His elevation.[2] R was a close relative, moreover, of the creed of St Hippolytus's *Tradition*: certainly the latter would scarcely have commended itself to the bishop if it had seemed susceptible of an Adoptionist interpretation. Still less easy is it to square such an interpretation with the presence of Monogenes in the same article. The unmistakable implication of this word, deliberately inserted as it was at the time of or a little previous to R's final redaction, was that there was a super-historical element in the Person of the Son of Mary. If Holl's theory of the connection between the clause and *Lk.* 1, 35 were to be deemed acceptable, we should be better advised to regard it as expressing the belief that Jesus Christ was the incarnation of divine Spirit, and that what originated with the birth from the Virgin was not His supernatural status but His Sonship. There is plenty of evidence for the existence in Rome in the late second and early third

---

[1] *Sitzungsberichte der Preussischen Akademie*, 1919, I, 7 f.

[2] Cf., e.g., St Hippolytus, *Ref. omn. haer.* 7, 35; 10, 23 (Wendland 3, 222; 282).

century of a Christology which, while fully admitting the full deity of the Saviour, was inclined to deny His pre-natal Sonship.[1]

But if we reject Holl's hypothesis, as we did in the last chapter, we are no longer obliged to read the clause as tracing Christ's Sonship, along the lines of *Lk.* 1, 35, to the historical birth. While there are advantages in this, it undoubtedly reduces our chances of determining what precisely was the Christology of the creed at the time of its redaction. There are no obvious indications pointing to any one kind of doctrine. Certainly there is no overt hint of a Logos theory, though there is equally nothing that is inconsistent with one. On the whole, however, since baptismal creeds were compendia of popular teaching rather than manifestos of the *théologie savante*, and since the Logos doctrine as formulated by St Hippolytus was encountering opposition from Popes Zephyrinus and Callistus as late as the first decades of the third century, it would be rash to claim that it underlies R. On the other hand, there is nothing to exclude the idea of pre-existent Sonship. On the contrary, that Christ was the Son of God and that, as the Only-begotten, He pre-existed as Son, seems to be the clear implication of the words immediately preceding our clause. We should be on our guard, however, against looking for a Christology in line with the conceptions of later orthodoxy. We have already hinted that the second-century fathers had not altogether made up their minds as to the identity of the Holy Spirit in the incarnation. A view which had considerable currency, and with which the learned theologians felt constrained to harmonize their more sophisticated speculations, was that what had become incarnate in the Blessed Virgin, as narrated by St Matthew and St Luke, was divine Spirit. We have a clear assertion of this in a well-known passage of St Justin,[2] where the Spirit mentioned in *Lk.* 1, 35 is identified with the Logos. A similar teaching was put forward, though more hesitantly, by St Irenaeus[3]; and Tertullian[4] and St Hippolytus[5] were also among

---

[1] Cf the important article by H. J. Carpenter, *J.T.S.* xl, 1939, 31 ff.

[2] *Apol.* I, 33 (E.J.G., 49).

[3] E.g., *Epideixis* 71; 97 (Robinson, 131 f.; 149). For an examination of his teaching, see Robinson, op. cit. 31 ff.

[4] E.g., *Adv. Prax.* 26 f. (*C.C.L.* 2, 1196 ff.).

[5] *Con. Noet.* 4; 16 (Nautin, 243; 259–61).

its exponents. In St Callistus[1] it reappeared couched in a form hostile to the Logos teaching. The fact that so many theologians of different schools reflected this Spirit-Christology encourages the suspicion that it was the most widespread view in the Roman church of the late second century.[2] If we are inclined to ascribe R's redaction to this period, we should be prepared to look for ideas akin to those described behind the wording of its second article.

While the individual items in the remainder of the Christological section do not call for elaborate discussion, a few comments should be made. Practically all of them go back to the primitive kerygma of the apostolic age, and find parallels in the earliest creed material. An exception is the dating UNDER PONTIUS PILATE. The words occur in 1 *Tim.* 6, 13, but have no place in the earliest summaries of the kerygma. The same formula, however, or something approximating to it, becomes almost routine in St Ignatius[3] and St Justin,[4] as well as in St Irenaeus[5] and Tertullian.[6] It is at first sight rather puzzling that Pontius Pilate should have been vouchsafed a position in the Church's confession of faith. We know that the imagination of second-century Christians busied itself to an astonishing extent with the figure of Pilate, usually with the object of making him testify to Christ's innocence and so, by implication, to the harmlessness of the Church. People have suspected that the desire to combat Docetism inspired the insertion of his name into the rule of faith. It is significant that in all the Ignatian contexts in which the dating UNDER PONTIUS PILATE occurs the writer is pressing home, as against Docetic denials, the reality of Christ's experiences. So, too, the first of the extracts of St Irenaeus cited above (*Adv. haer.* 2, 32, 4) is avowedly aimed at heretics who allege that Christ wrought His miracles "in appearance". Yet if a few passages can be quoted with such an unambiguous anti-Docetic bias, it is impossible to detect any such innuendo in the great majority of

---

[1] In St Hippolytus, *Ref. omn. haer.* 10, 27 (Wendland 3, 283).
[2] For the evidence, see, e.g., Robinson, loc. cit.; J. Lebreton, *Histoire du dogme de la Trinité*, Paris, 1927, I, 334; H. J. Carpenter, *J.T.S.* xl, 1939, 32 ff.
[3] *Magn.* 11; *Trall.* 9; *Smyrn.* 1 (Bihlmeyer, 91; 95; 106).
[4] *Apol.* I, 13; 61; II, 6; *Dial.* 30; 76; 85 (E.J.G., 34; 71; 124; 186; 197).
[5] *Adv. haer.* 2, 32, 4; 3, 4, 2; 3, 12, 9; 5, 12, 5 (*P.G.* 7, 829; 856; 902; 1155).
[6] *De virg. vel.* 1 (*C.C.L.* 2, 1209).

them. Even where it is present in a passage taken as a whole, it remains doubtful whether UNDER PONTIUS PILATE should be taken as contributing to it. On the other hand, no anti-Docetic argument was directly and explicitly founded on the words in such second-century writings as have come down to us. The real explanation of the presence of Pontius Pilate in the creed lies elsewhere—in the fact that the saving story of which the creed is a recapitulation is rooted in history. A date was called for so as to bring out that these events did not happen anywhere or at any time, and that the Gospel is not simply a system of ideas. For once Rufinus succeeded in hitting upon the truth when he remarked[1]: "Those who handed down the creed showed great wisdom in underlining the actual date at which these things happened, so that there might be no chance of any uncertainty or vagueness upsetting the stability of the tradition." Without anyone saying so in so many words, the instinct of the Church recognized the need for a historical reference. Thus, while the final form in which the dating crystallized was always UNDER PONTIUS PILATE, alternative forms were possible. St Ignatius, for example, in *Smyrn.* 1 speaks of Christ as "truly nailed for us in the flesh in the times of Pontius Pilate and Herod the tetrarch", while St Justin[2] has "under Pontius Pilate, who was governor in Judaea in the days of Tiberius Caesar".

The claims of the remaining elements in this section to belong to the apostolic kerygma are undisputed. WAS BURIED was cited by St Paul[3] as an item in the catechetical instruction he had received. That it was already an independent article of faith and that importance was attached to it is obvious from the fact of his prefixing "that ($\acute{o}\tau\iota$)" to it. So, too, preaching[4] at Antioch in Pisidia, he singled out the fact that "they took Him down from the tree and laid Him in the tomb". We may be certain that the reason for admitting the clause to the catechetical tradition had nothing to do with its guaranteeing the reality of the Lord's death. There was no need for an anti-Docetic

---

[1] *Comm. in symb. apost.* 16 (*C.C.L.* 20, 152).
[2] *Apol.* I, 13 (E.J.G., 34).
[3] 1 *Cor.* 15, 4. Cf. also *Rom.* 6, 4, which singles out the Lord's burial as a significant moment in His passion.
[4] *Acts* 13, 29.

polemic in the first two or three decades of the Church's history. What is more to the point is that Christ's burial plays a prominent part in the Gospel narrative. No doubt Christians dwelt on it and exploited the details surrounding it because it was the necessary prelude to His resurrection. It is to this interest that we must attribute the presence of the clause in the creed. At all events it is impossible to argue that the burial was treasured because it figured in ancient prophecy. Later theologians, like St Justin[1] and St Cyril of Jerusalem,[2] were hard put to it to unearth prophecies in the Old Testament showing that it was preordained. Others were frankly at a loss to explain its purpose in the creed, and Rufinus, for example, suggested[3] that the insertion of HE DESCENDED TO HELL was intended to elucidate the enigmatic clause.

The rest of the article can be dismissed in a summary paragraph. ON THE THIRD DAY ROSE AGAIN FROM THE DEAD formed the kernel of the apostolic preaching from the inauguration of the Christian mission. Closely linked with it and with one another are the two clauses ASCENDED INTO THE HEAVENS and SITS AT THE RIGHT HAND OF THE FATHER. We observe them both conjoined in 1 *Pet.* 3, 22 : "Who is on the right hand of God, having gone up to heaven." Other parallel passages which can be cited are *Rom.* 8, 34, *Col.* 3, 1, *Eph.* 1, 20, *Hebr.* 1, 3 and 13, as well as *Acts* 2, 31 ff., 5, 30 f., 7, 55. Ultimately the ideas contained in these clauses go back to *Ps.* 110, 1: "The Lord said unto my Lord, Sit thou at my right hand, until I make thine enemies thy footstool," which according to St Mark[4] Jesus Himself quoted in the course of His teaching in the temple. Though it is not explicitly affirmed, the Ascension and the Session, as the words of the psalm indicate, meant much more than might seem apparent on the surface. The first- and second-century Christian who expressed his faith in them understood them as implying that Christ had beaten down the hostile powers opposed to Him, and consequently to His Church. The natural sequence of the glorious victory was proclaimed in the words WHENCE HE WILL COME TO JUDGE

[1] Cf. *Dial.* 97; 118 (E.J.G., 211; 236): he relies on *Is.* 53, 9; 57, 2.
[2] Cf. *Cat.* 13, 34 and 14, 3 (*P.G.* 33, 813 and 828).
[3] *Comm. in symb. apost.* 16 (*C.C.L.* 20, 152 f.).
[4] 12, 35 f.

THE LIVING AND THE DEAD. Here again we are face to face with the apostolic kerygma. The phrase was already stereotyped when 1 *Pet.* 4, 5 was written: it appears in St Peter's speech at Caesarea as reported in *Acts* 10, 42, and again in 2 *Tim.* 4, 1. Thus in the whole of this section the Old Roman Creed faithfully reflects the feelings of the primitive Church—its exultation in Christ's triumph over death and the evil forces arrayed against Him and in the Father's marvellous vindication of His Son, and its excited anticipation, eager and at the same time apprehensive, of the Saviour's Second Coming on the clouds of heaven, as He Himself had foretold, to exercise judgment as the vicegerent of His Father.

4. *The Holy Spirit*

The third article of R (I BELIEVE IN THE HOLY SPIRIT, THE HOLY CHURCH, THE FORGIVENESS OF SINS, THE RESURRECTION OF THE FLESH) is singular in that it consists of a string of miscellaneous credenda. In later ages, when the metaphysical doctrine of the Holy Trinity had been worked out and was consciously read into the creed, it occasioned embarrassment in certain quarters to find a series of lesser items ranged alongside the Person of the Holy Spirit.[1] Both the texts of creeds and the candid comments of preachers and expositors betray the efforts made to escape from what were now recognized to be awkward implications. Rufinus, for instance, insisted[2] that the preposition IN properly went with the first clause, THE HOLY SPIRIT, only. It is reasonable, he contended, to speak of "believing in" when the object of belief is one of the divine Persons; but where creatures or the mysteries of our religion are concerned, it would be more accurate to say that we believe them than that we believe in them. St Faustus of Riez,[3] arguing that the words "I believe in the Holy Spirit" carry with them belief in His deity, repudiated a possible objection that by such a process of reasoning the Church itself must be regarded as

---

[1] Useful material bearing on this point has been assembled by J. E. L. Oulton in *J.T.S.* xxxix, 1938, 239 ff.

[2] *Comm. in symb. apost.* 34; 37 (*C.C.L.* 20, 169 f.; 171 f.).

[3] *De Spir. sanct.* 1, 2 (*C.S.E.L.* 21, 103 f.).

divine. We believe that the Church exists, he distinguished; we do not, in the proper sense, believe in the Church :

All that in the creed follows THE HOLY SPIRIT is to be construed without reference to the preposition IN, so that our belief concerning the holy Church, the communion of saints, etc., is stated with reference to God, i.e. we confess that these things have been ordered by God and maintain their existence by Him.

The Irish creed of Bangor, as we shall later see, inserted the infinitive IS (*esse*) before CATHOLIC CHURCH and thereby transformed HOLY into a predicate, probably under the influence of similar scruples. To return to a much earlier period, it is an interesting fact that a number of versions[1] of the creed in St Hippolytus's *Tradition* made the third interrogation run, "Dost thou believe also in the Holy Spirit in the holy Church . . .?" This is probably the correct reading, and we should regard as mistaken those scholars[2] who seek to explain the third article as expressing belief in the Holy Spirit as operating *within* the Church *with a view to* the resurrection of the flesh. As we have seen, there was no mention of the resurrection of the flesh in St Hippolytus's original, and these varying texts illustrate in their several ways the difficulty of coordinating the Church and other saving mysteries with the Third Person of the Godhead.

No such uneasiness, we may surmise, troubled the framers of R in the second century. There were precedents for stringing several clauses together, as the creed of the *Epistula Apostolorum*[3] confirms. Moreover, though R was consciously constructed on the basis of the threefold baptismal formula, the Trinitarian pattern was more important to it than the full-blown Trinitarian theology of later ages. To draw the conclusion, however, as many have done,[4] that the Holy Spirit could not, at the epoch of the creed's composition, have been regarded as a divine Person coordinate with the Father and the Son, but

---

[1] Cf. Ar., Eth. and Sah. versions (Dix, 37): also *Apost. Const.* 7, 41, 7 (Funk I, 446). *Test. Dom.* (Rahmani, 129) agrees with H. See p. 91 above.

[2] Cf. P. Nautin, *Je crois à l'esprit saint* (UNAM SANCTAM XVII), Paris, 1947. He has been criticized by B. Botte in *Mélanges J. de Ghellinck*, 1951, 189–200.

[3] Cf. above, p. 82.

[4] E.g., A. Harnack in his early pamphlet *Das apostolische Glaubensbekenntnis*, 1892, 26.

must have been treated as a mere gift or power, is to construct a rather artificial and anachronistic dilemma. When R was pieced together, a great deal of confusion and sheer perplexity prevailed concerning Him, and it is obvious that we must not attempt to squeeze out of the creed the developed theology of the Spirit which commended itself to fourth-century orthodoxy. To be assured of this the reader need only consult such second-century Roman writers as Hermas and St Justin. But the language of St Clement of Rome[1] at the close of the first century clearly suggested the separateness and divine status of the Spirit. The Apologists generally, for all their haziness and inexactitude when judged by later standards, explicitly asserted[2] that Christians venerated Him. For St Irenaeus, although he did not call the Spirit God, He was the Wisdom of God, present with God before creation alongside the Son, and could be described as one of the two "hands" (the other was the Son) by which God made man.[3] The mind of the Church, moreover, was more illuminatingly revealed in its doxologies and liturgical formulae than in the writings of its theologians, and the former were prevailingly triadic. We may therefore be confident that when the baptizand was asked in the words of R whether he believed in the Holy Spirit, his interrogators had in mind a divine Being Who could be distinguished from the Father and His Son Jesus Christ and of Whose special operation they were sensible.

Though it is tempting to try to define more precisely how they conceived of the Person of the Holy Spirit, it is sobering to realize that no completely satisfactory answer can be expected to our questions. Many currents of speculation about the Spirit intermingled in the second century. It is impossible to identify the affirmation of the creed with any one of them, partly because the actual circle in which it originated is no longer discoverable, and partly because it must have been appropriated and turned to their own purposes by Christians of many schools of thought. In any case an obsession with this aspect of the Spirit, which was not necessarily the one which

[1] *Ad Cor.* 46, 6; 58, 2 (Bihlmeyer, 60; 66).
[2] Cf., e.g., St Justin, *Apol.* I, 6; 13; St Athenagoras, *Leg. pro Christ.* 10 (E.J.G., 29; 34; 325).
[3] Cf., e.g., *Adv. haer.* 4, *praef.* 4; 4, 20, 1; etc. (*P.G.* 7, 975; 1032).

most interested the framers of the creed, is unhistorical, and is liable to blind us to the real meaning which this clause in their confession of faith had for them. Whatever conjectures he may have hazarded about the status of the Spirit in relation to the Godhead, there were certain thoughts, we may be sure, which were present in the believer's mind as he stepped down to the waters of baptism. He could scarcely forget, at this moment of solemn vows, that it was the Holy Spirit Who sanctified the faith of the community and enlightened it with knowledge of the truth.[1] It was the Spirit too, he had been taught in his catechetical preparation, Who had been active in the ancient prophets and had foretold through them, down to the smallest detail, the coming and career of the Saviour.[2] Least of all was the realization likely to have been far from his thoughts that it was the Spirit Who filled the Church, Who guaranteed him immortality and eternal life, Who gave efficacy and power to the sacraments, and Who could be bestowed upon him ("renewing man unto God", as St Irenaeus phrased it[3]) in the great process of baptism which he was now undergoing.

5. *The Spirit in Action*

When we turn to the remaining three clauses, we are at once faced with a problem which we have not encountered before. How are we to explain their presence in the creed? It is easy enough to see the appropriateness of their being appended to the mention of the Holy Spirit, for the realities they represent could be, and were, regarded as the fruits of the Spirit in action. Hermas[4] goes so far as to identify the Spirit with the Church, under the figure of an old lady; and the preacher of the homily known as 2 *Clement* seems almost to envisage the Church, like Christ, as an incarnation of eternal Spirit.[5] Speaking in a more sober strain,

[1] So, e.g., St Irenaeus, *Adv. haer.* 4, 33, 7 (*P.G.* 7, 1077); Tertullian, *De praescr.* 13; *Adv. Prax.* 2 (*C.C.L.* 1, 198; 2, 1160).
[2] Cf. St Justin, *Apol.* I, 13; 61 (E.J.G., 34; 71); St Irenaeus, *Adv. haer.* 1, 10, 1 (*P.G.* 7, 549); *Epideixis* 6 (Robinson, 75).
[3] *Epideixis* 6 (Robinson, 75).
[4] *Sim.* 9, 1, 1 f.: cf. *Vis.* 3, 1–13 (*G.C.S.* 48, 76; 7–19).
[5] Ch. 14 (Bihlmeyer, 77 f.).

St Irenaeus emphasized[1] the intimate liaison between the two.

"This gift of God", he said, "was entrusted to the Church that all the members might receive of Him and be made alive; and none are partakers of Him who do not assemble with the Church but defraud themselves of life. For where the Church is, there is the Spirit of God; and where the Spirit of God is, there is the Church and all grace."

Parallel ideas can be found abundantly in the major writers of the second and early third centuries. The forgiveness of sins, too, was clearly the effect of the bestowal of the Spirit in baptism. Finally, the resurrection of the flesh was the eschatological crown of the possession of the Spirit which the Christian might hope to gain in the Church. It is the Spirit, St John had declared,[2] Who revivifies. It is by the Spirit, St Irenaeus added in so many words,[3] that the dead will rise and will become spiritual bodies possessing everlasting life. Expounding 1 *Cor.* 15, 50, he agreed[4] that, properly speaking, the flesh would not inherit the kingdom, but rather those who had received the Spirit; and in another context[5] he put the matter succinctly in the sentence, "It is by virtue of the Spirit that believers will rise again when the body is anew united to the soul."

The logic of attaching these items in immediate association with the Holy Spirit is thus easy enough to follow. What is more difficult to understand is the motive for mentioning them in the creed at all. The problem is constituted by the fact that, while these doctrines were of course part of the Church's teaching from the start, none of them figured, so far as we can judge, in the earliest strata of creed material. We discovered no trace of them in the embryonic "creeds" discernible in the New Testament, any more than in those passages of the Apostolic Fathers, St Justin and St Irenaeus which have a formulary ring. Some older scholars[6] were confident that the Church at any rate must have been mentioned in the creed with which, they thought, Marcion was acquainted in the 'forties of the second century. They relied on a quotation from the heretic

---

[1] *Adv. haer.* 3, 24, 1 (*P.G.* 7, 966).   [2] 6, 63.
[3] *Adv. haer.* 5, 7, 2 (*P.G.* 7, 1141).   [4] *Adv. haer.* 5, 9, 4 (*P.G.* 7, 1146 f.).
[5] *Epideixis* 42 (Robinson, 107).
[6] E.g., Th. Zahn in *Das apostolische Symbolum*, Erlangen and Leipzig, 1893, 33.

made by Tertullian [1] in which he speaks of "the holy Church, to which we have given our pledge (*in quam repromisimus sanctam ecclesiam*)." But it is highly unlikely that this tag—which echoes Marcion's version of the text of *Gal.* 4, 26—is an excerpt from a creed at all. The phrase "we have given our pledge (*repromisimus*)" is suggested by St Paul's words, "But he who was from the free woman, by promise (*per repromissionem*)." All that is implied is that we have voluntarily engaged ourselves to the Church. But if this passage is eliminated, the earliest occurrence of the Church in a creed is in *Epistula Apostolorum* 5 : its presence in Tertullian's own baptismal interrogations is ensured by his remark[2] that "when the pledge of loyalty and the guarantee of salvation were exchanged in the presence of three witnesses, a mention of the Church was of necessity added." But if these items entered the creed at a comparatively late date, it is reasonable to look for an explanation. It remains a distinct possibility, of course, that they gained admission for no more recondite a reason than the spontaneous urge of the community to proclaim the vital facts of Christian experience associated with baptism. But it is equally possible that something in the theological climate of the times, not necessarily the positive desire to give the lie to heresy, prompted their inclusion.

The first of our three clauses announces the Christian's belief in the existence of THE HOLY CHURCH. The term "Church" (ἐκκλησία) was borrowed from the Septuagint, where it was used to translate the Hebrew *qahal*, the title commonly given to the chosen people of Israel solemnly assembled before God.[3] As appropriated by Christians, it gave expression to their claim to be the new Israel, the heir of all the promised blessings of the age to come, and this notion was fully exploited by theologians of the second as well as of the first century.[4] A good illustration of more general second-century thought about the Church is provided by St Justin,[5] who identified it with the queen mentioned in *Ps.* 45 and says it is composed of all who believe in Jesus Christ and form a single soul, a single synagogue,

---

[1] *Adv. Marc.* 5, 4 (*C.C.L.* 1, 673).
[2] *De bapt.* 6 (*C.C.L.* 1, 282).   [3] But cf. J. Y. Campbell in *J.T.S.* xlix, 1948, 130 ff.
[4] Cf., e.g., 1 *Pet.* 1, 1; *Jam.* 1, 1; 1 *Clem.* 29 (Lightfoot, 20); St Justin, *Dial.* 123 (E.J.G., 242 f.); St Irenaeus, *Adv. haer.* 4, 8, 1 (*P.G.* 7, 993).
[5] *Dial.* 63 (E.J.G., 169).

a single Church. Writers like Hermas[1] and the author of 2
Clement[2] liked to emphasize the spiritual aspect of the Church,
asserting that it was founded before the world and comprised
the elect in heaven as well as those on earth. The majority of
writers, like St Clement of Rome, St Ignatius and St Polycarp
placed the chief stress on its concrete, institutional character.

For St Irenaeus the Church was the great Church standing
out among the sects, filled with the Spirit of God and admitting His people to the blessings of the kingdom. It was
a world-wide society which was clearly demarcated from its
rivals by a common acceptance of the doctrine long ago proclaimed by the prophets of the old dispensation, preached by
the Son of God Himself, and transmitted to later ages by His
apostles and others charged to safeguard the precious deposit.
When a catechist was expounding this clause of the creed to a
convert, we may be satisfied that he dwelt upon all these
aspects of the divine society.

About the middle of the century "holy" was becoming a
stock epithet to describe the Church. St Paul had used it once,[3]
and it occurs once in each of St Ignatius's letters and in the
Martyrium Polycarpi[4]: otherwise it is not to be found among
the early writers. Like "Church" itself, the adjective "holy
(ἅγιος)" goes back to the Old Testament, where it could be
applied to whatever concerned or belonged to God. In particular
it became attached to the Chosen People to indicate their
special relation to Him. For example, when God renewed His
covenant, He instructed Moses to inform the people that they
would be to Him "a royal priesthood and a holy nation (ἔθνος
ἅγιον)".[5] Twice *Deuteronomy*[6] uses the expression "Thou art
an holy people (λαὸς ἅγιος) unto the Lord thy God." Several
times in the Law[7] God commanded His people to be holy, and
Isaiah[8] announced of the Remnant, "He that is left in Zion,
and he that remaineth in Jerusalem, shall be called holy." In

---

[1] Cf. *Vis.* 2, 4, 1; 3, 5, 1 (*G.C.S.* 48, 7; 11 f.).
[2] Ch. 14 (Bihlmeyer, 77 f.).
[3] *Eph.* 5, 27.
[4] Cf., e.g., *Trall. prooem.*; *Mart. Pol. prooem.* (Bihlmeyer, 92; 120).
[5] *Ex.* 19, 6.
[6] *Deut.* 7, 6; 26, 19.
[7] E.g., *Lev.* 11, 44; 19,2; 21, 6; *Num.* 15, 40.
[8] *Is.* 4, 3.

a later age the faithful people came to be designated simply
"the saints".[1] These and other passages were eagerly seized
upon by Christians and transferred to themselves. Everyone
knows St Peter's assurance[2] to his correspondents, "Ye are a
chosen generation, a royal priesthood, an holy nation, a
peculiar people." St Justin supplies[3] a typical illustration from
the second century:

> We are not only a people, but we are a holy people, as we have
> already showed—"And they shall call them the holy people, re-
> deemed by the Lord".[4] Therefore we are not a people to be despised,
> nor a barbarous race . . . but God has even chosen us, and He has
> become manifest to those who asked not after Him. . . . For this is
> that nation which God of old promised to Abraham, when He
> declared that He would make him the father of a mighty nation.

The connotation of the word "holy", like that of the parallel
word "saints" so frequent in New Testament Christian parlance, has nothing to do, in the first instance at any rate, with
de facto goodness of character or moral integrity. The Church
is described as HOLY in the creed because it has been chosen
by God, because He has predestined it to a glorious inheritance,
and because He dwells in it in the Person of the Holy Spirit.

Even where the word "Church" was not explicitly used, as
in the illuminating passage of St Justin quoted above, the idea
of the elect people of God was prominent in Christian thought
from the earliest times. It might not therefore seem necessary
to hunt out special reasons for the inclusion of a mention of
the Church in the creed: such a clause embodied one of those
saving verities of which Christians were always conscious, and
which it was particularly natural for them to recall at the
moment of sacramental initiation. Nevertheless we cannot
overlook the fact that the doctrine of the Church was beginning
to assume a much more distinctive role in the middle of the
second century as the difference between "the great Church"
and the sects became more and more marked. We can observe
the tension between the two at close quarters in the writings
of St. Irenaeus. The heretics, he reported,[5] despised "those who

---

[1] E.g., 1 *Macc.* 10, 39 and 44; *Wis.* 18, 19.
[2] 1 *Pet.* 2, 9.   [3] *Dial.* 119 (E.J.G., 237).
[4] He is quoting *Is.* 62, 12.   [5] *Adv. haer.* 1, 6, 2 (*P.G.* 7, 505).

belong to the Church" as material-minded; they branded[1] them as "ecclesiastical", and went so far as to revile the sacred name of the Church.[2] To counter their propaganda he developed the view that membership of the Church was necessary to salvation. "He will judge all those who are outside the truth, that is, outside the Church."[3] Again he remarked,[4] "All those who keep outside the Church . . . bring condemnation on themselves"; and we recall his teaching that it is only within the Church that the Holy Spirit can be received. When it is remembered that the earliest credal appearance of HOLY CHURCH is in the formula contained in the *Epistula Apostolorum*, an anti-Gnostic treatise, it is difficult to resist the conclusion that its presence in the Old Roman Creed, while not directly polemical (there is little proof of that), is a by-product of that enhanced and self-conscious emphasis on the Church as an institution which was becoming characteristic of orthodox theology in the second half of the century.

Hard on the heels of the mention of the Church comes THE REMISSION OF SINS. This did not stand, as we have seen, among the baptismal interrogations in St Hippolytus's *Tradition*. On the other hand, it seems to have had a place in Tertullian's creed-material, for in a well-known passage of the *De baptismo*[5] he raised the question why Jesus Himself did not baptize and, to demonstrate the folly of the suggestion, asked rhetorically what He would have baptized people into—"the remission of sins? Himself? the Holy Spirit? the Church?" The five-clause creed of the *Epistula Apostolorum* included a mention of it. In Eastern creeds, as we shall shortly see, it was a regular item in the third article. Sometimes, as in the *Apostolic Constitutions*,[6] it coincided with the Western form, but more often it was closely conjoined with baptism, a typical wording being ONE BAPTISM UNTO THE REMISSION OF SINS.[7]

Probably this supplies a clue to the original bearing of the clause in R. One of the grand convictions of Christians was that in baptism all their past sins were washed away once and

---

[1] *Adv. haer.* 3, 15, 2 (*P.G.* 7, 918).   [2] *Adv. haer.* 1, 25, 3 (*P.G.* 7, 682).
[3] *Adv. haer.* 4, 33, 7 (*P.G.* 7, 1076).   [4] *Adv. haer.* 1, 16, 3 (*P.G.* 7, 633).
[5] *De bapt.* 11 (*C.C.L.* 1, 286).   [6] *Apost. Const.* 7, 41, 7 (Funk I, 446).
[7] Cf., e.g., the old creed of Jerusalem (see pp. 183 f.) and the creed of Constantinople (our "Nicene Creed").

for all. We recall St Peter's dramatic words,[1] "Repent and be baptized every one of you in the name of Jesus Christ unto the remission of sins", and St Paul's indignant rebuke to the back-sliding Corinthians,[2] "But you were washed, you were sanctified, you were justified." So the second-century author of the *Epistle of Barnabas* remarked,[3] "We go down into the water full of sins and uncleanness, and come up bearing fruit in our hearts," and Hermas[4] wrote in a similar strain, "We went down into the water and received remission of our past errors." St Justin's famous account[5] of baptism delineates its object as being "that we may obtain remission of our former sins", and he assured[6] the Jew Trypho that the one way to secure this boon was to acknowledge Jesus as Messiah and undergo the bath prophesied by Isaiah. What all this language envisages, of course, is sin committed prior to baptism. As regards sin committed after baptism, the usual remedies suggested were prayer, repentance, confession and good works.[7] But presumably these availed only for minor sins: the possibility of Christians being guilty of, and being absolved by the sacraments of the Church from, acts of grievous sin was only beginning to be taken into consideration in the second century.

We are therefore justified in concluding that in practice, at the time it obtained entrance to the Old Roman Creed, THE REMISSION OF SINS must have conveyed the idea of the washing away of past offences and the opening up of a new life through the instrumentality of baptism. There is no serious argument in favour of the suggestion[8] that the clause was a direct reflection of the controversy at Rome in the reign of Pope Callistus over the Church's power to absolve its members from major sins. Apart from other considerations, it is manifest that the words had worked their way into the recognized creed material long before the outbreak of this dispute. In confirmation of our view it is worth noticing that in the *Epistula Apostolorum* the

[1] *Acts* 2, 38. [2] i *Cor.* 6, 11.
[3] *Ep. Barn.* 11 (Bihlmeyer, 24). [4] *Mand.* 4, 3, 1 (*G.C.S.* 48, 28).
[5] *Apol.* I, 61 (E.J.G., 70). [6] *Dial.* 44 (E.J.G., 141).
[7] Cf., e.g., 1 *Clem.* 51; 2 *Clem.* 8; 13; 16; 19; *Ep. Barn.* 19, 10–12 (Bihlmeyer, 62 f.; 74 f.; 76 f.; 78 f.; 80; 32).
[8] Cf. F. J. Badcock, *The History of the Creeds*, 2nd ed. 1938, 133.

remission of sins, mentioned in the five-clause summary of
faith, is closely associated with baptism[1]; and in Eastern creeds
the remission of sins was usually stated in so many words to be
the result of baptism. No doubt there was a special appropriateness in the catechumen's avowing his belief in the cancellation
of past trespasses which was the most obvious and practical
effect of the baptism he was on the point of receiving. At the
same time it is possible to discern a marked heightening in the
emphasis laid in the second half of the second century on the
release from the burden of sin brought about by baptism, and
this comes to light especially in the catechetical instruction
preceding the sacrament. As F. Kattenbusch pointed out,[2]
there is curiously little talk about it in the earlier writers,
though of course they assume it. But even in St Justin's time,
when the catechumenate was still relatively unorganized, we
are told that candidates for initiation were instructed to pray
during their novitiate specifically for the remission of their sins,
and that their prayers were supported by the united intercession of the community.[3] When we come to St Hippolytus's
Tradition, the situation is completely transformed. The prominence of the remission of sins is now so great that the phrase
is virtually a synonym for baptism itself.[4] In the prayer which
the bishop pronounces at the imposition of hands immediately
after the immersions, it is "the forgiveness of sins by the
laver of regeneration" which succinctly describes what has
been accomplished in the action so far.[5] What is much more
significant, however, the whole elaborate catechumenal preparation, when analysed, is seen to be "a vast sacramental
dominated by the idea of exorcism".[6] The devil is conceived
as having taken up his habitation almost physically in the
candidate, and this is patently the effect of sin. So powerful has the sense of the separation caused by sin between
the Christian and the non-Christian become! We can readily

[1] Cf. ch. 27 Eth., 23 Copt. and ch. 42 Eth., 33 Copt. (in C. Schmidt's *Die Gespräche Jesu*, 1919).
[2] II, 706.
[3] *Apol*. I, 61 (E.J.G., 70).
[4] Cf. *Ap. Trad*. xix, 2, in the Arab. and Sahid. versions (Dix, 30).
[5] *Ap. Trad*. xxii, 1 (Dix, 38).
[6] Cf. Dom B. Capelle's important article in *Rech. théol. anc. méd.* v, 1933, 129 ff. This is the conclusion he reaches on p. 148.

conceive how eager was the yearning for release which the catechumen experienced. Against this background the installation of an acknowledgement of THE REMISSION OF SINS in the credal questions to which he had to assent becomes easily intelligible.

When we come to the final clause of the Old Roman Creed, THE RESURRECTION OF THE FLESH, we can afford to dispense with any elaborate examination of its meaning. A belief in the resurrection of the body had been integral to Christianity from the beginning. In 1 *Cor.* 15 we find St Paul assuming the doctrine: he recalls that the foundation of our faith in it is the resurrection of Christ Himself, "the first-fruits of them that sleep", and settles down to the much more difficult problem contained in the question, "With what body will they come?" Anyone turning over the pages of the early fathers will gain a vivid impression of the immense importance the resurrection-hope had for the second-century Church. To cite a few examples at random, the authors of 2 *Clement* and the *Epistle of Barnabas* insist on the necessity of our rising in the very flesh we now possess in order that we may receive the due reward of our deeds.[1] St Clement of Rome[2] hazarded an explanation of the marvellous fact by appealing to the analogy of seed bearing fruit out of corruption, and combining it with the classical legend of the phoenix and the doctrine of the divine omnipotence. Most of the theologians and apologists of the period deployed their dialectics in defending it against the strictures and open mockery of pagan critics.[3]

About the middle of the century, however, they had to shift their tactics. Evidently there were groups of Christians, or pseudo-Christians, who denied the resurrection of the body. St Polycarp, we may recall, has a passing rebuke in his letter[4] for those who say there is no resurrection or judgment. St

---

[1] 2 *Clem.* 9; *Ep. Barn.* 5, 6 f.; 21, 1 (Bihlmeyer, 75; 15; 33).

[2] *Ad Cor.* 24–6 (Bihlmeyer, 49 f.).

[3] Cf., e.g., Tatian, *Adv. Graec.* 6; Theophilus Antioch., *Ad Autolyc.* 1, 7 f. (E.J.G., 272 f.; *P.G.* 6, 1033).

[4] *Ad Phil.* 7 (Bihlmeyer, 117). A date near the middle of the century, as is proposed for this part of the letter by P. N. Harrison (*Polycarp's Two Epistles*, Cambridge, 1936), would agree very well with the argument.

Justin in an important passage discloses[1] the existence of sects of such people :

> I have told you that men who call themselves Christians but are atheistical and impious heretics teach things which are absolutely blasphemous. . . . If you meet with people who describe themselves as Christians . . . but dare blaspheme the God of Abraham, of Isaac and of Jacob, and affirm that there is no resurrection of the dead . . . do not recognize them as Christians. . . .

According to the apocryphal correspondence[2] between the Corinthian church and St Paul, which belongs to the latter half of the century, and was for long treated as canonical Scripture in the Syrian church, blasphemers who repudiated the resurrection were abroad upsetting the minds of the faithful. St Irenaeus, in whose theology the doctrine of the resurrection was a theme of prime importance, introduces us to these Gnostic-minded persons who, believing that matter is essentially evil, deny the physical resurrection.[3] Salvation, they plead, belongs to the soul alone, and the body, derived as it is from the earth, is incapable of participating in it. His own rejoinder is to insist that "salvation belongs to the whole man, that is, soul and body" : this is the universal Catholic teaching.[4] Tertullian, too, aimed his *De resurrectione mortuorum* (written 208–11) against Gnostics of precisely this outlook. They dwell at length, he complains,[5] on the vileness of the flesh and on its sordid origin, uses and end, and twist the doctrine of the resurrection into an imaginary sense of their own invention, identifying it either with the effects of baptism or with the spiritual awakening which they suppose to crown the acceptance of their principles.[6] His own reply takes the form of an eloquent panegyric of the flesh.

This being the theological atmosphere of the times, we need have little hesitation in explaining the presence of the clause in the creed as due to the very natural desire to be assured of the soundness of the catechumen's attitude to this vital point

[1] *Dial.* 80 (E.J.G., 192).
[2] Cf. E. Hennecke, *New Testament Apocrypha* (E.T. 1965) II, 357; 373; 376.
[3] *Adv. haer.* 1, 22, 1; 1, 27, 3; 5, 2, 2 (*P.G.* 7, 669 f; 689; 1124).
[4] *Adv. haer.* 1, 10, 1; 5, 20, 1 (*P.G.* 7, 549; 1177).
[5] *De res. mort.* 4 (*C.C.L.* 2, 925).
[6] *De res. mort.* 19 (*C.C.L.* 2, 944 f.).

of Christian doctrine. The controversial background, we may infer, was also responsible, in part at any rate, for the choice of the word FLESH, as against the less provocative "resurrection of the dead (ἀνάστασις νεκρῶν)" preferred by the New Testament and some of the earlier writers. Quite under-standably, in view of their opponents' caustic jibes about the materiality of the flesh as such, the champions of orthodoxy made it a point of honour to use the word with all its realistic associations. The heretics, St Irenaeus does not flinch from admitting,[1] fall back on the Pauline text, " Flesh and blood cannot inherit the kingdom of God"; but his own reply in defence of "God's handiwork" is that what St Paul meant was the flesh considered by itself (καθ' ἑαυτήν), i.e. con-sidered apart from the Spirit, in other words unsanctified. Tertullian, arguing that "all flesh and blood, with their proper qualities, will rise again", grapples with the same objection, pointing out that the Apostle did not withhold the resurrection as such, but only the kingdom of God, from flesh and blood. For entrance into the kingdom the Spirit is necessary; and so, while all the dead will rise again with their physical bodies, only those who have been sanctified by the Spirit will actually inherit the kingdom.[2] Except in circles with more spiritualizing tendencies, such as that of Origen, this vigorous, full-blooded realism was to set the pattern for later orthodox thought on the subject.

With this affirmation of the resurrection of the flesh the Old Roman Creed reached its climax. As a compendium of popular theology it might seem curiously defective, and modern people with their special interests have sometimes wondered why it contains no reference (to select three points at random) to the teaching of Jesus, or to the Atonement, or to the Holy Eucharist. It should be remembered, however, that creeds, as they emerged historically, were never intended to be complete summaries of the Christian faith in all its aspects. Their pattern was dictated by the Lord's threefold baptismal command, and their content was limited to those fundamental truths about God the Father, Christ Jesus His Son, and the Holy Spirit

---

[1] *Adv. haer.* 5, 9, 1 and 3 (*P.G.* 7, 1144; 1145).
[2] *De res. mort.* 50 (*C.C.L.* 2, 992 f.).

which the Church had either inherited from Judaism or herself received in the Gospel revelation. The clearest proof of the authenticity of the Old Roman Creed lies in the way in which, while some of its clauses have received a sharper definition and others a heightened emphasis from the controversial atmosphere of the second century, they one and all hark back to the primitive kerygma of the apostolic age.

CHAPTER VI

CREEDS WESTERN AND EASTERN

1. *The Paucity of Creeds*

THE information at our disposal about the "creeds" of the second and early third century Roman church is, relatively speaking, extraordinarily rich. Thanks to it, we can write at least a tentative history of the beginnings of the Old Roman Creed. If it is a history with several gaping lacunae, and if the historian has to rely more often than he would choose upon his imagination, we can at least discern in shadowy outline the process by which R came into being. The local creeds of other churches fared less fortunately. Apart from those with Roman connections, the embryonic formulae of the second and early third centuries glanced at in Chapter III make a pretty meagre harvest. In this chapter our object will be to provide some account of Western baptismal creeds other than R and of Eastern baptismal creeds in the following two centuries. The reader would be well advised not to pitch his hopes too high. Even when full-blown declaratory creeds begin to take the stage, the examples we can reconstruct with confidence are few and far between, and the story of their earlier development remains wrapped in mystery.

The reasons for this state of affairs, which might seem singular to a newcomer to this field, are not really difficult to conjecture. For one thing, the Roman church was probably a pioneer in the production of crystallized credal forms. The liturgy at Rome had made big strides in the direction of fixity (though, of course, the goal had not by any means been reached) well before St Hippolytus drafted his *Tradition* as a model. Other churches lagged behind, and the East was if anything slower than the West to stereotype its liturgical rites and prayers. Credal summaries of faith, whether interrogatory or declaratory, were a by-product of the liturgy and reflected its fixity or plasticity. In

particular, all the indications point to the West as the birthplace
of the ceremonies of the "handing-out (*traditio*)" and "giving
back (*redditio*)" of the creed. These were, as we observed
before,[1] the logical precondition of the canonization of official
declaratory creeds in each locality. In the West itself it was
Rome,[2] probably, which took the initiative in establishing them.
We ought not to be surprised, in consequence, to find that formal
creeds emerged first in Rome, and we should be prepared to
find Rome supplying more abundant signs of a vigorous creed-
making activity than other churches in the second and early
third centuries.

At the same time, it must be remembered, there were other
influences at work which tended to cast a veil over whatever
local formularies were given positions of authority whether in
the East or in the West. What we have in mind is the ecclesiastical practice which, ever since the phrase was coined in the
seventeenth century by the Protestant scholar Jean Daillé (Dal-
laeus), has been known as the *disciplina arcani*, or rule of secrecy.
By this is understood the convention according to which the
inner mysteries of the Church, particularly the sacraments of
baptism and the Holy Eucharist, were treated as hidden from
the uninitiated and disclosed only to the instructed faithful. St
Augustine sounded[3] a typical note with his remark, "What is
it that is secret and not public in the Church? The sacrament
of baptism; the sacrament of the Eucharist." The Lord's Prayer
and the baptismal creed eventually came to be reckoned among
the hallowed tokens which could be imparted to none but the
faithful. St Cyril of Jerusalem, lecturing to candidates for
baptism, was careful not to quote the text of the creed he was
expounding, and was profuse in his warnings that it should not
be written down but should be engraved in his auditors'
memories.[4] St Ambrose's caution,[5] "Beware of imprudently
divulging the mystery of the Lord's Prayer and the symbol",

---

[1] See above, p. 49.
[2] For the prominence and solemnity of the *redditio symboli* at Rome, cf. St
Augustine, *Confess.* 8, 2 (*P.L.* 32, 751) and Rufinus, *Comm. in symb. apost.* 3 (*C.C.L.* 20,
136).
[3] *Enarr. in psalm.* 103, 14 (*P.L.* 37, 1348).
[4] Cf. *Procat.* 12; *Cat.* 5, 12; 6, 29 (*P.G.* 33, 352 f; 520 f.; 589).
[5] *De Cain et Abel* 1, 9, 37 (*P.L.* 14, 335).

was in tune with this, as were the references[1] by St Augustine and Rufinus to the impropriety of setting the creed down on paper. As late as the middle of the fifth century the historian Sozomen[2] was dissuaded by pious friends from writing out the text of the Nicene creed, "which only the initiated and the mystagogues (μύσταις καὶ μυσταγωγοῖς μόνοις) have the right to recite and hear". He continued: "For it is not suitable that any of the uninitiated (τῶν ἀμυήτων) should light upon this document." His scruples were probably rather old-fashioned at this date, for his contemporary Socrates[3] had no hesitation about publishing the selfsame formula, any more than had on occasion St Athanasius, St Basil and Eusebius.

There has been much heated controversy as to the dates within which we may presume the rule of secrecy to have been practically effective, and its underlying motives have also been debated.[4] To one school of historians it has seemed only another example of the ever-growing assimilation of the Christian cultus to the rites of the Hellenistic mystery religions. As a complete explanation this view may be dismissed as fantastic, although the atmosphere of holy awe with which the sacraments were sometimes invested, as well as the wholesale borrowing of mystery religion terminology which prevailed in some circles, suggests that motives like this were not wholly lacking. There can be no doubt, however, that, while they have sometimes been exaggerated,[5] the ties connecting the discipline with the catechumenate were at least equally important. Its introduction coincided with the establishment of the developed catechumenate involving the careful grading of catechumens, and it lapsed into obsolescence after the fifth century, when infant baptism had become the rule and the catechumenate proper had lost its meaning. The real problem, however, is to determine when it originated. Everyone is agreed that it was in full swing in the middle of the fourth century, for St Cyril of Jerusalem took it for granted in his *Catechetical Lectures*. As there

---

[1] St Aug., *Serm.* 212, 2 (*P.L.* 38, 1060); Ruf., *Comm. in symb. apost.* 2 (*C.C.L.* 20, 135). Among Greek fathers, cf., e.g., St Basil, *De Spir. sanct.* 66 (*P.G.* 32, 188 f.).
[2] *Hist. eccl.* 1, 20 (*P.G.* 67, 920 f.). [3] *Hist. eccl.* 1, 8 (*P.G.* 67, 68).
[4] Cf. *Reallexikon für Antike und Christentum* I, 667–79.
[5] E.g., by P. Batiffol in his important essay in *Études d'histoire et de théologie positive*, I, Paris, 6th ed. 1919.

is no hint there of its being a novelty, we are justified in carrying it at least a couple of generations back. Some scholars[1] have contended that its roots lie in the first decades of the second century, if not earlier, and imagine that they can trace glimpses of it in St Justin's works. This is extravagant, however: St Justin not only has no word that could be twisted into an allusion to it, but he felt not the slightest compunction about describing the sacraments in detail in a treatise designed for pagan eyes. A reticence of sorts when speaking of the sacraments can be observed in Tertullian and Origen. The former upbraided[2] contemporary heretics for admitting both the faithful and catechumens indiscriminately to their services, implying that in the Catholic Church (he had not yet become a Montanist) the sacraments were fenced about. Origen too, arguing with Celsus, had to admit[3] that Christianity had certain esoteric mysteries. In one of his homilies[4] he expressly declined to explain the significance of Christ's Body and Blood before a mixed audience: "Let us not linger on these matters, which are well known to initiates but cannot be revealed to the uninitiated." But the practice was obviously only at an embryonic stage. St Hippolytus, writing in Tertullian's lifetime, felt at liberty to publish the baptismal and eucharistic liturgies. Moreover, nothing goes to show that in the times of Tertullian and Origen this reserve extended to the Church's doctrinal norms. Tertullian, like St Irenaeus, was continually quoting, on occasion quite faithfully, quasi-credal summaries of the rule of faith. Origen, in the first of the two passages mentioned above, ridiculed the idea of Christian doctrine being a secret. To drive his point home, he rehearsed several articles of what sounds like a creed, declaring that the whole world was familiar with them. St Hippolytus set down his baptismal questions in full with the rest of the rite, and nowhere so much as hinted at the handing out of a carefully guarded formula to the catechumens. Christian teachers and apologists of this period, as is well known, made a special point of taxing heretics with the secrecy in which they wrapped their doctrines, and claimed that the best

[1] E.g., F. X. Funk, *Das Alter der Arkandisziplin*, Paderborn, 1907, 42–55.
[2] *De praescr. haer.* 41: cf. *Ad ux.* 2, 5 (*C.C.L.* 1, 221; 389).
[3] *Con. Cels.* 1, 7 (Koetschau 1, 60).
[4] *Hom. in Lev.* 9, 10 (Baehrens, 438).

guarantee of the apostolicity of their own was that they were, and always had been, public.

Evidently the rule of secrecy was of gradual growth. At first it covered the sacraments, only later the creed. Even when it reached its heyday, as we know, the creed was not regarded as quite such an esoteric mystery as the sacraments. Whereas the fuller teaching about these was reserved until after baptism, the creed was handed to the catechumens in the final stage of their preparation. We shall not be far wrong if we place its extension to the creed somewhere in the second half of the third century. It cannot have been much earlier than that: later it would be hazardous to date it in view of the testimony of St Cyril of Jerusalem. The effect of its introduction (and this is what is of importance to us) must have been to impose a virtual censorship on the direct quotation of baptismal creeds. Even the influential Roman creed fell under this. The reader must have felt surprised that there should be such a dearth of evidence for its existence in the third and fourth centuries. Marcellus is the only writer between St Hippolytus and Rufinus who quotes it directly. Even he was scrupulously careful not to attach an explicit identification-label to it. Rufinus, too, did not reproduce the full text of either the Aquileian or the Roman creed: we have to piece them together like jig-saw puzzles. Practically all the other contemporary local creeds were lost to sight in the same deliberate black-out. The complete text of one or two Eastern creeds has survived for special reasons, but in no single case have we a direct, continuous quotation of a Western formula. Fortunately a number, both Western and Eastern, can be reconstructed, mostly out of sermons or expository essays. But for this very reason, if for none other, it would be dangerous to claim anything like absolute certainty for their wording.

The sparseness of material available is disappointing for other reasons than the fragmentary knowledge of actual creeds which it permits. It means that there are few, if any, of the wider questions about creeds in this period to which we can return satisfactory answers. One of these is the precise date of the establishment of the rites of the tradition and reddition of the creed in different districts. Again, was it only the larger

churches which possessed creeds of their own, or did comparatively small ones enjoy the liberty of admitting their own local
variations? When did the exact wording of the creeds come to
be regarded as sacrosanct? And how rigorously at different
periods was the principle of a fixed text interpreted? We can
only guess at the right answers to these and other queries. If
only we had more creeds to draw upon, we would perhaps be
in a position to understand more thoroughly the mutual
influence of creed on creed. As it is, the enforced reticence of
preachers and writers puts a barrier between us and the knowledge we seek.

2. *Daughter-creeds of R*

In this section we shall glance at the principal Western baptismal creeds, from the fourth to the sixth century, which we
can recover with a degree of certainty sufficient for our purpose.
The spade-work in this field was carried out last century by
Caspari, Kattenbusch and Hahn, and though subsequent
scholars (notably Dom G. Morin) have made valuable contributions, they have only seen reason to dissent from the earlier
conclusions in matters of detail.

In addition to the Old Roman Creed and the baptismal
questionnaire of St Hippolytus's *Tradition*, the creeds of four
Italian churches can be reconstituted, all of them belonging to
the last generation of the fourth century and the first two of
the fifth. It is unquestionable, of course, that they all derive
from much earlier dates, for the documents which reproduce
them treat them as authoritative and established. The creed
of Milan in the latter half of the fourth century can be extracted
from St Augustine's three sermons [1] on the delivery of the creed,
and also from the treatise *Explanatio symboli ad initiandos*,[2] which
probably consists of notes taken from a lecture by St Ambrose.
Although he was preaching to his North African flock, St
Augustine used a formula which differed from the characteristic African creeds, and since it is practically identical with R
and the creed of the *Explanatio*,[3] we can be satisfied that it was

[1] *Sermm.* 212, 213 and 214 (*P.L.* 38, 1058–72).
[2] *P.L.* 17, 1155–60.
[3] *Explan. symb.* says that its creed is the form used by the Roman church: cf. St
Ambrose, *Ep.* 42 (*P.L.* 16, 1125).

the form of the church of his own baptism. Perhaps he felt entitled to use it as his sermons were intended for a wider public than the church at Hippo.

MILAN (Aug.)	MILAN (Amb.)
Credo in deum patrem omnipotentem;	Credo in deum patrem omnipotentem;
Et in Iesum Christum, filium eius unicum, dominum nostrum,	Et in Iesum Christum, filium eius unicum, dominum nostrum,
qui natus est de Spiritu sancto et Maria virgine,	qui natus est de Spiritu sancto ex Maria virgine,
passus est sub Pontio Pilato, crucifixus et sepultus,	sub Pontio Pilato passus, et sepultus,
tertia die resurrexit a mortuis,	tertia die resurrexit a mortuis,
ascendit in caelum,	ascendit in caelum,
sedet ad dexteram patris,	sedet ad dexteram patris,
inde venturus est iudicare vivos et mortuos;	inde venturus est iudicare vivos et mortuos;
Et in Spiritum sanctum, sanctam ecclesiam, remissionem peccatorum, carnis resurrectionem.	Et in Spiritum sanctum, sanctam ecclesiam, remissionem peccatorum, carnis resurrectionem.

I believe in God the Father almighty;
And in Jesus Christ His only Son our Lord,
Who was born from the Holy Spirit and (*or* from) the Virgin Mary,
suffered under Pontius Pilate, was crucified (*not in Amb.*) and buried,
on the third day rose again from the dead, ascended to heaven, sits at the right hand of the Father,
thence will come to judge the living and the dead;
And in the Holy Spirit, the holy Church, the remission of sins, the resurrection of the flesh.

Our three other Italian creeds are those of Aquileia, Ravenna and Turin. Rufinus[1] is the authority for the first: he used it, as we saw, as the basis of his commentary on the Apostles' Creed. Some fifty years later, in the reign of St Leo the Great, we come across the other two. One of them is contained in each of six sermons[2] by the Pope's friend St Peter Chrysologus, bishop of Ravenna between 433 and 450, the other in a homily[3] by his contemporary St Maximus, bishop of Turin, the famous preacher. There will be no need to print translations of these or the other Western creeds which have to be quoted. Their broad general sense is the same as that of R and the creed of

---

[1] *Comm. in symb. apost.* in *C.C.L.* 20, 135 ff.
[2] *Sermm.* 57–62 (*P.L.* 52, 357 ff.).
[3] *Hom.* 83 *de trad. symb.* (*P.L.* 57, 433 ff.).

Milan, and a translation tends to obscure minute linguistic differences.

<table>
<tr><td>AQUILEIA</td><td>RAVENNA</td></tr>
<tr><td>Credo in deo patre omnipotente invisibili et impassibili;</td><td>Credo in deum patrem omnipotentem;</td></tr>
<tr><td>Et in Christo Iesu, unico filio eius, domino nostro,</td><td>Et in Christum Iesum, filium eius unicum, dominum nostrum,</td></tr>
<tr><td>qui natus est de Spiritu sancto ex Maria virgine,</td><td>qui natus est de Spiritu sancto ex Maria virgine,</td></tr>
<tr><td>crucifixus sub Pontio Pilato et sepultus,</td><td>qui sub Pontio Pilato crucifixus est et sepultus,</td></tr>
<tr><td>descendit ad inferna,</td><td></td></tr>
<tr><td>tertia die resurrexit a mortuis,</td><td>tertia die resurrexit,</td></tr>
<tr><td>ascendit ad caelos,</td><td>ascendit in caelos,</td></tr>
<tr><td>sedet ad dexteram patris,</td><td>sedet ad dexteram patris,</td></tr>
<tr><td>inde venturus est iudicare vivos et mortuos;</td><td>inde venturus est iudicare vivos et mortuos;</td></tr>
<tr><td>Et in Spiritu sancto, sanctam ecclesiam, remissionem peccatorum, huius carnis resurrectionem.</td><td>Credo in Spiritum sanctum, sanctam ecclesiam, remissionem peccatorum, carnis resurrectionem, vitam aeternam.</td></tr>
</table>

TURIN

Credo in deum patrem omnipotentem;
Et in Iesum Christum filium eius unicum, dominum nostrum,
qui natus est de Spiritu sancto ex Maria virgine,
qui sub Pontio Pilato crucifixus est et sepultus,
tertia die resurrexit a mortuis, ascendit in caelum, sedet ad dexteram patris
inde venturus iudicare vivos et mortuos;
Et in Spiritum sanctum, sanctam ecclesiam, remissionem peccatorum,
carnis resurrectionem.

From the Balkan province of Upper Moesia one fairly early creed is forthcoming. It can be pieced together from the fragmentary *Instructionis libelli VI*,[1] the author of which can be safely identified with the Nicetas who lived roughly from 335 to 414 and was bishop of Remesiana (the modern Bela-Palanka, in Yugoslavia, 30 km. S.E. of Nish) for a lengthy span. A successful missionary, he was the friend of St Paulinus of Nola, who made him the subject of one of his poems. Gennadius of Marseilles[2] is the authority for his having composed the six *libelli*. One of them, the fifth, is a commentary on the

[1] *P.L.* 52, 847–76. On the whole question of Nicetas and his creed, see A. E. Burn, *Niceta of Remesiana*, Cambridge, 1905. More recent scholarship has not altered his conclusions.
[2] *De vir. illustr.* 22 (*P.L.* 58, 1073 f.).

baptismal creed, the separate clauses of which are expounded consecutively, and while the precise wording sometimes remains doubtful there is little difficulty in reconstructing the general outline of the formula.

REMESIANA

Credo in deum patrem omnipotentem, [caeli et terrae creatorem];
Et in filium eius Iesum Christum [dominum nostrum?],
natum ex Spiritu sancto et ex virgine Maria,
passum sub Pontio Pilato, crucifixum, mortuum,
tertia die resurrexit vivus a mortuis,
ascendit in caelos,
sedet ad dexteram patris,
inde venturus iudicare vivos et mortuos;
Et in Spiritum sanctum, sanctam ecclesiam catholicam, communionem sanctorum, remissionem peccatorum, carnis resurrectionem et vitam aeternam.

Among the interesting features of this formula are (*a*) the omission of ONLY with SON, (*b*) the use of participles (BORN, SUFFERED, etc.) in the second member, possibly as a result of Nicetas's having translated it from a Greek original, (*c*) the possible addition of CREATOR OF HEAVEN AND EARTH (the text does not make this absolutely certain), (*d*) the term ROSE LIVING FROM THE DEAD, characteristic of Spanish creeds, and (*e*) the addition of COMMUNION OF SAINTS and ETERNAL LIFE.

For specimens of African creeds we are indebted to St Augustine, who was bishop of Hippo from 396 to 430, to an anonymous and slightly younger contemporary of his who is possibly to be identified with the Quodvultdeus who was bishop of Carthage when it fell to the Vandals, and to St Fulgentius, bishop of Ruspe in the province of Byzacena (part of modern Tunisia), with an interval of exile, from 508 to 533. St Augustine's *Sermon* 215,[1] on the reddition of the creed, comments on the formula which the baptized candidates have just recited, and this fact, as well as the internal peculiarities by which it is marked, confirms that it is a local African form. The creed which we have attributed to the church of Carthage can be extracted from four discourses[2] of great importance for the liturgy of baptism which were traditionally, but erroneously, ascribed to St Augustine. Dom Morin[3] has reconstituted the

---

[1] *P.L.* 38, 1072–6.   [2] Cf. *P.L.* 40, 637–52; 651–60; 659–68; 42, 1117–30.
[3] Cf. *R. Bén.* xxxi, 1914, 156 ff.; xxxv, 1923, 233 ff. For African creeds see also P. C. Eichenseer, *Das Symbolum Apostolicum beim heiligen Augustinus*, St Ottilien, 1960.

creed which they presuppose, and has argued a convincing case for Quodvultdeus, the pupil and friend of St Augustine who became bishop of Carthage in 437, having been their author. St Fulgentius's creed can be collected from the fragments[1] which survive of his ten books *Contra Fabianum*. All three formulae are linked together by certain peculiarities, notably the fulsome wording of the first article, the threefold repetition of I BELIEVE, their contrast between BY THE HOLY SPIRIT and FROM THE VIRGIN MARY, their use of ETERNAL LIFE, and their placing of THE HOLY CHURCH at the end with the preposition THROUGH before it.

HIPPO	CARTHAGE
Credimus in deum patrem omnipotentem, universorum creatorem, regem saeculorum, immortalem et invisibilem;	Credo in deum patrem omnipotentem, universorum creatorem, regem saeculorum, immortalem et invisibilem;
Credimus et in filium eius Iesum Christum dominum nostrum,	Credo et in filium eius Iesum Christum,
natum de Spiritu sancto ex virgine Maria,	qui natus est de Spiritu sancto ex virgine Maria,
crucifixum sub Pontio Pilato, mortuum, et sepultum,	crucifixus est sub Pontio Pilato et sepultus,
[qui] tertia die resurrexit a mortuis,	tertia die a mortuis resurrexit,
ascendit ad caelos,	assumptus est in caelos,
sedet ad dexteram dei patris,	et ad dexteram patris sedet,
inde venturus est iudicare vivos et mortuos;	inde venturus est iudicare vivos et mortuos;
Credimus et in Spiritum sanctum, remissionem peccatorum, resurrectionem carnis, vitam aeternam per sanctam ecclesiam.	Credo et in Spiritum sanctum, remissionem peccatorum, carnis resurrectionem, in vitam aeternam per sanctam ecclesiam.

RUSPE

Credo in deum patrem omnipotentem, universorum creatorem, regem saeculorum, immortalem et invisibilem;
Credo in Iesum Christum, filium eius unicum, dominum nostrum,
qui natus est de Spiritu sancto ex virgine Maria,
crucifixus est [sub Pontio Pilato] et sepultus,
tertia die resurrexit [a mortuis],
in caelum ascendit,[2]
et in dextera dei sedit,
inde venturus est iudicare vivos et mortuos;
Credo in Spiritum sanctum, remissionem peccatorum,
carnis resurrectionem et vitam aeternam per sanctam ecclesiam.

[1] Cf. esp. *Frag.* xxxvi: *Frag.* xxxii is also helpful (*C.C.L.* 91A, 854 ff.; 831 f.). On this creed, see Caspari, *Quellen* II, 245 ff.
[2] So *De fid. ad Petrum* 63 (xx) (*C.C.L.* 91A, 751).

The oldest surviving Spanish creed is the one quoted by Priscillian,[1] the founder of the heretical sect which bears his name, who was executed in 385. The see of which he was bishop was Avila. It is possible[2] that the tract containing the creed was really the work of another Priscillianist named Instantius, but its ascription to Priscillian himself is on the whole more likely. Another Spanish creed, probably much earlier than the date of its citation, has been collected out of various Spanish writings of the sixth and seventh centuries.[3] Yet a third specimen is to be found in the Mozarabic liturgy.[4]

PRISCILLIAN	SPAIN VI CENT.
[Credentes] unum deum patrem omnipotentem . . .;	Credo in deum patrem omnipotentem;
Et unum dominum Iesum Christum . . .	Et in Iesum Christum, filium eius unicum, deum et dominum nostrum,
natum ex Maria virgine ex Spiritu sancto . . .	qui natus est de Spiritu sancto et Maria virgine,
passum sub Pontio Pilato, crucifixum . . . sepultum,	passus sub Pontio Pilato, crucifixus et sepultus,
	descendit ad inferna,
tertia die resurrexisse . . .	tertia die resurrexit vivus a mortuis,
ascendisse in caelos,	ascendit in caelos,
sedere ad dexteram dei patris omnipotentis,	sedet ad dexteram dei patris omnipotentis,
inde venturum et iudicaturum de vivis et mortuis;	inde venturus iudicare vivos et mortuos;
[Credentes] in sanctam ecclesiam, sanctum Spiritum, baptismum salutare . . . [credentes] remissionem peccatorum . . . [credentes] in resurrectionem carnis . . .	Credo in sanctum Spiritum, sanctam ecclesiam catholicam, remissionem omnium peccatorum, carnis resurrectionem et vitam aeternam.

MOZARABIC LITURGY

Credo in deum patrem omnipotentem;
Et in Iesum Christum, filium eius unicum, dominum nostrum,
natum de Spiritu sancto ex utero Mariae virginis,
passus sub Pontio Pilato, crucifixus et sepultus,
tertia die resurrexit vivus a mortuis,

[1] *Tract.* 2 (ed. by G. Schepss in *C.S.E.L.* xviii, 36 f.).
[2] Cf. G. Morin, *R. Bén.* xxx, 1913, 153 ff.
[3] St Martin of Braga, *De correct. rustic.* (ed. C. P. Caspari, Christiania, 1883); St Ildefonsus of Toledo, *De cognit. bapt.* 36 ff. (*P.L.* 96, 127 ff.); Etherius and Beatus, *Ad Elipand. ep.* I, 22 (*P.L.* 96, 906).
[4] *P.L.* 85, 395 f.

ascendit in celum,
sedet ad dexteram dei patris omnipotentis,
inde venturus iudicaturus vivos et mortuos;
Credo in sanctum Spiritum, sanctam ecclesiam catholicam,
  sanctorum communionem, remissionem omnium peccatorum,
  carnis huius resurrectionem et vitam eternam. Amen.

Again we notice kindred features in these creeds. Priscillian's curious placing of HOLY SPIRIT after the Virgin Mary and the Church respectively no doubt reflects a nuance of his personal teaching. But such traits as the repetition of I BELIEVE before the first and the third articles, the insertion of LIVING after ROSE AGAIN, the full form AT THE RIGHT HAND OF GOD THE FATHER ALMIGHTY, the preference for the future participle TO JUDGE (*judicaturus*) and for the emphatic ALL SINS, the placing of *sanctum* before *Spiritum*, and the use of CATHOLIC and ETERNAL LIFE are all characteristic.

Three Gallic creeds belonging to our period have come down to us in something approaching a reliable form. The earliest is that of St Faustus of Riez, the British-born abbot of Lérins and bishop of Riez, who acquired renown in the south of France as a hammer of the Arians in the 'seventies and 'eighties of the fifth century. His creed is derived from two homilies *De symbolo* and his *Tractatus de symbolo*[1] : the third article is further attested by his book *De Spiritu sancto*.[2] Next we have the baptismal creed of St Caesarius, the eloquent bishop of Arles (503–543). We are indebted to Dom G. Morin for having demonstrated,[3] on the ground of stylistic peculiarities, that the sermon on the exposition or tradition of the creed (beginning *Sermo et sacramentum*) in the so-called Missale Gallicanum Vetus[4] is really by St. Caesarius. Thirdly, we have a fragmentary creed in an apologetic letter by St Cyprian of Toulon, the disciple and friend of St Caesarius, who died in the 'forties of the sixth century.[5]

[1] For the homilies, see Caspari, *Quellen* II, 185 ff. and 191 ff. For the tractate, see his *A. und N.Q.*, 262 ff. All three are doubtful works.
[2] *De Spir. sancto*, I, 2 (Engelbrecht, 103 f.). This is genuine.
[3] *R. Bén.* xlvi, 1934, 178–89: for text cf. *Serm.* 9 (*C.C.L.* 103, 47).
[4] Cf. Mabillon, *De liturgia Gallicana*, Paris, 1685, 339–42. But the best and most accessible text of the sermon is that printed in Dom Morin's article in *R. Bén.* xlvi, 1934; it is based on a photograph of the Vatican MS *Palat. Lat.* 493 (foll. 20v.–26v.).
[5] Edited by W. Gundlach in *Mon. Germ. Hist.*, *Epp.* III, 435.

RIEZ

Credo in deum patrem omnipotentem;

Et in filium eius dominum nostrum Iesum Christum,
qui conceptus est de Spiritu sancto, natus ex Maria virgine,
crucifixus et sepultus,

tertia die resurrexit,
adscendit ad caelos,
sedet ad dexteram dei patris omnipotentis,
inde venturus iudicare vivos et mortuos;
Credo et in Spiritum sanctum, sanctam ecclesiam, sanctorum communionem, abremissam peccatorum, carnis resurrectionem, vitam aeternam.

ARLES

Credo in deum patrem omnipotentem, creatorem caeli et terrae;
Credo et in Iesum Christum filium eius unigenitum sempiternum,
qui conceptus est de Spiritu sancto, natus est de Maria virgine,
passus est sub Pontio Pilato, crucifixus, mortuus et sepultus, descendit ad inferna,
tertia die resurrexit a mortuis,
ascendit ad caelos,
sedit ad dexteram dei patris omnipotentis,
inde venturus iudicare vivos et mortuos;
Credo in sanctum Spiritum, sanctam ecclesiam catholicam, sanctorum communionem, remissionem peccatorum, carnis resurrectionem, vitam aeternam. Amen.

TOULON

Credo in deum patrem omnipotentem;
Credo et in Iesum Christum, filium eius unigenitum, dominum nostrum,
qui conceptus de Spiritu sancto, natus ex Maria virgine,
passus sub Pontio Pilato, crucifixus et sepultus,
tertia die resurrexit a mortuis,
ascendit in coelos,
sedet ad dexteram patris,
inde venturus iudicaturus vivos ac mortuos. . . .

The formulae printed above comprise most of the surviving baptismal creeds of the West between the fourth and the sixth centuries. Their kinship with one another and with the Old Roman Creed leaps to the eye at once. They all exhibit precisely the same ground-plan and structure as R, and precisely the same brand of teaching, and they are couched in practically identical language. Some, like the creeds of Milan, are almost indistinguishable: they differ only in the word-order JESUS CHRIST, the inclusion of SUFFERED, the omission of WHO before SUFFERED, and the substitution of THENCE for WHENCE. Others, like the African and Gallic formulae, can boast of several supplementary clauses. But whether the divergences are few or numerous, they amount to no more than superficial embroidery, and cannot conceal the underlying identity. Plainly they form a family group on their own, including a number of regional sub-groups with their own local idiosyncrasies, but clearly demarcated from all other contemporary formularies. The question therefore arises whether they are parallel forms, which have grown up independently of one another but have acquired this astonishing mutual similarity through cross-influence, or whether they all derive from a common basic stock. If the latter is the case, the only conceivable claimant for the position is R. Not only would it be hard to believe that the Roman church at this period accepted its baptismal creed from a provincial church, but we have already produced evidence for its very early activity in the composition of creeds and for the antiquity of R.

The suggestion that they are sister forms with R, unlikely in itself when we reflect on the immense distances of the several churches from each other, is ruled out by the extraordinary linguistic similarity of the creeds. These extend to minute refinements of verbal expression, such as the use of *unicum* (practically never *unigenitum*) for ONLY SON, *ascendere* for ASCEND, *ad dexteram* (*in dextera* has better Vulgate[1] authority) for AT THE RIGHT HAND, *venturus* (never the more ordinary *veniet*) for WILL COME, etc., and to peculiarities of word-order, such as *Maria virgine* and the chiastic structure of the original four items of the final article. Secondly, while the provincial creeds all contain additions to R, they do not show any material omissions. R is the irreducible skeleton which lurks, very near the surface, in all of them. The divergences themselves are fewest in certain fourth-century creeds hailing from churches geographically near to Rome, and they multiply in number in proportion to their lateness and their distance from the capital. Finally, none of the divergences points to a basic form different from R, or even to a different Latin version of the original Greek R than the one we know.

This last point has been fastened upon[2] as enabling a corollary of considerable importance to be established. Since all the provincial creeds descend from the Latin translation which became official, they must themselves date from the time when Latin was the liturgical language of the Roman church. That

---

[1] Cf. *Hebr.* 8, 1; 10, 12; 12, 2; 1 *Pet.* 3, 22; etc.
[2] Cf. H. Lietzmann in *Z.N.T.W.* xxi, 1922, 5.

is, they cannot be prior to the middle of the third century. But so stated the argument is not really tenable. The recognized Latin translation of the creed, as we observed in Chapter IV,[1] may well have been made some time before Latin had become officially adopted for use at Roman services, for there must always have been numerous Latin-speaking converts asking for baptism. The conclusion itself, however, may be accepted, though on rather different grounds. The dependence of the provincial creeds on R shows that they must have come into existence when R had acquired its position of unique prestige. This cannot have been, on the most optimistic estimate, much before the second generation of the third century. For our immediate purposes, however, this is a relatively minor point. The remarkable and absolutely certain datum which the evidence assembled in this section has impressed upon us is the fact that all Western baptismal creeds were directly descended from the creed of the Roman church.

3. *Eastern Creeds*

An examination of the baptismal creeds of the East confronts us with a very different state of affairs. No single Eastern formula stands out, in respect either of early origin or of paramount influence, in a way analogous to the Roman creed. On the other hand, while Western creeds other than the Roman symbol are hardly forthcoming in the third century, the East can produce one or two well attested forms which probably go back to that epoch. There are several, also, which derive from the fourth and early fifth centuries. Some of these, as we shall observe, have been interlarded with the famous catchwords of the Nicene theology (OF ONE SUBSTANCE WITH THE FATHER, etc.), and thus probably represent early baptismal creeds which have been brought up to date.

The appropriate starting-point for a survey of Eastern formularies is " the statement concerning belief ($\dot{\eta}$ περὶ πίστεως γραφή) "[2] which Eusebius, the scholarly bishop of Caesarea

---

[1] See above, p. 112.

[2] St Athanasius added it as an appendix to his *De decret. Nic. syn.* It is printed in *P.G.* 20, 1537 and in Opitz, *Urk.* 22. Cf. also Socrates, *Hist. eccl.* 1, 8 (*P.G.* 67, 68); Theodoret, *Hist. eccl.* 1, 12 (Parmentier, 48 ff.).

from *c.* 314 to 339 or 340, submitted at the council of Nicaea (325). He set it down himself in the letter of self-justification which he subsequently thought it prudent to despatch to his flock. An important item in the statement read out before the emperor Constantine and the council (we shall have an opportunity of discussing it more fully in the next chapter) was a creed, the text of which runs as follows :

CAESAREA

Πιστεύομεν εἰς ἕνα θεόν, πατέρα, παντο-κράτορα, τὸν τῶν ἁπάντων ὁρατῶν τε καὶ ἀοράτων ποιητήν.

Καὶ εἰς ἕνα κύριον Ἰησοῦν Χριστόν, τὸν τοῦ θεοῦ λόγον, θεὸν ἐκ θεοῦ, φῶς ἐκ φωτός, ζωὴν ἐκ ζωῆς, υἱὸν μονογενῆ, πρωτότοκον πάσης κτίσεως, πρὸ πάντων τῶν αἰώνων ἐκ τοῦ πατρὸς γεγεννημένον, δι' οὗ καὶ ἐγένετο τὰ πάντα, τὸν διὰ τὴν ἡμετέραν σωτηρίαν σαρκωθέντα καὶ ἐν ἀνθρώποις πολιτευσάμενον, καὶ παθόντα, καὶ ἀνα-στάντα τῇ τρίτῃ ἡμέρᾳ, καὶ ἀνελθόντα πρὸς τὸν πατέρα, καὶ ἥξοντα πάλιν ἐν δόξῃ κρῖναι ζῶντας καὶ νεκρούς.

Πιστεύομεν δὲ καὶ εἰς ἓν πνεῦμα ἅγιον.

We believe in one God, the Father, almighty, maker of all things visible and invisible;

And in one Lord Jesus Christ, the Logos of God, God from God, light from light, life from life, Son only begotten, first-begotten of all creation, begotten before all ages from the Father, through Whom all things came into being, Who because of our salvation was incarnate, and dwelt among men, and suffered, and rose again on the third day, and ascended to the Father, and will come again in glory to judge living and dead;

We believe also in one Holy Spirit.

This creed, possibly with a fuller final section, is almost certainly Eusebius's own: the creed, that is, of the local community at Caesarea. Some critics[1] have shown scepticism on this point, thinking that he could never have had the impertinence to foist a formulary of his own on the grand ecumenical council. Its basic structure, they argue, may well have been borrowed from the Caesarean model, but its contents were probably an amalgam of baptismal creeds in general. But conjectures like this are wide of the mark, and spring from a misunderstanding of the actual situation as well as from an extravagant measure of scrupulous caution. As a matter of historical fact (we shall develop this point later) Eusebius did not bring the creed forward with a view to its being adopted by the council, but in vindication of his own orthodoxy, which at the time lay under a cloud. Its apologetic value would have dimin-

---

[1] So, e.g., A. Harnack in his article *Apostolisches Symbolum* in Hauck's *Realen-cyklopaedie*, 3rd ed., I.

ished in proportion as it was a mere *ad hoc* generalization of creeds in the Catholic East. But his own statement to the council makes the position absolutely clear. He introduced the formula with the words : "As we received from the bishops before us, both in our catechetical instruction and when we were baptized (ἐν τῇ κατηχήσει καὶ ὅτε τὸ λουτρὸν ἐλαμβάνομεν) . . . so also we believe now and submit our belief to you." The inference that the creed which he then proceeded to insert was the creed of his own baptism, and so of Caesarea, is the only one which does justice to his words. Since Eusebius, who was born *circa* 263, had been brought up as a Christian, we are justified in concluding that a recognized baptismal formulary on these lines must have been current at Caesarea in the latter half of the third century.

A second example of a local Eastern creed of fairly early date is the baptismal creed of Jerusalem. We owe our knowledge of it to St Cyril of Jerusalem, who while still a priest (or possibly as bishop) commented on its clauses in the catechetical lectures he delivered *circa* 350. Naturally St Cyril did not quote the text *in extenso*; the discipline of reserve prevented that. But most of it can be reconstructed confidently, as A. A. Stephenson has shown, from excerpts in his lecture expositions, and the rest (printed below in square brackets) very precariously from allusions in the lectures.[1] A point worth noticing is that St Cyril, although prepared to do battle with Acacius of Caesarea over the privileges granted by the council of Nicaea to the see of Jerusalem, declined to incorporate anything of the Nicene doctrine into the creed which he handed out to his catechumens. Like many others he was suspicious,[2] at this period of his life at any rate, of the new-fangled Nicene term OF ONE SUBSTANCE, and shunned the new orthodoxy almost as much as Arianism.

JERUSALEM

Πιστεύομεν εἰς ἕνα θεόν, πατέρα, παντοκρά- We believe in one God, the Father, al-
τορα, ποιητὴν οὐρανοῦ καὶ γῆς, ὁρατῶν   mighty, maker of heaven and earth,
τε πάντων καὶ ἀοράτων.   of all things visible and invisible;

[1] Cf. *Cat.* 7–18 (*P.G.* 33, 605–1060); A. A. Stephenson, *Studia Patristica* III, 303–13 (Berlin, 1961): his reconstruction is followed here.
[2] For St Cyril's theological position cf. I. Berten, *Revue des sciences phil. et théol.* lii, 1968; A. A. Stephenson, *St Cyril of Jerusalem*, 1969, vol. I, 34 ff.

Καὶ εἰς ἕνα κύριον Ἰησοῦν Χριστόν, τὸν υἱὸν τοῦ θεοῦ τὸν μονογενῆ, τὸν ἐκ τοῦ πατρὸς γεννηθέντα θεὸν ἀληθινὸν πρὸ πάντων τῶν αἰώνων, δι᾽ οὗ τὰ πάντα ἐγένετο, [τὸν σαρκωθέντα καὶ] ἐνανθρωπήσαντα, [τὸν σταυρωθέντα καὶ ταφέντα καὶ] ἀναστάντα [ἐκ νεκρῶν] τῇ τρίτῃ ἡμέρᾳ, καὶ ἀνελθόντα εἰς τοὺς οὐρανούς, καὶ καθίσαντα ἐκ δεξιῶν τοῦ πατρός, καὶ ἐρχόμενον ἐν δόξῃ κρῖναι ζῶντας καὶ νεκρούς, οὗ τῆς βασιλείας οὐκ ἔσται τέλος.

Καὶ εἰς ἓν ἅγιον πνεῦμα, τὸν παράκλητον, τὸ λαλῆσαν ἐν τοῖς προφήταις, καὶ εἰς ἓν βάπτισμα μετανοίας εἰς ἄφεσιν ἁμαρτιῶν, καὶ εἰς μίαν ἁγίαν καθολικὴν ἐκκλησίαν, καὶ εἰς σαρκὸς ἀνάστασιν, καὶ εἰς ζωὴν αἰώνιον.

And in one Lord Jesus Christ, the only begotten Son of God, Who was begotten from the Father as true God before all ages, through Whom all things came into being, Who [was incarnate and] became man, [Who was crucified and buried and] rose again [from the dead] on the third day, and ascended to the heavens, and sat down at the right hand of the Father, and will come in glory to judge living and dead, of Whose kingdom there will be no end;

And in one Holy Spirit, the Paraclete, Who spoke in the prophets, and in one baptism of repentance to the remission of sins, and in one holy Catholic church, and in the resurrection of the flesh, and in life everlasting.

While these creeds have been preserved in a relatively secure form, the ancient baptismal creed of Antioch can only be reconstructed conjecturally. In 430 or 431 John Cassian, at the request of the deacon who was later to become Pope Leo the Great, wrote a treatise against the heresiarch Nestorius. In the sixth book[1] of this he argued that Nestorius could be refuted out of his own mouth since his teaching disagreed so glaringly with the "Antiochene creed (symbolum Antiochenum)" which he had professed at his baptism. He then quoted the Antiochene creed, which we thus have in his Latin translation.

ANTIOCH

Credo in unum et solum verum deum, patrem, omnipotentem, creatorem omnium visibilium et invisibilium creaturarum;
Et in dominum nostrum Iesum Christum, filium eius unigenitum et primogenitum totius creaturae, ex eo natum ante omnia saecula et non factum, deum verum ex deo vero, homousion patri, per quem et saecula compaginata sunt et omnia facta, qui propter nos venit et natus est ex Maria

I believe in one only true God, the Father, almighty, creator of all creatures visible and invisible;
And in our Lord Jesus Christ, His only-begotten Son and first-begotten of all creation, born from Him before all ages and not made, true God from true God, of one substance with the Father, through Whom also the ages were framed and all things were made, Who because of us came and

[1] Con. Nest. 6, 3 (Petschenig I, 327).

virgine, et crucifixus sub Pontio Pilato, et sepultus, et tertia die resurrexit secundum scripturas, et ascendit in caelos, et iterum veniet iudicare vivos et mortuos;

Et reliqua.

was born from the Virgin Mary, and was crucified under Pontius Pilate, and was buried, and on the third day rose again according to the Scriptures, and ascended to heaven, and will come again to judge living and dead;

And the rest.

John Cassian broke off abruptly because it was not to his purpose to cite the third article. But there are two passages [1] in a sermon by St John Chrysostom, who himself had been baptized at Antioch and now was preaching there, which make specific reference to this. His words clearly indicate that it contained at any rate the clauses AND IN THE REMISSION OF SINS, AND IN THE RESURRECTION OF THE DEAD, and AND IN LIFE EVERLASTING (καὶ εἰς ἁμαρτιῶν ἄφεσιν, καὶ [εἰς] νεκρῶν ἀνάστασιν, καὶ εἰς ζωὴν αἰώνιον). Furthermore, the accuracy of Cassian's version of the central section is confirmed by the quotation of it in an *Obtestatio*, written by Eusebius of Dorylaeum,[2] about 429–30, against Nestorius and preserved among the *acta* of the council of Ephesus.[3] This refers explicitly to "the creed of the church of Antioch (τοῦ μαθήματος τῆς ἐκκλησίας Ἀντιοχέων)", and gives the following brief excerpt:

... θεὸν ἀληθινὸν ἐκ θεοῦ ἀληθινοῦ, ὁμοούσιον τῷ πατρί, δι' οὗ καὶ οἱ αἰῶνες κατηρτίσθησαν καὶ τὰ πάντα ἐγένετο, τὸν δι' ἡμᾶς ἐλθόντα [al. κατελθόντα] καὶ γεννηθέντα ἐκ Μαρίας τῆς ἁγίας παρθένου [al. τῆς ἁγίας τῆς ἀειπαρθένου] καὶ σταυρωθέντα ἐπὶ Ποντίου Πιλάτου— καὶ τὰ ἑξῆς τοῦ συμβόλου.

... true God from true God, of one substance with the Father, through Whom also the ages were framed and all things came into being, Who because of us came (*al.* came down) and was born from Mary the holy Virgin (*al.* the holy, the ever-virgin), and was crucified under Pontius Pilate ... and the rest of the creed in order.

On the other hand, the text as reproduced by Cassian and Eusebius of Dorylaeum has plainly had the key-phrases of Nicene orthodoxy superimposed upon it—AND NOT MADE, TRUE GOD FROM TRUE GOD, OF ONE SUBSTANCE WITH THE FATHER. Even when these are removed, however, Cassian's confession has a

[1] *Hom.* 40 *in* 1 *Cor.* 15, 29 (*P.G.* 61, 348 and 349).
[2] So Leontius of Byzantium in *Con. Nest. et Eutych.* 3, 43 (*P. G.* 86, 1389).
[3] *A.C.O. Tom.* I, *vol.* 1, i, 102 (Mansi IV, 1009 gives a text less consonant with Cassian's).

suspicious air about it. In the Christological section we observe how he has silently altered the Greek FROM MARY THE HOLY VIRGIN, attested by Eusebius, to FROM MARY THE VIRGIN, presumably to bring it into line with the Roman usage. A similar motive may have inspired the substitution of I BELIEVE for the more usual WE BELIEVE, of OUR LORD JESUS CHRIST for ONE LORD JESUS CHRIST, and ON THE THIRD DAY ROSE AGAIN for ROSE AGAIN ON THE THIRD DAY. Despite these touchings up, however, we have every reason to identify the underlying form as being, like the Jerusalem creed which it resembles, an ancient baptismal symbol.

Another Syrian creed, also used at baptism but much longer and more detailed, is found in the *Apostolical Constitutions* in the account [1] there given of the ritual of initiation. The treatise itself was probably compiled in Syria or Palestine towards the end of the fourth century.

APOSTOLICAL CONSTITUTIONS

Καὶ πιστεύω καὶ βαπτίζομαι εἰς ἕνα ἀγέννητον μόνον ἀληθινὸν θεόν, παντοκράτορα, τὸν πατέρα τοῦ Χριστοῦ, κτίστην καὶ δημιουργὸν τῶν ἁπάντων, ἐξ οὗ τὰ πάντα.

Καὶ εἰς τὸν κύριον Ἰησοῦν τὸν Χριστόν, τὸν μονογενῆ αὐτοῦ υἱόν, τὸν πρωτότοκον πάσης κτίσεως, τὸν πρὸ αἰώνων εὐδοκίᾳ τοῦ πατρὸς γεννηθέντα οὐ κτισθέντα, δι᾽ οὗ τὰ πάντα ἐγένετο τὰ ἐν οὐρανοῖς καὶ ἐπὶ γῆς, ὁρατά τε καὶ ἀόρατα, τὸν ἐπ᾽ ἐσχάτων τῶν ἡμερῶν κατελθόντα ἐξ οὐρανῶν καὶ σάρκα ἀναλαβόντα, ἐκ τῆς ἁγίας παρθένου Μαρίας γεννηθέντα, καὶ πολιτευσάμενον ὁσίως κατὰ τοὺς νόμους τοῦ θεοῦ καὶ πατρὸς αὐτοῦ, καὶ σταυρωθέντα ἐπὶ Ποντίου Πιλάτου, καὶ ἀποθανόντα ὑπὲρ ἡμῶν, καὶ ἀναστάντα ἐκ νεκρῶν μετὰ τὸ παθεῖν τῇ τρίτῃ ἡμέρᾳ, καὶ ἀνελθόντα εἰς τοὺς οὐρανοὺς καὶ καθεσθέντα ἐν δεξιᾷ τοῦ πατρός, καὶ πάλιν ἐρχόμενον ἐπὶ συντελείᾳ τοῦ αἰῶνος μετὰ δόξης κρῖναι ζῶντας καὶ νεκρούς, οὗ τῆς βασιλείας οὐκ ἔσται τέλος.

And I believe, and am baptized, in one unbegotten, only, true God, almighty, the Father of the Christ, creator and framer of all things, from Whom are all things;

And in the Lord Jesus the Christ, His only-begotten Son, the first-begotten of all creation, Who before ages was born, not created, by the good pleasure of the Father, through Whom all things came into being, in heaven and upon the earth, visible and invisible, Who in the last days came down from heaven and took flesh, born from the holy virgin Mary, and lived in holy wise according to the laws of God His Father, and was crucified under Pontius Pilate, and died for us, and rose again from the dead, after His passion, on the third day, and ascended to heaven, and sat down on the Father's right hand, and will come again at the end of the age with glory to judge living and dead, of Whose kingdom there will be no end;

[1] *Ap. Const.* 7, 41 (ed. of F. X. Funk, I, 444 ff.).

Βαπτίζομαι καὶ εἰς τὸ πνεῦμα τὸ ἅγιον, τουτέστι τὸν παράκλητον, τὸ ἐνεργῆσαν ἐν πᾶσι τοῖς ἀπ' αἰῶνος ἁγίοις, ὕστερον δὲ ἀποσταλὲν καὶ τοῖς ἀποστόλοις παρὰ τοῦ πατρὸς κατὰ τὴν ἐπαγγελίαν τοῦ σωτῆρος ἡμῶν καὶ κυρίου Ἰησοῦ Χριστοῦ, καὶ μετὰ τοὺς ἀποστόλους δὲ πᾶσι τοῖς πιστεύουσιν ἐν τῇ ἁγίᾳ καθολικῇ καὶ ἀποστολικῇ ἐκκλησίᾳ, εἰς σαρκὸς ἀνάστασιν καὶ εἰς ἄφεσιν ἁμαρτιῶν καὶ εἰς βασιλείαν οὐρανῶν καὶ εἰς ζωὴν τοῦ μέλλοντος αἰῶνος.

I am baptized also in the Holy Spirit, that is the Paraclete, Who worked in all the saints from the beginning, and afterwards was sent to the apostles also from the Father according to the promise of our Saviour and Lord Jesus Christ, and after the apostles to all believers within the holy Catholic and apostolic church ; in the resurrection of the flesh and in the remission of sins and in the kingdom of heaven and in the life of the age to come.

Another interesting creed which has come to light recently is the one used at baptism by Theodore of Mopsuestia (in Cilicia). He was ordained priest at Antioch in 383 (circa), and exercised his ministry there until he was consecrated bishop of Mopsuestia in 392 : he died in 428. In his catechetical lectures,[1] which have survived in Syriac, he expounded the baptismal creed to his neophytes, citing its several clauses textually many times over, and thus it is possible to piece the formula together as a whole. It bears a remarkable resemblance, it is worth recalling, to a Syrian creed used by the Nestorians which Caspari reconstructed[2] in what must have been approximately its Greek form. As it stands it bears obvious signs of having developed in the controversial atmosphere of the fourth century, but its basis is no doubt ancient. We reproduce the creed below in English along with a retranslation into Greek made by Père J. Lebon.[3]

MOPSUESTIA

We believe in one God, the Father, almighty, maker of all things visible and invisible ;
And in one Lord Jesus Christ, the only-begotten Son of God, the first-begotten of all creation, Who was begotten from His Father before all ages, not made, true God from true God, of one substance with His Father, through Whom the ages

Πιστεύομεν εἰς ἕνα θεόν, πατέρα, παντοκράτορα, πάντων ὁρατῶν τε καὶ ἀοράτων ποιητήν.
Καὶ εἰς ἕνα κύριον Ἰησοῦν Χριστόν, τὸν υἱὸν τοῦ θεοῦ τὸν μονογενῆ, τὸν πρωτότοκον πάσης κτίσεως, τὸν ἐκ τοῦ πατρὸς αὐτοῦ γεννηθέντα πρὸ πάντων τῶν αἰώνων, οὐ ποιηθέντα, θεὸν ἀληθινὸν ἐκ θεοῦ ἀληθινοῦ, ὁμοούσιον τῷ πατρὶ αὐτοῦ, δι' οὗ οἱ αἰῶνες κατηρτίσθησαν

[1] Published for the first time (the Syriac with an English translation) by A. Mingana in *Woodbrooke Studies* V (Cambridge, 1932).
[2] Caspari, *Quellen* I, 116 and 118. Cf. also Hahn 132. The text survives only in Syriac.
[3] *R.H.E.* xxxii, 1936, 836.

were fashioned and all things came
into being. Who because of us men
and because of our salvation came
down from heaven and was incarnate
and became man, being born from
the Virgin Mary, and was crucified
under Pontius Pilate, was buried and
rose again on the third day according
to the Scriptures, ascended to heaven,
sits on the right hand of God and
will come again to judge living and
dead;
And in one Holy Spirit, Who proceeds
from the Father, a life-giving Spirit.
[We confess] one baptism, one holy
Catholic church, the remission of
sins, the resurrection of the flesh, and
life everlasting.

καὶ τὰ πάντα ἐγένετο, τὸν δι᾽ ἡμᾶς τοὺς
ἀνθρώπους καὶ διὰ τὴν ἡμετέραν
σωτηρίαν κατελθόντα ἐκ τῶν οὐρανῶν
καὶ σαρκωθέντα καὶ ἄνθρωπον γενόμενον,
γεννηθέντα ἐκ Μαρίας τῆς παρθένου, καὶ
σταυρωθέντα ἐπὶ Ποντίου Πιλάτου,
ταφέντα καὶ ἀναστάντα τῇ τρίτῃ ἡμέρᾳ
κατὰ τὰς γραφάς, ἀνελθόντα εἰς τοὺς
οὐρανούς, καθεζόμενον ἐκ δεξιῶν τοῦ
θεοῦ, καὶ πάλιν ἐρχόμενον κρῖναι ζῶντας
καὶ νεκρούς.

Καὶ εἰς ἓν πνεῦμα ἅγιον, τὸ ἐκ τοῦ πατρὸς
ἐκπορευόμενον, πνεῦμα ζωοποιόν. [ὁμο-
λογοῦμεν] ἓν βάπτισμα, μίαν ἁγίαν
ἐκκλησίαν καθολικήν, ἄφεσιν ἁμαρτιῶν,
ἀνάστασιν σαρκὸς καὶ ζωὴν αἰώνιον.

All these formularies have a Syro-Palestinian or Cilician
background,[1] but there is evidence too for Egyptian creeds.
We glanced in an earlier chapter at Origen's references to "the
rule of faith" and "the ecclesiastical preaching", and we
studied the brief creed of the Dêr Balyzeh Papyrus. There are
unmistakable echoes of a creed in the letter[2] of St Alexander,
bishop of Alexandria (313–328), to Alexander, bishop of Constantinople, at the outbreak of the Arian controversy. After
attacking the false positions of the heretics, St Alexander stated
the orthodox doctrine concerning the Father and the Son, and
went on:

ALEXANDRIA

46 Περὶ ὧν ἡμεῖς οὕτως πιστεύομεν, ὡς τῇ
ἀποστολικῇ ἐκκλησίᾳ δοκεῖ· εἰς μόνον
ἀγέννητον πατέρα . . .
καὶ εἰς ἕνα κύριον Ἰησοῦν Χριστόν, τὸν
υἱὸν τοῦ θεοῦ μονογενῆ, γεννηθέντα οὐκ
ἐκ τοῦ μὴ ὄντος ἀλλ᾽ ἐκ τοῦ ὄντος
πατρός. . .
53 Πρὸς δὲ τῇ εὐσεβεῖ ταύτῃ περὶ πατρὸς
καὶ υἱοῦ δόξῃ, καθὼς ἡμᾶς αἱ θεῖαι
γραφαὶ διδάσκουσιν, ἐν πνεῦμα ἅγιον
ὁμολογοῦμεν τὸ καινίσαν τούς τε τῆς
παλαιᾶς διαθήκης ἁγίους ἀνθρώπους καὶ

46 Concerning Whom we so believe as
seems good to the apostolic church,
i.e. in one only unbegotten Father . . .
and in one Lord Jesus Christ, the
only-begotten Son of God, begotten
not from that which is not but from
the Father Who is . . .
53 In addition to this pious doctrine
concerning the Father and the Son,
as the divine Scriptures teach us, we
confess one Holy Spirit, Who made
new both the saints of the old coven-

[1] Dom R. H. Connolly attempted (*Z.N.T.W.* vii, 1906, 202 ff.) to reconstruct
early Syrian creeds from the writings of Aphraates, etc., but the results were too
fragmentary and conjectural to be reliable.
[2] See Theodoret, *Hist. eccl.* 1, 4, 46 ; 53 ; 54 (Parmentier, 20 ; 22 ; 23): but
H. G. Opitz (*Urk.* 14) gives the best text.

τοὺς τῆς χρηματιζούσης καινῆς παι-
δευτὰς θείους, μίαν καὶ μόνην καθολικὴν
τὴν ἀποστολικὴν ἐκκλησίαν.

54 Μετὰ τοῦτον ἐκ νεκρῶν ἀνάστασιν
οἴδαμεν, ἧς ἀπαρχὴ γέγονεν ὁ κύριος
ἡμῶν Ἰησοῦς Χριστός, σῶμα φορέσας
ἀληθῶς καὶ οὐ δοκήσει ἐκ τῆς θεοτόκου
Μαρίας, ἐπὶ συντελείᾳ τῶν αἰώνων εἰς
ἀθέτησιν ἁμαρτίας ἐπιδημήσας τῷ γένει
τῶν ἀνθρώπων, σταυρωθεὶς καὶ ἀπο-
θανών, . . . ἀναστὰς ἐκ νεκρῶν, ἀναλη-
φθεὶς ἐν οὐρανοῖς, καθήμενος ἐν δεξιᾷ
τῆς μεγαλωσύνης.

ant and the inspired teachers of the so-
called new covenant, one and only
one Catholic apostolic church . . .

54 After this we acknowledge a resurrection from the dead, of which our
Lord Jesus Christ was the first-
fruits, Who was truly and not in
appearance clothed in a body derived
from Mary the mother of God, Who
at the consummation of the ages
dwelt among the race of men for the
destruction of sin, was crucified and
died, . . . rose again from the dead,
was taken up into heaven, sits on the
right hand of the majesty.

It can scarcely be doubted that the writer had a credal formula,
of an official character, in mind, although he only singled out
those parts of it which seemed relevant to his immediate
purposes. The clear implication in particular of the words,
"As seems good to the apostolic church", is that he was appealing to a form endorsed by ecclesiastical authority.

Side by side with this must be placed two other creeds connected with Egypt. The first is the formula which Arius and
Euzoius submitted to the emperor Constantine in 327 in the
hope of being readmitted to the Church, and which in fact
secured their rehabilitation.[1]

ARIUS AND EUZOIUS

Πιστεύομεν εἰς ἕνα θεόν, πατέρα, παντο-
κράτορα.

Καὶ εἰς κύριον Ἰησοῦν Χριστόν, τὸν υἱὸν
αὐτοῦ, τὸν ἐξ αὐτοῦ πρὸ πάντων τῶν
αἰώνων γεγεννημένον θεὸν λόγον, δι' οὗ
τὰ πάντα ἐγένετο, τά τε ἐν τοῖς οὐρανοῖς
καὶ τὰ ἐπὶ τῆς γῆς, τὸν κατελθόντα καὶ
σαρκωθέντα καὶ παθόντα καὶ ἀναστάντα,
ἀνελθόντα εἰς τοὺς οὐρανούς, καὶ πάλιν
ἐρχόμενον κρῖναι ζῶντας καὶ νεκρούς.

Καὶ εἰς τὸ ἅγιον πνεῦμα, καὶ εἰς σαρκὸς
ἀνάστασιν, καὶ εἰς ζωὴν τοῦ μέλλοντος
αἰῶνος, καὶ εἰς βασιλείαν οὐρανῶν,
καὶ εἰς μίαν καθολικὴν ἐκκλησίαν τοῦ
θεοῦ τὴν ἀπὸ περάτων ἕως περάτων.

We believe in one God, the Father,
almighty;
And in the Lord Jesus Christ, His Son,
the God-Logos Who was begotten
from Him before all the ages, through
Whom all things came into being,
things in heaven and things on earth,
Who came down and took flesh and
suffered and rose again, ascended to
heaven, and will come again to judge
living and dead;
And in the Holy Spirit, and in the resurrection of the flesh, and in the
life of the coming age, and in the
kingdom of heaven, and in one
catholic church of God from end to
end of the earth.

[1] Cf. Socrates, *Hist. eccl.* 1, 26 (*P.G.* 67, 149); Sozomen, *Hist. eccl.* 2, 27 (*P.G.*
67, 1012); Opitz, *Urk.* 30. For a discussion of the creed, see G. Bardy, *Recherches
sur saint Lucien d'Antioche et son école*, Paris, 1936, 274 ff.

Arius went on to assert that this faith of his was based on the holy Scriptures, in which the Lord had commanded His disciples to go and teach all nations, baptizing them in the threefold Name. Yet it can scarcely be claimed that his formula was more than distantly related to current baptismal forms. Sozomen reports [1] the opinion of some that it was "an artificial concoction (τεχνικῶς συγκεῖσθαι)", and certainly the body of it seems to have been based on the Nicene creed, though carefully excluding the latter's distinctive teaching. The historical passage in the central section, it will be observed, is an abbreviation of the Nicene wording. It is the concluding article which sounds convincingly like a local Egyptian creed. The Nicene formula confined itself to a mention of the Holy Spirit, and it is not easy to imagine any special reasons why Arius, if he wanted to continue, should have improvised out of his own head. Moreover, the omission of HOLY with the Church recalls Alexander's creed. while the unusual elaboration of the future life aligns the formula with the creed of the *Apostolical Constitutions*.

Our other Egyptian creed is the formula known as the creed of St Macarius. The description is not very apt, for, if the evidence on which our knowledge of it depends is well founded, it is not his creed at all but the official formula of some Egyptian church. According to one of the stories appended to a ninth century Viennese codex of the so-called *Apophthegmata Macarii*, the saint was called upon by a local bishop in the neighbourhood of Arsinoe to assist him in dealing with a heretical monk.[2] The monk wanted to recite his faith, but St Macarius objected, "Let not an evil faith be so much as named before the people, but let us pronounce the Catholic faith of the Church," and persuaded the bishop to recite it. The following is the creed.

ST. MACARIUS

Πιστεύω εἰς ἕνα θεόν, πατέρα, παντοκράτορα.
I believe in one God, the Father, almighty;

Καὶ εἰς τὸν ὁμοούσιον αὐτοῦ λόγον, δι' οὗ ἐποίησε τοὺς αἰῶνας, τὸν ἐπὶ συντελείᾳ
And in His consubstantial Word, through Whom He made the

---

[1] *Hist. eccl.* 2, 27 (*P.G.* 67, 1012).
[2] For the story, and the text of the creed printed below, see Kattenbusch II, 242 ff.

τῶν αἰώνων εἰς ἀθέτησιν τῆς ἁμαρτίας ἐπιδημήσαντα ἐν σαρκί, ἣν ἐκ τῆς ἁγίας παρθένου Μαρίας ἑαυτῷ ὑπεστήσατο, τὸν σταυρωθέντα καὶ ἀποθανόντα καὶ ταφέντα, καὶ ἀναστάντα τῇ τρίτῃ ἡμέρᾳ καὶ καθεζόμενον ἐν δεξιᾷ τοῦ πατρός, καὶ πάλιν ἐρχόμενον ἐν τῷ μέλλοντι αἰῶνι κρῖναι ζῶντας καὶ νεκρούς.

Καὶ εἰς τὸ πνεῦμα τὸ ἅγιον τὸ ὁμοούσιον τῷ πατρὶ καὶ τῷ λόγῳ αὐτοῦ. πιστεύωμεν δὲ καὶ εἰς ἀνάστασιν ψυχῆς καὶ σώματος καθὼς λέγει ὁ ἀπόστολος, «σπείρεται σῶμα ψυχικόν, ἐγείρεται σῶμα πνευματικόν», κ.τ.λ.

ages, Who at the consummation of the ages with a view to the destruction of sin sojourned in flesh, which He took from the holy Virgin Mary, Who was crucified and died and was buried, and rose again on the third day, and sits on the right hand of the Father, and will come again in the coming age to judge living and dead; And in the holy Spirit, Who is consubstantial with the Father and His Word. Let us believe also in the resurrection of soul and body, as the Apostle says, "It is sown a natural body, it is raised a spiritual body", etc.

A slightly different version, omitting the word SOJOURNED, mentioning the ascension to heaven, and making a few changes of wording and word-order, is given in a Paris MS.[1] The details of the story are quite realistic, and there seems no reason to doubt that it represents a genuine reminiscence, embroidered with the miraculous in hagiographical fashion, of St Macarius, who died in 390 at the age of 90. The creed itself reveals some striking points of contact with the creed of St Alexander of Alexandria, such as the sentence AT THE CONSUMMATION OF THE AGES WITH A VIEW TO THE DESTRUCTION OF SIN SOJOURNED, and the sequence of participles CRUCIFIED AND DIED . . ., without mention of Pontius Pilate in either case. It also resembles the creed of Arius, e.g. in the short first article without allusion to the Father as maker of heaven and earth, in the description of Christ as Logos followed immediately by the reference to Him as the agent of creation, and in the clause WILL COME TO JUDGE without any mention of glory. These points not only serve to confirm the inference that St Macarius's creed is an authentic Egyptian one, but also add weight to our previous argument in favour of the view that Alexander had a creed in mind and that Arius was basing his apology on an Egyptian formula.

The above are a number of specimens of local creeds used by churches of the East. The selection has been deliberately

[1] This MS was followed by E. Preuschen in his *Palladius und Rufinus*, Giessen, 1897, 127.

confined to local creeds or formulae deriving from them: the symbols framed by ecclesiastical assemblies have been excluded from consideration for the moment. Even so, the list should not be regarded as complete. Some, possibly the majority, of the conciliar creeds of the fourth century are local creeds wearing a thin disguise. Besides these, however, there are several other formularies which have been passed over in the meantime because they make no special contribution to the present discussion and will be more fittingly examined in a subsequent chapter. Among these are the so-called creed [1] of Lucian the Martyr (died 312), which is supposed to underlie the second formula of the synod of Antioch (341), and the two creeds [2] of St Epiphanius. The present selection should be sufficient for our purpose. The reader should now be in a position to form some general idea of the character of Eastern creeds. He should also have gained some impression of the number and variety of confessions of which the Eastern churches could boast.

It will not escape notice that they are widely distributed over the Christian East, and that some of them must go well back into the third century. The harvest, we are led to suppose, would have been much fuller if the discipline of reserve had not been in operation. The importance of this is far-reaching. Some of the older critics, under the impression that Rome had an official creed in the second century and unable to discover any parallel in the East, took the view that baptismal creeds were in fact a novelty there and did not exist as formal documents before the last generation of the third century. Thus Harnack [3] and Kattenbusch, [4] the leaders of credal research in their day, thought they could trace the two earliest Eastern creeds, those of Caesarea and Jerusalem, to Antioch. Their theory was that the Old Roman Creed was adopted there after the deposition of Paul of Samosata, about 272, and that after undergoing radical revision to comply with the special requirements of the East at the time became the parent of all Eastern creeds. This latter hypothesis will be considered later, but for the moment we must be content with observing the weakness

---

[1] Cf. St Athanasius, *De syn.* 23 (*P.G.* 26, 721 ff.).
[2] *Ancoratus*, 118 and 119 (Holl I, 146–149).
[3] Cf. art. *Apostolisches symbolum* in Hauck's *Realencyk.*, 3rd ed., I, 749.
[4] I, 380 ff.; II, 194 ff.

of the premisses on which its depends. First, it involves a serious error about the date and manner of the emergence of declaratory creeds. Even at Rome it is unlikely, as we have seen, that there was a single authoritative creed of this kind until the middle of the third century. Before then the baptismal creed proper had been the interrogation regarding belief, and we have ample evidence that this existed in the East as well as the West. Dionysius of Alexandria, for example, in the middle of the third century knew of [1] "the faith and the confession preceding baptism", and of "the questions and answers". Firmilian of Caesarea, a little before Dionysius, could speak[2] of "the established and churchly interrogation" and "the customary and established words of the interrogation". Secondly, so far as summaries of faith are concerned, we possess such early Eastern examples as the profession of the presbyters of Smyrna [3] and the creed of the *Epistula Apostolorum*.[4] Thirdly, it seems highly likely that several of the creeds listed above derive from a period well before the council of Nicaea. This applies at anyrate to the creeds of Caesarea and Jerusalem, and very probably to the underlying basis of others too.

In view of this evidence, and the absence of any facts pointing in the opposite direction, the only natural conclusion is that Eastern creeds followed a course of development closely analogous to that of Western creeds, with the difference that the peculiar position of the Roman church secured a special role for the formula it finally adopted. At the primitive stage there were the ancient baptismal questions and answers, and at the same time more or less fixed catechetical summaries were coming extensively into use. Later, in the third century, with the elaboration of the catechumenate and of the baptismal rite itself, declaratory creeds were introduced and speedily became regular.

4. *Comparison of Eastern and Western Creeds*

The local Eastern formularies at which we glanced in the preceding section make a motley crowd. The first general

---

[1] In Euseb. *Hist. eccl.* 7, 8 and 7, 9 (Schwartz, 275; 276).
[2] Cf. St Cyprian, *Ep.* 75, 10 f. (Hartel I, 818).
[3] See above, p. 82.   [4] See above, p. 82.

impression likely to be conveyed by such a survey is one of immense productivity and bewildering variety. The East, it would appear, treated its creeds with the same freedom and readiness to improvise as it treated its liturgy generally. Nevertheless, a certain unity is seen to pervade what at first sight looks like complete diversity. In particular, the creeds of the Eastern churches exhibit a broad similarity of pattern and content when compared with contemporary Western formularies. If R is taken as the representative of the latter, it becomes possible to speak of an Eastern as distinct from a Western type, and to define the differences between them.

It has become, for example, a commonplace to say that Eastern creeds differ from Western in being "more theological". Or the divergence is said to lie in the fact that "Eastern creeds deal with ideas while Western creeds deal with facts".[1] The theological interest is naturally in the foreground in the conciliar creeds of the East which we shall be examining in later chapters: we are here concerned with the ordinary baptismal confessions. It is true that the impress of theological speculation is more obvious and more on the surface in them than in contemporary Western forms. They bring out, for example, the truth that God is creator of things visible and invisible, they tend to use the theological term Logos as a description of Christ, they call Him FIRST-BEGOTTEN and emphasize His pre-cosmic origin, they underline the fact that He was the Father's agent in creation, and they frequently indicate the motive of His incarnation by such a phrase as FOR US MEN AND FOR OUR SALVATION. But it must be remembered that theological motives were at work in R too, and that it was not just a summary of "facts". The first article announced the creative activity and sovereignty of God, the second consisted of a gospel as well as a narrative of events, and the items included in the third represented the faith and hope of the baptized Christian. A more satisfactory way of putting the matter, therefore, would be to say that both types of creed are theological through and through, but that in Western creeds the centre of interest is the primitive kerygma about the Saviour, whereas in Eastern creeds the cosmic setting of the drama obtrudes itself more obviously.

[1] Cf. Burn, 70.

But the differences between Western and Eastern formularies can be catalogued more precisely. So far as the first article is concerned, R stands apart from later creeds because of its failure to emphasize the oneness of God the Father. The creeds of the Dêr Balyzeh Papyrus, of St Hippolytus's *Tradition*, and of the Syrian *Testamentum Domini* share this peculiarity with it, but scarcely count since they belong to the same family. What is more noteworthy, the creeds of St Justin and of the *Epideixis* also lack ONE. R is also marked off from the typical Eastern creeds by its avoidance of any mention of the Father as the author of creation. Almost without exception the Eastern practice is to assert belief in ONE GOD THE FATHER ALMIGHTY, and to describe Him as MAKER OF ALL THINGS VISIBLE AND INVISIBLE or something of the kind. The main exceptions to the latter point are the Egyptian creeds of Arius, St Macarius and, possibly, of St Alexander of Alexandria ; and it is not surprising to find the Egyptian church reflecting Roman liturgical oddities.

When we turn to the second article, the first thing that leaps to the eye is the unanimity of Eastern creeds in teaching explicitly the Father's pre-cosmic begetting of the Son. In R the doctrine is probably implied, but what characterizes it is the prominence given to the birth of Jesus from the Holy Spirit and the Blessed Virgin. The idea of His birth from the Virgin is occasionally taken up in Eastern creeds, possibly out of regard for the Bible story, but the cooperation of the Holy Spirit is almost invariably left out. Eastern creeds are also united against R in asserting that the Son was the Father's agent in the work of creation. At the same time the general construction of the article in Eastern creeds contrasts markedly with R. As against R's AND IN CHRIST JESUS HIS ONLY-BEGOTTEN SON OUR LORD, they generally have something like AND IN ONE LORD JESUS CHRIST, THE ONLY-BEGOTTEN SON OF GOD. They also underline, again in distinction from R, the Son's incarnation as such, using some such words as WAS MADE FLESH (σαρκωθέντα) and WAS MADE MAN (ἐνανθρωπήσαντα), and more often than not they add BECAUSE OF OUR SALVATION. The mention of Pontius Pilate, so striking in R, is rare in the earlier Eastern formularies. Almost invariably, too, they prefer the bare term ROSE AGAIN

(ἀναστάντα) for Christ's resurrection, as opposed to R's ROSE
AGAIN FROM THE DEAD. A small point is that they all express
the ascension by the Greek ἀνελθόντα as against R's characteristic ἀναβάντα. R is also exceptional in stringing together the
various items in this section of the creed without any connecting particle (Eastern creeds repeat the conjunction AND between
WAS INCARNATE, SUFFERED, etc.), and in prefacing its account
of the Second Coming with WHENCE (other Western creeds have
THENCE, whereas Eastern creeds generally read AND WILL COME
AGAIN).

The third article presents still further material for contrasting
the two types of creed. Some of the Eastern forms represent a
transitional stage at which its contents were limited to a bare
mention of the Holy Spirit: so the creeds of Caesarea, Nicaea,
and possibly the first creed of the council of Antioch (341).[1]
The majority, however, elaborate the third article much more
fully than R does, as often as not referring explicitly to baptism
and subordinating THE REMISSION OF SINS to it, and usually
describing the Church as ONE and CATHOLIC (sometimes APOS-
TOLIC as well), and adding LIFE EVERLASTING or LIFE OF THE
COMING AGE.

5. *The Descent of Eastern Creeds*

The accumulation of characteristics common to Eastern
creeds which we listed in the preceding section is sufficient to
justify us in speaking of an Eastern type. The problem we now
have to face is whether we can take a further step and assert that
all Eastern creeds belong to one family and actually descend
from a single stock. The analogy of the lineal connection
between all later Western formularies and their ancestor the
Old Roman Creed has naturally been tempting to scholars. It
would be highly satisfying if a similar course of development
could be posited for the East on the basis of the undoubted resemblances between all Eastern creeds. This was the assumption on which the majority of older students worked. With
Kattenbusch and Harnack, of course, it was an integral part

---

[1] See below, p. 265. Cf. its curious words, "But if something must be added,
we believe also concerning the resurrection of the flesh and eternal life."

of their theory that Eastern creeds derived from the revision of the Old Roman Creed carried out, as they supposed, at Antioch about 272. Others who did not share their view of the Western basis of Eastern creeds were equally confident that, behind the mass of local variations and conciliary revisions of the fourth century, they could descry a common plan. The question was reopened, with characteristic thoroughness, by H. Lietzmann about half a century ago. He devoted the third of his famous *Symbolstudien*[1] to an exhaustive analysis and collation of all the principal Eastern formularies. As the fruit of his researches he drew up a simple creed of three articles which he felt sure must represent the original confession underlying all Eastern creeds, and which he accordingly labelled O.

Πιστεύω εἰς ἕνα θεόν, πατέρα, παντο-κράτορα, πάντων ὁρατῶν τε καὶ ἀοράτων ποιητήν.	I believe in one God, the Father, almighty, maker of all things visible and invisible;
Καὶ εἰς ἕνα κύριον Ἰησοῦν Χριστόν, τὸν υἱὸν τοῦ θεοῦ τὸν μονογενῆ, τὸν ἐκ τοῦ πατρὸς γεννηθέντα πρὸ πάντων τῶν αἰώνων, δι' οὗ τὰ πάντα ἐγένετο, τὸν [διὰ τὴν ἡμετέραν σωτηρίαν] ἐναν-θρωπήσαντα, παθόντα, καὶ ἀναστάντα τῇ τρίτῃ ἡμέρᾳ καὶ ἀνελθόντα εἰς τοὺς οὐρανούς, καὶ [πάλιν] ἐρχόμενον κρῖναι ζῶντας καὶ νεκρούς.	And in one Lord Jesus Christ, the only begotten Son of God, Who was begotten from the Father before all ages, through Whom all things came into being, Who [because of our salvation] became man, suffered, and rose again on the third day and ascended to heaven, and will come [again] to judge living and dead;
Καὶ εἰς τὸ ἅγιον πνεῦμα.	And in the Holy Spirit.

In this formula, or something very closely resembling it, he argued, we have "the common archetype out of which the Eastern confessions grew".[2]

The value of Lietzmann's meticulous sorting out of Eastern credal forms cannot be rated too highly. The third of his *Symbolstudien* is a painstaking piece of work which will remain indispensable to students for many years to come. His skill and ingenuity, too, in seizing upon the recurrent Eastern traits and reassembling them in O deserve acknowledgement. Whether O ever had historical actuality or is merely a scholar's artefact, it certainly remains the model Eastern creed. It represents

---

[1] *Z.N.T.W.* xxi 1922, 5–22.
[2] See his article on creeds in *Encyclopædia Britannica*, 14th edition, Vol. VI, 657, col. 2.

a common pattern which reveals itself with surprising frequency behind the diversity of Eastern confessions. Yet it is difficult to repress the conviction that he made a mistake in deciding to set out upon the path trodden by so many previous scholars with ill success. The analogy of the history of creeds in the West may have been tempting, but it was deceptive. There is, on the face of it, no reason why the course of development should have been similar in the East, and almost every reason why it should have been different. The status and authority of the Roman church, it should be remembered, were quite peculiar: there was nothing remotely parallel to them in the East. Because of its prestige, aided by the relative lateness of the rise of other local churches, the Roman church was able to exercise a quite extraordinary influence on the liturgy in the areas which acknowledged her suzerainty. Even apart from the testimony of actually recorded creeds, we should from the start have been prepared to find the Western churches looking to Rome for an authoritative liturgical confession. On the other hand, unless faced with very compelling considerations to the contrary, we should naturally be predisposed to believe that the Eastern churches developed their credal forms in some measure of independence of each other.

The whole presupposition of a common archetype for Eastern creeds seems to rest upon a misconception of the way in which creeds took shape in the context of the baptismal service. So far as our evidence goes, the questions and answers at the moment of baptism were the creed in embryo. These questions and answers, however, together with the catechetical summaries with which they were connected, were as much part of Eastern as they were of Western practice in the second and third centuries. Consequently, each local church must have possessed, virtually from the start, the beginnings of a creed or creeds as part of its liturgical apparatus. There is no need to posit an *Urform* or *Grundtypus* at all, so far as the East is concerned, much less one so elaborate and patently mature as O. The fact which is singular is the position of R *vis-à-vis* other Western creeds, but that is explicable in the light of its early origin and the extraordinary pre-eminence enjoyed by the Roman church.

Our doubts are redoubled when we turn to the text and compare the Eastern creeds marshalled and surveyed by Lietzmann with one another and with O. Striking as are the resemblances which they display, they exhibit none of that underlying identity which was so obvious a feature in Western formularies. No one who examines them is likely to conclude at once that they are all variants of a common form. On the contrary, side by side with the similarities there are equally impressive divergences. Thus the general agreement over the first article hardly amounts to more than we should expect in view of the common Christian teaching. Lietzmann himself admitted that the second half of it, which appears in O as MAKER OF ALL THINGS VISIBLE AND INVISIBLE, could not be reconstructed with any certainty. In addition to the form he selected for inclusion in O, there were traditions which read THE CREATOR ($\kappa\tau\iota\sigma\tau\acute{\eta}\nu$) AND MAKER OF THE UNIVERSE,[1] or which expressed the same thought by the Pauline "from Whom are all things".[2] There may also have been a tradition, represented by Egyptian creeds, which omitted all reference to the Father's creative work. Again, while in the second article the mention of ONE LORD JESUS CHRIST was practically universal, there were some important creeds[3] from which ONE was significantly absent. Others again[4] diverged from O in describing the Son as FIRST-BEGOTTEN OF ALL CREATION, a credal tradition at least as old as St Justin.[5] A notable discrepancy with O is the appearance of the session at the Father's right hand in a great number of Eastern creeds. Their independence in this respect from R is proved by their preference for the Greek $\kappa\alpha\theta\epsilon\zeta\acute{o}\mu\epsilon\nu o\nu$ or $\kappa\alpha\theta\acute{\iota}\sigma\alpha\nu\tau\alpha$ to R's $\kappa\alpha\theta\acute{\eta}\mu\epsilon\nu o\nu$. Lastly, a wider background than O's curt AND IN THE HOLY SPIRIT must surely be sought for the third article. In some creeds it was no doubt confined to a bare mention of the Spirit, but we know, from St Justin and from St Irenaeus, as well as from others, that an expanded third article had won a footing quite early.

[1] Cf. the third creed of Antioch in St Athan., *De syn.* 24 (*P.G.* 26, 724 f.); see *infra*, p. 266 f.
[2] Cf. the formula of Nicé (359) given by Theodoret, *Hist. eccl.* 2, 21 (Parmentier, 145 f.).
[3] Cf. the creeds of Antioch, *Apost. Const.*, and Egypt given above.
[4] Cf. the creeds of Caesarea, Antioch, *Apost. Const.*, Mopsuestia.
[5] Cf. *Dial.* 85 (E.J.G., 197).

These are but a few signal examples of the inadequacy of O for the role of archetype of Eastern creeds. It is important to recall the very much stronger claims of R in the West. The Western formularies we studied were, one and all, manifest examples of R thinly disguised by local peculiarities. In the case of all of them the shape of R could be plainly discerned beneath the embroidery. Their agreements with R extended to the most trivial idiosyncrasies of language. We were thus amply justified in inferring that they were direct descendants of R. Eastern creeds, as we have discovered, had nothing quite corresponding with this unmistakable identity, and it is therefore far-fetched (in view of the general unlikelihood of the hypothesis) to assume that they derive from a common stock. Nor is it a point of small importance that, whereas R actually exists and the scholar to-day can lay hands upon it, the formulary we are invited to acknowledge as the historical basis of Eastern creeds can only be at best inferred.

It is true that there still remains, pervading their rich diversity, enough real similarity between Eastern creeds to warrant us in classifying them as a distinct type. But this may be accounted for in a much simpler and more natural way than by the hypothesis of a single ancestor. Creeds grew up in the baptismal rite, their ground-plan being prescribed by the threefold questionnaire and triple immersions. Their content was supplied from the Trinitarian and Christological outlines of basic Christian truths imparted in catechetical instruction. The shape of the baptismal act, including the baptismal confessions, was thus fixed in every church. A broad similarity of structure and content in creeds was thus to be expected in any case. In addition there was plenty of intercourse, and therefore of opportunity for cross-influence, between the churches of the East. We are familiar with the tendency of creeds in local churches of one district or region to become assimilated to one another. The creeds of Egypt, or the creeds of Rome itself at the beginning of the third century, provide examples; and we noticed that the creeds of Africa or of Spain tended to develop distinctive characteristics. The same tendency must have been at work as between the formularies of churches belonging to different regions. Consequently, we should not be surprised to find most Eastern creeds exhibiting a broad similarity of pattern and content, while at the same time preserving traces of independent traditions. This is exactly what we do find. It is considerations like these, coupled with the general demarcation between East and West, which sufficiently explain the emergence of two distinct types, Eastern and Western, of baptismal creeds.

6. *Relation of Eastern and Western Creeds*

The view which we would press is that, if the framework within which credal formulae were constructed was the baptismal act and if this, under the influence of the Dominical command in St Matthew's Gospel, was everywhere the same, all discussion about common stocks and the like becomes unnecessary and indeed meaningless. It will be useful to test our theory from another, slightly different angle of approach. It is commonly held that there must have been some definite relation between the Western and the Eastern types of creeds. We have already mentioned the contention, supported by Harnack and Kattenbusch, that R was adopted at Antioch in 272 after the deposition of Paul of Samosata, and after drastic alteration became the parent of all later Eastern formularies. Their view is the most important of those which derive the Eastern type from the Western. Others take the opposite line, attributing priority to the Eastern type and seeing R as a deviation from it. Yet a third school refuses priority to either type, and concludes that both stem from a common stock which is older than either. H. Lietzmann identified himself with this viewpoint. He was persuaded that all creeds, Eastern and Western alike, could be traced back to a common formula, based on the Pauline "creed" in 1 *Cor.* 8, 6, which was current somewhere in the East.

It is easy to demonstrate the weakness of all these hypotheses. To start with the Harnack-Kattenbusch doctrine, it seems extremely unlikely that creeds of the Eastern type sprang directly from R. To substantiate that, we should have to maintain that the people who took over R deliberately hacked it about in ways which defy rational explanation. They must have cut out, for example, all the affirmations in the third article, with the exception of the Holy Spirit, in the case of certain credal traditions. Again, they must have decided that the birth from the Holy Spirit and the Virgin, the explicit mention of the crucifixion, and the session at the Father's right hand had all to be expunged. The motives for such a procedure are hard to fathom, the more so as later generations apparently repented of it and considered that the excised clauses were worthy of re-insertion. Yet if R reached the East as a fully established norm of belief and was adopted at Antioch or elsewhere, its prestige must presumably have been immense in the eyes of its new adherents. All the more astonishing is it that they thought it desirable to make these drastic alterations, as well as the numerous lesser ones which a comparison of creeds of the two types uncovers.

The contrary hypothesis, that R was descended from a creed or creeds of the Eastern type, fares no better in the light of such a comparison. For one thing, its very antiquity is a weighty argument in favour of its originality and independence, especially as it is impossible to point to any Eastern creeds which flourished at so early a date. Again, it is hard to explain, on the basis of this assumption, such a feature as the absence of ONE from the first article. Some of the older students, we may recall, held that ONE must have been cut out because it might give colour to Sabellian propaganda. It has always seemed odd that such a fundamental Christian affirmation (granted it really had a place in the creed) should have been scrapped in the interest of passing controversy, and we can point to creed-forms other than R (possibly Roman in origin), like those of St Justin, which apparently never had ONE. A really serious objection, however, is the fact that the short Trinitarian baptismal formula from which we saw that R itself must have been descended probably lacked ONE, and this must have taken shape at an epoch prior to the time when Sabellianism assumed a menacing aspect. Even harder to account for, on the theory that R was derived from a creed of the O type, would be the erasure of MAKER OF HEAVEN AND EARTH. Even granting that the title FATHER implied God's creative role, there would appear to have been every motive for retaining the full and

precise assertion of it if it had at any time been ensconced in
the creed. Lastly, while the Gospel narrative provided the
most ample authority for proclaiming Christ's birth from the
Holy Spirit and the Virgin, it remains an enigma why it
should have been deliberately substituted for a declaration of
His pre-cosmic begetting.

H. Lietzmann's suggestion of a common root for both the
R type and the O type of creed might seem to hold greater
attractions. He hazarded the guess that, somewhere in the
East, there arose on the basis of the Pauline text ("But for us
there is one God the Father, from Whom are all things, and we
to Him, and one Lord Jesus Christ, through Whom are all
things, and we through Him") a Trinitarian creed adapted to
the needs of baptism. It must have run somewhat as follows:

I believe in one God, the Father, almighty, from Whom are all things;
And in one Lord Jesus Christ, the only-begotten Son of God, through Whom
    are all things;
And in the Holy Spirit.

"Out of this creed", he remarked,[1] "there was developed in
Rome, through excisions, interpolations, and the disciplined
ordering of its structure, that very nine-clause formula with
which we are already acquainted." By the use of such drastic
methods it would be possible to prove almost anything. Certainly there is nothing in R itself, much less in the brief
Trinitarian formula which underlies it, to suggest that either of
them was a rehash of Lietzmann's hypothetical Pauline creed.
If such had been their origin, the deliberate erasure of the
reference to Christ's work as the agent of creation demands a
more satisfactory explanation than the needs of symmetry. In
any case, the claim of the Pauline text to be the nucleus of all
more developed confessions is exposed to serious question.
Many early creeds, it must be admitted, show the influence of
it, but there are many others which are entirely free from it,[2]
and it is arbitrary to try to force them all into the same mould.
The Lord's Trinitarian baptismal command was the creative
model on which the baptismal questions, and so baptismal
creeds, were constructed, and where hints of the Pauline text

---

[1] Cf. *Geschichte der alten Kirche*, Berlin and Leipzig, 1936, II, 108.
[2] E.g. the creeds of St Justin, of the *Epideixis*, and of the Dêr Balyzeh Papyrus.

occur we may suspect that they were imposed as an inspired after-thought upon material much more primitive.

The failure of attempts like these to find a direct relationship between Eastern and Western creeds throws us back with renewed confidence on our own hypothesis. We can find further confirmation of it in the decisive period of the second century, when the chief types of creeds had not yet clearly separated themselves from each other. An impressive witness, for example, is St Irenaeus. Some of his formularies, notably the little creed in *Epideixis* 3, are thoroughly Western in flavour. On the other hand, his summaries of the rule of faith (e.g. *Adv. Haer.* 1, 10, 1) are marked with the typical Eastern traits. Tertullian, as we saw, seems to have known R, or a creed closely resembling it, but he also worked with credal summaries of an Eastern pattern. St Justin's creeds are also illuminating. The baptismal questionnaire suggested by *Apol.* 1, 61 has points of kinship with R, e.g. in the omission of ONE and in the emphasis on the crucifixion under Pontius Pilate; and the reference to Pontius Pilate as well as the choice of ἀναβαίνω (="ascend") in his famous Exorcism formula [1] also seem to re-echo R. At the same time, the mention of God as the Lord of the universe, the citation of *Col.* 1, 15 ("first-begotten of all creation"), and the words "begotten through the Virgin"[2] without allusion to the Holy Spirit, are all Eastern features. Thus formularies of different types were existing side by side in friendly competition, and no one type had the monopoly. This is exactly the situation which we should expect at this early date on the assumption that there was no one original stock from which all creeds derived, but that their roots were embedded in the act of baptism and the catechetical rule of faith.

[1] *Dial.* 85, 2 (E.J.G., 197).
[2] Cf. Apol. I, 31, 7; 46, 5; *Dial.* 63, 1; 85, 2 (E.J.G., 46; 59; 168; 197).

CHAPTER VII

THE CREED OF NICAEA

1. *Creeds as Tests of Orthodoxy*

PRIOR to the beginning of the fourth century all creeds and summaries of faith were local in character. It was taken for granted, of course, that they enshrined the universally accepted Catholic faith, handed down from the Apostles. But they owed their immediate authority, no less than their individual stamp, to the liturgy of the local church in which they had emerged. Moreover, while creed-like formularies were to be found in the Eucharist, in the rite of exorcism and elsewhere, those in the main line of development were confined to baptism and the catechetical preparation leading up to it. A great revolution now takes place with the introduction of synodal or conciliar creeds. The custom becomes established, beginning with the council of Nicaea, for ecclesiastics meeting in solemn conclave to frame formularies giving utterance to their agreement on matters of faith. These new creeds were intended, of course, to have a far more than local authority. Sometimes including anathemas, they were put forth not merely as epitomes of the beliefs of their promulgators, but as tests of the orthodoxy of Christians in general. Hence they were theological in the special sense that they were implicated in the theological controversies of the times. It was not in the mind of their signatories, at first at any rate, to supersede the existing local baptismal confessions. As C. H. Turner once put it,[1] "the old creeds were creeds for catechumens, the new creed was a creed for bishops." It was devised as the touchstone by which the doctrines of Church teachers and leaders might be certified as correct.

The early fourth century is acclaimed as having inaugurated the transition to this new type of formulary, but like most other historical transitions it was not in fact quite so abrupt as it has

---

[1] *History and Use of Creeds and Anathemas*, London, 1910, 24.

seemed. The motive of obtaining an assurance about the soundness of a man's beliefs was implicit in baptismal confessions in their most primitive form. The catechetical summaries which in the second century formed the wider context of the questions and answers were known by such names as "the rule of faith", "the canon of the truth", etc. Expressions such as these carried with them the idea of the exclusion of error, and the writers who used them were obviously very conscious of possessing the monopoly of the orthodox, apostolically certified deposit in contradistinction to the false speculations of heretical sects. We can even point to an early example of a creed, or something approximating to a creed, being deliberately brought forward in attestation of orthodoxy. This procedure was adopted, according to the story recorded by St Hippolytus[1] and St Epiphanius,[2] by the presbyters of Asia at their famous interview (*circa* 180) with the patripassian heretic Noetus. Similarly the ninth canon of the council of Arles (314), as we noticed before,[3] laid it down that heretics desiring to attach themselves to the Church should be "asked the creed" (*interrogent eum symbolum*, where *symbolum* probably denotes the baptismal questions). As the Arian controversy was coming to a head, Arius himself, along with his companions, concocted a creed-like summary[4] of their theological position and sent it to St Alexander, bishop of Alexandria. St Alexander in his turn included a creed, interspersed with theological comments and explanations, in the letter which he wrote to Alexander of Byzantium[5] justifying his attitude in the face of Arian misrepresentations. Creeds, it would appear, even creeds properly designed for use at baptism, were coming to be employed in detachment from the baptismal service as a means of demonstrating that the man who professed them was above reproach theologically.

Admittedly this motive began by being secondary and, strictly, exceptional: the baptismal purpose naturally loomed in the foreground. In the new type of creed the motive of testing

---

[1] *Con. Noet.* 1 (Nautin, 235).
[2] *Pan. haer.* 57 (Holl II, 345).
[3] See above, p. 57. For the canon, see *C.C.L.* 148, 10 f.
[4] Cf. St Athanasius, *De syn.* 16 (*P.G.* 26, 708 ff.). Cf. also Opitz, *Urk.* 6.
[5] Cf. Theodoret, *Hist. eccl.* 1, 4, 46 ff. (Parmentier, 20 ff.) ; Opitz, *Urk.* 14. There is a difficulty about the addressee, for Alexander was not bishop of Byzantium at this time : Opitz suggests Alexander of Thessalonica.

orthodoxy was primary: the creeds were deliberately framed with this object in view. The common opinion is that at all events this new and drastic step was first taken at the council of Nicaea. We may agree that this is substantially correct. The creed of Nicaea was the first formula to be published by an ecumenical synod: consequently it was the first which could claim universal authority in a legal sense. Its anathemas excommunicating, in the name of the Catholic Church, those who dissented from its definitions sounded a new note in the history of the Church as an institution. Even this, however, was no more than the logical development of a practice which had been gaining ground in the preceding two or three generations. Thus the six bishops who assembled at Antioch in 268 to deal with the case of Paul of Samosata included a "statement of faith" (notice the technical Greek term ἔκθεσις τῆς πίστεως) in their united letter to him. This long rambling document[1] was not a creed, nor was it constructed on the basis of a contemporary baptismal creed. Its authors claimed, however, that it represented "the faith handed down from the beginning and preserved in the holy Catholic Church from the blessed Apostles' times". They condemned anyone who disagreed with it as "outside the ecclesiastical rule (ἀλλότριον τοῦ ἐκκλησιαστικοῦ κανόνος)", and were confident that it was endorsed by "all Catholic churches". They closed by peremptorily asking Paul whether he was prepared to subscribe it with them. Doubtless their interest was limited to points of doctrine on which the archheretic was suspect. They dwelt at length, for example, on Christ's pre-existence as a person (and not just in the Father's foreknowledge), on His manifestations in the Old Testament, and on His identity before and after the Incarnation. But the ideas of a formula drawn up by bishops in synod, of the invocation of the support of the Church universal, and of the summoning of suspected persons to affix their signatures were all present in their action. We are justified in regarding it as a kind of rehearsal or anticipation of what was shortly to become the routine procedure of the Church in matters of theological dispute.

[1] See Hahn 151; Mansi I, 1033 ff. Cf. also F. Loofs, *Paulus von Samosata*, Leipzig, 1924, 108 ff.; 265 ff.

The council held at Antioch in the early weeks of 325[1] furnishes a much more overt and instructive example of synodal creed-making prior to Nicaea. This gathering of fifty-nine bishops from Palestine, Arabia, Phenicia, Coele-Syria, Cilicia and Cappadocia had Ossius of Cordoba (as H. Chadwick has shown) as chairman, and coincided with the need to fill the vacant see of Antioch. But they took advantage of their meeting together to condemn the Arian heresy and to publish a full-dress declaration of their own position. Possibly they were aware of Constantine's determination himself to settle a controversy which was becoming a festering sore in the Church's body, and wanted to anticipate by a *fait accompli* any chance there might be of the imperial decision going the wrong way.[2] A synodal letter announcing their resolutions and setting out their faith in credal form was issued at the same time. It reported that three bishops—Theodotus of Laodicea, Narcissus of Neronias, and Eusebius of Caesarea—had withheld their signatures, and had in consequence been provisionally excommunicated, with an opportunity of changing their minds before the forthcoming "great and hieratic synod" to be held at Ancyra. The letter was given wide publicity, and secured the hearty approval at any rate of the bishops of Italy.

Our detailed knowledge of the affair[3] and of the credal document has only been obtained this century. It rests, first, on the Syriac text of the synodal letter preserved in a Paris MS (*Cod. Par. Syr.* 62), the Vatican *Cod. Syr.* 148, and Mingana *Cod. Syr.* 8 (Selly Oak); and, secondly, on the Syriac canons of the synod of 325 itself, which occur somewhat later in the Paris MS. It was E. Schwartz who first lighted upon this letter, guessed that it was connected with the synod of 325, and substantiated his guess with argument.[4] Both A. von Harnack and the French scholar F. Nau vigorously contested the identification. Schwartz found a laborious and persuasive advocate to plead his cause in Erich Seeberg.[5] The twin pillars on which their argument was

[1] For the date (not 324) cf. H. G. Opitz, *Z.N.T.W.* xxxiii, 1934, 151.
[2] Cf. N. Baynes, *Journal of Roman Studies* xviii, 1928, 219.
[3] For English discussions of the council, cf. F. L. Cross, *Church Quarterly Review* cxxviii, 1939, 49 ff.; H. Chadwick, *J.T.S.* NS ix, 1958, 292–304.
[4] *Zur Geschichte des Athanasius* VI, in *Nachricht. Gött.* 1905, 271 ff., and *Ibid.* 1908 (*Zur Geschichte* VII), 305 ff.
[5] See his *Die Synode von Antiochien*, Berlin, 1913.

supported were, first, the intrinsic character of the documents, which presuppose a situation prior to the decisions of the Nicene council, and, secondly, the illumination which the events of the synod, on the assumption that they followed the course mapped out in the documents, throw on the procedure of the ecumenical council itself. Both scholars admitted that there were obscurities which puzzled them, but since then solutions have been provided for most of these. To-day an all but unanimous[1] consensus of opinion is prepared to accept the Syrian texts as supplying a reliable picture of what happened at the synod of 325.

Despite its great length, the creed appended to the circular letter sent round by the bishops deserves, because of its intrinsic interest, to be reproduced here; the following, therefore, is a translation of Schwartz's Greek retroversion.

"The faith is", say the writers, "as follows: to believe in one God, Father, almighty, incomprehensible, immutable and unchangeable, protector and ruler of the universe, just, good, maker of heaven and earth and of all the things in them, Lord of the law and of the prophets and of the new covenant; and in one Lord Jesus Christ, only begotten Son, begotten not from that which is not but from the Father, not as made but as properly an offspring, but begotten in an ineffable, indescribable manner, because only the Father Who begot and the Son Who was begotten know (for 'no one knows the Father but the Son, nor the Son but the Father'), Who exists everlastingly and did not at one time not exist. For we have learned from the Holy Scriptures that He alone is the express image, not (plainly) as if He might have remained unbegotten from the Father, nor by adoption (for it is impious and blasphemous to say this); but the Scriptures describe Him as validly and truly begotten as Son, so that we believe Him to be immutable and unchangeable, and that He was not begotten and did not come to be by volition or by adoption, so as to appear to be from that which is not, but as it befits Him to be begotten; not (a thing which it is not lawful to think) according to likeness or nature or commixture with any of the things which came to be through Him, but in a way which passes all understanding or conception or reasoning we confess Him to have been begotten of the unbegotten Father, the divine Logos, true light, righteousness, Jesus

---

[1] For an acute, well-argued critique of the generally accepted view, and of the inferences drawn from it, see D. H. Holland, *Z. für KG* II, 1970, 163–81.

Christ, Lord and Saviour of all. For He is the express image, not of the will or of anything else, but of His Father's very substance (ὑποστάσεως). This Son, the divine Logos, having been born in flesh from Mary the Mother of God and made incarnate, having suffered and died, rose again from the dead and was taken up into heaven, and sits on the right hand of the Majesty most high, and will come to judge the living and the dead. Furthermore, as in our Saviour, the holy Scriptures teach us to believe also in one Spirit, one Catholic Church, the resurrection of the dead and a judgment of requital according to whether a man has done well or badly in the flesh. And we anathematize those who say or think or preach that the Son of God is a creature or has come into being or has been made and is not truly begotten, or that there was when He was not. For we believe that He was and is and that He is light. Furthermore, we anathematize those who suppose that He is immutable by His own act of will, just as those who derive His birth from that which is not, and deny that He is immutable in the way the Father is. For just as our Saviour is the image of the Father in all things, so in this respect particularly He has been proclaimed the Father's image.

The patently anti-Arian tone of this tortuous compilation, combined with its transparent ignorance of the Nicene theological solutions, is a powerful argument for its authenticity. All the emphasis is on the assertion that the Son was not created out of nothing, but was begotten in an ineffable way, and that He is the express image of the Father in every respect. Yet there is no mention of the technical phrases FROM THE SUBSTANCE OF THE FATHER or OF ONE SUBSTANCE or anything equivalent. If the creed which Arius submitted to St Alexander is set alongside it, the close relationship between the two documents becomes at once visible. The anathemas at the end deal point by point with matters raised in Arius's *Thalia*,[1] branding such typical theses of his as that Christ was a creature, that there had been a time when He was not, and that His immutability was due to the exercise of His will. The drift of its language, moreover, seems to re-echo that of St Alexander and the creed he sent to his namesake of Byzantium.[2] For us its striking importance lies in the fact that it is the forerunner of all synodal

[1] See E. Seeberg, *Op. cit.* 147.
[2] Cf. E. Schwartz, *Nachricht. Gött.* 1905, 288: he says that it is "im Wesentlichen eine Paraphrase von Alexanders Tomos".

creeds. Despite its diffuseness (not without abundant parallels in the formulas of later councils), it is constructed as a creed and has the unmistakable ground-plan of one. Its basis, manifestly, was some already existing creed, most probably one in use locally. The transformation was effected, by methods afterwards to be exploited by creed-framers at Nicaea and elsewhere, by freely interpolating passages bearing on the controversy into the underlying framework. The anathemas are particularly interesting, for they anticipate, with closer attention to the genuine thought of Arius, the ones to be adopted by the Nicene fathers. Altogether the discovery of this document has conferred an immense boon on the student of creeds. The synod of Antioch was evidently an overture to the council of Nicaea, and some of the themes which were to be taken up there were played over with effect at Antioch first.

2. *The Promulgation of N*

The ecumenical council met a few months later, at Nicaea instead of Ancyra.[1] According to the historian Socrates,[2] its opening session was held on 20 May 325, but it has been shown that the true date was 19 June.[3] The full discussion of the proceedings, with the many fascinating and often unanswerable problems which they raise, belongs rather to the field of Church history proper than to the study of creeds. Here it is sufficient to emphasize the point that Constantine's object in summoning the council (or, if it was already planned or at least in the air, in taking it over and enlarging its scope)[4] was to consolidate the Church, which represented in his eyes the spiritual aspect of his empire, on the basis of the widest possible measure of doctrinal unity. His carefully phrased inaugural address, if we can trust the account given by Eusebius,[5] fastened on the perils of intestine strife in the Church, and voiced his ardent longing for peace and unity among the bishops. None of his audience could

---

[1] For a fragment of a letter of the emperor's explaining the change, see E. Schwartz, *Nachricht. Gött.* 1905, 289; Opitz, *Urk.* 20.
[2] *Hist. eccl.* 1, 13 (*P.G.* 67, 109).
[3] Cf. E. Schwartz, *Zur Geschichte des Athanasius III* (*Nachricht. Gött.* 1904, 398).
[4] So N. Baynes in the article cited above.
[5] *De vit. Const.* 3, 12 (Heikel I, 82 f.).

have been left in any doubt as to what was expected, and the
part the emperor played in the day-to-day debates was of a
piece with this. In view of the growing precedent indicated in
the last section, however, it would be an exaggeration to conceive of him as actually imposing on the assembled bishops
the obligation of finding a formula which might serve as a
criterion for the admission of clergy to, or their exclusion from,
the new state Church.[1] While doubtless he looked to the council
to manufacture a creed, and was not behindhand in giving a
lead to the drafting committee, there is no evidence that the
initiative came from him. The bishops themselves must have
assumed from the start that the circumstances called for an
agreed statement of faith. In itself there was nothing novel or
revolutionary in their decision, which merely reflected what
was becoming normal practice. What made it momentous in
import was the ecumenical character of the gathering, and the
altogether new position of the Church *vis-à-vis* the state.

The actual course of events which led to the formulation of
the creed is bafflingly obscure, thanks to the absence of a
reliable and consecutive account of the proceedings of the
council. Official minutes, or *acta*, either were never recorded
or for some reason have not come down to us. Nevertheless
there survive three illuminating glimpses of the council's
activity in regard to its creed from the pens of three personages
who were eye-witnesses of, or even protagonists in, the proceedings. They consist of (*a*) a fragmentary reminiscence[2] of
St Eustathius of Antioch (who possibly presided over the debates
as chairman), (*b*) some chapters[3] of St Athanasius written a
generation after the events described, and (*c*) the famous
letter[4] by which Eusebius of Caesarea informed his church of
what had happened at the council and attempted to justify
his own conduct there. All three passages are tendentious in
tone, and therefore must be used with caution.

The Eustathian fragment would suggest that the Eusebian

[1] So E. Schwartz. *Kaiser Constantin*, Leipzig, 2nd ed., 1936, 28. He consistently
exaggerated the degree of the Church's absorption in Constantine's "Reich".
[2] In Theodoret, *Hist. eccl.* 1, 8, 1–5 (Parmentier, 33 f.).
[3] *De decret. Nic. syn.* 19 and 20 (written 350–54); *Ep. ad Afr. episc.* 5 and 6 (written
369) (*P.G.* 25, 448–452; 26, 1036–1040).
[4] *P.G.* 20, 1535–1544. The best edition is still H. G. Opitz, *Urkunden* 22.

or Arian party made the first move to get a creed adopted, but that their overtures collapsed ignominiously. The passage runs:

When they began to inquire into the nature of the faith (ὡς δὲ ἐζητεῖτο τῆς πίστεως ὁ τρόπος), the formulary of Eusebius [i.e. most probably of Nicomedia][1] was brought forward, which contained undisguised evidence of his blasphemy. The reading of it before all occasioned great grief to the audience on account of its divergence from the faith, while it inflicted irremediable shame on the writer. After the Eusebian gang had been clearly convicted, and the impious writing had been torn to shreds in the sight of all, some people concerted together and, on the plea of preserving peace, imposed silence on those who were accustomed to speaking most ably.

On the other hand, the dramatic chapters of St Athanasius indicate that when the fathers came to draw up their own formulary, their original intention was that it should express what they took to be the truth in scriptural language. This proved, however, impossible. Whatever turns of phrase were proposed—that the Son was "from God", that He was "the true Power and Image of the Father", that He was "indivisibly in God", etc.—the Arians managed somehow to twist them round so as to chime in with their own notions. In the end, says St Athanasius, there was nothing for it but to interpolate the precise, utterly unambiguous, but non-scriptural, clauses FROM THE SUBSTANCE OF THE FATHER and OF ONE SUBSTANCE WITH THE FATHER.

We shall later recur to both these important and revealing passages. In the meantime it should be observed that neither of them gives us more than the most fleeting glimpse of the sequence of events culminating in the adoption of the creed, or throws any light on the identity of the text canonized. For information on these points we must turn to Eusebius's apologetic letter, although in view of its length only a summary of it can be given here. The bishop opens by telling his correspondents that he is going to describe to them exactly what took place at the council in case they should get a misleading impression through gossip and hearsay. He then reproduces verbatim a lengthy document which, he says, he had read out

[1] I find it hard to accept the suggestion (cf. A. H. M. Jones, *Constantine and the Conversion of Europe*, 1948, London, 158 f.) that it was Eusebius of Caesarea.

at one of the sessions in the presence of the emperor himself. This began with a short preface declaring that the faith which he now believed, and which he was now submitting to the council, was the faith in which he had been instructed as a catechumen and had been baptized, and which he had himself taught both as a priest and as a bishop. There followed immediately after this what was manifestly a baptismal creed, in all likelihood, in view of the previous statements, that of the church of Caesarea.[1] In its turn the creed was followed by a brief theological explanation and elaboration of its clauses, asserting in the plainest terms the continued separate existence of each of the three divine persons ("the Father is in truth the Father, the Son in truth the Son, the Holy Spirit in truth the Holy Spirit"), although tactfully avoiding Eusebius's favourite and characteristic description "three hypostases". To conclude the memorandum came an assurance of his unswerving attachment to these doctrines in the future as in the past. Eusebius then resumes his letter proper, remarking that "when this faith had been set forth by us, there was no room to gainsay it. Our beloved emperor himself was the first to testify that it was entirely orthodox, and that he himself held exactly the same opinions. He instructed the others to sign it and to assent to its teaching, with the single addition of the word 'consubstantial (ὁμοούσιος)'".

Apparently Constantine added his own interpretation of this contentious word in language designed to counter possible objection in advance. "He explained that ὁμοούσιος was not used in the sense of bodily affections, for the Son did not derive His existence from the Father by means of division or severance, since an immaterial, intellectual and incorporeal nature could not be subject to any bodily affection. These things must be understood as bearing a divine and ineffable signification." The council, however, on the pretext of adding CONSUBSTANTIAL (προφάσει τῆς τοῦ ὁμοουσίου προσθήκης) "produced this formulary"—and then follows the creed of Nicaea with its anathemas. Eusebius brings his letter to a close with a long passage explaining how he insisted on scrutinizing the creed, and refused absolutely to append his signature until

[1] For the text of this, see above, p. 182.

a satisfactory explanation had been put upon every clause both of the symbol itself and of the anathemas at the end.

As well as supplying precious hints regarding the origin of the creed of Nicaea, the letter is a fundamental authority for its text. In addition to the appendix to his *De decret. Nic. syn.*, St Athanasius quoted the creed again in his letter to the Emperor Jovian.[1] Other important witnesses to the authentic text are Socrates the historian,[2] and St Basil.[3] The creed was reproduced, of course, by many other Greek authors in the century following the council, and numerous Latin versions of it were current.[4] A text based on these authorities is printed below with an English translation. Its accuracy is supported by what took place more than a hundred years later at the council of Chalcedon (451). At the second session, held on 10 October, the assembled bishops caused the creed of Nicaea to be read out in their hearing. According to the very full account preserved in the Acts of the council, this was done by Eunomius, bishop of Nicomedia. E. Schwartz held[5] that the choice of this dignitary, metropolitan of Bithynia (in which Nicaea was situated), was dictated by the desire to have the creed recited in its authentic, original text. While this is unlikely, he showed, as editor of the Chalcedonian *acta*, that the text read out must have differed only in minute particulars from the one printed below.

NICAEA

Πιστεύομεν εἰς ἕνα θεόν, πατέρα, παντο-κράτορα, πάντων ὁρατῶν τε καὶ ἀοράτων ποιητήν.

Καὶ εἰς ἕνα κύριον Ἰησοῦν Χριστόν, τὸν υἱὸν τοῦ θεοῦ, γεννηθέντα ἐκ τοῦ πατρὸς μονογενῆ, τουτέστιν ἐκ τῆς οὐσίας τοῦ πατρός, θεὸν ἐκ θεοῦ, φῶς ἐκ φωτός, θεὸν ἀληθινὸν ἐκ θεοῦ ἀληθινοῦ, γεννη-θέντα οὐ ποιηθέντα, ὁμοούσιον τῷ πατρί, δι' οὗ τὰ πάντα ἐγένετο, τά τε ἐν τῷ

We believe in one God, the Father, almighty, maker of all things visible and invisible;

And in one Lord Jesus Christ, the Son of God, begotten from the Father, only-begotten, that is, from the substance of the Father, God from God, light from light, true God from true God, begotten not made, of one substance with the Father, through

---

[1] *Ep. ad Iov. imp.* 3 (*P.G.* 26, 817).
[2] *Hist. eccl.* 1, 8, 29 (*P.G.* 67, 68).
[3] *Ep.* 125, 2 (*P.G.* 32, 548).
[4] G. L. Dossetti, *Il simbolo di Nicea e di Costantinopoli*, Rome etc., 1967, gives an exhaustive critical survey of all the witnesses.
[5] *Z.N.T.W.* xxv, 1926, 51. For a more correct evaluation of the text read out, see Dossetti, *op. cit.*, 77 f. The text printed follows Dossetti's.

οὐρανῷ καὶ τὰ ἐν τῇ γῇ, τὸν δι᾽ ἡμᾶς
τοὺς ἀνθρώπους καὶ διὰ τὴν ἡμετέραν
σωτηρίαν κατελθόντα καὶ σαρκωθέντα,
ἐνανθρωπήσαντα, παθόντα καὶ ἀναστάντα
τῇ τρίτῃ ἡμέρᾳ, ἀνελθόντα εἰς οὐρανούς,
ἐρχόμενον κρῖναι ζῶντας καὶ νεκρούς.

Whom all things came into being,
things in heaven and things on earth,
Who because of us men and because
of our salvation came down and became incarnate, becoming man,
suffered and rose again on the third
day, ascended to the heavens, will
come to judge the living and the
dead;

Καὶ εἰς τὸ ἅγιον πνεῦμα.

And in the Holy Spirit.

Τοὺς δὲ λέγοντας· ἦν ποτε ὅτε οὐκ ἦν, καὶ
πρὶν γεννηθῆναι οὐκ ἦν, καὶ ὅτι ἐξ οὐκ
ὄντων ἐγένετο, ἢ ἐξ ἑτέρας ὑποστάσεως ἢ
οὐσίας φάσκοντας εἶναι, ἢ τρεπτὸν ἢ
ἀλλοιωτὸν τὸν υἱὸν τοῦ θεοῦ, ἀναθεματίζει
ἡ καθολικὴ καὶ ἀποστολικὴ ἐκκλησία.

But as for those who say, There was
when He was not, and, Before being
born He was not, and that He came
into existence out of nothing, or who
assert that the Son of God is of a
different hypostasis or substance, or
is subject to alteration or change—
these the Catholic and apostolic
Church anathematizes.

At this point we leave Eusebius's letter, and to reconstruct
the rest of the story must rely on fragmentary reminiscences in
other writers. The bishops were invited to vote on the symbol
which was now laid before them.[1] There was apparently much
embarrassment, much heart-burning. The emperor's laboured
explanations were not calculated to allay the bishops' suspicions
of what appeared to them a new direction in theological interpretation. Arius and his friends were given the choice of signing
or being sent into exile[2]: they chose the latter. But they were
a small company. Apart from the heresiarch himself, only
Secundus of Ptolemais and Theonas of Marmarica declined
to give their signatures. Even Eusebius of Nicomedia and the
local prelate, Theognis of Nicaea, were found prepared to
conform. The idea that they subscribed a text in which the
word ὁμοούσιος (="of the same substance") was replaced by
ὁμοιούσιος (="of like substance")[3] is an ingenious fiction
invented so as to save their honour. In fact they limited
their opposition to a refusal to endorse the official condemnation of Arius himself, their argument being that his
teaching had been grossly misrepresented in the formal
accusations.

---

[1] Philostorgius, *Hist. eccl.* I, 9 (Bidez, 10).
[2] Philostorgius, *Hist. eccl.* I, 9a (Bidez, 10).
[3] Philostorgius, *Hist. eccl.* I, 9 (Bidez, 10 f.).

3. Comparison of N and CAES.

The twofold problem confronting the student of creeds concerns the identity and intention of the short formula (technically known as N) which was thus canonized by the ecumenical council. What is the history of this creed which Constantine succeeded in persuading the three hundred and eighteen bishops to accept, and what fine shades of meaning attached to its disputed clauses? The solution to the first of these problems which held the field until recently, and which may still be met with in many text-books of Church history and authoritative encyclopaedia articles, is based upon a simple, rather one-sided reading of the apologetic letter of Eusebius referred to and summarized above. N, it was argued, is none other than the local creed of Caesarea (hereafter designated CAES.) revised in the light of the emperor's instructions. The committee appointed to carry out the revision inserted, as admonished, the word ὁμοούσιος (=OF ONE SUBSTANCE), and took advantage of the opportunity, while they were at it, to make several other changes in the same direction. This is the view which was carefully worked out and energetically defended by the English scholars F. J. A. Hort[1] and A. E. Burn,[2] and which A. von Harnack[3] maintained for most of his life.

These scholars were well aware that the divergences between CAES. and N. were rather more numerous and far-reaching than Constantine's encouragement, to judge by the accepted reading of Eusebius's letter, might appear to have warranted. But they had ingenious and ably worked out explanations ready to hand. Thus, according to Hort, the clauses FIRST-BEGOTTEN OF ALL CREATION (πρωτότοκον πάσης κτίσεως) and BEFORE ALL AGES (πρὸ πάντων τῶν αἰώνων), which appear in CAES. but not in N, were "possibly dropped because of the danger that they might play into the hands of the heretics, who liked to appeal to the former as suggesting that Christ was a creature, and who could interpret the latter as implying that 'there was when He was not'." The title SON (υἱός) was substituted in N for LOGOS

---

[1] Cf. *Two Dissertations*, Cambridge, 1876, 54–72.
[2] Cf. *Introduction to the Creeds*, 76 ff. He continued to hold the same view in *The Council of Nicaea*, London, 1925.
[3] Cf. *Realencykl.*, 3rd ed., XI, 15 f. D. L. Holland (*art. cit.*, 180) agrees.

in CAES. because of its Biblical associations, and because the
latter word had been discredited by Arian misuse of it. Hort
indeed went further, and in contradiction to popular misrepresentations of his viewpoint insisted that other creeds than
CAES. made their contributions to N. The insertions and modifications in the second article, he noticed, correspond fairly
exactly to the phraseology of extant Syrian and Palestinian
creeds. The inference he drew was that, despite Eusebius's
silence on the point, the leaders of other great churches must
have been invited to collaborate in drafting the new formulary.
Yet these admissions did not shake his conviction, based upon
what seemed to him the unmistakable meaning of Eusebius's
words, that N "might with equal correctness be described as
the creed of Caesarea with additions".[1]

Yet, however we take it, this description hardly tallies with
the facts. The truth of the matter is, as anyone can discover for
himself who cares to make an exhaustive comparison, that
CAES. and N differ far more radically than Hort and his followers, even in their most liberal moments, were prepared to
concede. It is not just a question of the manipulation of a few
technical slogans. If the two formularies are placed side by
side, it can be seen at a glance what clauses in N are specifically
anti-Arian insertions. Manifestly the sentence THAT IS, FROM
THE SUBSTANCE OF THE FATHER (τουτέστιν ἐκ τῆς οὐσίας τοῦ
πατρός) is one of them. The clauses BEGOTTEN NOT MADE
(γεννηθέντα οὐ ποιηθέντα) and OF ONE SUBSTANCE WITH THE
FATHER (ὁμοούσιον τῷ πατρί) fall equally obviously into the
same category. So too, it is apparent, do the words TRUE GOD
FROM TRUE GOD (θεὸν ἀληθινὸν ἐκ θεοῦ ἀληθινοῦ), which
assert the fullness of the Son's deity. If these items are removed,
and at the same time (for argument's sake) the clauses in CAES.
stigmatized by Hort as possibly suspect are restored, we should
expect to come face to face with the Caesarean formulary.
Actually what confronts us is a creed broadly resembling CAES.,
but also diverging from it in a number of particulars, minute
and important.[2] In the first article, for example, N has for

---

[1] *Op. cit.* 58.
[2] In this discussion I have relied largely on the masterly collation of the two
creeds given by H. Lietzmann in *Z.N.T.W.* xxiv, 1925, 196 ff.

MAKER OF ALL THINGS VISIBLE AND INVISIBLE the Greek πάντων ὁρατῶν τε καὶ ἀοράτων ποιητήν, as against CAES.'s τὸν τῶν ἀπάντων ὁρατῶν τε καὶ ἀοράτων ποιητήν. In the third article N reads καὶ εἰς τὸ ἅγιον πνεῦμα (AND IN THE HOLY SPIRIT), while CAES. offers πιστεύομεν καὶ εἰς ἓν πνεῦμα ἅγιον (N.B. ONE HOLY SPIRIT). Admittedly these are insignificant differences for which it is not easy to conjecture a motive. But, from our point of view, their very insignificance makes them all the more impressive. Why should people have bothered to make such changes, especially the change in the third article from a superior to a much inferior form? In the first of these divergences from CAES., it should be noticed, N is in line with the second creed of St Epiphanius, while in its omission of ONE from the third article it agrees with his first creed.[1]

But it is in the structure of the second article that N stripped of the anti-Arian sentences reveals itself most strikingly as alien to CAES. Thus while CAES. separates ONLY-BEGOTTEN SON (υἱὸν μονογενῆ) and BEGOTTEN FROM THE FATHER (ἐκ τοῦ πατρὸς γεγεννημένον), and places the latter towards the end of the first half of the article, N joins them together and pushes them forward to the very beginning. N also uses the aorist participle γεννηθέντα instead of the perfect γεγεννημένον for BEGOTTEN. There is nothing in N to correspond to the theologically colourless LIFE FROM LIFE (ζωὴν ἐκ ζωῆς) of CAES. Coming to the second half, we observe that CAES.'s δι' οὗ καὶ ἐγένετο τὰ πάντα (THROUGH WHOM ALL THINGS CAME INTO BEING) re-appears in N as δι' οὗ τὰ πάντα ἐγένετο. The following lines (on the basis of the theory under discussion) abound in similar, to all seeming pointless, changes and additions, such as the clumsy insertion of THINGS IN HEAVEN AND THINGS ON EARTH (τά τε ἐν τῷ οὐρανῷ καὶ τὰ ἐν τῇ γῇ), the insertion of BECAUSE OF US MEN AND (δι' ἡμᾶς τοὺς ἀνθρώπους καὶ), and the insertion of CAME DOWN (κατελθόντα), the omission of a couple of AND's as well as (for what conceivable reason?) of IN GLORY (ἐν δόξῃ), and the changes of TO THE FATHER (πρὸς τὸν πατέρα) to TO THE HEAVENS (εἰς οὐρανούς), and of the participle ἥξοντα (WILL COME) to ἐρχόμενον. The net result[2] is the definite

---

[1] For St. Epiphanius's creeds, see his *Ancoratus*, 118 and 119 (Holl I, 146–149).
[2] Cf. Harnack, *Realencykl.*, 3rd ed., XI, 15.

assimilation of N to the Jerusalem-Antioch type of creed, and Harnack even argued that these alterations could be regarded as "undogmatic concessions" made by the drafting committee to the powerful patriarchs of those sees. Actually we have no reason to believe that people were so interested as all that in the exact phrasing of their local creeds at this date. If they were, it is extremely odd that personages so weighty should have been content with such insignificant concessions.

4. *The Letter of Eusebius*

The effect of the above considerations is inevitably to cast grave doubts on the Hort-Harnack hypothesis that N was the result of a recasting of CAES. They compel the question whether in fact that hypothesis is necessitated by the testimony of Eusebius's letter. And here it is worth noticing that none of the authorities who preserve the letter so much as hints that it implies any lineal connection between CAES. and N. St Athanasius's object in reproducing it was frankly enough avowed[1]: he wanted the world to know that even Eusebius, who had resisted stoutly until the eve of Nicaea, had eventually come round to admit that the Nicene teaching represented the faith of the Church and the tradition of the fathers. His letter was thus at once a confession of the error of his former ways and a repudiation of Arianism. Similarly both Socrates[2] and Theodoret,[3] knowing the prestige which Eusebius enjoyed and the way the Arians had of exploiting it, were glad to use the letter, with its admission, albeit reluctant, that the Nicene formula could be interpreted in an acceptable sense, as a stick with which to beat the heretics. These facts deserve to be recalled because the modern scholar unconsciously slips into the assumption that the interest of ancient chroniclers coincided with his own, and forgets that, while the letter throws valuable light on the composition of N, it only does so indirectly.

A point of decisive importance to be noted at the outset is that Eusebius himself nowhere claims in his letter that N was,

---

[1] *De decret. Nic. syn.* 3 (*P.G.* 25, 428 f.).
[2] *Hist. eccl.* 1, 8 (*P.G.* 67, 65 ff.).
[3] *Hist. eccl.* 1, 11–12 (Parmentier, 48 ff.).

or was intended to be, the result of a revision of the *creed* of his native church. The key sentence comes at the very beginning, where he announces that he is going to quote, first, "the statement about my beliefs which I submitted (τὴν ὑφ' ἡμῶν προτεθεῖσαν περὶ πίστεως γραφήν)", and then the second "writing (γραφήν)" which the bishops had produced "after making additions to my words (ταῖς ἡμετέραις φωναῖς προσθήκας ἐπιβαλόντες)". Here Eusebius's "statement about my beliefs", to which additions were made, cannot have been simply the creed of Caesarea. The description must refer to the whole exposition which follows, and which (as was pointed out previously) included, as well as the creed, both his personal declaration that he had been brought up in this faith and had himself loyally taught it, and (what is directly relevant) the theological elucidation appended to the creed. If this is so, then "my words", to which he complained that additions had been made, cannot be taken, as is commonly done, as being equivalent to the Caesarean creed. They cannot refer to any text as such, but must refer to the general theological position expressed in the whole passage. The emphasis, in other words, is on the old inherited faith of the Church, taught by the bishops preceding him and ultimately derived from the Lord Himself, much more than on the Caesarean creed considered as a document. It is this traditional teaching to which, by his account, the bishops listened so respectfully and which the emperor himself so generously applauded, commanding that it should be incorporated in a formal profession containing the word *homoousios*. There is no suggestion that either Eusebius or Constantine expected the final document to be the actual Caesarean creed with the Nicene key-word inserted. What Eusebius implies that he had a right to expect was that it would give expression to the *doctrine* which he had professed to the satisfaction of the council, the only fresh feature being the nuance introduced by the use of *homoousios*.

A similar and parallel misunderstanding vitiates the current interpretation put upon the other key-passage. This is the sentence by which Eusebius introduced the creed of the council: "But they, on the pretext of adding *homoousios* (προφάσει τῆς τοῦ ὁμοουσίου προσθήκης), produced this document." Some scholars[1] have helped to obscure the meaning of the words by mistranslating προφάσει ("on the pretext of") as "with a view to", thereby making it easy to take them as evidence supporting the Hort-Harnack hypothesis. As a matter of fact, if Eusebius had the actual texts of creeds in mind at all, the sentence meant for him something very different. What he was asserting, on this interpretation, was that the committee exploited the opportunity given them to insert *homoousios* by devising an entirely new formulary, diverging from CAES. in the minutiae of its wording. This is H. Lietzmann's[2] exegesis of the passage, and it may be correct that Eusebius's bitter tail-words, "this document!", betray his disgust that, instead of his favourite creed-form, the responsible authorities had foisted on the council a quite alien symbol. Even this, however, seems to misconceive the essential point of his complaint, and to depict him as pedantically concerned about the texts of different local creeds as if he were a modern student of the subject. The truth of the matter surely is that he was not primarily interested, here any more than elsewhere in the letter, in the mere texts of creeds as such, still less in the claims of different local creeds. The ground of his disappointment was not that the new creed N had some creed other than his darling and familiar CAES. as its basis (that other creed, it may be remarked, was not *dogmatically* so very dissimilar to CAES.). It was that, irrespective of what creed they had adopted as their framework, the committee had gone much further than Constantine's mandate gave Eusebius and his friends reason to expect. Not only had they embodied *homoousios* in their formulary, but the whole theological bias of the resultant document was out of harmony with his own teaching, especially in view of the string of anathemas which they had appended. This last point is important, for the force of the passage will be lost if it is forgotten that the indignant "this document!" referred not simply to N, but to N dressed out with its anathemas.

The remainder of the letter coheres admirably with this conception of Eusebius's attitude. If, as Lietzmann suggested,

---

[1] E.g. B. J. Kidd, *Documents Illustrative of the History of the Church*, London, 1932, II, 23.
[2] *Z.N.T.W.* xxiv, 1925, 201 f.

the sentence quoted above must be taken as giving vent to his annoyance that the text of his own Caesarean formula had been tampered with, it is strange that no reference to this appears in the paragraphs in which he expatiated on how he sifted the newly devised formula to the last grain. Actually these paragraphs make plain what was the real ground of his complaint. Eusebius, it appears, would have been prepared to swallow the bare word *homoousios* : we notice how he underlined the emperor's injunction "with the sole addition of one word *homoousios* (ἑνὸς μόνου προσεγγραφέντος ῥήματος τοῦ ὁμοουσίου) ". He could all the more easily afford to do so in view of the vagueness and evasiveness of the explanations which Constantine had provided for the term. But the committee, given an inch, had taken an ell : at least, that was Eusebius's verdict on its behaviour. It was one thing to insert the bare word into a formula giving expression to the sort of teaching professed by Eusebius in his own creed and its appended theological elucidation. It was quite another thing to devise a creed heavily loaded with homoousian catchwords and, so far from allowing the least loophole to the theology of the three hypostases favoured by himself, actually equating *hypostasis* with *ousia*. Consequently he felt obliged, so he assures his Caesarean constituents, to go through the bristling mass of additional clauses and anathemas with a fine critical comb, so as to satisfy himself that each and all were susceptible of an interpretation which agreed with what he and they would regard as sound theology.

This is all very well, the reader may object, but surely the whole suggestion of the letter (whatever motives St Athanasius and the rest may have had in preserving it) is that Eusebius brought forward his creed as a basis for the formula of faith to be drawn up by the council. Surely the whole point of the approval with which it was greeted by the bishops and by Constantine himself was that it seemed to them to be the ideal creed for adoption. What else is the meaning of the words, "Our beloved emperor himself was the first to testify that it was most orthodox, and that he himself held exactly the same opinions. He instructed the others to assent to it and to subscribe to its doctrines and to hold the same views"? Even if an explicit statement to this effect is lacking, it is surely easy to read between the lines and follow the course of events.

There might possibly be a difficulty here if we were in the dark concerning the situation which preceded the council. Thanks, however, to the information which has been unearthed about the synod held at Antioch a few months previously and to which reference was made in the opening section of this chapter, we are no longer under the necessity of resorting to an otherwise improbable explanation of Eusebius's behaviour. If the evidence of the Syriac sources is reliable, we now know that a provisional ban [1] had been placed on him at that council, although he was to be given an opportunity of clearing himself at the forthcoming ecumenical gathering. As the communiqué ran: "We, fellow-ministers at the synod, have determined not to hold communion with these [i.e. Theodotus, Narcissus and Eusebius], judging that they are not fit for communion . . . but we have granted them the great and hieratic synod at Ancyra as a place for repentance and for coming to a knowledge of the truth."

We can accordingly now appreciate the true significance of the episode recalled in the letter. The scene from which it lifts the curtain a few tantalizing inches was none other than the formal rehabilitation of the bishop of Caesarea and his re-admission to Catholic communion. Naturally Eusebius himself did not think it necessary to throw this aspect of the affair into high relief. So far as he and his flock were concerned, his temporary condemnation was best forgotten as soon as possible, and his object in writing was not to dwell upon it but to explain to his anxious correspondents how he had come to sign a formula so manifestly at variance with his well known teaching. It was important for him to mention that that teaching had received the formal, and spontaneous, endorsement of the council. But that in fact his orthodoxy was being vindicated and the temporary ban of the Antiochene fathers removed, we need not doubt. In the light of this realization we can understand the point of his repeated assertion, in the document read out to the assembled bishops, that this orthodox faith was what he had been taught from his youth upwards and what he would go on

[1] See E. Seeberg, *Die Synode von Antiochien*, 151 ff.

teaching till his dying day. We can also perceive the real meaning underlying the words, "When this statement of our faith had been put forward, there was no room to gainsay it. Our divinely favoured emperor himself was the first to testify that it was most orthodox." In other words, Constantine himself out of his own mouth gave him a certificate to the soundness of his theological views. It was the emperor's plan to secure as wide an area of agreement as possible at the council, and there was nothing whatever to be gained by excluding so important and representative a leader as Eusebius.

On the other hand, there is nothing in his further remarks, read in this setting, to suggest that Constantine seriously proposed that the actual Caesarean text should constitute the basis of the council's creed. It should be manifest, if the account we have given of the proceedings is at all plausible, that the Caesarean formulary would scarcely have stood much chance of being selected to become, with the addition of some safeguarding clauses, the new ecumenical formula. Ancient and orthodox though it was, the circumstances of its production before the assembly were hardly propitious to its being chosen for that honour. In any case, what the emperor had approved was Eusebius's teaching, not his creed as such, and this comes to light in the statement that he counselled the bishops to subscribe the same *doctrines* (τοῖς δόγμασι . . . τούτοις αὐτοῖς). It seems probable that in using these words he was not thinking of the later act of framing a conciliar creed at all, but was merely urging the company to acquiesce in Eusebius's restoration. But if he was looking ahead, to the stage of drawing up definitions, his meaning may be paraphrased as amounting to saying, "I personally accept the theological position he has expounded, and would advise that we all accept it; but for the sake of greater sureness let us include the word *homoousios* and the idea it stands for."

We must now sum up our argument, even if it involves a certain amount of repetition. It is no longer possible to assume that Eusebius's production of his creed had in the first instance anything to do with the council's formulation of its own faith. The once popular reconstruction [1] of the scene, according to

---

[1] Cf., e.g. A. E. Burn, *Introduction to the Creeds*, 77.

which the Arians first presented their formula as a basis, only to see it indignantly rejected, and then the venerable bishop of Caesarea stepped forward with the baptismal confession of his church amid the general applause, must be discarded. His real object in submitting a creed, it would appear, was to clear himself of the taint of heresy and so to obtain his theological rehabilitation. If this be so, the episode must have occurred at a preliminary stage of the agenda, whereas the creed-making probably came much later. Not only is this the case, however, but Eusebius's letter, if read aright, nowhere suggests (contrary to the widespread notion) that he ever claimed that the Caesarean text as such had been selected as the working basis of the official formulary, much less that he ever complained that the creed-drafting committee failed to adopt it as their basis. His disappointment is obvious, but its cause was not the committee's cavalier tampering with, or disregard of, his own Caesarean creed. The verbal differences between CAES. and N were apparent to every careful eye, but he was apparently not interested in them. The real ground of his disappointment was the theological tone of the new creed, as he showed by the way in which he scrutinized every specifically theological clause in the formula itself and its anathemas. The gist of his complaint was that, whereas the emperor had commended the traditional teaching of which the statement submitted by himself had provided a sample, and had simply urged that greater precision be given to it by incorporating the one word *homoousios*, the committee had exceeded his injunctions and had completely distorted the teaching. They had introduced, not so much a new creed, as what looked dangerously like a new theology, which Eusebius was only able to accept (so he assured his correspondents) after he had tested every article of it. Only a misreading of his language, and the disappearance of the records of the synod of Antioch, have led scholars to take his reminiscences as evidence for a direct relationship between CAES. and N. Properly interpreted, they do not, as we have seen, support such a conclusion. Indeed, they do not give the least colour to the idea that he was even interested in the problems which naturally exercise modern credal research.

5. *The Basis of N*

If the commonly accepted theory of the relationship of CAES. and N is rejected, the question of N's background must be tackled afresh. The most obvious approach is to inquire what is this basic creed which, as we saw, stands revealed when the palpably Nicene insertions are stripped off. What remains, it is worth emphasizing, is not just a mutilated torso, but a complete and, to all appearances, independent formulary. The Nicene alterations, on our new assumption, can be restricted to (*a*) the clause THAT IS, FROM THE SUBSTANCE OF THE FATHER, and (*b*) the longer passage TRUE GOD FROM TRUE GOD, BEGOTTEN NOT MADE, OF ONE SUBSTANCE WITH THE FATHER. There is now no need to suppose that LOGOS once stood where the Nicene fathers wrote SON, or that LIFE FROM LIFE and BEFORE ALL AGES were for some reason struck out, or that other modifications were introduced for subtle motives such as those suggested by Hort and Harnack. It was long ago observed that N bore a striking resemblance at certain points to creeds of the Syro-Palestinian type. H. Lietzmann followed [1] up this hint, and argued that the creed underlying N, into which the Nicene tags were interpolated, must have been one belonging to the Jerusalem family. The creeds to which its kinship is most marked are the first of the two quoted by St Epiphanius [2] and the one used by St Cyril of Jerusalem in his catechetical lectures. [3] The actual creed which the drafting committee used, thought Lietzmann, has not survived, and it is impossible now to guess the church to which it belonged.

This is an attractive suggestion, and it holds water even if, as is probable, we should be driven to conclude that the present text of St Epiphanius's first creed has been intruded into the manuscripts by the carelessness or misplaced zeal of later scribes. [4] The Palestinian traits in N are unmistakable, as anyone can perceive who takes the trouble to collate it with creeds from Syria and Palestine. It is also possible on this view to account for any resemblances which N may be thought to have to CAES., for CAES. too is presumably a creed of the same Syro-Palestinian family. N and CAES. are therefore related, not, however, as

---

[1] *Z.N.T.W.* xxiv, 1925, 203.
[2] Cf. *Ancoratus*, 118 (Holl I, 146).
[3] See above, p. 183 f.
[4] See below, p. 318 ff.

offspring to parent, but as two denizens of one and the same ecclesiastical region. There is nothing intrinsically improbable in the committee's having recourse to a Palestinian formulary as a working draft. The alternative hypothesis, that they did not use an existing creed as a working draft but improvised their formulary *de novo*, has not much to be said for it. The procedure seems unlikely in itself, and the creed which is left when the patently Nicene passages are removed has all the air of being an independent formulary.

Harnack, however, though persuaded towards the end of his life of the untenability of the hitherto conventional theory, which he himself had once supported, of the relation of Caes. to N, found Lietzmann's substitute proposal too difficult to digest. His objections [1] were, first, that the whole existence of this lost Palestinian creed was chimerical; secondly, that the suggested picture of the course of events scarcely does justice to Eusebius's narrative; and, thirdly, that it fails to account for the stylistic peculiarities of N. Eusebius may have been wrong, wilfully or unconsciously, in postulating that Caes. was intended by the emperor to be the sole source of the new conciliar formulary, but his argument implies that there must be *some* kinship between Caes. and N. Consequently he argued that, once the council was agreed that a new creed containing the homoousian catchwords was to be promulgated, a number of bishops of the orthodox and central parties, among them Eusebius, probably produced their creeds. The official or officials appointed to compose a draft of the new symbol had, therefore, no option but to piece together a composite document reflecting a variety of ecclesiastical traditions; and since in addition last-minute suggestions were probably thrust upon them, it is little wonder that the formula was clumsily written. As a result, Eusebius, and several other bishops too, could with some show of justification claim that their creeds had been impressed to play a part in the manufacture of the Nicene formulary.

This compromising solution has secured support in certain quarters,[2] but is open to serious criticism. If the interpretation

---

[1] *Z.N.T.W.* xxiv, 1925, 203. His remarks are added as a "kritischer Epilog" to No. 13 of Lietzmann's *Symbolstudien.*

[2] E.g. from F. J. Badcock (2nd ed.) and D. L. Holland (*art. cit.,* 180).

of Eusebius's letter which was developed in the preceding section is correct, there is no ground for supposing that he ever claimed any relationship between CAES. and N. Thus the keystone of Harnack's arch collapses. Quite apart from this, however, it is not true that the existence of the underlying formula is a matter of pure guesswork. As has been pointed out, the Nicene technical catchwords are obvious in N to every eye. If they are detached from the body of the creed to which they adhere so loosely, they leave behind a complete and, to all appearances, independent formulary. It is difficult to see how we are to explain this on the basis of Harnack's reconstruction of the course of events. Moreover, if the editor or editors were piecing together an entirely new creed out of elements contributed from a variety of sources, it remains, in spite of Harnack, a mystery why they did not do their job better. One would expect the resultant formulary to be a homogeneous whole. Instead, as we have seen, we have a complete creed of the familiar Eastern type with the anti-Arian clauses added, to all seeming, almost as an afterthought. They have been interpolated with a gaucherie and disregard for stylistic grace which are hard to reconcile with Harnack's picture of a new formula built up from the foundations by the drafting committee. If, on the other hand, the plea is put forward that the very variety of competing claims rendered their task difficult and conduced inevitably to clumsy workmanship, it must still be asked why this clumsiness should make itself manifest only in respect of the anti-Arian passages. The rest of the creed, these clauses removed, runs smoothly enough.

Harnack's objections thus fall to the ground. There is no need to examine them further, or to inquire what evidence he had for his theory that the bishops of several sees must have proffered creeds to an embarrassed drafting committee. His reconstruction of what happened was clearly conjectural. We are left with the meagre conclusion that N consists of some local baptismal creed, of Syro-Palestinian provenance, into which the Nicene keywords were somewhat awkwardly interpolated. To go beyond this and attempt to identify the underlying formula would be an unprofitable exercise. The drafting committee was probably left a fairly free hand, subject to the

result of its labours proving satisfactory to the body of the
council, and we have no means of guessing what lines they
worked upon. There was a tradition, recalled many years later
by St Basil [1] but in itself quite unobjectionable, that the leading
spirit responsible for actually writing the creed was a Cappa-
docian priest called Hermogenes, a stalwart opponent of Arius
who was destined to become bishop of Caesarea (in Cappadocia). Even if we accept it as reliable, however, it must
remain an open question whether his achievement was confined
merely to proposing the specifically anti-Arian clauses, or
whether he also suggested the local formula into which they
were inserted. In any case, we may surmise, he and his colleagues were much more concerned to bolt the door firmly
against Arianism than worried about the rival claims of different
credal texts.

[1] Cf. *Epp.* 81; 244, 9; 263, 3 (*P.G.* 32, 457; 924; 977).

CHAPTER VIII

THE MEANING AND USE OF THE NICENE CREED

1. *The Arian Theology*

IN the last chapter we were so much taken up with the literary problem of the Nicene creed that we had to leave several other important questions virtually untouched. In particular, the theological significance of the creed and the motives, doctrinal or otherwise, which lay behind the characteristic terminology in which it was expressed, deserve rather more extensive treatment than was then possible. We shall therefore in this chapter attempt to elucidate its crucial clauses in a way which will bring out their dogmatic tendency. It will also help to clear up some common and widely prevalent misconceptions if we devote some attention to the use made of the formula in the decades following the ecumenical council. As the principal aim of those who manufactured the creed was to call a halt, once and for all, to the Arian heresy, our discussion will have to be prefaced by a brief account of the heretics' main positions. The reader who desires detailed and authoritative information should resort to the full-sized histories of doctrine or, better still, to the fundamental documents of the controversy, such as the surviving fragments of Arius's own writings.[1] The sketch which is all that can be provided here will confine itself to emphasizing points with a bearing on the creed.

The outbreak of the Arian debate is probably to be placed somewhere in 318,[2] when Arius was presiding as priest over the church of Baucalis. The broad lines of his system, which was a model of dovetailed logic, are not in any doubt. Its key-

---

[1] The most convenient collection of these, as of the fragments of Asterius the Sophist, is to be found in G. Bardy's *Recherches sur saint Lucien d'Antioche*, Paris, 1936, 226 ff. For the documents in general, see Opitz, *Urkunden*.

[2] This traditional date, instead of autumn 323 as proposed by E. Schwartz (*Nachricht. Gött.* 1905, 297), has been shown still to be best supported (cf. H. G. Opitz, *Z.N.T.W.* xxxiii, 1934, 131 ff.; N. H. Baynes, *J.T.S.* xlix, 1948, 165–8).

stone was the conviction of the absolute transcendence and perfection of the Godhead. God (and it was God the Father Whom he had in mind) was absolutely one: there could be no other God in the proper sense of the word beside Him. The carefully drafted profession of faith[1] which he sent to bishop Alexander from Nicomedia,[2] always recognized as classic authority for his teaching, opened with the emphatic words: "We acknowledge one God, Who is alone unbegotten, alone eternal, alone without beginning, alone true, alone possessing immortality, alone wise, alone good, alone ruler, alone judge of all, etc." This God was unengendered, uncreated, from everlasting to everlasting: Himself without source, He was the source and origin of whatever else existed. The being, substance, essence ($o\mathring{v}\sigma\acute{\iota}a$, $\tau\grave{o}$ $\mathring{\epsilon}\chi\epsilon\iota\nu$) of the unique God was absolutely incommunicable. For God to communicate His essence or substance to another being would imply that He was divisible and subject to change. Moreover, if another being were to share the divine nature in any valid sense, there would be a plurality of divine Beings, whereas God was by definition unique. Thus everything else that existed must have come into existence by an act of creation on His part, and must have been called into being out of nothing.

The inescapable corollary of this was the drastic subordination of the Son or Word. God desired to create the world, and for this purpose He employed an agent or instrument. This was necessary because, as one of the exponents of the Arian theology, Asterius the Sophist, put it,[3] the created order could not bear the weight of the direct action of the increate and eternal God. Hence God brought into existence His Word. But, first of all, the Word was a creature, a $\kappa\tau\acute{\iota}\sigma\mu a$ or $\pi o\acute{\iota}\eta\mu a$, as the Arians were for ever reiterating, Whom the Father had brought into existence by His fiat. True, He was a perfect creature, and was not to be compared with the other creatures, but that He was to be ranged among other derivative and dependent beings they had no doubt. He was "the first-begotten of all creation",

---

[1] Cf. St Athan., *De syn.* 16 (*P.G.* 26, 708 f.); Opitz, *Urk.* 6, 2.

[2] W. Telfer has rendered Arius's flight to Nicomedia doubtful (*J.T.S.* xxxvii, 1936, 60 ff.).

[3] Cf. St Athan., *Or. con. Ar.* 2, 24; see also *De decret. Nic. syn.* 8 (*P.G.* 26, 200; 25, 437).

the Pauline text being interpreted to mean that He was included among creation. And, like all other creatures, He had
been created out of nothing (ἐξ οὐκ ὄντων).[1] The suggestion
that He participated in God's essence, Arius hinted mischie-
vously, smacked of the Manichaean conception of the Saviour
as a consubstantial portion of the divine light.

Secondly, as a creature the Word must have had a beginning,
only the Father being without beginning (ἄναρχος). "He came
into existence before the times and the ages", said Arius in his
letter to Eusebius of Nicomedia[2]: naturally, because He was
the creator of "the times and the ages" just as much as of all
the rest of the contingent order, and so was "begotten outside
time (ἀχρόνως γεννηθείς)". But, continued Arius, "before
He was begotten or created or defined or established, He was
not". Having been created by God, He was necessarily posterior
to God. Hence the familiar and repeatedly used Arian slogan,
"There was when He was not (ἦν ποτε ὅτε οὐκ ἦν)." Hence,
too, their exasperated protests against the orthodox counter-
cry, "God from everlasting, the Son from everlasting; the
Father and the Son together always (ἀεὶ Θεός, ἀεὶ υἱός· ἅμα
πατήρ, ἅμα υἱός)",[3] and their rejection out of hand of the
idea that the Son could eternally coexist with the Father.
Thirdly, it followed from all this that the Son could have no
real knowledge of His Father. Being Himself finite, He could
not comprehend the infinite God: indeed He had no full comprehension of His own being. "The Father", remarked Arius
in a passage cited [4] by St Athanasius, "remains ineffable to the
Son, and the Word can neither see nor know His Father
perfectly and accurately . . . but what He knows and sees, He
knows and sees in the same way and with the same measures
as we know by our own powers." The same point was rammed
home on many occasions.[5] A fourth consequence was that the
Son was liable to change and sin (τρεπτὸς καὶ ἀλλοιωτός).

---

[1] P. Nautin (*Analecta Boll.* 67, 1949, 131 ff.) argued that Arius did not teach that
the Son was "out of nothing". For criticism of his position cf. M. Simonetti, *Studi
sull' Arianesimo* (Rome, 1965), ch. 2.

[2] In St Epiphan., *Pan. haer.* 69, 6 (Holl III, 157); Opitz, *Urk.* 1.

[3] Cf. the letter to Eusebius just cited.

[4] *Ep. ad episc. Aeg. et Lib.* 12 (*P.G.* 25, 565).

[5] Cf. St. Athan., *Or. con. Ar.* 1, 6; *De syn.* 15; St Alexander in Socrates, *Hist.
eccl.* 1, 6, (*P.G.* 26, 24; 708; 67, 48).

Arius himself in his more formal writings [1] seems to have declared that the Word remained immutable and morally impeccable, but he more than once let it out that it was by His own resolute act of will that He retained His moral perfection. [2]

It might be asked in what sense the Word was God's Son if He was cut off from Him and subordinated to Him in all these ways. Arius and his friends continued to use the words "begotten", "Son", etc. They even exploited the ideas they conveyed in order to insinuate the necessary priority of the Father to the Son, and drew full profit [3] from the current confusion between "begotten ($\gamma\epsilon\nu\nu\eta\tau\acute{o}s$)", which it was agreed on all hands that the Son was, and "contingent ($\gamma\epsilon\nu\eta\tau\acute{o}s$)", which the orthodox denied the Son was. But they declined to draw the inference which the orthodox drew, that if He was really Son, the Word must share to the full His Father's nature. In fact, they did not attach more than a metaphorical significance to the term. The Word, in Arius's eyes, was not the authentic but the adoptive Son of the Father: "He is called Son or Power by grace." [4] He had been promoted to that position because the Father had foreseen the meritorious and perfect life He would, by His own free acts of will, lead. The net result was that the Trinity, or divine Trias, was described, in speciously Origenistic language, as consisting of three Persons ($\tau\rho\epsilon\hat{\iota}s$ $\acute{\upsilon}\pi o\sigma\tau\acute{a}\sigma\epsilon\iota s$). [5] But the three Persons were three utterly different beings, and did not share in any way the same substance or essence as each other. Only the Father was "true God", the title being ascribed to the other two in an almost figurative sense.

2. *The Reply of the Nicene Creed*

Such in outline was the Arian theological position. With its main features before us, we can begin to appreciate the full

---

[1] Cf. his letter to St Alexander (in St Athan., *De syn.* 16: *P.G.* 26, 708 f.; Opitz, *Urk.* 6).

[2] Cf., e.g., St Athan., *Or. con. Ar.* 1, 5 (*P.G.* 26, 21).

[3] Cf. his letter to Eusebius of Nicomedia (in St Epiphan., *Pan. Haer.* 69, 6; Holl III, 157): ὁ υἱὸς οὐκ ἔστιν ἀγέννητος οὐδὲ μέρος ἀγεννήτου κατ' οὐδένα τρόπον. See Opitz, *Urk.* 1.

[4] In St Athan., *Or. con. Ar.* 1, 9 (*P.G.* 26, 29).

[5] Cf. ὥστε τρεῖς εἰσιν ὑποστάσεις in Arius's letter to St Alexander (in St Athan., *De syn.* 16: *P.G.* 26, 709; Opitz, *Urk.* 6).

import of the special clauses in the Nicene creed, at least in so far as they sought to rebut Arianism. We may pass over ONLY-BEGOTTEN (μονογενῆ), although much ink has been expended in the discussion of it,[1] because it was accepted by all parties in the Arian quarrel and no special dogmatic significance was read into it. Let us look, however, at the first of the anti-Arian interpolations, the clause THAT IS, FROM THE SUBSTANCE OF THE FATHER (τουτέστιν ἐκ τῆς οὐσίας τοῦ πατρός), which was inserted immediately after the words BEGOTTEN FROM THE FATHER, ONLY-BEGOTTEN, and was clearly intended to give a more precise interpretation to BEGOTTEN FROM THE FATHER. What we have here is a deliberately formulated counter-blast to the principal tenet of Arianism, that the Son had been created out of nothing and had no community of being with the Father. The Arians had been perfectly willing to acquiesce in the description "begotten from the Father", so long as they were at liberty to interpret it in a sense consistent with their theory of the Son's origin by a creative fiat of the Godhead. To exclude any such interpretation, our clause nails up the thesis that, so far from being produced like the creatures out of nothing, the Son was generated out of the Father's very substance or being. The implication which this carried with it was that He shared the divine essence to the full. This latter thought was driven home in the all-important phrase OF THE SAME SUBSTANCE AS THE FATHER (ὁμοούσιον τῷ πατρί), which was inserted a couple of lines further down.

At the council, if we can rely on the vivid picture drawn many years later by St Athanasius[2] and referred to in the previous chapter, the fathers would have preferred a more patently biblical expression to mark the impropriety of the suggestion that the Son was created out of nothing. Such a description as "from God", which the Saviour Himself had used of His own Person in St John's Gospel (8, 42), might have seemed to the majority of them admirably suitable. They soon perceived, however, that they were playing into the hands of the Arian minority, who gleefully noted that St Paul[3] had said

---

[1] E.g. by F. J. A. Hort in *Two Dissertations*, Cambridge and London, 1876, Pt. I.
[2] *De decret. Nic. syn.* 19; *Ep. ad Afr.* 5 (*P.G.* 25, 448 f.; 26, 1037).
[3] 1 *Cor.* 8, 6; 2 *Cor.* 5, 18.

that all things were "from God". They were therefore forced to trespass outside the vocabulary of the Bible to make their point clear beyond any risk of misunderstanding. The phrase FROM THE SUBSTANCE OF THE FATHER was not, however, an entire novelty. The sentence, "He is sprung from the Father's substance (ἐκ τῆς τοῦ πατρὸς οὐσίας ἔφυ)", had been used, as St Athanasius himself later pointed out,[1] towards the end of the third century by Theognostus in his *Hypotyposes*. Moreover, the idea it conveyed was one which the Arians had strenuously and persistently denied, often in language approximating to that now employed. Arius himself, in his well-known letter to St Alexander, had branded the proposition that the Son was *homoousios* with the Father as savouring of Manichaeism, and in his *Thalia* had sung:[2] "He is not equal to Him [the Father], nor for that matter of the same substance (ὁμοούσιος) . . . the Father is alien to the Son in substance". Again, he had said:[3] " He is not from the Father, but came into existence out of nothingness, and Himself has nothing in common with the Father's substance (οὐκ ἔστιν ἴδιος τῆς οὐσίας τοῦ πατρός)"; and, "The substances of the Father and of the Son and of the Holy Spirit are different and have no share in each other (ἀλλότριοι καὶ ἀμέτοχοί εἰσιν ἀλλήλων)".[4] He was always insisting that the Word was utterly unlike (ἀνόμοιος κατὰ πάντα) the Father's essence or being. His great friend and champion, Eusebius of Nicomedia, was entirely at one with him, and in his letter[5] to Paulinus of Tyre had repudiated the very words "derived from His essence (ἐκ τῆς οὐσίας αὐτοῦ γεγονός)".

The next anti-Arian clause is TRUE GOD FROM TRUE GOD (Θεὸν ἀληθινὸν ἐκ Θεοῦ ἀληθινοῦ). It has already been stated that the absolute uniqueness of the divine Father was one of the staple Arian articles. To bring out His uniqueness the heretics pressed the Saviour's words in *Jn.* 17, 3, "This is life eternal, that they should know Thee the only true God", into

[1] *De decret. Nic. syn.* 25 (*P.G.* 25, 460). Cf. M. J. Routh, *Reliquiae Sacrae*, Oxford, 1846, III, 411.
[2] In St Athan., *De syn.* 15 (*P.G.* 26, 708).
[3] In St Athan., *Or. con. Ar.* 1, 9 (*P.G.* 26, 29).
[4] *Ibid.* 1, 6 (*P.G.* 26, 24).
[5] In Theodoret, *Hist. eccl.* 1, 6 (Parmentier, 28). Cf. Opitz, *Urk.* 8.

their service, trying to squeeze out of them every drop of meaning. Eusebius of Caesarea, who quoted the text with effect in a letter,[1] added that the suggestion of the words was "not that the Father alone is God, but that He alone is true God, and the addition of the word 'true' is most necessary". The Word of God, he admitted, was "God", but not "true God". Arius too, according to a report of St Athanasius,[2] had remarked, "Nor is the Word true God ($\Theta \epsilon \delta s \ \dot{a}\lambda\eta\theta\iota\nu\delta s$). If He is called God, He is none the less not true God, but is God by favour ($\mu\epsilon\tau o\chi\hat{\eta} \ \chi\dot{a}\rho\iota\tau os$), like all the others, and is called so in name only." Our clause had the effect of laying it down that the Son was truly God in whatever sense the Father was God. As a matter of fact, however, it was not much appealed to by either side in the controversy. When pressed, the Arians were prepared to concede that the Son was "true God", for that He was God in a certain sense they readily agreed, and that He was "true" was obvious from the fact that He was a real existent. St Athanasius drew attention to this quibbling interpretation of theirs when criticizing the way they wriggled out of every attempt to tie them down to an orthodox definition:[3]

The sentence BEGOTTEN NOT MADE ($\gamma\epsilon\nu\nu\eta\theta\acute{\epsilon}\nu\tau a \ o\dot{v} \ \pi o\iota\eta\theta\acute{\epsilon}\nu\tau a$), which was the next characteristically Nicene article, was not one from the implications of which the Arians could escape so easily. They were, as has been previously indicated, eager enough to employ such language as BEGOTTEN, but the meaning they put upon it was indistinguishable from MADE. The Word was a creature, a perfect creature admittedly and in a class altogether apart from other creatures, but He had been brought into existence by the divine decree out of nothing. To suggest that He had in any real sense been born implied subjecting the Godhead to a kind of necessity. They liked to stress that his coming into being had depended on an act of the Father's will.[4] The orthodox rejoinder was to insist on taking the word BEGOTTEN in its full acceptation, and to point out[5] that it was

[1] To Euphration, cited at Sess. V of the Second Council of Nicaea. See Mansi XIII, 317. It is printed by H. G. Opitz as *Urkunde* 3.
[2] *Or. con. Ar.* 1, 6 (*P.G.* 26, 24).
[3] *Ep. ad Afr.* 5 (*P.G.* 26, 1040).
[4] Cf., e.g., $\dot{v}\pi o\sigma\tau\acute{\eta}\sigma a\nu\tau a \ \dot{\iota}\delta\acute{\iota}\omega \ \theta\epsilon\lambda\acute{\eta}\mu a\tau\iota$ in Arius's letter to St Alexander (*P.G.* 26, 709: Opitz, *Urk.* 6).
[5] Cf., e.g., St Athan., *Or. con. Ar.* 3, 62 ff. (*P.G.* 26, 453 ff.).

nonsense to talk of God being subjected to necessity if His very nature was to beget. In answer to the objection that then the Father must, since it is natural for fathers so to be, be prior to the Son, they had recourse to Origen's well-known teaching of the eternal generation of the Son by the Father. The Godhead had never been without His Word or His Wisdom: so the Father had never been other than Father, and had never been without His Son. The Son and the Father must therefore have coexisted from all eternity, the Father eternally begetting the Son.

But it was in the fourth characteristic phrase of the creed, the words OF ONE SUBSTANCE WITH THE FATHER (ὁμοούσιον τῷ πατρί), that the full weight of the orthodox reply to Arianism was concentrated. The previous history and use of the word will be studied in the next section, as will the motives for its selection for insertion in the creed. Here it will be sufficient to point out that it completely traversed the Arian position by asserting the full deity of the Son. The Son, it implied, shared the very being or essence of the Father. He was therefore fully divine: whatever belonged to or characterized the Godhead belonged to and characterized Him. The word itself, as well as the idea it contained, had been explicitly repudiated by the Arian leaders, and it aroused objection in quarters outside the heretical camp. There were four chief grounds for this hostility to it, and each of them carried different degrees of weight with different people. First, there were many who thought that the term must entail a materialistic conception of the Deity, the Father and the Son being regarded as parts or separable portions of a concrete substance. Secondly, if the Father and the Son were taken as being of one substance, it seemed to many that Sabellianism with all its perils must lurk round the corner. Thirdly, the Semi-Arians made the point at the council of Ancyra (358) that the word had already been condemned by sound and orthodox bishops at the Antiochene synod (268) which had dealt with Paul of Samosata. Fourthly (and this consideration worked upon the minds of many who were far removed from Arianism proper), the word CONSUBSTANTIAL, no more than the phrase FROM THE SUBSTANCE OF THE FATHER, was not to be found in Holy Scripture, and thus the tradition that the binding formulae contained in the Church's creeds should be expressed in inspired language was violated. The orthodox had their answers to all these cavils. They would have preferred a more Scriptural term, but they had discovered that every Scriptural title or image that was put forward was immediately twisted by the Arian minority to suit their own purposes. St Athanasius was later to argue[1] that, if the word did not appear in Holy Writ, the meaning it stood for did (εἰ καὶ μὴ οὕτως ἐν ταῖς γραφαῖς εἰσιν αἱ λέξεις, ἀλλὰ τὴν ἐκ τῶν γραφῶν διάνοιαν ἔχουσι). As for the Antiochene fathers who had anathematized Paul's use of the word, they had understood it, he argued, in a purely materialistic sense.[2] He vigorously denied that the word implied that the essence of the Father was divided, or that the Son was a portion of the Father, on the analogy of human generation. The divine essence was, of course, indivisible, and as such it must be wholly possessed by the Son.

As if the Arian theology had not been placed under a total ban in the creed itself, the anathemas return to the attack with renewed vigour and particularization. All the phrases singled out for condemnation are typical Arian catchwords or slogans: most of them had been repeated again and again by Arius himself in his ill-fated *Thalia*. To a certain extent they repeat the analogous anathemas appended to the profession of faith published by the council held at Antioch earlier in the year. The first proposition pilloried, "There was when He was not (ἦν ποτε ὅτε οὐκ ἦν)", pithily summed up the Arian denial of the Son's eternity and asserted His posteriority to the Father. It crops up so frequently in the literature of the Arian controversy that detailed references are unnecessary.[3] Origen, it is worth noticing, had long ago given the direct negative to speculations along these lines, declaring[4] in so many words that "there was not when He was not (*non est quando Filius non Filius fuit*)". St Dionysius of Rome, too, had remarked,[5] "For if the Son came into being, then there must have been

[1] *De decret. Nic. syn.* 21 (*P.G.* 25, 453).
[2] *De syn.* 45 (*P.G.* 26, 772).
[3] Cf., e.g., St Athan., *De decret. Nic. syn.* 15; 18; *Or. con. Ar.* I, 11; 14; *De syn.* 14; 36 (*P.G.* 25, 449; 456; 26, 33; 40; 705; 757).
[4] *In ep. ad Hebr. frag.* (*P.G.* 14, 1307). Cf. *In ep. ad Rom.* 1, 5 (*P.G.* 14, 849); *De princip.* 4, 4, 1 (28) (Koetschau, 350).
[5] In St Athan., *De decret. Nic. syn.* 26 (*P.G.* 25, 464).

when He was not. But He has been from everlasting (ἀεὶ δὲ ἦν), if indeed He is in the Father, as He Himself says." The second formula condemned, "Before He was begotten He was not (πρὶν γεννηθῆναι οὐκ ἦν)", is not much more than another method of expressing the thought contained in the first. Arius had used it in his letter [1] to St Alexander, and again in his letter [2] to Eusebius of Nicomedia. Judged by orthodox standards, its error lay in conceiving of the Father's generation of the Son as a temporal act, or at least as an act which had had a beginning at a particular point in eternity. The orthodox view was that represented by Origen in his ninth Homily on Jeremiah [3] that the Father for ever begets the Son. Eusebius, it may be pointed out, seems to have been guilty of a curious (and, we may be sure, wilful) misunderstanding of the intention of the creed. In recounting his attitude to the anathemas, he says that he had no objection to this one, for everyone was agreed that the Son of God existed prior to the fleshly generation. In other words, he was taking "begotten" in the sense, never heard of in the controversy, of Christ's historical birth. In the next paragraph he recalls that Constantine himself, when explaining the anathemas, had urged the point that the Father, as changeless God, must always have been Father, and that the Son must therefore be conceived as having existed "potentially (δυνάμει)" and "without generation (ἀγεννήτως)" with the Father before He began to exist "actually (ἐνεργείᾳ)". This was an ingenious attempt to get round the Nicene teaching, which was that the Son had been really begotten from all eternity and had always existed in the fullest sense as Son.

The remaining anathemas carry on the same theme. "He came into existence out of nothing (ἐξ οὐκ ὄντων ἐγένετο)" needs no special comment after all that has already been said. A generation later the banned phrase became the watchword of the Anomoean party, who in consequence were dubbed "Exoukontians".[4] The words "Of another hypostasis or substance (ἐξ ἑτέρας ὑποστάσεως ἢ οὐσίας)" are more important,

---

[1] In St Athan., De syn. 16 (P.G. 26, 709). Cf. Opitz, Urk. 6.
[2] In St Epiph., Pan. haer. 69, 6 (Holl III, 157). Cf. Opitz, Urk. 1.
[3] Hom. in Ierem. 9, 4 (Klostermann, 70).
[4] Cf. St. Athan., De syn. 31 (P.G. 26, 749); Socrates, Hist. eccl. 2, 45 (P.G. 67, 360).

not so much for their doctrine (they merely re-echo the Arian cliché that the Son was not of the Father's substance), but because they show the terms *hypostasis* and *ousia* employed as equivalents. The history of the relation of these two key-words can hardly be set forth afresh here. It will be enough to remind the reader that, while their separate applications were settled at the synod of Alexandria (362), their confusion prior to that had been a source of endless trouble. After 362 the meaning assigned to *hypostasis* in regard to the Trinity was "person": its role was to stress the individuality of each of the three modes or forms in which the divine essence existed. *Ousia* was reserved for the divine essence or substance itself, the very being of the Godhead. Earlier the etymology of *hypostasis* (ὑφεστάναι="lie under") had made it susceptible of the meaning "substratum", and so it had approximated to *ousia*. Origen had attempted to discriminate between them along the lines which were later adopted, but without success. In the controversy between St Dionysius of Rome and St Dionysius of Alexandria, one of the chief causes of misunderstanding had been uncertainty as to the precise sense in which the terms were being used. The Pope, for example, suspected his Alexandrian namesake of virtual tritheism when he spoke of "three *hypostases*", while his own preference for "one *ousia*" must have looked like Sabellianism to the bishop. At the time of the council of Nicaea the West, Egypt and the orthodox party were inclined to identify the terms, describing God as one *ousia* or one *hypostasis* indifferently.[1] St Athanasius maintained this usage until the end of his life, and in his *Ep. ad Afros episcopos*, written probably in 369, remarked,[2] "*Hypostasis* is *ousia*, and means nothing else than 'being'." But in the East generally about this time the meaning "individual existent" or "person" for *hypostasis* was the current one. We saw that Eusebius himself, in the profession of faith which he submitted to the council, tactfully avoided the formula τρεῖς ὑποστάσεις (three *hypostases*), but it was the one he normally employed and which expressed his theology. The treatment of the two terms as having the same meaning was, therefore, another token of the

[1] Cf. St Athan., *Tom. ad Ant.* 6 (*P.G.* 26, 803 f.).
[2] *Ep. ad Afr.* 4 (P.G. 26, 1036).

victory of the "Western" group, and the inclusion of the phrase must have added considerably to the embarrassment of men like Eusebius.

We need not spend much time over the closing anathemas. The ban on describing the Son as "created ($\kappa\tau\iota\sigma\tau\acute{o}\nu$)", though printed by many editors, is probably not authentic, being absent (*inter alia*) from the version of the creed read out at the second session of Chalcedon; but if it is, it merely stigmatizes another of Arius's catchwords. In any case its point has been made sufficiently clear in what has already been said. So, too, the ban on "morally changeable or peccable ($\tau\rho\epsilon\pi\tau\grave{o}\nu$ $\mathring{\eta}$ $\mathring{a}\lambda\lambda o\iota\omega\tau\acute{o}\nu$)" was intended to rule out one of the drastic corollaries the Arians drew from their general position. According to St Alexander's encyclical letter,[1] they were asked the question, "Could the Word of God be changed ($\tau\rho\alpha\pi\mathring{\eta}\nu\alpha\iota$) as the devil was changed?", and were not afraid to answer, "Yes, He could. For He is of a nature capable of change, being a contingent being and capable of change ($\tau\rho\epsilon\pi\tau\mathring{\eta}s$ $\gamma\grave{a}\rho$ $\phi\acute{v}\sigma\epsilon\omega s$ $\mathring{\epsilon}\sigma\tau\iota$, $\gamma\epsilon\nu\eta\tau\grave{o}s$ $\kappa\alpha\grave{\iota}$ $\tau\rho\epsilon\pi\tau\grave{o}s$ $\mathring{v}\pi\acute{a}\rho\chi\omega\nu$)". In his *Thalia* Arius himself had said,[2] "He is not incapable of change ($\mathring{a}\tau\rho\epsilon\pi\tau os$), like the Father, but He is by nature mutable, like the creatures." If He remained sinless, it was by the stubborn effort of His will. Another fragment[3] of the *Thalia* put the matter even more clearly: "By nature the Word Himself, like all others, is capable of change, but He remains good ($\kappa\alpha\lambda\acute{o}s$) by His own act of will ($\tau\mathring{\omega}$ $\mathring{\iota}\delta\acute{\iota}\omega$ $\alpha\mathring{v}\tau\epsilon\xi ov\sigma\acute{\iota}\omega$), so long as He wills to be so. But when He wills so, He can change, exactly as we can, for He is of a mutable nature."

3. *The Homoousion*

What has been said so far should have brought out something of the character of the Nicene creed. The reader should perhaps be warned that our interpretation of some of its clauses has been the "orthodox" one, based on the exposition of them given by St Athanasius in such later writings as his *De decretis Nicaenae synodi* (350–54). Nevertheless, it can scarcely be

---

[1] In Socrates, *Hist. eccl.* 1, 6 (*P.G.* 67, 48): Opitz, *Urk.* 4b.
[2] In St Athan., *Or. con. Ar.* 1, 9 (*P.G.* 26, 29).
[3] In St Athan., *Or. con. Ar.* 1, 5 (*P.G.* 26, 21).

disputed that it contained much more than a denial, point by point, of the principal Arian contentions. Not satisfied with merely demolishing the heretics' positions, it affirmed the full divinity of the Son in language which implied, if it did not explicitly assert, the doctrine of identity of substance between Him and the Father. The chief vehicle of this was the term *homoousios*, which was in consequence destined to be for ever associated with the council. It is plain, however, that this was a strange, novel term, in the company of which no great body of churchmen felt entirely at home. Eusebius of Caesarea in his letter to his flock did not disguise the consternation into which theologians of his school were thrown when it was put forward. Even after the careful explanations which the emperor and others furnished, his suspicions were not wholly at rest, and the interpretation [1] of it which he personally adopted, that it implied that the Son was "from the Father" and "like the Father in all respects", fell a long way short of what we have taken to be the Nicene teaching. St Athanasius himself for many years showed a noticeable reluctance to use it, preferring "like in substance ($\mathring{o}\mu o \iota o s \ \kappa a \tau' \ o \mathring{v} \sigma \acute{\iota} a \nu$)", and only took it up in a convinced, wholehearted fashion after his long exile in the West. We are, therefore, justified in devoting a special section to an investigation (a rather cursory one, it is to be feared) of its background and of the motives behind its selection by the framers of the ecumenical creed.

Homoousios is, of course, a compound adjective with *ousia*, or "substance", as its principal element. There were few words in Greek susceptible of so many and so confusing shades of meaning as *ousia*. Its fundamental significance can be at once defined as "being", "essence", "reality", but these synonyms only bring out the cause of the ambiguity. The precise meaning attached to *ousia* varied with the philosophical context in which it occurred and the philosophical allegiance of the writer. Let us instance only three of the possible meanings which had to be distinguished. Sometimes the term was generic: it stood for the universal, the class to which a number of individuals belonged. This was what Aristotle had called $\delta \epsilon \upsilon \tau \acute{\epsilon} \rho a \ o \mathring{v} \sigma \acute{\iota} a$, or "secondary substance". Sometimes, however, the dominant

[1] See his letter in *P.G.* 20, 1535 ff. and H. G. Opitz, *Urk.* 22.

meaning was "individual". An *ousia* was a particular entity regarded as the subject of qualities: what Aristotle had intended by πρώτη οὐσία, or "primary substance". Thus St Athenagoras stated [1] that Thales had defined demons as "psychic *ousiai*". But, thirdly, to people of a Stoic cast of thought (and the impact of Stoicism on the mind of the ancient world was a powerful one) *ousia* might suggest just matter, stuff, nothing more or less. All these various meanings, with finer nuances which cannot be enumerated here, reappear in the theological usage of the word. Of great importance, for example, all down the patristic period was its employment with the meaning of individual substance, Aristotle's πρώτη οὐσία. Though rarely, if ever, strictly identical with it, *ousia* was quite frequently treated as, for all practical purposes, equivalent to *hypostasis*, i.e. "object" or "person", in discussions about the Trinity. Thus, according to Marcellus of Ancyra,[2] Narcissus told Ossius that, on the basis of Holy Scripture, he was obliged to maintain that there were three *ousiai* in the Godhead; and St Basil[3] himself found it possible to speak of the Trinity as three *ousiai*. At the same time the emphasis in *ousia*, even when used in this sense, was always more on the internal characteristics or relations than on metaphysical reality. When, however, this latter aspect was to the fore, the purport of the word was rather different. Then it referred to the being of the Godhead, or of one of the divine Persons, from the point of view of its content, substance, or essence. Since it could boast of all these meanings, we must not be surprised if we discover that *homoousios* too reflected a corresponding multiplicity of possible interpretations.

The word had apparently a certain currency in philosophical circles. The Neo-Platonist Porphyry, for example, spoke[4] of the souls of animals as being *homoousioi* with ours; while Plotinus used[5] the same adjective to describe the kinship between the disembodied soul and the divine nature. Here the sense is generic: the beings compared belong to the same class,

[1] *Leg. pro Christ.* 23, 2 (*P.G.* 6, 941).
[2] In Eusebius, *Con. Marcell.* 1, 4, 25 (Klostermann, 26).
[3] *Hom.* (23) *in Mam.* 4 (*P.G.* 31, 597).
[4] *De abstin.* 1, 19 (Nauck, 99).
[5] *Enn.* 4, 7, 10 (Bréhier 4, 206).

their membership of it resulting from similarity of nature. Its first occurrence among Christian writers was in Gnostic circles, where it apparently enjoyed some popularity. When Tertullian translated it, he had recourse to *consubstantialis* or *consubstantivus*.[1] Typical is the remark of Ptolemaeus[2] in his letter to Flora that it was of the nature of God to produce objects "similar to Himself and *homoousia* with Himself". So, too, it was the doctrine of the Valentinians, as quoted by St Irenaeus,[3] that the spiritual part of the world was *homoousion* with Achamoth, who originated from and consisted of a like *ousia*, whereas the material man (τὸν ὕλικον) was made after the image of God and was nearly like, but not *homoousios* with, Him; while Heracleon[4] believed that a certain number of souls were consubstantial with the devil. Here again the dominant meaning is the generic one. The several entities brought together belong to one family or class as sharing the same sort of substance. It was this signification which, it would seem, Origen had in mind when he used the term, as he did at least once, in regard to the relations of the Persons of the Trinity. He argued[5] that there was a community of substance (*communio substantiae*) between Father and Son because an emanation was *homoousios* with, that is of the same substance as, the body from which it was an emanation or vapour. Presumably what he was affirming was, not that the Father and Son were identical in substance, but that they participated in the same kind of essence. Eusebius of Caesarea was presenting a sadly watered down version of this when he accepted the *homoousion* with the proviso that it indicated "that there is no similarity between the Son of God and the creatures, but that He has been made in all respects like to the Father alone Who begat Him, and that He is not derived from any other *hypostasis* or *ousia* but from the Father".[6]

On the other hand, the Arians clearly understood *homoousios*, in all good faith, in a material sense. The heresiarch himself

[1] *Adv. Hermog.* 44; *Adv. Valent.* 12; 18; 37 (*C.C.L.* 1, 433; 2, 764; 767; 778).
[2] In St Epiphan., *Pan. haer.* 33, 7, 8 (Holl I, 457).
[3] *Adv. haer.* 1, 5, 1 and 5 (*P.G.* 7, 492 and 500).
[4] Cf. Origen, *In Ioann.* xx, 20 (18), 120 (Preuschen, 352).
[5] *Frag. in ep. ad Hebr.* (*P.G.* 14, 1308).
[6] See his letter.

brushed aside [1] the insinuation that the Son was a "consubstantial portion (μέρος ὁμοούσιον)" of the Father: it seemed to him, as many contexts show, to imply a division of substance. Eusebius of Nicomedia was envisaging precisely the same idea when, in his letter to Paulinus of Tyre,[2] he angrily exclaimed that they had never heard of two ingenerate beings (ἀγέννητα) nor of one divided into two or subjected to any bodily experience. That many more than the out-and-out Arians took this view of *homoousios* is clear from the fact that, according to Eusebius's famous letter, Constantine felt it necessary to explain that the word carried no quasi-physical implications and must not be taken as suggesting any division or severance from the Father's substance.

A most illuminating illustration of yet another current interpretation of *homoousios* was provided by the affair of the two Dionysii in the 'sixties of the third century.[3] Bishop Dionysius of Alexandria, it will be recalled, had been put to much trouble by an outbreak of Sabellianism in the Libyan Pentapolis. When he took forceful measures to eradicate it, the leaders of the dissident group made a formal complaint to the Roman pontiff, alleging among other things that the bishop of Alexandria declined to say that the Son was *homoousios* with God.[4] Dionysius, it appears, was a keen protagonist of the Origenist theology. There is little doubt that the Sabellians stood for that ancient and, in popular circles at any rate, widely established brand of Monarchianism which regarded Jesus Christ as the earthly manifestation of the divine Being. To them the Origenist approach, with its distinction of the three hypostases and its tendency to subordinate the Son, was anathema. When they appealed to *homoousios* as their watchword, they meant by it that the being or substance of the Son was identical with that of the Father. The way in which they invoked *homoousios* in their complaint to the Pope is thus highly significant. It suggests, first, that it was already becoming in certain circles a

---

[1] See his letter to St Alexander in St Athan., *De syn.* 16 (*P.G.* 26, 709): Opitz, *Urk.* 6.

[2] In Theodoret, *Hist. eccl.* 1, 6 (Parmentier, 28); Opitz, *Urk.* 8.

[3] The most convenient edition of the correspondence is that of C. L. Feltoe (Cambridge, 1904). My references are to it.

[4] See Feltoe, 188.

technical term to describe the relation of the Father and the Son, and, secondly, that they expected it would be recognized and approved at Rome. It is equally significant that St Dionysius abstained from pressing the necessity of using it upon his namesake. His formal reply [1] condemned the views reported to him, in particular the separation of the divine Being into "three powers and unrelated hypostases and three divinities", and took a markedly Monarchian line. St Dionysius of Alexandria made an extremely skilful defence of himself. While maintaining all the essentials of the Origenist position, he explained that he had not used *homoousios* because it was not a Scriptural word, but had really intended the doctrine it enshrined. To prove this he claimed that he had produced as illustrations of the relation of the Father and the Son such images as the relation of parent to child, of seed to plant, and of the well to the stream which flows from it, all these being examples of entities which were "of the same nature ($\delta\mu o\gamma\epsilon\nu\hat{\eta}$)". Of course, this was quite a different exegesis of *homoousios* than the Sabellians wanted, and a quite different one too from what the Pope may have had in mind. We are back again at the generic meaning of the word favoured by Origen and the Valentinian Gnostics before him. It is possible that St Dionysius of Alexandria proved too subtle and expert a dialectician for his Roman brother, and that his profession of willingness to accept the formula counted for more than his carefully argued exposition of Trinitarian doctrine.

The next occasion on which the term cropped up was, apparently, at the synod of Antioch in 268 which condemned Paul of Samosata. Though there is no record in the surviving documents relating to the council, and though the whole episode was completely lost sight of until the Semi-Arians dragged it out of obscurity at the council of Ancyra (358), it seems certain that Paul's application of the description *homoousios* to the relation of the Father and the Son was condemned by his judges. The question which faces us is what he can have meant by it. [2] Some modern scholars, [3] basing themselves on

---

[1] See Feltoe, 177 ff.

[2] For this difficult question cf. G. Bardy, *Paul de Samosate*, 2nd ed., Louvain, 1929, 333 ff.; H. de Riedmatten, *Les Actes du procès de Paul de Samosate*, Fribourg en Suisse, 1952, ch. vi.

[3] E.g. G. L. Prestige in *God in Patristic Thought*, London, 2nd ed. 1952, Ch. X (a most valuable chapter).

St Athanasius's report[1] of the matter, have thought that what was thus put under the bishops' ban was a possible interpretation of *homoousios* quoted by Paul in a *reductio ad absurdum* argument which he used. According to this view, Paul had argued that, unless Christ "from man became God", He must have been *homoousios* with the Father, and this would involve the assumption of a third antecedent *ousia* shared by and prior to both. Yet St Athanasius is not really the most trustworthy witness in the matter. An exile at the time, he was not *au courant* with the situation of the Semi-Arian party, and his reply was couched in fairly general terms and betrayed how ill at ease he felt. A more reliable clue is supplied by St Hilary, who obviously had a first-hand knowledge of the Semi-Arian objections and dealt with them much more thoroughly. According to him,[2] Basil of Ancyra and his associates understood Paul to have meant by *homoousios* that Father and Son formed a single, undifferentiated being (*solitarium atque unicum sibi esse patrem et filium praedicabat*). In other words, when he had used the term he was developing his familiar teaching that the Son was in the Father as logos in man, and that Christ the Logos was merely a λεκτικὴ ἐνέργεια, i.e. something like the speech which issues from a man's mouth. Naturally such a doctrine must have given a severe shock to the Origenist bishops who met in council to decide his case. They could not but anathematize it and declare that the Son was not *homoousios*, at any rate in this sense of the word, but was a separate hypostasis. Their ban no doubt risked annoying the Roman Pope, who had silently approved the term in the case of the appeal from the Sabellians of Alexandria, and there is evidence that they were disposed to maintain good terms with him. But we have already pointed out that St Dionysius had been careful himself not to adopt or insist upon the term *homoousios*. The Antiochene bishops must have trusted that, since he held no brief for the official canonization of the word, he would observe that the doctrine condemned was one which he must join with them in execrating.

The net result of our survey, therefore, is that *homoousios* was a word with a variety of meanings. At the time of the Arian controversy it was viewed in very different lights by different

---

[1] *De syn.* 45 (*P.G.* 26, 772).   [2] *De syn.* 81 (*P.L.* 10, 534).

groups. According to the historian Sozomen,[1] the Meletians who engineered the assault on Arius's orthodoxy were vociferous in their demand for the recognition of the divine Logos as coeternal and *homoousios* with the Father. Clearly the meaning it had on their lips approximated to the one around which their predecessors who had caused so much trouble to Dionysius had rallied, i.e. that the Son was of one and the same nature as the Father and shared His substance. True to the tradition of the unsophisticated masses of the Libyan Pentapolis, they were registering their protest against the Origenist teaching of the three hypostases, with its dangerous bias towards subordinationism. On the other hand, every loyal adherent of Origenism tended to view it so interpreted, like Dionysius of Alexandria and the bishops who sentenced Paul, with intense suspicion. If we are to trust his letter, Eusebius of Caesarea could only be induced to accept it on the understanding that its meaning was that "the Son of God bears no resemblance to creatures, but is in every way like His Father who begat Him, and is not derived from any other subsistence or essence, but from the Father". To the Arian-minded, however, it was a bogy of sinister omen. Arius himself, in his profession of faith[2] submitted to St Alexander, poured scorn on what he cunningly alleged to be its Manichaean implications. In his *Thalia*[3] he had roundly declared that the Son was "not equal to, nor for that matter *homoousios* with, the Father". Eusebius of Nicomedia, who in his letter[4] to Paulinus of Tyre had repudiated the description "derived from the essence of the Father", held the word *homoousios* itself up to contumely in the memorandum, now lost, which (if we are justified in linking together a reminiscence[5] of St Eustathius of Antioch and a story told by St Ambrose[6]) was read out and torn to shreds at the council. His actual words are reported to have been, "If we describe Him as true Son of God and increate, we are beginning to say He is *homoousios* with the Father."

The question must therefore be faced how it came to be

---

[1] *Hist. eccl.* 1, 15 (*P.G.* 67, 905).
[2] In St Athan., *De syn.* 16 (*P.G.* 26, 709): Opitz, *Urk.* 6.
[3] See St Athan., *De syn.* 15 (*P.G.* 26, 708).
[4] In Theodoret, *Hist. eccl.* 1, 16 (Parmentier, 28): Opitz, *Urk.* 8.
[5] Cf. Theodoret, *Hist. eccl.* 1, 8 (Parmentier, 34).
[6] *De fid.* 3, 15, 125 (*P.L.* 16, 614).

incorporated in the creed. The explanation which formerly attracted most support[1] was that the responsibility rested exclusively with Constantine. The theory could appeal to the witness of Eusebius, who in his letter represented the emperor as taking the initiative in proposing the word, and it harmonized well with current interpretations of his ecclesiastical policy. What chiefly commended *homoousios* to him, it was argued, was its extreme ambiguity. Being concerned above everything else with unity, he welcomed an expression which was the badge of no party and which was wide enough in its range of possible connotation to include groups of every colour. Much play was made with the fact that St Athanasius himself avoided using it until the early 'fifties, and the suggestion was advanced that he at first regarded it with suspicion, and only came round to a wholehearted acceptance of it after his theology had undergone a significant development. We shall have occasion to examine the validity of these last statements in the following section. In the meantime we can freely acknowledge the importance of the role played by the emperor at the council. It was his influence alone, we need not doubt, which succeeded in suppressing the opposition, if not the interior qualms, of the considerable body of central churchmen of which Eusebius was the representative. It is worth recalling Eusebius's reminiscence in his letter that, so far as the positive elucidation of *homoousios* was concerned, Constantine was content to lay it down that "these things must be understood as bearing a divine and ineffable signification". Clearly he had nothing to gain from pushing a new and difficult theology: what he wanted was a creed which as many different schools of thought as possible could embrace and make some kind of sense of.

So much may be granted. But to pretend to discover the complete explanation of the choice of *homoousios* in Constantine's political manoeuvres is surely paradoxical. The creed contained much more than the enigmatic term itself: alongside it stood THAT IS, FROM THE SUBSTANCE OF THE FATHER, and in the anathemas the identification of *ousia* and *hypostasis*. It is

---

[1] Cf., e.g., E. Schwartz's brilliant study *Kaiser Constantin und die christliche Kirche*, 2nd ed., Leipzig and Berlin, 1936, and F. Loofs's article *Das Nicänum* in the *Festgabe für K. Müller*, Tübingen, 1922.

hard, also, to believe that St Alexander, supported as he was by his deacon St Athanasius, would have been persuaded to acquiesce in a terminology about whose precise connotation there were doubts. As a matter of fact, however various the senses which *homoousios* was capable of bearing, its use in the earlier stages of the controversy must have fastened a fairly definite meaning upon it in the eyes of theologians, if not of the emperor. In any case, to suppose that St Athanasius, after being at first extremely uneasy about this key-word, was subsequently transformed into its enthusiastic champion, puts a considerable strain upon the historical imagination. There are reasons for believing, moreover, that Constantine did not act entirely on his own in Church matters at this time. He leaned very heavily on the advice of his ecclesiastical confidant, Ossius of Cordoba, and had already used him as a special informant on the Arian crisis itself. The older tradition, which saw the hand of Ossius behind the emperor's patronage of *homoousios*, has still a great deal to be said for it on general grounds, and it in no way clashes with a full recognition of the importance of Constantine's personal intervention. We may recall that St Athanasius, though his language is not as explicit as we could wish, seems to have singled out Ossius as responsible for the creed. There is a well-known passage[1] in which, explaining why Ossius (now an aged man) should be victimized by the Arians, he exclaimed: "When was there a council held when he did not take the lead and win all over by his sound words!" In another passage[2] he was perhaps more to the point: "It was he [Ossius] who put forth the faith accepted at Nicaea (οὗτος τὴν ἐν Νικαίᾳ πίστιν ἐξέθετο)." The anti-Arian writer Phoebadius seems to give some support to this view in a sentence[3] of his *Liber c. Arianos* (written 356 or 357). There was every reason why Ossius should regard the acceptance of *homoousios* as the best possible solution of the present troubles. Even if the word was not, as has often been alleged, an accepted piece of Western theological terminology, it was admirably suited to describe the particular type of Trinitarian theology, with its strong emphasis on the divine monarchy, which had long been fashionable in the West.

---

[1] *De fug.* 5 (*P.G.* 25, 649).   [2] *Hist. Ar.* 42 (*P.G.* 25, 744).
[3] *Con. Ar.* 23 (*P.L.* 20, 30).

Another valuable link in the chain of evidence is provided by a story told by the historian Philostorgius [1] to the effect that Ossius and St Alexander reached an understanding together in Nicomedia, before the council, on the use of the very term *homoousios*. The fact that Arius repudiated it so forcefully in his letter to St Alexander might be read as an indication of his awareness that his bishop's mind was veering in its direction. The course of events thus adumbrated would suggest a wider, more complex background for the formulation of the creed than those who regard it as merely a unifying device of the emperor's are prepared to admit. F. Loofs [2] sharply criticized Philostorgius's report on the ground that St Alexander, to judge by his encyclical letter [3] and his letter [4] to Alexander of Byzantium, had pitched his tent in the moderate Origenist camp. The theology he there expounded, Loofs argued, was markedly Origenist in complexion, with its stress on the eternal generation of the Son, its predilection for "like in all things", and its insistence that Father and Son were two hypostases. But it is misleading to place this exclusive emphasis on one aspect of St Alexander's thought, which was very far from being a logically coherent system. Side by side with the Origenist strain there was a strong, not always clearly worked out, conviction of the inseparable unity formed by Father and Son. This came to light in such statements as that the Father could not be conceived to have ever been without His Word and His Wisdom (ἄλογος καὶ ἄσοφος),[5] that the Son (cf. *Jn.* 10, 15) had a perfect knowledge of the Father [5] and was His perfect Image,[6] that the Father and the Son were two inseparable beings between Whom no interval could be thought (ἀλλήλων ἀχώριστα πράγματα δύο), and that the Son, if not ἐκ τῆς οὐσίας τοῦ πατρός, was ἐξ αὐτοῦ τοῦ ὄντος πατρός.[6] With ideas like these in his head,[7] and with his special knowledge of the way the Arians reacted to the claim that the Son was

[1] *Hist. eccl.* 1, 7 (Bidez, 8 f.).
[2] *Festgabe für K. Müller*, Tübingen, 1922, 78 f.
[3] In Socrates, *Hist. eccl.* 1, 6 (*P.G.* 67, 44 ff.) : Opitz, *Urk.* 46.
[4] In Theodoret, *Hist. eccl.* 1, 4 (Parmentier, 8 ff.) : Opitz, *Urk.* 14.
[5] See *Ep. encyc.*
[6] See *Ep. ad Alex. Byz.*
[7] Though not altogether sympathetic to St Alexander, Harnack brought out the essentials of his teaching in *Lehrbuch der Dogmengeschichte*, 5th ed., II, 204 ff.

homoousios with the Father, we can readily perceive that the way was clear for an agreement between Ossius and the bishop of Alexandria.

Shrouded as they are in obscurity, it is impossible now to pick one's way with any confidence through the deliberations of the council. One thing which may be regarded as fairly established, however, is that the precise way in which the homoousian formula was to be used had not been finally determined in advance by the personages who guided the proceedings. This is borne out by the strong tradition, which St Athanasius recalls,[1] and which is in itself most probable, that the original intention was to frame a definition in language borrowed from Scripture. This was only abandoned when it was seen that every conceivable text or biblical turn of phrase could be ingeniously distorted by the Arians to look like evidence in support of their speculations. St Ambrose tells a story,[2] which has already been cited, that Eusebius of Nicomedia was himself responsible for throwing the word *homoousios* into the debates. He goes on to say that "when his letter had been read out, the fathers inserted this word into their definition of faith because they observed that it struck terror into their adversaries' hearts. They thought it an excellent idea to sever the head of the foul heresy with the very sword which they had themselves unsheathed." Loofs thought[3] this a "feeble hook" on which to hang such a momentous happening, but there is nothing intrinsically unlikely in the reminiscence, although St Ambrose may have been giving a rather generalized account of what took place. Ossius and his confederates may well have judged that the enemy was playing into their hands, and that a handle had been given them, at the opportune moment, to spring the prearranged word on the assembly. After the blasphemies of Eusebius of Nicomedia, the atmosphere was bound to be more favourable than they had dared hope. And the emperor had been won over to be their mouthpiece.

Thus the different parties present at the ecumenical council understood its creed in very different ways. For Constantine himself the theological issue was not the primary one: he

---

[1] See above, p. 213. [2] *De fid.* 3, 15, 125 (*P.L.* 16, 614).
[3] *Festgabe*, 80.

was interested in re-establishing unity in the Church, and somehow or other he had persuaded himself, or been persuaded, that this formula was likely to promote it. He was less concerned about the interpretation people put upon it than about getting them to append their signatures to it. The great mass of conservative-minded bishops must have been taken aback to read the creed they were expected to accept. Eager enough to ostracize Arianism proper, they had no desire to be saddled with an un-Scriptural term suggestive of a theology which appeared to strike at the roots of the doctrine of the three divine hypostases which was prevalent over most of the Eastern Church. They must have been relieved to hear the minimizing explanation Constantine gave of it, and to observe that it was their signatures that he wanted more than anything else. Even the Arians, including Eusebius of Nicomedia, when they became aware of the emperor's attitude, found it consistent with conscience to sign. Only a comparatively small group, consisting of the handful of Western bishops, St Alexander, St Eustathius of Antioch, Marcellus of Ancyra and a few others, wholeheartedly welcomed the language of the creed, realizing that it entailed, at anyrate implicitly,[1] that theory of identity of substance between Father and Son which they wanted to push into the foreground.

4. *After Nicaea*

Such was the symbol proposed and ratified at the first ecumenical council. Not unnaturally it has often been assumed, in learned as well as popular circles, that a formula published under such auspices must have been surrounded with extraordinary éclat and must have at once secured widespread diffusion and claimed overriding authority. That the theological controversy was by no means settled, and that long decades of acrimonious debate had still to come, is of course recognized. The brute facts of history stare us in the face. But the usual attitude towards these involved, protracted struggles tends to be coloured by the initial assumption about the status of the Nicene creed. The new formula, it has often been taken for granted, must have been at once the theological strong-

---

[1] For this distinction see esp. I. Ortiz de Urbina, *El símbolo Niceno*, 207 f.

point fiercely defended by the "orthodox" and the target of equally violent assaults by their "Arianizing" opponents. It is precisely at this point that the student comes up against what at first sight looks like an enigma. For as much as a whole generation after the council one hears singularly little, either from the "orthodox" or from the "Arianizing" camp, of the creed which bears its name. So far from occupying a position in the foreground of controversy, the symbol and its characteristic key-word are rarely mentioned and practically never quoted in the literature of the period. Only in the 'fifties of the fourth century did they begin to emerge from their obscurity and play a prominent role as the rallying-point of the Athanasian party.

An explanation which has sometimes been proposed for these curious facts is the special character of the creed. The Nicene symbol, it is correctly pointed out, was first and foremost a definition of orthodox faith for bishops. It was propounded to smooth over a particular crisis in the Church. No one intended it, in the first instance at any rate, to supersede the existing baptismal confessions. Bristling with anti-Arian clauses and armed at the tail with polemical anathemas, it was hardly suited to be the solemn formula in which the catechumen would avow his adhesion to the Christian revelation. So in the West, as we saw in a previous chapter, the old baptismal creeds based on R continued to flourish without rivals. Not a trace of Nicene influence appeared in their wording. There was no creed in the fourth century, so far as we know, which was modified even to the extent of admitting *homoousios* or its Latin equivalent. In the East, too, the professions of belief recited at baptism continued to be the old ones handed down in the local churches. The creed of St Cyril of Jerusalem, for example, which belongs to 348, and the creed of the late fourth-century *Apostolical Constitutions*, both reveal an entire independence of N. To account for the former it might be suggested that St Cyril at this stage of his career still retained sympathetic leanings towards Arianism. Even if the doctrine [1] of the *Catechetical Lectures* themselves, especially that of the eleventh, which treats

---

[1] J. Lebon's studies in *R.H.E.* xx, 1924, 181 ff.; 357 ff. need to be corrected by I. Berten's article in *Revue des sciences phil. et théol.* lii, 1968.

directly of the Godhead of the Son, gives no support to such a theory, it remains arguable that St Cyril's theological position fell somewhere between that of St Athanasius and that of Arius; it is also true that, like many of his contemporaries, he was distinctly uneasy about employing the Nicene terminology. However that may be, even when this reluctance had disappeared and when the Nicene faith was being outspokenly promoted after 362, the Nicene creed itself was never, so far as we know, used at baptism. The practice which was universally adopted in the East was to carry on with the existing local baptismal formulae, but to bring them into line with Nicene orthodoxy by interpolating the crucial phrases of the council. We saw examples of this treatment in the fragments of the creed of Antioch quoted by John Cassian and in the creed of Theodore of Mopsuestia.[1]

The fact that N was a conciliar and not a baptismal creed is an important one and deserves careful notice. But it has really nothing to do with the disconcerting phenomena we are trying to understand. It may be well to instance a few of the points we have in mind. They certainly throw a very illuminating light upon the position of N in the years immediately subsequent to the council, and they are not rendered any less surprising by the recognition that of course no one dreamed of substituting N for the current baptismal symbols. First, we have the fact that, for some time at any rate after the council, the manufacture of new conciliary creeds was apparently not frowned upon either by the Eusebians or, what is much more revealing, by the orthodox themselves. When synods set about framing credal confessions, as they did with considerable zest and frequency, the criticism of the latter, as we shall see in the next chapter, was initially not directed so much at the disloyalty of daring to go behind the Nicene council as at the substance of the new creeds themselves. The first protest we hear, the first hint that the Church ought to be satisfied with the Nicene formulary, comes in St Athanasius's account[2] of the council of Serdica (343). According to him he succeeded in persuading his colleagues not to publish a creed but to stay content with the Nicene decisions. Whether in fact

---

[1] See above pp. 184 f. and 187 f.   [2] *Tom. ad Antioch.* 5 (*P.G.* 26, 800).

he adopted this line, or whether he was merely viewing what happened in the light of his later campaign on behalf of Nicaea, it is not without significance that the formulary, in the composition of which the great Ossius of Cordoba and Protogenes took the lead, was completely devoid of reference to the Nicene council, its creed and the homoousion. A point worth bearing in mind is that, at any rate until the emergence of a virulent form of Arianism in the 'fifties, the great majority of bishops who took part in these councils and joined in framing their creeds were not men animated by conscious disloyalty to Nicaea. Though often branded as Arians, they were not really such, but were prepared to join with Nicaea in outlawing anyone truly deserving that label.

A second and even more striking fact calling for explanation is the attitude of St Athanasius himself towards the Nicene symbol. The popular myth has always delighted to represent him as the adventurous paladin of Nicene orthodoxy, bearing N emblazoned challengingly on his shield from the very moment it was subscribed by the 318 bishops. But the picture which forms itself in the reader's mind after a study of his works in their chronological order seems, at first at any rate, to tell a very different story.[1] Nicaea and its sacrosanct watchword *homoousios* are not so much as mentioned in his earlier theological writings *Contra gentes* and *De incarnatione*, despite the fact that they appear to have been written in deliberate, if unspoken, competition with Eusebius's *Theophania* (after 323; possibly 333)[2]. Even more astonishing is it that there is an almost equally profound silence regarding Nicaea and its technical terms in the three great discourses *Contra Arianos*, written in the full heat of the controversy. The term *homoousios* crops up at the very beginning of the first, but disappears entirely after that. The same goes for the earlier Festal Letters and other writings of his early period. On the other hand, we are amazed to read in the *Contra Arianos* and elsewhere of the Son being "like" the Father, or "like in all respects", or "like

---

[1] The argument was well stated by F. Loofs in Hauck's *Realencykl.*, 3rd ed., II, 195 ff. (s.v. *Athanasius von Alexandria*).

[2] I accept E. Schwartz's argument that they date from 335–337 (see his *Der s.g. Sermo maior de fide des Athanasius* in *Sitzungsberichte der Bayer. Akad. der Wiss.*, Munich, 1925, 41). The usual date given is 318–320.

in substance ". All these formulae were later to be branded as Arian or Semi-Arian in their bias. Yet at this stage St Athanasius apparently preferred to employ them, and consciously (it must have been consciously) kept himself clear of *homoousios*. It was only in the early 'fifties, when he wrote the *De sententia Dionysii* and the *De decretis Nicaenae synodi*, that he came out into the open as the champion of the Nicene formulae.

To be linked with these two points is a third, the extraordinary ignorance about the documents of the Arian controversy which apparently prevailed for many years in the West.[1] It is interesting to note that the Western churches had no firsthand knowledge of the principal texts expounding the Arian position—such texts as the letters of Arius and the letter of Eusebius of Nicomedia—until little short of a quarter of a century after the council of Nicaea. The year 355 is probably the earliest date to which the publication of the first Latin translations can be ascribed. Even more remarkable, however, is the fact that the corresponding orthodox documents were equally slow in coming to the notice of Western churchmen. No doubt there was a general knowledge of what had taken place at Nicaea, and of course the papal chancellery, and probably the archives of other great sees too, possessed authentic copies of the creed and the canons in Greek with Latin translations. But it was St Hilary of Poitiers who abolished the blackout and introduced the West generally to the crucial texts of the Arian controversy. Even before his exile in 356 he had published some: in his *De synodis*, addressed in 359 to the bishops of Germany, Gaul and Britain, he carried on the good work. But the real measure of the ignorance in which the Western churches were still enveloped is disclosed by a confession which he made in his *De synodis*[2] regarding his own acquaintance with the Nicene symbol. "Though I had been baptized", he remarked, "some time previously and had been a bishop quite a while, I did not hear of the Nicene creed until I was about to set forth to exile (*fidem Nicaenam nunquam nisi exsulaturus audivi*)." Yet, as a modern scholar[3] has aptly commented, "Poitiers was not at this time

---

[1] Cf. G. Bardy, *L'occident et les documents de la controverse arienne*, in *Revue des sciences religieuses* xx, 1940, 28 ff.
[2] *De syn.* 91 (*P.L.* 10, 545).   [3] G. Bardy, *art. cit. ad fin.*

a town lost in the depths of a desert and inaccessible to sounds from outside."

We have here a body of, at first sight, startling facts which suggest that the status of the Nicene creed was very different in the generation or so following the council from what many have been brought up to believe. One is perhaps tempted to sympathize with the somewhat radical solution of the problem provided by that school of historians[1] which treats the Nicene symbol as a purely political formula representative of no strain of thought in the Church but imposed on the various wrangling groups as a badge of union. If this reconstruction of the situation is accepted, all the awkward facts seem to fall at once into place. St. Athanasius's reticence about the homoousion ceases to be at all mysterious once it is agreed that, so far from being one of the instigators of its adoption at the council, he was still at an Origenist phase of his theological development,[2] attached to the doctrine of three hypostases and highly suspicious of the emperor's chosen term. The apparent disregard for the council and its work becomes explicable in the light of the realization that it was not conceived as having prescribed a positive theology, but merely as having passed sentence on Arianism in its original form and as having attempted to restore unity in the divided Church. Just as there were no Nicene theologians, there were no anti-Nicene theologians: all were united in acknowledging its achievement in the sense described.

There are certainly valuable and true features in this bold attempt to elucidate the course of events, but it is marred by the determination to make the picture altogether too clear-cut. The insistence on eliminating the Nicene group of theologians, and particularly St Athanasius, is its most disastrous weakness. Far too much has been made in certain quarters of his abstention from using the term *homoousios*, as of the alleged drastic development of his theology which is associated with it. As stated by Loofs, the theory depended, it may be pointed out in passing, on his being able to assign the three *Orationes contra Arianos* to an extremely early date, 338 or 339: only so was he

---

[1] An excellent example of a book written on these lines is H. Lietzmann's *A History of the Early Church*, vol. 3 (E.T. London, 1950).
[2] So F. Loofs in *Realencykl.* II, 202 f.

able to plot out their author's supposed theological progression. If the date 356–362[1] proposed by the Maurine editors, or even the date 347–350,[2] should be preferred, his argument would collapse. We should then have St Athanasius before our eyes studiously avoiding *homoousios* at the very time when he was composing, or even after he had published, the *De decretis Nicaenae synodi* and the *De sententia Dionysii*. Leaving this on one side, however, it may be suggested that his silence is susceptible of another, altogether more plausible explanation. St Athanasius was as conscious as anyone of the evil odour under which *homoousios* lay. It was in accord neither with his desires nor with his interest to flaunt the word provocatively before a largely hostile public. It was not that he was personally unhappy about it, but that he wanted above all things to promote the doctrine for which it stood. That this doctrine was his own all along, and that his thought did not undergo any significant theological evolution, is borne out by a careful study of his vocabulary. If in many of his writings he steered clear of *homoousios*, he had no compunction about using periphrases like "His oneness with the Father (τὴν πρὸς τὸν πατέρα ἑνότητα)",[3] "the single and indivisible nature of Father and Son (ἡ φύσις μία καὶ ἀδιαίρετος)",[4] "offspring intimately united with the Father's substance (ἴδιον τῆς τοῦ πατρὸς οὐσίας γέννημα)",[5] "intimately united with the Father's substance (ἴδιος τῆς οὐσίας τοῦ πατρός)",[6] "identity of Godhead and oneness of substance (τὴν μὲν ταὐτότητα τῆς θεότητος, τὴν δὲ ἑνότητα τῆς οὐσίας)",[7] and many more equally expressive. Descriptions like these are really synonyms for the Nicene teaching: they attempt to get it across in language which their author considered would be more palatable to his audiences than the formulae of the creed.

The at first sight puzzling reticence of St Athanasius was

---

[1] See O. Bardenhewer, *Geschichte der altkirchlichen Literatur*, Freiburg im Breisgau, 2nd ed., 1923, III, 55.

[2] So F. Cavallera, *St Athanase*, Paris, 1908, xi f.

[3] *In Mt.* 11, 27: c. 3 (*P.G.* 25, 213).

[4] *Ibid.* c. 5 (*P.G.* 25, 217).

[5] Cf. *Or. con. Ar.* 1, 9 (*P.G.* 26, 28), etc.

[6] This phrase is so frequent that references are unnecessary.

[7] *Or. con. Ar.* 3, 3 (*P.G.* 25, 328). On this subject, but especially with regard to the equivalence of ἴδιος τῆς οὐσίας to ὁμοούσιος, cf. C. Hauret, *Comment le "Défenseur de Nicée" a-t-il compris le dogme de Nicée?*, Univ. Pontif. Gregor., 1936. See also J. Lebon's review in *R.H.E.* xxxiii, 1937, 351 ff.

the most formidable aspect of the problem we had to tackle. Once we grasp the fact that it was the result of his fine theological tact, it becomes easier to bring its other aspects into focus. And here we may point out that, for all its initial strangeness, the ignorance which the churches of the West evinced in regard to the Nicene creed is not, after all, so very difficult to account for. In the first place, all the important documents of the Arian controversy, including the creeds, were in Greek. Popular dissemination of them was therefore out of the question, unless some special reason made it indispensable. But, in the second place, the West was not deeply engaged in the Arian troubles at the time of the Nicene council or for many years afterwards. Having a theology which broadly coincided with that of the council, it had at first no interest in the subtle disputes which set Eastern theologians at such bitter odds. Hence we should not initially expect a first-hand knowledge of the controversial texts in the West. Whatever the position and status of the Nicene creed, there was no occasion to set it up as a standard of orthodoxy, since the particular doctrines it sought to maintain seemed in no danger of being compromised in the West. St Augustine, for example, who wrote much about the Trinity, and cannot be accused of disinterest in the Nicene theology, scarcely ever referred to the creed in his treatises.[1]

There still remains the problem of the attitude of the Eastern Church, to which explanations along lines similar to these have no application. At this point the strong element of truth in the hypothesis that the emperor alone took the initiative in formulating the creed comes into its own. Its characteristic teaching, as we have several times emphasized, did not correspond to any strong body of opinion in the East. The great majority of bishops, while horrified by the bold statements of Arius, were too deeply entrenched in a pluralistic, mildly subordinationist Trinitarian theology to take kindly to the homoousion, with its wholly un-Scriptural flavour and its apparently Sabellian bias. But Constantine's idea was that it should prove a formula of union, and he was not anxious to stipulate any particular interpretation of it. Within certain limits he achieved his object.

[1] Cf., e.g., *Con. Max. Ar. Ep.* 2, 14 ff. (*P.L.* 42, 772 ff.).

Very soon, once his real intentions became clear, men of every brand of theological allegiance were found ready to endorse the Nicene decisions. The emperor left it to them to read their own meaning into the formula provided they were ready to attach their names to it, and he steadfastly set his face against authorizing any one official exposition of it. Thus it was not long before Arius and Euzoius made their peace with him,[1] and he was able to assure St Alexander that they had bowed the knee to Nicaea.[2] Eusebius of Nicomedia and Theognis also petitioned, it would seem with equal success, to be taken back, and the former indicated in his letter that, on examining the sense of *homoousios*, he had found it quite acceptable.[3] In the light of this we can understand that, when councils were held, it was not, in the early days at anyrate, the decisions of the ecumenical synod that were in question. It was taken for granted that they were there: occasionally an act of reverence was offered to them. The Dedication Council of Antioch (341), for example, repudiated in its encyclical letter the innuendo that it adhered to the teaching of Arius, and reproduced the Nicene anathemas in a modified form. Arianism, in the true and original sense of the word, was considered to have been outlawed and to be as good as dead. The council of Nicaea was held to have disposed of it. Its creed was thus understood, even accepted, in a negative sense, and it is significant that later synods, while avoiding the homoousion, did not hesitate to repeat its anathemas. But since this was the light in which it was regarded, there was no occasion to be for ever appealing to its authority. The council was an affair of the past: the debate was now moving (so the majority of churchmen, for a time at any rate, thought) along different lines.

[1] Cf. Socrates, *Hist. eccl.* 1, 26 (*P.G.* 67, 149 f.): Opitz, *Urk.* 30.
[2] Cf. his letter in Gelasius of Cyzicus, *Hist. Eccl.* 3, 15, 1 (Loeschcke-Heinemann, 164 f.); Opitz, *Urk.* 32. I am accepting E. Schwartz's reconstruction of events.
[3] Cf. Socrates, *Hist. eccl.* 1, 14 (*P.G.* 67, 110 ff.): Opitz, *Urk.* 31.

CHAPTER IX

THE AGE OF SYNODAL CREEDS

1. *The Dedication Council*

HOWEVER high Constantine's hopes may have been of healing the rifts in the Church by his great ecumenical council, they were foredoomed to disappointment. A full half-century of bitter dissension had still to be endured before some kind of final accord was patched up between the factions he had striven to reconcile. The secular historian Ammianus Marcellinus, a cold and detached observer of Christianity, commenting on the character of Constantius, drily noted[1] that in his reign the efficiency of the imperial transport system was dislocated by bishops hurrying to and from ecclesiastical synods. A feature of the period between the councils of Nicaea (325) and Constantinople (381) was certainly the large number of controversial assemblies of bishops which were summoned by one party or the other or by the emperors themselves. Many of these drafted and published formularies of faith, and it is of these that we shall proceed to give some account in this chapter. The reader must be prepared, it is to be feared, for an irritatingly episodic and unsatisfactory exposition. Only in the setting of a full-dress history of the protracted doctrinal debates, for which there is no space in a book of such limited scope as this, could the full significance of the creeds be properly brought out. Their intrinsic interest, however, is so great, and the illumination they shed on the evolution of Church doctrine so instructive, that no study of creeds could afford to bypass them. To us they have an additional importance because their detailed examination serves to illustrate in the most striking way the vicissitudes of the Nicene creed itself. In the previous chapter we had perforce to be content with generalizations. Now, as we pick our way among the synods of the mid-fourth century and their credal manifestos, we should be able to note,

[1] *Rerum gest. lib.* xxi, 16, 18 (Gardthausen I, 263).

with something more approaching precision, the varying position of N in the eyes of the contending groups.[1]

The first creeds which it falls to us to investigate are the four traditionally associated with the Dedication Council held at Antioch in the summer of 341. Ninety-seven bishops, all Eastern and all adherents of the Eusebian way of thinking, met in conclave at this synod, and the emperor Constantius imitated the precedent set by his father by being present in person.[2] The immediate and ostensible object of the gathering was to celebrate the dedication (hence the Greek title of the council, ἡ ἐν τοῖς ἐγκαινίοις) of the golden church founded ten years previously by Constantine and now brought to completion by his son. In fact, the ecclesiastical ceremony proved to be no more than a convenient pretext, and the real motives at work were not long in disclosing themselves. St Athanasius, we may recall, had been deposed by the council of Tyre (335), and Marcellus of Ancyra by the council of Constantinople (336). On the death of Constantine both had been permitted to return to their episcopal thrones, but the Eusebians had taken speedy steps to extrude them once more. They had taken refuge in Rome, and the synod convoked by Pope Julius I in the spring of 341[3] had pronounced them guiltless and readmitted them to communion. One of the chief concerns of the Dedication Council was obviously to present a united front to this Western insult, and to reply to the letter,[4] full of remonstrances and accusations, which Pope Julius had sent announcing the Roman decisions. But doctrinal issues came to the fore as well. Eusebius and his friends had evidently been cut to the quick by St Athanasius's reiterated charges that they were virtually Arians and by the Pope's insinuation, put forward at St Athanasius's instigation, that they were being disloyal to Nicaea. Hence among the first measures of the council (the exact order of events cannot be reconstructed) was the promulgation of a solemn statement protesting that they were not Arian ("How, being bishops,

---

[1] For excellent, full discussions of most of the creeds here considered, cf. M. Meslin, *Les Ariens d'Occident 335–430*, Paris, 1967, 253–91.

[2] So St Athan., *De syn.* 25 (*P.G.* 26, 725).

[3] The date is Schwartz's: the one more usually given is 340.

[4] For the letter, see St Athan., *Apol. con. Ar.* 21–35 (*P.G.* 25, 281–308).

should we follow a priest?"), and that, so far from taking him as their teacher, they had only received Arius back into communion after rigorously testing his orthodoxy. To clinch this they appended a creed,[1] which opened: "For we have been taught from the beginning

Εἰς ἕνα θεόν, τὸν τῶν ὅλων θεόν, πιστεύειν, τὸν πάντων νοητῶν τε καὶ αἰσθητῶν δημιουργόν τε καὶ προνοητήν.

To believe in one God, the God of the universe, the creator and controller of all things intelligible and perceptible;

Καὶ εἰς ἕνα υἱὸν τοῦ θεοῦ μονογενῆ, πρὸ πάντων αἰώνων ὑπάρχοντα καὶ συνόντα τῷ γεγεννηκότι αὐτὸν πατρί, δι' οὗ τὰ πάντα ἐγένετο, τά τε ὁρατὰ καὶ τὰ ἀόρατα, τὸν καὶ ἐπ' ἐσχάτων ἡμερῶν κατ' εὐδοκίαν τοῦ πατρὸς κατελθόντα καὶ σάρκα ἐκ τῆς παρθένου ἀνειληφότα, καὶ πᾶσαν τὴν πατρικὴν αὐτοῦ βούλησιν συνεκπεπληρωκότα, πεπονθέναι καὶ ἐγηγέρθαι, καὶ εἰς οὐρανοὺς ἀνεληλυθέναι, καὶ ἐν δεξιᾷ τοῦ πατρὸς καθέζεσθαι, καὶ πάλιν ἐρχόμενον κρῖναι ζῶντας καὶ νεκρούς, καὶ διαμένοντα βασιλέα καὶ θεὸν εἰς τοὺς αἰῶνας.

And in one only-begotten Son of God, before all ages subsisting and coexisting with the Father Who begat Him, through Whom all things came into being, things visible and invisible, Who in the last days, according to the Father's good pleasure, came down and was incarnate of the Virgin, and fulfilled all His Father's will, suffered and was raised again, and ascended to heaven, and sits on the Father's right hand, and will come again to judge living and dead, and abides king and God for the ages;

Πιστεύομεν δὲ καὶ εἰς τὸ ἅγιον πνεῦμα.

We believe also in the Holy Spirit;

Εἰ δὲ δεῖ προσθεῖναι, πιστεύομεν καὶ περὶ σαρκὸς ἀναστάσεως καὶ ζωῆς αἰωνίου.

And if something must be added, we believe also concerning the resurrection of the flesh and life everlasting."

St Athanasius, who quoted this creed along with the other creeds of the Dedication Council in his *De synodis*, inserted the ungenerous innuendo that they were proof of the "Arians'" passion for novelty and their general indecision. But there is really nothing to show that this, the so-called First Creed of Antioch, was formulated as an official confession of the council at all. The protest about their not being Arians with which the bishops prefaced it suggests, even in the fragmentary form of St Athanasius's citation, that it was in fact simply an extract from the apologetic letter which the council prepared as an answer to Pope Julius. As it stands the formula contains nothing particularly striking. In pattern and substance it is a creed of the recognizable Eastern type, and is no doubt a baptismal form modified to suit the requirements of the

[1] St Athan., *De syn.* 22 (*P.G.* 26, 720 f.).

council. J. F. Bethune-Baker gave a misleading impression of it when he said [1] that "it was 'Arianizing' not only in its avoidance of any expression which Arians could not have accepted, but also in its explanation of ONLY-BEGOTTEN and in its marked attribution of the work of the Incarnate Son to the good pleasure and purpose of the Father ". The term *homo-ousios*, admittedly, does not feature in it, and to this extent it silently evades the full Nicene theology. But Arianism in the proper sense of the word is deliberately ruled out by the affirmation that the Son existed before all ages and coexisted with the Father. At the same time the bishops seized the opportunity to make a shrewd thrust at their much-hated foe Marcellus of Ancyra, against whom the statement about the Son's everlasting kingdom and divinity was aimed. It was a characteristic article in his teaching [2] that Christ's lordship must one day be terminated, as St Paul himself seemed to imply when he said (1 *Cor.* 15, 25), "For He must reign until He set all His enemies under His feet." Thus the divine Monad, which in the historical revelation had unfolded Itself successively so as to form a triad, would eventually return, by an ordered reversal of the process, to Its original unity, and God would be all in all. By thus excluding the extremes represented by Arius and Marcellus, the creed was choosing the middle way preferred by most conservative churchmen.

There is another formulary which, despite being misleadingly called the Third Creed of Antioch, has really no title to be an official statement of faith promulgated by the council. So far from emanating from the assembly itself, it was the formula which a certain bishop, Theophronius of Tyana, in Cappadocia, thought it prudent to deposit with his colleagues. Possibly he had been suspected of heresy, and was conscious of the desirability of clearing himself. His creed [3] opened with an unusually solemn adjuration, "God knows, Whom I call to witness to my soul, that thus I believe :

Εἰς θεὸν, πατέρα, παντοκράτορα, τὸν τῶν ὅλων κτίστην καὶ ποιητήν, ἐξ οὗ τὰ πάντα.

In God, the Father, almighty, the creator and maker of the universe, from Whom are all things;

[1] *Early history of Christian doctrine*, 5th ed., London, 1933, 172.
[2] Cf. *Fragg.* 111 ff. in Klostermann's appendix to his Eusebius IV, 208 ff.
[3] See St Athan., *De syn.* 24 (*P.G.* 26, 724 f.).

Καὶ εἰς τὸν υἱὸν αὐτοῦ τὸν μονογενῆ, θεόν,
λόγον, δύναμιν καὶ σοφίαν, τὸν κύριον
ἡμῶν Ἰησοῦν Χριστόν, δι' οὗ τὰ πάντα,
τὸν γεννηθέντα ἐκ τοῦ πατρὸς πρὸ τῶν
αἰώνων, θεὸν τέλειον ἐκ θεοῦ τελείου,
καὶ ὄντα πρὸς τὸν θεὸν ἐν ὑποστάσει,
ἐπ' ἐσχάτων δὲ τῶν ἡμερῶν κατελθόντα
καὶ γεννηθέντα ἐκ τῆς παρθένου κατὰ
τὰς γραφάς, ἐνανθρωπήσαντα, παθόντα
καὶ ἀναστάντα ἀπὸ τῶν νεκρῶν, καὶ
ἀνελθόντα εἰς τοὺς οὐρανούς, καὶ καθεσθέντα ἐκ δεξιῶν τοῦ πατρὸς αὐτοῦ, καὶ
πάλιν ἐρχόμενον μετὰ δόξης καὶ δυνάμεως
κρῖναι ζῶντας καὶ νεκρούς, καὶ μένοντα
εἰς τοὺς αἰῶνας.

Καὶ εἰς τὸ πνεῦμα τὸ ἅγιον, τὸν παράκλητον, τὸ πνεῦμα τῆς ἀληθείας, ὃ καὶ
διὰ τοῦ προφήτου ἐπηγγείλατο ὁ θεὸς
ἐκχέειν ἐπὶ τοὺς ἑαυτοῦ δούλους καὶ ὁ
κύριος ἐπηγγείλατο πέμψαι τοῖς ἑαυτοῦ
μαθηταῖς· ὃ καὶ ἔπεμψεν, ὡς αἱ πράξεις
τῶν ἀποστόλων μαρτυροῦσιν.
Εἰ δέ τις παρὰ ταύτην τὴν πίστιν διδάσκει
ἢ ἔχει ἐν ἑαυτῷ, ἀνάθεμα ἔστω, † καὶ
Μαρκέλλου τοῦ Ἀγκύρας, ἢ Σαβελλίου,
ἢ Παύλου τοῦ Σαμοσατέως, ἀνάθεμα
ἔστω καὶ αὐτὸς καὶ πάντες οἱ κοινω-
νοῦντες αὐτῷ.

And in His only-begotten Son, God, the Word, Power and Wisdom, our Lord Jesus Christ, through Whom are all things, Who was begotten from the Father before the ages, perfect God from perfect God, and Who exists as a person with God, and in the last days came down and was born from the Virgin according to the Scriptures, became man, suffered and rose again from the dead, and ascended to heaven, and sat down on the right hand of His Father, and will again come with glory and power to judge living and dead, and abides for the ages; And in the Holy Spirit, the Paraclete, the Spirit of truth, Which God through the prophet promised to pour out upon His servants and the Lord promised to send to His disciples, Which also He sent, as the Acts of the Apostles testify. But if anyone teaches or holds in his heart anything other than this faith, let him be anathema . . . of Marcellus of Ancyra, or of Sabellius, or of Paul of Samosata, let both him and all who share with him be anathema."

This creed apparently satisfied the company, and all the bishops subscribed it. Like the first one, it plainly represents a remodelled baptismal confession, although the alterations and interpolations are probably far more numerous in this case. Perhaps this is what St Athanasius had in mind when he said[1] that the formula was the composition of Theophronius himself. It is chiefly noteworthy for its strong insistence that the Son is a hypostasis, and therefore, presumably, not a mere function of the Father. Both Paul of Samosata and Marcellus had denied this, and therefore are anathematized at the end along with Sabellius. The words AND ABIDES FOR THE AGES applied to Christ reigning in glory represent another cut at Marcellus. It was his teaching, it would seem, that the council viewed with particular apprehension. It is likely that the cloud under

[1] De syn. 24 (P.G. 26, 724): συνθεὶς καὶ αὐτός.

which Theophronius stood was because of his supposed leanings in that direction. The bishops probably welcomed the opportunity of signing the disclaimer contained in the creed, and of thereby recording their disapproval of the neo-Sabellianism which Marcellus in their eyes represented.

The only official statement of faith ratified by the Dedication Council in its own name was the so-called Second Creed of Antioch.[1] According to St Athanasius's not wholly unprejudiced account, the bishops had repented of, or changed their minds about, their earlier definition (μεταγνόντες ἐπὶ τοῖς προτέροις). St Hilary gave the story a different, and more credible, twist by saying that the suspected heresy of one of their number prompted the composition of the creed (cum in suspicionem venisset unus ex episcopis quod prava sentiret). If this is correct, the guilty man may well have been Theophronius of Tyana, for the main tendency of the creed is anti-Sabellian and anti-Marcellan. It is a long, rambling document, having as a basis a typical Eastern baptismal confession greatly expanded with biblical phrases of theological import and terminating in a group of anathemas. There is an ancient tradition that the creed of Lucian of Antioch underlies this formula, and the possibility that it has some link with him cannot be dismissed.[2] Our creed runs :

Πιστεύομεν ἀκολούθως τῇ εὐαγγελικῇ καὶ ἀποστολικῇ παραδόσει εἰς ἕνα θεόν, πατέρα, παντοκράτορα, τὸν τῶν ὅλων δημιουργόν τε καὶ ποιητὴν καὶ προνοητήν, ἐξ οὗ τὰ πάντα.

Καὶ εἰς ἕνα κύριον Ἰησοῦν Χριστόν, τὸν υἱὸν αὐτοῦ τὸν μονογενῆ θεόν, δι' οὗ τὰ πάντα, τὸν γεννηθέντα πρὸ τῶν αἰώνων ἐκ τοῦ πατρός, θεὸν ἐκ θεοῦ, ὅλον ἐξ ὅλου, μόνον ἐκ μόνου, τέλειον ἐκ τελείου, βασιλέα ἐκ βασιλέως, κύριον ἀπὸ κυρίου, λόγον ζῶντα, σοφίαν ζῶσαν, φῶς ἀληθινόν, ὁδόν, ἀλήθειαν, ἀνάστασιν, ποιμένα, θύραν, ἄτρεπτόν τε καὶ ἀναλλοίωτον, τῆς θεότητος οὐσίας τε καὶ βουλῆς καὶ δυνάμεως καὶ δόξης τοῦ πατρὸς ἀπαράλλακτον εἰκόνα, τὸν πρωτότοκον πάσης

Agreeably with the evangelic and apostolic tradition we believe in one God, the Father, almighty, the creator and maker and controller of the universe, from Whom are all things; And in one Lord Jesus Christ, His Son, only-begotten God, through Whom are all things, Who was begotten before the ages from the Father, God from God, whole from whole, sole from sole, perfect from perfect, King from King, Lord from Lord, living Word, living Wisdom, true Light, Way, Truth, Resurrection, Shepherd, Door, unalterable and unchangeable, exact Image of the Godhead, substance, will, power and

[1] See St Athan., De syn. 23 (P.G. 26, 721 ff.) ; St Hil., De syn. 29 (P.L. 10, 502 ff.).
[2] For a full discussion, see G. Bardy, Recherches sur saint Lucien d'Antioche, Paris, 1936, 85 ff.

κτίσεως, τὸν ὄντα ἐν ἀρχῇ πρὸς τὸν θεόν,
λόγον θεὸν κατὰ τὸ εἰρημένον ἐν τῷ
εὐαγγελίῳ «καὶ θεὸς ἦν ὁ λόγος», δι'
οὗ τὰ πάντα ἐγένετο καὶ ἐν ᾧ τὰ πάντα
συνέστηκε· τὸν ἐπ' ἐσχάτων τῶν ἡμερῶν
κατελθόντα ἄνωθεν, καὶ γεννηθέντα ἐκ
παρθένου κατὰ τὰς γραφάς, καὶ ἄνθρωπον γενόμενον, μεσίτην θεοῦ καὶ
ἀνθρώπων, ἀπόστολόν τε τῆς πίστεως
ἡμῶν, καὶ ἀρχηγὸν τῆς ζωῆς, ὡς φησιν
ὅτι «καταβέβηκα ἐκ τοῦ οὐρανοῦ, οὐχ
ἵνα ποιῶ τὸ θέλημα τὸ ἐμόν, ἀλλὰ τὸ
θέλημα τοῦ πέμψαντός με», τὸν παθόντα
ὑπὲρ ἡμῶν, καὶ ἀναστάντα τῇ τρίτῃ
ἡμέρᾳ καὶ ἀνελθόντα εἰς οὐρανούς, καὶ
καθεσθέντα ἐν δεξιᾷ τοῦ πατρός, καὶ
πάλιν ἐρχόμενον μετὰ δόξης καὶ δυνάμεως κρῖναι ζῶντας καὶ νεκρούς.

Καὶ εἰς τὸ πνεῦμα τὸ ἅγιον, τὸ εἰς
παράκλησιν καὶ ἁγιασμὸν καὶ τελείωσιν
τοῖς πιστεύουσι διδόμενον, καθὼς καὶ ὁ
κύριος ἡμῶν Ἰησοῦς Χριστὸς διετάξατο
τοῖς μαθηταῖς, λέγων· «πορευθέντες
μαθητεύσατε πάντα τὰ ἔθνη, βαπτίζοντες
αὐτοὺς εἰς τὸ ὄνομα τοῦ πατρὸς καὶ τοῦ
υἱοῦ καὶ τοῦ ἁγίου πνεύματος», δηλονότι
πατρὸς ἀληθῶς πατρὸς ὄντος, υἱοῦ δὲ
ἀληθῶς υἱοῦ ὄντος, τοῦ δὲ ἁγίου πνεύματος ἀληθῶς ἁγίου πνεύματος ὄντος, τῶν
ὀνομάτων οὐχ ἁπλῶς οὐδὲ ἀργῶς κειμέν-
ων, ἀλλὰ σημαινόντων ἀκριβῶς τὴν
οἰκείαν ἑκάστου τῶν ὀνομαζομένων ὑπό-
στασίν τε καὶ τάξιν καὶ δόξαν, ὡς εἶναι τῇ
μέν ὑποστάσει τρία, τῇ δὲ συμφωνίᾳ ἕν.

Ταύτην οὖν ἔχοντες τὴν πίστιν, καὶ ἐξ
ἀρχῆς καὶ μέχρι τέλους ἔχοντες, ἐνώπιον
τοῦ θεοῦ καὶ τοῦ Χριστοῦ πᾶσαν αἱρετικὴν
κακοδοξίαν ἀναθεματίζομεν. καὶ εἴ τις
παρὰ τὴν ὑγιῆ τῶν γραφῶν ὀρθὴν πίστιν
διδάσκει, λέγων ἢ χρόνον ἢ καιρὸν ἢ αἰῶνα
ἢ εἶναι ἢ γεγονέναι πρὸ τοῦ γεννηθῆναι τὸν υἱόν, ἀνάθεμα ἔστω. καὶ εἴ
τις λέγει τὸν υἱὸν κτίσμα ὡς ἓν τῶν
κτισμάτων ἢ γέννημα ὡς ἓν τῶν γεν-
νημάτων ἢ ποίημα ὡς ἓν τῶν ποιημάτων,
καὶ μὴ ὡς αἱ θεῖαι γραφαὶ παραδέδωκαν
τῶν προειρημένων ἕκαστον [ἀφ'ἑκάστον],
ἢ εἴ τι ἄλλο διδάσκει ἢ εὐαγγελίζεται

glory of the Father, the first-begotten
of all creation, Who was in the beginning with God, God the Word
according to what was said in the
gospel, 'And the Word was God',
through Whom all things came into
being and in Whom all things consist, Who in the last days came down
from above, and was born from a
Virgin according to the Scriptures,
and became man, mediator of God
and men, and Apostle of our faith,
and Prince of life, as He says, 'I
came down from heaven, not to do
my own will but the will of Him Who
sent me', Who suffered for us, and
rose again on the third day and ascended to heaven, and sat down on
the Father's right hand, and will
come again with glory and power to
judge living and dead;

And in the Holy Spirit, Who is given
to believers for comfort and sancti-
cation and initiation, as also our
Lord Jesus Christ enjoined His disciples, saying, 'Go, teach all nations,
baptizing them in the name of the
Father and of the Son and of the
Holy Spirit', i.e. of a Father Who
is truly Father, and a Son Who is
truly Son, and of the Holy Spirit
Who is truly Holy Spirit, the names
not being given without meaning or
effect, but denoting accurately the
peculiar subsistence, rank and glory
of each that is named, so that they
are three in subsistence, and one in
agreement.

Holding then this faith, and holding it
from the beginning to the end, in the
sight of God and of Christ we anathematize every heretical heterodoxy.
And if anyone teaches contrary to the
sound and right faith of the Scriptures, that time or season or age
either is or has been before the generation of the Son, let him be anathema.
Or if anyone say that the Son is a
creature as one of the creatures, or
an offspring as one of the offsprings,
or a work as one of the works, and
not as the divine Scriptures have

παρ' ὃ παρελάβομεν, ἀνάθεμα ἔστω. ἡμεῖς γὰρ πᾶσι τοῖς ἐκ τῶν θείων γραφῶν παραδεδομένοις ὑπό τε προφητῶν καὶ ἀποστόλων ἀληθινῶς τε καὶ ἐμφόβως καὶ πιστεύομεν καὶ ἀκολουθοῦμεν.

handed down each of the aforesaid articles, or if he teaches or preaches besides what we have received, let him be anathema. For all that has been handed down in the divine Scriptures, whether by prophets or apostles, we do truly and reverently believe and follow.

This formula, the authentic creed of the council, is remarkable for the light it throws on current controversies as well as on the general theological position for which the Eusebian party was fighting. The intensely Scriptural tone is unmistakable. Not only is its doctrine expressed as far as possible by extracts from the Bible, but the signatories themselves claim biblical authority for their teaching and ostracize all who presume to deviate from the narrow Scriptural path. Arianism proper is excluded, and the creed piles up descriptions of the Son as UNALTERABLE AND UNCHANGEABLE and WHO WAS IN THE BEGINNING WITH GOD, as well as putting a ban on several Arian doctrines in the concluding section of the anathemas. It will be recalled, however, that Arius had had a sense of his own which he was prepared to put upon UNALTERABLE AND UNCHANGEABLE. Moreover, the Arians could have quite easily got round such a description as A CREATURE AS ONE OF THE CREATURES, for the prudent form of their teaching was that the Son, while a creature, was a perfect one and not like other creatures.[1] In fact, there are several points of resemblance between this creed and the formulary which Arius and Euzoius submitted to Constantine to secure their rehabilitation. As regards the anathemas, the addition of TIME OR SEASON OR AGE robbed the Nicene ban of much of its force, seeing that the Arians were ready to concede that the creation of time and the ages was to be attributed to the Word.

In its main drift, however, the creed is resolutely anti-Sabellian, anti-Marcellan. This comes out forcibly in the exegesis attached to the baptismal command of *Mt.* 28, 19. With its insistence on the separation of the three hypostases and on the fact that they are not just three names, it re-echoes teaching

[1] Cf. Arius's formal profession sent to St Alexander and reproduced by St Athan., *De syn.* 16 *P.G.* 26, 709): Opitz, *Urk.* 6.

which Eusebius of Caesarea had put forward at Nicaea[1] and which he later repeated specifically against Marcellus.[2] The latter had taken Asterius the Sophist, the disciple of Lucian, to task for precisely this teaching.[3] The string of descriptive phrases from the Bible (GOD FROM GOD . . . EXACT IMAGE), not to mention a number of other passages, is strongly reminiscent of language which Asterius had used and Marcellus had vigorously denounced.[4] Marcellus had asserted that such titles as "exact image of the Father", "Life", "Way", "Resurrection", "Door", etc. belonged only to the incarnate Christ,[5] whereas the creed pointedly applies them to Him in His preincarnate state. Positively it has a markedly Origenist flavour, as indeed its use of *Col.* 1, 15 shows. Its guiding conception is of three quite separate hypostases, each possessing its own subsistence and rank and glory, but bound into a unity by a common harmony of will. This reproduces exactly what Origen had taught when he spoke[6] of the Father and the Son as being "two things in subsistence, but one in agreement and harmony and identity of will (ὄντα δύο τῇ ὑποστάσει πράγματα, ἓν δὲ τῇ ὁμονοίᾳ καὶ τῇ συμφωνίᾳ καὶ τῇ ταυτότητι τοῦ βουλήματος)". Nothing could be more opposed than this hierarchically constructed Trinity to the Monarchianism recently approved at Rome and represented in its extreme form by Marcellus. The synod was working with a theology which, while by no means sympathetic to Arianism, was subordinationist and pre-Nicene. In avoiding the homoousion it must not be assumed that the bishops were consciously anti-Nicene. St Athanasius himself considered it politic at this period to employ other terms to express his meaning. They resented, and probably sincerely, any insinuation that they were undermining the Nicene decisions. Their real object was to steer a middle course between Arianism and the Sabellianism they dreaded.

A fourth symbol is traditionally connected with the

---

[1] See his letter to his church.
[2] *Con. Marcell.* 1, 1 (Klostermann IV, 4).
[3] Cf. *Fragg.* 65; 72; 74 (Klostermann IV, 197 ; 198; 199).
[4] Cf. *Frag.* 96 (Klostermann IV, 205 f.).
[5] Cf. *Frag.* 43 (Klostermann IV, 192).
[6] *Con. Cels.* 8, 12 (Koetschau II, 229 f.).

Dedication Council, though its actual origin is somewhat obscure. Its text, as given by St Athanasius and Socrates,[1] runs as follows:

Πιστεύομεν εἰς ἕνα θεόν, πατέρα, παντο-κράτορα, κτίστην καὶ ποιητὴν τῶν πάντων, ἐξ οὗ πᾶσα πατριὰ ἐν οὐρανοῖς καὶ ἐπὶ γῆς ὀνομάζεται.

Καὶ εἰς τὸν μονογενῆ αὐτοῦ υἱόν, τὸν κύριον ἡμῶν Ἰησοῦν Χριστόν, τὸν πρὸ πάντων τῶν αἰώνων ἐκ τοῦ πατρὸς γεν-νηθέντα, θεὸν ἐκ θεοῦ, φῶς ἐκ φωτός, δι' οὗ ἐγένετο τὰ πάντα, ἐν τοῖς οὐρανοῖς καὶ ἐπὶ τῆς γῆς, τὰ ὁρατὰ καὶ τὰ ἀόρατα, λόγον ὄντα καὶ σοφίαν καὶ δύναμιν καὶ ζωὴν καὶ φῶς ἀληθινόν, τὸν ἐπ' ἐσχάτων τῶν ἡμερῶν δι' ἡμᾶς ἐνανθρωπήσαντα καὶ γεννηθέντα ἐκ τῆς ἁγίας παρθένου, τὸν σταυρωθέντα καὶ ἀποθανόντα καὶ ταφέντα καὶ ἀναστάντα ἐκ νεκρῶν τῇ τρίτῃ ἡμέρᾳ, καὶ ἀναληφθέντα εἰς οὐρανόν, καὶ καθεσθέντα ἐν δεξιᾷ τοῦ πατρός, καὶ ἐρχόμενον ἐπὶ συντελείᾳ τοῦ αἰῶνος κρῖναι ζῶντας καὶ νεκροὺς καὶ ἀποδοῦναι ἑκάστῳ κατὰ τὰ ἔργα αὐτοῦ, οὗ ἡ βασιλεία ἀκατάλυτος οὖσα διαμένει εἰς τοὺς ἀπείρους αἰῶνας· ἔσται γὰρ καθεζόμενος ἐν δεξιᾷ τοῦ πατρὸς οὐ μόνον ἐν τῷ αἰῶνι τούτῳ, ἀλλὰ καὶ ἐν τῷ μέλλοντι.

Καὶ εἰς τὸ πνεῦμα τὸ ἅγιον, τουτέστι τὸν παράκλητον, ὅπερ ἐπαγγειλάμενος τοῖς ἀποστόλοις μετὰ τὴν εἰς οὐρανοὺς αὐτοῦ ἄνοδον ἀπέστειλε διδάξαι αὐτοὺς καὶ ὑπομνῆσαι πάντα, δι' οὗ καὶ ἁγιασ-θήσονται αἱ τῶν εἰλικρινῶς εἰς αὐτὸν πεπιστευκότων ψυχαί.

Τοὺς δὲ λέγοντας ἐξ οὐκ ὄντων τὸν υἱόν, ἢ ἐξ ἑτέρας ὑποστάσεως καὶ μὴ ἐκ τοῦ θεοῦ, καὶ ἦν ποτε χρόνος ὅτε οὐκ ἦν, ἀλλοτρίους οἶδεν ἡ καθολικὴ ἐκκλησία.

We believe in one God, the Father, almighty, creator and maker of all things, from Whom every family in heaven and earth is named;

And in His only-begotten Son our Lord Jesus Christ, Who was begotten from the Father before all ages, God from God, light from light, through Whom all things came into being, in heaven and on earth, visible and invisible, being Word and Wisdom and Power and Life and true Light, Who in the last days because of us became man and was born from the holy Virgin, Who was crucified and died and was buried, and rose again from the dead on the third day, and was taken up to heaven, and sat down on the Father's right hand, and will come at the end of the age to judge living and dead and to reward each accord-ing to his works, Whose reign is in-dissoluble and abides for endless ages; for He will be sitting on the Father's right hand not only in this age but also in the coming one;

And in the Holy Spirit, that is the Paraclete, Whom He sent as He promised to the Apostles after His ascent to heaven to teach them and to remind them of all things, through Whom also the souls of whose who have sincerely believed in Him will be sanctified.

But those who say that the Son is from nothing, or is from another hypostasis and is not from God, and that there was a time when He was not, the Catholic Church regards as alien.

St Athanasius's account of the matter is that, some months after they had published their first three formulae, the bishops felt dissatisfied with their work, and being indecisive in mind drew up yet a fourth statement of faith. This they despatched

[1] *De syn.* 25; *Hist. eccl.* 2, 18 (*P.G.* 26, 725 ff.; 67, 221 ff.).

to Gaul by the hands of four of their number (Narcissus of Neronias, Maris of Chalcedon, Theodore of Heraclea, and Mark of Arethusa) and delivered to the emperor Constans (he was orthodox in the Athanasian sense) at his court at Trèves. Socrates tells the more picturesque story that the four envoys who had been sent to the West with the official creed of the Dedication Council concealed it at the last moment in their clothes, and delivered this one, of their own composition, to the emperor. It remains a mystery what prompted this strange embassy of Eastern prelates to the Augustus of the West: Socrates's confused explanation that it was in response to Constans's own request for further information about the deposition of St Athanasius and Paul of Constantinople scarcely rings true. Probably E. Schwartz was right in discerning in the delegation a manoeuvre on the part of the East to satisfy Constans that a general council (for which the Western emperor was pressing, but which they were anxious to avoid) was unnecessary.[1] At any rate the intrinsic character of the formulary suggests an attempt at rapprochement between East and West. For the most part it has the air of being an old-fashioned baptismal creed. It abstains from laying down the law on the separateness of the divine hypostases, and the questionable formulae of Asterius have disappeared. It does not, of course, mention the homoousion, but there was nothing provocative about such reticence. The condemnation of Arianism is much more outspoken, and from the Western point of view much more satisfactory, than anything that had appeared in the other formularies. The insistence in the anathemas that the Son had not come into existence out of nothing, and that He was not of another hypostasis but from God, cut the ground from under any kind of Arianism. On the other hand, the authors felt free to let themselves go in their onslaught on Marcellus, whose doctrine of the limited reign of Christ was repudiated with unusual thoroughness. As a theological statement it differed substantially from the official creed of the council, and if passions had not been so excited and if the issue had not been complicated by theologically irrelevant factors, it might not have proved so unpalatable to the West.

[1] *Gesch. Athan.* IX (*Nachricht. Gött.* 1911, 514 f.).

So much for the creeds of the Dedication Council. In one well known and widely used history of doctrine[1] they are described as attempts to supersede the Nicene creed. But such an account of them misses the point in a most misleading way. It is perfectly true that all four symbols turned their back on the homoousion. The doctrine they taught or implied was a faithful replica of the average theology of the Eastern Church, the theology of which Eusebius of Caesarea was a spokesman. But to interpret this as disloyal to Nicaea is to misconceive the situation. The homoousion had not yet become a brand of discord. If the Antiochene bishops steered clear of it, St Athanasius himself apparently thought it wise to do so too. Pope Julius made no stipulation about the use of the word, and even Marcellus of Ancyra did not garnish the apology[2] he prepared for the Roman synod with it. On the other hand, though Constantine was dead, the bishops seem to have been perfectly sincere in resenting the charge of going behind Nicaea. Like everyone else, they accepted the authority of the council: only they took a negative view of its achievement as consisting in the repudiation of Arianism proper. With that rejection they themselves were ready to concur. Their *bête noire*, it would seem, was the theology of Marcellus: it was this which in every creed was seized upon with almost fanatical vituperation. The real battle at this period was between two misrepresentations of the truth, an Athanasian caricature of the Eusebians as unadulterated Arians, and an Eastern caricature of the Athanasian position as indistinguishable from that of Marcellus.

2. *From Serdica to Sirmium*

The next milestone in the history of fourth-century creeds is the council of Serdica (the present-day Sofia), held in 342, or, more probably, 343.[3] The initiative for this came from the Western emperor, the "orthodox" Constans. The Western

---

[1] J. F. Bethune-Baker, *op. cit.* 172.

[2] Cf. St Epiphan., *Pan. haer.* 72, 3 (Holl III, 258).

[3] The date is disputed. E. Schwartz, on the basis of St Athan., *Apol. ad Const.* 4 and the Collection of Theodosius the Deacon, has argued for 342 (*Gesch. Athan.* IX, *Nachricht. Gött.* 1911, 516); but J. Zeiller (*Les origines chrétiennes dans les provinces danubiennes*, Paris, 1918, 228 ff.), F. Loofs (*Theologische Studien und Kritiken*, 1909, 292 f.) and H. Hess (*The Canons of the Council of Sardica*, Oxford, 1958) give 343.

episcopate had been clamouring for a general synod of the Church for some time, and the flat refusal of their Eastern brethren to attend the Roman council in 341 had been something of a diplomatic defeat. Constans, won over to their point of view, seems to have persuaded his brother Constantius that, if the widening rift between East and West was to be closed, a united synod of both empires should be convened to settle, once and for all, the question of the deposition of St Athanasius and his colleagues, and also the question of the faith. Serdica was chosen as the meeting-place as being an important city on the frontier between the two empires and just inside the Western territory. From the first, however, the council was a fiasco so far as conciliation and collaboration were concerned. For one thing, the Eusebian party sent only 76 delegates, although they could usually muster some hundreds for such an occasion. For another, they were adamant that the bishops they had deposed, St Athanasius, Marcellus and the rest, should not have seats at the council. The aged Ossius of Cordoba, who headed the Western delegation, tried hard to secure a compromise, but all to no effect. The Orientals stuck to their guns, and eventually (they had never been happy about the general council) quitted Serdica in a body on the pretext that they had heard news of a notable victory gained by Constantius over the Persians and wanted to present their congratulations.

Before departing for Philippopolis, the Eastern bishops formed their own rival assembly and drew up an encyclical letter[1] addressed to the whole episcopate, clergy and laity of the Church. The largest part of it was occupied with recapitulating the story of St Athanasius, Marcellus and their companions, and justifying their deposition. It expressed astonishment that, notwithstanding their excommunication, they should be sitting as recognized bishops at Serdica, and condemned Julius, Ossius and the leading Westerns who had been responsible for their restoration. But a profession of faith was appended. This was none other than the so-called Fourth Creed of Antioch,[2] the formula which had been presented a few months previously to

---

[1] Cf. St Hilary, *Frag. hist.* 3, 1–29; *de syn.* 34 (*P.L.* 10, 659–78; 507 f.). H. Hess (op. cit. 16–8) argues that they drafted the letter etc. at Serdica before leaving.
[2] See above, p. 272.

Constans at Treves, expanded by some additional anathemas at the end. These run:[1]

'Ομοίως καὶ τοὺς λέγοντας τρεῖς εἶναι θεούς, ἢ τὸν Χριστὸν μὴ εἶναι θεόν, ἢ πρὸ τῶν αἰώνων μήτε Χριστὸν μήτε υἱὸν αὐτὸν εἶναι θεοῦ, ἢ τὸν αὐτὸν εἶναι πατέρα καὶ υἱὸν καὶ ἅγιον πνεῦμα, ἢ ἀγέννητον υἱόν, ἢ ὅτι οὐ βουλήσει ἢ θελήσει ἐγέννησε ὁ πατὴρ τὸν υἱόν, ἀναθεματίζει ἡ ἁγία καὶ καθολικὴ ἐκκλησία.

Likewise also those who say that there are three Gods, or that the Christ is not God, or that before the ages He is neither Christ nor Son of God, or that Father and Son and Holy Spirit are one and the same, or that the Son is unbegotten, or that the Father did not beget the Son by His choice or will, the holy and catholic Church anathematizes.

The first ideas here condemned, that there are three Gods and that Christ is not God, were scarcely positions to which any body of Christians was committed, but the Origenist doctrine of three hypostases in the divine Triad was dreaded by many as virtual tritheism. The Eastern bishops wanted to clear themselves of any suspicion on this score. The other additional anathemas were directed against Marcellus. We know, for example, that Marcellus considered such appellations as "Christ" and "Son of God" only applicable to the Word after the incarnation. To Eastern minds, moreover, his teaching seemed to involve the Sabellian view that Father, Son and Spirit constituted an identical unity, the Persons being mere names. The ban on the suggestion that the Son is unbegotten (ἀγέννητον in Greek) refers to the reluctance of Marcellus and his more extreme followers to ascribe birth in any real sense to the Word: the only "birth" was that of the historical Jesus. As for the final anathema, Marcellus belonged to those who declined to admit that the Father's "choice and will" were operative in the begetting of the Son:[2] to have said that they were would have seemed to him tantamount to saying that the Father was prior to the Son, and this bordered on Arianism. Even more significant, St Athanasius himself held that the expression "by the Father's will" was inappropriate. Since the Son was naturally the Son of the Father from all eternity, His generation transcended any act of will.[3]

[1] Only the Latin text of the complete creed survives (in St Hil., *Frag. hist.* 3, 29), but the Greek of the anathemas reappears in the *Ecthesis Macrostichos* in St Athan., *De syn.* 26 (*P.G.* 26, 728 ff.).

[2] Cf., e.g., *Frag.* 34 (Klostermann IV, 190).

[3] Cf. *Or. con. Ar.* 3, 62 (*P.G.* 26, 453 ff.).

On the whole the stand made by the Eastern bishops was moderate, if not eirenical. Apart from their determination to outlaw Marcellus's theology, they were evidently not going to put themselves in the wrong by being the aggressors. Their Western brethren were in no mood to imitate them. Under the chairmanship of Ossius and the local bishop Protogenes, they settled down to the task of rehabilitating St Athanasius, Asclepas of Gaza, and Marcellus. Then they excommunicated a long list of Eastern bishops on the ground of their alleged Arianism. These agreeable tasks having been accomplished, they gathered the results together in an encyclical letter, and appended to it a theological manifesto stating the views of the council on the doctrinal questions at issue and, in particular, defining its attitude to "Arianism". This frank, by no means lucid, pronunciamento, in the main the work of Ossius and Protogenes, is known as the Western creed of Serdica.[1]

Unlike most conciliar creeds of the period, it is a long, rambling document bearing hardly any relation to the ordinary baptismal confessions. A polemical broadside, it was once described by Harnack[2] as "the most unambiguous expression of Western thought on the subject" of the Trinity. As such it is worth careful analysis.[3] Professing to be an attack on Arianism (the extremist bishops Valens and Ursacius were pilloried by name in the opening paragraph as "two vipers begotten from the Arian asp"), the doctrine which it anathematized was scarcely that of Arius himself, but included any teaching which admitted three hypostases in the Godhead and ascribed to the Logos or Son of God an independent personal existence side by side with the Father. Herein lies its great importance, for such an official declaration of war on the Origenist theology was unprecedented. The doctrine positively inculcated was that there is only one divine hypostasis, "which the heretics themselves term *ousia*". There is but one God, one Godhead of Father, Son and Holy Spirit, one hypostasis. The hypostasis of

---

[1] For the text cf. Theodoret, *Hist. eccl.* 2, 8, 37–52 (Parmentier, 112–118). F. Loofs gives a critical edition of it in his article in *Abhandlungen der Preussischen Akademie*, 1909, 3–39. It is too long to print here.

[2] *Lehrbuch der Dogmengeschichte*, 5th ed., II, 246 n.

[3] F. Loofs has given one in the article referred to above, though not all his conclusions are acceptable.

the Son is one and the same as that of the Father. Yet the Father and the Son are not identical. "We do not say that the Father is the Son, or again that the Son is the Father: the Father is Father, and the Son of God is Son." As Logos of the Father, the Son is His power (δύναμις) and wisdom (σοφία). The technical terms employed by Marcellus were studiously avoided, and it was even asserted against him that "the Son reigns endlessly with the Father, and His kingdom has neither term nor passing-away". The theology, nevertheless, betrayed his influence at the crucial points. The Father, it was conceded, is greater than the Son, but "not because He is another hypostasis or in any way different, but because the name of Father is superior to that of Son". The explanation that They are one in virtue of harmony of will (διὰ τὴν συμφωνίαν καὶ τὴν ὁμόνοιαν), the formula borrowed from Origen by the Second Creed of Antioch,[1] was stigmatized as blasphemous and corrupt. But the way in which They are separate Persons in any comprehensible sense was not made clear.

This was, it must be obvious, an extreme and highly provocative statement, and the abusive language in which it was couched did not render it any more acceptable. In itself the theology involved was difficult enough for even moderate men in the Eastern camp to view with sympathy, but it finally slammed the door in their face by coming down decisively in favour of the formula "one hypostasis". There has been much debate as to how far it can fairly be described as the official creed of the council. All agree that it was probably the composition of Ossius and Protogenes, but the general opinion has been that the synod never in fact stamped it with its official approval. It wanted to do so, but St Athanasius, who appreciated its firebrand character, persuaded the majority to be content with the Nicene creed. But the chief authority for this version of the affair is St Athanasius[2] himself. He was writing at a time (362) when much in the Serdican creed was distinctly embarrassing to him (its insistence on "one hypostasis" did not square with the decisions of the synod of Alexandria regarding the use of *hypostasis* and *ousia*), and when it had become

---

[1] See above, p. 269 ; 271.
[2] *Tom. ad Antioch.* 5 (*P.G.* 26, 800).

his policy to uphold the Nicene symbol as the sole authoritative criterion of orthodoxy. On the other hand, it is evident that the Eustathians of Antioch to whom St Athanasius wrote about the creed supposed that it was the symbol of the council. Theodoret was of the same opinion.[1] Moreover, we have a letter [2] from Ossius to Pope Julius assuring him that the creed was not intended to dethrone the Nicaenum. It is odd that he should have taken the trouble to write such an apology for a formula which was of a purely private nature and which the synod had deliberately decided not to endorse. The true account of the matter is probably given by the historian Sozomen.[3] According to him, the creed formed, despite the embarrassment it was later to cause to St Athanasius, an authentic part of the encyclical letter. Ossius and Protogenes thought it advisable to write to Pope Julius in case he should suspect them of being disloyal to Nicaea, and the defence they pleaded was that they wanted, for the sake of clarity, to give a fuller exposition of N.[4]

Two more creeds fall to be mentioned here as belonging to this phase of the great dogmatic controversy, both of them the handiwork of the Eastern party. The first of them, the famous *Ecthesis Macrostichos*, or Long-lined Creed,[5] was carried to Milan in 345 by four bishops charged with the task of explaining the Eastern theological standpoint to their Western colleagues and the emperor Constans. The tide had meantime been flowing in favour of St Athanasius, and Constantius himself had been showing him and his supporters unwonted favour. Naturally enough, therefore, the creed breathed the spirit of appeasement. Composed probably at Antioch, it consisted of the Eastern creed of Serdica, i.e. the Fourth Creed of the Dedication Council along with the additional anathemas,[6] expanded to several times its original size by eight elucidatory paragraphs addressed to Western churchmen.[7] The most noteworthy feature of these was the scrupulous avoidance of the misleading and contentious words *hypostasis* and *ousia* and of the formula, so

---

[1] *Hist. eccl.* 2, 8, 53 (Parmentier, 118).
[2] In the collection of Theodosius the Deacon (*P.L.* 56, 839 f.).
[3] *Hist. eccl.* 3, 12, 6 (*P.G.* 67, 1065).
[4] See the discussion by F. Loofs in *Theologische Studien und Kritiken*, 1909, 291 ff.
[5] See St Athan., *De syn.* 26 ; Socrat., *Hist. eccl.* 2, 19 (*P.G.* 26, 728 ff.; 67, 224 ff.).
[6] See above, pp. 272 and 276.   [7] For text cf. Hahn 159.

much disliked in the West, "three hypostases". Instead the commentary described the three Persons as "three things and three *prosôpa* (τρία πράγματα καὶ τρία πρόσωπα)", repudiating the suggestion that this could fairly be taken as compromising the unity of the Godhead. It proclaimed the Son as "like the Father in all things", following the example of St Athanasius in his earlier works, and affirmed that the two were inseparable. The insistence on this unity was very strongly worded: "Yet in saying that the Son exists in Himself and both lives and subsists in a manner like to the Father, we do not separate Him from the Father, conceiving of space and gaps between Their unity after the fashion of bodies. For we believe that They are united with each other without mediation or distance, and that They exist inseparable, the whole of the Father embracing the Son, and the whole of the Son attached and adhering to the Father, and alone resting on the Father's bosom continually." While the language sometimes has a slightly subordinationist flavour, its assertion of belief in "the all-perfect Triad (τὴν παντέλειον τριάδα)" and "one dignity of Godhead (ἐν . . . τῆς θεότητος ἀξίωμα)" was quite unambiguous. At the same time it did not flinch from using outspoken language about Marcellus and his even more audacious disciple Photinus (a native of Ancyra who had been reared in the school of Marcellus and now occupied the see of Sirmium), or from relegating them to the execrated company of Paul of Samosata.

Unfortunately, the Western bishops who assembled in synod at Milan in 345 were not disposed to respond to this conciliatory gesture. For the moment the wind was blowing too steadily in favour of their point of view for them to be content with anything less than unconditional surrender. The one concession they were prepared to make (it must have been a matter of great satisfaction) was to condemn Photinus as a heretic.[1] It was now plain that his extravagant teaching was a serious embarrassment to them, and the sacrifice was not difficult. They insisted, however, as the price of peace that the doctrine of the three hypostases should be renounced. This seemed to them the basic error, the essential Arianism: as such they had

[1] St Hil., *Frag. hist.* 2, 19 (*P.L.* 10, 645 f.).

outlawed it at Serdica. Since the four bishops could not take that step, they were obliged to depart with their mission unaccomplished.

The second creed which must be mentioned is the one ratified at the second council of Sirmium in 351 (the first had met in 347 and had given the Eastern bishops an opportunity of registering formally their condemnation of Photinus, who, we recall, was bishop of Sirmium). This synod, which met at the bidding of Constantius (now sole emperor), was attended solely by Eastern delegates. It condemned Photinus anew, after a debate between him and Basil of Ancyra,[1] and at last succeeded in removing him from the see in which he had managed to maintain his position in spite of successive excommunications. It also published a creed,[2] known as the First Creed of Sirmium, which was none other than the now familiar Fourth Creed of the Dedication Council,[3] this time enlarged with twenty-six additional anathemas (perhaps reproducing the series of points debated between Photinus and Basil). A few of these, like the original first anathema, were aimed against Arianism or that caricature of it which was the bogy of the West. The second, for example, anathematized the statement that the Father and the Son are two Gods, just as the twenty-third condemned the notion of three Gods, and the twenty-fourth outlawed the affirmation that "the Son of God came into existence, like one of the things which have been made, by God's act of will". The great majority, however, passed the typical positions associated with Marcellus and Photinus in review and proscribed them. Among these were the assertions that the Son of God did not collaborate with the Father in the work of creation (No. 3: cf. No. 27); that the Word was not really begotten from the Father before all ages and that the birth from Mary was the real one (Nos. 4, 5, 9, 10, 27); that Scripture proves that the Only-begotten did not exist before the ages (No. 11); that the Word underwent change and suffering in the incarnation (Nos. 12, 13); that the Old Testament does not testify to the existence and activity of the Son prior to the

---

[1] Cf. St Epiphan., *Pan. haer.* 71, 1 ff. (Holl III, 250 ff.).
[2] Cf. St Athan., *De syn.* 27; Socrat., *Hist. eccl.* 2, 30 (*P.G.* 26, 736 ff; 67, 280 ff.); St Hil., *De syn.* 38 (*P.L.* 10, 509 ff.). For text cf. Hahn 160.
[3] See above, p. 272.

incarnation (Nos. 14, 15, 16, 17); that the three Persons of the Trinity form one *prosôpon* (No. 19); that the Holy Spirit is God unbegotten or is identical with the Son or is part of the Father or the Son (Nos. 20, 21, 22); that the Father's will was not involved in the begetting of the Son (No. 25: cf. No. 18); that the Son is unbegotten and without beginning (No. 26); and that the titles of Christ and Son only belong to the Word after the birth from Mary (No. 27). The philosophical jargon which the heretics used was also put under a ban. Thus such affirmations as that "the essence of God expands or contracts (τὴν οὐσίαν τοῦ θεοῦ πλατύνεσθαι ἢ συστέλλεσθαι)" (No. 6), or that "the Son makes the substance of God become expanded (πλατυνομένην τὴν οὐσίαν τοῦ θεοῦ ποιεῖν)", or that He is "the expansion of God's substance (τὸν πλατυσμὸν τῆς οὐσίας αὐτοῦ)" (No. 7), were anathematized. There was a certain ungraciousness about this exaggerated emphasis, for the leaders of the Western Church had washed their hands of Photinus in 345 at Milan (and again in 347), and it would appear that St Athanasius and his circle, while not cutting off communion with Marcellus, had severed relations with him shortly after.[1] At the same time, however, the creed strove to maintain the unity of the Godhead, which in Western eyes might have seemed imperilled by the wholesale elimination of Marcellus's safeguards, by dwelling on the fact that the Father is the one unconditioned principle (μίαν ἄναρχον τῶν ὅλων ἀρχήν). Taken as a whole, its tone was conciliatory; if the distinction of Persons was maintained, there was again no mention of three hypostases. It is not surprising that St Hilary was afterwards able to give a favourable interpretation of it.[2]

This rapid survey of the creeds published within a decade strengthens the impressions left by our study of the earlier phase. The controversy was still moving on the same plane as at the Dedication Council. The opposing forces were still, on the one side, the traditional Western Trinitarianism, with its strong sense of the unity of God and its bias in favour of Marcellus (the dangers of whose theology St Athanasius and the West generally were slow to appreciate), and, on the other,

---

[1] Cf. St Hil., *Frag. hist.* 2, 21 (*P.L.* 10, 650).
[2] *De syn.* 39 ff. (*P.L.* 10, 512 ff.).

the conservative Eastern conception of the Godhead as three hierarchically ordered hypostases. The West consistently saw this as incipient tritheism and consistently, if unfairly, branded it as Arianism. The East, equally unfairly, was for ever terrified that Western theology was slipping over into Sabellianism. There was still very little overt discussion, on the one side or the other, of the Nicene creed and its watchword *homoousios*. It is a striking fact that even the Western formula of Serdica, so often designated the "homoousian" creed, is completely innocent of reference either to Nicaea or to *homoousios*. The council of Nicaea had, of course, not been forgotten: Ossius and Proto-genes felt it necessary to reassure the Pope that the new Serdican confession was not intended to displace its creed. The East, too, was understandably impatient of the oft-repeated charge of Arianism, with its implication of disloyalty to Nicaea, and tried to make its position clear by reiterating the Nicene anathemas. But N was still in the background, neither the public rallying-point of the one party nor the target of the other's assaults.

3. *The Triumph of Arianism*

A new chapter in the history of creeds, as of the great doctrinal argument itself, opened with the final triumph of Constantius over Magnentius in August 353. Henceforth until his death in 361 he reigned as sole emperor over both East and West. As a consequence the ascendancy passed rapidly, and for a space decisively, to the anti-Athanasian, anti-Western sections of the Church. So complete was their victory, for the moment at any rate, that scruples were thrown aside and for the first time the Nicene faith began to be openly attacked. After a brief interval a powerful left wing, reviving the almost forgotten ideas of Arius himself and restating them in radical terms, emerged into prominence, and passed under the leader-ship of extremists like Aetius and Eunomius. They became known as Anomoeans, because of their teaching that the Son was unlike (ἀνόμοιος) the Father. The very sharpness of the con-flict, however, caused a rift in the ranks of those who had hitherto been suspicious of the homoousion. A door was opened for a reconciliation between the moderates in the Eastern camp, who were appalled to discover the lengths to which their more headstrong allies were prepared to go, and the Homoousians, as they were beginning to be called. The chief stumbling-block had been the close cooperation which had existed between St Athanasius and Marcellus, but these two had long since parted company. Thus, after 361, when Constantius died and agreement over terminology was reached at the council of Alexandria (362), the achievement of full mutual understanding was only a matter of time.

From our point of view one of the main points of interest in the period is the focusing of attention on the Nicene creed. The first hint of the new role it was beginning to play comes in the letter[1] which Pope Liberius addressed to Constantius in 354 in reply to the sentence pronounced on St Athanasius at the council of Arles a short time previously (353). He demanded that the emperor should convoke a universal synod with the object not only of settling the question of personalities, but also of confirming the decisions taken at Nicaea. In the following year (355), when the proposed gathering assembled at Milan, Eusebius of Vercelli, representing the Western party, produced a copy of the Nicaenum and urged that, before getting down to the rest of the business, the delegates should register their doctrinal unanimity by subscribing the Nicene faith.[2] Valens of Mursa, it is related, intervened with dramatic violence, snatching the pen from the grasp of a prelate who was about to sign, and protesting that no progress was possible by such methods. Incidents like this suggest that the Athanasian party, provoked by the ascendancy won by their opponents and the increasing extravagance of their views, had decided openly to adopt the Nicene council and its creed as their standard of orthodoxy. It will be recalled that it was about this time that St Hilary, by his own admission,[3] first became acquainted with the text of the Nicene creed. It was only a short time before this, moreover, that St Athanasius himself had begun to come out into the open with the full-blooded homoousian teaching

---

[1] St Hil., *Frag. hist.* 5, 6 (*P.L.* 10, 685 f.).
[2] Cf. St Hil., *Ad Const. Aug.* 1, 8 (*P.L.* 10, 562 f.).
[3] *De syn.* 91 (*P.L.* 10, 545): see above, p. 258.

and terminology; while just a little later we find Marius Victorinus, the famous convert, stoutly championing the Nicene doctrine in the most explicit way.[1]

The altered atmosphere was not long in making itself felt. An illuminating document is the creed[2] drawn up, in the emperor's presence, at the synod held at Sirmium (the third to meet there, attended mainly by Western bishops) in the autumn of 357, and immediately circulated to all churches. By this time the fortunes of the Athanasian party were at the lowest ebb, St Athanasius himself having been ejected with violence from his see (356) and the Western episcopate generally having abandoned him and yielded to the pressure of events. The leading spirits were the politically minded prelates Ursacius of Singidunum (Belgrade) and Valens of Mursa (Osijek), who had become Constantius's theological confidants, and the local bishop Germinius. It is unnecessary to print the Latin original of their profession of faith, for it does not conform to any of the usual creed patterns, but in translation it runs as follows:

Since there was thought to be some dispute concerning the faith, all the questions were carefully dealt with and examined at Sirmium, in the presence of our holy brothers and fellow-bishops Valens, Ursacius and Germinius. It is agreed that there is one God, almighty and Father, as it is believed throughout the whole world, and His only begotten Son Jesus Christ the Lord, our Saviour, begotten from Him before the ages. But we cannot and ought not to preach that there are two Gods, for the Lord Himself said, "I shall go to My Father and to your Father, to my God and to your God." Therefore there is one God over all, as the Apostle has taught, "Is He God of the Jews only? Is He not of the Gentiles also? Yes, He is of the Gentiles too. For there is one God, Who justifies the circumcision from faith and the uncircumcision through faith." And in all else they were in agreement and would admit of no discrepancy. But inasmuch as some or many were troubled about substance (*substantia*), which in Greek is called *usia*, that is, to make it more explicit, *homousion* or the term *homoeusion*, there ought to be no mention of these at all and no

---

[1] Cf., e.g., *Adv. Ar.* 1, 28; 2, 9; 2, 12 (*P.L.* 8, 1061; 1095; 1098); also his *Tract. de Homoous. recip.* (*P.L.* 8, 1137 ff.). The dates given for these books are 358 and 359 respectively.

[2] Cf. St Hil., *De syn.* 11 (*P.L.* 10, 487 ff.); St Athan., *De syn.* 28 (*P.G.* 26, 740 ff.). M. Meslin (*op. cit.*, 276–8) gives an excellent analysis.

one should preach them, for the reason and ground that they are not contained in inspired Scripture, and because the subject is beyond the knowledge of man, and no one can explain the nativity of the Son, regarding Whom it is written, "Who shall explain His generation?" For it is plain that only the Father knows how He begat the Son, and the Son how He was begotten by the Father. There is no question that the Father is the greater. For it can be doubtful to none that the Father is greater than the Son in honour, dignity, splendour, majesty, and in the very name of Father, the Son Himself testifying, "He Who sent Me is greater than I." And no one is ignorant that it is Catholic doctrine that there are two Persons of the Father and the Son, and that the Father is greater and the Son subordinated to the Father, together with all those things which the Father has subjected to Himself, and that the Father has no beginning and is invisible, immortal and impassible, but that the Son has been begotten from the Father, God from God, light from light, and that the generation of this Son, as has already been said, no one knows except His Father. And that the Son of God Himself, our Lord and God, as we read, took flesh or body, that is, man, from the womb of the Virgin Mary, as the angel foretold. And as all the Scriptures teach, and especially the Apostle, the doctor of the Gentiles himself, He took from the Virgin Mary manhood, through which He shared in suffering. The whole faith is summed up and is secured in this, that the Trinity must always be preserved, as we read in the gospel, "Go, baptize all nations in the name of the Father and of the Son and of the Holy Spirit." Complete, perfect is the number of the Trinity. But the Paraclete, the Spirit, is through the Son: He was sent and came according to the promise so as to instruct, teach and sanctify the apostles and all believers.

The most noteworthy things about this creed are its extraordinary emphasis on the oneness of God the Father, and its explicit prohibition of the use both of *homoousios* and *homoiousios*. St Hilary shrewdly observed that the former of these points was made at the expense of the full divinity of the Son, and went on to point out that the agnosticism professed regarding the Son's generation left the door open to believing that He was born either from nothing or from some other substance than God the Father. It is little wonder that he described the document as "the blasphemy".[1] Apart from this, it is full of

---

[1] *De syn.* 10 (*P.L.* 10, 486).

suspicious statements about the Son's subordination, and it even hints that, as opposed to the impassibility of the Father, He was in some way passible through association with the man Jesus. We may note the significant fact that, while every creed of the central Eastern party devised since the Dedication Council had contained anathemas of Arianism as a matter of course, such anathemas are for the first time conspicuously absent here. The Nicene watchword, while not declared false, is put under a ban, as one might expect in a virtually Anomoean formula. The Finnish scholar J. Gummerus gave an accurate estimate of its character when he wrote[1]: "Without directly preaching Arianism, the formula was an edict of tolerance in its favour, while the Nicene party found itself excluded from that tolerance." The Nicene creed, towards which all sections of the Church had hitherto observed a correct and tactful attitude, suddenly found itself declared unorthodox and unlawful. Ossius of Cordoba, one of the original promotors of N, now an aged man, was present at the synod, and the framers of the "Blasphemy", in their eagerness to arm their creed with as much prestige as possible, did not scruple[2] to force him, broken man as he was, to attach his signature to it too.

Put forward as a formula of peace (such the emperor naïvely supposed it might prove), the Second Creed of Sirmium was "a trumpet which was heard from one end of the empire to the other".[3] In the West it raised an immense stir, being a Western document composed in the main by Western bishops, and the result was a strengthening of the position of the Nicene creed. Shortly afterwards, for example, we find Phoebadius of .Agen describing the latter as "the perfect rule of Catholic faith",[4] and attacking the "Blasphemy". A Gallic synod attacked it too about the same time, and formally condemned it.[5] In the East the effect of the publication of the Sirmian manifesto, with the contemporaneous emergence of the extreme teachings of Aetius and Eunomius (the leaders of the Anomoean

[1] *Die homöusianische Partei bis zum Tode des Konstantius*, Leipzig, 1900, 57.
[2] Sozom., *Hist. eccl.* 4, 6 and 12 (*P.G.* 67, 1121 and 1144).
[3] H. M. Gwatkin, *Studies of Arianism*, 2nd ed., Cambridge, 1900, 162.
[4] *Con. Ar.* 6 (*P.L.* 20, 17).
[5] St Hil., *De syn.* 2 and 8 (*P.L.* 10, 481 and 485).

party), was to open the eyes of the great body of central church-men or "Semi-Arians" to the menace involved in the new, more virulent Arianism. A crisis meeting was held at Ancyra in 358 under the chairmanship of Basil, the local bishop, and the reaction was vividly expressed in the synodal letter[1] which announced its decisions. While failing to mention Nicaea and in fact condemning *homoousios* (the word, they pointed out, had been rejected by the council which sentenced Paul of Samosata), the Semi-Arians were outspoken in their hostility to the Anomoeans and insisted upon the doctrine that the Son was like the Father in substance (ὁμοιούσιος). When delegates of the synod of Ancyra, led by Basil, made contact with Con-stantius at Sirmium a little later in the same year, they suc-ceeded in winning him over to sympathy with the Semi-Arian, or homoeousian, standpoint and obtained his agreement to the drafting of a formulary reflecting it, the so-called Third Creed of Sirmium.[2] This consisted of the First Creed of Sir-mium (i.e. the second creed of the Dedication Council with anathemas directed against Paul of Samosata and Photinus) augmented with a number of anathemas which figured in the Ancyran letter.

Flushed with his success and confident of being able to steer a course between the Anomoean teaching and the troublesome homoousion, Basil of Ancyra now pressed the emperor to summon a general council which might legislate a final settle-ment. After some changes of plan and consequent delay, which the Anomoeans skilfully exploited so as to recover much of the ground they had lost, Constantius granted his request, but the dénouement proved, as the creeds which we shall now consider will show, very different from what Basil had expected. The arrangement which Constantius finally sanctioned, at the sug-gestion of the Anomoeans, was that two parallel councils should be held, one of the Western church at Rimini on the Adriatic coast of North Italy, and another of Eastern bishops at the sea-board town of Seleucia in Cilicia. Meanwhile, in May 359, a small committee met at Sirmium and, in the emperor's presence, drafted the following formulary as a working basis to be sub-

---

[1] See St Epiphan., *Pan. haer.* 73, 2–11 (Holl III, 268–284).
[2] Cf. Sozomen, *Hist. eccl.* 4, 15 (*P.G.* 67, 1152).

mitted to both councils for their discussion and, it was hoped, approval:[1]

Πιστεύομεν εἰς ἕνα τὸν μόνον καὶ ἀληθινὸν θεὸν, πατέρα, παντοκράτορα, κτίστην καὶ δημιουργὸν τῶν πάντων.

Καὶ εἰς ἕνα μονογενῆ υἱὸν τοῦ θεοῦ, τὸν πρὸ πάντων τῶν αἰώνων καὶ πρὸ πάσης ἀρχῆς καὶ πρὸ παντὸς ἐπινοουμένου χρόνου καὶ πρὸ πάσης καταληπτῆς οὐσίας γεγεννημένον ἀπαθῶς ἐκ τοῦ θεοῦ, δι' οὗ οἵ τε αἰῶνες κατηρτίσθησαν καὶ τὰ πάντα ἐγένετο· γεγεννημένον δὲ μονογενῆ, μόνον ἐκ μόνου τοῦ πατρός, θεὸν ἐκ θεοῦ, ὅμοιον τῷ γεννήσαντι αὐτὸν πατρὶ κατὰ τὰς γραφάς· οὗ τὴν γένεσιν οὐδεὶς ἐπίσταται εἰ μὴ μόνος ὁ γεννήσας αὐτὸν πατήρ. τοῦτον ἴσμεν τοῦ θεοῦ μονογενῆ υἱὸν νεύματι πατρικῷ παραγενόμενον ἐκ τῶν οὐρανῶν εἰς ἀθέτησιν ἁμαρτίας, καὶ γεννηθέντα ἐκ Μαρίας τῆς παρθένου, καὶ ἀναστραφέντα μετὰ τῶν μαθητῶν, καὶ πᾶσαν τὴν οἰκονομίαν πληρώσαντα κατὰ τὴν πατρικὴν βούλησιν, σταυρωθέντα καὶ ἀποθανόντα, καὶ εἰς τὰ καταχθόνια κατελθόντα, καὶ τὰ ἐκεῖσε οἰκονομήσαντα, ὃν πυλωροὶ ᾅδου ἰδόντες ἔφριξαν, καὶ ἀναστάντα ἐκ νεκρῶν τῇ τρίτῃ ἡμέρᾳ, καὶ ἀναστραφέντα μετὰ τῶν μαθητῶν, καὶ πᾶσαν τὴν οἰκονομίαν πληρώσαντα, καὶ τεσσαράκοντα ἡμερῶν πληρουμένων ἀναληφθέντα εἰς τοὺς οὐρανούς, καὶ καθεζόμενον ἐκ δεξιῶν τοῦ πατρός, καὶ ἐλευσόμενον ἐν τῇ ἐσχάτῃ ἡμέρᾳ τῆς ἀναστάσεως τῇ δόξῃ τῇ πατρικῇ ἀποδιδόντα ἑκάστῳ κατὰ τὰ ἔργα αὐτοῦ.

Καὶ εἰς τὸ ἅγιον πνεῦμα, ὃ αὐτὸς ὁ μονογενὴς τοῦ θεοῦ Ἰησοῦς Χριστὸς ἐπηγγείλατο πέμψαι τῷ γένει τῶν ἀνθρώπων, τὸν παράκλητον, κατὰ τὸ γεγραμμένον «ἀπέρχομαι πρὸς τὸν πατέρα μου καὶ παρακαλέσω τὸν πατέρα, καὶ ἄλλον παράκλητον πέμψει ὑμῖν, τὸ πνεῦμα τῆς ἀληθείας· ἐκεῖνος ἐκ τοῦ ἐμοῦ λήψεται καὶ διδάξει καὶ ὑπομνήσει ὑμᾶς πάντα».

We believe in one only and true God, the Father, almighty, creator and framer of all things;

And in one only-begotten Son of God, Who was begotten impassibly from God before all ages and before all beginning and before all conceivable time and before all comprehensible essence, through Whom the ages were fashioned and all things came into existence, begotten only-begotten, alone from the Father alone, God from God, like the Father Who begat Him according to the Scriptures, Whose generation no one knows save only the Father Who begat Him. We know that this only begotten Son of God, at the Father's bidding, came from heaven for the abolition of sin, and was born from the Virgin Mary, and consorted with the disciples, and fulfilled all the economy according to the Father's will, was crucified and died, and descended to hell, and regulated things there, Whom the gatekeepers of hell saw and shuddered, and rose again from the dead on the third day, and consorted with the disciples, and fulfilled all the economy, and when forty days were completed was taken up to heaven, and sits on the right hand of the Father, and will come on the last day of the resurrection with the glory of the Father, rendering to each according to his deeds;

And in the Holy Spirit, Whom the Only-begotten of God, Jesus Christ, Himself promised to send to the race of men, the Paraclete, as it is written, 'I go to My Father, and I shall pray the Father, and He will send you another Paraclete, the Spirit of truth: He shall take of Mine, and shall teach and remind you of all things.'

---

[1] In St Athan., De syn. 8 (P.G. 26, 692 f.). Socrates, in Hist. eccl. 2, 37 (P.G. 67, 305), reports that the original was Latin.

Τὸ δὲ ὄνομα τῆς οὐσίας διὰ τὸ ἁπλούστερον ὑπὸ τῶν πατέρων τεθεῖσθαι, ἀγνοούμενον δὲ ὑπὸ τῶν λαῶν σκάνδαλον φέρειν, διὰ τὸ μήτε τὰς γραφὰς τοῦτο περιέχειν, ἤρεσε τοῦτο περιαιρεθῆναι καὶ παντελῶς μηδὲ μίαν μνήμην οὐσίας ἐπὶ θεοῦ εἶναι τοῦ λοιποῦ, διὰ τὸ τὰς θείας γραφὰς μηδαμοῦ περὶ πατρὸς καὶ υἱοῦ οὐσίας μεμνῆσθαι. ὅμοιον δὲ λέγομεν τὸν υἱὸν τῷ πατρὶ κατὰ πάντα, ὡς καὶ αἱ ἅγιαι γραφαὶ λέγουσί τε καὶ διδάσκουσιν.

But whereas the term 'substance' has been adopted by the fathers in simplicity, but being unknown by the people gives offence, because neither do the Scriptures contain it, it has seemed good to remove it, and that there should be no further mention of substance in regard to God, because the divine Scriptures nowhere refer to the substance of the Father or the Son. But we say the Son is like the Father in all things, as the holy Scriptures themselves declare and teach.

Because of the elaborate dating prefixed to it ("in the consulate of the most illustrious Flavians, Eusebius and Hypatius, on the eleventh day before the calends of June"), this creed, the Fourth of Sirmium, became known, rather sardonically, as the Dated Creed. Its critics thought it ridiculous to suggest that the Catholic faith could be dated.[1] The final drafting of it is supposed to have been the work of Mark of Arethusa. It seems to have been based upon a baptismal creed of the conventional pattern, although the alterations and interpolations have completely disrupted the ground-plan. Some features in the underlying text hint at a kinship with the creed of Antioch. Such clauses as ONE ONLY AND TRUE GOD and THROUGH WHOM THE AGES WERE FASHIONED, etc. recall the very similar terminology employed in the symbol quoted in Latin by John Cassian.[2] Again, this creed stands out as being the first to give official recognition to the Descent to Hell. But its real importance is theological. It was a mediating manifesto, designed as far as possible to please everybody, and it gave expression to the new "Homoean" formula of compromise proposed by Acacius of Caesarea and accepted by the emperor—LIKE IN ALL RESPECTS—and strictly avoided technical terms. The "orthodox", it was thought, could note with satisfaction that it proclaimed the Son's generation in a way incompatible with Arianism. The new Arians for their part could congratulate themselves that the use of *ousia*, and with it the homoousion, was condemned: the Son could not be described even as LIKE IN SUBSTANCE.

[1] Cf. St Athan., *De syn.* 3 (*P.G.* 26, 685).
[2] See above, p. 184 f.

Basil of Ancyra and his influential party would have liked to have seen LIKE IN SUBSTANCE sanctioned, but had to be content with LIKE IN ALL THINGS. At least that went further than Valens and Ursacius wanted, with their belief that the Son was like the Father "in will and energy", but unlike Him in substance. When it came to appending their signatures, the leaders of the several groups could not conceal their disgruntlement. Valens, we are told, tried to write simply LIKE, leaving out IN ALL THINGS, and had to be pulled up by Constantius. Basil, too, in the copy which Valens was to take to Rimini with him, added a lengthy postscript expounding his own interpretation of the creed and emphasizing that the Son was like the Father "in all things, and not just in will, but in hypostasis and in existence and in substance".[1]

This creed appears again, in a dress slightly but significantly altered so as to bring it more into harmony with the taste of Valens and Ursacius, as the formulary signed on 10 October, 359 in the Thracian town of Niké by a delegation of Western bishops from the council sitting at Rimini.[2] This crowded assembly (over four hundred bishops are said to have attended) had shown itself ardently Homoousian, had acclaimed the Nicene creed and the use of "substance", had deposed and excommunicated Ursacius, Valens and their coadjutors, and had sent an embassy to Constantius to acquaint him with their decisions. The emperor, as we can appreciate, was by no means pleased that his draft Homoean creed had been so hastily brushed aside. The envoys were directed to Niké, where they were gradually worn down by the protracted delay as well as by the propaganda and threats to which they were subjected.[3] Eventually, contrary to their instructions, they consented to sign a revision of the Dated Creed, which was now put forth as "Nicene". Most of the alterations were purely verbal and of little consequence. Of greater moment, however, as betokening a substantial weakening of the draft creed agreed at Sirmium, were (a) the omission of IN ALL THINGS with LIKE, and (b) the prohibition not only of *ousia* but also of "one hypostasis" in the

---

[1] For these details, see St Epiphan., *Pan. haer.* 73, 22 (Holl III, 295).
[2] For text see Theodoret, *Hist. eccl.* 2, 21, 3–7 (Parmentier, 145 f.) ; Hahn 164.
[3] St Hil., *Frag. hist.* 8, 4 (*P.L.* 10, 701 f.).

doctrine of the Trinity ("nor of the *prosôpon* of the Father and of the Son and of the Holy Spirit must the phrase ONE HYPO-STASIS be used").

The subscription of this creed was a demonstration that the Arians were cleverly exploiting the new Homoean compromise to their own advantage. Meanwhile events were taking a not dissimilar course at the parallel Eastern council at Seleucia. The great majority were Homoeousians, led by George of Laodicea, and wanted to endorse officially the Second Creed of the Dedication Council. Indeed, they ratified it at the second session (28 September) behind closed doors, the minority of Homoeans led by Acacius having withdrawn. At the next session, however, on 29 September the minority returned and, with the imperial commissioner Leonas acting as their spokesman, put forward their creed.[1] It opened with a short preface which declared that they did not reject the authentic faith published at the Dedication Council, but that trouble had arisen since then because of the words *homoousios, homoiousios,* and *anomoios.* "We accordingly repudiate *homoousios* and *homoiousios* as alien to Holy Scripture, and we anathematize *anomoios.*" The doctrine to be accepted was that the Son was "like the Father", as the Apostle had said of Him that He was the image of the invisible God. Then followed their creed, which was in effect the Dated Creed of Sirmium with some minor alterations. The crucial words IN ALL THINGS were, however, omitted after LIKE. There followed a protracted debate as to what exactly was implied by "like", and in the end Leonas dissolved the council without the matter having been put finally to the vote. Like the council at Rimini, both groups sent delegations to the emperor at Constantinople to report their decisions, but Constantius was determined that the Homoeousians, no less than the Western Homoousians, should sign his Homoean draft creed. After a long struggle lasting well into the night he wrung their signatures from them on 31 December, 359.[2] Thus the Homoean victory was complete, and it was this sequence of events which St Jerome had in mind when he wrote that "the

---

[1] Cf. St. Athan., *De syn.* 29; Socrat., *Hist. eccl.* 2, 40 (*P.G.* 26, 744 f.; 67, 337 ff.); St. Epiphan., *Pan. haer.* 73, 25 (Holl III, 298 f.).
[2] Cf. Sozomen, *Hist. eccl.* 4, 23 (*P.G.* 67, 1188).

whole world groaned and wondered to find itself Arian (*ingemuit totus orbis, et Arianum se esse miratus est*)".[1]

From the official point of view, therefore, the faith of the Church was now Homoean. To complete the work, however, it was necessary to bring the decisions of the delegates of Rimini and Seleucia before a great united council and obtain its final ratification for them. To this end a synod,[2] dominated by Homoeans and consisting largely of bishops from Bithynia, was held in Constantinople in January 360. The following is the creed which it promulgated[3]:

Πιστεύομεν εἰς ἕνα θεόν πατέρα, παντοκράτορα, ἐξ οὗ τὰ πάντα.

Καὶ εἰς τὸν μονογενῆ υἱὸν τοῦ θεοῦ, τὸν πρὸ πάντων αἰώνων καὶ πρὸ πάσης ἀρχῆς γεννηθέντα ἐκ τοῦ θεοῦ, δι' οὗ τὰ πάντα ἐγένετο, τὰ ὁρατὰ καὶ τὰ ἀόρατα, γεννηθέντα δὲ μονογενῆ, μόνον ἐκ μόνου τοῦ πατρός, θεὸν ἐκ θεοῦ, ὅμοιον τῷ γεννήσαντι αὐτὸν πατρὶ κατὰ τὰς γραφάς, οὗ τὴν γένεσιν οὐδεὶς γινώσκει, εἰ μὴ μόνος ὁ γεννήσας αὐτὸν πατήρ. τοῦτον οἴδαμεν μονογενῆ θεοῦ υἱὸν πέμποντος τοῦ πατρὸς παραγεγενῆσθαι ἐκ τῶν οὐρανῶν ὡς· γέγραπται, ἐπὶ καταλύσει τῆς ἁμαρτίας καὶ τοῦ θανάτου, καὶ γεννηθέντα ἐκ πνεύματος ἁγίου, ἐκ Μαρίας τῆς παρθένου τὸ κατὰ σάρκα ὡς γέγραπται, καὶ ἀναστραφέντα μετὰ τῶν μαθητῶν, καὶ πάσης τῆς οἰκονομίας πληρωθείσης κατὰ τὴν πατρικὴν βούλησιν, σταυρωθέντα καὶ ἀποθανόντα καὶ ταφέντα καὶ εἰς τὰ καταχθόνια κατεληλυθότα, ὅντινα καὶ αὐτὸς ὁ ᾅδης ἔπτηξεν, ὅστις καὶ ἀνέστη ἀπὸ τῶν νεκρῶν τῇ τρίτῃ ἡμέρᾳ καὶ διέτριψε μετὰ τῶν μαθητῶν, καὶ πληρωθεισῶν τεσσαράκοντα ἡμερῶν ἀνελήφθη εἰς οὐρανοὺς καὶ καθέζεται ἐν δεξιᾷ τοῦ πατρός, ἐλευσόμενος ἐν τῇ ἐσχάτῃ ἡμέρᾳ τῆς ἀναστάσεως ἐν τῇ πατρικῇ δόξῃ, ἵνα ἀποδῷ ἑκάστῳ κατὰ τὰ ἔργα αὐτοῦ.

We believe in one God, the Father, almighty, from Whom are all things; And in the only begotten Son of God, Who was begotten from God before all ages and before all beginning, through Whom all things came into existence, visible and invisible, begotten only-begotten, alone from the Father alone, God from God, like the Father Who begot Him according to the Scriptures, Whose generation no one knows save alone the Father Who begot Him. We know that this only-begotten Son of God, the Father sending Him, came from heaven as it is written for the destruction of sin and death, and was born from the Holy Spirit, from the Virgin Mary as regards the flesh as it is written, and consorted with the disciples, and having fulfilled all the economy according to the Father's will was crucified and died, and was buried and descended to the lower world (at Whom hell itself quailed): Who also rose again from the dead on the third day, and sojourned with the disciples, and when forty days were fulfilled was taken up to heaven, and sits on the Father's right hand, purposing to come on the last day of the resurrection in the Father's glory so as to render to each according to his deeds.

[1] *Dial. con. Lucif.* 19 (*P.L.* 23, 172).
[2] For this synod, see Sozomen, *Hist. eccl.* 4, 24 (*P.G.* 67, 1188 ff.).
[3] Cf. St Athan., *De syn.* 30 (*P.G.* 26, 745 ff.).

Καὶ εἰς τὸ ἅγιον πνεῦμα, ὅπερ αὐτὸς ὁ μονογενὴς τοῦ θεοῦ υἱὸς ὁ Χριστὸς ὁ κύριος καὶ θεὸς ἡμῶν ἐπηγγείλατο πέμπειν τῷ γένει τῶν ἀνθρώπων παράκλητον, καθάπερ γέγραπται «τὸ πνεῦμα τῆς ἀληθείας», ὅπερ αὐτοῖς ἔπεμψεν ὅτε ἀνῆλθεν εἰς τοὺς οὐρανούς.

Τὸ δὲ ὄνομα τῆς οὐσίας, ὅπερ ἁπλούστερον ὑπὸ τῶν πατέρων ἐτέθη, ἀγνοούμενον δὲ τοῖς λαοῖς σκάνδαλον ἔφερε, διότι μηδὲ αἱ γραφαὶ τοῦτο περιέχουσιν, ἤρεσε περιαιρεθῆναι καὶ παντελῶς μηδεμίαν μνήμην τοῦ λοιποῦ γίνεσθαι, ἐπειδήπερ καὶ αἱ θεῖαι γραφαὶ οὐδαμῶς ἐμνημόνευσαν περὶ οὐσίας πατρὸς καὶ υἱοῦ, καὶ γὰρ οὐδὲ ὀφείλει ὑπόστασις περὶ πατρὸς καὶ υἱοῦ καὶ ἁγίου πνεύματος ὀνομάζεσθαι. ὅμοιον δὲ λέγομεν τῷ πατρὶ τὸν υἱὸν ὡς λέγουσιν αἱ θεῖαι γραφαὶ καὶ διδάσκουσι. πᾶσαι δὲ αἱ αἱρέσεις αἵ τε ἤδη πρότερον κατεκρίθησαν καὶ αἵτινες ἐὰν καινότεραι γένωνται ἐναντίαι τυγχάνουσαι τῆς ἐκτεθείσης ταύτης γραφῆς, ἀνάθεμα ἔστωσαν.

And in the Holy Spirit, Whom the only-begotten Son of God Himself, Christ our Lord and God, promised to send as a Paraclete to the race of men, as it is written, 'The Spirit of truth', Whom He sent to them when He had ascended to heaven. But as for the name 'substance', which was adopted simply by the fathers, but being unknown to the people occasioned offence, because the Scriptures themselves do not contain it, it has pleased us that it should be abolished and that no mention at all should be made of it henceforth, since indeed the divine Scriptures nowhere have made mention of the substance of Father and Son. Nor indeed should the term hypostasis be used of Father and Son and Holy Spirit. But we say the Son is like the Father, as the divine Scriptures say and teach. But let all the heresies which have either been condemned previously, or have come about more recently and are in opposition to this creed, be anathema.

This is the last of the long line of creeds promulgated in this era so prolific in their manufacture. The synod which ratified it expressly rejected all previous symbols, and forbade the formulation of new ones in the future. In itself the new creed represented the complete triumph of that Homoean compromise which attempted to drive a mediating road between the irreconcilable positions of the Anomoeans on the one hand, and of the Homoousians and the Homoeousians on the other. It is, of course, the creed of Niké, and so the Dated Creed of Sirmium, in a slightly altered dress. It became the official formula of what was henceforth to be known as Arianism, especially among the barbarians on the outskirts of the empire. It was not for nothing that Ulfilas, the national bishop of a colony of Goths established on the banks of the Danube, whom chance had brought to the imperial city, shared in the deliberations of the council.[1] Arianism, it will be appreciated, is really a misnomer, for the creed asserts none of the articles

[1] Cf. Socrates, *Hist. eccl.* 2, 41; Sozomen, *Hist. eccl.* 4, 24 (*P.G.* 67, 349; 1189).

of the old heresy and explicitly condemns Anomoeanism. Its deliberate vagueness, however, made it capable of being recited by Christians with very different sets of ideas. Comprehension was Constantius's aim, and the term LIKE, without any qualification or addition, seemed better adapted to achieve this than question-begging phrases which were tied up 'with elaborate systems of speculative theology. The creed was circulated to all the bishops of Christendom with an imperial letter commanding them either to sign it or take the consequences.[1]

At this point our survey may be fittingly brought to a close. It is not for a book like this, devoted solely to the study of credal formulae and concerned only indirectly with the history of doctrine, to trace the stages by which in the course of the next twenty years the Nicene faith reasserted itself and made it possible for a creed giving expression to the homoousian doctrine to oust and supersede the speciously neutral formula of Constantinople.

---

[1] Cf. Socrates, *Hist. eccl.* 2, 43; Sozomen, *Hist. eccl.* 4, 26 (*P.G.* 67, 353; 1197).

CHAPTER X

THE CONSTANTINOPOLITAN CREED

1. *The Tradition about C*

BY far the most influential credal product of the fourth century was the formula which is sometimes technically called the Niceno-Constantinopolitan creed.[1] Ordinary Christians are familiar with it as the creed of the Holy Eucharist, where it is misnamed the Nicene creed. Its hybrid title combines the popular but erroneous tradition that it is none other than the true Nicene creed enlarged with the theory, widely held since the middle of the fifth century at any rate, that the occasion of its enlargement was the second general council, held at Constantinople in 381. Of all existing creeds it is the only one for which ecumenicity, or universal acceptance, can be plausibly claimed. Unlike the purely Western Apostles' Creed, it was admitted as authoritative in East and West alike from 451 onwards, and it has retained that position, with one significant variation in its text, right down to the present day. So far from displacing it, the Reformation reaffirmed its binding character and gave it a new lease of life and an extended currency by translating it into the vernacular tongues. It is thus one of the few threads by which the tattered fragments of the divided robe of Christendom are held together. Yet the circumstances of its composition and promulgation, as well as the course of its history, are far from clear. It will be the business of this and the following chapter to attempt to unravel the tangled skein of problems which they raise.

First of all, the original text of the creed, known as C for short, must be established. Its first appearance, at all events as an official formulary, was at the council of Chalcedon (451). At the second session of the council, on 10 October, the Nicene

---

[1] The name seems to have been first applied to it by Joh. Benedikt Carpzov (Carpzovius) in the middle of the seventeenth century. Cf. his *Isagoge in libros ecclesiarum Lutheranarum symbolicos*, Leipzig, 3rd ed., 1690, 57.

creed having been publicly read and acclaimed, the imperial commissioners ordered "the faith of the 150 fathers" to be read out too.[1] The description they used was the one popularly applied to the council of Constantinople of 381. Aetius, the archdeacon of the capital city, immediately got up and recited our creed from a written document. It again played a prominent part at the fifth and sixth sessions,[2] on 22 and 25 October, when it was incorporated along with the Nicene creed in the definition adopted by the council. On the latter occasion the definition embodying it was signed, in the presence of the emperor Marcian, by the papal legates and all the bishops present. The minutes, or *acta*, of the council of Chalcedon, which survive in full, thus constitute our primary source for the creed. The Greek text printed below, along with a translation, reproduces the version read out at the second session as it appears in the magisterial edition of G. L. Dossetti.[3]

Πιστεύομεν εἰς ἕνα θεόν, πατέρα, παντο-κράτορα, ποιητὴν οὐρανοῦ καὶ γῆς, ὁρατῶν τε πάντων καὶ ἀοράτων.

We believe in one God, the Father, almighty, maker of heaven and earth, of all things visible and invisible;

Καὶ εἰς ἕνα κύριον Ἰησοῦν Χριστόν, τὸν υἱὸν τοῦ θεοῦ τὸν μονογενῆ, τὸν ἐκ τοῦ πατρὸς γεννηθέντα πρὸ πάντων τῶν αἰώνων, φῶς ἐκ φωτός, θεὸν ἀληθινὸν ἐκ θεοῦ ἀληθινοῦ, γεννηθέντα οὐ ποιη-θέντα, ὁμοούσιον τῷ πατρί, δι' οὗ τὰ πάντα ἐγένετο, τὸν δι' ἡμᾶς τοὺς ἀνθρώπους καὶ διὰ τὴν ἡμετέραν σωτη-ρίαν κατελθόντα ἐκ τῶν οὐρανῶν καὶ σαρκωθέντα ἐκ πνεύματος ἁγίου καὶ Μαρίας τῆς παρθένου καὶ ἐνανθρωπή-σαντα, σταυρωθέντα τε ὑπὲρ ἡμῶν ἐπὶ Ποντίου Πιλάτου, καὶ παθόντα καὶ ταφέντα, καὶ ἀναστάντα τῇ τρίτῃ ἡμέρᾳ κατὰ τὰς γραφάς, καὶ ἀνελθόντα εἰς τοὺς οὐρανούς, καὶ καθεζόμενον ἐν δεξιᾷ τοῦ πατρός, καὶ πάλιν ἐρχόμενον μετὰ δόξης κρῖναι ζῶντας καὶ νεκρούς · οὗ τῆς βασιλείας οὐκ ἔσται τέλος.

And in one Lord Jesus Christ, the only-begotten Son of God, begotten from the Father before all ages, light from light, true God from true God, begotten not made, of one substance with the Father, through Whom all things came into existence, Who because of us men and because of our salvation came down from heaven, and was incarnate from the Holy Spirit and the Virgin Mary and became man, and was crucified for us under Pontius Pilate, and suffered and was buried, and rose again on the third day according to the Scriptures and ascended to heaven, and sits on the right hand of the Father, and will come again with glory to judge living and dead, of Whose kingdom there will be no end;

---

[1] *A.C.O.* II, I, ii, 79 f. G. I. Dossetti (*Il simbolo di Nicea e di Costantinopoli*, 76 n.) shows that this was the second, not (as Schwartz held) the third, session.
[2] *A.C.O.* II, I, ii, 128 and 141. [3] *Op. cit.*, 244–50.

Καὶ εἰς τὸ πνεῦμα τὸ ἅγιον, τὸ κύριον καὶ ζωοποιόν, τὸ ἐκ τοῦ πατρὸς ἐκπορευόμενον, τὸ σὺν πατρὶ καὶ υἱῷ συμπροσκυνούμενον καὶ συνδοξαζόμενον, τὸ λαλῆσαν διὰ τῶν προφητῶν· εἰς μίαν ἁγίαν καθολικὴν καὶ ἀποστολικὴν ἐκκλησίαν. ὁμολογοῦμεν ἓν βάπτισμα εἰς ἄφεσιν ἁμαρτιῶν· προσδοκῶμεν ἀνάστασιν νεκρῶν καὶ ζωὴν τοῦ μέλλοντος αἰῶνος. ἀμήν.

And in the Holy Spirit, the Lord and life-giver, Who proceeds from the Father, Who with the Father and the Son is together worshipped and together glorified, Who spoke through the prophets; in one holy Catholic and apostolic Church. We confess one baptism to the remission of sins; we look forward to the resurrection of the dead and the life of the world to come. Amen.

There can be no doubt that the text of C, as of N, publicly recited at the second Chalcedonian session and reproduced above represents the primitive, authentic shape of the creed. Whether or not it was actually composed and ratified in 381 (we shall spend some time sifting this tradition a little later), its connection with Constantinople was apparently taken for granted. Thus the motive for inviting the archdeacon of the imperial city, Aetius, to read it out (whatever the motive for calling on Eunomius to read out N) was plainly to make sure of an accurate version. The texts to which the assembly listened had been extracted from the archives in which the original documents were presumed to have been deposited. It should be observed that the texts embodied in the Definition appear to have differed in several respects from those recited at the second session, and that E. Schwartz once suggested[1] that they were deliberately modified, at the request of Marcian and the Empress Pulcheria, so as to be brought into closer harmony with each other. Whatever the final verdict on this difficult question may be,[2] we may rest content that it can do nothing to upset our confidence in the antiquity and authority of the version of C quoted at the second session. It is interesting to notice that the creed was formally rehearsed and subscribed on 16 September, 680, at the eighteenth session of the sixth general council, the third of Constantinople, and that it is the form printed above that the recorded minutes preserve.[3]

Having settled the text, let us now turn to the problem of C's identity. Reference has already been made to the universal

---

[1] Z.N.T.W. xxv, 1926, 38 ff.
[2] For criticism of Schwartz cf. J. Lebon, R.H.E. xxxii, 1936, 809 ff.; Dossetti, op. cit., 296 ff.
[3] Cf. Mansi XI, 633.

tradition that it was the symbol of the council of Constantinople. At Chalcedon it was introduced as such, and the fathers apparently (we shall consider their attitude more closely later) accepted the description without demur. In the form prevalent from the sixth century onwards the tradition asserted that C was simply N elaborated by the interpolation of clauses designed to counter heresies which had cropped up subsequently to Nicaea. There are hints in the minutes of the council of Chalcedon that the theory of a revision of N was already in the making. At the first session,[1] for example, Eusebius of Dorylaeum and Diogenes of Cyzicus jumped up and accused Eutyches (whose case, it will be recalled, was under investigation) of falsehood in denying that the faith of the Nicene council could receive any additions. "The creed received additions", cried Diogenes, "from the holy fathers on account of the perverse notions of Apollinarius and Valentinus and Macedonius and men like them. The words WHO CAME DOWN AND WAS INCARNATE FROM THE HOLY SPIRIT AND THE VIRGIN MARY were inserted into the creed, but Eutyches has left them out because he is an Apollinarian. . . . For the expression which the holy fathers at Nicaea used, viz. WAS INCARNATE, the holy fathers who came later clarified by adding FROM THE HOLY SPIRIT AND THE VIRGIN MARY." Though he did not explicitly mention C, it is probable that Diogenes had it in mind when he spoke of an expanded version of N. His statement was not allowed to pass unchallenged. The Egyptian bishops at once protested against the idea of anything having been added to the creed of the Nicene fathers, and declared that Eutyches had done right to quote it in its original form. But the episode is proof that, even at this relatively early date, C was being regarded as an expansion of N carried out by the 150 fathers.

The same point of view came to the fore on several occasions at Chalcedon. For example, at the fourth session, when members were giving their testimony to the agreement of St Leo's *Tome* with N and C, Florentius of Adrianopolis in Pisidia characterized our creed as "proclaiming clearly that our Lord Jesus Christ was incarnate by the Holy Spirit and the Virgin

[1] *A.C.O.* II, I, i, 91.

Mary".[1] In the Definition itself the council spoke of "the decisions ratified by the 150 fathers at Constantinople with a view to the destruction of the heresies which had then sprung up as well as for the confirmation of our same Catholic and apostolic faith".[2] Finally, there is the memorandum which the council addressed to the emperor justifying their acceptance of St Leo's *Tome* against the charge of innovating in matters of faith. In this they pointed out[3] that it had proved necessary in the past to make explanatory additions to the rule of faith with a view to rebutting heresy, and as an illustration they instanced the words AND IN THE HOLY SPIRIT from the Nicene creed. Sound believers, they said, would have found this perfectly adequate, but current attacks on the status of the Spirit had determined "those who came after" (οἱ μετὰ ταῦτα: the routine phrase for the Constantinopolitan fathers) to describe Him as "Lord and God, and having His procession from the Father". Here again we have a transparent clue to their conception of C.

In subsequent centuries the accepted theory of C's origin conformed to this pattern, with a growing emphasis on the basic identity of the two creeds. A very instructive example is provided by the Monophysite usurper Basiliscus, who obtained possession of the imperial throne in 475. One of his first acts was to publish an encyclical setting aside the council of Chalcedon and the *Tome* of Pope Leo, and affirming that the one and only valid formula was the Nicene creed of the 318 fathers. At the same time he prescribed that the definitions drawn up by the 150 fathers as a reply to calumniators of the Holy Spirit should continue to hold good, and plainly regarded the council of 381 as having "sealed (ἐπεσφράγισαν)" N and elucidated its meaning.[4] Zeno revealed precisely the same attitude in the *Henoticon*, or edict of union, which he published in 482. He insisted that the only symbol which should be professed was that of the 318 fathers, "which the 150 assembled at Constantinople confirmed".[5] The viewpoint of Justinian was

---

[1] *A.C.O.* II, I, ii, 106.
[2] *A.C.O.* II, I, ii, 127.
[3] *A.C.O.* II, I, iii, 111.
[4] Evagrius, *Hist. eccl.* 3, 4 (*P.G.* 86, 2600 f.).
[5] Evagrius, *Hist. eccl.* 3, 14 (*P.G.* 86, 2621).

exactly the same as that of these Monophysites, and in a decree
of 533[1] he affirmed his loyalty to "the holy instruction or symbol
. . . set forth by the 318 holy fathers, which the 150 holy
fathers in this royal city explained and clarified". When next
it comes before our notice, at the council held at Constantinople
in 536,[2] and then at the fifth ecumenical council (also held at
Constantinople) in 553, the theory seems to be established that
C is an improved version of N. According to the minutes of
the latter,[3] "the same holy fathers [the 150], while following
the orthodox faith as expounded by the 318 holy fathers, added
an explanation regarding the deity of the Holy Spirit and gave
a complete account of the dispensation of the incarnate Word".
In the middle ages the original difference of C from N was
forgotten and in most circles it became known as the Nicene
creed. Wherever the difference was recalled, however, C was
treated as identical with N save for the insertion of material
demanded by the emergence of later heresies. For example, at
the provincial synod of Forum Iulii (Cividale del Friuli, in
Venetia), which St Paulinus of Aquileia convened in 796 or
797, C was published (in its Latin dress, of course) with the
addition of the clause AND FROM THE SON (*filioque*) of the procession of the Holy Spirit. In his explanatory discourse St
Paulinus sought to justify the inclusion of the novel clause, and
appealed to the precedent of the fathers of Constantinople.
They too, he pointed out, had been obliged by the circumstances of their age to amplify the original creed of the Nicene
council and, in particular, to make its teaching about the Holy
Spirit more precise.[4]

2. *Comparison of C with N*

Such is the complex tradition which we have now to examine.
The following chapter will contain a section devoted to analys-
ing the special teaching of C, and we can therefore postpone

[1] Cf. P. Krüger, *Codex Iustinianus*, Berlin, 1877, I, 1, 7.   Justinian seems frequently to have used the title "Nicene creed" of C.
[2] Cf. Mansi VIII, 1051; 1059; 1063.
[3] Mansi IX, 179.
[4] Mansi XIII, 836. A better text, along with reasons for amending Mansi's
dating 791 to 796 or 797, is given by A. Werminghoff, *Mon. Germ. Hist.*, *Concilia*,
II, 177 ff.

for the moment a consideration of the ways in which it can be regarded as having supplemented the Nicene faith. The section after this will begin to tackle the baffling problem of C's connection with Constantinople. In this one we shall simply concern ourselves with a single strand in the tradition, that one which affirms that, certain additions for the purpose of clarification and precision apart, C is substantially identical with N. If this is to be taken literally (the possibility cannot, of course, be ruled out that the ancients did not intend their words to be taken in all strictness), it is an affirmation with which few students will find it easy to rest satisfied. The case against it was stated long ago with masterly thoroughness and skill, first by F. J. A. Hort,[1] and then by A. Harnack.[2] Here we shall content ourselves with summarizing their argument, which has been universally accepted. Essentially it consists in making a meticulous comparison between the two creeds. If this is done, the admittedly additional matter of the third article being disregarded, the result is to demonstrate conclusively that they are in fact two entirely different documents.

The points to be noticed are the following. First, there are certain notable omissions from C which are not easy to account for on the assumption that it is a modified version of N. These are (a) the words THAT IS FROM THE SUBSTANCE OF THE FATHER; (b) GOD FROM GOD; (c) THINGS IN HEAVEN AND THINGS ON EARTH (of the Son's creative work, in the second article); (d) the anathemas. It might be argued, of course, that the anathemas were no longer appropriate, for they envisaged a form of Arianism which now was obsolete and employed language inconsistent with the newly settled distinction between *hypostasis* and *ousia*; and also that the erasure of the clause labelled (c) was a dogmatically unimportant stylistic improvement. But these excuses do not avail in the case of the other two omissions, which comprise key-formulae of Nicene orthodoxy. Whoever was instrumental in carrying out the alleged modification of N must have acted very oddly in excising phrases which gave such clear-cut expression to the Nicene position.

---

[1] *Two Dissertations*, Cambridge and London, 1876, 73 ff.
[2] Hauck's *Realencykl.*, 1902, XI, 19 ff.

Secondly, C contains a series of words and clauses, some of them of little or no significance, which are not present in N. These include, (a) MAKER OF HEAVEN AND EARTH in the first article; (b) the words BEFORE ALL AGES with BEGOTTEN in the second article; (c) the words FROM THE HEAVENS with CAME DOWN; (d) the sentence FROM THE HOLY SPIRIT AND THE VIRGIN MARY with WAS INCARNATE; (e) the clause AND WAS CRUCIFIED FOR US UNDER PONTIUS PILATE with the connecting particle AND before SUFFERED; (f) the words AND WAS BURIED after SUFFERED; (g) the words ACCORDING TO THE SCRIPTURES after ROSE AGAIN ON THE THIRD DAY; (h) the clause AND SITS ON THE RIGHT HAND OF THE FATHER after ASCENDED TO HEAVEN; (i) the phrase AGAIN WITH GLORY with WILL COME; and, of course, (j) OF WHOSE KINGDOM THERE WILL BE NO END. The majority of these have little, if any, bearing on current theological discussion, and only (d) and (j) can be plausibly explained as inspired by polemical considerations. The clause BEFORE ALL AGES represents not only a deviation but a recession from the strict Nicene standpoint. The latter's champions were consistently reluctant to use language which might seem to define the time of the Son's generation because of the misinterpretations to which any such definition, however guarded, could give rise. The point of (d), on the theory under examination, is clear enough, if it was thought desirable to make the orthodox position clear against Apollinarianism (this will be discussed in the next chapter[1]). (j) too was obviously intended to guard against any resurgence of the ideas of Marcellus of Ancyra. But why the other alterations which have been listed should ever have been made passes comprehension.

Thirdly, there are a number of differences, many of them trivial in themselves but for that reason all the more striking, between C and N in matters of word-order and sentence-construction. Thus (a) the first article, which describes God as creator of all things, while exactly the same in content in both, is built up rather differently in C. In C we read ὁρατῶν τε πάντων καὶ ἀοράτων as against N's πάντων ὁρατῶν τε καὶ ἀοράτων. Again, (b) in C ONLY-BEGOTTEN (μονογενῆ) with the definite article stands in apposition to THE SON OF GOD, whereas in N it is placed alongside of BEGOTTEN FROM THE FATHER without the article. (*c*) So, too, N's γεννηθέντα ἐκ τοῦ πατρός is reproduced in C as τὸν ἐκ τοῦ πατρὸς γεννηθέντα. (*d*) With the exception of σταυρωθέντα (CRUCIFIED), the several members of the second article in C are linked together by AND. (*e*) In the third article the simple καὶ εἰς τὸ ἅγιον πνεῦμα (AND IN THE HOLY SPIRIT) of N reappears in C as καὶ εἰς τὸ πνεῦμα τὸ ἅγιον. It is difficult to conjecture why the supposed reviser of N should have gone to the trouble of making these, for the most part trifling, alterations.

This statistical comparison makes it certain that, whatever else C may be, it cannot accurately be described as a modified version of N. The two are really two utterly different texts, resembling each other in a broad, general way, but to no greater extent than any other pair of Eastern formularies. Hort summed the matter up with convincing succinctness when he pointed out[1] that of the 178 (approx.) words in C only 33, or about a fifth, can be plausibly derived from N. If C had a direct relationship with any fourth-century creeds, it was certainly not with N, but with certain others which have not so far been mentioned. It is interesting to observe, in passing, that it is practically identical with the first symbol quoted by St Epiphanius towards the end of his *Ancoratus*[2]—that is, if the MS evidence can be trusted. The only respects in which the latter differs from it are in the inclusion of (*a*) THAT IS FROM THE SUBSTANCE OF THE FATHER, (*b*) THINGS IN HEAVEN AND THINGS ON EARTH, and (*c*) the Nicene anathemas. C also bears a certain resemblance to a curious Latin creed found in the collection of Theodosius the Deacon, in Codex Verona LX (58), under the obviously unsuitable title *Synbolus sanctae synodi Sardici*.[3] With its interesting divergences scholars have sometimes claimed this as an important precursor of C, perhaps Antiochene in background; but in fact it seems to be nothing more than an adaptation of C itself for baptismal purposes. A discussion of these texts, however, raises large issues which can only be satisfactorily treated against the background of the main problem, viz. the

---

[1] *Two Dissertations*, 107 n. Cf. Harnack, *op. cit.*, 119.
[2] *Ancor.* 118 (Holl I, 146 f.).
[3] For the text and a summary of theories about it, see Dossetti, *op. cit.*, 186–90.

relation of C to the council of Constantinople of 381. To this we must now turn, but we can do so with the full assurance that the tradition is in error at least in its identification of the basic stock of C with N.

3. *The Case Against the Tradition*

The universal tradition, as we have already noted, dating at least from the time of the council of Chalcedon (451), is that C was the creed ratified by the 150 bishops who formed the council of Constantinople (May–July 381), and who had been summoned, along with some 36 bishops of Macedonian sympathies who later withdrew, by the emperor Theodosius I for the threefold purpose of finally establishing the Nicene faith and eliminating all heresies, appointing an orthodox bishop for the imperial city, and settling other current problems. Until recently the great majority of modern scholars have been united in their rejection of this ancient view of C's origin. The objections against supposing that C was composed and promulgated by the council of 381 have seemed overwhelming, both in number and in weight. One or two notable scholars have stood their ground, but the general opinion has been that the Chalcedonian fathers were just as much mistaken about C's original ratification as they, or at any rate their successors, were about its relationship to N. So far from being the authoritative formulary, or *ekthesis*, of the bishops assembled at Constantinople, it must be some local baptismal creed which somehow or other (at this point the suggestions mooted differ markedly) became connected with the council. Some such theory, it is held, would explain how a creed which manifestly could not have been the official pronouncement of the council nevertheless succeeded in persuading uncritical generations of churchmen that it was.

The considerations which have been regarded as fatal to the tradition deserve detailed recapitulation.[1] First, such first-hand evidence as we have of the activities of the council of Constantinople has seemed innocent of reference to C. The official

---

[1] See, e.g., F. J. A. Hort, *Two Dissertations*, 73ff.; A. Harnack in *Realencykl.*, 3rd ed., XI, 17 ff.; J. Kunze, *Das nicänisch-konstantinopolitanische Symbol*, Leipzig, 1898, 5 ff.

minutes have not been preserved, possibly because the council
was not reckoned as ecumenical until much later. On the other
hand, there is no mention of a creed in the four canons which
the council sanctioned or in the letter which, on completing
its labours, it despatched to Theodosius with the canons.[1]
True, later collections include three additional canons with
our creed appended, but it is agreed that both they and it are
intruders.[2] The first of the genuine canons confines itself to
confirming the Nicene faith in the words:

The faith of the 318 fathers who met at Nicaea in Bithynia must
not be set aside but must be maintained as binding, and every heresy
must be anathematized, and in particular that of the Eunomians, or
Anomoeans, and that of the Arians, or Eudoxians, and that of the
Semi-Arians, or Pneumatomachians, and that of the Sabellians, and
that of the Marcellians, and that of the Photinians, and that of the
Apollinarians.

The letter to Theodosius epitomizing the council's work simply
says: "After that we published some concise definitions
(συντόμους ὅρους ἐξεφωνήσαμεν), ratifying the faith of the
Nicene fathers and anathematizing the heresies which had
sprung up against it." It is difficult, the critics think, to take
this as an allusion to C, not least because C is devoid of anathemas. Very nearly the same company of bishops foregathered
again in Constantinople in the following year (382), and sent
a famous synodical letter[3] to Pope Damasus excusing themselves on various grounds from accepting his invitation to an
ecumenical council to be held in Rome. In the course of it,
after summarizing their theological views, they referred their
correspondent for a fuller exposition of them to "the statement
(τῷ τόμῳ) of the synod of Antioch" (which had been sent to
the Pope in 379), and also to "the statement which was last
year published by the ecumenical synod held at Constantinople,
in which documents we have confessed our faith more fully
(ἐν οἷς πλατύτερον τὴν πίστιν ὡμολογήσαμεν), and have in
written form anathematized the heresies which have been

---

[1] For the letter and canons, see Mansi III, 557 ff.
[2] Cf. Mansi III, 567, for the creed.
[3] Cited by Theodoret, *Hist. eccl.* 5, 9 (Parmentier, 289 ff. The relevant section
is 13, on p. 293).

recently invented". Here again, it is argued, there can be no reference to a newly formulated or recently ratified *creed*. The *tomos* of Constantinople, like that of Antioch, must have been an extended theological manifesto with anathemas subjoined.

Secondly, the external evidence of historians and other writers has every appearance of being in accord with this version of what took place at the council. Socrates,[1] for example, in his account of the proceedings, describes how, after the secession of the Macedonian bishops, the fathers settled down to the re-affirmation of the Nicene faith (ἐβεβαίωσαν αὖθις τὴν ἐν Νικαίᾳ πίστιν). Earlier in the same chapter he had remarked that the object of the council was "to ratify the Nicene faith". Sozomen[2] and Theodoret[3] tell the same tale, using almost identical language. Harnack was convinced that St Gregory of Nazianzus, who had actually been president of the council for a time, must also have taken the view that its work was limited to ratifying the Nicene creed. Shortly after the council he wrote a letter[4] to Cledonius in answer to his request for "a concise definition and rule of our belief", remarking in it :

We for our part have never esteemed, and never can esteem, any doctrine preferable to the faith of the holy fathers who assembled at Nicaea to destroy the Arian heresy. We adhere with God's help, and shall adhere, to this faith, supplementing the gaps which they left concerning the Holy Spirit because this question had not then been raised.

The natural implication of this, the German scholar argued, was that St Gregory admitted only the Nicene creed, despite his consciousness of its deficiency in certain particulars. He could not have written in such terms had he been aware that a fully satisfactory alternative formula had already been solemnly promulgated a few months before.[5]

The third and most impressive objection is the seemingly absolute silence regarding a Constantinopolitan creed which apparently reigned from 381 to 451. This silence is particularly striking for the various synods which met in the period, at which some allusion to such a creed, had it existed, might have

[1] *Hist. eccl.* 5, 8 (*P.G.* 67, 576 ff.).   [2] *Hist. eccl.* 7, 9 (*P.G.* 67, 1436 ff.).
[3] *Hist. eccl.* 5, 8 (Parmentier, 288).   [4] *Ep.* 102 (*P.G.* 37, 193).
[5] Cf. Hauck's *Realencykl.*, 3rd ed., XI, 18.

been expected. At the third general council, at Ephesus in 431, the creed which played the authoritative role and which was entered in the minutes was N.[1] A vote was even passed to the effect that nobody should be allowed "to bring forward or to compose or to put together any other faith than that which has been defined by the holy fathers who assembled at Nicaea under the guidance of the Holy Spirit".[2] C was even passed over in silence at the synod which Flavian held at Constantinople in 448 to pass judgment on Eutyches, although if in fact it had been sponsored by the council of 381 one might have expected it to be held in honour in its own city. The authorities appealed to at the meetings of the council itself,[3] in the imperial rescript read out at the seventh session,[4] and in Flavian's own letter to Pope Leo acquainting him with the proceedings,[5] were always the Nicene faith, the council of Ephesus, and St Cyril's letters. A few months later, at the beginning of 449, writing to the emperor in response to a request for an exposition of his faith, Flavian said in similar vein: "Our views are orthodox and blameless, for we always conform to the divine Scriptures and the official statements of the holy fathers who met at Nicaea, and of those who met at Ephesus in the time of Cyril of blessed memory."[6] The words "and in Constantinople", which occur in many MSS and which point to a creed of Constantinople, are rejected by historians of this school as an intrusion on the true text.

The evidence of the "Robber Synod" of Ephesus (449) points in exactly the same direction. Both the parties meeting there were apparently equally ignorant of C and equally united in their recognition of N as the sole authoritative formula. The emperor, in his official letter to the synod, made reference to "the orthodox faith set out by the holy fathers of Nicaea which the holy synod of Ephesus confirmed";[7] and Eutyches himself asserted that he had been exposed to many dangers because, in harmony with the resolutions adopted at the previous council at Ephesus, he had determined "not to

---

[1] For references to it, cf. A.C.O. I, I, iii, 38 ; v, 121; 122; 127; 128; 132; 134–135.

[2] A.C.O. I, I, vii, 105.
[3] Cf. A.C.O. II, I, i, 101; 120.
[4] A.C.O. II, I, i, 138.
[5] Cf. Ep. Leonis 22, 3 (P.L. 54, 724).
[6] A.C.O. II, I, i, 35.
[7] A.C.O. II, I, i, 73 and 82.

think otherwise than in accordance with the faith expounded by the holy fathers".[1] Apart from councils, however, the same reticence regarding the alleged ratification of C at Constantinople in 381 is reflected in the writings of theologians of all schools in the period under review. A detailed survey of the evidence would demand more space than can be spared at this point. It is noteworthy, however, that Nestorius, who was patriarch of Constantinople till 431 and was the first to introduce the creed into Christological controversy in his first letter[2] to Pope Celestine, consistently spoke of "the faith of Nicaea". Although the text he used often diverged markedly from N in its purity, it did not coincide with C and it apparently never occurred to him that any other formulary was authoritative than that sanctioned by the 318 fathers. St Cyril, too, was acquainted with only one valid and binding symbol, which he called the faith set forth by the fathers of Nicaea. He was indeed a stickler for its pure, unadulterated text, and on one occasion poured heavy scorn on Nestorius for suggesting that it contained the clause WAS INCARNATE FROM THE HOLY SPIRIT AND THE VIRGIN MARY.[3] In the West St Leo made a number of references to the creed in handling the case of Eutyches. Sometimes he meant by it the Apostles' creed, but at other times he explicitly mentioned the faith or decisions of Nicaea.[4] But nowhere did he betray the least knowledge of a Constantinopolitan formulary.

The fact is, so Harnack once ventured to claim,[5] there is not the slightest trace, in the period 381–451, whether in the official records of synods Eastern or Western, or in the writings of theologians orthodox or heterodox, of the existence of C, much less any hint of its being the *ekthesis* sponsored by the fathers of Constantinople. It might be contended, of course, that this conspiracy of silence was merely the result of the fact that the council of Constantinople was not recognized as ecumenical until 451 at the earliest. There is force in this contention, for we know that only Eastern bishops were present at it, and in fact

[1] *A.C.O.* II, I, i, 90 f.
[2] Written in 429. For the text see F. Loofs, *Nestoriana*, Halle, 1905, 165 ff.
[3] *Adv. Nest.* 1, 8 (*P.G.* 76, 49).
[4] Cf., e.g., *A.C.O.* II, IV, 11; 15; 29–31.
[5] *Realencyckl.* XI, 18.

most of the delegates came exclusively from sees in Thrace, Asia Minor and Syria. Its decisions were repudiated from the start in the West and by Church leaders in Egypt. Nevertheless, for all its unpopularity in certain quarters, the work of the council was not entirely overlooked, as the preservation of its canons and the allusions of Church historians show. Moreover, the obscurity in which C is wrapped extends not only to the West and to Egypt, where it is perhaps explicable, but to the East as well, and even to Constantinople itself.

The weight of external evidence has thus seemed to many to be massively ranged against the traditional account of C's origin. In the eyes of most critics, however, the *coup de grâce* seemed to be the fact, to which a passing reference was made in the preceding section, that C was evidently in existence several years before the council of Constantinople. The creed which St Epiphanius, towards the end of his tract *Ancoratus*,[1] recommended as a baptismal formula to the presbyters at the church of Syedra, in Pamphylia, is practically identical with our text. The tract may be assigned with absolute confidence to the year 374, for the author prefaces his second creed, in the following chapter, with an elaborate dating. If the identification be admitted, it may very well be that C has some connection with the council of 381, but it manifestly cannot have been drafted by it. The most that can be claimed is that the council took over and ratified an existing local baptismal creed, but the critics in question have thought this an extremely doubtful procedure.

The preceding paragraphs have given a résumé of the case against the tradition. The majority of scholars in the past found it absolutely decisive, and turned their attention to subsidiary but closely related topics. First, what is this creed which St Epiphanius reproduces? After setting it down, he proceeded to describe it in the enigmatic words: "This faith was handed down from the holy Apostles and in the Church, the holy city, by all the holy bishops, more than 310 in number, gathered there on that occasion." The answer, suggested first by G. J. Voss[2] and fully worked out by F. J. A. Hort,[3] is that what we

---

[1] 118 (Holl I, 146 f.).
[2] *Dissertationes tres de tribus symbolis*, Amsterdam, 1642, 32 ff.
[3] *Two Dissertations*, 76 ff ; 84 ff.

have in it is the old creed of Jerusalem[1] revised in a Nicene direction. If the characteristic Nicene clauses are removed, the whole of the first article and of the second as far as BEFORE ALL AGES is verbally identical with the creed recoverable from St Cyril's *Catechetical Lectures*. The second article seems Jerusalemite in its basis, but the Nicene key-phrases and certain more precise historical statements have been inserted—FROM THE HOLY SPIRIT AND THE VIRGIN MARY, ON BEHALF OF US UNDER PONTIUS PILATE, AND SUFFERED, ACCORDING TO THE SCRIPTURES, AGAIN . . . WITH GLORY. In the third article the underlying plan is either pure Jerusalemite or can be vouched for in creeds related to Jerusalem; and the additional matter about the Holy Spirit finds its prototype in the letters of St Athanasius to St Serapion of Thmuis (356–362). Hort carried the case a stage further by arguing, with extreme ingenuity and learning, that St Cyril himself was probably the author of the revision of the original Jerusalem creed, and by emphasizing the possible historical links between St Cyril and St Epiphanius.

The second problem to be solved, if the tradition is to be discarded, concerns the connection between the revised creed of Jerusalem and the council of 381. Some connection there must have been, or else it would have been impossible to represent it with any degree of plausibility as the *ekthesis* of the 150 fathers. Once again F. J. A. Hort was the propounder of a widely accepted solution.[2] He drew attention to the fact that, though St Cyril was present in person at the council of Constantinople, his orthodoxy was not above suspicion in the eyes of Western theologians, for he had long belonged to the anti-Nicene party. Indeed the hostility of the West to the council was in large measure due to the prominent part played in its deliberations by men about whose theology there was reason to be doubtful. Above all, the bishop who for a time was president of the council, Meletius of Antioch, hardly counted as an orthodox person at all in the West. The Eastern Church fully understood the dogmatic attitude of the West. Nothing could therefore have been more natural than for St Cyril to present a creed

---

[1] See above, p. 183 f.
[2] *Two Dissertations*, 97 ff.

as the proof of his theological correctness; and the creed which he would present would be the revised creed of Jerusalem. This would be entered in the minutes of the council, and many years later, when people had forgotten the precise order of events, may well have come to be regarded as in fact the creed promulgated by the council.

An alternative solution was advanced by J. Kunze in an important monograph,[1] and in its main features has been given fresh support by E. Molland.[2] This is the view that C may have been used at the baptism and episcopal consecration of Nectarius, praetor of the city, who was elected bishop of Constantinople in the course of the council and, in consequence, became its third president. At the time of his election he is known to have been a layman and unbaptized. It is probable, argued Kunze, that he received both baptismal instruction and the sacrament itself at the hands of Diodore of Tarsus, who had sponsored his candidature. The fact that C first comes to light in Cyprus (Salamis was St Epiphanius's see-city), and passed thence to Syedra in Pamphylia, seemed to Kunze to make its adoption by the church of Tarsus, in Cilicia, a distinct possibility. Its use at the baptism and ordination of Nectarius would therefore be perfectly natural if Diodore was the bishop who administered them. Granting that it was so used, C would inevitably be associated thereafter with the council, the more so as Nectarius probably made it the official creed of Constantinople thereafter. Among other pieces of evidence which seemed to Kunze to tally with his conjecture is a curious note embedded in the minutes recording the voting at Chalcedon on the question whether N and C agreed with Leo's *Tome*. As he cast his vote, Callinicus of Apamea in Bithynia, a town not too far removed from Constantinople, described the council of 381 as having been held "at the consecration of the most pious Nectarius".[3] There was evidently some connection in his mind between the creed which formed part of the Definition and the elevation of Nectarius to the episcopate.

[1] *Das nicänisch-konstant. Symbol*, 32 ff.
[2] See *Opuscula Patristica*, Oslo-Bergen-Tromsö, 1970, 236.
[3] *A.C.O.* II, I, ii, 104.

4. *The Tradition Re-considered*

The considerations listed in the foregoing section combine to confront the traditional ascription of C to the council of Constantinople with an embarrassing question-mark. We cannot casually brush aside such facts, if facts they are, as (*a*) the absence of any hint in contemporary documents that the council made itself responsible for anything more enterprising than the re-affirmation of N, (*b*) the unquestioning assumption in the long span between Constantinople and Chalcedon that N was the sole authoritative formula, and (*c*) the evidence for C's vogue as a purely local baptismal creed almost a decade before the 150 fathers met. It is not surprising that many scholars have found the case overwhelming. On the other hand, there have always been a minority who have refused to bow the knee. Caspari, it may be noted, steadily adhered to the tradition, despite his appreciation of the difficulties it entailed. Even in the hey-day of the Hort-Harnack hypothesis, voices could be distinctly heard questioning its validity. Amongst these conservative stalwarts may be numbered the German scholar W. Schmidt,[1] the Russian ecclesiastical historian A. P. Lebedev,[2] and the Greek archbishop Chr. Papadopoulos.[3] The English F. J. Badcock[4] later joined their ranks. More recently still Eduard Schwartz[5] added his powerful influence to the defence of the tradition in its most uncompromising form. So great is the prestige of his learning and, in particular, of his knowledge of the day-to-day working of the synods of the early centuries, that the position which he espoused, once abandoned as untenable in most quarters, has evidently begun to be taken seriously again.

It is easy to sympathize with the dissatisfaction of these more cautious students. There were grave weaknesses in the Hort-Harnack hypothesis which its brilliant façade could not conceal. Not every student, for example, will be prepared to admit its

---

[1] Cf. *Neue Kirchliche Zeitschrift* x, 1899, 935 ff.
[2] For a summary of his views, see *J.T.S.* iv, 1903, 285 ff.
[3] See Ἐπιστημονικὴ ἐπετηρὶς τῆς θεολογικῆς σχολῆς τοῦ Ἀθήνῃσι πανεπιστημίου. Athens, 1924.
[4] Cf. *J.T.S.* xvi, 1915, 205 ff., and his book (2nd ed.), 186 ff.
[5] *Z.N.T.W.* xxv, 1926, 38 ff.

starting-point, the identification of C as the creed of Jerusalem revised by St Cyril. Prudence bids us remember that the formulary known as the creed of Jerusalem is an artificial construction based on St Cyril's *Catechetical Lectures*, and that the text of a portion of the Christological section cannot be pronounced as certain. Furthermore, the points of difference between J (=Jerusalem) and C are numerous and far-reaching. If the first articles of both coincide, the second article of C contains several items which are not present in J, such as BECAUSE OF US MEN AND BECAUSE OF OUR SALVATION, FROM HEAVEN (and probably CAME DOWN as well), FROM THE HOLY SPIRIT AND THE VIRGIN MARY, FOR US UNDER PONTIUS PILATE, ACCORDING TO THE SCRIPTURES, and AGAIN. Some of these are dogmatically pointless, and so it is not clear why St Cyril should have inserted them. Again, while J reads SAT (καθίσαντα) and IN GLORY (ἐν δόξῃ), C has SITS (καθεζόμενον) and WITH GLORY (μετὰ δόξης); and since J's forms have Scriptural authority, it is not easy to understand why they should have been altered. In the third article, even if we leave the anti-Macedonian passages on one side, the modifications are so sweeping as to amount to virtual re-writing. Among the more inexplicable phenomena, on the assumption that C resulted from a revision of J, are the erasure of J's ONE with THE HOLY SPIRIT, the disappearance of J's THE PARACLETE, the alteration of J's IN THE PROPHETS to THROUGH THE PROPHETS, and the change of LIFE EVERLASTING to LIFE OF THE WORLD TO COME.[1] Hort's attempt to connect the transformation involved in these changes with the evolution of St Cyril's theological views was a *tour de force* of ingenious conjecture, but was a study in the possible rather than the probable.

Furthermore, the general case developed by Hort and Harnack was more successful in drawing attention to the difficulties facing the tradition than in furnishing an alternative explanation of the facts. Beyond question there must be some point of contact between C and the council of 381, or else the Chalcedonian fathers would never have swallowed the description of it foisted upon them so confidently. Yet it is hard to read with

[1] For a fuller statement of these points, see E. C. S. Gibson, *The Three Creeds*, London, 1908, 169 ff.

patience the theories propounded to account for this. Let us glance first at Hort's suggestion that C was handed in at the council in token of St Cyril's orthodoxy. The assumption that the 150 fathers felt the need to rehabilitate its leading figures in the eyes of the Western Church is pure guesswork. There is no positive evidence to support it, and the decision to appoint Meletius of Antioch as chairman of the council is scarcely indicative of a desire to be conciliatory. In any case it remains a mystery why St Cyril, and apparently St Cyril alone, should have felt it necessary to clear himself. As a matter of fact, as A. E. Burn recognized, St Cyril's orthodoxy had not been under a cloud for a decade at least, and he had suffered exile thrice at the hands of the Arians for his acceptance of the orthodox point of view. There is nothing at all to be said for the idea that he must have submitted a theological testimonial at the council. Much the same verdict must be passed on Kunze's alternative proposal, that C became associated with the council through its use at the baptism and consecration of Nectarius. The only information we have is that the pious layman Nectarius was baptized and consecrated at the council, and that Diodore of Tarsus was his sponsor. There are no solid grounds for supposing that Diodore catechized and baptized him, much less that the creed employed was the creed of Tarsus. If C was used at Nectarius's baptism, which in itself is quite conceivable, this would rather suggest that it was already somehow associated with the council.

There is, however, a consideration far more weighty than the exposure of the inner weaknesses from which these conjectures suffer. Even granting that in themselves they were absolutely water-tight, and that C may well have been employed either at the baptism and consecration of Nectarius or in vindication of St Cyril's orthodoxy, or on some other occasion at the council, is it really conceivable that it should have been described as the *ekthesis*, or as *ta ektethenta*, of the 150 fathers on the basis of such a slender and almost accidental connection? The Chalcedonian bishops who accepted such language used of C were strongly opposed to the fabrication of new creeds. They would surely have resisted to the uttermost a barefaced attempt to palm off on them a formula which was entirely without synodical endorsement. The matter is so important that it will be worth our while to recall in detail the references made to C in the course of the proceedings.

C was first mentioned, at the very close of the first session, by the imperial commissioners. They invited all the bishops present to set out their faith in writing, without fear and in the knowledge that the emperor's own beliefs were "in accord with the *ekthesis* of the 318 holy fathers at Nicaea and the *ekthesis* of the 150 who met subsequently".[1] At the opening of the second session, when the commissioners were urging the assembly to get down to the task of "setting forth the faith purely" (they wanted a new creed drafted), they again explained that, along with the emperor, "they adhered loyally to the orthodox faith delivered by the 318 and by the 150 and by the other holy and illustrious fathers".[2] In the discussion which ensued the bishops demurred to propounding a new creed, saying that the teaching of the fathers should prevail, and those who spoke appealed consistently to N, never so much as mentioning C. Eventually in response to a motion from Cecropius of Sevastopol, N was read out, and was received with immense applause. The commissioners then ordered "the *ekthesis* of the 150" to be read out too, and this was done.[3] The applause which greeted it was noticeably less cordial, but no dissenting voice was raised. Shortly afterwards the meeting was adjourned, and we next hear of C at the beginning of the fourth session. In answer to the commissioners' inquiry what the synod had decided about the creed, the papal legate Paschasinus replied on his own and his colleagues' behalf that the synod adhered to the rule of faith published by the 318 fathers at Nicaea, which selfsame faith "the synod of the 150 assembled at Constantinople in the time of Theodosius the Great of blessed memory confirmed", and the creed of which the council of Ephesus had endorsed, and that they did not propose to add anything to it or subtract anything from it.[4] Applause followed these remarks, and the commissioners proceeded to inquire whether "the *ekthesis* of the 318 fathers who met long ago at Nicaea and of those who assembled thereafter in the royal city" was in

[1] *A.C.O.* II, I, i, 195 f.   [2] *A.C.O.* II, I, ii, 78.
[3] *A.C.O.* II, I, ii, 79 f.   [4] *A.C.O.* II, I, ii, 93.

harmony with Pope Leo's *Tome*. In the voting which followed[1] practically all the bishops, beginning with Anatolius of Constantinople and the papal legates, explicitly mentioned C side by side with N as the standard with which the *Tome* was in agreement. Only the Egyptian bishops and a few others confined their references to N, the council of Ephesus and St Cyril, although it became plain in the debates that their real opposition was to the *Tome* rather than to C.[2] Finally, at the fifth session C was incorporated in the Definition with the significant words:

. . . we have renewed the unerring faith of the fathers, proclaiming to all the symbol of the 318, and, in addition, accepting as our own fathers those who received that statement of orthodoxy, the 150 who subsequently met together in great Constantinople and themselves set their seal to the same creed.[3]

The impression left by a study of the Chalcedonian *acta* is unambiguously clear. When C was introduced to the fathers at the first session, it was evidently quite unfamiliar to the great majority of them, and probably took them completely by surprise. We can only surmise the motives which prompted the imperial commissioners and their supporters at the council to push the claims of C, but there can be little doubt that the manoeuvre fitted in with the policy of magnifying the prestige of "new Rome". The fathers' reticence, however, on the subject of a Constantinopolitan creed at the second session is significant: it suggests that, while reluctant to question the formulary which the commissioners declared represented the emperor's personal faith, they were by no means prepared to treat it as on a level with so unique and venerable a creed as N. Even after the second session, when the history and identity of C must have been fully explained to them, they could not bring themselves to show the same enthusiasm towards it as towards N. Such reserve is perfectly comprehensible when we remember the extremely dubious status of the council of 381 in the eyes of many of the bishops. What is really noteworthy, however, about the attitude of the fathers towards C is that,

---

[1] *A.C.O.* II, I, ii, 94-109.   [2] *A.C.O.* II, I, ii, 118 f.
[3] *A.C.O.* II, I, ii, 126 f.

in spite of their understandable detachment and even coolness, no one was apparently disposed to cast doubts on its *bona fides*. We should bear in mind that they were men of spirit, quite courageous enough, as in the case of their refusal to draw up a new creed, to stand out against the plainly expressed wishes of the emperor. The implication is that they must have been satisfied that it had a real and substantial connection with the council of Constantinople. To suppose that they abstained from questioning its credentials, or that when they questioned them they allowed themselves to be hoodwinked by Anatolius and Aetius, reveals an extravagant measure of scepticism. The only reasonable conclusion to draw, in view of their initial bewilderment and their eventual readiness to canonize C along with N, is that in the meantime trustworthy evidence had been produced showing that it could claim to be in some real sense a creed of the council of 381.

The failure of the Hort-Harnack hypothesis to explain the attitude and language of the Chalcedonian fathers is its fundamentally unsatisfactory feature. In the light of it the attempt of some scholars recently to discover ways and means of rehabilitating the tradition is not surprising. One great obstacle in their way has been the presence of C, or a creed remarkably like it, in a treatise of St Epiphanius's written several years before 381. We should perhaps remind the reader that the implications of this argument have sometimes been carried too far. Granting it its full weight, it would still be possible to hold that the fathers of 381, even if they could no longer be reckoned as C's authors, may nevertheless have adopted it as a suitable expression of their teaching. The obstacle, however, seemed unsurmountable to many until, as a result of a closer analysis of the text of St Epiphanius, certain facts were disclosed which, if solidly established, disposed of it once and for all. The scholars to whom this discovery is due are Lebedev, Papadopoulos and Schwartz.[1]

To state their conclusion in a sentence, there are grounds for believing that the creed originally occupying the place at present held by *Ep*. I in *Ancoratus* 118 was not C but N. The reasons for making this inference are two. First, the language

---

[1] See their works cited on p. 313.

which St Epiphanius himself used in the surrounding context
is more consistent with the creed's being N than C ; and,
secondly, the intrinsic character of the creed which follows in
119, known as *Ep*. II, seems to presuppose N rather than C.
As regards the former point, St Epiphanius commended his
creed to the people of Syedra as one belonging to the whole
Church: he spoke of it as "this holy faith of the Catholic
Church, as the holy and only virgin of God received it from
the holy Apostles of the Lord as a trust to be preserved". After
setting it down in full, he went on explicitly to ascribe it to
Nicaea in the words: "This faith was handed down from the
holy Apostles and ⟨*was published?*⟩ in the Church, the holy
city, by all the holy bishops, above three hundred and ten in
number, gathered together then." The older interpretation of
these enigmatic words, which took them as implying that the
creed embodied apostolic, Jerusalemite and Nicene elements,
overlooked the true reference of "the holy city". As K. Holl
pointed out in the Berlin edition of the *Ancoratus*,[1] the phrase
was commonly used by St Epiphanius to describe, not the
earthly city of Jerusalem, but the heavenly Jerusalem of the
Church. What he was really saying in his complicated way
was that the creed he had just quoted was the Nicene creed.
In harmony with this he terminated it with the Nicene anathemas, which undoubtedly look somewhat out of place at
the end of *Ep*. I as it stands in the text at present. Secondly,
when he proceeded to write out a fuller creed (*Ep*. II) in
ch. 119, he announced in so many words that it would conform
with "the faith enjoined by those holy fathers", but would take
account of the various heresies which had raised their heads
since they had published it. But when *Ep*. II is studied closely,
it is seen to add little or nothing to the anti-heretical content
of *Ep*. I : the most that can be said is that its language is slightly
stiffer and more precise. If N originally stood where *Ep*. I now
stands, *Ep*. II must have provided a valuable supplement to
it, but after *Ep*. I it was virtually superfluous. Moreover (and
this is the really startling point), *Ep*. II is in no sense a re-
modelling of *Ep*. I, but consists of the ancient Nicene creed,
N, enlarged with an anti-Apollinarian, anti-Macedonian

---

[1] See note *ad loc.*

running commentary, and with the third article elaborated along different lines from the third article of *Ep*. I. The conclusion is irresistible that the only way of explaining this queer assortment of facts is to assume that the position now usurped by *Ep*. I rightfully belongs to N, and that the present situation came about through the misplaced zeal of some scribe in substituting, or adding as a marginal gloss, the form which he took to be the fully developed, authorized Nicene creed. Since at this point the *Ancoratus* depends on a single, not very accurate MS, no objection against this inference can be convincingly raised from that quarter.

Another obstacle facing the champions of the tradition was, as we saw, the complete absence of any suggestion in surviving records that the council of Constantinople had been responsible for a creed of its own. Yet the question has been asked recently whether this represents an altogether fair account of the evidence. First, E. Schwartz and his supporters have called for a reconsideration of the letter, preserved by Theodoret,[1] which the synod of Constantinople of 382 despatched to the Western bishops assembled at Rome. In this, we remember, there was a reference to "the *tomos* of the synod of Antioch" and "the *tomos* which was last year published by the ecumenical council held at Constantinople, in which documents we have confessed our faith more fully". There is nothing far-fetched, it is argued, in taking *tomos* in this passage as a description of C. The verb "we have confessed" is precisely the one used for setting out one's faith in a creed. Secondly, a parallel reconsideration of the letter which Flavian sent the emperor in 449 has been demanded.[2] It has been asked whether the reasons for excising "and in Constantinople" from the text are valid. The words have the backing of some important MSS, and the summary of his faith which Flavian gives in the following sentences seems to presuppose a fuller creed than N.

Thirdly, in addition to these obscure and much disputed possible allusions, there are a number of quite unambiguous patristic passages which suggest that the Constantinopolitan fathers were known to have made alterations in the Nicene

---

[1] *Hist. eccl.* 5, 13 (Parmentier, 293).
[2] *A.C.O.* II, I, i, 35.

creed. Thus one of the pseudo-Athanasian dialogues *De Trinitate*[1] represents Macedonius, who stands for the heresy called after his name, as being accused by one Orthodoxus of being dissatisfied with the Nicene creed and of having made additions to it. He counters the charge by inquiring whether the orthodox too had not been guilty of the same offence. Orthodoxus has to admit that they have added to N, but pleads that their additions were not inconsistent with the Nicene creed and concerned matters which had not been raised at the time of Nicaea. The date and authorship of the dialogue are uncertain, but it must have been written prior to the outbreak of the Nestorian controversy, and recent scholarship has produced an impressive case for attributing it to Didymus the Blind (313–398).[2] It may therefore well belong to the decade immediately following the council of 381. Again, Theodore of Mopsuestia, in his commentary on the Nicene creed,[3] after ascribing the whole of it down to the words AND IN THE HOLY SPIRIT to the Nicene fathers, declared that the more developed teaching about the Spirit which followed was due to "the fathers who came after them". The initiative, he said, was taken by a synod of Western bishops, but was confirmed by a later gathering of Eastern bishops. A few pages later[4] he repeated his point, again affirming that "the doctors of the Church, who assembled from all parts of the earth and who were the heirs of the first blessed fathers," endorsed the Nicene faith but added clauses about the Holy Spirit. We noticed above that Diogenes of Cyzicus took the same line, though with regard to a different clause of C, at Chalcedon, saying that FROM THE HOLY SPIRIT AND THE VIRGIN MARY had been inserted by "the holy fathers who came later".[5] The same tradition, as we saw earlier, regarding the activities of the 150 fathers was maintained in orthodox and Monophysite circles after Chalcedon.

It is not surprising, in the light of these and similar considerations, that the traditional theory that the council of 381 was

---

[1] *Dial. de sanc. trin.* 3, i (*P.G.* 28, 1204).
[2] Cf. E. Stolz, *Theologische Quartalschrift* lxxxvii, 1905, 395 f., and the very thorough study by Anselm Günthör, O.S.B., in *Studia Anselmiana* XI, Rome, 1941.
[3] Cf. A. Mingana's edition, *Woodbrooke Studies* V (*Cambridge*, 1932), 93.
[4] *Ibid.* 101 f.
[5] See above, p. 299 (*A.C.O.* II, I, i, 91).

responsible for promulgating C has come to be seriously can-
vassed once more. The chief difficulty still remains the blanket
of silence which, despite the occasional hints we have mentioned,
seems to overhang it until Chalcedon. Many would think that
the failure of the Constantinopolitan synod to achieve recognition as ecumenical provides a sufficient explanation. E.
Schwartz, however, gave an individual twist of his own to this
version of the course of events. Part of his object in the important article already referred to[1] was to magnify the council
of 381. According to his interpretation, Theodosius I regarded
himself as wearing the mantle of Constantine, and in summoning the council he desired it to play the same august role of
unifying the Church which the Nicene fathers had played. C
may well have been deliberately overlooked in the West, but
its position was admitted in the East. There it ranked, as the
council which had framed it intended, as the juridical equal
of N. Naturally, however, the see of Alexandria was ranged
with Rome in opposing the council which had elevated Constantinople to the second rank. Hence it was St Cyril who
fostered the idea that no creed could claim equality with N.
Both in his writings and at the council of Ephesus, where he
was the leading spirit, he sedulously propagated this doctrine,
and it is to him more than to anyone else that the obscurity
of C is due. Nevertheless the fact that it was ratified by the
150 fathers, Schwartz thought, could not be concealed.

5. Towards a Solution

The foregoing sections have, in effect, presented the substance of the arguments first against, and then in favour of,
the traditional account of C's origin. The reader may well
feel that he has reached an impasse. The fathers at Chalcedon
seemed content with, if not enthusiastic about, the description of C as the *ekthesis* of the 150 Constantinopolitan
fathers; yet the weight of contemporary evidence, as well as
the reports of historians, would suggest that the latter simply
endorsed the Nicene faith. The silence about C between 381
and 451 is a puzzling problem, and the obscure allusions to

[1] *Z.N.T.W.* xxv, 1926, 38 ff.

the work of the fathers subsequent to Nicaea do not provide
a complete solution. Yet if C was not the product of the council,
how did it ever come to be associated with it? It is time to
attempt a more positive approach to this age-old crux of credal
studies. The key is supplied, we would suggest, by an important
fact to which neither party to the controversy has hitherto
drawn sufficient attention.

The fact is one which has been casually touched upon
previously. It is a circumstance of immense significance that,
from the time of Constantinople and probably before it, and
also after Chalcedon, the description "the faith of Nicaea", or
"the faith, symbol or *ekthesis* of the 318 fathers", was not
necessarily applied solely to N in its pure, authentic form. It
could equally well be used of a creed, local or otherwise, which
was patently Nicene in its general character, while differing
from N in much of its language. It is true, as we noticed before,
that St Cyril seems to have resisted this flexibility of usage. For
reasons of his own (Schwartz may be right in his diagnosis of
them), he always invoked N in its pure, unadulterated form,
and his influence secured that the council of Ephesus followed
suit. His careful attitude, however, was not reflected generally
in the writings of the fifth century.

The evidence bearing out what has just been said cannot be
set out in full detail, but a few typical examples should suffice.
Theodore of Mopsuestia is a case in point. We saw in an earlier
chapter[1] that it is possible to piece together a complete creed
from his catechetical instructions. Manifestly it was the baptismal confession in use in his church. In language and content
it closely resembled N, and yet at several points it parted company with the Nicene creed strikingly. Similarly it had a
certain kinship with C, and yet there were places where it
differed from C. Even the third article, which Theodore admitted to be the work of the fathers subsequent to Nicaea, did
not reproduce C faithfully. Yet this composite formula was described in the instructions as the Nicene creed. Exactly the
same looseness of language is observable in the case of Nestorius.
References to what he called "the faith of the Nicene fathers"
occur over and over again in his surviving writings, both in the

[1] See above, p. 187 f.

fragments collected by F. Loofs in his volume *Nestoriana* and in the *Bazaar of Heracleides*.[1] Yet the creed he had in view, so far as it can be reconstructed, was much fuller than N, although it did not overlap exactly with C. St Cyril took him to task, we know, for using a text (which he doubtless regarded in all good faith as Nicene) containing the words FROM THE HOLY SPIRIT AND THE VIRGIN MARY. An interesting case is that of Charisius, the presbyter of Philadelphia, who at the sixth session of the council of Ephesus complained of some Lydian converts who had been received into the Church with an illegitimate symbol and not with the Nicene creed. He quoted his own creed, which he evidently regarded as loyally Nicene, but again it diverged markedly from N.[2] Similarly Theodoret of Cyrus showed he was prepared to give the title of Nicene creed to a formula containing non-Nicene elements,[3] and applied the description "the faith set forth at Nicaea by the holy and blessed fathers" to the creed used for catechetical instruction and baptism.[4] Yet another witness to the same usage is Isaac the Great (Sahak), Catholicos of the Armenians (†439), who when acknowledging receipt of the *Tome* of Proclus gave a résumé of the faith in his letter, assuming that it was the Nicene creed. In fact it was not N in its pure form, but a freer, fuller version bearing many resemblances to C.[5]

A revealing illustration, from a rather different point of view, of the readiness of fifth-century churchmen to apply phrases like "the faith of Nicaea" rather loosely is provided by the third session of Chalcedon. When the Nicene creed in its original wording had been recited, the assembled fathers hailed it with excited shouts: "In this we were baptized, in this we baptize." It is still an open question how far N was used as a baptismal creed. Some think that it was employed fairly regularly for this purpose, whereas others (with whom this book is inclined to agree) conclude that it was hardly ever, if indeed ever, so used. But nobody could possibly believe that it was at any stage the exclusive baptismal formula of the Church. Hence the meaning of the fathers' acclamation must be that

[1] Cf. *Nestoriana* 167; 171; 187; 295; *Bazaar of Heracleides* (Driver and Hodgson), 141 ff.
[2] *A.C.O.* I, I, vii, 97.   [3] *Dial.* 3 (*P.G.* 83, 280 f.).
[4] *Ep.* 145 (*P.G.* 83, 1377).   [5] Cf. *Vienna Oriental Journal* xxvii, 1913, 425 ff.

they used creeds broadly agreeing with the true Nicene creed at baptism. The creeds they in fact used were almost certainly, in most cases at any rate, the local baptismal creeds filled out at the appropriate points with the characteristic Nicene phrases. These evidently seemed to them to serve the same purpose, and therefore to qualify for the same title, as the genuine Nicene symbol.

With this important discovery as our guide, we can perhaps begin to descry a way out of the impasse. Perhaps the best procedure will be to sketch in advance the solution we would venture to propose, leaving its elaboration to subsequent paragraphs. The only satisfactory explanation of the apparently contradictory facts, we would suggest, is the following one. The council of Constantinople did in fact, at some stage in its proceedings, endorse and use C, but in doing so it did not conceive of itself as promulgating a new creed. Its sincere intention, perfectly understood by contemporary churchmen, was simply to confirm the Nicene faith. That it should do this by adopting what was really a different formula from that of Nicaea may appear paradoxical to us, until we recall that at this stage importance attached to the Nicene teaching rather than to the literal wording of N. It is improbable that the council actually composed C. The whole style of the creed, its graceful balance and smooth flow, convey the impression of a liturgical piece which has emerged naturally in the life and worship of the Christian community, rather than of a conciliar artefact. C was probably already in existence when the council took it up, though not necessarily in exactly the form it now wears: the fathers may well have touched it up to harmonize with their purposes. In settling upon C as a suitable formulary the council assumed unquestionably that it was reaffirming the Nicene faith, but it was no doubt guided in its choice by the conviction that this particular formulation of the Nicene teaching, as modified by whatever additions it thought fit to make, was peculiarly well adapted to meet the special situation with which it was dealing. Whether the creed occurred as an illustrative document in that "fuller statement" to which the council which reassembled in 382 made reference in its synodical letter is doubtful. If it did, it was perhaps incorporated *en passant* in the body of the statement, just as the Old Roman Creed was inserted with seeming casualness by Marcellus of Ancyra in his own theological apologia, while the manifesto itself consisted of a forthright reassertion, against the various schools of heretics, of the sacrosanct Nicene faith.

A hypothesis of this kind (the details, of course, are only put forward as tentative guesses) coheres at every point with the fourth- and fifth-century accounts of what happened at Constantinople. There was general agreement among historians and others that the 150 fathers had been content with re-affirming the faith of Nicaea; and the first of the canons is in full accord with this. The general tradition from Theodore of Mopsuestia onwards, which found an echo at Chalcedon itself, was that, so far as the main body of the creed was concerned, the 150 fathers had simply endorsed the Nicene faith: their personal contribution consisted in the elaboration of the third article, or possibly (so Diogenes of Cyzicus) the insertion of FROM THE HOLY SPIRIT AND THE VIRGIN MARY. The tradition, we should notice, never claimed the manufacture of C for the 150 fathers: its most consistent and regular theme was that C was N re-interpreted and elucidated at certain critical points. This mass of evidence constitutes a weighty argument against the assumption that an entirely fresh creed was promulgated by the council. The suggestion of Schwartz that the *tomos* mentioned in the synodical letter of 382 must be the creed does not hold water. Not only is the word much more naturally understood of a full-dress theological statement, but the letter links the *tomos* of 381 with that of the previous synod at Antioch, which as far as we know did not produce a creed. On the other hand, there is no need to interpret the tradition as sanctioning the conclusion that N was re-affirmed at Constantinople in its pure, original form. The difficulties which that hypothesis has to meet have been seen to be at least equally formidable. If we conclude that the Nicene faith was ratified in the shape of C, we have an explanation of the course of events which seems to account fully for all the facts.

For all the facts except one: for there still remains the final, vitally important question what form of endorsement the council gave C, and at what stage in its proceedings, as a result of which that formula could be plausibly described as its creed. Hitherto scholars have had to be content with vague, general suppositions, but recently an attractive and satisfying solution of the problem has been propounded by A. M. Ritter. Briefly, his proposal[1] is that the creed was officially put forward at the council during discussions with the delegation of Macedonian or Pneumatomachian bishops led by Eleusius of Cyzicus who have already been mentioned twice.[2] The object of these discussions, according to the historians Socrates and Sozomen,[3] was to bring about an accommodation between the orthodox majority, who accepted the divinity and consubstantiality of the Holy Spirit, and the Macedonians, who contested this doctrine; and Ritter has given good reasons[4] for believing (a) that they should be placed, not at the very commencement of the council (as has been generally supposed), but after the death of St Meletius when St Gregory of Nazianzus was acting as president, and (b) that the initiative both for getting them going and for framing the line to be followed must have lain with Theodosius himself. Flying in the face of all practical probability, he must have hoped that at least the less intransigent Macedonians could be won over; and to this end he must have induced the reluctant Meletian majority to hold out to them an olive branch.

That this is not guess-work but fact, and that in all likelihood the olive branch took the form of C, Ritter has effectively argued by drawing attention to a striking passage in the long autobiographical poem which St Gregory of Nazianzus composed in his retirement, and which (although its importance has been generally neglected) constitutes in the relevant sections an eye-witness, if heavily prejudiced, account of events at the council. In this passage[5] St Gregory bitterly complains that at the council he had been obliged to witness "the sweet and beauteous spring of our ancient faith, which gathered in unity the adorable nature of the Trinity, being wretchedly befouled with briny infusions poured into it by double-minded men

---

[1] See his *Das Konzil von Konstantinopel und sein Symbol*, esp. 189–91.
[2] See pp. 305 and 307 above.
[3] Socrates, *Hist. eccl.* 5, 8; Sozomen, *Hist. eccl.* 7, 7, 2–5 (*P.G.* 67, 576 f.; 1429).
[4] *Op. cit.*, 78–85.
[5] *Carm. hist.* xi, 1703–14 (*P.G.* 37, 1148 f.).

sharing the beliefs favoured by the Majesty who claim to be mediators—how admirable if they really were mediators, and not blatantly adherents of the contrary cause!" Stripped of diplomatic and poetic obscurities, the obvious implication of these lines is that the Nicene creed, the palladium of orthodox Trinitarianism, had been tampered with and, in the supposed interests of unity and to satisfy the imperial will, had had additions forced upon it which, in Gregory's opinion, were unsatisfactory to the point of blasphemy. That these mediating concessions were designed to placate Macedonians is clearly implied by St Gregory's later statement[1] that as a result the Church had now opened its doors to "Moabites and Ammonites", for this is a description he elsewhere[2] applies specifically to the contentious people who query the divinity of the Holy Spirit. As is well known, he himself not only firmly believed in the divinity and consubstantiality of the Spirit (as did the other Cappadocians), but was content with nothing less than their full and frank proclamation.[3]

We may conclude, then, that in the course of the discussions with the Macedonians the council put forward, as a statement of belief which might be acceptable to all parties, a version of "the Nicene creed" modified by additional matter concerning the Holy Spirit which fell short of what St Gregory (who was fully aware[4] that N needed supplementing at this point) deemed adequate. From this it is an easy step, as Ritter has persuasively argued, to identify the formula proposed with C, which by studiously refraining from calling the Spirit "God" and "consubstantial" might seem to be stretching out an eirenical hand to Christians, like the Macedonians, who questioned His fully divine status. To be sure, St Gregory did less than justice to its sponsors by condemning it so sharply as a betrayal of the true faith. As we shall discover, for all its eirenical avoidance of controversial terms, C contained a pneumatology which was in substance all that St Gregory could have desired. But its lack of outspokenness and deceptive

---

[1] *Carm. hist.* xi, 1737 f. (*P.G.* 37, 1151).
[2] *Or.* 42, 18 (*P.G.* 36, 480).
[3] Cf., e.g., *Or.* 6, 11; 21, 34; 31, 10 (*P.G.* 35, 726; 1124; 36, 144).
[4] Cf. his remarks quoted on p. 307 above.

air of ambiguity on this cardinal article were sufficient to damn it in his eyes.

If this identification (which, incidentally, is supported by the reference, already noted,[1] in the pseudo-Athanasian *De Trinitate* to the enlargement of N by the orthodox) is accepted, we can readily agree that C was in a real, though rather special, sense the creed of the 150 fathers. The negotiations broke down (as might have been expected), the dissatisfied Macedonians packed their bags and departed, and the creed lost its original *raison d'être*; but since the council had adopted and used it in the unsuccessful discussions, it was the council's creed. This account of the matter also provides an adequate explanation of the curious silence about C as an independent creed. If the council really had formulated a new creed and had really published it as such under its own name, it is inconceivable that every trace of so momentous a happening should have disappeared. Such few references to it as can be collected do not speak unambiguously of a Constantinopolitan creed. At the most they suggest that the 150 fathers brought certain articles of the Nicene faith up to date. It is true, of course, that the council of Constantinople was slow in acquiring ecumenical status, and this fact may to some extent explain the curious silence. What it fails to explain is that the work of the 150 fathers was several times alluded to, but never with any acknowledgement that they had composed and published a new creed. On the other hand, if what the council did was to re-affirm the Nicene faith in the form of C in the context of its negotiations with the Macedonian delegation—negotiations, moreover, which eventually broke down—everything becomes clear. We should not expect to come across separate references to C, at any rate until the authentic text of N began to be disentangled from the ambiguous formula "the faith of the 318 Nicene fathers". It is clear from the writings of Theodore of Mopsuestia, Nestorius and others that this did not happen for some time. Broadly speaking, it was not until the council of Ephesus, in 431, that the pure text of N began to be clearly distinguished from C, although the habit of designating

---

[1] See p. 321 above. The context shows that the "additions" of which Macedonius complained concerned the Holy Spirit.

any orthodox formula constructed on Nicene principles as "the faith of Nicaea" was never eradicated.

Furthermore, our explanation is in complete accord with the treatment of C at Chalcedon. As has been insisted upon previously, the repeated recognition of it as the *ekthesis* of the 150 fathers is fatal to any hypothesis which proposes a merely accidental connection between it and the council. On the other hand, the Chalcedonian minutes do not really indicate that N and C enjoyed, as Schwartz tried to show, juridical equivalence. It is clear that the majority of members were surprised to hear of "the faith of the 150 fathers", and it is not unlikely that they demanded to be satisfied about its credentials. Moreover, there can be no doubt that they considered N as their principal instrument. In the prologue to the Definition they used significant language:

This in fact we have accomplished, having by a unanimous vote driven away misleading doctrines, and having renewed the unerring faith of the fathers, proclaiming to all the creed of the 318, and in addition accepting as our fathers those who received this statement of orthodoxy, the 150 fathers who subsequently met together in great Constantinople and set their seal to the same faith.

Again they wrote:

We decree that the exposition of the right and blameless faith of the 318 holy and blessed fathers, assembled at Nicaea in the time of the emperor Constantine of pious memory, should be pre-eminent (προλάμπειν μέν), while the decisions of the 150 holy fathers . . . should also hold good[1].

Later still in the Definition they declared that the council

has decreed primarily that the creed of the 318 holy fathers should remain inviolate; and on account of those who contend against the Holy Spirit, it ratifies the teaching subsequently set forth by the 150 holy fathers assembled in the royal city concerning the essence of the Spirit, not as adducing anything left lacking by their predecessors, but making distinct by Scriptural testimonies their conception concerning the Holy Spirit against those who were trying to set aside His sovereignty.[2]

---

[1] *A.C.O.* II, I, ii, 126 f.   [2] *A.C.O.* II, I, ii, 128f.

"We get the impression", remarked Père J. Lebon,[1] "that, except for special reasons, the Chalcedonian fathers would have preferred to have recalled simply the Nicene creed. . . . Their special reason for according an express and distinct mention to the intervention of the Constantinopolitan fathers is given by the bishops of Chalcedon in the very terms in which they define the nature of the work of the second general council in regard to the formula of faith. For them the Constantinopolitan fathers received the symbol of the 318 and set their seal on the same faith, but they also, against the Pneumatomachi, clarified their thought, with appropriate Scriptural references, about the Holy Spirit."

The conclusion to which we are thus drawn is one which, while rejecting the Hort-Harnack hypothesis of a purely accidental association of C with the council of 381, avoids the radical alternative espoused by Eduard Schwartz and such English scholars as Badcock, viz. the theory that the council formally propounded a new creed of its own and elevated it to a position parallel to that of N. It seems clear that the council's primary object was to restore and promote the Nicene faith in terms which would take account of the further development of doctrine, especially with regard to the Holy Spirit, which had taken place since Nicaea. This it did in its first canon and also, more circumstantially and without any attempt at eirenical compromise (there was no need for that now), in the dogmatic *tomos* which, according to the synodal letter[1] of 382, it published. Nevertheless, at a critical juncture in its proceedings it had adopted C and used it as a negotiating instrument. In consequence C could with some justification claim to be the creed of the 150 fathers, and all the more so as they had promulgated no other.

---

[1] *R.H.E.* xxxii, 1936, 860.   [2] Theodoret, *Hist. eccl.* 5, 13 (Parmentier, 293).

CHAPTER XI

THE TEACHING AND HISTORY OF C

1. *C and Apollinarianism*

WHATEVER the circumstances of its origin, the Constantino-politan creed had a glittering destiny in store for it. We have now to recount the successive stages, so far as they are still discernible, by which it became the sole baptismal confession of the East and the eucharistic creed of Christendom. But before we settle down to this, we must devote two sections to the special doctrines which its original authors or sponsors were concerned to press home. Like the Nicene creed of which they regarded it as a legitimate expansion, C bears the marks of theological controversy, although they have tended to become blurred with the passage of centuries. The Christian who repeats it or hears it sung to-day at the holy mysteries is rarely conscious of the deeper theological intention which lies concealed beneath certain of its majestic clauses.

More probably than not, the framework of the creed was a local baptismal confession in current use in the 'seventies of the fourth century, and the likelihood is that it belonged to either the Antioch or the Jerusalem family. Like many similar baptismal formularies in the epoch following the synod of Alexandria (362), it had been modified in a Nicene direction by the inclusion of the homoousion. Its revisers, however, failed to incorporate the Nicene clause THAT IS, FROM THE SUBSTANCE OF THE FATHER, and this fact deserves special attention. Harnack seized[1] upon it as confirming his well-known theory that the new orthodoxy which came to the fore after 362 and triumphed at Constantinople in 381 was Nicene only in name. "It was not the homoousion which finally won the day," he wrote, "but the homoeousian doctrine which had come to terms with the homoousion." The homoeousian "half-

[1] Cf. *Lehrbuch der Dogmengeschichte*, 5th ed., Tübingen, 1931, II, 261 f.

friends of the Nicaenum" and the Cappadocians, he argued, found the homoousion itself quite acceptable because it could without any trouble be interpreted as "like in substance". As their writings reveal, however, they felt much more uncomfortable about FROM THE SUBSTANCE OF THE FATHER, which struck them as an open invitation to Sabellianism.[1] The final verdict on this hotly debated question belongs to the historian of doctrine:[2] all we shall say here is that a careful analysis of the theology of the Cappadocians does not bear out Harnack's re-reading of history. So far as the real Homoeousians were concerned, their attitude was precisely the opposite of that described by Harnack. While rejecting the homoousion, they found the ἐκ τῆς οὐσίας perfectly acceptable, even including it in their manifesto, their reason being that by itself it did not convey identity of substance. Those whom Harnack's general argument fails to convince need not attach any special significance to the omission of the clause in question from the creed. The creed was, above all, a formula for liturgical purposes, and while it was desirable to bring it into line with Nicene orthodoxy, it was unnecessary to incorporate all the Nicene phrases.

The first passage in C which, according to the ancient tradition, owed its insertion to dogmatic motives is the clause FROM THE HOLY SPIRIT AND THE VIRGIN MARY. These words, elaborating the bare BECAME INCARNATE of N, are said to have been added with a view to making the opposition of the creed to Apollinarianism clear. Our primary authority for this is that episode of the intervention of Diogenes, bishop of Cyzicus, at the first Chalcedonian session which has already come before us more than once. Provoked by Eutyches's reported attachment to the pure text of N, Diogenes protested that the Nicene creed had received additions from the holy fathers because of the perverse notions of Apollinarius and Valentinus and Macedonius and men like them. He continued: "The creed had added to it WHO CAME DOWN AND BECAME INCARNATE FROM THE HOLY SPIRIT AND THE VIRGIN MARY. Eutyches has passed these words

[1] *Op. cit.* 277.
[2] For a criticism of Harnack's point of view, cf. J. F. Bethune-Baker, *The Meaning of Homoousios in the 'Constantinopolitan' Creed* (*Texts and Studies* VII, 1), Cambridge, 1901; Ritter, 291 f.
[3] Cf. Epiphanius, *Pan. haer.* 73, 6 (Holl III, 276): cited by Ritter.

over because he is an Apollinarian. Apollinarius himself accepts the holy synod of Nicaea, interpreting its definitions in accordance with his own wrongheaded ideas. But he evades FROM THE HOLY SPIRIT AND THE VIRGIN MARY so as to avoid confessing the union of the flesh (ἵνα πανταχοῦ μὴ τὴν ἕνωσιν τῆς σαρκὸς ὁμολογήσῃ)."[1] We may compare with this Justinian's statement in a decree published in 533, in which, after declaring his loyalty to the creed of the 318 fathers which the 150 had clarified and explained, he added: "Not as though there was anything lacking to it, but because the enemies of the faith had some of them presumed to undermine the divinity of the Holy Spirit, while others had denied the true incarnation of the Word of God, from holy Mary, ever-virgin, mother of God."[2]

The real heresy of Apollinarius, we know, consisted in his refusal to admit the completeness of the Lord's humanity. The Word, he thought, could not have assumed a free, intelligent human soul without introducing a disastrous duality into the Saviour's being. At first he based himself on a dichotomist anthropology and taught that Christ's human nature consisted simply of a body, the place of the soul being usurped by the Word. Later, becoming trichotomist, he admitted that Christ possessed an animal soul (ψυχή) in addition to a body, but denied Him a human rational soul (νοῦς). In either case his doctrine was that Christ had but a single nature, and that the flesh was something, as it were, adventitious and added to the divinity. Very soon, however, all sorts of bizarre, not to say mutually inconsistent, distortions of his ideas were in circulation, as we can vividly see in St Athanasius's *Letter to Epictetus* (written in 370 or 371). According to this, the Apollinarians were thought to teach that the body born of Mary was consubstantial with the divinity of the Word, that the Word was transformed into flesh, that the Saviour had a body only in appearance and not by nature, that His divinity itself underwent the human experiences, that Jesus did not assume a passible body from the Blessed Virgin but formed one out of His own substance, that His body was coeternal with His

[1] *A.C.O.* II, I, i, 91.
[2] Cf. P. Krüger, *Codex Iustinianus*, Berlin, 1877, I, 1, 7. Justinian seems to stress the birth from the Virgin in his decrees.

divine nature, and so on.[1] Much the same picture, or rather caricature, of Apollinarianism is provided by St Epiphanius,[2] who reproduced St Athanasius's letter, and by the anonymous author of the pseudo-Athanasian *Libri II contra Apollinarium*.[3] Apollinarius himself and his follower Timothy of Berytus were condemned at Rome by Pope Damasus in 377,[4] and the sentence was confirmed in 378 by a council at Alexandria and in 379 by one at Antioch.[5] The council of Constantinople solemnly re-affirmed the ban.

The question we have to decide is whether the tradition was well grounded which discerned an anti-Apollinarian intent in our clause of the creed. Several considerations, it can be said with confidence, compel a negative answer. First, the belief that the Constantinopolitan fathers interfered with the creed at this point was not very widely or firmly held. While a whole series of witnesses testified to their contribution to the section dealing with the Holy Spirit, only two or three explicitly suggested that their handiwork was to be seen in the article about the Incarnation too. Secondly, there seems to be nothing distinctively anti-Apollinarian in the clause as it stands: it consists, in fact, of an excerpt from the primitive kerygma. Thirdly, St Epiphanius's second creed, *Ep.* II, shows the kind of precise wording that was called for if Apollinarianism proper was to be ruled out. Expanding N with a view to excluding the heresy, he wrote: ". . . came down and became incarnate, that is, was perfectly ($\tau\epsilon\lambda\epsilon\iota\omega\varsigma$) born from holy Mary ever-virgin through the Holy Spirit; became man, that is, assumed a complete man, animal soul and body and rational soul."[6] Fourthly, the Apollinarians had apparently no qualms about affirming the birth from the Virgin. Apollinarius himself included the words ". . . was born from Mary according to the flesh" and "He therefore Who was born from the Virgin Mary . . ." in the profession of faith which he sent to Jovian;[7] and

[1] *Ep. ad Epict.* 2 (*P.G.* 26, 1052 f.).
[2] *Pan. haer.* 77 (Holl III, 416–451). He was writing in 377.
[3] *P.G.* 26, 1093 ff. The date usually given for them is 380.
[4] Cf. *Ep. Dam.* 2, *frag.* 2, and *Ep.* 7 (*P.L.* 13, 352 and 370 f.).
[5] Rufinus, *Hist. eccl.* 2, 20 (*P.L.* 21, 527).
[6] *Ancor.* 119 (Holl I, 148).
[7] Originally attributed to St Athanasius. It is printed in *P.G.* 26, 25 ff. and H. Lietzmann's *Apollinaris von Laodicea*, Tübingen, 1904, 250 ff.

his disciple Vitalis, according to St Epiphanius,[1] admitted at a conference held at Antioch that Jesus Christ had been born from the holy Virgin Mary without seed of man and through the Holy Spirit.

Finally and most convincingly, if the account of the original function of C sketched in the previous chapter is correct, it seems highly unlikely that in formulating it the 150 fathers were concerned to rebut Apollinarianism. Their sole object at this stage was to reach an accommodation with the Macedonians, and the Apollinarian issue was totally irrelevant to this. Admittedly, one of the purposes of the council was to place a ban on Apollinarianism, but it had no motive for doing this in an indirect or imprecise fashion, using language which, whatever its profounder implications, was (as we have noted) perfectly acceptable to the heretics. Had it followed this line, it would undoubtedly have earned another stinging rebuke from St Gregory of Nazianzus in his autobiographical poem, for he was as unyielding and as outspoken in his opposition to Apollinarianism as he was in his espousal of the full deity of the Holy Spirit; but the poem contains, as Ritter has acutely observed,[2] no trace of such a rebuke. As a matter of fact, the fathers roundly condemned Apollinarianism in their first canon; and we have every reason to suppose that they did so in greater detail, and in precise and effective terms, in their dogmatic *tomos*. At anyrate the summary of the latter which survives in the synodal letter of 382 makes no bones about the heresy, declaring[3] unambiguously that "we preserve unperverted the doctrine of the incarnation of the Lord, accepting the tradition that the dispensation in the flesh was neither without soul nor without rational mind nor incomplete, and fully recognizing that God the Word was perfect before the ages, and in the last days became perfect man for our salvation".

The only plausible conclusion, therefore, is that there was no anti-Apollinarian thrust in the clause FROM THE HOLY SPIRIT AND THE VIRGIN MARY; the words are present in C for the simple reason that the fathers found them in the formula they used as

---

[1] *Pan. haer.* 77, 22 (Holl III, 435).
[2] *Op. cit.*, 193 f.
[3] Theodoret, *Hist. eccl.* 5, 9, 12 (Parmentier, 292 f.).

their basis. Nevertheless it remains an indisputable fact of history that Diogenes of Cyzicus, and others both at the time of Chalcedon and later, firmly believed that they had been inserted into the creed with a view to excluding Apollinarianism. False though it appears to be, we have to explain how this tradition arose, and different solutions have been proposed. According to A. M. Ritter,[1] the clue is to be found in the use which Leo the Great had made of the Roman baptismal creed in his refutation of Eutyches. The very words of the creed, he had claimed,[2] "in which the whole company of the faithful professes belief . . . in Jesus Christ, His only Son, our Lord, *Who was born from the Holy Spirit and Mary the Virgin*, . . . are sufficient to destroy the machinations of practically all heretics". Among these heretics he had especially Eutyches in mind, but the same appeal to the credal statement would be equally valid against Apollinarianism, the two heresies being now hopelessly mixed up with each other.

This is an interesting and constructive suggestion; its weakness, as M. Santer has pointed out,[3] is that it fails to take account of Diogenes's quite explicit assertion that the clause had been added to the creed for clarification by "the holy fathers who came after" Nicaea. Santer's own attractive explanation is that the tradition of its anti-Apollinarian bias is much older than Pope Leo, being traceable in all probability to Nestorius's polemic a generation before against St Cyril of Alexandria. In Nestorius's view St Cyril's position was indistinguishable from Apollinarianism, and like Apollinarianism was refuted by the statement of the Nicene fathers that Christ was incarnate from the Holy Spirit and the Virgin Mary. He was mistaken, as St Cyril was quick to point out, in implying that the authentic text of the Nicene creed contained any statement to that effect. Nevertheless it was apparently during the Christological controversy that the idea gained credence that the clause was originally anti-Apollinarian, and it was natural that people believing this should attribute its insertion to the 150 fathers, who were known to have expanded N's third article.

[1] *Op. cit.*, 194.   [2] *Ep. 28 ad Flav.* 2 (*P.L.* 54, 757 ff.).
[3] *J.T.S.* NS xxii, 1971, 163. For Santer's alternative proposal, and the detailed references to Nestorius, St Cyril, etc., see the rest of this suggestive article.

2. *The Holy Spirit in C*

While the alleged anti-Apollinarian bias of the clause about Christ's birth must be rejected, there can be no doubt as to the polemical bearing of the next clause in C to elaborate and extend the teaching of the original Nicene creed. This is, of course, the sentence OF WHOSE KINGDOM THERE SHALL BE NO END. These words, taken bodily from St Luke (1, 33), were aimed at the doctrine, attributed to Marcellus of Ancyra, that the relationship of Sonship in the Godhead was limited to the Incarnation, and would disappear when the purposes for which the Word became incarnate had been accomplished. The Word would then again become, what He had been from all eternity, immanent in the Father, Who would be all in all.[1] We saw in Chap. IX that anti-Marcellan clauses, expressed in these or similar terms, were incorporated in most of the Eastern conciliar creeds constructed in the 'forties and 'fifties of the fourth century: they testify to the dread in which Marcellus's views were held. The words themselves made an appearance in the creed commented upon by St Cyril of Jerusalem, who gave his animosity against the heretic full rein: "If ever you hear anyone saying that there is an end to the kingship of Christ, hate the heresy. It is another head of the dragon which has sprouted lately in the region of Galatia."[2] Marcellus died in 374, and the excitement over his dangerous doctrines had to a large extent passed away. Yet so late as 377 St Basil's letters reveal that they were still feared, and that there was opposition to restoring to communion too easily those who shared them.[3] The Marcellians and the Photinians (followers of Marcellus's extremist disciple and ally) were among the heretics singled out for condemnation in the first canon of the council of Constantinople. The council's object, manifestly, was to dispose once and for all of all the various heresies by which the pure teaching of the Nicene faith had been embarrassed since its formulation, and since it was placing the Arians and their successors under its ban, it was fitting that those whose

---

[1] See above, p. 266 f.
[2] *Cat.* 15, 27 (*P.G.* 33, 909).
[3] Cf. *Epp.* 263, 5; 265, 3 (*P.G.* 32, 981; 988 f.).

error lay on the Sabellian side should be proscribed as well. In all probability the clause OF WHOSE KINGDOM, etc., already stood in the creed which the 150 fathers took over and made their own. It was an item in St Cyril's creed as early as 348, and it must have spread to other creeds of the Jerusalem and related families.

The ban on Marcellus's doctrine has seemed to some scholars, not altogether justly, as a mere *pro forma* re-enactment of anathemas which had become conventional. But the third article of the Constantinopolitan Creed beyond question represented a development of and advance on the teaching of N which the controversies of the hour made imperative. Several of the credenda listed in it—the Church, baptism, the remission of sins, the resurrection of the dead, the life of the world to come —were perfectly normal constituents of the third article of Eastern baptismal formularies. The clauses which should be regarded as the distinctive contribution of the second general council are those concerned with the doctrine of the Holy Spirit.

The heretics against whom they were directed were the Pneumatomachians, otherwise known as Macedonians. (The latter name, which later historians liked to use, was scarcely appropriate: the Semi-Arian Macedonius, who had been bishop of Constantinople between 342 and his deposition in 360, was not really the founder of the party called after him.) While the Arian controversy was at its height, the problems raised by the status of the Holy Spirit had been kept in the background, although neither Arius himself nor his followers had concealed their view that the third Person of the divine Trinity, like the second, was to be ranked with the creatures. In the late 'fifties, however, of the fourth century His true nature and position began to be matters of public discussion. About this time, as we learn from the letters[1] which St Athanasius addressed (356-362) to St Serapion, bishop of Thmuis in the Nile delta, the theory was being put forward even by Christians who believed in the divinity of the Son that the Spirit was a creature or, to be more precise, one of the ministering spirits or angels. In his reply St Athanasius vigorously defended the

[1] *P.G.* 26, 529-676.

view that His consubstantiality with the Father and the Son was as indispensable as the consubstantiality of the Father and the Son with each other. In 362 the council of Alexandria expressly declared that only those could be received into communion who, accepting the council of Nicaea, rejected the thesis of the creation of the Spirit.[1] From now onwards the issue was a burning one, although when it came to the positive formulation of doctrine great uncertainty prevailed in the Nicene camp itself. St Basil, for example, thought it prudent to refrain from proclaiming openly the divinity of the Spirit; and it was only after his rupture in 373 with his former friend Eustathius of Sebaste, who henceforth became "the protagonist of the Pneumatomachians",[2] that he and the other Cappadocians began to speak out with greater confidence. Meanwhile the Macedonian opposition, the right wing of which was orthodox on the doctrine of the Son while the left wing slipped more and more down the Anomoean slope, was clearer as regards the Holy Spirit in its negations than in its affirmations. What seems certain, however, is that its more moderate leaders took refuge in Scripture, refusing to admit the full divinity of the Spirit, but at the same time recoiling from the old Arian idea that He was a creature. The words which Socrates[3] put into the mouth of Eustathius were probably typical of most of them: "For my part, I neither choose to name the Holy Spirit God, nor should presume to call Him a creature."

When the council of Constantinople met in 381, one of its express objects was to bring the Church's teaching about the Holy Spirit into line with what it believed about the Son. Several years before, it is interesting to observe, St Basil had reached the conclusion that, while not the smallest addition must be made to the Nicene faith in general, an exception was the doctrine of the Holy Spirit. In their creed the 318 fathers had only touched upon Him in passing, for He had not yet become the subject of disputes.[4] Quite understandably, there-

[1] Cf. St. Athan., *Tom. ad Antioch.* 3 (*P.G.* 26, 800).
[2] Cf. St Basil, *Ep.* 263, 3 (*P.G.* 32, 980).
[3] *Hist. eccl.* 2, 45 (*P.G.* 67, 360).
[4] Cf. his letter to St Epiphanius, dated 376: *Ep.* 258, 2 (*P.G.* 32, 949).

fore, the council of 381 anathematized the Pneumatomachians
in its first canon, and, to judge by the letter of the synod of
382,[1] proceeded to assert the full deity and consubstantiality
of the Holy Spirit, and His existence as a separate hypostasis.
Nevertheless, at the stage in its proceedings when it sponsored
C, it was adopting, at the request of Theodosius, a deliberately
less aggressive, more conciliatory line. Even so it failed to reach
agreement with the Macedonian delegation led by Eleusius of
Cyzicus, who according to the historian Socrates[2] preferred to
break off discussions rather than become a party to the homoousion of the Spirit. Hence it was to be expected that the
creed, while embodying a doctrine which the sharp-sighted
Macedonians inevitably found unpalatable, would be clothed
in language much more moderate and less provocative than the
synodical decisions later ratified.

We notice in the first place the Scriptural flavour of the
language employed. St Paul had used the word LORD of the
Spirit in 2 *Cor.* 3, 17 f. He had also spoken of the Spirit as "the
Spirit of life" (*Rom.* 8, 2), and the epithet LIFE-GIVER ($\zeta\omega o\pi o\iota\acute{o}\nu$)
in its verb-form ($\zeta\omega o\pi o\iota\epsilon\tilde{\iota}\nu$) had been used of Him in *Jn.* 6, 63
and 2 *Cor.* 3, 6. The description PROCEEDING FROM THE FATHER
was borrowed from the Lord's own words, "The Spirit of truth,
Who proceeds from the Father", recorded in *Jn.* 15, 26, with
only a change of preposition ($\dot{\epsilon}\kappa$ for $\pi a\rho\acute{a}$) ; and even that change
of preposition was authorized by St Paul's language ("the
Spirit Who is from God") in 1 *Cor.* 2, 12. The words WHO SPOKE
THROUGH THE PROPHETS, which of course had a long history in
creeds and went back to the primitive kerygma of Christendom,
recalled the verse of 2 *Pet.* 1, 21, "For no prophecy ever came
by the will of man, but men spake from God, being moved by
the Holy Spirit."

In the second place, it is obvious that the creed was intended
to convey the conception of the divinity of the Holy Spirit,
though in language which was guarded and calculated to give
no more offence than was unavoidable. The Greek word LORD
($\tau\grave{o}\nu$ $\kappa\acute{v}\rho\iota o\nu$) was the Septuagint equivalent of the Hebrew
Yahweh, though its use was too widespread in the Hellenistic

---

[1] In Theodoret, *Hist. eccl.* 5, 9, 11 (Parmentier 292).
[2] *Hist. eccl.* 5, 8 (*P.G.* 67, 577).

world for it to be decisive. The all-important clause, however, was WHO WITH THE FATHER AND THE SON IS TOGETHER WORSHIPPED AND TOGETHER GLORIFIED. The expressions used almost reproduced St Athanasius's own choice of words, "Who is glorified with the Father and the Son."[1] Even more strikingly did it reflect St Basil's usage. He had spoken of "that sound doctrine according to which the Son is confessed as homoousios with the Father, and the Holy Spirit is numbered together with Them and worshipped together with Them with identical honour (ὁμοτίμως συναριθμεῖται τε καὶ συνλατρεύεται)".[2] He had also written:[3] "Glorifying the Holy Spirit with the Father and the Son because of the conviction that He is not alien from the divine nature. For that which is foreign in nature could not have shared in the same honours." The starting-point of his treatise De Spiritu sancto was his desire to demonstrate the legitimacy of a doxology giving glory to the Father "with the Son and with the Holy Spirit". The burden of its central section[4] was the demonstration of the identity of honour (ὁμοτιμία) enjoyed by the Spirit with the Father and the Son. For St Basil these phrases "conglorification" and "identity of honour" had a very definite meaning: they were the equivalent of "consubstantial" since their applicability was based on identity of being.[5]

A feature of this article about the Spirit which is often thought somewhat puzzling is the comparative mildness of its tone. The council of Constantinople, our records say, took its stand on the full consubstantiality of the Holy Spirit with the Godhead. It was because they could not stomach this, apparently, that the Macedonian representatives decided to take their departure. Yet the clause we are studying scrupulously avoids the term homoousios and contents itself, apart from the mention of the worship and honour due to the Spirit, with biblical phrases which, however unexceptionable if pressed, could be accepted by the Macedonians in their own sense.

[1] Cf. Ad Serap. 1, 31; Ad Iov. ad fin. (P.G. 26, 601; 820).
[2] Ep. 90, 2 (P.G. 32, 473).
[3] Ep. 159, 2 (P.G. 32, 621).
[4] Chaps. 9–24 (P.G. 32, 108–173).
[5] For a full discussion of St Basil's position and the significance for him of homotimos, see the edition of De Spiritu sancto by B. Pruche, O.P., 12 ff. (Éditions du Cerf, Paris, 1946).

Scholars have pointed to this fact as conclusive evidence that this article could not be the work of the council, which must have expressed itself in much more decisive language if it had made a credal pronouncement on the Spirit. Yet such arguments betray a curious failure to understand the historical situation. The aim of Theodosius at this phase of the council was genuinely conciliatory, and he had insisted on including a quota of Macedonian bishops in his invitation. According to Socrates,[1] "the emperor and the bishops who shared the same faith spared no efforts to bring Eleusius and his party into unity with them". Renewed efforts to win them over were to be made a couple of years later[2] : hopes ran high that the Church might be reunited on the basis of the Nicene faith. At the same time it must be remembered that not all in the orthodox ranks felt completely easy about the frank description of the Holy Spirit as God and as consubstantial with the Father and the Son which was becoming *de rigueur*. Their leaders generally, starting with St Athanasius, had deliberately exercised restraint in their language about the Spirit. St Basil, in particular, practised a diplomatic caution which was sometimes harshly judged in more uncompromising circles,[3] and even in the *De Spiritu sancto*, while in effect pleading for the doctrine of consubstantiality, had desisted from using the term. There is a revealing passage in one of the sermons of St Gregory of Nazianzus, preached almost contemporaneously with the council, in which, expatiating on the prevailing uncertainty about the real status of the Holy Spirit, he admitted that some of those who held Him to be God kept this as a pious opinion to themselves.[4]

Bearing these points in mind, we can appreciate that C's firm but temperately worded theology of the Spirit corresponded, so far as its substance was concerned, to the real convictions of the 150 fathers, and in its expression went so far as they deemed prudent to meet the susceptibilities of the Macedonians. It is little wonder that Eleusius and his colleagues

---

[1] *Hist. eccl.* 5, 8 (*P.G.* 67, 577).
[2] Socrat., *Hist. eccl.* 5, 10 (*P.G.* 67, 588 ff.).
[3] Cf. the anecdote told by St Greg. Naz., *Ep.* 58 (*P.G.* 37, 116). See also his *Orat.* 43, 68 (*P.G.* 36, 588).
[4] *Orat.* 31, 5 (*P.G.* 36, 137).

soon decided that no worth-while compromise was likely to be reached on this basis, for the concessions offered were largely verbal. Indeed some of the language used, for all its Biblical sound, was patently anti-Pneumatomachian in content, e.g. PROCEEDING FROM THE FATHER. As Ritter has shown,[1] the Pneumatomachians were strenuously hostile to the idea of the Spirit's derivation from the Father, holding that this derogated from the honour of the Only-begotten Son; in the interests of a graded Triad they argued for the Spirit's direct dependence on the Son. Thus the contrast between the relative mildness of the creed and the forthrightness of the *tomos* is explained by the very different situations in which they were framed.

3. *The Baptismal Use of C*

As canonized by the council of Constantinople and re-affirmed in the Chalcedonian Definition, C, like the original Nicene creed, appeared in the guise of a formal test of orthodox belief. There is every reason to suppose, however, that it was also employed from early times as a baptismal confession. Such had probably been its original function before the 150 fathers appropriated it, and its smooth-flowing style and balanced theological content marked it out for liturgical use. It is not unlikely that it was established in Constantinople and the surrounding region before 451 as the official baptismal creed. It would be natural for Constantinople, a city whose church life had been presided over mainly by Arians since St Alexander's death, to adopt the orthodox creed of 381 for catechetical purposes. This would help to explain the marked eagerness with which the imperial commissioners and the ecclesiastical spokesmen of Constantinople pressed its claims at Chalcedon. That after 451 it was the baptismal creed of the Constantinopolitan church scarcely admits of doubt. As illustrations of the fact we may note that Basiliscus, in his encyclical issued in 475, declared that he and all the faithful before him had been baptized with the Nicene creed; while Zeno in his Henoticon (482) spoke of the creed of the 318 fathers as confirmed by the 150 fathers as the only symbol

---

[1] *Op. cit.*, 300 (with useful references).

with which Christians were baptized.[1] Yet the context makes it plain that they were thinking of C as the complete, definitive form of the Nicene creed. When shortly afterwards C was interpolated into the Eucharist at Constantinople, we are distinctly told that hitherto it had been used as the baptismal creed.[2]

In process of time, however, C was destined to become the sole baptismal creed of all the Eastern churches. A few communities detached from the central stream of Orthodoxy, such as the Jacobite church of Syria,[3] and the Nestorian,[4] Armenian[5] and Abyssinian[6] churches, continue to employ creeds marked with traits drawn from N. But, broadly speaking, C, to all intents and purposes in its original form, has enjoyed a monopoly of baptism since the sixth century. The stages of its progress to this unique position cannot now be traced in detail, but it is apparent that they were not accomplished all at once. At first the practice in the East was to insert the Nicene key-words into the framework of local baptismal creeds: the creed of Antioch cited by John Cassian is an obvious example. Later, in the fifth century prior to Chalcedon, formularies were in use at baptism which bore a remarkable resemblance to C, as we saw when we studied the creeds of Nestorius and Theodore of Mopsuestia. There is no real basis for the widespread view that N in its pure form was frequently used at baptism, or indeed that it was ever used at all. The assumption that it was has to explain how a creed so manifestly defective, particularly in its meagre third article, could ever have lent itself to catechetical purposes. What has given currency to this view is the failure to appreciate that it was regular to describe any formulary which was loyal to the Nicene tradition as "the faith of Nicaea". After Chalcedon the process of bringing local creeds into line with C was accelerated, although the writings of Philoxenus of Hierapolis (Mabbug)[7] and Severus of Antioch[8] show that

---

[1] Evagrius, *Hist. eccl.* 3, 4 and 14 (*P.G.* 86, 2600 and 2624).
[2] Cf. Theodorus Lector, *Hist. eccl.* 2, *frag.* 32 (*P.G.* 86, 201).
[3] Hahn 128.   [4] Hahn 132.   [5] Hahn 136.   [6] Hahn 141.
[7] He died *circa* 523. Cf. his *De uno e sancta Trinitate incorporato et passo dissert.* I (*Patrol. Orient.* XV, 489 f.).
[8] He died in 538. Cf. his *Lib. con. imp. gramm.* 3, 11 (*Corp. script. Christ. Orient.*, *Script. Syr.*, *Ser.* IV, *Tom.* v, 149: ed. J. Lebon, Louvain, 1929).

forms far from identical with C continued in use. At the fifth general council, held at Constantinople in 553, both N and C were quoted in full,[1] and after this date the latter's position was assured. As the creed of the metropolis of the patriarchate, it was, after all, only a matter of time before it was adopted wherever the writ of Constantinople ran.

There is nothing surprising or out of the ordinary in this development: we should in any case have expected C eventually to oust all other creeds in the East. What is more likely to take the student's breath away is the fact (for fact it seems to be) that C actually became the baptismal creed of Rome and certain other churches in the West for a time. At first, as was only natural, C did not enjoy any great esteem in the regions which fell under the jurisdiction of the Roman Pope. It shared in the general disfavour with which the council of Constantinople (the third canon of which had sought to elevate the see of Constantinople to a position second only to that of Rome) was regarded in the West. St Leo the Great, for example, while insistent that the Chalcedonian Definition should be kept inviolate[2] and while acquainted with the pure text of N,[3] was always significantly silent about any creed of the 150 fathers of Constantinople. Harnack was probably correct in claiming that the first direct and unambiguous allusion to it in Western writings occurs in the encyclical letter of Pope Vigilius of 552.[4] Nevertheless the facts which point to its use in the Roman baptismal office are inescapable. In the first place, both the Gelasian Sacramentary[5] and the Sacramentarium Gellonense[6] provide for the use of C in its original Greek at the tradition of the creed by Greek-speaking candidates. There is nothing striking about this, however, for it merely implies that C was recognized in the West as the baptismal creed of the Greek world. But, in the second place (and this is what is really significant), both the Gelasian Sacramentary[7] and the Ordo

---

[1] Mansi IX, 179.
[2] Cf. his four letters, written 21 March 453, in *A.C.O.* II, iv, 67–71.
[3] Cf. his letter to the emperor Leo of 17 August 458, in *A.C.O.* II, iv, 114.
[4] Mansi IX, 50–55.
[5] Cf. H. A. Wilson's edition, Oxford, 1894, 53 f.
[6] Such seems to be the implication of the rite described by E. Martène, *De antiquis ecclesiae ritibus*, Rouen, 1700, I, 100.
[7] Wilson, *op. cit.* 55.

Romanus VII [1] indicate that the creed handed out at the tradition to Latin-speaking candidates, and presumably rendered back by them at the reddition, was none other than C in a Latin dress. At the moment of baptism the interrogations continued to be the old ones, closely approximating in form and content to R, though abbreviated. We may add that in the jumble of baptismal rites in the *Ordo Romanus antiquus* [2] (tenth century) C is the creed of most regular occurrence, while in Codex Sessorianus 52 [3] C is prescribed for the *redditio symboli* on Holy Saturday. It would seem that C was still being used in the Roman baptismal liturgy early in the ninth century, for at the conference held in 810 between Leo III and Charlemagne's three ambassadors the Pope's language implied that C had an instructional, i.e. a catechetical, role. [4]

It must be admitted that the whole matter is extremely mysterious; the subject calls for a great deal more study and research. As the evidence stands, however, the only possible inference, though many scholars are reluctant to draw it, is the one indicated above. Apparently the Roman church, which had been so proud of its age-long use of the same baptismal confession, laid it aside at some date in the sixth century and substituted C. Some other Western churches, for example those of Spain, followed suit. Despite the obscurity of the circumstances in which this startling revolution in practice took place, certain facts are available to throw light upon it and explain the motives at work. First, the replacement of R by C in the baptismal office followed speedily on the abandonment by Rome of her attitude of suspicion to the council of Constantinople. Secondly, the Roman church had recently been grievously threatened by Arianism. For some time the Goths, Arian in religion, had been pouring into the empire, and Odoacer and the Ostrogoths had obtained control of Italy and brought the menace to the gates of the capital. It is practically certain that, if the Roman authorities were induced to adopt C as the creed for the instruction of candidates for baptism, they were moved

[1] *P.L.* 78, 997 f.
[2] See below, p. 428 f. for an account of this.
[3] See below, p. 429 f.
[4] Cf. the account by the abbot Smaragdus in *P.L.* 102, 975. Also see below, pp. 354 f. and 365 f.

by the thought that it provided a more satisfactory repudiation of the heresy of the hour. Last but not least, the change must be viewed as a significant by-product of that subservience to Byzantium to which the Roman church found itself reduced in the middle of the sixth century.[1]

4. C in the Holy Eucharist

The victorious career of the Constantinopolitan Creed was not to be confined within the limits of the baptismal service. Important as was its role in the initiation of Christian catechumens, this was destined to be overshadowed by a function still more impressive and more intimately bound up with the believer's daily life. C was promoted, in the short space of a few decades in the East, and in the West by a series of moves spread over several centuries, from Baptism to the Holy Eucharist, and so became the creed *par excellence* of Christian worship. This was a revolutionary innovation, for in its original and authentic shape the eucharistic liturgy had contained no formal, independent confession of belief. When circumstances prompted the inclusion of one, C with its majestic phrases and stately rhythm seemed almost pre-ordained for the role.

The first occasion of the interpolation of the creed into the eucharistic service was hardly, it would seem, an edifying one. The Monophysites, the reader should be reminded, were bitterly disappointed by the verdict of the council of Chalcedon, and waged ceaseless war against its Definition. One of the chief planks in their propaganda was that, thoroughly unsound in its teaching, it was also an unwarranted superimposition on the one and altogether sufficient creed. An isolated, anonymous sentence [2] which somehow found its way into the collected fragments of Theodore the Reader records that Peter the Fuller, the runaway monk who sat four several times on the patriarchal throne of Antioch, "instituted . . . the recitation of the creed at every synaxis". A fanatical Monophysite, he had seen his

---

[1] So Harnack: cf. *Realencykl.* XI, 25.

[2] Cf. Theodorus Lector, *Eccl. hist.* 2, *frag.* 48 (*P.G.* 86, 208 f.). Dom B. Capelle has shown conclusively (in *Cours et conférences des semaines liturgiques* VI, Louvain, 1928, 174 f. I am deeply indebted to him for sending me a copy of an otherwise unobtainable publication) that the author of this fragment is most unlikely to be Theodore himself.

Chalcedon-minded predecessor Calendion driven into exile (484), had himself signed Zeno's Henoticon (which indirectly condemned the council of 451), and was enjoying the heady wine of personal and party triumph. If the story is true, his action was no doubt intended as an elaborate gesture of obeisance to the Nicene faith and, by implication, of insult to the Definition which had sought to go beyond it. A few years later, in 511 or shortly after, the orthodox patriarch of Constantinople, Macedonius II, was extruded by the machinations of the emperor Anastasius I, and the Monophysite Timothy, who had been a minor functionary in Santa Sophia, was set upon the patriarchal throne in his place. According to a report of the historian Theodore the Reader,[1] himself a contemporary of the events, Timothy "ordered that the symbol of the 318 fathers should be recited at every service in disparagement of Macedonius, as if he did not accept the creed; for it had previously been said only once a year, on the occasion of the catechetical instructions given by the bishop on Good Friday". The two accounts have been held to be inconsistent, and the preference has been given to the second as more circumstantial and as coming from the pen of a reliable witness.[2] But it should be observed that Theodore did not state that Timothy was the inaugurator of the custom, but merely that it was new at Constantinople.

The practice started by heretics in such a dubious atmosphere seems to have taken root at once, and not to have been displaced when orthodoxy once again gained the upper hand in the imperial city. A striking illustration of the way in which it was accepted as a matter of course is furnished by the vivid narrative of the events succeeding the deaths of the patriarch Timothy (5 April 518) and the Monophysite emperor Anastasius I (9 July 518) preserved in the acts of the council held at Constantinople by the patriarch Mennas in 536. This document paints an exciting picture of the tumultuous services over which the new archbishop John presided in Santa Sophia on Sunday

---

[1] *Eccl. hist.* 2, *frag.* 32 (*P.G.* 86, 201).

[2] So Dom B. Capelle in *Cours et conférences des semaines liturgiques* VI. But even if the story about Peter the Fuller is anonymous, it is not necessarily apocryphal. There is nothing intrinsically improbable in it, and no apparent reason why it should have been invented.

and Monday, 15 and 16 July. It describes [1] how, on the latter occasion, the orthodox enthusiasm of the multitude passed all bounds, and includes the significant words: "After the reading of the gospel, the divine liturgy taking its usual course and the doors having been shut, and the holy creed ($\mu\acute{a}\theta\eta\mu a$) having been recited *according to custom* . . ." Apparently, the crowd took the creed for granted in the service, despite the Monophysite initiative in placing it there. Its position, which corresponded to that which it occupies in the Eastern rite to-day, was after the offertory and before the Pax. Half a century later its use in the Eucharist was still further regularized by an ordinance of the emperor Justin II, issued in 568, to the effect that the faith should be sung in every Catholic church before the Lord's Prayer. [2] If the position in the rite implied by this was meant seriously, it must soon have become a dead letter, for in all Eastern liturgies the creed precedes the anaphora.

It is sometimes supposed that the creed thus introduced into the liturgy was the original Nicene symbol. Theodore the Reader himself spoke of the creed of the 318 fathers when recounting the innovation of Timothy at Constantinople. A theory has accordingly been developed by modern students [3] which sees the real point of the moves of Peter the Fuller and Timothy in their determination to get behind C and go right back to the authentic Nicene definition N. C, they think, was suspect in Monophysite eyes, partly because its more precise teaching about the incarnation was not to their taste, and still more because it had been sponsored by the Chalcedonian fathers. Thus what happened was that Peter and Timothy started the fashion of having N sung at the Eucharist, the custom caught on and could not be abolished without offence, and so the orthodox kept it up when they regained power but cunningly substituted C for N. But the basic assumption of this reconstruction, that the Monophysites were consistently hostile to C, is quite unfounded. Basiliscus's encyclical and Zeno's Henoticon, as we observed before, [4] characteristic Monophysite documents as they were, treated C with deferential

---

[1] Mansi VIII, 1057–1065.
[2] Cf. Johannes Biclarensis, *Chronicon* (*P.L.* 72, 863)
[3] So, e.g., A. E. Burn, 114.
[4] See above, p. 300.

respect, and leading Monophysite writers, like Severus of Antioch,[1] were fully acquainted with, and evinced no disapprobation of, the contribution of the Constantinopolitan fathers. Furthermore, while admittedly Theodore the Reader said it was the creed of the 318 that Timothy introduced into the Eucharist, he testified in the very next breath that it was the formulary used in the Lenten catechizings; and this cannot have been N, as Theodore, who was a reader in Santa Sophia, must have known. What has misled modern critics has been the persistent failure to recognize that the designation "the faith of the 318 fathers" was a very loose one, and was habitually employed to indicate, not only N in its purity, but the improved version of N which the fathers of 381 had endorsed.

In the West the creed installed itself in the Eucharist more gradually. The first stage of the development was accomplished in Spain at the famous third council of Toledo, held in 589, which was to prove a noteworthy landmark in the history of Spanish Catholicism. It was at this council that Reccared, king of the Visigoths, who had come under the influence of his saintly uncle, Leander of Seville, formally renounced Arianism on behalf of himself and his people. The second canon promulgated on this occasion ordered the creed to be recited in all churches on Sundays. The exact words ran as follows:[2]

Out of reverence for the most holy faith and to strengthen the vacillating minds of men, the holy synod has resolved, on the advice of the religious and glorious king Reccared, that in all the churches of Spain and Gaul the symbol of the council of Constantinople, that is, of the 150 bishops, shall be recited according to the use of the Eastern churches, so that before the Lord's Prayer is said the creed shall be chanted aloud by the congregation, testimony thereby being borne to the true faith and the people being enabled to draw near and partake of Christ's body and blood with hearts cleansed by the faith.

Several points in this account deserve notice. First, the motive for adopting the creed was clearly as a gesture of repudiation of Arianism. Reccared, in his own address to the council, said the object of the new move was "to confirm the

---

[1] Cf. the text cited above, p. 345.
[2] Mansi IX, 992 f.

recent conversion of our people".[1] Thus the Spanish innovation was linked with the probable admission of C into the Roman baptismal liturgy a few decades previously. Secondly, the now well-established custom of Eastern Orthodoxy was frankly acknowledged to be the model. The conjecture has been made[2] that the moving spirit behind the reform may have been John, abbot of Biclaro, who spent seventeen years as a young man at Constantinople, was highly esteemed by Reccared, and was elevated by him in 592 to the see of Gerona. He was interested in the use of the creed at the Eucharist, for he was careful to note the emperor Justin's efforts to extend it.[3] But while this is an ingenious theory, it is quite unnecessary. Contacts between Spanish Christianity and the Greek Church were neither infrequent nor remote in the sixth century. As recently as 554 Justinian, in response to an appeal from the noble Goth Athanagild, had sent an expeditionary force to Spain, as a result of which Cartagena, Malaga, Cadiz and possibly Seville were reattached to the empire. Commercial relations were in full swing. A general familiarity with Greek liturgical customs was inevitable, and the Mozarabic rite in fact betrays numerous traces of Byzantine influence. Thirdly, the position assigned to the creed was a peculiar one, well after the canon and just before the Lord's Prayer. The object of this was to make the solemn profession of belief a prelude to communion. The creed continued to be rehearsed at this point in the Mozarabic rite.

The immediate result of the council's decisions was to establish the eucharistic use of the creed in Spain generally and in the Spanish provinces north of the Pyrenees: the sway of the Visigoths reached as far as the Rhône. At that point its advance was halted so far as the continent was concerned. The Irish church, however, with its liturgical eclecticism, seems to have shown itself more hospitable to the new fashion. The Stowe Missal, written according to its most recent editor[4] within the first decade of the ninth century, prescribed the singing of the

---

[1] Mansi IX, 990.
[2] A. E. Burn, 115 (following E. B. Pusey).
[3] *Chronicon* (*P.L.* 72, 863).
[4] Cf. G. F. Warner, *The Stowe Missal* (H. Bradshaw Society XXXI and XXXII, 1915) II, xxxiv.

creed after the gospel.[1] Scholars formerly saw in this an imitation
of the interpolation of the creed in the mass at the court of
Charlemagne after 798; but the early date of the Missal, combined with certain traits in the text of the creed itself, makes
this highly unlikely. By far the most plausible explanation is
the one put forward recently by Dom B. Capelle in a brilliant
article,[2] that the presence of the creed in the Stowe Missal is a
sample of Spanish liturgical influence in Ireland. We know
that the golden age for such influence was the period of the
seventh and eighth centuries, and the extent of the Irish
borrowings was very great.[3] The Irish monks showed characteristic originality by inserting the creed at a different point
in the service from the one favoured in Spain. Thus it would
seem that the custom of singing the creed at mass was well
established in Ireland in the eighth century, and there is
evidence that it passed from there to England. The text of C
with which Alcuin, a Northumbrian by birth and upbringing,
worked was closely akin to that of the Stowe Missal, and even
before the court at Aachen had introduced the creed into the
Eucharist he seems to have been familiar with the usage.[4]
Probably he had had experience of it at home in the north of
England, where the form of the creed employed was that which
had been brought across from Ireland.[5]

For the next stage in the incorporation of C into the Western
rite, the scene shifts from the Visigothic metropolis at Toledo
and the Irish monasteries to the court of Charlemagne at
Aachen. The evidence for it is rather obscure and, at first sight,
conflicting. Thus several of the most trustworthy liturgical
authorities in Gaul of the ninth century, such as Amalarius of
Metz[6] († 850 or 851), Hrabanus Maurus of Mainz[7] († 856)
and Remigius of Auxerre[8] († circa 908), maintain a steady silence
in their authentic works about the creed and its presence in the

---

[1] Cf. fol. 20 r. of the Missal, which is kept in the Library of the Royal Irish
Academy, Dublin (Press-mark D. II, 3).
[2] Rech. théol. anc. méd. vi, 1934, 249 ff.
[3] Cf. E. Bishop in Liturgica Historica, Oxford, 1918, 165–202.
[4] Cf. Ep. ad Felic. 3 (P.L. 101, 121), written 793.
[5] So B. Capelle in art. cit.
[6] Cf. his De eccl. offic. III (P.L. 105, 1101 ff.): written 820.
[7] Cf. his De cleric. instit. I (P.L. 107, 297 ff.): not later than 819.
[8] Cf. De divin. offic. 40 (P.L. 101, 1246 ff.): falsely ascribed to Alcuin.

mass. On the other hand, Aeneas of Paris († 871), writing about the middle of the same century,[1] speaks of "the Catholic faith, which on Sunday the entire church of the Gauls chants at mass". There are two outstandingly important passages, however, which point the way to the true solution. The first is by Walafrid Strabo, abbot of Reichenau († 849), and deserves to be reproduced in full.[2]

"The symbol of the Catholic faith", he wrote, "is rightly rehearsed in the solemnities of the mass after the gospel, so that by means of the holy gospel we may believe with the heart unto righteousness, and by means of the creed confession may be made with the lips unto salvation. And it is worth noting that the reason why the Greeks transposed that creed (rather than another) which we, in imitation of them, have adopted in the mass into a musical chant, was because it was the peculiar confession of the council of Constantinople. Perhaps also it seemed more suitable for setting to music than the Nicene creed, which was prior in time. Furthermore, they wanted the piety of the faithful, at the celebration of the sacraments, to counter the poisons of heretics with the medicine concocted in the imperial city itself. From there the usage is believed to have passed to the Romans. Among the Gauls and Germans, however, the same creed began to be repeated more widely and frequently (*latius et crebrius*) in the eucharistic offices after the deposition of the heretic Felix, who was condemned in the reign of the glorious Charles, ruler of the Franks."

Our second important context is an account, preserved by the abbot Smaragdus,[3] of a conference held in 810 between Pope Leo III and three delegates, or *missi*, sent to Rome by Charlemagne. The passage is too long to print in full, and in any case the barbarousness of the Latin does not conduce to elegance of translation. The real topic of discussion was the legitimacy of including the words AND FROM THE SON in the creed in the clause about the procession of the Holy Spirit. Indeed, the purpose of Charlemagne's embassy to the Pope may well have been to extract from him some sort of official endorsement for the inclusion of the controversial phrase in the creed. The gist of the Pope's reply was that, while he had

---

[1] *Adv. Graec.* 93 (*P.L.* 121, 721).
[2] *De eccl. rerum exord. et increm.* 22 (*P.L.* 114, 947).
[3] *P.L.* 102, 971 ff.; also *Mon. Germ. Hist., Concil.* II, 240 ff.

given his licence for the singing of the creed in the royal chapel at Aachen and elsewhere in Gaul, he had never sanctioned AND FROM THE SON. The interesting point which emerges, so far as we are concerned at the moment, is that the singing of the creed in the Frankish rite had been approved in Pope Leo's reign, i.e. at some date after 795. This agrees exactly with Walafrid's independent statement that the custom began after the deposition of Felix the heretic. Felix, we know, was the famous Adoptionist bishop of Urgel in Spain (there was a great outbreak of Adoptionism in Spain in the closing decades of the eighth century), who was finally condemned and obliged to make his submission at a council which met at Aachen in October 798. We may observe, in passing, that the position assigned to the creed by the Franks was that which it now occupies in the West, viz. immediately after the gospel. Evidently they were aware that they were breaking with the practice elsewhere (e.g. in Spain), for Walafrid thought it proper to supply an edifying justification for the Frankish position.

We have not yet, however, exhausted the importance of Walafrid's evidence. It need not be supposed that he had merely a chronological intent in citing the deposition of Felix. The unmistakable innuendo of his words is that the Adoptionist controversy gave an impetus to the liturgical innovation. Confirmation of his insinuation cannot be looked for in the acts of the council of Aachen, for they are lost. But there are strong reasons for supposing that St Paulinus of Aquileia, who took a leading part with Alcuin in crushing the Adoptionist outbreak, deliberately fixed upon the Constantinopolitan Creed as the most effective instrument for suppressing the heresy. In all this he had Alcuin behind him. For example, at his synod at Cividale del Friuli in 796 or 797, after inveighing eloquently against Adoptionism, he advised the assembly that the best nostrum against errors of this kind was the creed of Constantinople. He declared in so many words that the true doctrine with which to counter Adoptionism was inculcated much better by the creed than by anything else, and he enjoined the learning of the creed by heart on his clergy.[1] A close analysis of

---

[1] *Mon. Germ. Hist., Concil.* II, 180 f.; 189.

the Carolingian text of the creed, which is approximately that used in the West to-day, shows that it is identical with the one promulgated on that occasion by St Paulinus. In the light of this acknowledged policy of his, and the fact that the text circulated in Charlemagne's dominions was drafted under his influence, it is difficult to resist the conclusion that the chief, if not the only, motive for bringing the creed into the mass was the desire to roll back the menace of Adoptionism.[1] The practice, it should be pointed out, would not have struck people as at all revolutionary. The Carolingian empire extended far down into Spain, and thus included provinces where the creed had been chanted at mass since the days of king Reccared; and it is highly likely that the custom prevailed in the north of England too. It is this fact which explains Walafrid's otherwise puzzling statement that the repetition of the creed became "more widespread and frequent" after the deposition of Felix. The placing of the creed in the Frankish service after the gospel probably betrays the influence of Alcuin. Coming from Northumbria, where the creed may have been sung at this point, he was probably responsible for the preference being given to it rather than to the Spanish position.

Meanwhile the Roman church, with the whole ecclesiastical region subject to its liturgical sway, held aloof with characteristic conservatism and refrained from falling into line with the new fashion. The student should be on his guard against taking too literally statements like that of Walafrid that "from there (i.e. Constantinople) the usage is believed to have passed to the Romans". Probably this represents what Frankish liturgists wanted to think, and perhaps sincerely did think, although the qualifying word *creditur* reads like a twinge of misgiving. We should be cautious, too, about such a reference as that of Amalarius of Metz, in his *Eclogae de officio missae*,[2] to the Roman custom of saying the creed. The book is probably a tenth-century compilation; and, in any case, what the author had in mind was not the practice of the Roman church itself, but the *Ordo Romanus* which Pope Leo's predecessor, Hadrian I,

---

[1] On all this see the very suggestive article by Dom B. Capelle in *Rech. théol. anc. méd.* i, 1929, 7 ff.
[2] *P.L.* 105, 1323.

had sent to the Gallic church at the request of Charlemagne,[1]
and into which rubrical directions regarding the creed had
probably crept. All the really solid evidence (e.g. Smaragdus's
report of the interview between the *missi* and Pope Leo) leaves
the clear impression that the recitation of the creed at mass
was frowned on at Rome.

Two hundred years had to pass before another emperor,
perhaps a less famous figure in European history than Charlemagne, but the bestower of favours on the Pope which the latter
may well have felt obliged to repay, succeeded in inducing one of
Leo's successors to bring the Roman usage into conformity with
the rest of Christendom. Abbot Berno of Reichenau, who
was himself an eyewitness, tells the story of how the emperor
Henry II, visiting Rome in 1014 for his coronation, was
shocked to discover that the mass celebrated there still lacked
a creed.[2]

"If we," wrote Berno, "as is often stated, are forbidden to sing the
angelic hymn on feast-days because the Roman clergy do not sing
it, we may in like manner leave unsaid the creed after the gospel,
because the Romans never sang it even up to the time of the emperor
Henry of blessed memory. But being asked by the said emperor in
my presence why this was their practice, I heard them give an
answer of this nature, that the Roman church had never been
tainted with any dregs of heresy, but remained unshaken in the
soundness of the Catholic faith according to the teaching of St Peter,
and so it was more needful for that symbol to be sung frequently by
those who might be sullied by any heresy. But the Lord emperor did
not desist until with general consent he persuaded the apostolic Lord
Benedict that they should chant the symbol at the public mass."

The Pope was already heavily in Henry's debt for assistance
in overcoming the rival pseudo-pope Gregory in 1012, and in
general his position *vis-à-vis* the emperor made compliance
with his requests sound common-sense in matters like this. In
any case Rome was at this period very much under the liturgical influence of the German church, and the adoption of the
creed was merely the climax of a long series of borrowings.[3]

---

[1] For the Pope's letter, see *Mon. Germ. Hist., Epp.* III, 626.
[2] Cf. his *Libell. de quibusdam rebus ad miss. offic. pertin.* (*P.L.* 142, 1060 f.).
[3] Cf. Th. Klauser, *Historisches Jahrbuch* liii, 1933, 169 ff.

5. *The Filioque*

Curiously intertwined with the series of incidents by which the creed worked its way into the Eucharist is the problem of the fateful interpolation in the third article which, ever since the eighth century, has been one of the most explosive topics of debate between the churches of East and West. For many hundreds of years the text of C accepted in the Latin church and its daughter communions has contained the clause PRO-CEEDING FROM THE FATHER AND THE SON (*filioque*) of the Holy Spirit. The Orthodox churches of the East have remained fiercely, even fanatically, attached to the more primitive PRO-CEEDING FROM THE FATHER. A full discussion of the portentous addition in all its implications would necessitate an examin-ation of at least three questions—the theology of the double procession, the history of the insertion of the *filioque*, and the history of the long-standing quarrel between East and West over it. Here we shall be mainly concerned with the second, although a few remarks about the first must be set down by way of preface. The third belongs by rights to the field of church history proper rather than the study of creeds.

So far as theology is concerned, the doctrine that the third Person derives His being equally and coordinately from the first and the second was characteristic, in its fully developed form, of Western Trinitarianism and, in particular, of St Augustine's presentation of it. From the days of Tertullian[1] the typical formula had been, "From the Father through the Son". In the fourth century, however, the deeper implication was extracted from this that the Son, conjointly with the Father, was actually productive of the Holy Spirit. The text to which appeal was regularly made was the Lord's statement in *Jn*. 16, 14, "He (i.e. the Spirit) will receive of mine." Here the pioneers were St Hilary (cf. his *Patre et Filio auctoribus*)[2] and Marius Victorinus[3] (not St Ambrose[4], whose texts refer to the Spirit's *external* mission), but both these avoid speaking directly

---

[1] Cf. *Adv. Prax.* 4 (*C.C.L.* 2, 1162): *spiritum non aliunde puto quam a patre per filium.*
[2] *De trin.* 2, 29: cf. 8, 20; 8, 26 (*P.L.* 10, 69; 250 f.; 255).
[3] E.g. *Adv. Ar.* 1, 13; 1, 16; *Hymn.* 1, 62 f. (Henry, 216; 224; 624).
[4] For fuller discussion, see J. N. D. Kelly, *The Athanasian Creed*, London, 1964, 86–90.

of His procession from the Son. St Augustine felt no need for reserve. His Trinitarianism did not start with the Father as the source of the other two Persons, but with the idea of the one, simple Godhead Which in Its essence is Trinity. The logical development of his thought involved the belief that the Holy Spirit proceeded as truly from the Son as from the Father, and he did not scruple to expound it with frankness and precision on numerous occasions.[1] He admitted that, in a primordial sense (*principaliter*), the Spirit proceeded from the Father, because it was the Father Who endowed the Son with the capacity to produce the Holy Spirit.[2] But it was a cardinal premiss of his theology that whatever could be predicated of one of the Persons could be predicated of the others. So it was inevitable that he should regard the denial of the double procession as violating the unity and simplicity of the Godhead.

This way of thinking became universally accepted in the West in the fifth and sixth centuries: there could be no more illuminating instance of the hold the great African had on Latin Christianity. Greek theology, however, was by no means prepared to take the bold step which seemed so easy and natural to St Augustine. Many passages can be cited from the Eastern fathers, and have been cited in the course of the long, embittered controversy, which appear to approximate to the doctrine of the double procession. One or two writers, like St Epiphanius,[3] may even have succumbed to the influence of their Latin associates so far as to echo their language. Generally speaking, however, they never lost sight of the idea, which St Gregory of Nyssa brought out forcibly at the close of his *Quod non sunt tres dii*,[4] that what accounted for the distinctions in the Trinity was the fact that one of the Persons stood in the relation of cause (τὸ αἴτιον) to the other two. Thus they found no difficulty in saying that the Spirit proceeded *from* the Father *through* the Son, the Son being considered the Father's instrument or agent. But they treated it as axiomatic that the Father alone was the source or fountain-head of Deity, and that both

[1] Cf., e.g., *Con. Max. Ar.* 2, 14, 1 ; 2, 17, 4 ; *De trin.* 2, 4, 7 ; 4, 20, 29 (*P.L.* 42, 770 ; 784 f ; 824 ; 908).
[2] Cf. *De trin.* 15, 17, 29 ; 15, 26, 47 (*P.L.* 42, 1081 ; 1095).
[3] Cf. *Ancor.* 7, 8 (Holl I, 15).
[4] *P.G.* 45, 133.

the Son and the Spirit derived, in the only legitimate sense of the word, from Him, the one by generation and the other by procession. Their steadfast refusal to fall into line with the Latins was not the fruit of mere obstinacy, but sprang from an instinctive sense of the deep principle involved. What really divided East and West in their acrimonious and often unsavoury quarrel over the *filioque* was a fundamental difference of approach to the problem of the mystery of the triune Godhead.

Naturally the leaders of Western Christianity, while fully accepting and teaching the doctrine of the double procession, were far too cautious and diplomatic to flaunt it as an official dogma in the face of Eastern theologians. Gatherings held far from the centre, like the third council of Toledo (589) and the English synod of Hatfield (680),[1] might proclaim the doctrine and anathematize its deniers, but the papacy deliberately resisted the temptation to commit itself. To take but one example, the procession of the Spirit from the Son as well as from the Father was expressly taught by St Gregory the Great[2] (590–604), but the formula expressing it was carefully omitted from the profession of faith put out almost a century later (680) by Pope Agathon in the name of a synod held at Rome.[3] So far as creeds are concerned, the double procession made its first appearance, it would seem, in Spain, in a series of local formulae directed against the Priscillianist heresy. One of the most ancient of these is the so-called creed of Damasus,[4] in its original form ascribed to St Jerome, which A. E. Burn identified as the Pope's reply to the treatise addressed to him by Priscillian of Avila in 380. K. Künstle[5] hazarded the guess that its actual compilation was the work of the synod of Saragossa, which condemned the heretic in the same year, and which may have sent it to Damasus for his approval. Markedly anti-Priscillianist in tone, it contains the statement: "We believe . . . in the Holy Spirit, not begotten nor unbegotten, not created nor made, but proceeding from the Father and the Son." Another example is the creed with twelve anathemas

---

[1] Cf. Bede, *Hist. eccl.* 4, 17 (*P.L.* 95, 198 f.).
[2] Cf. *Moral.* 1, 22, 30 ; *Hom.* 26, 2 (*P.L.* 75, 541 ; 76, 1198).
[3] *Ep.* 3 (*P.L.* 87, 1220).
[4] For text see Hahn 200. Cf. A. E. Burn, 245 ff.
[5] *Antipriscilliana*, Freiburg im Breisgau, 1905, 46 ff.

which has often been fathered on the first council of Toledo (400),[1] but which Dom Morin suggested [2] might be the long-lost *Libellus in modum symboli* of Pastor, bishop of Gallicia in 433. Here, too, belief is expressed in "the Spirit, the Paraclete, Who is neither the Father Himself nor the Son, but proceeds from the Father and the Son". Many other similar texts might be quoted, and the student might be tempted to infer that there was something particularly deadly to Priscillianism in the *filioque*. The true explanation, however, is that Priscillianism was marked with a deep strain of Sabellianism, and the refutation of it demanded a detailed exposition of Trinitarian teaching. The presence of the *filioque* in Spanish creeds of this period merely testifies to the popularity of the doctrine in this section of the Western church.

A vivid illustration of the hold the double procession had on Spanish Christianity is provided by the record of events at Reccared's council at Toledo in 589. At the opening session the king addressed the assembled bishops and notables, dwelling at length on his own conversion and his earnest desire to do what he could to set forth the true faith.[3] Thereupon he proceeded to recite an exposition of it, in the course of which the following statement occurred:

In equal degree must the Holy Spirit be confessed by us, and we must preach that He proceeds from the Father and the Son and is of one substance with the Father and the Son: moreover, that the Person of the Holy Spirit is the third in the Trinity, but that He nevertheless shares fully in the divine essence with the Father and the Son.

Evidently the doctrine was regarded as clinching the case against Arianism. It implied that the Son, as the source equally of the Spirit, was in no sense inferior to the Father, and that all three Persons were completely coordinate and participated equally in the divine essence. The council followed Reccared's lead enthusiastically, and drafted the third of its anathemas in the form: "Whoever does not believe in the Holy Spirit, or does not believe that He proceeds from the Father and the

---

[1] For text see Hahn 168; also Mansi III, 1003.
[2] *R. Bén.* x, 1893, 385 ff.
[3] Mansi IX, 977 ff.

Son, and denies that He is coeternal and coequal with the
Father and the Son, let him be anathema."[1] The suggestion
of this language is that, while the doctrine was considered indispensable, it did not strike the council as revolutionary, but
rather as an accepted article of orthodoxy.

It has often been held that the interpolation of the word
filioque into the actual text of the creed must date from this
occasion. King Reccared formally recited the Nicene creed,
with its anathemas, and the Constantinopolitan Creed as embodying the faith of the first four general councils. It has seemed
incredible that, after his own forceful language on the subject
of the double procession and the enthusiasm with which the
council took it up, the term symbolizing the doctrine should
not have been incorporated in the creed. The evidence of the
MSS, however, is not free from ambiguity on the point. Many
years ago A. E. Burn drew attention to the fact that several
important MSS containing the acts of the council either lack
the crucial word or exhibit it inserted by a later hand.[2] The
matter still requires investigation, but the conclusion seems
inescapable that, as originally recited at the council of Toledo,
the text of C was the pure one without *filioque*. Nevertheless it
was inevitable that, with the growing stress laid on the doctrine,
the word should speedily creep into the creed. Spanish MSS of
the subsequent centuries give abundant illustrations of the
process at work.

The rest of the story is familiar enough. The use of the
filioque spread from Spain to Gaul, where, even before it
installed itself in the creed, it found a niche in some rites in
the Preface of the mass.[3] At first the West seems to have been
genuinely unaware that the doctrine of the double procession
represented a definite advance on, or certainly clarification of,
the teaching of earlier centuries. Thus the synod of Hatfield,
summoned to stabilize the Church against the presumed
Eutychian tendencies of Monotheletism, expressed its loyal

---

[1] Mansi IX, 985.
[2] Cf. his brief article in *J.T.S.* ix, 1908, 301 f. Unfortunately no one seems to
have followed up and confirmed his researches.
[3] Cf. the first *contestatio* of the third of the Gallican masses of Mone (*P.L.* 138,
867), inscribed on a Reichenau palimpsest dating from *circa* 650: the Spirit is
addressed as "subsisting by mystic procession from the Father and the Son".

adherence to the decisions of the first five ecumenical councils and of the Lateran synod held in 649 under Pope Martin I. But the profession of faith which it published ran as follows:

We acknowledge and glorify our Lord Jesus Christ as they (i.e. the fathers of the general councils) glorified Him, neither adding nor subtracting anything, and we anathematize with heart and voice those whom they anathematized, and we acknowledge those whom they acknowledged, glorifying God the Father without beginning, and His only-begotten Son, begotten of the Father before all ages, and the Holy Spirit proceeding in an inexpressible manner from the Father and the Son, as those holy apostles and prophets and doctors taught whom we have mentioned.[1]

Language like this reads all the more strangely when it is remembered that archbishop Theodore, who presided at the synod, had once been a monk at Tarsus and so presumably was familiar with the true text of the creed. Sooner or later, however, a clash between East and West was bound to come. The first round seems to have been fought at the council of Gentilly, at Easter 767. The immediate subjects under discussion were the worship of images and the return of territories in Italy, to which Constantinople felt it had a claim, but it is reported[2] that "the question about the Trinity was ventilated between the Greeks and the Romans, and whether the Holy Spirit proceeds from the Son in the same way as He proceeds from the Father". Apparently what happened was that the Western delegates accused the ambassadors of the emperor Constantine V (Copronymus) of neglect in the matter of the worship of images, and they retorted with a reproach about the impropriety of inserting *filioque* into the creed.

The dispute which had thus flared up almost accidentally was not long in developing into a steady blaze. Pippin, king of France, who had been present at the council of Gentilly, died in 768, and his son and successor, Charlemagne, took up the *filioque* with something like fervour, using every opportunity to parade it before the horrified East and trying his best to induce the papacy to lend him its moral and practical support. A

[1] Bede, *Hist. eccl.* 4, 17 (*P.L.* 95, 199).
[2] Mansi XII, 677; Ado Viennensis, *Chron.* (*P.L.* 123, 125).

good example was the remonstrance he addressed to Pope Hadrian I in 794. The Patriarch of Constantinople, Tarasius, had circulated a letter to the clergy of Antioch, Alexandria and Constantinople giving a creed expressing belief in the procession of the Holy Spirit from the Father alone, and it appeared that Hadrian had given his assent to this confession at the seventh general council held at Nicaea in 787. Charlemagne rebuked the Pope for admitting such erroneous doctrines as those of Tarasius, "who professes that the Holy Spirit proceeds not from the Father and the Son, according to the faith of the Nicene symbol, but from the Father through the Son". The Pope in his reply, written also in 794, defended the Patriarch, arguing that his theology was not his own, but was consonant with the teaching of many ancient fathers and with the practice of the Roman church.[1]

In the same year the *filioque* received great publicity at the synod of Frankfurt-on-Main, which met to condemn the Adoptionist heresy and its chief supporters, Elipandus of Toledo and Felix of Urgel. Charlemagne was present in person, and the Pope was represented by legates. Among the documents read out was the *Libellus* of the Italian bishops against Elipandus, which was probably the work of St Paulinus of Aquileia. Here the doctrine of the double procession was vigorously asserted.[2] Later in the proceedings a letter of Charlemagne's to Elipandus and the other Spanish bishops was read out, and appended to this was a form of creed in which he, too, proclaimed belief in the double procession.[3] Two years later, in 796 or 797, at the synod of Cividale which St Paulinus summoned, the symbol set forth was C with the *filioque* in the third article.[4] In his inaugural address St Paulinus skilfully justified its insertion: it no more violated the principle that new creeds must not be framed than did the alterations which the fathers of 381 had felt obliged to make in N. It had become necessary to interpolate AND FROM THE SON "on account of those heretics who whisper that the Holy Spirit is of the Father alone".[5] We need not doubt that the form in which the creed was sung in

[1] *Mon. Germ. Hist.*, *Epp.* V, 7 ff. [2] *Mon. Germ. Hist.*, *Concil.* II, 136.
[3] *Mon. Germ. Hist.*, *Concil.* II, 163. [4] *Mon. Germ. Hist.*, *Concil.* II. 187.
[5] *Mon. Germ. Hist.*, *Concil.* II, 182.

the royal chapel at Aachen, and in the Frankish dominions generally after 798, also contained the disputed clause.

Nevertheless the papacy had not been won over to accept it, and Charlemagne, who saw the *filioque* as a trump-card against the Eastern empire, could not rest until he had persuaded Rome to fall into line with his policy. He made a strong attempt to do so on the occasion of the troublesome incident which took place at Jerusalem in 808. There was a convent of Latin monks settled on Mount Olivet, and these were treated as heretics and threatened with expulsion by their Orthodox neighbours because they chanted the Constantinopolitan Creed at mass with the addition of AND FROM THE SON. Naturally they resisted, protested their rights in the matter, and addressed a letter[1] to Leo III complaining and inquiring what they should do. They requested him to inform Charlemagne, for it was in his chapel that they had heard the creed sung with the *filioque*. The Pope, it appears, first of all sent them a profession of faith aimed at the Eastern churches and affirming the procession of the Holy Spirit from the Father and the Son.[2] Then he informed the emperor of the affair. It was as a result of these happenings that Charlemagne, who assumed the role of protector of Christians in the Holy Land, commissioned Theodulphus of Orleans to write his treatise *De Spiritu sancto*[3] and assembled a council at Aachen in 809–10. The delegates present approved and endorsed Theodulphus's book, pronounced in favour of the *filioque*, and possibly even enjoined its addition to the creed.[4] It was as a consequence of this gathering that Charlemagne sent that embassy to Leo III of which abbot Smaragdus preserved an account. As his report of the conversation still shows, the envoys used all their arts on the Pope without avail. With Roman conservatism, and a shrewd sense that if he yielded he would put himself in an awkward position *vis-à-vis* the East, he parried their ingenious arguments. The doctrinal truth conveyed by the *filioque*, he freely admitted, was essential to orthodoxy, but not all essential truths were enshrined in the creed. He admitted, too, that he

---

[1] Cf. *Ep. peregrin. monach.* (*P.L.* 129, 1257 ff.).
[2] Cf. *Ep.* 15 (*P.L.* 102, 1030 ff., and 129, 1260 ff.).
[3] *P.L.* 105, 239 ff.
[4] *Mon. Germ. Hist., Concil.* II, 235 f.

had sanctioned the singing of the creed in the Frankish territories, but his permission had not been intended to cover an
amended form of it. He went on to say that, if they wanted his
candid opinion, all this trouble would have been avoided if
they had adhered to the custom of the Roman church, where
the creed was not sung at mass but only used for instructional
purposes. His advice therefore was to drop the creed from the
Eucharist altogether by gradual stages, making a start with
the royal chapel.[1]

Leo III thus emerged victorious from the encounter. He
seems to have desired, however, to make a more public and
permanent record of his determination to cleave steadfastly to
the primitive version of the creed. The chronicler Anastasius
tells the story of how he caused two silver shields inscribed
with the creed, one in Greek and the other in Latin, to be
fixed up in the basilica of St Peter's.[2] In the eleventh century
St Peter Damian and others noticed the striking monument
and reproduced part of the inscription. Their report makes it
clear that the third article read PROCEEDING FROM THE FATHER.[3]

At the beginning of the ninth century, therefore, although
the doctrine of the double procession was taught everywhere
in the Western Church and the clause *filioque* was ensconced in
the creed in Spain, France, Germany, and at any rate North
Italy, Rome herself declined to tamper with the authorized
text. No doubt sturdy traditionalism was one motive: reluctance
to follow in the footsteps of provincial churches may have been
another, although the period of Roman borrowing from the
Gallican liturgy was beginning. There must also have been a
very understandable determination on the part of the papacy
not to put itself and the Western Church irretrievably in the
wrong in the eyes of Constantinople. It was one thing for
churches on the fringe to naturalize the controversial clause in
their creeds: for the Holy See it involved far more to take the
irrevocable step. It seems that the popes maintained this attitude for two full centuries more. Even during the Photian
controversy, in the middle of the ninth century, when the

---

[1] *Mon. Germ. Hist., Concil.* II, 240 ff.; also *P.L.* 102, 971 ff.
[2] *P.L.* 128, 1237–38.
[3] *De process. Spir. sancti* 2 (*P.L.* 145, 635).

patriarch of Constantinople was hurling violent accusations of heresy against the whole Western Church and, in particular, charging it with admitting the double procession, there is nothing to show that the creed at Rome had been altered. At what precise date and in what circumstances Rome received the *filioque* into the creed remains a mystery. The theory which has been widely accepted is that the decisive occasion was the day when, overborne by the persuasions of the emperor Henry II, Benedict VIII consented to have the Constantinopolitan Creed sung at the Holy Eucharist. The guess is plausible: it is hard to believe that the Pope could have been so tactless as to flourish in the emperor's face a text of the symbol which lacked the phrase to which the church of Charlemagne and his successors attached so much importance.

CHAPTER XII

THE APOSTLES' CREED

1. *The Received Text*

NEXT to the Constantinopolitan Creed, the most important confessional formulary in Christendom is the so-called Apostles' Creed. Except in Anabaptist circles, its authority was generally recognized at the Reformation, Martin Luther singling it out as one of the three binding summaries of belief, and both Calvin and Zwingli including it among their doctrinal norms. The English church has given it unusual prominence by requiring its recitation twice daily at morning and evening prayer. It has never ranked among the theological standards, and consequently has no place in the liturgy, of the Eastern Orthodox churches, but the suspicion with which they once regarded it has long disappeared. In the twentieth century its prestige has been enhanced and extended by its acknowledgement by several ecumenical gatherings as a uniquely authoritative statement of Christian belief. In 1920, for example, it was put forward by the Lambeth Conference, in its famous Appeal to all Christian people, as one of the four pillars (the Holy Scriptures, the two dominical sacraments, and the ministry were the others) on which the visible unity of the Church might be erected.[1] Similarly, at the World Conference on Faith and Order which met at Lausanne in 1927, churchmen from the East as well as the West recited it in unison at the opening session, and joined in acclaiming it as a fitting expression of the Christian message[2].

The text of the Apostles' Creed, in its Latin and its English dress, is printed below. The Latin corresponds exactly with the form given by Melchior Hittorp, canon of Cologne, in the

---

[1] See Section VI of the Appeal, which formed the ninth of the Resolutions adopted by the Conference (p. 28 of the Report, published 1922).

[2] Cf. G. K. A. Bell, *Documents of Christian Unity*, 2nd ser., 1930, 9. The Orthodox representatives safeguarded their traditional attitude by a cautious footnote.

so-called *Ordo Romanus antiquus*, which he made the opening section of his influential *De divinis catholicae ecclesiae officiis ac ministeriis*, published in his cathedral city in 1568.[1] It is identical with the one which was authoritative in the West in the later middle ages, and which the reformers themselves adopted as their norm—except that Luther read CHRISTIAN for CATHOLIC.

TEXTUS RECEPTUS

Credo in deum patrem omnipotentem, creatorem coeli et terrae;
Et in Iesum Christum, filium eius unicum, dominum nostrum, qui conceptus est de Spiritu sancto, natus ex Maria virgine, passus sub Pontio Pilato, crucifixus, mortuus et sepultus, descendit ad inferna, tertia die resurrexit a mortuis, ascendit ad coelos, sedet ad dexteram dei patris omnipotentis, inde venturus est iudicare vivos et mortuos;
Credo in Spiritum sanctum, sanctam ecclesiam catholicam, sanctorum communionem, remissionem peccatorum, carnis resurrectionem, et vitam aeternam. Amen.

I believe in God the Father almighty, creator of heaven and earth;
And in Jesus Christ, His only Son, our Lord, Who was conceived by the Holy Spirit, born from the Virgin Mary, suffered under Pontius Pilate, was crucified, dead and buried, descended to hell, on the third day rose again from the dead, ascended to heaven, sits at the right hand of God the Father almighty, thence He will come to judge the living and the dead;
I believe in the Holy Spirit, the holy Catholic Church, the communion of saints, the remission of sins, the resurrection of the flesh, and eternal life. Amen.

First, we should notice (the fact has never been denied) that what we have here is simply a rather elaborate variant of the Old Roman Creed (R) which we identified and studied in Chapters III and IV. For ease of reference the conventional label T (=*textus receptus*) is customarily attached to it. We observed in Chapter VI that the creeds used in the Western Church in the early centuries for instructing catechumens and administering baptism were always variant forms of R. We glanced at creeds of this description hailing from North Italy, the Balkans, North Africa, Spain and Gaul. In all of them the core was R, and they were distinguished from one another and from R either by minor modifications of phrasing or by the inclusion of additional matter. In the case of T the characteristic trimmings, all told, amount to eleven—(*a*) T adds CREATOR OF HEAVEN AND EARTH (*creatorem coeli et terrae*); (*b*) T alters R's

---

[1] Cf. p. 73 of the 1568 edition. See also *Maxima bibliotheca veterum patrum et antiquorum scriptorum ecclesiasticorum*, Lugduni, 1677, XIII, 696, where the *Ordo Romanus antiquus* is conveniently reprinted.

distinctive word-order CHRIST JESUS to the more common JESUS CHRIST; (c) T gives precision to R's BORN FROM THE HOLY SPIRIT AND THE VIRGIN MARY by reading CONCEIVED BY THE HOLY SPIRIT, BORN FROM THE VIRGIN MARY; (d) T adds SUFFERED (passus) before UNDER PONTIUS PILATE; (e) T inserts DEAD (mortuus); (f) T inserts DESCENDED TO HELL (descendit ad inferna) after BURIED; (g) T expands R's AT THE RIGHT HAND OF THE FATHER to AT THE RIGHT HAND OF GOD THE FATHER ALMIGHTY (ad dexteram dei patris omnipotentis); (h) T changes R's WHENCE (unde) to THENCE (inde); (i) T adds CATHOLIC (catholicam) to R's description of the Church as HOLY; (j) T interpolates COM-MUNION OF SAINTS (sanctorum communionem) as an article of belief; (k) T adds ETERNAL LIFE (vitam aeternam).

Secondly, we should recall in passing that, although the milieu in which R and its daughter creeds grew up was mainly catechetical and baptismal, T was from its formation called upon to discharge much more extensive functions. Its primary role, of course, has always been to serve as the declaratory creed at baptism. In that capacity it has featured in the baptismal rites of the Latin West since the eighth century, and in that of the Roman church, in conjunction with the shorter and more primitive interrogations, since a date only a little later which we shall have to discuss in the following chapter. But almost contemporaneously with its final redaction T obtained a foothold in the divine office too, and this it has retained ever since. Long before that happened, when their creeds were still fluctuating and immature variants of R, St Ambrose and St Augustine were speaking of the *symbolum fidei* as a talisman to be memorized and recited at stated intervals. "Say the creed daily," the latter advised his flock.[1] "When you rise, when you compose yourself to sleep, repeat your creed, render it to the Lord, remind yourself of it, be not irked to say it over." At this early period the regular repetition of the creed had nothing, so far as we know, of canonical obligation about it, but was a matter of private devotion. In the middle of the seventh century, however, we find St Fructuosus († *circa* 665), archbishop of Braga, assigning the creed a place in compline,

---

[1] *Serm.* 58, 11 (*P.L.* 38, 399 f.). Cf. St Ambrose, *De virg.* 3, 4; *Explan. symb. ad init.* (*P.L.* 16, 225; 17, 1155 and 1160).

and laying it down that the brethren in a monastery, at the close of their night prayers, "should all together with a united voice recite the symbol of the Christian faith." [1] We have to wait until much later for definite evidence of its use at mattins and prime. Alcuin does not mention the practice in his liturgical writings, and the first to prescribe the use of the creed *before* mattins and prime, as *after* compline, are St Benedict of Aniane († 821), the great reformer of monasteries under Charlemagne and Louis the Pious,[2] and Amalarius of Metz.[3] But the presence of the creed in early psalteries proves that its insertion into the morning offices can be safely carried back a good way before their epoch. By this time all the other derivative versions of R had given place to T, and it thus fell to it, as the mature flower of Western credal development, to inherit an impressive role in the daily worship of the Church.

There are several closely connected problems which T raises and which it will be our task in this and the followng chapter to examine. One big question to which we must attempt to supply an answer concerns its identity and provenance. Is T a provincial creed, a cousin of all those others which flourished so prolifically all over Western Europe and North Africa after the third century? If it is, to what region must we assign its birthplace, and by what fateful sequence of events are we to suppose that it came to be promoted to a paramount position even at Rome? Alternatively, is it in fact a revision of R carried out by the Roman church itself? Parallel with this literary and historical inquiry is the problem of the meaning of the additional matter which represents the difference between R and T. What were the motives for its incorporation, and to what extent was the teaching of the creed altered by its presence? For the moment we shall limit our investigation to the theological and doctrinal aspect of the Apostles' Creed. This is so intricate and important that the whole of the present chapter will be taken up with it. In the final chapter we shall turn to the even knottier problem of T's origin and emergence as an independent creed of European authority.

---

[1] *Reg. monach.* 2 (*P.L.* 87, 1099).
[2] Cf. *Vita S. Bened. Anian.* (*Bolland. Acta SS.*, Antwerp, 1658: Tom. IV, 618).
[3] Cf. *De eccl. offic.* 4, 2 (*P.L.* 105, 1168). It was published not long after 820.

2. *Changes in the First Article*

The first article need not detain us long. It has already been pointed out in Chapter V that the original import both of FATHER and of ALMIGHTY very early faded into the background. After the fourth century, if not before, exegetes and expositors almost always interpreted the Fatherhood as referring to the special relation of the first to the second Person within the Holy Trinity. Once the theological conception of the triune Godhead had begun to become explicit, it was inevitable that churchmen should come to regard the creed as a compendious exposition of current Trinitarianism. A typical comment was that of St Faustus of Riez (fl. 450)[1]: "How excellently throughout the whole creed the separate Persons are distinguished. How manifestly in all these the Trinity is unfolded." Almost a century before him Nicetas of Remesiana had characterized the creed, apart from the articles following THE HOLY SPIRIT, as "this profession of the Trinity",[2] despite the fact that it had been far from the intentions of R's framers to make it such. So GOD was regularly understood as connoting the one Godhead, and FATHER as pointing to the Father of Jesus Christ. ALMIGHTY, too, gradually lost its primitive sense, suggested by the Greek παντοκράτωρ, of "all-ruling", and under the influence of the Latin *omnipotens* was taken to imply the ability to do all things.

The only novel clause which appears in T's first article is CREATOR OF HEAVEN AND EARTH. Some predicate like this, stressing God's creative activity, was an almost invariable element in Eastern creeds. Its absence from R was one of the most characteristic features of that formulary. Western theologians always taught the doctrine, of course, and catechetical expositions of the rule of faith no doubt always explained and elaborated the first article by dwelling on God's work in the creation of the universe: it was a truth which marked Christianity off from all other religions. So Novatian, in the middle of the third century, demanded that we believe "first of all, in God the Father and almighty Lord, that is, the all-perfect

---

[1] Cf. *Hom.* I *de symb.* in Caspari, *Quellen* II, 188.
[2] *De symb.* 8; 9; 10 (Burn, 46; 47; 48).

framer of all things, Who suspended the heavens aloft, established the solid earth, etc."[1] Nicetas accumulated a whole row of adjectives which, he said, belonged to God—"unbegotten . . . invisible . . . incomprehensible . . . unchangeable . . . good and just, framer of heaven and earth".[2] Rufinus in passing described God as "Himself without author, the author of all things".[3] But overt references to this aspect of His being were infrequent and late in Western creeds. North African formularies were the first in the field with them, if we can judge from the words CREATOR OF ALL THINGS (*universorum creatorem*) in the text handed down to us by St Augustine.[4] The identical phrasing of our Apostles' Creed is attested by the creed of St Caesarius of Arles.[5] The choice of words is curious. For long the Western tradition seems to have hovered between CONDITOREM and CREATOREM, while FACTOREM (always preferred in Latin translations of the Constantinopolitan Creed) failed to win much support. What may have unconsciously determined the ultimate selection of CREATOREM may have been the fact that the Vulgate version of *Gen.* 1, 1 read: "In the beginning God *created* (*creavit*, notwithstanding the LXX ἐποίησεν) heaven and earth."

Did any special considerations prompt the interpolation of the clause? Some have overheard the rumbling of anti-heretical polemic in it. It is well known that the Church did not hesitate to use its inherited dogma that God had made earth as well as heaven as a powerful weapon against the Gnostic denial that the material order could have owed its existence to the good God. But this was in the second and third centuries, when Western creeds were as yet innocent of allusion to God's creativity. In a later age Priscillianism might have furnished the occasion for a pointed declaration that God was the author of matter no less than spirit, for (to judge by the anathematisms pronounced against it by the council of Braga of 563[6]) there was a strongly Manichaean strain in its teaching. It refused to admit that flesh was the handiwork of God, preferring to

[1] *De trin.* 1 (*P.L.* 3, 913).
[2] *De symb.* 2 (Burn, 39 f.). This clause *may* have figured in his creed. See above, pp. 174 f.
[3] *Comm. in symb. apost.* 4 (*C.C.L.* 20, 137 f.).
[4] *Serm.* 215 (*P.L.* 38, 1072).
[5] See above, p. 179.
[6] Mansi IX, 774 ff. Cf. especially Nos. 4, 5, 7, 8, 11, 12, 13, and 14.

attribute its origin to bad angels. But there is not the slightest suggestion in the commentaries of Western theologians that they regarded the clause as a bulwark against this or any other form of error. It is just conceivable that the example of Eastern creeds, in particular of C, exerted some influence. What makes one sceptical about this, however, is the fact that CREATOREM, not FACTOREM (the regular Latin translation of the term ποιητήν in C), was the word chosen to express the idea. The most likely explanation would seem to be that the clause has crept into the creed quite casually and spontaneously. In the second century, it will be remembered, the thought of God as the source and origin of the universe was considered to be contained in FATHER. But when that title came to be explained as meaning the Father of Jesus Christ, those whose task it was to expound and comment on the creed may well have become conscious of an awkward gap in its teaching. As the fact that God was creator of all things was an item which lay ready to hand in the routine catechetical instruction provided in the Church, the insertion of a reference to it was merely a matter of time.

3. *Some Minor Modifications*

As it reappears in the traditional Apostles' Creed, the second article of R has been expanded by some six or seven additions or modifications. Several of them are of little or no dogmatic significance and can be passed over almost without comment. The word-order CHRIST JESUS, for example, which was a peculiar feature of R, gave place in process of time to the much more common JESUS CHRIST. With the fading of the realization that CHRIST was a title and meant Messiah, this alteration was bound to be made sooner or later. Nothing need be said either about the substitution of THENCE (*inde*) for R's WHENCE (*unde*) before the mention of the Second Coming. THENCE was in all the local creeds, and R's choice of WHENCE stood quite isolated (the creed of St Hippolytus's *Tradition* had no conjunction). The addition of SUFFERED and DEAD, with consequential alterations in the structure of the sentence, seems equally without doctrinal import. Both words had an established place among the stereotyped credal tags of the second century, and the latter could claim the authority of St Paul's paradosis,[1] "that Christ died on behalf of our sins". There are a number of contexts in St Justin,[2] St Irenaeus,[3] and Tertullian [4] where SUFFERED is preferred to CRUCIFIED. Among writers whose rule of faith contained DEAD after either CRUCIFIED or SUFFERED were St Ignatius,[5] St Justin,[6] and Tertullian.[7] Some have thought[8] that the addition of SUFFERED at any rate may have been inspired by the example of the Nicene Creed. As they have pointed out, it made its first appearance (to judge by surviving formularies) in local variants of R (e.g. the creed of Milan) dating from post-Nicene times. But both words had obviously belonged to the stock-in-trade of the catechetical schools from the earliest times. If special influences need to be sought to explain their presence in creeds, it seems much more plausible to look, so far as SUFFER is concerned, to such Biblical texts as *Mk.* 8, 31 (".The Son of Man must *suffer* many things") and *Acts* 3, 18 ("God . . . announced beforehand through the mouth of all the prophets that His Christ would *suffer* . . .").

The addition of GOD . . . ALMIGHTY to AT THE RIGHT HAND OF THE FATHER had no far-reaching implications. Eastern creeds, it is interesting to recall, where they mentioned the Session, adhered to the simple form characteristic of R. In the West the creed of Priscillian is the first to show both GOD and ALMIGHTY[9]: St Faustus of Riez is the earliest witness from Gaul.[10] The addition of GOD alone was more frequent, and is the one we should be inclined to look for first. FATHER invited completion: and the New Testament prototypes of the clause about the Session invariably read "on the right hand of God", or its equivalent.[11] Once GOD had ensconced itself, the attachment of ALMIGHTY as well must have followed as a matter of course, GOD THE FATHER ALMIGHTY having become a stereotyped phrase.

---

[1] I *Cor.* 15, 3.
[2] *Dial.* 126 (E.J.G., 246).
[3] *Adv. haer.* 1, 10, 1; 3, 4, 2; 3, 16, 5; 3, 18, 3 (*P.G.* 7, 549; 856; 924; 933).
[4] *Adv. Marc.* 1, 11 (*C.C.L.* 1, 452).
[5] *Trall.* 9 (Lightfoot 118).
[6] *Dial.* 63 (E.J.G., 168).
[7] *De carne Christi* 5; *adv. Prax.* 2 (*C.C.L.* 2, 880; 1160).
[8] E.g. Kattenbusch II, 890.
[9] See above, p. 177.
[10] See above, p. 179.
[11] Cf. *Mk.* 16, 19; *Acts* 2, 33; *Rom.* 8, 34; *Col.* 3, 1 ; etc.

A rather more interesting elaboration of R's original text is the reading WHO WAS CONCEIVED BY THE HOLY SPIRIT, BORN FROM THE VIRGIN MARY, so characteristic of the Apostles' Creed. The earliest formulary to exhibit this is the one alleged by St Jerome to have been drafted by the orthodox party at Rimini in 359 (this was their own creed, not the one their representative signed at Nicé), which has been attributed to one of their leading members, Phoebadius of Agen.[1] About the same period we come across echoes of the wording in St Hilary.[2] A century later St Faustus of Riez vouches for its currency in Provence: he treated it as an accepted article of his creed.[3] The sentence has often been printed in one of St Augustine's sermons, but the reading is almost certainly faulty.[4] Both his other sermons and his writings generally imply that the text he was familiar with approximated to R at this point. We may notice that, while the opening article of the orthodox formula of Rimini was obviously improvised with an eye to the theological issues of the hour, its Christology has all the air of having been extracted bodily from a baptismal creed of the R-type. It is plausible to conjecture that, if Phoebadius really had any hand in its composition, he made use of a form which was familiar to him in his own church.

There is nothing to indicate that, as originally propounded, the modification was consciously anti-heretical in tendency. Yet that it had the object of conveying a subtle doctrinal nuance and correcting possible misunderstandings seems likely. It was evidently considered important to distinguish between the respective roles of the Holy Spirit and the Blessed Virgin in the incarnation. Thus, where R (in agreement with *Mt.* 1, 20) used the simple preposition FROM (*ex*), most of its local variants preferred two prepositions, BY (*de*) to mark the operation of the Holy Spirit, and FROM to express the birth from our Lady. The addition we are examining carries this tendency a step further in harmony with the emphasis on the conception in *Lk.* 1, 31 and 35. It has been proposed that, if the original Christology of the creed was one implying the incarnation of

[1] For the text, see St Jerome, *Dial. adv. Lucifer.* 17 (*P.L.* 23, 170 f.), and Hahn 166.
[2] *De trin.* 10, 20 (*P.L.* 10, 358).
[3] Cf. *De Spir. sanct.* 1, 3; *Ep.* 7 (Engelbrecht, 105 f; 205).
[4] *Serm.* 213 (*P.L.* 38, 1061).

divine Spirit, it may well have occasioned uneasiness to later theologians, with their formulated theory of the personal and eternal distinction of the Son from the Spirit.[1] The burden of this suggestion may be accepted, even if the underlying Christology is very different from the one proposed. The introduction first of separate prepositions, and then of the fresh participle CONCEIVED, may well have been determined by the instinctive desire to throw what the fully developed theology of the Trinity considered the true perspective into the sharpest relief. This explanation derives some support from the patristic discussion of the clause. Rufinus, for example, whose text read BY and FROM but not CONCEIVED, was at pains to emphasize that the Son was eternally Son in the heavens, and that BORN BY THE HOLY SPIRIT merely meant that He (the Son) had built a temple for Himself in the Virgin's womb.[2] St Hilary repeatedly underlined the fact that the role of the Spirit was to conceive.[3] St Augustine, whose creed apparently lacked the distinction between CONCEIVED and BORN, was fully aware that BORN FROM THE HOLY SPIRIT AND THE VIRGIN MARY might lead to the travesty that Jesus was in effect the Son of the Spirit. His solution[4] of the problem was to suggest that Jesus is not literally born from the Holy Spirit: He is the Son of God the Father, but can be described as born from the Spirit, just as we, who of course are sons of God by adoption and grace, can legitimately be described as born of water and the Holy Spirit.

Several centuries afterwards the nice distinction between the conception and the birth was to equip the champions of orthodoxy with a useful weapon against the heresies of their day. In combating the outbreak of Adoptionism in the closing years of the eighth century, Alcuin made frequent appeal to the Lord's conception by the Holy Spirit as the clinching proof that, even as man, He was more than an adoptive Son (*filius adoptivus*). Since He had been actually conceived by the Holy Spirit, it was plain that He had never at any moment of His earthly existence been anything else than God, and so it was out of the question

[1] Cf. H. J. Carpenter in *J.T.S.* xl, 1939, 36.
[2] *Comm. in symb. apost.* 8 (*C.C.L.* 20, 144 f.).
[3] Cf., e.g., *De trin.* 2, 24; 10, 17 ff.; 10, 35 (*P.L.* 10, 66; 356 ff.; 371).
[4] *Enchir.* 37–40 (*P.L.* 40, 251 f.).

for Him to be raised to that status by adoption.[1] "What but God", he inquired, "could have been born from God?"[2]

4. *The Descent to Hell*

None of the modifications of R we have so far considered can be reckoned as of decisive importance. There is one, however, which really adds something of substance to the second article of the creed, and which involves exegetical difficulties of no mean order—HE DESCENDED TO HELL (*descendit ad inferna*[3]). The first variant of R to exhibit it is the Aquileian creed commented upon by Rufinus: he remarked that the clause was not to be found in either the Roman creed or in Eastern formularies. It occurs in some Spanish creeds of the sixth century, and was a feature of the Gallican creeds of the seventh and eighth centuries, beginning with that of St Caesarius of Arles in the sixth. Rufinus himself had not much light to shed on its interpolation: he merely remarked that it seemed to have much the same implications as BURIED,[4] while in a later chapter he connected it with 1 *Pet.* 3, 19 (how Christ "went and preached to the spirits in prison"), which he regarded as explaining "what Christ accomplished in the underworld"[5] In view of his silence it is improbable that the clause was a recent addition to the Aquileian creed. In any case its first credal appearance was in the Fourth Formula of Sirmium, the Dated Creed of 359,[6] which affirmed (with an allusion to *Job* 38, 17) that the Lord had "died, and descended to the underworld (εἰς τὰ καταχθόνια κατελθόντα), and regulated things there, Whom the gatekeepers of hell saw and shuddered". The Homoean synods which met about the same time, at Niké (359) and at Constantinople (360), published creeds armed with similar statements. Both these, of course, were modifications of the Fourth Formula of Sirmium, and it is interesting to recall that, according to the historian Socrates,[7] its author had been Mark of Arethusa, a Syrian. There is a good deal of evidence pointing

---

[1] Cf. e.g. *Adv. haer. Felic.* 37; 70 f. (*P.L.* 101, 102; 117 f.).
[2] *Adv. Felic.* 4, 8 (*P.L.* 101, 182).
[3] The form *inferos* is nowadays preferred as indicating that the place of the departed, not the damned, is meant: so the Roman Breviary.
[4] *Comm. in symb. apost.* 16 (*C.C.L.* 20, 153).   [5] *Op. cit.* 20 (*C.C.L.* 20, 161).
[6] See above, p. 289 f.   [7] *Hist. eccl.* 2, 30 (*P.G.* 67, 280).

to the probability that the Descent figured very early in Eastern creed material. The doxology of the Syrian *Didascalia*, for example, contained the sentence: "Who was crucified under Pontius Pilate and departed into peace, in order to preach to Abraham, Isaac and Jacob and all the saints concerning the ending of the world and the resurrection of the dead." This seems to echo credal language. Even more to the point is the fact that the creed of Aphraates, the Persian sage (fl. 340), so far as it can be pieced together from his Homilies, seems to have included an article WENT DOWN TO THE PLACE OF THE DEAD. A reference to the Descent occurs seven or eight times in the works of Aphraates, twice in the third-century *Acts of Thomas*, and a number of times in other sources for Syrian creeds.[1] Thus, although it never caught on in official Eastern creeds (St Cyril of Jerusalem, however, reckoned[2] it among the Church's *credenda*), it is very likely that the West admitted it to its formularies under Eastern influence.

The belief that Christ spent the interval between His expiry on the cross and His resurrection in the underworld was a commonplace of Christian teaching from the earliest times. Apart from the possibility of its having been in the minds of New Testament writers,[3] the Descent was explicitly mentioned by St Ignatius,[4] St Polycarp,[5] St Irenaeus,[6] Tertullian,[7] and others. According to one strain of patristic exegesis,[8] the Lord Himself had hinted at it in His prophecy (*Mt.* 12, 39 f.) that the Son of Man would spend three days and three nights in the heart of the earth (ἐν τῇ καρδίᾳ τῆς γῆς). St Paul's remarks in *Rom.* 10, 7, as well as *Col.* 1, 18, were widely interpreted as involving a visit of Christ to the place of the departed. So, too, St Peter's speech in *Acts* 2, 27–31, transferring to Christ the words of *Ps.* 16, 8 ff. ("Thou wilt not leave my soul in hell" etc.), was taken as a clear pointer in the same direction, as were the famous texts 1 *Pet.* 3, 19 and 4, 6, suggesting that He

---

[1] On this see R. H. Connolly's important article in *Z.N.T.W.* vii, 1906, 213 ff.
[2] *Cat.* 4, 11 (*P.G.* 33, 469).
[3] F. Loofs detected allusions in *Hebr.* 11, 39 f.; 12, 22 f.; 10, 20, as well as in *Mt.* 27, 51–53: see *H.E.R.E.* IV, 662.
[4] *Magn.* 9 (Bihlmeyer, 91).   [5] *Ad Philipp.* 1 (Bihlmeyer, 114).
[6] *Adv. haer.* 4, 27, 2; 5, 31, 1; 5, 33, 1 (*P.G.* 7, 1058; 1208; 1212).
[7] *De anima* 55 (*C.C.L.* 2, 862 f.).
[8] E.g. St Cyprian, *Testim.* 2, 25 (Hartel, 92).

had preached to "the spirits in prison". (After St Augustine, it should be remarked, the prevailing Western fashion was to explain 1 *Pet.* 3, 19 as testifying to a mission of Christ's to the contemporaries of Noah long prior to His incarnation.) In its original significance the doctrine had nothing to do with pagan mythology, though numerous superficially apt parallels can be adduced. It was no more than the natural corollary of Judaeo-Christian ideas about the condition of the soul after death. To say that Jesus Christ had died, or that He had been buried, was equivalent to saying that He had passed to Sheol. The unquestioned premiss, for example, of the lengthy passage in Tertullian's *De anima* 50 ff. is that all souls descend to Hades immediately after death, and that

Christ our God, Who because He was man died according to the Scriptures, and was buried according to the same Scriptures, satisfied this law also by undergoing the form of human death in the underworld, and did not ascend aloft to heaven until He had gone down to the regions beneath the earth.[1]

In view of the early popularity of the Descent in Syriac-speaking regions, it is worth noticing that, as R. H. Connolly has pointed out,[2] the Syriac translation for "from the dead ($\dot{\epsilon}\kappa\ \nu\epsilon\kappa\rho\hat{\omega}\nu$)", so frequent in the New Testament of the risen Lord, was ambiguous: it could mean either "from the dead", or "from the place, or house, of the dead". In harmony with this the Peshitta version of *Rom.* 10, 6 f. introduced an explicit mention of Sheol.

A full study[3] of the meaning of the conception in the eyes of the early Church would divert us into irrelevant, if attractive, by-paths. Two broad, often intermingling streams of interpretation can be distinguished. According to one, Christ was active during the mysterious three days preaching salvation, or else administering baptism, to the righteous of the old Covenant, according to the other He performed a triumphant act of liberation on their behalf. The former found representatives in

---

[1] *De anima* 55 (*C.C.L.* 2, 862 f.).
[2] Cf. *Z.N.T.W.* vii, 1906, 213 f.
[3] Cf. A. Grillmeier's two detailed articles in *Z. für Kath. Th.* 71, 1949.

the author of the *Gospel of Peter*,[1] St Justin,[2] St Irenaeus,[3] and Origen.[4] St Hippolytus added the pleasing detail that John the Baptist acted as the Lord's precursor in the underworld as on earth,[5] while Hermas suggested that the Apostles and teachers who had passed away carried on His ministry below and baptized their converts.[6] The main difficulties facing this line of thought were that the Old Testament saints scarcely needed illumination, since they had foreseen Christ's coming, and that it seemed inappropriate that the unconverted should receive a second opportunity for repentance in the other world. Hence the alternative view, which placed the accent on the deliverance of the saints and the defeat of Satan, gained ground and established itself in the West, where indeed the doctrine that Christ had liberated any others than those holy persons, primarily Jews, who had either foreseen His coming or kept His precepts by anticipation, was afterwards branded as heretical.[7] What is important for us to observe, however, is that by the time the Descent became an accepted article in the creed, a rather different complex of ideas was being associated with it according to which Christ's activity consisted in completely subjugating hell and the ruler of the underworld. Clear traces of this occur as early as the Paschal Homily (68; 102) of Melito of Sardis and Hippolytus's anaphora. We can see it taking shape in the thought of Rufinus, who argued that Christ consented to die in order that He might spoil death, and expatiated on His victorious combat in the underworld with the Devil.[8] For him, it would appear, the underworld meant hell, and the Descent was coming to be viewed as the occasion of the redemption, not just of the patriarchs of old, but of mankind in general. The older tradition that it was simply the natural corollary of the Lord's death,[9] or that its object was the release of the Old Testament saints, still persisted.[10] But for an

---

[1] Vv. 41 f.   [2] *Dial.* 72 (E.J.G., 182).

[3] *Adv. haer.* 3, 20, 4; 4, 22, 1 (*P.G.* 7, 945; 1046 f.); *Epideix.* 78 (*P. Or.* 12, 717); etc.

[4] *Con. Cels.* 2, 43 (Koetschau I, 166).

[5] *De Christo et anti-Christo* 45 (*G.C.S.* 1, 2, 29).

[6] *Sim.* 9, 16, 6 f., 5–7 (*G.C.S.* 48, 90).

[7] Cf. St Augustine, *De haer.* 79; St Gregory, *Ep.* 15 (*P.L.* 42, 45; 77, 869 f.).

[8] *Comm. in symb. apost.* 14 f. (*G.C.L.* 20, 151 f.).

[9] The fact that it was so understood probably explains why it was so often passed over in silence in creed-expositions.

[10] Cf., e.g., St Faustus of Riez, *Hom.* I (Caspari, *Quellen* II, 190).

illustration of the ideas which captured the popular imagination we need only refer to St Caesarius of Arles, who declared,[1] "Because this Lion, that is, Christ, of the tribe of Judah, descended victoriously to hell, snatching us from the mouth of the hostile lion. Thus He hunts us to save us, He captures us to release us, He leads us captive to restore us liberated to our native land." It was probably St Caesarius who in another sermon[2] remarked: "He descended to hell in order to rescue us from the jaws of the cruel dragon." So an African preacher could declaim: "He, so merciful and blessed, mercifully visited the region of our misery, so as to escort us to the region of His blessedness."[3]

A pertinent question, though it is not easy to work out a satisfactory answer to it, concerns the motives at work in the insertion of the Descent into the creed. A theory which enjoyed considerable influence in the past was that it had an anti-Apollinarian bias.[4] It is true that developments in Christology were reflected in the changing interpretations put upon the doctrine.[5] Thus in the earlier period Christ's death and Descent were understood in terms of the separation of His human soul from His body (so, e.g., Tertullian and Origen). Among the exponents of the Word-flesh Christology it was naturally the Logos alone, disjoined from the Lord's body, Who was conceived of as descending to the underworld (so Arius, St Athanasius, Eusebius of Caesarea, etc.). In the struggle against Apollinarianism, however, the older tradition that it was in His human soul that Christ descended reasserted itself. Yet it would be hazardous to infer that anti-Apollinarian motives prompted the insertion of the Descent into the creed. As we have seen, it was established in Syrian creed-material long before Apollinarius began to teach. Even more flimsy is the suggestion, which has sometimes been put forward, that the intention behind the clause was to bolster up the doctrine of Purgatory. If it is legitimate to seek polemical motives at all for its interpolation,

---

[1] *Serm.* 119 (*C.C.L.* 103, 498).
[2] Pseudo-Aug., *Serm.* 44, 6 (*P.L.* 39, 1834).
[3] Pseudo-Fulgentius: cf. *R. Bén.* xxxv, 1923, 238.
[4] Cf., e.g., Peter, Lord King, *The History of the Apostles' Creed*, 5th ed., London, 1737, 169 ff.
[5] See A. Grillmeier, *arts. cit.*: also *Lex. f. Theol. u. Kirche* 5, 452–4.

the only heresy which can conceivably be envisaged is Docetism.[1] It is just possible that the details of the Lord's experiences were elaborated so as to underline the reality of His death. In the passage of Tertullian already cited,[2] for example, we can overhear a note of insistence that Christ's descent to the underworld proved His participation in the fulness of human experience. An objection to this is that, although the doctrine was frequently mentioned, it is hardly ever possible to read an anti-Docetic intention into the references to it. This is not to imply that the clause entered the creed fortuitously and was devoid of dogmatic significance. If it secured admittance first in a Syrian-speaking locality, it was no doubt regarded initially as no more than a more colourful equivalent of DEAD and BURIED. But when it travelled Westwards, it may have been welcomed for several distinct reasons. The imagination of Christians delighted to dwell on the Saviour's experiences in the underworld, as we can see from the numerous and often fantastic attempts to portray them in art. The clause, moreover, provided the creed with something which had hitherto been lacking and of which the need may have been keenly, if inarticulately, felt, a mention of the act of redemption wrought by Christ. It is significant that, as has already been hinted, about the time when the Descent was beginning to appear in creeds, the ancient notion of Christ's mission to the patriarchs was fading more and more into the background, and the doctrine was coming to be interpreted as symbolizing His triumph over Satan and death, and, consequently, the salvation of mankind as a whole.

5. *The Third Article Reinterpreted and Revised*

By the time the Apostles' Creed assumed its final shape, the third article had come to be understood in the light of the Church's developed doctrine of the Trinity. Thus the interpretation read into THE HOLY SPIRIT represented the words as affirming belief in the third Person of the Godhead, coeternal, coequal and consubstantial with the Father and the Son. As Rufinus put it succinctly: "Thus with the mention of the Holy

[1] So H. B. Swete, *The Apostles' Creed*, Cambridge, 1894, 61; Kattenbusch II, 901.
[2] *De anima* 55 (*C.C.L.* 2, 862 f.).

Spirit the mystery of the Trinity is completed."[1] The clause about the forgiveness of sins, also, which had originally referred to the cleansing effect of baptism, was explained after the middle of the fourth century as including the forgiveness obtained through confession and absolution. "Since we have to live in this world," St Augustine commented on our clause,[2] "in which life without sin is impossible, the remission of sins does not consist solely in the washing of holy baptism"; and he went on to inculcate the regular use of the Lord's Prayer, with its petition for forgiveness, as a kind of daily baptism. In another sermon expounding the creed,[3] he enumerated three methods of obtaining remission of sins in the Church—baptism, prayer, and "the greater humbling of oneself in penitence (*humilitate maiore penitentiae*)". Later theologians, like St Fulgentius of Ruspe († 532)[4] and St Ildefonsus of Toledo († 667),[5] dwelt at length on the penitential discipline of the Church, while St Ivo of Chartres († 1117) briefly expounded the clause,[6] "not only of those sins which are remitted by baptism, but also of those which are purged by making suitable amends after humble confession".

Apart from these reflections of a later, more mature theology, the third article of T boasts three features which differentiate it from the Old Roman Creed. One of these, the clause THE COMMUNION OF SAINTS, presents certain difficulties of interpretation, and we shall defer discussion of it for the moment. The other two, the adjective CATHOLIC describing the Church, and the clause THE LIFE EVERLASTING, can be dealt with in a few paragraphs.

Everyone knows that the original meaning of CATHOLIC was "general" or "universal". Zeno the Stoic wrote a book about universals, which he called καθολικά; Polybius[7] spoke of "universal history (τῆς καθολικῆς καὶ κοινῆς ἱστορίας)"; and St Justin[8] applied the word to the resurrection (ἡ καθολικὴ

---

[1] *Comm. in symb. apost.* 33 (*C.C.L.* 20, 169).
[2] *Serm.* 213, 8 (*P.L.* 38, 1064 f.).
[3] *Serm. ad catech.* 8 (*P.L.* 40, 636).
[4] E.g. *Ep.* 7; *De remiss. peccat.* II (*C.C.L.* 90, 244–54; 91A, 678–707).
[5] *Lib. de cognit. bapt.* 81 f. (*P.L.* 96, 140 f.).
[6] *Serm.* 23 (*P.L.* 162, 606).
[7] *Hist.* 8, 2, 11 (Büttner-Wobst II, 335).
[8] *Dial.* 81 (E.J.G., 194).

ἀνάστασις). It is in St Ignatius that we first come across it as a predicate of the Church. "Wherever the bishop shows himself," he said,[1] "there shall the community be, just as wherever Christ Jesus is, there is the Catholic Church." Here there is no thought of the antithesis between the one orthodox Church and the dissident conventicles. The writer was comparing the universal Church, directed by Christ, with the local churches presided over by the bishops; and his point was that the local community only had reality, life and power in proportion as it formed part of the universal Church with its spiritual head. Precisely the same sense attaches to the adjective in the passages of the *Martyrdom of St Polycarp* where it occurs.[2] This meaning always remained primary, so that St Cyril of Jerusalem could say of the Church (while adding other, more fanciful reasons): "It is denominated Catholic because it is spread throughout the whole world from one end to the other."[3] On the other hand, after the middle of the second century it began to acquire a new connotation, designating "the great Church" (to use a phrase of Celsus's[4]) in contrast to the numerous heretical sects. Probably the first instance of its employment with this meaning is in the Muratorian Canon, which enumerated the sacred books which were, or were not, "received in the Catholic Church". In harmony with this usage Pope Cornelius (†253) complained in a letter that his rival Novatian was ignorant that "there ought to be but one bishop in a Catholic church".[5] About the same date (250), when the martyr Pionius was asked by his judges what he was called, he replied, "A Christian"; and when the inquiry was pressed, "To what church do you belong?", he answered, "To the Catholic Church."[6]

It was in the late fourth century that CATHOLIC began to appear in Western creeds. The first reliable witness to it that we can produce is Nicetas of Remesiana. Later it became a favourite item in Spanish and Gallic creeds. Eastern creeds had always manifested a predilection for it, and some have

---

[1] *Smyrn.* 8, 2 (Bihlmeyer, 108).
[2] *Inscr.* 8, 1; 19, 2 (Bihlmeyer, 120; 124; 130).
[3] *Cat.* 18, 23 (*P.G.* 33, 1044).
[4] Origen, *Con. Cels.* 5, 59 (Koetschau II, 62).
[5] In Eusebius, *Hist. eccl.* 6, 43, 11 (Schwartz, 263).
[6] For the *Martyrium Pionii* see R. Knopf, *Ausgewählte Märtyrerakten*, 3rd ed., 1929, 45 ff.

suspected Eastern influence behind its adoption in the West. If such an explanation is required, we can at once rule out the suggestion that C set the fashion: if the West had taken C as a model, we should have expected APOSTOLIC as well. It is just possible that the immense prestige of St Cyril's *Catechetical Lectures*, which presuppose a formulary lacking APOSTOLIC but containing CATHOLIC, may have influenced Western creed-makers. But the word CATHOLIC had become such a routine term in Western theological parlance that it is unnecessary to search for recondite reasons for its incorporation in the creed. What is interesting to observe is that in the mind of Nicetas it connoted primarily the one orthodox Church as opposed to the sects. He spoke of "the one Catholic Church established throughout the whole world, to whose communion you ought to hold fast", and contrasted it with "other pseudo-churches" which believed and acted in a way inimical to Christ and His apostles.[1] It was natural that this significance should be prominent in an age when Arianism, Donatism and other heresies were rife and were propagating rival churches. As time went on, however, it tended to become secondary, though it was never lost sight of. Most of the sermons and expositions of the creed explain the word, the origin of which was sometimes mysterious to Latin-speakers, as synonymous with "universal". "What is the Catholic Church," asked St Faustus of Riez, "save the people dedicated to God which is diffused throughout the world?";[2] and the author of a sermon in the pseudo-Augustinian appendix echoed these words in his curt paraphrase of CATHOLIC as "spread throughout the whole world".[3] As an illustration of both meanings held together, we have the statement of St Ildefonsus of Toledo that CATHOLIC means "universal", followed immediately by the claim that it is precisely in this respect that the true Church is distinguished from "the conventicles of heretics", which only flourish locally.[4]

The insertion of CATHOLIC thus gave expression to the Church's consciousness of its uniquely authoritative position *vis-à-vis* the dissident sects. THE LIFE EVERLASTING, which

[1] *De symb.* 10 (Burn, 48).
[2] See his *Tract. de symb.* in Caspari, *A. und N.Q.*, 272 f.
[3] *Serm.* 242, 4 (*P.L.* 39, 2193).
[4] *Lib. de cognit. bapt.* 73 (*P.L.* 96, 138).

seems to have secured its earliest mention in African formularies, met a more specifically religious need. It is evident that many people wanted more than the assurance that they would one day rise from the dead: mere resurrection was compatible with dying again. St Augustine had their difficulties in mind when, expounding (probably in 421) his own personal beliefs, he remarked: "Now with regard to the resurrection of the flesh (which is not like that of certain persons who have risen from the dead but have afterwards died, but is like the resurrection of Christ's flesh, that is, to life everlasting), I do not see how I can explain matters briefly."[1] So, in a sermon attributed to him, he admitted in so many words that the clause TO THE LIFE EVERLASTING was added so as to exclude the assumption that the resurrection of believers would follow the precedent of that of Lazarus rather than that of Christ.[2] Again, in one of his letters, when discussing a number of questions propounded by a pagan, he revealed that many were worried as to whether the resurrection bestowed on the faithful would resemble Lazarus's or Christ's.[3] Anxieties on this score were apparently not confined to Africa, for St John Chrysostom deemed it advisable to counter them in one of his homilies.

"After you have said FORGIVENESS OF SINS," he declared, "you go on to confess THE RESURRECTION OF THE DEAD. . . . After that, since a mention of the resurrection does not suffice to bring out the whole doctrine (for many men who have arisen from the grave have died again, as the example of Old Testament personages, of Lazarus, and of the people who rose at the time of the crucifixion shows), you are also bidden to affirm, AND IN THE LIFE EVERLASTING."[4]

The glimpses which passages like these permit of popular speculation about the resurrection justify us in inferring that the clause owed its place in the creed to the desire to quieten troubled minds. Corroboration may be derived from the form of wording in which it is occasionally set out, TO THE LIFE EVERLASTING, which suggests that it was understood as bringing out the full significance of RESURRECTION OF THE FLESH. This reading, as we noticed in the preceding paragraph, was characteristic of the Augustinian *Sermo ad catechumenos,* and there is some

[1] *Enchir.* 84 (*P.L.* 40, 272).   [2] *Serm. ad catech.* 9 (*P.L.* 40, 636).
[3] *Ep.* 102 *ad Deograt.* (*P.L.* 33, 371 ff.).   [4] *Hom.* 40, 2 (*P.G.* 61, 349).

MS evidence that Nicetas, too, had TO THE LIFE EVERLASTING in his creed. Yet an independent, more positive complex of ideas was not slow in attaching itself to the clause. St Cyril of Jerusalem, for example, while disposing of LIFE EVERLASTING quite briefly, did indicate that it stood for something more than mere continuance of life: it pointed, he said, to "the real, veritable life (ἡ ὄντως ζωὴ καὶ ἀληθῶς)", which was God Himself.[1] For Nicetas LIFE EVERLASTING was life with Christ in heaven, eternal and blessed life, the fruit of faith and right conversation, a life which neither the pagan nor the unbelieving Jew could possess, but which was reserved for the faithful who lived chastely here on earth.[2] Thus the emphasis was transferred from the idea of protracted existence to the blessed quality of the life of the world to come. Thus when the Pelagians, anxious to justify their practice of baptizing children, tried to draw a distinction between life everlasting or salvation (which sinful men of course need) and the kingdom of heaven (which was what they thought innocent babes might acquire in baptism), they were met with an indignant protest from St Augustine. It was a blasphemous novelty, he urged,[3] to say that life everlasting differed in any way from the kingdom of heaven. So, too, in the middle ages the stress in LIFE EVERLASTING was on the positive state of blessedness enjoyed by the redeemed. As St Thomas Aquinas put it, the first truth about eternal life is that a man there finds union with God, Who is the reward and end of all our labours, and crowns all our desires.[4]

6. *The Communion of Saints*

Finally, we come to an additional clause of the Apostles' Creed which has aroused immense discussion, THE COMMUNION OF SAINTS (*sanctorum communionem*). The first surviving creed to attest its presence is the formulary commented on by Nicetas of Remesiana. Before Nicetas, however, if Dom G. Morin's conjecture can be accepted as correct, it would seem to have featured in the so-called "Faith of St Jerome",[5] which ends

[1] *Cat.* 18, 28 ff. (*P.G.* 33, 1049 ff.).
[2] *De symb.* 12 (Burn, 51).
[3] *Serm.* 294, 2 f. (*P.L.* 38, 1336 ff.).
[4] Cf. *Expos. sup. symb. apost. ad fin.* (Vol. III of 1634 Paris edition, 133).
[5] Cf. *Anecdota Maredsolana* III, iii, 199 f.

with I BELIEVE IN THE REMISSION OF SINS IN THE HOLY CHURCH, THE COMMUNION OF SAINTS, THE RESURRECTION OF THE FLESH, AND LIFE EVERLASTING. An old Armenian creed quoted by Caspari also speaks of belief in THE FORGIVENESS OF SINS IN THE HOLY CHURCH AND THE COMMUNION OF SAINTS.[1] Perhaps too much uncertainty surrounds the origins of these two formularies for us to be able to build much upon them alone. But the phrase unquestionably occurs[2] (a) in an imperial rescript of 388 banning Apollinarians, among other things, *a communione sanctorum*; (b) in a canon of a synod held at Nîmes in 394 or 396. Henceforth it was to feature in creeds, but almost exclusively in South Gaul.

This fact might seem to favour the inference that Nicetas probably borrowed COMMUNION OF SAINTS in the first place from Gaul, with which he had close personal ties as the friend of St Paulinus of Nola, and which he visited on more than one occasion. Harnack, however, questioned this, and contended that the exchange was more likely to have been in the reverse direction, Nicetas deriving the idea from St Cyril of Jerusalem. But there is nothing to indicate that St Cyril had any knowledge of COMMUNION OF SAINTS: the passages Harnack cited from the *Catechetical Lectures* in support of his theory are altogether too vague.[3] There are, however, more persuasive pointers to the importation of the clause from the East. (a) If the *Fides Hieronymi* identified by G. Morin really is the creed subscribed by St Jerome in the desert of Chalcis in 377/8, it must have been an Antiochene formula, and this is borne out by other Eastern traits in it.[4] (b) Nicetas himself was subject to influences from the East, as is shown by the degree to which his creed commentary was inspired by the *Catecheses* of St Cyril of Jerusalem. Further, while he did not visit Paulinus in Nola until 398, it is accepted that in his life-time there was a strong current of influence from the East to South Gaul through his Balkan homeland. (c) While the expression SANCTORUM COMMUNIO was rare and its meaning fluctuating in the West, the Greek equivalent, viz. κοινωνία τῶν ἁγίων, and related phrases were firmly estab-

[1] See *Quellen* II, 11; Hahn 138.
[2] For these texts see Codex Theod. xvi, 5, 4; *C.C.L.* 148, 50.
[3] *Cat.* 18, 26, *fin*; 27; 28 (*P.G.* 33, 1048 ff.).
[4] Cf., e.g., G. Morin, *R. Bén.* xvi, 1904, 1 ff.

lished in the East and bore the clear-cut sense of "participation in the holy things", i.e. the eucharistic elements.[1] This makes it highly probable that the idea and the language expressing it originated in the East.

The acutest controversy, however, has centred round the doctrinal content of *sanctorum communio*, and the motives for its insertion into the creed. The traditional interpretation, if it may for convenience be so described, is that it means "fellowship with holy persons", the word *sanctorum* being taken either in a narrow sense of the saints proper and martyrs, or in the broader, more primitive sense of the faithful generally, living as well as departed.[2] In rivalry with this an alternative exegesis, suggesting that the words should bear in the creed the sense their Greek equivalents undoubtedly bore, viz. "participation in the eucharistic elements", has gained increasing support since the late nineteenth century.[3] The word *sanctorum*, it should be observed, may be either masculine or neuter. Yet a third school of interpretation would read a concrete meaning into *communio*, translating the phrase as "fellowship, i.e. community, consisting of holy persons", and so would understand it as a further description of HOLY CATHOLIC CHURCH. It was inserted into the creed, it is claimed, as a protest against Donatist rigorism, which delighted to criticize the Catholic Church for welcoming goats as well as sheep within its fold.[4] It is conceivable that the words were sometimes used to signify "fellowship of holy persons" in the concrete sense.[5] The real controversy, however, at all events so far as the bearing of the clause in the creed is concerned, lies between the two former interpretations and the various sub-forms of them: it can scarcely be doubted that COMMUNION OF SAINTS means much more than "Church" in the creeds. A powerful argument against trying to find an anti-Donatist bias in the words is the fact that they never obtained a foothold in any of the creeds of North Africa,

---

[1] For illustrative texts, cf. W. Elert, *art. cit.* below.

[2] Cf., e.g., J. P. Kirsch, *Die Lehre von der Gemeinschaft der Heiligen im Christlichen Altertum*, Mainz, 1900 (Eng. trans. 1910).

[3] Cf. Th. Zahn, *Das apost. Symbolum*, Erlangen-Leipzig, 1893, 88 ff.; W. Elert, *Theol. Literaturzeitung* lxxiv, 1949, 578 ff.; S. Benko, *The Meaning of Communion of Saints*, London, 1964.

[4] So H. B. Swete, *The Apostles' Creed*, 1894, 30.

[5] Cf., e.g., St Aug., *Enarr. in psalm.* 36, 2, 20; *Serm.* 52, 2; *Ep. Donat. ad Flav. Marcell.* (*P.L.* 36, 379; 38, 357; 43, 835). Other interpretations are preferable.

although it was only in that region that Donatism exercised any serious influence.

The most profitable method of approaching the problem (an insoluble one, perhaps) of the original bearing of the words is to study them as they are found in their credal setting. Here at any rate we have solid handrails to grasp and need not poise ourselves unsupported in the dizzy air of conjecture. There can be no question, for example, what Nicetas was thinking about when he quoted our clause.

"What is the Church," he inquired, "but the congregation of all saints? From the beginning of the world patriarchs, prophets, martyrs, and all other righteous men who have lived or are now alive, or shall live in time to come, comprise the Church, since they have been sanctified by one faith and manner of life, and sealed by one Spirit and so made one body, of which Christ is declared to be head, as the Scripture says. Moreover, the angels, and the heavenly virtues and powers too, are banded together in this Church. . . . So you believe that in this Church you will attain to the communion of saints."

Manifestly COMMUNION OF SAINTS is here interpreted as standing for that ultimate fellowship with the holy persons of all ages, as well as with the whole company of heaven, which is anticipated and partly realized in the fellowship of the Catholic Church on earth. On the other hand, the reference was narrowed down by St Faustus of Riez (he was elected bishop there about 452) to the saints in the technical acceptation of the word.

"Let us believe", he said,[1] "in the communion of saints, but let us venerate the saints, not so much in place of God, as for God's honour and glory. . . . Let us worship in the saints the fear and love of God, not His divinity. Let us worship the merits of the saints, not merits which they have from themselves, but which they have earned for their devotion. Thus they deserve to be venerated worthily, forasmuch as they infuse into us, through their contempt of death, the worship of God and the yearning for the life to come."

Faustus was clearly trying to defend, while at the same time controlling and keeping within common-sense bounds, the growing cult of martyrs which was a feature of Gallican religion

[1] Cf. *Hom.* II in Caspari, *Quellen* II, 197.

at the time, and which the Aquitanian priest Vigilantius had recently sought in vain to check.[1] The tractate on the creed which is also attributed to St Faustus girded against the followers of Vigilantius with much less temperate language. "This article", it declared, "puts to shame those who blasphemously deny that the ashes of the saints are to be held in honour, and refuse to believe that the memory of the blessed martyrs ought to be celebrated by paying respect to their monuments."[2]

Kindred conceptions, though not always restricted to the saints in the technical sense of the word, are to be found associated with the clause in other Gallican expositions of the creed where no polemical note is audible. Thus *Sermo pseudo-August.* 242 makes the comment[3]: "COMMUNION OF SAINTS: that is, we are bound in fellowship and the communion of hope with those saints who have passed away in this faith which we have embraced." The reference is plainly to all departed Christians. *Sermo pseudo-August.* 240 remarks that in eternity the gifts of the Spirit, which are here distributed differently to different individuals, will be the common property of all, and each of the saints will find his own deficiencies made up by the virtues of others.[4] Here the fellowship envisaged is again that of believers generally, although the realization of it is altogether transferred to the future life. *Sermo pseudo-August.* 241 has often been appealed to as a witness to the sacramental interpretation, asserting as it does that we believe in the communion of saints because where there is holy faith, there is holy communion (*sancta communio*).[5] But this, some claim, is to miss the preacher's real point, which is that because we believe in the holy Catholic Church, and because faith brings holy fellowship, we therefore enjoy the fellowship of saints, and so ought to believe in the resurrection and the remission of sins even while we are in the body. However that may be, Hrabanus Maurus reproduced almost verbally the teaching of *Sermo pseudo-August.* 242,[6] as did the author (Alcuin?) of the ninth-century *Disputatio puerorum*.[7]

---

[1] St Jerome wrote his tract against Vigilantius (*P.L.* 23, 339 ff.) in 406; but he seems to have lived on, and his heresy apparently took root.

[2] See Caspari, *A. und N.Q.*, 273 f.   [3] *P.L.* 39, 2193.

[4] *P.L.* 39, 2189.   [5] *P.L.* 39, 2191.

[6] *P.L.* 112, 1226.   [7] *P.L.* 101, 1142.

There can be no doubt that, so far as concerns Western creeds, this was the interpretation of COMMUNION OF SAINTS which had the longest and most continuous history. Yet we may freely admit that the words were often taken, even in the West, as referring to the sacrament. This was undoubtedly their meaning in the rescript of Theodosius referred to above, and also in a letter[1] of St Jerome's (a translation, actually, of a Greek original). Again, although the text of the canon of Nîmes is badly mutilated (it runs "*in primis quia multi de ultimis orientis partibus venientis presbyteros et diaconos se esse confingunt . . . sanctorum communione speciae simulatae religionis impraemunt: placuit nobis si qui fuerint eiusmodi . . . ad ministerium altarii non admittantur*"), there can be little doubt that exclusion from communion is envisaged. If the evidence of *Sermo pseudo-August.* 241 is considered doubtful, a quite unambiguous allusion to the sacraments crops up in the sermon *Symbolum Graeca lingua est*,[2] which dates from the Carolingian era. This explains the clause as meaning "holy communion through the invocation of the Father, the Son and the Holy Spirit, in which all the faithful ought to participate every Lord's day". In the middle ages, while *sanctorum* was usually taken as masculine in gender, the word *communio* was often regarded as equivalent to "the communion which the saints enjoyed", that is, the holy sacrament of the altar. St Ivo of Chartres, for example, understood the clause as pointing to "the truth of the Church's sacraments, in which the saints participated who have passed out of this life in the unity of the faith";[3] while Abelard remarked of it, "that is, that communion by which the saints are made saints and are confirmed in their sanctity, by participation in the divine sacrament."[4] It should be noted, however, that Abelard immediately added that *sanctorum* could also be taken in a neuter sense (*neutraliter*) as referring to the consecrated bread and wine of the Blessed Sacrament. In harmony with this an oft-quoted Norman-French version of the creed translated our article "*la communiun des seintes choses*".[5] It

---

[1] *Ep.* 92, 3 (*P.L.* 22, 764 f.): *a communione sanctorum . . . separatus.*
[2] In Codex Sessorianus 52: see below, p. 428 ff.
[3] *Serm.* 23 (*P.L.* 162, 606).
[4] *Expos. in symb. apost.* (*P.L.* 178, 629 f.).
[5] See Hahn 74. The text is 12th cent.

was a variant of this exegesis which St Thomas Aquinas espoused in his short essay on the Apostles' Creed.[1] "Because all the faithful form one body," he wrote, "the benefits belonging to one are communicated to the others. There is thus a sharing of benefits (*communio bonorum*) in the Church, and this is what we mean by *sanctorum communio*." The goods shared, he went on to explain, comprise everything worth while done on earth by the saints (*sancti*), but particularly the seven sacraments, which convey to us the virtue of Christ's passion, He being the head of the body. According to most scholars, St Thomas took *sanctorum* here as neuter and as precisely equivalent to *bonorum*, i.e. "benefits", but this seems most improbable. Such an interpretation consorts ill with the stress on the faithful as donors and recipients of the benefits, or with the explicit mention of "all the saints" further down in the chapter, or with the inclusion of blessings other than the Church's sacraments among the benefits under discussion. It should be evident that what St Thomas actually understood by the clause was "that sharing or participation which the saints enjoy". At the same time other medieval writers applied it strictly to the Church as a corporate society. Amalarius of Trèves († *circa* 816), for example, paraphrased it as the fellowship of the saints which is held together by the Spirit,[2] while Magnus of Sens explained it as meaning, "that is, the congregation of all the faithful in Christ".[3]

Our review provides an illuminating picture of the fluctuating meanings which were read into *sanctorum communio* in the patristic and medieval periods. Yet the inescapable conclusion to which it points is that, so far as the creed is concerned, the dominant conception, at any rate between the fifth and eighth centuries, was "fellowship with holy persons". The sacramental exegesis came later in time, and has all the air of being secondary: even where it did occur, *sanctorum* itself was most often understood in a masculine sense. The strength of Th. Zahn's case was drawn from considerations which were either à priori or far removed in their bearing from the history of the Western

---

[1] *Expos. sup. symb. apost.* (Vol. III of the 1634 Paris edition, 132).
[2] *Ep. de caer. bapt.* (P.L. 99, 896).
[3] *Libell. de myst. bapt.* in Martène's *De antiquis ecclesiae ritibus*, Antwerp, 1736, 170.

creed. Thus he and his followers argued that a reference to the sacraments was surely called for in the official summary of the Church's faith. No doubt there is force in this: and we may conjecture that it was the instinctive consciousness of a lacuna in the formulary which, among other factors, moved the theologians of later ages to read an allusion to the sacraments into it. But it would be foolhardy to work on the assumption that the criterion of what ought to have been embodied in the creed supplies the key to what actually was embodied in it. Again, they placed great reliance on analogies drawn from Greek usage, appealing to the frequent presence of a sacramental reference in such words as κοινωνία and τὰ ἅγια. But it must be pointed out that true parallels to *sanctorum communionem* are hardly to be found in Greek, and that in any case it is hazardous to assume that Greek and Latin linguistic usage necessarily overlapped. While τὰ ἅγια in Greek regularly meant the consecrated elements of the Eucharist, there is no unambiguous evidence until very late that *sancta* had the same technical sense in Latin. In the few absolutely incontrovertible instances that can be collected of the word's being used in this way, the meaning seems to be quite untechnical and general, and the context places the reference to the sacraments beyond any reasonable doubt.[1] The relevance and value, moreover, of Greek parallels become even more questionable when we recall that, for all its Eastern origin, the clause never established itself in official Greek creeds, and that the very ambiguity of the Latin encouraged different interpretations.

For these reasons the older, traditional understanding of the phrase seems much more likely to be the original one. When later the sacramental interpretation began to thrust itself to the fore, it may have been in some degree the response to the felt need for some mention of the sacraments; and the growing tendency to include the sacrament of Penance under THE REMISSION OF SINS may have helped to focus attention on the gap. The term *communio* itself, which was coming to be increasingly appropriated as a terse description of the sacrament

---

[1] Cf. St Augustine, *In Joh. evang. tract.* 6, 15; *De fid. et op.* 8 (*P.L.* 35, 1432; 40, 202). In *Ep.* 98, 5 (*P.L.* 33, 36), sometimes cited in this connection, *sanctis* probably means "saints".

of the altar, very easily lent itself to, if it did not actually suggest, the novel explanation. When the question is asked, however, what particular situation or crisis prompted the interpolation, a confident answer does not come so readily to the lips. Harnack at one point [1] (he later refused to commit himself) proposed that the new clause must be regarded as the orthodox rejoinder to the attacks made by Vigilantius and like-minded critics on the growing cult of the saints which was such a feature of the late fourth and early fifth century. Yet it should be obvious that COMMUNION OF SAINTS already enjoyed a secure position, and carried with it no odour of controversy, when Nicetas cited it. For him SAINTS had a wider connotation than the saints and martyrs, comprising as it did the patriarchs of old, the present members of the Church, and all the righteous of future generations. In any case, had polemical considerations motivated the addition of the words, we should have expected them to be much more precise and definite in their bearing.

On the other hand, the essential element of truth contained in Harnack's suggestion should not be ignored, even if we cannot agree that the particular controversies he had in mind provoked the orthodox to add COMMUNION OF SAINTS to the creed. The fourth century witnessed an enormous expansion of the devotion which the Church had paid to its saints and illustrious dead from the earliest times. Even at the beginning of the third century the author of the *Passion of Perpetua and Felicitas* [2] assured his readers that his purpose in writing out what had happened was to enable them to enjoy communion with the holy martyrs (*ut . . . communionem habeatis cum sanctis martyribus*), and through them with Jesus Christ. During the fourth century popular enthusiasm for the martyrs and the treasuring of their relics, and with these the demand for their prayers, were everywhere on the upgrade. Sometimes the ideas presupposed were of extraordinary crudity. We have, for example, worked up in the shape of a short treatise, the sermon which St Victricius of Rouen preached in 396 when welcoming a gift of martyrs' relics sent to his episcopal city by St Ambrose. [3]

---

[1] *Das apost. Glaubensbek.*, 31 f.
[2] *Ch.* 1 (in *Texts and Studies* I, 2, 62 f.). The author was probably Tertullian.
[3] *De laud sanct.* (*P.L.* 20, 443 ff.).

His glowing language reveals that he and his auditors regarded the relics as conveying with them the veritable and gracious presence of the martyrs themselves, and through them of the Godhead with Whom they were united. But extravagances of this order merely represented the popular side of an ever-developing sense of the intimate fellowship which the Church on earth felt itself privileged to enjoy with the elect who had already passed beyond the veil. "While dwelling in this Church," remarked St Hilary, "we shall dwell also in that other Church, for this Church is the form of that one. . . . That is the Church of innumerable hosts of angels; it is the Church of the ancient ones, the Church of the spirits established in the Lord."[1] A few lines further down the same page he claimed that the angels and saints, the apostles, patriarchs and prophets surrounded the Church on earth with their watchful guard. Thoughts like these were still further elaborated in St Augustine's writings. It is evident that in the fourth century the consciousness of communion with the redeemed in heaven, who had already tasted of the fulness of the glory of Christ, was as real and as rich in hope to the theologians as to circles of ordinary Christians. With the devotional and doctrinal atmosphere charged with such ideas, it calls for but a slight effort of the imagination to understand how easy it must have been for some formal testimony to their influence to find its way into the creed. Thus, although it involved no polemical *arrière pensée*, COMMUNION OF SAINTS gave expression to conceptions which were very vividly present to the minds of fourth and fifth century churchmen, particularly in those regions of Western Europe where, as we shall shortly discover, the Apostles' Creed was moulded into its final shape.

---

[1] *Tract. in psalm.* 124, 4 (*P.L.* 9, 681 f.).

CHAPTER XIII

THE ORIGINS OF THE APOSTLES' CREED

1. *Texts Approximating to T*

IT was made plain at the beginning of the preceding chapter that the formulary now known in the West as the Apostles' Creed came into existence as one of many variants of the ancient baptismal confession of the Roman church. We have already observed how much more detailed and theologically mature it is as a statement of belief than R, but nothing has so far been said about the complicated and difficult problem of its origin. The issues which this raises are of great interest and importance, and we shall devote this chapter to a discussion of them. Our first task, it is clear, must be to summarize the evidence for the earliest appearance of T (=*textus receptus*), and about this there is no serious doubt. A text to all intents and purposes identical with it is found in the tract *De singulis libris canonicis scarapsus*, written by St Priminius, founder and first abbot of the famous monastery of Reichenau, near Lake Constance. St Priminius (his name has usually been spelt Pirminius, but both philology and the preponderant MS tradition support our form[1]) was a notable Benedictine missionary who arrived in the neighbourhood of Lake Constance about 724, established the abbey of Reichenau under the protection and with the patronage of Charles Martel, organized monastic institutions in S.W. Germany generally, and awakened a new religious and scholarly life by the banks of the Upper Rhine. He wrote his *Scarapsus*[2] at some date which cannot now be determined between 710 and 724. It is a kind of compendious handbook of Christian doctrine, compiled out of Holy Scripture and

---

[1] On the spelling of his name, and its implications for the question of his background and origin, see G. Morin, *Revue Charlemagne* i, 1911, 2-4.

[2] *P.L.* 89, 1029 ff. By far the best edition of the text is that printed in G. Jecker's *Die Heimat des heiligen Pirmin*, Münster in Westf., 1927.

recognized ecclesiastical authors, and was designed to assist him and his disciples in their missionary enterprises. Later he fell into disfavour with the local authorities, was expelled and took refuge in Alsace, and after a further period of energetic labour ended his days in the abbey of Hornbach (near Zweibrücken), another of his foundations, probably in 753.

Priminius quoted the Apostles' Creed in three separate contexts in his missionary manual. In the first of these (chap. 10) he recounted the familiar story of how the Twelve, being filled with the Holy Spirit, composed a summary of belief. The creed which results from piecing together the twelve clauses which he cited coincides exactly with T, except that it reads SAT (*sedit*) instead of SITS (*sedet*) of Christ's session at the Father's right hand. The third (chap. 28) consists of a hortatory instruction on faith and morals, and reproduces the creed in a loose, inexact fashion. By far the most interesting is the second (chap. 12), in which St Priminius reminded his readers of the solemn occasion of their own baptism.

"Thus we recall to your memories, brothers," he wrote, "the pact we made with God in the baptistery itself: that is, how, when we were severally asked by the priest our names and how we were called, either you yourself answered, if you were already of an age to answer, or at all events he who was undertaking the vow for you and lifted you up from the water answered and said, 'He is called John,' or some other name. And the priest inquired, 'John, do you renounce the devil and all his works and all his shows?' You replied, 'I renounce, that is, I despise and relinquish, all evil and diabolic works.' After that renunciation of the devil and all his works, you were also asked by the priest, 'Do you believe in God the Father almighty, creator of heaven and earth?' You replied, 'I believe.' And again, 'Do you believe in Jesus Christ, His only Son, our Lord, Who was conceived by the Holy Spirit, born from the Virgin Mary, suffered under Pontius Pilate, was crucified, dead and buried, descended to hell, on the third day rose again from the dead, ascended to heaven, sat at the right hand of God the Father almighty, thence He will come to judge the living and the dead?' And you replied, 'I believe.' And the priest asked a third time, 'Do you also believe in the Holy Spirit, the holy Catholic Church, the communion of saints, the remission of sins, the resurrection of the flesh, eternal life?' Either you or your god-father for you replied, 'I believe.'

See what manner of pact and promise or confession on your part is binding between you and God. And believing you were baptized in the name of the Father and of the Son and of the Holy Spirit unto the remission of all your sins, and were anointed by the priest with the chrism of salvation unto eternal life, and your body was clothed with a white garment, and Christ clothed your soul with heavenly grace, and a holy angel was assigned to you as your guardian."[1]

This, we observed, is the first appearance of a creed practically identical with T: its only divergence is SAT (*sedit*) for T's SITS, and this is hardly significant in view of the popularity of SITS in Western creeds. Formularies almost as similar to T are to be found in certain other roughly contemporary liturgical documents. One of these is the seventh, or early eighth, century missal sometimes called the Gallican Sacramentary, but nowadays more commonly designated the Missal of Bobbio[2] (Cod. Lat. 13246 in the Bibliothèque Nationale at Paris). Here the creed puts in no fewer than four appearances.

(A) On the first occasion[3] it is prefixed to the sermon at the delivery of the creed, just after the ceremony of the "opening of the ears", i.e. the ritual handing out to the candidates of the first words of each of the four gospels. While fairly close to T, it differs from it in several particulars, notably in substituting I BELIEVE for AND at the opening of the second article and ONLY-BEGOTTEN EVERLASTING[4] for T's ONLY, in omitting OUR LORD, in writing CONCEIVED, BORN, CRUCIFIED, DEAD and BURIED as participles in the accusative, and in using the past SAT for SITS. The position of HOLY with the Spirit also deserves notice. (B) Another text can be reconstructed out of the sermon which follows on immediately afterwards expounding the clauses of the creed.[5] Though allusive and not necessarily complete, it presupposes an acquaintance with ONLY and OUR LORD, as well as with the reading WHO WAS CONCEIVED . . . BORN . . . .

---

[1] For a photographic reproduction of the passage as contained in Cod. Einsidlensis, 199, fol. 237 r. (late 8th or early 9th century: the best of the three MSS of *Scarapsus*), see A. E. Burn, *Facsimiles of the Creeds*, Plate X (H. Bradshaw Society XXXVI, 1909).

[2] For the text, see H. Bradshaw Society LIII, 1917 (a complete photographic facsimile), and LVIII, 1920 (a complete transcription).

[3] H.B. Soc. LVIII, 56: in MS fol. 88 r.

[4] Kattenbusch (II, 776 n. 28) saw the influence of the Te Deum vv. 12 and 15 in this peculiarity.

[5] H. B. Soc. LVIII, 56 f.: in MS foll. 88 v.–90 v.

(C) Yet a third creed crops up,[1] this time interrogatory in form, in the service of baptism provided for Easter Even, directly after the renunciation and before the immersions. Again it approximates closely to T, the main differences being that CONCEIVED, BORN, etc. are expressed by participles in the accusative, that DEAD is lacking, that SAT replaces SITS, and that ETERNAL LIFE is greatly elaborated. (D) Lastly, an isolated text of the creed figures in a collection of miscellaneous addenda attached to the end of the missal.[2] It consists of a fragment attributing the several clauses to their presumed apostolic authors, and exhibits a number of peculiar divergences from T. For example, it lacks CREATOR OF HEAVEN AND EARTH, it speaks of HIS ONLY SON OUR GOD AND LORD, it has no CONCEIVED but reads instead BORN FROM THE VIRGIN MARY THROUGH THE HOLY SPIRIT, it omits DEAD, FROM THE DEAD and CATHOLIC, it adds THROUGH HOLY BAPTISM to REMISSION OF SINS, and closes with RESURRECTION OF THE FLESH TO ETERNAL LIFE. It has been wrongly identified as a formulary for use in the hour offices.[3] As a matter of fact, though there would be nothing out of the way in the presence of a creed in the hour services at this date, the context of the passage, as well as the attribution of the articles to the twelve Apostles, suggests that the compiler's interest was in the main catechetical.[4] The Latin of the first and third of these variants of T (A and C), with all their carelessnesses of spelling and grammar, is printed below :

BOBBIO A

Credo in deum patrem omnipotentem, creatorem celi et terrae.
Credo in Iesu Christo filium eius unigenitum sempiternum, conceptum de Spiritu sancto, natum ex Maria virgene, passus sub Poncio Pilato, crucifixum, mortuum et sepultum, discendit ad inferna, tercia die resurrexit a mortuis, ascendit ad celus, sedit ad dexteram dei patris omnipotentis, inde venturus iudicare vivos et mortuos.

BOBBIO C

Credis in deum patrem omnipotentem, creatorem celi et terre?
Credit et in Iesu Christo filium eius unicum, dominum nostrum, conceptum de Spiritu sancto, natum ex Maria virgene, passo sub Poncio Pilato, crucifixum et sepultum, discendit ad inferna, tercia die resurrexit a mortuis, ascendit in celis, sedit ad dexteram dei patris omnipotentis, inde venturus iudicare vivos ac mortuos?

---

[1] H.B. Soc. LVIII. 74 f.: in MS foll. 117 v.–118 r.
[2] H.B. Soc. LVIII, 181: in MS fol. 298 r. and v.
[3] E.g. by Kattenbusch I, 55; II, 747 n. 34; 881 n. 14.
[4] See A. Wilmart in H.B. Soc. LXI, 1923, 43.

Credo in sancto Spiritu, sancta aeclesia catolica, sanctorum comunione, remissione peccatorum, carnis resurreccioniem, vitam aeternam.	Credit in sancto Spiritu, sancta aeclesia catholica, sanctorum comunione, remissione peccatorum, carnis resurreccionis, vitam abere post mortem, in gloriam Christi resurgere.

So much for the Bobbio Missal. Secondly, we should turn to the Antiphonary of Bangor, which contains a credal text which is at once reminiscent of T and related to the formulae we have just been studying. This famous Irish MS, now preserved in the Ambrosian Library at Milan (press-mark C. 5 *inf.*), was written at the great monastery founded in 559 by St Comgall near Belfast: its date, 680–691, is fixed by references to the name of the contemporary abbot.[1] On fol. 19 r. and v., among a collection of anthems and prayers and immediately preceding the Pater Noster, the following creed is quoted:

Credo in deum patrem omnipotentem invisibilem, omnium creaturarum visibilium et invisibilium conditorem.

Credo et in Ihesum Christum filium eius unicum, dominum nostrum, deum omnipotentem, conceptum de Spiritu sancto, natum de Maria virgine, passum sub Pontio Pylato, qui crucifixus et sepultus discendit ad inferos, tertia die resurrexit a mortuis, ascendit in caelis seditque ad dexteram dei patris omnipotentis, exinde venturus iudicare vivos ac mortuos.

Credo et in Spiritum sanctum, deum omnipotentem, unam habentem substantiam cum patre et filio, sanctam esse aecclesiam catholicam, abremissa peccatorum, sanctorum commonionem, carnis resurrectionem. Credo vitam post mortem et vitam aeternam in gloria Christi. Haec omnia credo in deum.

The striking peculiarities which at once leap to the eye here are (*a*) the use of FRAMER OF ALL CREATURES etc. as well as INVISIBLE with FATHER ALMIGHTY, (*b*) the introduction of GOD ALMIGHTY after the mention both of the Son and of the Spirit, (*c*) the insistence on the consubstantiality of the Spirit, and (*d*) the form of the final clause about the future life. The omission of DEAD should also be noticed. Apart from these points, however, the creed is broadly similar to T, and where it parts company with it recalls features in the creeds of the Bobbio Missal. Among kindred traits we may single out (*a*) the repetition of I BELIEVE before the second article, (*b*) the use of participles in the accusative for CONCEIVED, etc., (*c*) the use of

[1] Cf. the magnificent photographic edition prepared for the H. Bradshaw Society (IV and X) in 1893 and 1895 by F. E. Warren.

SAT for SITS, (*d*) the ablative *in caelis* for TO HEAVEN, and (*e*) the phrase THE GLORY OF CHRIST in the final clause.

A third liturgical document which we may adduce as witnessing to a creed-form resembling T is the so-called Missale Gallicanum Vetus.[1] In the view of experts the MS containing it (Cod. Vat. Pal. 493) comprises the remains of two separate sacramentaries which have been bound up together. The sections which concern us were, it would seem, connected with the diocese of Auxerre, in France, were written early in the eighth century, and came from Burgundy to Lorsch in the ninth by way of one of the Burgundian cloisters which had relations with Germany.[2] On foll. 16 r. and v. and 17 r. a form of the creed is to be found at the beginning of a sermon for delivery at the *traditio symboli*.[3] The sermon itself comments on the clauses of the creed individually, but in our codex breaks off suddenly at *credo in filio eius* because of the disappearance of several leaves. The creed set out in full at the beginning is substantially identical with T, and so need not be printed here. The only points of discrepancy are that it omits DESCENDED TO HELL, interpolates VICTOR before TO HEAVEN, reads SAT for SITS, and preserves the old Gallican reading ABREMISSION OF SINS. The complete text of the defective sermon, it is interesting to observe, is to be found in Cod. Lat. Monacensis (Munich) 6298 of *Sermo pseudo-August*. 242 (an eighth century MS from the monastery of St Emmerus, in the diocese of Freising). The creed to be extracted from it again approximates to T, but omits ONLY, OUR LORD, DEAD, DESCENDED TO HELL, and all mention of the Session. These omissions are paralleled in old Gallican creeds, and the threefold repetition of I BELIEVE is also a Gallican trait. Possibly this represents the original form of the creed as used in the liturgy, while the text reproduced *in extenso* at the beginning is the one familiar to the eighth-century copyist. A second creed-form, it should be noted, appears on fol. 20 v. of the Gallican Missal: it is the one which we identified on p. 179 as the formulary of St Caesarius of Arles, and is again very close to T.

---

[1] See J. Mabillon, *De liturgia Gallicana libri* III, Paris, 1685; J. M. Neale and G. H. Forbes, *Ancient Liturgies of the Gallican Church*, Burntisland, 1855.

[2] So L. Traube, the famous palaeographer, in A. E. Burn's *Facsimiles of the Creeds*, 48.

[3] Cf. J. Mabillon, *Op. cit.* 348; A. E. Burn, *Facsimiles of the Creed*, Plates V–VII.

Lastly, T occurs in practically its complete form in the so-called Sacramentary of Gellone. The MS containing this (the richly illustrated Cod. Lat. 12048 in the Bibliothèque Nationale at Paris) dates from the last decades of the eighth century. Attempts have been made[1] to trace its origin to the abbey of Gellone or St Guilhem-du-Désert (near Aniane, to the N.W. of Montpellier), where it undoubtedly found a home early in the ninth century. But the considerations connecting it with northern France, either with Rebais[2] in the diocese of Meaux or with Cambrai,[3] remain far more impressive. In many of its spelling forms, abbreviations and illuminations it hints at Spanish influence. As a sacramentary it belongs to the Gelasian class, and provides two orders of baptism. In the first the *interrogationes de fide* consist of an interrogatory creed even more meagre than R—"Do you believe in God the Father almighty? And in Christ Jesus His only Son our Lord? Do you believe also in the Holy Spirit, the holy Catholic Church, the remission of sins, the resurrection of the flesh?" In the second order the creed makes two appearances,[4] first in a declaratory and later in an interrogatory form. The former comes after the *apertio aurium* (fol. 181 r.), the priest making a short prefatory speech and inviting the acolyte to declare the creed on behalf of the infant candidate. The text at this point is identical with T, except that it gives SAT for SITS and omits *est* with *venturus*. The latter (fol. 181 v.) forms part of the baptism of a sick catechumen, and again coincides with T save for the interrogatory form, the addition of DO YOU ALSO BELIEVE? at the opening of the second article, the omission of MAKER OF HEAVEN AND EARTH, and the substitution of SAT for SITS.

2. *T's Redaction Not Roman*

Such in the main is the earliest evidence for the existence of T and of creeds closely allied to it. With this material before us our task is now to attempt to determine where T originated.

[1] Cf. P. de Puniet, *Le sacramentaire romain de Gellone*, Rome, 1938 (an off-print of articles in *Ephemerides Liturgicae*), 6 ff.
[2] So L. Traube in A. E. Burn, *Facsimiles of the Creeds*, 49.
[3] Cf. Dom A. Wilmart's article in *R. Bén.* xlii, 1930, 210–222.
[4] Cf. A. E. Burn's *Facsimiles of the Creeds*, Plates VIII and IX.

And here the hypothesis which claims first consideration is obviously the one which maintains that the thorough-going redaction of R of which T was the result was carried out in Rome itself. This was the theory which G. L. Hahn[1] and A. E. Burn[2] defended more than fifty years ago. Though A. E. Burn afterwards compromised so far as to admit that R may have undergone its actual metamorphosis into T elsewhere,[3] he steadfastly refused to budge from his position that its adoption at Rome must have taken place well before 700, and that it was from Rome that it spread. An examination of his arguments, which have often been set aside but have never been thoroughly sifted, makes the most convenient method of approaching the whole question of T's origin.

In pleading for Rome as T's birthplace, or at least as the ecclesiastical centre responsible for its wide diffusion, Burn relied on several independent considerations. First, he appealed to a MS preserved in the library of Corpus Christi College, Cambridge, the *Psalterium Latino-Graecum* (No. 468), which he believed bore the further description *Papae Gregorii*. The MS itself, he admitted, was probably of English penmanship, and dated from no earlier than the fifteenth century. But, following in the footsteps of Caspari,[4] he connected its contents with Pope Gregory III (731–741). A creed figures in this MS, and its text is identical with T except for a couple of trifling variations (the omission of *est* with *venturus*, and of AND before THE HOLY SPIRIT). Burn therefore felt justified in reckoning this as evidence for the existence of T at Rome *circa* 700.

Secondly, he professed to find the use of T by St Priminius highly significant. The great Benedictine missionary, he argued, spoke in his *Scarapsus* of the delivery of the creed to the catechumens immediately after their renunciation of the devil and all his works and shows, and this was a distinctively Roman custom. He also cited the renunciation itself in what Burn took to be its Roman form, and introduced a reference to the Roman prayer of anointing. Furthermore St Priminius was, according

---

[1] Cf. *Bibliothek* 24, n. 20.
[2] Cf. *An Introduction*, 233 ff.
[3] Cf., e.g., *Facsimiles of the Creeds*, 1908, 12; *Encyclopædia Britannica*, 11th ed., VII, 395.
[4] *Quellen* III, 215 f.

to Burn, the friend and fellow-worker of St Boniface, who we know received explicit instructions from Pope Gregory II to use the official Roman baptismal order. In a famous letter[1] the Pope admonished the new missionary to adhere loyally to the usages of the Holy See.

"We desire", he wrote, "that you should apply the sacramental ritual, which you aim at observing in the initiation of those who through God's grace will come to believe, in accordance with the prescribed form of the offices of our holy apostolic see, and this we have despatched for the sake of your instruction."

Admittedly, it is impossible to demonstrate that St Boniface in actual fact adopted T as his baptismal creed, but Burn considered it unlikely that he would have used a text different from that favoured by his collaborator St Priminius. But if T was used by St Boniface, the enthusiastic propagator of Roman ways, the probability that it was a Roman form is vastly increased.

In the third place, Burn found valuable confirmation of his views in certain of the replies sent to the questionnaire which Charlemagne put out in 812 (we shall recur to this later) as to the form of the baptismal rite prevalent in his empire. The most important of the answers which have survived is that of Amalarius of Trèves, and the text of the creed which it seems to presuppose was almost certainly T or something very close to it. His covering remarks were read by Burn as implying that he used the Roman order of baptism, creed and all.

"At the scrutiny," Amalarius wrote, "we make the sign of the cross over the children, as we find it laid down in the Roman order, and we also make a genuflexion and an adjuration, and we instruct the godfathers and godmothers in the Lord's Prayer, so that they may do likewise with the charges for whom they stand sponsors. Similarly we instruct them in the creed, which in our language is translated *sign*."[2]

Burn deduced from his words that all the items specified must have been equally modelled on current Roman practice. The presence of T in the various contemporary Gallican missals

---

[1] *Ep.* 1 (*P. L.* 89, 496).   [2] *P.L.* 99, 894.

and sacramentaries he regarded as clinching his case, since everyone recognizes that these liturgies, as a consequence of the deliberately Romanizing policy of the latter part of the eighth century, embodied considerable Roman elements side by side with Gallican ones. Finally, he brought forward a more general reflection, the extreme unlikelihood of Rome's having borrowed such an important liturgical instrument as the baptismal creed from strangers. "It is impossible to believe that the Church, which in the ninth century refused to insert the *filioque* in N to please an emperor, should during that very period have accepted from outside a brand new recension. All analogy points to a process of gradual growth."[1]

Such was A. E. Burn's case. While conscious of the futility of dogmatism on such a subject, scholars have on the whole not been satisfied with it. There were grave weaknesses in all his arguments, as we shall see if we examine them in order, and some of them were based on sheer blunders. A glaring example of the latter sort was his reliance (in the company, it may be said in extenuation, of a host of other students) on the Cambridge *Psalterium Latino-Graecum*. It is a mystery how this MS ever came to be linked up with a Pope Gregory. On fol. ii r. it bears the inscription "*psalterium grecum prioris Gregorii*". According to M. R. James, it was probably written in the thirteenth century, and he hazarded the conjecture that it was the property of Gregory of Huntingdon, Prior of Ramsey (fl. *circa* 1250).[2] Whether he was right or not, the MS had nothing to do with Pope Gregory, and the tenuous thread which in the eyes of Burn and others connected its contents with Rome was purely imaginary.

Burn undoubtedly made too much also of the supposed friendship and collaboration of St Priminius with St Boniface. The only recorded occasion of contact between the two great missionaries of Germany was when St Priminius lay on his death-bed at Hornbach and, according to his ninth-century biographer[3] (not too trustworthy a witness), received a visit

---

[1] *An Introduction*, 239.

[2] Cf. M. R. James, *A Description of the MSS in the Library of Corpus Christi College, Cambridge*, Cambridge, 1912, II, 399 ff.

[3] Cf. *Vit. et mirac. S. Pirminii* 9 (ed. of E. O. Holder-Egger in *Mon. Germ. Hist., Script.* XV, 28 f.).

from St Boniface. If the incident ever took place (it is edifyingly recounted, and St Boniface's own well-informed biographers are silent about it), it must have been a passing visit as St Boniface was returning to Mainz from the anointing of Pippin as king of the Franks. The name of St Priminius does not crop up in the surviving correspondence of St Boniface, in spite of their belonging to the same Benedictine Order, and while the two men must have been aware of each other's existence, they appear to have kept out of each other's way. Thus, although St Boniface was commissioned by Pope Gregory III in 738 as his legate in both Bavaria and Alamannia, he seems to have studiously abstained from developing his mission in Alamannia, no doubt so as to avoid interfering with the work of St Priminius.[1] The assumption that they were friends and operated as associates or even colleagues is entirely without historical basis.

Thus it involves more than one risky leap into the dark to conclude that, since St Priminius used T, St Boniface must likewise have used it, with the implication in mind that St Boniface's use of it suggests, in the light of his well-known devotion to Roman practice, that T was a Roman form. As a matter of plain fact, not a trace of the creed which he employed for baptismal purposes survives in St Boniface's writings.[2] In any case, it is hazardous to take it for granted that his creed-form must have been identical with the Roman one, for while the Roman authorities undoubtedly insisted on the main scheme of their baptismal office being observed, there is nothing to show that they were particularly concerned about the wording of the creed. If the mission of St Augustine of Canterbury to England more than a century earlier furnishes any analogy, the inference would be that they were not. In the reign of St Gregory the Great the Roman church almost certainly employed C as its baptismal creed, at any rate for domestic purposes. St Augustine, we know, was a stickler for Roman precedent, and in particular stipulated that "the ministry of baptism, by which we are reborn to God, should be fulfilled according to the manner of the holy Roman and apostolic church."[3] Yet all the

---

[1] On all this, see G. Jecker, *Die Heimat des hl. Pirmin*, 14.
[2] Kattenbusch brought this out (II, 821 ff.).
[3] Cf. Bede, *Hist. eccl.* 2, 2 (*P.L.* 95, 83).

evidence seems to point to the conclusion that R was the creed which the British church was persuaded to adopt. Burn's further point that St Priminius himself followed Rome both in the position of the creed and in the form of the renunciation cannot be taken seriously. It is not really possible to reconstruct the precise order of ceremonies from St Priminius's selective summary. So far as we can, however, it is manifest that he is referring, not to the formal recitation of the creed at the *redditio*, as Burn's argument presupposes, but to the interrogations at the actual moment of baptism. The fact that the credal questions known to St Priminius were cast in the form of T is a proof of the decidedly un-Roman character of his baptismal rite. The questions used at this point in the authentic Roman service were always much briefer than T, as we know from the Gelasian Sacramentary, as well as from the service as it is performed to-day.

Burn was also guilty of trying to squeeze too much out of his texts when he interpreted Amalarius as implying in his reply to Charlemagne that his creed-form (again T) was Roman as well as the ceremonies he used at baptism. The most that can be deduced from the context of his letter is that he arranged for the order of ceremonies to reproduce the Roman scheme. He was no more referring to a specifically Roman wording of the creed than he was implying that the Holy See had a distinctive version of the Lord's Prayer. It is in any case dangerous, when picking one's way through Frankish liturgies of this period, to build too much on the description of a rite as Roman. The Carolingians, especially Charlemagne himself, were no doubt determined Romanizers, and fostered the adoption of the Roman liturgy by every means within their power. But what emerged as a result of their efforts, and passed for "Roman", was usually a transparent conflation of Roman with Gallican elements. The general plea that the Rome which declined to accept the *filioque* from Charlemagne cannot be credited with meek acquiescence in the Gallican form of the baptismal creed can be dismissed out of hand. It is highly improbable that Leo III's motives for repudiating the *filioque* had anything to do with his concern for ancient texts as such, or even with the disdain a Roman pontiff might be supposed to feel for being dictated to in liturgical matters by a Frankish emperor. It is not difficult to perceive that what deterred him was really the statesmanlike instinct that he must on no account put himself and the Holy See in the wrong in the eyes of Eastern Orthodoxy. Relations between East and West were quite delicately enough balanced as it was without the Pope gratuitously placing trump cards in the hands of the Oriental bishops. As a matter of fact, as we shall later observe, the tide of liturgical influence had already begun to turn, and if in the eighth century the Roman rite was spreading throughout France and Germany, in the ninth Rome itself was becoming the borrower. So far from the Holy See being too proud in the ninth century to be a debtor to the Gallican church, Gallican elements were beginning to appear with increasing frequency, with her free consent, in her service-books.

So far these are mainly negative considerations. If they suffice to undermine the positive case advanced in favour of T's alleged Roman origin, they still leave the hypothesis of such an origin a possible one. The argument which has inclined most scholars to reject it has still to be mentioned: it divides into three parts. First, there are strong grounds for supposing that, in so far as a creed of this type was known and used at Rome before the ninth century, it was R and not T. Leo the Great († 461) and Gregory the Great († 604), it has been shown,[1] while both apparently ignorant of T, both knew and availed themselves of R or a creed very similar to it. The appearance of R, and not T, in the Codex Laudianus of *Acts*, a late sixth- or seventh-century MS brought to England by Roman missionaries (possibly by Theodore of Tarsus, 669–690), and in the Psalter of Aethelstan (ninth century) points in the same direction. Secondly, it is difficult to escape the impression, as was pointed out in the previous chapter, that the Roman church used C as its baptismal creed, for its own local purposes at any rate, for some hundreds of years. Thirdly, it must have struck readers of the last section that all the earliest documents testifying to T's existence or to the existence of creeds akin to T are Gallican. Whatever mysteries there may be about their precise provenance, they cannot by any stretch of imagination be associated

[1] By Kattenbusch, II, 807 ff.

with Rome directly. The majority of them date from before the middle of the eighth century. The significance of this is that it was not until after the middle of that century that that deliberate Romanizing of the Gallican service-books which was such a feature of Carolingian liturgical policy really got under way.

3. T's Hispano-Gallic Origin

If the theory that T originated in and emanated from Rome is discarded, its source must plainly be sought in one of the provincial centres. A useful method of approach to the problem is to examine the different types of local creed, so far as they can be ascertained, and compare them with T. Although it is obvious that creed-forms were not rigidly fixed, it is equally obvious that the texts used in different localities tended to be marked by distinctive traits. There is *prima facie* much plausibility in the hypothesis that T must have taken its rise in the region where formularies closely approximating to it were current.

If this is the approach adopted, it becomes clear at once that certain regions can be decisively ruled out. No one, perhaps, is likely to propose Africa as the milieu in which T was born, but it is interesting to note that such creeds as we can identify as African diverge emphatically from T. Let us take the formulae quoted on pp. 175 f. as representative African creeds. Of the eleven provincialisms listed in the first section of Chapter XII only five appear in them—the word-order JESUS CHRIST, DEAD, THENCE, CATHOLIC and ETERNAL LIFE; and of these neither DEAD nor CATHOLIC (only in St Augustine) seems to have secured a firm hold. At the same time, in striking contrast to T, they have unusual features like KING OF THE AGES, IMMORTAL, and THROUGH THE HOLY CHURCH. On the other hand, it has occasionally been argued that T may be a North Italian form. The presence of a closely similar text in the Bobbio Missal has been hailed as proof of this, but (quite apart from the unlikelihood of the Bobbio Missal being in fact a North Italian document) the theory derives little or no support from the creeds belonging to that region. They are, as we saw on pp. 173 f., much nearer to R than to T.

The claim of the Spanish churches must be rated much higher. Spain seems to have possessed a fairly stable version of the creed from the times of St Martin of Braga († 580) down to the eighth century, and this agreed with T in a host of particulars. Naturally all Spanish creeds of this period had the word-order JESUS CHRIST. But in addition the clauses SUFFERED, DESCENDED TO HELL, GOD THE FATHER ALMIGHTY in the passage about the Session, CATHOLIC and ETERNAL LIFE all had a place in them.[1] The Mozarabic liturgy could even boast COMMUNION OF SAINTS. Yet it must be noticed that, notwithstanding the use of the Constantinopolitan Creed at mass in Spain since 589, the words MAKER OF HEAVEN AND EARTH were uniformly lacking. So, too, was the important distinction CONCEIVED BY . . . BORN FROM . . . .

A creed of some interest in determining T's provenance is necessarily the late fourth-century formula of Nicetas of Remesiana, in what is now called Yugoslavia.[2] The text which can be extracted from his *De symbolo* agrees with T extraordinarily closely. Beyond any shadow of doubt Nicetas was familiar with the variant forms JESUS CHRIST, SUFFERED, DEAD, CATHOLIC, and ETERNAL LIFE, and spoke of Christ as sitting on the right hand of THE FATHER (omitting ALMIGHTY). Although slightly less certain, it is highly probable that he knew CREATOR OF HEAVEN AND EARTH. A most striking feature of his creed was, of course, its inclusion of COMMUNION OF SAINTS. The chief points of divergence between it and T were its failure to mention CONCEIVED BY and DESCENDED TO HELL. It is worth recalling that Nicetas's agreements with T do not stand alone, for we can point to other well-known creeds deriving from the Eastern districts of the Western empire and the neighbouring provinces of the Eastern empire which have similar points of contact with T. The Fourth Creed of Sirmium and the related creed of Nicé both contained DEAD and DESCENDED TO HELL. The so-called "Faith of St Jerome", whatever its actual relation to the saint, combined Nicene elements with elements drawn from local creeds (possibly from Pannonian creed-forms current around Stridon), and revealed an acquaintance with CREATOR OF HEAVEN AND EARTH (the text

[1] See above, pp. 177 f.   [2] See above, p. 174 f.

reads OF THINGS VISIBLE AND INVISIBLE), DESCENDED to HELL, and COMMUNION OF SAINTS.[1]

It remains an indisputable fact, however, that creeds practically identical with T began to appear in South Gaul, and particularly in Provence, from the fifth century onwards. The creed of St Faustus of Riez, we may recall, already contained the characteristic wording CONCEIVED BY THE HOLY SPIRIT, BORN FROM THE VIRGIN MARY, and could also boast of the clause COMMUNION OF SAINTS, in the middle of the fifth century.[2] Very important is the creed recently identified by Dom G. Morin as that of St Caesarius of Arles († 542).[3] This contained CREATOR OF HEAVEN AND EARTH, the distinction CONCEIVED BY . . . BORN FROM . . ., the clauses SUFFERED, DEAD, DESCENDED TO HELL, FATHER . . . ALMIGHTY, THENCE, and COMMUNION OF ˹ INTS, and, of course, JESUS CHRIST, CATHOLIC and ETERNAL L.. ᴇ. It was distinguished from T only by a few minor peculiarities—the use of ONLY-BEGOTTEN for ONLY, the omission of OUR LORD and the insertion of ETERNAL after ONLY-BEGOTTEN, the insertion of an additional I BELIEVE at the opening of the second article, and the inverted word-order *sanctum Spiritum*. St Caesarius's disciple and younger contemporary St Cyprian of Toulon had a formulary closely resembling this. The surviving fragments do not show CREATOR OF HEAVEN AND EARTH (any more than St Caesarius's creed does in the body of his expository sermon), or DEAD, or ALMIGHTY in the clause about Christ's session, but they add OUR LORD and leave ETERNAL out after ONLY-BEGOTTEN.[4] At the same time, as we saw earlier in this chapter, there are certain liturgical documents, notably the Missal of Bobbio and the Missale Gallicanum Vetus, as well as the slightly later Sacramentary of Gellone, which testify to forms hardly differing from T, and which are almost certainly to be connected with Gaul.

The evidence thus strongly suggests that T's place of origin is to be sought in South Gaul. On the whole, scholars have been inclined to look to Burgundy because of the apparent connection

---

[1] Cf. G. Morin, *Anecdota Maredsolana* III, iii, 199 f.
[2] See above p. 179.
[3] See above p. 179. This is the creed which appears in Missale Gallicanum Vetus, fol. 20 v.
[4] See above p. 179.

of the relevant liturgical documents, as well as of St Priminius's missionary activities, with that region.[1] On the other hand, there are a number of considerations which point to a rather different part of the Frankish dominions as T's probable birthplace. That part is the South-Western district of France stretching from the Pyrenees to the Rhône, with its capital at Narbonne, which in ancient times was known as Septimania, and which from the fifth to the eighth century was under the domination and influence of Visigothic Spain. It will be worth devoting a few pages to an examination of the hypothesis that T derives from this part of the world.

First, and of primary importance, there is the evidence of St Priminius. He is undoubtedly the first literary witness to T's existence. The suggestion that he got his creed-form from Rome has been rejected. It might be proposed, as an alternative to this, that the most natural formulary for him to use would have been that of the district in which he worked. But Alamannia was not at this time a country with a flourishing Christian life: liturgical practice must have been at an embryonic stage of development. The letters of St Boniface to the Holy See give a shocking picture of the barbarism of the people to whom he carried the gospel, and of the deplorable level of their sacramental and liturgical standards. St Priminius's lot is not likely to have been cast in an environment with a livelier and better equipped tradition. On the whole, the idea that he must have relied for his baptismal creed on the local customs of the people to whom he preached must be dismissed as resting on a misconception of the situation. A more decisive objection to this view, however, is the fact that it seems highly probable, judging from the nature of his literary sources, that he composed his *Scarapsus* before actually starting his missionary labours in Alamannia. Thus, on all grounds, the most plausible theory is that he used the form of creed with which he had grown up in his native land.

The all-important question is to determine what this was, and formerly there were all sorts of guesses (they scarcely merited a more serious name) on the subject. St Priminius has

---

[1] E.g. Kattenbusch, II, 790 ff.; F. Loofs, *Symbolik*, Tübingen and Leipzig, 1902, 39; Badcock, 148 ff.

been claimed for Ireland, for England, even for Denmark. It has now been established, however, with something approaching certainty that he was really of Romanic descent, and that his origins lay in the Visigothic region of France which for centuries was subject to the control and cultural impact of Spain.[1] This may seem a daring hypothesis, but it is the one upon which several distinct lines of evidence converge. The philology of his name is one: it can be traced to Latin, but not to German, Anglo-Saxon or Irish, roots. The analysis of his literary sources is also suggestive: it reveals that his reading lay almost exclusively in Spanish authors, such as St Martin of Braga, St Isidore of Seville and St Ildefonsus of Toledo. His theological and liturgical interests were fully in harmony with this, pointing to a Spanish background; and the type of organization he set up in the many religious houses he founded was marked by traits reminiscent of practice in the far South-West. The tradition was that he had been an exile from his own country. If it is true that he was originally a native of the district around Narbonne, a flood of light is thrown on the reasons for his departure from Septimania and for his undertaking a long career of missionary wandering. It was in 718 that the Saracens, under the leadership of the terrible El-Hurr, burst through the Pyrenees with their hordes, spreading devastation wherever they went: Narbonne itself fell to them in 720. Churches, with their furnishings and treasure, and the clergy who looked after them were the chosen objects of their attack, and St Priminius may well have been one of those who fled for their lives before the onslaught.

Secondly, the use by St Caesarius of Arles († 542) of a creed strikingly similar to T two hundred years before St Priminius provides powerful support for our hypothesis. Arles was, of course, on the Eastern bank of the Rhône. But its ecclesiastical attachments, unlike those of Vienne (which were with the Burgundians), were with the Visigoths who dominated Pro-

---

[1] Cf. G. Morin, *D'où est venu St Pirmin?* in *Revue Charlemagne* i, 1911, 87 ff; D. U. Berlière, *R. Bén.* xxxiv, 1922, 388; D. J. Pérez, *Boletín de la Real Academia de la Historia* (Madrid) lxxvii, 1920, 132–150; G. Jecker, *Die Heimat des hl. Pirmin*; W. Levison, *Neues Archiv* xlv, 1924, 385 f. Against this point of view, cf. M. J. Fleskamp, *Z. für KG.* xlvi, 1925, 199–202; but the case he develops for an Irish extraction for St Priminius is quite inadequate.

vence, and in 514 Pope Symmachus granted St Caesarius himself the power to settle questions of faith arising in Spain and Gaul alike.[1] His own relations with the rulers of the Goths, despite moments of extreme tension (he suffered exile on more than one occasion), were intimate and issued in a great deal of skilful collaboration. It is interesting to observe that the creed which we have agreed with Dom Morin in attributing to him,[2] and which bears unmistakable tokens of kinship with T, recalls Spanish formularies in a number of particulars. The adjective ONLY-BEGOTTEN (*unigenitum*), for example, has Spanish precedent in the *libellus fidei* of St Gregory of Elvira in the fourth century.[3] It recurs again in St Theodulphus of Orléans round about 800[4]; and he was a Goth from Spain. It comes also, as we have already noticed, in the creed of St Cyprian of Toulon. Again, the inversion of noun and adjective in HOLY SPIRIT (*sanctum Spiritum*) is found in St Gregory of Tours († 594),[5] and is probably Spanish: at any rate it reappears in the creed of the Mozarabic liturgy.[6]

Thirdly, the chief creed of the Bobbio Missal, formula A, seems to be really identical with this creed (to be found also, we may remind the reader, on fol. 20 v. of the Missale Gallicanum Vetus) which we have accepted as the faith of St Caesarius. The Bobbio version agrees with St Caesarius's text in substituting ONLY-BEGOTTEN EVERLASTING (*unigenitum sempiternum*) for *unicum* of T. Both have *inde venturus iudicare* (THENCE WILL COME TO JUDGE) without *est*, the inversion of adjective and noun in HOLY SPIRIT, and certain important clauses (DESCENDED TO HELL, etc.) which make them witnesses to T and its origins. The only discrepancies between them spring from certain instances of barbarous handwriting in the Bobbio Missal which belong to the age and circle in which it was produced, or consist of minutiae of wording (the omission in Bobbio A of *et* after the second *credo*, the use of *ex Maria* for St Caesarius's *de Maria*, the substitution of accusative participles for St Cae-

---

[1] Cf. the Pope's letter (*Ep.* 9), *P.L.* 62, 66.
[2] See above p. 179 (cf. *R. Bén.* xlvi, 1934, 178 ff.).
[3] Cf. *P.L.* 20, 49 f. (usually assigned to Phoebadius of Agen).
[4] Cf. *Lib. de ord. bapt.* 7 (*P.L.* 105, 227): also Hahn 69.
[5] Cf. *Hist. eccl. Franc.* 1, *prol.* (*P.L.* 71, 161 ff.); also Hahn 63.
[6] See above, p. 178.

sarius's finite verbs). The noting of these facts at once raises the question of the place of origin of the Bobbio Missal. Mabillon denied[1] its connection with the North Italian town whose name it bears: he considered it a Gallican document, and traced it to the monastery at Luxeuil. Duchesne,[2] followed by Dom Cagin,[3] went back on this and argued for its composition in the neighbourhood of Bobbio: according to them it was a unique representative of the liturgy of North Italy from the ninth century. S. Bäumer,[4] F. Probst[5] and E. Bishop[6] discerned in it the work of Irish missionaries settled on the continent. In his latest study of the Missal Dom A. Wilmart[7] returned to Mabillon's conjecture, though he readily admitted the Irish influences. A book of this character, he thought, must have been written in, and circulated from, some Burgundian monastery which was near neighbour to some centre of Irish influence like Luxeuil. Among all the guesses proposed, however, by far the most solidly grounded and attractive is that of Dom G. Morin. Both in 1914 and in 1934 he laid stress on the impressive part played in the Missal by Spanish and Mozarabic elements.[8] The presence of these elements, he pointed out, was best explained by the assumption that the Bobbio Missal was put together in the S.W. region of France. As for the numerous traces of Irish influence, which he was in no way concerned to cover up, they fitted in perfectly with the theory he was advocating. Where, he asked, in Gaul were there not Irish settlements towards the end of the seventh century or in the early part of the eighth? He went on:

On les retrouve partout, ces "peregrini" insulaires, depuis le Quercy et l'Aquitaine jusqu'aux milieux monastiques de la Belgique, des rives de l'océan Atlantique jusqu'au delà du Rhin; et il n'est point douteux qu'ils n'aient pénétré en une foule de milieux au sujet desquels les documents nous font défaut.[9]

---

[1] *Museum Italicum*, 273; 276: *Praef.* n. i, ix.
[2] *Christian Worship* (Eng. trans.), London, 1931, 158 f.
[3] *Te Deum ou Illatio?*, 1907, 29 n. 1.
[4] *Z. für Kat. Theol.* xvi, 1892, 485 f.
[5] *Die abendländische Messe*, 1896, 37 ff., 359 ff.
[6] *J.T.S.* iv, 1903, 566 and viii, 1907, 293.
[7] H. Bradshaw Society LXI, 1923, 38 f.
[8] *R. Bén.* xxxi, 1914, 326 ff., and xlvi, 1934, 187 ff.
[9] *R. Bén.* xxxi, 1914, 328.

Dom Morin had been much occupied in reconstituting the homiletical works of St Caesarius. He was led by these studies to observe, with ever-growing conviction, how close were the bonds of union between the old Gallican sacramentary and the liturgy presupposed by St Caesarius in his sermons, and particularly in his biblical catechetical instructions preparatory to the Easter baptisms.[1] It really seems that the solution he proposed has cleared up the age-long riddle of the place of origin of the Missal of Bobbio.

A further fact which makes the picture which is now taking shape more convincing is the appearance of a creed virtually identical with T in the Sacramentarium Gellonense. Liturgical authorities are agreed that the MS containing this was written in the closing years of the eighth century, and the probability is that it was written for some religious house in the neighbourhood of Meaux (not far from Paris, to the East). Its most recent editor, Dom P. Puniet, as was remarked above, has argued for Gellone itself, in the neighbourhood of Montpellier in S. France, as its birthplace, but his case is not likely to convince everyone. The abbey of St Guilhem-du-Désert at Gellone was not founded until 804, which is rather a late date for the MS; and one cannot overlook the repeated mentions in the martyrology, in the original hand, of the abbey of Rebais (in the diocese of Meaux). Dom A. Wilmart's discovery[2] that the same hand that wrote the Sacramentary worked on another eighth-century MS belonging to the chapter at Cambrai, while not implying that the Sacramentary was made for Cambrai, strengthens the case for its connection with North France. From our point of view the interesting thing is that tradition has linked St Priminius with Meaux. According to his biographer,[3] the Benedictine missionary did not go straight to Alamannia. He took refuge first, probably, in Aquitania, and then travelled on to Austrasia, where "he exercised a pastoral episcopate blamelessly" for a spell at a place called Castellum Melcis. There has been some controversy over the situation of this mysterious place. Dom G. Morin conjectured (for reasons, it must be feared, more

[1] R. Bén. xlvi, 1934, 187.
[2] See R. Bén. xlii, 1930, 210–222: the MS concerned is No. 300 in the municipal library at Cambrai.
[3] Cf. Vit. et mirac. S. Pirmin. I (Mon. Germ. Hist., Script. XV, 21 f.).

patriotic than well grounded) that it must have been Mels-broeck, formerly Meltburch, near Brussels. His guess was rendered possible, though hardly plausible, by his insistence on reading, against the evidence of all the best MSS, Meltis for Melcis.[1] On the whole scholarship has come down decidedly in favour of identifying Castellum Melcis with Meaux.[2] Certainly this is on general grounds the most likely theory in view of the ancient ecclesiastical tradition that St Priminius was once bishop of Meaux. It is therefore possible that the presence of a creed identical with T (the creed, be it remembered, of St Priminius) in the Sacramentary of Gellone is in some way a relic of the influence which the Benedictine refugee from Narbonne must have wielded there during his stay two or three generations previously. The MS, it should be noted, has a number of other Spanish traits.

The hypothesis that T originated in S.W. France, in the region once known as Septimania, and that it attained its present shape there in the seventh century, is one which deserves serious consideration. Its superiority to the Burgundian hypothesis scarcely needs to be emphasized: there is no connecting link between St Priminius and Burgundy, and the association of the relevant liturgical MSS with Burgundy is purely accidental. So far from being an objection to it, the appearance of similar creeds in the Latin Balkans comparatively early, e.g. in the writings of Nicetas of Remesiana, supplies it with useful confirmation. There were close ties between the Eastern districts of the Western empire on the one hand and Gaul and Spain on the other. To take an example, St Martin of Tours († 397) was not only born in Pannonia (at Szombathely, in Hungary), but worked there for a long period. St Martin of Braga († 580) was also a Pannonian. The Visigoths, who after 419 subdued S. Gaul and then Spain, and about 470 infected a section of the Burgundians with Arianism, had settled for a considerable time in Dacia and its neighbourhood. The Ostrogoths, who ruled Provence for more than a generation after 510, came from Pannonia. Hence a certain borrowing of credal

---

[1] Cf. *R. Bén.* xxix, 1912, 262–273.
[2] See B. Krusch, *Neues Archiv* xxxix, 1914, 550 ff., and *Göttinger Nachr. Phil-Hist. Kl.*, 1916, 231 ff. See also W. Levison, *Neues Archiv* xxxviii, 1913, 351 f.

clauses is easily accounted for. Relations were equally close between Ireland and both Spain and Gaul, and if Irish missionaries streamed over Europe in the train of St Columban, Ireland in its turn was indebted to Western Europe for a good deal of its culture and liturgical art. Thus the acquaintance of Irish churchmen with T can also be explained.

4. Charlemagne and the Creed

Whatever may be the final verdict on the claims of S.W. France to be the birthplace of the *textus receptus* of the Apostles' Creed, very few will be likely to deny that its origin is to be sought somewhere north of the Alps at some date in the late sixth or seventh century. Having established this fixed point, we should now be in a position to tackle the equally important and no less troublesome problem of its canonization as the sole baptismal creed of the Western Church. How did T come to be selected for this exalted role, and by what steps did it obtain an entry into the Roman liturgy? Two separate discussions will be necessary, for it would seem that T first became the authorized version of the creed in France and Germany, and then worked its way to supremacy at Rome itself. It may as well be admitted at the outset that we cannot hope to reconstitute with precise detail the stages by which these goals were reached. The scanty evidence available does not allow us to plot out a theory in terms of concrete happenings and hard-and-fast dates. Nevertheless, though the country we shall be exploring is thickly veiled in mist, it is possible to discern dimly the kind of development that must have taken place, and thus to reconstruct it in broad outline.

A fact which stands out with unmistakable clarity is that circumstances were uniquely favourable in the Frankish empire, in the late eighth and early ninth centuries, to the selection and ultimate enthronement of a single text of the baptismal creed. In the first place, the Frankish rulers, and Charlemagne in particular, deliberately gave liturgical uniformity a high place in their programme of cultural restoration. It was their consistent aim, after the pact of mutual support sealed between Pippin and Pope Stephen II in 754, to bring liturgical usage in their realms, marked as it was at the time by chaotic diversity, into some kind of order based on harmony with current Roman practice. Roman influences were already at work (e.g. missionaries like St Boniface were indefatigable Romanizers), but they must have received a powerful impulse when Pippin set Rome before the clergy as a model and endeavoured to supply himself with Roman liturgical books.[1] There is some question whether Pippin's reforms extended beyond the introduction of the Roman chant of the antiphonary and responsary.[2] Whatever may be thought of this technical question, there can be no doubt that Charlemagne energetically continued the same Romanizing ideal in the celebration of mass and the administration of the sacraments generally. In all this he received substantial aid from the pure Gregorian sacramentary which, in answer to his request, was sent to him in 785 or 786 by Pope Hadrian I by the hands of abbot John of Ravenna.[3] As disseminated throughout the Frankish territories, the copies made of this service-book were interpolated with lavish modifications designed to prevent it from clashing too violently with local usage. So far as the baptismal office was concerned, we have no reason to suppose that the policy had any drastic effect on the text of the creed. In view of the reluctance which Charlemagne and his adviser Alcuin showed to upsetting established usage more than necessary, we can appreciate that they would not be disposed to dethrone the T-type of baptismal creed in favour of the form C still employed in the Roman rite at the tradition and the reddition. But it is at least clear that the spirit which was in the air must have been hostile to the persistence of regional idiosyncrasy, and must have encouraged the development of uniform, officially recognized texts.

In the second place, alongside their general concern for uniformity of rites, the Frankish rulers laid great stress, as a matter of state policy, on the learning of the creed and the Lord's Prayer. In the deplorable breakdown of education,

---

[1] See M. Netzer, *Introduction de la messe romaine en France sous les Carolingiens*, Paris, 1910, 30 ff; E. Caspar, *Pippin und die Römische Kirche*, Berlin, 1914, 12–53; Th. Klauser, *Hist. Jahrbuch* liii, 1933, 169 ff.

[2] So, e.g., S. Bäumer, *Geschichte des Breviers*, Freiburg, 1895, 228 ff. But cf. Th. Klauser, *Hist. Jahrbuch* liii, 1933, 171.

[3] For the Pope's letter, cf. *Mon. Germ. Hist.*, *Epp.* III, 626.

culture, morals and religion with which they found themselves confronted, they seem to have seized upon these texts as admirably adapted for imposing at least a minimum standard of knowledge. Thus Carloman, in 742, sanctioning the decisions of a council presided over by St Boniface, took the step of ordaining that every year in Lent bishops should examine their parish clergy on the functions of their ministry, and chiefly on the ceremonies of baptism, on the prayers and ritual of the mass, and on the Catholic faith.[1] What was contemplated, no doubt, was an investigation into the priest's grasp of the essentials of Christian teaching, but both contemporary usage and the general ignorance of the clergy at the time suggest that the examination included the text of the creed.[2] Originally applicable only to the territory under Carloman's sway, Austrasia, this ordinance was accepted by Pippin at the council of Soissons in 744 for Neustria,[3] was affirmed by the general council of the Franks in 747,[4] and was repromulgated by Charlemagne for all his dominions in 769.[5] The immense importance he attached to teaching the true faith came out forcibly in the *Admonitio Generalis*[6] which he published on 23 March 789, and several of its capitula (e.g. 32, 82) almost read like paraphrases of the Apostles' Creed. Charlemagne never wearied of reiterating that what he wanted was instructed priests, meaning by that men with an exact knowledge of their liturgical functions, of baptism and mass in particular, and able to educate the people by sound commentaries on the Lord's Prayer and the creed.[7] Local councils gave practical force to his wishes by ratifying his programme of ecclesiastical studies. We possess an interesting questionnaire drafted, probably, for the use of a *missus* at some date between 803 and 813, which opens with a brusque inquiry addressed to the clergy, whether they know by heart and understand the creed and the Lord's

---

[1] Cf. A. Boretius, *Capitularia Regum Francorum* (*Mon. Germ. Hist., Legg.* II) 1, 25 (No. 3).
[2] Cf. E. Vykoukal, *R.H.E.* xiv, 1913, 90.
[3] *Mon. Germ. Hist., Concil.* II, 35 (No. iv).
[4] *Mon. Germ. Hist., Concil.* II, 47.
[5] A. Boretius, *Op. cit.* 45 (No. 8).
[6] A. Boretius, *Op. cit.* 52 ff.
[7] Cf. the material conveniently assembled by M. Andrieu, *Les ordines romani du haut moyen âge*, Louvain, 1931, I, 476 ff.

Prayer.[1] We also possess a list of items of knowledge which "all ecclesiastical persons are bidden to learn", which includes the Catholic faith of St Athanasius, the Apostles' Creed, and the Lord's Prayer.[2]

At the same time a series of parallel ordinances made the study of these basic texts obligatory on all the laity. To pick but two examples out of many, a letter of Charlemagne's has come down to us addressed to a bishop Garibaldus (Gerbald of Liège, 784–810), and giving expression to his solicitude for the religious instruction of the faithful.[3] No one is qualified to be a godfather or godmother, he insists, unless he knows by heart and can repeat the Lord's Prayer and the creed. In the same way, in a programme of questions drawn up for the benefit of Charlemagne's *missi*, it is laid down that all Christians are expected to know the Lord's Prayer and the creed, and to be able to teach them to others.[4] Decrees of this pattern could be multiplied indefinitely. Their implication would seem to be that the creed, like the Lord's Prayer, was a recognizable, official instrument; and if this was so, it is obvious that a large number of variant texts could not have been tolerated for long.

A turning-point in the development of a single official version of the creed may almost certainly be discerned behind an important measure which Charlemagne took in 811–813. It was probably about that time that he wrote to all the metropolitans in his realms demanding detailed information about the baptismal rites practised and the baptismal creed used in their dioceses. In his letter to Odilbert of Milan he said:[5]

Thus we desire to learn, either by letter from you or by word of mouth, in what manner you and your suffragans teach and instruct the priests of God and the people committed to your charge regarding the sacrament of baptism, that is, why a child is first made a catechumen, and what a catechumen is. After that, what you tell them about the other parts of the service in order—as regards the scrutiny, what the scrutiny is; as regards the symbol, what the term

---

[1] A. Boretius, *Op. cit.* 234. Cf. also C. De Clercq, *La législation religieuse Franque*, Louvain and Paris, 1936, 252.
[2] A. Boretius, *Op. cit.* 235.
[3] A. Boretius, *Op. cit.* 241. Cf. C. De Clercq, *Op. cit.* 222 f.
[4] A. Boretius, *Op. cit.* 109 f.
[5] A. Boretius, *Op. cit.* 246 f. Cf. also C. De Clercq, *Op. cit.* 216.

means according to the Latins; as regards belief (*de credulitate*), after what fashion they are supposed to believe in God the Father almighty, and in Jesus Christ His Son, Who was born and suffered, and in the Holy Spirit, the holy Catholic Church, and the other items which follow in the same creed; as regards the renunciation of Satan and all his works and shows, what the renunciation is, and what are the works and shows of the devil, etc.

We observe that the emperor here specifically mentions the creed. His object plainly was to secure uniformity in the baptismal service on the basis of the Roman type. The bishops' replies, a number of which have come down to us, must have revealed an appalling state of diversity, and we must assume that his worst suspicions were confirmed. Thus the councils held under his auspices in 813 insisted anew that the Roman rite must be the standard, and that the bishops should instruct the clergy along those lines. The ideal of uniformity was being eagerly pushed forward, and it is interesting for us to observe that the text of the baptismal creed was among the items about which the emperor was most concerned.

The results to which this survey points may not at first seem very exciting. But if we have nowhere come across any clear sign of a monopoly being granted to T, we should at least be in a position to appreciate how very propitious the atmosphere was to the emergence of a single official creed and the elimination of idiosyncrasy. It need not occasion surprise that the choice fell upon T. It must be remembered that T was unusually favourably placed for attaining pre-eminence. Originally a native of Septimania in S.W. France, it was in current use at Arles on the other side of the Rhône; and through the missionary wanderings of St Priminius it had become domiciled both in northern France and in parts of Germany. The abbey of Reichenau which its patron had established was a vigorous centre of liturgical influence. It was only to be expected that when the policy of liturgical uniformity pursued by the Carolingians, the elevation of the baptismal creed into an educational instrument, and the special solicitude of Charlemagne for the baptismal service, combined to hasten the adoption of a common form, that chosen form would be one which had already achieved a wide measure of diffusion and popularity.

At any rate it was about the beginning of the ninth century that T began to enjoy a practical monopoly in Western Europe. We noticed above that the form of creed which Amalarius of Trèves sent to Charlemagne in answer to his questionnaire was either T or something very close to it.[1] It would be interesting if we could discover what part, if any, was played in the development by the court schools at Aachen and Tours. An unsolved question is the authorship of the *Disputatio puerorum* which tradition ascribes to Alcuin.[2] In chapter 11 of this interesting little work the creed is quoted twice over, in the form of questions and answers, and both times it is the text of our Apostles' Creed. The *Disputatio* survives in a Salzburg MS (No. 67) of the end of the ninth century: the other works written out along with it there belong indisputably to Alcuin. Froben, the editor of Alcuin's collected works, accepted it as genuine, declaring that its style and manner corresponded exactly with Alcuin's, but scholarship has not pronounced a final verdict. If the tract is really by Alcuin, it would constitute a remarkable illustration of T's adoption as the official text of the baptismal creed by Charlemagne's leading theologians. As it is, there is nowhere else any trace of T in Alcuin's writings, although he alludes to both the Constantinopolitan Creed (which was for him the creed *par excellence*) and the "Apostles' Creed". Almost all the other ninth-century writers are equally silent about the text of the creed they knew and used. But there is one notable exception, Hrabanus Maurus. He was, it should be observed, a pupil of Alcuin's at Tours, and it is a fact that he quotes the creed, in the authentic form T, several times in his works.[3]

Another illustration of the special status which T was now acquiring is provided by its appearance in psalters. It was about this period, or a little earlier, that the creed began to be written out in psalters along with other kindred formularies, such as the Te Deum and the Quicunque Vult. It is a remarkable fact that, whenever the Apostles' Creed appears in ninth-century psalters, the text is the one we are studying. Probably the earliest of these service-books is the Vienna Psalter (No. 1861 in the

---

[1] See above, p. 406: cf. *P.L.* 99, 896.
[2] For the text, see *P.L.* 101, 1099 ff.
[3] Cf. esp. *Hom.* 13 and *De eccl. discip.* 2 (*P.L.* 110, 27; 112, 1225 f.).

Nationalbibliothek at Vienna), which according to tradition was ordered by Charlemagne from the copyist Dagulf for presentation to Pope Hadrian I. This would place it earlier than 795. Kattenbusch was inclined to doubt this very early dating, pointing out that the *Karolus* and *Hadrianus* referred to by the original scribe might equally well indicate Charles the Bald and Pope Hadrian II; but there is probably more to be said, on palaeographical as well as other grounds, for the traditional date.[1] Here we have T in a service-book produced to the orders of the king himself. T also features in the famous Utrecht Psalter, now in the library of the University of Utrecht, which goes back to the first decades of the ninth century.[2] Again it makes an appearance (fol. 167 r.) in the Psalter of Charles the Bald (Cod. Lat. 1152 of the Bibliothèque Nationale, Paris).[3] This was made for the king himself during the lifetime of Queen Hermentrude (842–869). We know that Charlemagne was concerned, in harmony with his insistence on propriety in other matters liturgical, that the clergy should be supplied with corrected psalters.[4] T must have had something of the status and prestige of an official form if it was selected for inclusion in psalters prepared for the royal house. Its presence in them, and probably in the corrected psalters used by the clergy, must be reckoned as one of the explanations of its rapid diffusion in the ninth century, for the saying and singing of the psalms, as a method of intercession and for other purposes, became a devotion of widespread popularity among clergy and laity in Carolingian times.

5. *The Acceptance of T at Rome*

The preceding section has attempted to assemble, it is to be feared in a rather selective and haphazard fashion, material throwing light on the process by which the Apostles' Creed in the form of T became current coin throughout the Frankish dominions. We are not in the least surprised to observe that it was treated as the authoritative version of the creed in the West

[1] Cf. H. Leclercq, *D.A.L.C.* iii, 703 f.
[2] Cf. H. Leclercq, *D.A.L.C.* xi, 1344 ff.
[3] Cf. H. Leclercq, *D.A.L.C.* iii, 843 ff.
[4] Cf. *Admonitio Generalis, capp.* 70 and 72 (A. Boretius, *Op. cit.* 59 f.).

generally in the eleventh and twelfth centuries. St Ivo of
Chartres († 1117), for example, wrote a sermon on the Apostles'
Creed, and it is certain that the text he had before him was T,
despite the fact that he passed over DESCENDED TO HELL without
mention.[1] So too Joslenus, or Gosienus, who was bishop of
Soissons in the first half of the twelfth century († 1152), presupposed T in his exposition of the creed.[2] The late twelfth-
century Spanish priest and monk of Léon, St Martinus Legion-
ensis († 1221), also used T as his standard,[3] as did Abelard
(† 1142) almost a century before him.[4] What is more interesting,
however, is the fact that, from the twelfth century onwards at
any rate, T was the official text of the creed at Rome itself. A
useful illustration of this is provided by Pope Innocent III
(† 1216) in his treatise on the Blessed Sacrament.[5] Discussing
the singing of the creed at mass, he quoted both the Apostles'
and the Constantinopolitan Creeds, the former in the shape of
T. From this time onwards trivial variations in the text disappear, and it is plainly T which is everywhere regarded as the
Apostles' Creed. Thus, when St Thomas Aquinas wrote his exposition of it, he adopted T as his basis as a matter of course.[6]

The question which must now be faced is when and how a
version of R which, as we have seen, in all probability reached
its final development in France, came to be adopted at Rome.
It will be recalled that the creed used for declaratory purposes
in the Roman baptismal rite since the sixth century had, almost
certainly, been C. The questionnaire addressed to the candidate
at the moment of baptism continued, of course, to be an abbreviation of R: precisely the same curtailed version is employed
at the same point in the service to-day. But both the Gelasian
Sacramentary and Mabillon's Ordo Romanus VII depict the
candidate or his sponsors as making their profession of faith in
the words, I BELIEVE IN ONE GOD, etc. There is nothing to show
that this practice had become obsolete, much less that T had
taken the place of C, at the beginning of the ninth century;

---

[1] *Serm.* 23 (*P.L.* 162, 604 ff.).
[2] *Expos. in symb.* (*P.L.* 186, 1479 ff.).
[3] *Serm.* 34 (*P.L.* 208, 1326 ff.).
[4] *Expos. symb.* (*P.L.* 178, 617 ff.).
[5] *De sacr. altar. myst.* 2, 50 (*P.L.* 217, 827 f.).
[6] *Expos. super symb. apost.* (Vol III of the 1634 Paris edition of his works).

indeed the evidence that does exist suggests that the catechetical use of C was in full swing at that time.[1]

The two earliest allegedly Roman documents which testify
to T's acceptance at Rome are (a) the *Ordo Romanus antiquus*,
edited by Melchior Hittorp in 1568 as the first part of his *De
divinis catholicae ecclesiae officiis*, and (b) the Codex Sessorianus 52
(now Codex 2096 in the Biblioteca Nazionale at Rome). The
former of these, described by the seventeenth-century Cardinal
Tommasi as "a hotchpotch of diverse rites according to various
customs", has been traced by recent students to the middle of
the tenth century.[2] It is one of the principal documents lying
behind the "Romano-German Pontifical" of the tenth century
which it has been the noteworthy achievement of M. Michel
Andrieu to disinter.[3] The Codex Sessorianus 52 is also a composite document, including pieces of the late eleventh and
twelfth centuries.[4] Of the four segments of which it is made up
foll. 1–103 and foll. 178–190 are, for the most part, of the
twelfth century, while foll. 104–177 and foll. 191–205 belong
to the end of the eleventh century. The whole seems to have
been written beyond any doubt in Italy. The MS was the
property in the thirteenth century (such is the implication of
a note jotted down on the *verso* of the last page) of the abbey
of Nonantola, situated 10 km. to the north-east of Modena.

The occurrence of T in both these important sources calls
for a more precise and detailed description. Many fragments
and excerpts from the baptismal rite are to be found chaotically
scattered up and down the *Ordo Romanus antiquus*. In all of them,
with a single exception, the creed presupposed is C. In this one
exception, however, which is printed on p. 73 of the 1568
edition, T is quoted as a declaratory creed, with the prefatory
rubric:

When the litany at the font is finished, all the clergy and people
standing in a circle round the font, silence is made and the Pope at

[1] See above pp. 346 ff.

[2] Cf. R. Mönchemeier, *Amalar von Metz*, 1893, 140; S. Bäumer, *Die Katholik*
i, 1889, 626.

[3] Cf. *Les ordines romani du haut moyen âge*, Louvain, 1931, and *Le pontifical romain
au moyen-âge* (*Studi e Testi* LXXXVI, 1938).

[4] The MS has been described by G. Morin, *R. Bén.* xiv, 1897, 481–488; P.
Grisar, *Analecta Romana* I, 214–216. Cf. M. Andrieu, *Op. cit.* 287 ff.

the ninth hour, as he is about to bless the font, as the custom is, pronounces the Lord's Prayer, *Pater noster*, etc., *Credo in deum*, etc.

In Codex Sessorianus 52 the creed T appears in two separate places. The first of these is on foll. 114 v. and 115 r., where the *traditio symboli* is described after the model of Mabillon's Ordo Romanus VII, but with certain significant changes. The chief of these are two, (*a*) that there is now no suggestion that the catechumen speaks Greek, and (*b*) that the text of the creed which the acolyte recites is no longer C but T. It is worth observing, however, that it is C which is recited at the *redditio symboli* on Holy Saturday. The second appearance of T is in the sermon expounding the creed which begins on fol. 161 v. and ends on fol. 163 r. Here the names of the apostles considered responsible for each clause are written in the margin. The reconstituted creed coincides exactly with T, except for the omission of BORN FROM THE VIRGIN MARY, which must have been left out by an oversight. There are other creed-texts in the MS as well as T: for example, on fol. 163 r. another exposition of the creed is given, and this yields a text (the preacher quotes it in full in his exordium) closely resembling R.

The *Ordo Romanus antiquus*, as we saw, was probably not compiled until the middle of the tenth century. Moreover, much of the material embodied in it is patently Gallican, and not Roman at all. It is doubtful in consequence whether, in spite of its name, it can be adduced as a witness to Roman practice at all. The special importance which, in the eyes of students, attaches to the Codex Sessorianus 52, depends on the possibility that it may give us a precious glimpse into Roman liturgical habits in the middle of the ninth century or a little later. As Dom Morin pointed out long ago, certain formulae which occur in much the same portion of the codex as the baptismal rite seem to be directly connected with this date. On fol. 126 r. are to be found certain solemn acclamations to be recited at papal masses on great festivals in honour of the Pope and the emperor. The names mentioned are Nicholas (*domno nostro Nicholao*) and Louis (*domno nostro Hludovico*). It seems natural to infer that the persons indicated must be Pope Nicholas I (858–867) and the emperor Louis II (850–875). The solemn acclamations are of a type which was frequent in the Carolingian epoch. Dom Morin also noted that the baptismal order was closely followed (foll. 128 v.–131 r.) by an order for the consecration of bishops which was clearly connected (cf. the reference to the consecrator as *domnus apostolicus*) with Rome.[1]

In view of these apparently decisive pointers to the date of the liturgies delineated in Codex Sessorianus 52, many scholars have felt justified in inferring that T must have been adopted into the Roman baptismal rite in the middle of the ninth century at least. Such was the conclusion of Dom Morin himself, and he was followed somewhat less confidently by Kattenbusch.[2] It is by no means impossible or far-fetched. The Roman liturgy, aided by the deliberate efforts of Pippin and Charlemagne, was making powerful inroads in the Frankish territories in the second half of the eighth century. At the beginning of the ninth, however, the tide was showing signs of flowing in the reverse direction. About this time Rome was making tentative borrowings from the Frankish church. Leo III, for example, for all his unwillingness to imitate the Gallican fashion of having the creed sung at mass, did not hesitate to introduce the Frankish rogation days before the feast of the Ascension at Rome.[3] A Roman *capitulare evangeliorum* used in Lucca in the second half of the ninth century already contained the Frankish festivals of the Apostles with their pericopes.[4] Instances like these may be isolated, but they were signs of the times: Frankish influence was soon to become a mighty flood, but the waves were already lapping the Roman shore. We cannot exclude the possibility that among the innovations which Rome took over from the Frankish empire in the early ninth century was the Frankish version of the Apostles' Creed.

Nevertheless the question may be asked whether too much has not been built upon the festal acclamations which undoubtedly form a striking feature in the Codex Sessorianus 52. On general grounds it would be preferable to date T's adoption

---

[1] See his article in *R. Bén.* xiv, 1897, 481 ff. *passim*.

[2] For his queries, see II, 801.

[3] See *Liber pontificalis* (edited by L. Duchesne, Paris, 1892), II, 12, with the note on p. 40.

[4] Cf. the capitulare in the Gospel MS Vatic. Lat. 7016. The example is borrowed from Th. Klauser's article in *Hist. Jahrbuch* liii, 1933, 183 f.

at Rome somewhat later. While Frankish liturgical influence
was beginning to make itself felt at Rome in the middle of the
ninth century, it did not sweep over Italy in full force until a
hundred years later. Moreover, the long survival of the memory
of C's use in the baptismal service (a use attested on several
occasions by the *Ordo Romanus antiquus* itself, as the reader will
recall) would be difficult to account for if C had surrendered
its place to T so early. Considerations like these bid one probe
rather more cautiously into the credentials of Codex Sessorianus
52 as a reliable witness to mid-ninth century practice at Rome.

Several points at once suggest themselves as calculated to
strengthen one's doubts. First, the part of the codex under discussion was not written, it is agreed on all hands, until the end
of the eleventh century. This fact immediately arouses one's
suspicions. It was a natural and almost irresistible temptation
to scribes, when copying out the creed *in extenso*, to reproduce
it in the form with which they were familiar. Assuming that the
rite depicted as a whole belongs to the ninth century, we have
therefore no guarantee that the declaratory creed is a faithful
replica of the original text; and the occurrence of C at the
redditio on Holy Saturday complicates matters still further.
Secondly, it is not altogether certain that the rite is necessarily
a ninth-century one. Codex Sessorianus 52 is a collection of
pieces deriving from a very wide range of dates. It cannot be
lightly assumed that all of them, or even all the *ordines* comprised in foll. 104–177, emanate from the same epoch. No
doubt the festal acclamations on fol. 126 are correctly attributed to the reigns of Pope Nicholas I and the emperor Louis II.
Other pieces, however, may come from much later dates. To
take one example, the rite for the consecration of a bishop (fol.
128 v.–130 r.) evinces extensive borrowings from Frankish
models, and this borrowing would be most easily understood
if it took place after the ninth century. It is perfectly conceivable
that the modified version of Ordo Romanus VII which forms
the baptismal service derives from a correspondingly late epoch.
Thirdly, we have really no right to assume that all the rituals
comprised in the codex are Roman in origin. The most recent
and authoritative discussion of the MS[1] has drawn attention to

[1] Cf. M. Andrieu, *Les ordines romani*, 484.

the close points of contact between it and the Romano-German pontifical compiled probably in Mainz about the middle of the tenth century. It inclines to the opinion that the codex, or the model on which it was based, must have seen the light only a short while before the definitive adoption of the pontifical at Rome, i.e. in the latter part of the tenth century. So far as its contents are concerned, it is clearly an amalgam of material derived from many sources, Frankish and Roman alike.

If the ultimate bearing of considerations like these is not altogether clear, they do at least emphasize very forcibly the danger of building too much on the occurrence of our received text of the creed in Codex Sessorianus 52. Quite a number of possibilities need to be weighed which did not enter into the purview of Dom Morin and Kattenbusch, and one would like to defer decisions until a properly noted edition of the codex is available. In the meantime, confidence in the theory that T supplanted C in the Roman baptismal service as early as the ninth century is seriously undermined. It may well have done so, but the evidence usually marshalled with a view to proving it is far from satisfactory. On the other hand, it is possible to propose an alternative date which has considerable intrinsic likelihood. This is the period when, as a result of political circumstances and its own disastrous internal weakness, the Roman church succumbed without resistance to Franko-German influence and, in particular, permitted its liturgy to undergo virtual transformation. This period lasted roughly from the restoration of the empire under Otto I in 962 to the opening of the reign of Pope Gregory VII (1073). During the whole of this century and more, as Pope Gregory himself observed, "*Teutonicis concessum est regimen nostrae ecclesiae.*"[1] Everything goes to show that the condition of the Church in Italy, and not least in the holy city, was deplorable in the tenth century. Ignorance and corruption were rife, and liturgical science and practice had fallen into pitiful decay. The emperor Otto I, who made the rehabilitation of ecclesiastical standards one of the main planks of his policy, made several protracted stays in Italy, and swarms of German ecclesiastics crossed the Alps in his train. It is no matter for wonderment that their

[1] Cf. G. Morin, *Anecdota Maredsolana* II, i, 460.

efforts to resuscitate sound liturgical usage resulted in a drastic
Gallicanization of the Roman rite. A step which must have
contributed largely to this was taken by Pope Gregory V in 998.
On 22 April of that year, apparently, on the intervention of
Otto III, he accorded special privileges to the abbey of
Reichenau, including that of having its abbot consecrated by
the Roman pontiff himself, but in return imposed on it the
duty of sending to the Holy See, on each occasion of the consecration of an abbot, one sacramentary, one epistle-book, one
gospel-book and two white horses.[1] This curious charge throws
an illuminating ray of light on the shocking level of cultural
life in central Italy at the time, if the Pope could not rely on
local *scriptoria* to produce the service-books that he needed.
At the same time it conveys a vivid impression of the liturgical
subjection of Rome, and illustrates one of the ways in which
the Franko-German rites penetrated beyond the Alps. The
missals and sacramentaries which the monks of Reichenau
despatched periodically to the Lateran palace must naturally
have conformed to the pattern of usage current at the time
in Alamannia and in the Frankish empire generally.

It must be admitted that no echo of the baptismal creed, no
whisper hinting at its varying fortunes, can be overheard in this
lengthy span of centuries. The change-over from the use of C
to the use of T may have been carried through at any one of
several possible dates. One thinks, for example, of the essay at
liturgical reform tried out in the second quarter of the tenth
century by Alberic, *Patricius Romanorum*, with the assistance of
St Odo, the venerable abbot of Cluny.[2] This resulted in the
blending of the Roman liturgy inherited from St Gregory and
pontiffs more ancient still with a number of important Gallican
elements. Again, the suspicion cannot be avoided that the
Benedictine monks at Reichenau may have played their part.
The baptismal orders which travelled south to the papal palace
from their *scriptorium* certainly contained the creed T which
had descended to them from their refugee founder.

[1] See A. Brackmann, *Germania Pontificia* (in *Regesta Pontificum Romanorum*) II,
Pt. I, 152, nr. 12. It was not a dead letter in 1083: cf. M. Andrieu, *Les ordines
romani*, 516.
[2] Cf. M. Andrieu, *Les ordines romani*, 512 ff., and *Rev. des sciences relig.* v, 1925,
251.

Amid much that is obscure and baffling, however, one broad conclusion stands out; and it remains equally true whether the earlier or the later date for the transformation of Rome's baptismal rite is preferred. The adoption of T into the Roman liturgy may be regarded as a by-product, small in itself but fraught with lasting significance, of the large-scale permeation of the Roman service-books with German influence after the beginning of the ninth century. The claim has been made[1] that "it was the Franko-German church which, at this critical epoch, saved the Roman liturgy for Rome and the Western world". If the argument of this chapter is well founded, these words may be applied in a special sense to the Apostles' Creed. In persuading Rome to accept a new baptismal confession, the church beyond the Alps was merely handing back to her, enriched and improved, that same venerable rule of faith which she herself had compiled in the second century as an epitome of the everlasting gospel.

[1] So Th. Klauser in *Hist. Jahrbuch* liii, 1933, 189.

INDEX

Aachen, 353, 365, 425; Council of (*798*), 355; Council of (*809–10*), 365
Abelard, 393, 427
Acacius of Caesarea, 290, 292
Achamoth, 245
Acta Iustini, 81 n.
Acts of St Thomas, 379
Admonitio Generalis, 422, 426 n.
Adoptionists; Adoptionism, 128, 129, 130, 147, 355, 356, 364, 377
Ado Viennensis, 363 n.
Aeneas of Paris, 354
Aetius (the Anomoean), 283, 287
Aetius (of Constantinople), 297 f, 318
African Church, 36, 44, 54, 85, 88, 93, 114, 116, 175 f.
Agathon, Pope, 360
Alamannia, 408, 414, 433
Alberic, *Patricius Romanorum*, 433
Alcuin, 353, 355, 356, 371, 377, 392, 421, 425
Alexander, St, 188, 190, 191, 206, 210, 232, 233 n, 234 n, 236, 240, 242, 246 n, 251, 252, 253 f, 262, 344
Alexander of Byzantium, 206, 210, 252
Alexandria, 92, 188 f, 322; Synod of (*362*), 241, 278, 284, 332, 340; Council of (*378*), 335
Amalarius of Metz, 353, 356, 371
Amalarius of Trèves, 394, 406, 409, 425
Ambrose, St, 1, 2, 36 f, 105 f, 168, 172 f, 249, 253, 337, 358, 370, 396
Ammianus Marcellinus, 263
Anastasius (Chronicler), 366
Anastasius I, Emperor, 349
Anathema Iēsous, 15
Anatolius of Constantinople, 317, 318
Ancoratus (St Epiphanius), 192 n, 219 n, 227 n, 304, 310, 318–20
Ancyra, 108, 109; Synod of (*358*), 238, 288
Andrieu, M., 422 n, 428, 431 n, 433 n.
Anomoeans, 240, 283, 287 f, 294, 295, 306, 340
Antioch, 34, 184–6, 197, 207, 279, 328; Council of (*268*), 201, 207, 238 f, 247; Council of (*325*), 208 f, 211, 224, 239; Dedication Council of (*341*), 110, 262, 263–74, 281, 282, 292; Council of (*379*), 306, 320, 335

Apollinarians; Apollinarianism, 303, 306, 333, 334, 335, 336, 337
Apollinarius, 299, 333, 334, 335, 336, 382
Apophthegmata Macarii, 190
Apostles, Composition of creed by, 1–6, 29, 53 f, 101, 105, 399, 401
Apostolical Constitutions, 2, 34, 39, 160, 186–7, 190, 255
Apostolic Tradition, 35, 45–49, 89–92, 97, 99, 100, 104, 114 ff, 122, 124, 129, 139, 147, 153, 160, 162, 167, 172, 195, 374
Aquinas, St Thomas, 3, 388, 394, 427
Arians; Arianism, 109, 188, 206, 208, 213, 220, 226, 230, 231–4, 235, 237, 238, 239, 242, 243, 245, 252 f, 254, 255, 257 f, 259, 261, 262, 265, 266, 270, 271, 273, 274, 277, 280, 283, 287, 288, 290, 292, 293, 294, 305, 306, 339, 344, 347, 351, 361, 419
Aristides, *Apology* of, 76
Aristotle, 243, 244
Arius, 189 f, 206, 210, 211, 216, 231–34, 236, 237, 240, 242, 249, 251 f, 258, 261, 262, 265, 270, 277, 283, 339, 382
Arles, 415 f, 424; Council of (*314*), 57, 60, 206; Council of (*353*), 284
Arnobius, 56, 58
Asclepas of Gaza, 277
Assemanus, J. A., 122 n.
Asterius the Sophist, 231 n, 232, 271, 273
Athanagild, 352
Athanasius, St, 51 n, 110 n, 169, 181 n, 206 n, 212, 213, 215, 220, 223, 232 n, 233, 235, 236, 237, 239, 241, 243, 250, 251, 253, 256, 264, 265, 267, 270 n, 271, 272 f, 274, 275, 276, 277, 278 ff, 282, 311, 336, 339 f, 342, 343, 382; attitude towards N. 257 f, 259, 260 f, 284 f.
Athenagoras, St, 154 n, 244
Augustine, St, 32, 36, 39, 55, 57, 61, 106, 125, 134 f, 138, 168, 169, 172, 175 f, 261, 358 f, 370, 373, 376 f, 380, 381 n, 384, 387 f, 395 n, 397
Augustine of Canterbury, St, 408

Badcock, F. J., 104–11, 161 n, 228 n, 313, 331, 414 n.

435